Frommer's®

London

from $95 a Day

10th Edition

by Donald Olson

Here's what the critics say about Frommer's:

"Amazingly easy to use. Very portable, very complete."

—Booklist

"Detailed, accurate, and easy-to-read information for all price ranges."

—Glamour Magazine

"Hotel information is close to encyclopedic."

—Des Moines Sunday Register

"Frommer's Guides have a way of giving you a real feel for a place."

—Knight Ridder Newspapers

Wiley Publishing, Inc.

Donald Olson is a novelist, playwright, and travel writer. His seventh novel, *Confessions of a Pregnant Princess,* was written under the pseudonym Swan Adamson and published by Kensington in 2005. An earlier Swan Adamson novel, *My Three Husbands,* has been translated into French and several other European languages. Donald Olson's novel *The Confessions of Aubrey Beardsley* was published in the U.K. by Bantam, and his play, *Beardsley,* was produced in London. His travel stories have appeared in the *New York Times, Travel & Leisure, Sunset, National Geographic* guides, and many other national publications. He is the author of *London For Dummies, Germany For Dummies,* and *England For Dummies,* which won the 2002 Lowell Thomas Travel Writing Award for "Best Guidebook."

Published by:

Wiley Publishing, Inc.

111 River St.
Hoboken, NJ 07030-5774

ISBN-13: 978-0-471-74702-4
ISSN-10: 0-471-74702-5

Editor: Elizabeth Heath
Production Editor: Melissa S. Bennett
Cartographer: Andrew Murphy
Photo Editor: Richard Fox
Production by Wiley Indianapolis Composition Services

For information on our other products and services or to obtain technical support, please contact our Customer Care Department within the U.S. at 800-762-2974, outside the U.S. at 317-572-3993 or fax 317-572-4002.

Wiley also publishes its books in a variety of electronic formats. Some content that appears in print may not be available in electronic formats.

Manufactured in the United States of America

5 4 3 2 1

Contents

5 Accommodations You Can Afford 74

6 Great Deals on Dining 114

7 Exploring London 159

List of Maps

An Invitation to the Reader

In researching this book, we discovered many wonderful places—hotels, restaurants, shops, and more. We're sure you'll find others. Please tell us about them, so we can share the information with your fellow travelers in upcoming editions. If you were disappointed with a recommendation, we'd love to know that, too. Please write to:

Frommer's London from $95 a Day, 10th Edition
Wiley Publishing, Inc. • 111 River St. • Hoboken, NJ 07030-5774

An Additional Note

Please be advised that travel information is subject to change at any time—and this is especially true of prices. We therefore suggest that you write or call ahead for confirmation when making your travel plans. The authors, editors, and publisher cannot be held responsible for the experiences of readers while traveling. Your safety is important to us, however, so we encourage you to stay alert and be aware of your surroundings. Keep a close eye on cameras, purses, and wallets, all favorite targets of thieves and pickpockets.

Frommer's Star Ratings, Icons & Abbreviations

Every hotel, restaurant, and attraction listing in this guide has been ranked for quality, value, service, amenities, and special features using a **star-rating system.** In country, state, and regional guides, we also rate towns and regions to help you narrow down your choices and budget your time accordingly. Hotels and restaurants are rated on a scale of zero (recommended) to three stars (exceptional). Attractions, shopping, nightlife, towns, and regions are rated according to the following scale: zero stars (recommended), one star (highly recommended), two stars (very highly recommended), and three stars (must-see).

In addition to the star-rating system, we also use **seven feature icons** that point you to the great deals, in-the-know advice, and unique experiences that separate travelers from tourists. Throughout the book, look for:

Finds	Special finds—those places only insiders know about
Fun Fact	Fun facts—details that make travelers more informed and their trips more fun
Kids	Best bets for kids and advice for the whole family
Moments	Special moments—those experiences that memories are made of
Overrated	Places or experiences not worth your time or money
Tips	Insider tips—great ways to save time and money
Value	Great values—where to get the best deals

The following **abbreviations** are used for credit cards:

AE	American Express	DISC	Discover	V	Visa
DC	Diners Club	MC	MasterCard		

Frommers.com

Now that you have the guidebook to a great trip, visit our website at **www.frommers.com** for travel information on more than 3,000 destinations. With features updated regularly, we give you instant access to the most current trip-planning information available. At Frommers.com, you'll also find the best prices on airfares, accommodations, and car rentals—and you can even book travel online through our travel booking partners. At Frommers.com, you'll also find the following:

- Online updates to our most popular guidebooks
- Vacation sweepstakes and contest giveaways
- Newsletter highlighting the hottest travel trends
- Online travel message boards with featured travel discussions

What's New in London

On July 6, 2005, Londoners exulted in the news that the International Olympic Committee had chosen London as the site of the 2012 Olympic games. The next day, July 7, terrorists detonated bombs in the London Underground and on a double-decker bus, killing 56 people, including themselves, and injuring hundreds more. A second attempted attack two weeks later was completely unsuccessful. As of press time, British police had arrested four men thought to be the would-be murderers.

It's with a heavy heart that I report this news because the last thing I want to do is discourage anyone from traveling to London. In the weeks following the attacks, London was, understandably, on edge. Police presence in the subways was dramatically increased, and packages and backpacks were searched. What's important to emphasize, however, is the way Londoners reacted. Jitters aside, they refused to be terrorized. A palpable sense of solidarity and determination was felt throughout the city. London's emergency hospital, police, and transportation services were able to respond quickly.

So life goes on, and London goes on, continuing to amaze, enchant, and provoke—all the more reason to visit the pulsating capital of the U.K. as soon as possible.

Why go now? Because after a decline in tourism following 9/11, visitors are flocking back. London has never been better. It's in the midst of an ongoing urban renaissance that has made it more roamable and visitor-friendly than ever. In the coming years, as the 2012 Olympics approach, the city will see even more exciting changes.

Ever since 1997, when Tony Blair's New Labour party put an end to the Tories' Thatcherite policies, people everywhere have been hailing Britain's capital as *the* happening place. Call it a multiethnic semi-European cultural epicenter. It's got the hottest fashion designers; the most mouthwateringly inventive dining scene; the most exciting theater, music, and dance; the greatest museums; an increasingly visible art world; fabulous shopping; and since it's a royal and celebrity hangout, it's a hotbed of gossip and scandal, all of which you can read about every day in London's many newspapers and tabloids (for a lowdown on recent royal scandals, see "London in Depth," appendix A).

Below I've summarized some of the newer events and experiences that await you in London.

PLANNING YOUR TRIP The U.K.'s national tourism agency has changed its name from the stern and rather forbidding British Tourist Authority to the snazzier and more forthright **VisitBritain** (**www.visitbritain.com**). It's closed its walk-in offices in Chicago and Canada, so in North America everything now gets filtered through the New York office (see "Visitor Information," in chapter 2 for contact information). You can still get all kinds of useful information from them, and the website is far more user-friendly.

London's "official" website is now **www.visitlondon.com**. The London Tourist Board closed its Tourist Information Centre in the forecourt of Victoria Station and moved over to share space in what is now the **Britain & London Visitor Centre**, 1 Regent St., SW1 (see "Visitor Information" in chapter 3 for contact information).

GETTING AROUND As of press time, all service had been restored to the London Underground, but security alerts—most of them caused by riders reporting unattended bags—were causing many delays. It serves as a reminder never to leave your luggage, bags, or packages unattended in an Underground station or in a train, bus, or ferry.

In general, London's public transportation system has seen steady improvement under Mayor Ken Livingstone. London Transport—the agency responsible for the Underground, buses, and ferries—has been reorganized and renamed **Transport for London,** with a comprehensive new website: **www.tfl.gov.uk**. For all questions regarding travel in London, call **© 020/7222-1234.**

Overall, there's less traffic congestion in London these days because of the "congestion charge" that went into effect in 2003. Drivers now pay £5 ($9) for the privilege of driving into Central London during specified times of the day; the fee is likely to increase in 2006.

If you're traveling on a budget, you'll be using public transportation rather than expensive taxis to get around this enormous city. With a money-saving **Visitor Travelcard** (see chapter 3 for details), you can go anywhere by bus or Underground without the hassle of buying individual tickets. The passes, which you can buy in London at any Underground station, are good for 1, 3, or 7 days, and they are a great value. In addition to unlimited Tube and bus travel, the cards get you a third off the price of Thames boat trips. That includes the "Tate to Tate" river shuttle between the two Tate galleries. See chapter 3 for more information on navigating London.

If you're arriving at Heathrow bear in mind that the **Heathrow Terminal 4 Underground station is closed until sometime in 2006** and a dedicated bus line carries visitors from Terminal 4 to Hatton Cross station on the Piccadilly line. This is a result of work on the gigantic new Terminal 5, scheduled to open in 2011. For more on arriving at Heathrow, see "Flying into Heathrow," in chapter 2.

To help you explore the South Bank, which is bursting with fresh energy, a new **Riverside RV1 bus service** travels between Waterloo Bridge and Tower Bridge, stopping at or near all the new South Bank attractions—like the British Airways London Eye, County Hall with the Saatchi Gallery, and the Shakespeare Globe Theatre & Exhibition. It's the same fare as all London buses (£1.20/$2.25), or you can use your Visitor Travelcard.

ACCOMMODATIONS In general, hotels and B&Bs held their prices steady between 2004 and 2005, and it's reasonable to expect they'll do the same in 2006. If the hotel prices look exorbitant, it's because of the shrinking dollar, not because of higher prices in London. Every hotel I visited while researching this edition of *London from $95 a Day* urged me to tell readers to check the hotel's website for special deals and promotions. Doing so may land you a much better rate than the standard nondiscounted "rack rates" I list. It's impossible to enumerate the ever-changing special deals that are offered throughout the year, but a little Web research can pay off handsomely. When booking your hotel room, remember to ask about specials.

Though it opened too late to be fully reviewed for this guide, budget travelers should take note that Central London now has its first easyHotel, 14 Lexham Gardens, W8 (www.easyHotel.com), just off the Cromwell Road between South Kensington and Earl's Court. Room rates start at an almost unbelievable £20 ($37) a night, but don't expect glamour or even a window for that matter. The hotel has 34 double rooms, all with double mattresses and a quilt, en suite bathrooms with towels, air-conditioning, and pay-as-you-go television at £5 ($9) per 24 hours. There is one disabled room, and only three of the rooms have windows. The rooms come in three sizes—small, very small, and tiny (or to be more precise, 80, 70, and 60 sq. ft. respectively). easyHotel has one member of staff permanently on-site, but there are no services other than accommodations and no common or public areas other than a manned reception desk.

A nice surprise for budget travelers who stay in the Victoria & Westminster area is the makeover of the **Luna Simone Hotel** (p. 108), 47–49 Belgrave Rd., SW1 (✆ **020/7834-5897;** www.lunasimonehotel.com). It now has a smooth contemporary look that makes it a real standout among mostly frumpy B&Bs.

Backpackers, take note: **St. Christopher's Village** (p. 112) recently opened a hostel on Shepherds Bush green (✆ **020/7407-1856;** www.st-christophers.co.uk), a scruffy neighborhood west of Notting Hill, home to the BBC and squads of young travelers from overseas. See chapter 5 for more places to lay your head without straining your wallet.

DINING The high cost of dining out in London makes even Londoners careful with their pounds. That said, there are still lots of places that are *almost* reasonable and good options for travelers on tight budgets. One of my favorite "dining" spots is actually a sandwich shop: **Pret a Manger** has locations all over London and offers fabulous, fresh, healthy sandwiches and salads for £3 to £5 ($5.50–$9). If you eat in, the cost is slightly higher than if you take away.

The South Bank is becoming more and more popular, and it's about time that visitors discovered the delights on the other side of the Thames, including the marvelous Thames-side path from Westminster Bridge down to Tower Bridge. There's been a move to reinvent down-market (and down-budget) Indian street food at **Masala Zone** (p. 138), 9 Marshall St., W1 (✆ **020/7287-9966**), and **Mela** (p. 148), 152–156 Shaftesbury Ave., WC2 (✆ **020/7836-8635**). This reaction against "see and be seen" dining is part of the waning popularity of the megarestaurants that were so hot in the booming '90s but are now looking a bit forlorn.

SIGHTSEEING When I said that London is more visitor-friendly than ever, I wasn't just blowing PR bubbles. Get this: All of London's national museums—world-class institutions like the British Museum, the Victoria & Albert, the Natural History Museum, the Science Museum, the Museum of London, the Tate Modern, and the Tate Britain—are now free. This opens up the cultural side of London as never before. Some of these places used to charge £8 ($14) admission. Now you can visit any of London's unforgettable treasure troves on a whim, and even take the entire family, without anxiously biting your nails over the cost.

In addition to that, the museums themselves have never looked spiffier or been more inviting. Marvelous new galleries have opened in the **Victoria & Albert Museum** (p. 174), Cromwell Rd., SW7 (✆ **020/7942-2000**); the **Tate Britain** (p. 172), Millbank, SW1 (✆ **020/7887-8000**); and the **Museum of London** (p. 187), 150 London Wall, EC2 (✆ **020/7600-3699**). A life-size animatronic T. Rex is the star of the revamped Dinosaur Galleries in the **Natural History**

Museum (p. 169), Cromwell Rd., SW7 (© **020/7942-5000**). The Natural History Museum has also opened its intriguing new **Darwin Centre,** which showcases the private collection of Charles Darwin, father of evolutionary theory, and houses the museum's huge collection of preserved specimens. The new Wellcome Wing in the **Science Museum** (p. 170), Exhibition Rd., SW7 (© **020/7942-4000**), is full of intriguing interactive exhibits. And then, of course, there's the "new" **British Museum** (p. 161), Great Russell St., WC1 (© **020/7323-8000**) with its stunning Great Court; the new covered courtyard at the **Wallace Collection** (p. 190), Manchester Sq., W1 (© **020/7563-9500**); and the fabulous **Tate Modern** (p. 172), Bankside, SE3 (© **020/7887-8000**), one of London's most popular attractions. Where else in the world could you have such incredible pickings for free?

The new **Museum in Docklands** (p. 193), No. 1 Warehouse, West India Quay, Hertsmere Road, E14 (© **0870/444-3856**), unlocks the history of London's river, port, and people. Originally used to house imports of exotic spices, rum, and cotton, the warehouse-turned-museum now holds a wealth of objects, from enormous whale bones to World War II gas masks, which provide glimpses of the people that have come and gone from the Docks over the last 2,000 years.

If you're returning to London after some time away, you'll be thrilled to see the transformation of **Trafalgar Square.** Formerly cut off from easy access by a hellishly busy street, the square has now been joined to the National Gallery, encouraging pedestrians to visit instead of making them dodge the roaring traffic. The first phase of this revamp was completed in 2003; there will be further cosmetic and symbolic changes made to Trafalgar Square in the coming years.

Architecturally, in addition to historic stars like the Tower of London, Westminster Abbey, and Buckingham Palace, London has a host of new glamorpuss buildings and structures, including Sir Norman Foster's environmentally "green" **City Hall,** his "glass gherkin" skyscraper in the City at 30 St. Mary Axe (where one of the windows fell out in 2005), and his sleek **Millennium Bridge** linking St. Paul's to the Tate Modern (the wobblies that forced the closure of the bridge the day after it opened have been repaired). Graceful new pedestrian walkways on **Hungerford Bridge** make walking from Embankment to the South Bank a real pleasure, day or night.

Americans will be interested to hear that the house where **Benjamin Franklin** lived between 1757 and 1775 is due to open to the public in 2006 after a lengthy and on-going restoration; to find out more, call © **020/7930-9121.**

See chapter 7 for details on all of London's museums and attractions.

SHOPPING **Spitalfields Market** is undergoing a complete metamorphosis, and the old streets around it are bustling with new activity. If you love traditional British foods and confectionery, one new "old" store worth checking out is **A. Gold,** 42 Brushfield St., E7 (© **020/7247-2487**; www.agold.co.uk). Old-fashioned and hard-to-find candies like the slightly medicinal-tasting Army and Navies and soft, mouth-puckering lemon sours share shelf space with all manner of U.K.-made treats.

AFTER DARK At press time, the newest hot ticket is the Elton John/Stephen Daldry musical version of the film **"Billy Elliott,"** which opened in May 2005 at the **Victoria Palace Theatre,** Victoria St., SW1 (© **0870/895-5577**). The other big musical hit, also based on a movie, is **"Mary Poppins,"** playing at **Prince Edward Theatre,** Old

Compton St., W1 (© **0870/850-9198**). It looks like both musicals will be running for a long time.

If you love symphony concerts, you'll love the new prices for tickets to hear the fabulous **London Symphony Orchestra** at the Barbican Centre, Silk St., EC2 (© **020/7638-8891;** www.lso.co.uk): all seats in this acoustically brilliant hall go for £5 to £20 ($9–$38). Similarly, opera fans who show up at 10am on the day of performance at the **English National Opera,** St. Martin's Lane, WC2 (© **020/7632-8300;** www.eno.org) are usually able to snag a ticket for £5 or £10 ($9–$18).

Speaking of the **English National (ENO)**, its home, the **London Coliseum,** has now completed the refurb of its public spaces and auditorium that began in 2000. A new glass-roofed bar area has enhanced the upper floors, and everything inside and out looks significantly fresher.

Royal Festival Hall, the 50-year-old music and arts complex on the South Bank (see "Major Arts Venues," in chapter 9), is currently in the midst of a major indoor/outdoor refurbishment that will continue into 2007. The big concert hall will remain open, but Queen Elizabeth Hall will be closed for part of 2006.

The **Royal Shakespeare Company** (p. 234), based in Stratford-upon-Avon, no longer performs in London at its old home in the Barbican. Instead, it utilizes West End theaters like the Gielgud on Shaftesbury Avenue for its London productions.

Club nights are still a big deal, but the days of superclubs being hot news just for being big is well over. It's impossible to track what the next faddy scene will be. Only in London will you find **School Disco.com** (p. 245), a Saturday nighter for which 2,000 allegedly cool kids dress up in school uniforms. A less-uniformy crowd heads for intimate club bars like **Cargo** (p. 247), Kingsland Viaduct, 83 Rivington St., EC2 (© **020/7739-3440**), where the cover for live music, DJs, dancing, and food is almost as cheap as a nightclub in the 1950s. See chapter 9 for more budget-friendly nightlife options.

1

The Best of London from $95 a Day

London is one of the most expensive cities in the world, but that doesn't mean you can't enjoy a marvelous, affordable vacation there. That's why this guidebook was written. Here are some of the best sightseeing, lodging, and dining options for travelers who want a great vacation without breaking the bank.

1 Frommer's Favorite London Moments

- **Roam Along the River.** I'm torn between two favorite strolls. A newly spruced-up walk runs uninterrupted along the south bank of the Thames from the British Airways London Eye, opposite the Houses of Parliament, to Southwark, past a score of must-visit sights, including the Tate Modern and the Millennium Bridge, to Tower Bridge and beyond. For a different but just as lovely pedestrian perspective on London, take the footpath heading west from Putney along the river. The luminous tunnel of trees leads past the world's largest urban wetland sanctuary to Hammersmith Bridge. Cross over there for a pint at one of the pubs between the string of north-bank boathouses.
- **Take to the Streets.** It's not just Covent Garden where strollers can watch great street entertainment while grazing. Millions have gone into refurbishing the courtyard at Somerset House, on the other side of the Strand, and there's nearly always something going on there. The summer cafe on the river terrace is one of the most delightful cheap lunch spots in town. Another favorite pastime is to pick up the Sunday paper and head to Soho for a late breakfast at one of the tempting patisseries. With the throngs of locals and visitors, it has a wonderful urban buzz.
- **Get a Rooftop View.** The giant British Airways London Eye (p. 160) slowly lifts you 135 feet in the air for a staggering 25-mile view across the city. There are also stunning panoramas from the dome of St. Paul's Cathedral, from the tower of Westminster Cathedral, and from the Wellington Arch at Hyde Park Corner. But you have to get out your wallet to enjoy all of these bird's-eye views. Savvy travelers head for an unofficial picnic spot—the glass-walled corner room on level 7—at our favorite freebie, Tate Modern (p. 172). For another great city profile, just walk across Tower Bridge.
- **Time-Travel into Pageantry from the Past.** The Brits have had centuries to practice their pomp and circumstance, which is why they've got ceremonies like the Changing of the Guard at Buckingham Palace and

Impressions

Anybody who enjoys being in the House of Commons probably needs psychiatric care.

—Ken Livingstone MP, now Mayor of London, in the *Evening Standard,* February 26, 1988

Horse Guards Parade down to a fine art (see the box "Changing of the Guard" on p. 161).

- **Take in a Show with "Auntie."** That's the nickname for the BBC among Brits of a certain generation. The Beeb, as it's also known, is always keen to recruit audiences for its TV and radio shows, and tickets are free. If you're a fan of quirky British humor, try to catch Radio4 favorites *The News Quiz* and *I'm Sorry I Haven't a Clue,* the latter hosted by famous jazzman Humphrey Littleton. Some of the references will be pretty obscure to out-of-towners, but you're guaranteed a good giggle. See "Entertainment on a Shoestring" in chapter 9.
- **Make like a Modern Mary Poppins.** Nannies have always taken their charges to the park for a dose of healthy fresh air before afternoon tea. Today, you're more likely to see stay-at-home dads in charge or young Aussie travelers earning money to hop over to another European country. They'll be heading for the scramble-on pirate ship at the Peter Pan playground in Kensington Gardens, a memorial to Princess Diana. The other Mary Poppins treat is watching the keepers feed the pelicans, descended from a pair given by the Russian ambassador in the 17th century, by the lake in St. James's Park. See "Parks & Gardens" in chapter 7.
- **Drool over Aspirational Antiques.** London is a fantastic place to browse for antiques. Go to a free preauction viewing of rare treasures and weird arcana at one of the big salerooms—Christie's, Sotheby's, Phillips, or Bonhams. Serious treasure-hunters should set their alarm clocks for a dawn raid on Bermondsey market, where dealers come to sniff out bargains at 5:30am. Portobello market is on Saturday—not quite such an early start, but bolt your breakfast to beat the tourist hordes. Camden Passage is best on Wednesday and Saturday when stalls set up outdoors. See "Auction Houses" and "Markets" under "Shopping A to Z" in chapter 8.
- **Label Yourself for Less.** If you love the traditional Burberry look—it even does tartan bikinis these days—but hate the astronomical prices, you'll do what price-busting locals do and head for the factory shop in Hackney (p. 221). For wannabe It-girls and -boys, there's one stop—Top Shop at Oxford Circus (p. 221). It has persuaded a gang of great designers to create exclusive collections that even show up in the pages of *Vogue*—in the cheap, cheap shopping section.
- **Be a Good Sport.** Horse racing is much less snobby than you might imagine from watching the Derby or Ascot on TV. A great way to spend a summer Monday evening is to take the boat up the river to Royal Windsor Racecourse (p. 256), with a picnic and a bottle of fake champagne—you can buy a glass of the real stuff there.
- **Steal a Musical Moment.** Lots of London's major arts venues do giveaways, perhaps to prove that they're

Central London

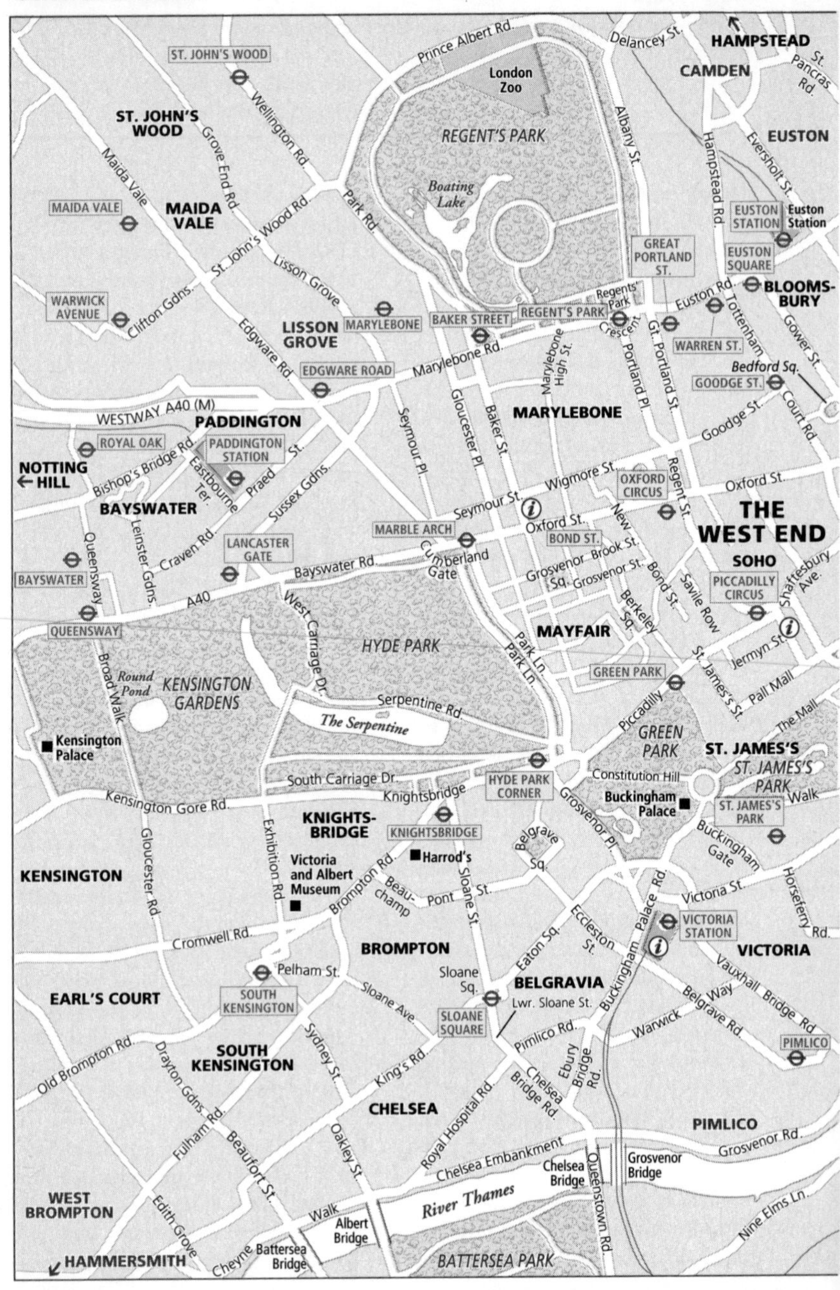

HAMPSTEAD
CAMDEN
EUSTON
Prince Albert Rd.
Delancey St.
St. Pancras Rd.
ST. JOHN'S WOOD
London Zoo
REGENT'S PARK
Boating Lake
ST. JOHN'S WOOD
Wellington Rd.
Grove End Rd.
Maida Vale
Albany St.
Hampstead Rd.
Eversholt St.
MAIDA VALE
MAIDA VALE
Park Rd.
St. John's Wood Rd.
EUSTON STATION
Euston Station
GREAT PORTLAND ST.
EUSTON SQUARE
BLOOMS-BURY
Lisson Grove
WARWICK AVENUE
Clifton Gdns.
St. John's Wood Rd.
Regents' Park Crescent
Euston Rd.
Tottenham
Gower St.
LISSON GROVE
MARYLEBONE
BAKER STREET
REGENT'S PARK
WARREN ST.
Edgware Rd.
Marylebone Rd.
Marylebone High St.
Portland Pl.
Gt. Portland St.
Bedford Sq.
EDGWARE ROAD
GOODGE ST.
Court Rd.
WESTWAY A40 (M)
PADDINGTON
Seymour Pl.
Gloucester Pl.
Baker St.
MARYLEBONE
Goodge St.
ROYAL OAK
PADDINGTON STATION
Bishop's Bridge Rd.
Eastbourne Ter.
Praed St.
Sussex Gdns.
NOTTING HILL
Wigmore St.
OXFORD CIRCUS
Regent St.
Oxford St.
BAYSWATER
Seymour St.
New Bond St.
THE WEST END
Leinster Gdns.
Craven Rd.
Oxford St.
MARBLE ARCH
BOND ST.
SOHO
Queensway
LANCASTER GATE
Cumberland Gate
Grosvenor Sq.
Brook St.
Grosvenor St.
Savile Row
PICCADILLY CIRCUS
Shaftesbury Ave.
BAYSWATER
Bayswater Rd.
A40
West Carriage Dr.
Berkeley Sq.
QUEENSWAY
HYDE PARK
MAYFAIR
Jermyn St.
Broad Walk
Round Pond
KENSINGTON GARDENS
Park Ln.
GREEN PARK
St. James's St.
Pall Mall
Serpentine Rd.
The Serpentine
Piccadilly
GREEN PARK
The Mall
Kensington Palace
ST. JAMES'S
ST. JAMES'S PARK
South Carriage Dr.
HYDE PARK CORNER
Constitution Hill
Kensington Gore Rd.
Knightsbridge
Buckingham Palace
Walk
Grosvenor Pl.
ST. JAMES'S PARK
KNIGHTS-BRIDGE
KNIGHTSBRIDGE
Exhibition Rd.
Gloucester Rd.
Belgrave Sq.
Buckingham Gate
Harrod's
KENSINGTON
Victoria and Albert Museum
Brompton Rd.
Beau-champ
Pont St.
Sloane St.
Horseferry Rd.
Palace Rd.
Victoria St.
VICTORIA STATION
Eccleston St.
Cromwell Rd.
Eaton Sq.
BROMPTON
VICTORIA
Pelham St.
Sloane Sq.
BELGRAVIA
EARL'S COURT
SOUTH KENSINGTON
Sloane Ave.
Lwr. Sloane St.
Buckingham
Vauxhall Bridge Rd.
Belgrave Rd.
Warwick Way
SLOANE SQUARE
Pimlico Rd.
PIMLICO
Old Brompton Rd.
Drayton Gdns.
SOUTH KENSINGTON
Sydney St.
King's Rd.
Ebury Bridge Rd.
Chelsea Bridge Rd.
Royal Hospital Rd.
CHELSEA
Fulham Rd.
Oakley St.
PIMLICO
Beaufort St.
Chelsea Embankment
Grosvenor Rd.
Chelsea Bridge
Queenstown Rd.
Grosvenor Bridge
WEST BROMPTON
River Thames
Nine Elms Ln.
Edith Grove
Walk
Albert Bridge
Cheyne
Battersea Bridge
BATTERSEA PARK
HAMMERSMITH

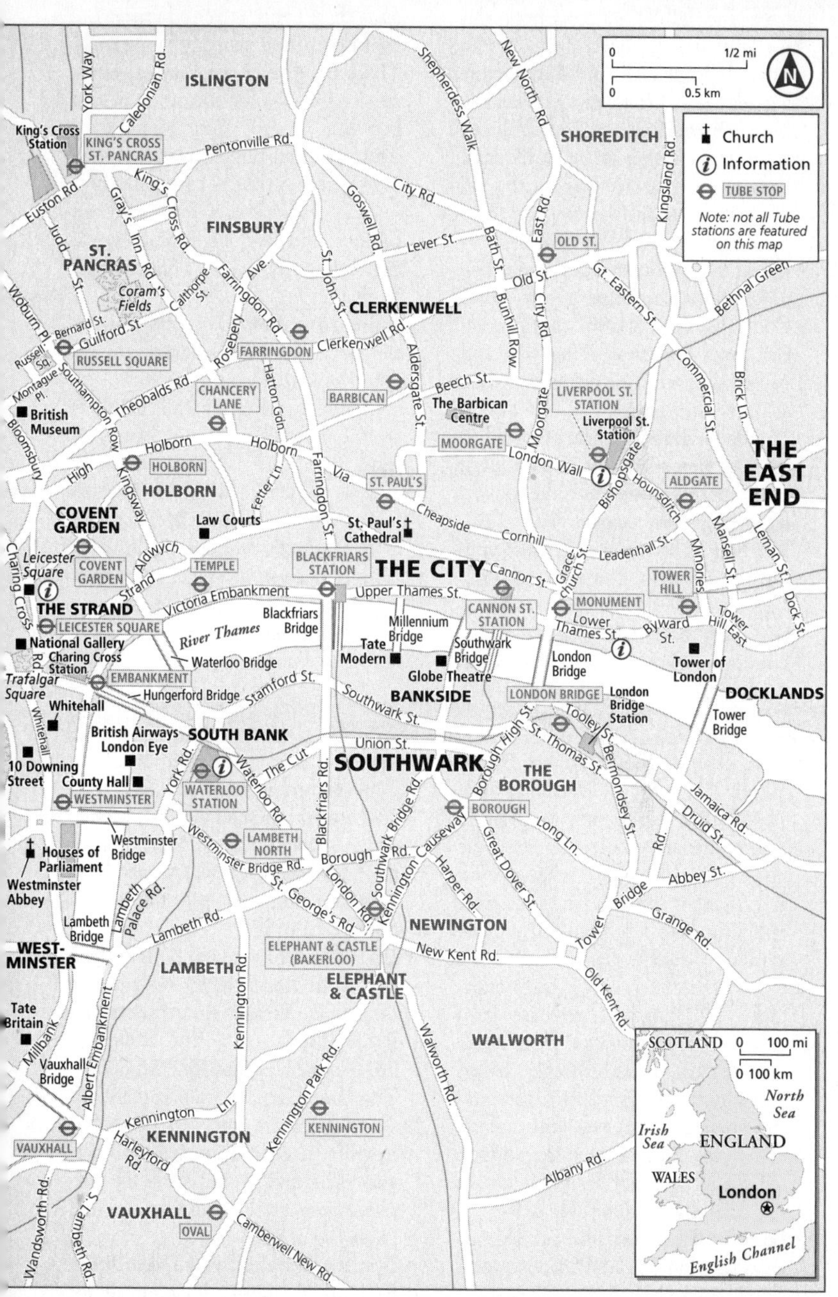
0 1/2 mi
0 0.5 km
N
Church
Information
TUBE STOP
Note: not all Tube stations are featured on this map
ISLINGTON
SHOREDITCH
FINSBURY
ST. PANCRAS
CLERKENWELL
HOLBORN
COVENT GARDEN
THE CITY
THE EAST END
THE STRAND
BANKSIDE
SOUTH BANK
SOUTHWARK
THE BOROUGH
DOCKLANDS
NEWINGTON
WEST-MINSTER
LAMBETH
ELEPHANT & CASTLE
WALWORTH
KENNINGTON
VAUXHALL
King's Cross Station
KING'S CROSS ST. PANCRAS
York Way
Caledonian Rd.
Pentonville Rd.
Shepherdess Walk
New North Rd
Kingsland Rd.
City Rd.
Goswell Rd.
Bath St.
East Rd.
OLD ST.
Lever St.
Old St.
Gt. Eastern St.
Bethnal Green
Euston Rd.
King's Cross Rd.
Gray's Inn Rd.
Judd St.
Coram's Fields
Calthorpe St.
Farringdon Rd.
Ave.
Rosebery
St. John St.
Bunhill Row
City Rd.
Woburn Pl.
Bernard St.
Guilford St.
Russell Sq.
RUSSELL SQUARE
Montague Pl.
Southampton Row
FARRINGDON
Clerkenwell Rd.
Aldersgate St.
Commercial St.
Brick Ln.
Theobalds Rd.
CHANCERY LANE
Hatton Gdn.
BARBICAN
Beech St.
The Barbican Centre
Moorgate
LIVERPOOL ST. STATION
Liverpool St. Station
British Museum
Bloomsbury
Holborn
HOLBORN
Farringdon St.
Via.
MOORGATE
London Wall
Bishopsgate
Houndsditch
ALDGATE
High
Kingsway
Fetter Ln.
ST. PAUL'S
Cheapside
Law Courts
St. Paul's Cathedral
Cornhill
Leadenhall St.
Minories
Mansell St.
Leman St.
Aldwych
TEMPLE
BLACKFRIARS STATION
Cannon St.
Gracechurch St.
Charing Cross
Leicester Square
COVENT GARDEN
Strand
Victoria Embankment
Upper Thames St.
CANNON ST. STATION
MONUMENT
TOWER HILL
Dock St.
LEICESTER SQUARE
Blackfriars Bridge
Millennium Bridge
Lower Thames St.
Byward St.
Tower Hill East
National Gallery
River Thames
Tate Modern
Southwark Bridge
London Bridge
Tower of London
Charing Cross Station
Waterloo Bridge
Globe Theatre
Trafalgar Square
EMBANKMENT
Stamford St.
LONDON BRIDGE
London Bridge Station
Hungerford Bridge
Southwark St.
Tooley St.
Tower Bridge
Whitehall
British Airways London Eye
Union St.
St. Thomas St.
Bermondsey St.
10 Downing Street
York Rd.
The Cut
Waterloo Rd.
Blackfriars Rd.
Borough High St.
County Hall
WATERLOO STATION
WESTMINSTER
Southwark Bridge Rd.
BOROUGH
Jamaica Rd.
Druid St.
Long Ln.
Westminster Bridge
Westminster Bridge Rd.
LAMBETH NORTH
Borough Rd.
Causeway
Great Dover St.
Harper Rd.
Rd.
Houses of Parliament
Westminster Abbey
St. George's Rd.
London Rd.
Kennington
Abbey St.
Bridge
Lambeth Palace Rd.
Lambeth Bridge
Lambeth Rd.
Grange Rd.
Tower
ELEPHANT & CASTLE (BAKERLOO)
New Kent Rd.
Old Kent Rd.
Kennington Rd.
Tate Britain
Millbank
Albert Embankment
Walworth Rd.
Vauxhall Bridge
Kennington Park Rd.
Kennington Ln.
KENNINGTON
Harleyford Rd.
VAUXHALL
Albany Rd.
Wandsworth Rd.
S. Lambeth Rd.
OVAL
Camberwell New Rd.
SCOTLAND
0 100 mi
0 100 km
North Sea
Irish Sea
ENGLAND
WALES
London
English Channel

worth all those millions of pounds from the public purse. Check out Commuter Jazz in the foyer of the Royal Festival Hall (p. 242) and the Monday lunchtime concerts at the Royal Opera House (p. 241). You can enjoy the summer opera at Holland Park Theater for free while sitting on the grass outside (see the box "Performers in the Park" on p. 238).

- **Invest in the Theatrical Future.** The productions you'll see at the Royal Court Theatre (p. 233) could be on Broadway next year. Why wait and pay astronomical ticket prices when all seats here go for £7.50 ($14) on Monday nights? If you're prepared to gamble, here's an even better deal: last-minute standbys at the downstairs stage cost a token 10p (18¢). The Soho Theatre (p. 237) also specializes in new writing and only charges £5 ($9) a seat on Mondays.
- **Go Early-Bird Clubbing.** Lots of London's nightspots start the evening as bars. Go before the DJ plugs in, and there's no cover charge. You could even find that it's happy hour. That's the deal at Bar Rumba, where drinks are two for the price of one between 5 and 9pm Monday to Thursday. You can even learn to salsa at the preclub classes. Later on, a hot-'n'-cool crowd comes for a different funky sound every night of the week. See "Entertainment on a Shoestring," in chapter 9.
- **Raise Your Elbow.** A pub-crawl is the best way to re-educate anyone who thinks beer is that anemic, aerated, and antarctically chilled yellow stuff. For a really good pint of real ale head for Jerusalem Tavern in Clerkenwell (p. 250), which is stocked with over 20 different brews to try from St. Peter's Brewery in Suffolk. If it's a pint of stout you're after, then crawl over to the always-crowded Toucan in Soho (p. 252).

2 Best Hotel Bets on a Budget

- **Best Overall Value: Arran House Hotel,** 77 Gower St., WC1 (© **020/7636-2186**), isn't a ritzy place at all. The rooms are simple, and some are quite small. But look at what it offers at extremely competitive rates: roses rambling across a beautiful private garden; double-glazed windows masking traffic noise; a truly enormous full English breakfast (two types of bacon, sausages, fried bread, French toast, scrambled eggs, baked beans, tomatoes, grapefruit, toast and jam, orange juice, tea, and coffee); use of the kitchen to make supper; self-service laundry facilities; and a very friendly welcome. See p. 97.
- **Best for Families:** The British Airways London Eye is right next door. The Houses of Parliament are on the opposite bank of the river. The London Aquarium is in the basement. And there's a restaurant with robotic waiters. Do not pass go. Head straight for **Travel Inn Capital, County Hall,** Belvedere Rd., SE1 (© **0870/242-8000**). See p. 111.
- **Best for Do-It-Yourself Travelers:** You won't find a better self-catering deal than **Astons Apartments,** 31 Rosary Gardens, SW7 (© **800/525-2810** in the U.S., or 020/7590-6000). The South Ken location is fabulous; the rooms are nice; the staff is friendly; there's daily maid service; and each unit comes with its own kitchenette, so you can save on food costs. See p. 82.
- **Best for Travelers with Disabilities:** Sadly, there aren't a lot of rivals for

this recommendation. **Regent Palace Hotel,** Piccadilly Circus, W1 (✆ **020/7734-0716**) has 32 units, and it is right in the thick of things. See p. 96. The **Citadines Trafalgar Square,** 18–21 Northumberland Ave., WC2 (✆ **0800/376-3898**), is a splurge but good for people on longer visits who prefer the flexibility of self-catering. It has 16 adapted studios and a one-bedroom apartment. See p. 105.

- **Best for Nonsmokers:** The filthy weed is banned outright at **Jenkins Hotel,** 45 Cartwright Gardens, WC1 (✆ **020/7387-2067**), where the strokeable Labradors are a good substitute if you're missing your four-legged friend. See p. 101.
- **Best for Romantics:** You may have to forge a marriage certificate, but it's worth it because honeymooners can sometimes jump the queue for a four-poster bed at **Wigmore Court Hotel,** 23 Gloucester Place, W1 (✆ **020/7935-0928**). See p. 95.
- **Best Jumbo Breakfast:** The Davies family cooks a huge fat-boy breakfast *and* gives guests free run at a buffet of fruit, yogurt, croissants, and cereals, at **Harlingford Hotel,** 61–63 Cartwright Gardens, WC1 (✆ **020/7387-1551**). See p. 100. For a local treat, check into **Vicarage Private Hotel,** 10 Vicarage Gate, W8 (✆ **020/7229-4030**). It's the only budget guesthouse I've seen with kippers (smoked herring) and porridge on the menu. See p. 83. As befits a Frommer's top tip, **Arran House** (see above) also sets out a bumper feast.
- **Best for Serious Shoppers:** Put a padlock on your wallet if you're staying at either of these. **The Willett Hotel** (✆ **800/270-9206**) is just round the corner from Peter Jones in Sloane Square and a 5-minute walk to Chelsea's King's Road. See p. 83. The **Ivanhoe Suite Hotel,** 1 St. Christopher's Place, W1 (✆ **020/7935-1047**), is in a little pedestrian enclave off Oxford Street, crammed with boutiques. See p. 95.
- **Best for Theater Buffs: The Fielding Hotel,** 4 Broad Court, WC2 (✆ **020/7836-8305**), is right by the Royal Opera House, in the heart of theatrical Covent Garden, which is why so many of its guests are performers and their groupies. See p. 107.
- **Best for Interior Design Tips:** The **Rushmore Hotel,** 11 Trebovir Rd., SW5 (✆ **020/7370-3839**), is an extravaganza of muraled ceilings and stage-set bedrooms. See p. 84. It is only rivaled for va-va-voom by a less refined, even more over-the-top splurge, **The Pavilion,** 34–36 Sussex Gardens, W2 (✆ **020/7262-0905**). See p. 93.
- **Best for Party Animals on a Shoestring:** For as little as £16 ($30) a night, **St. Christopher's Village,** 165 Borough High St., SE1 (✆ **020/7407-1856**), offers you a sauna and hot tub on the roof, a basement nightclub, and affordable grub. See p. 112.
- **Best for Net Addicts:** Guests get free, unlimited Web access at **InterneSt@ Portobello Gold,** 97 Portobello Rd., W1 (✆ **020/7460-4910**). The cyber bar at this old converted pub is right in the middle of the antiques stalls during the Saturday market. See p. 86.

3 Best Dining Bets on a Budget

- **Best Overall Value:** The name of Nico Ladenis has been synonymous with splurgey London dining for decades, so it's a shock and a delight to find that the ambrosial three-course lunch and early-bird menu at his new eatery, **Incognico,** 117 Shaftesbury Ave., WC2 (✆ **020/7836-8866**), costs a mere £13 ($23). Nico has retired from the kitchen, but this remains a classy budget blow-out.

- **Best Fixed-Price Bargain:** Indian food is the hot thing, so it seems fitting to split this accolade between a newer restaurant and an old friend. **Masala Zone,** 9 Marshall St., W1 (✆ **020/7287-9966**), restyles traditional street food, offering *thalis* from £6 ($11): this meal on a tray includes a curry, bowls of vegetables, dal, yogurt curry, rice, poppadums, chapattis, chutneys, and raita. See p. 138. Or try a South Indian feast at longtime budget favorite, **Diwana Bhel Poori House,** 121 Drummond St., NW1 (✆ **020/7387-5556**), for just £6.50 ($12), and you can bring your own wine with no charge. See p. 145.
- **Best for Families:** Talking drink trolleys circle the restaurant like R2D2 while the food circles on a long conveyor belt. So tell me **YO! Sushi** isn't kid heaven! The restaurant's many branches are heaven for Mom and Pop, too, because at most branches the kids eat for free from Monday to Friday. There are scaled down and toned down dishes for them, from chicken nuggets to fish fingers. See p. 136.
- **Best for a Grand Entrance:** The sweeping staircase down into the multileveled **Boxwood Café,** Berkeley Hotel, Wilton Place, SW1 (✆ **020/7235-1010**), could have been made for a royal entrance. And the £21 ($39) fixed-price lunch, though a splurge, is a delightful way to break up your Knightsbridge shopping spree. See p. 121.
- **Best of Britain I:** Lily Langtry and Edward VII used to tryst at **Rules,** 35 Maiden Lane, WC2 (✆ **020/7836-5314**), and this 200-year-old restaurant still specializes in feathered and furred game—farmed now, rather than blasted onto the plate with a 12-bore shotgun. See p. 150.
- **Best of Britain II:** Cabbies know everything, and they're always right, as you'll find out if you travel by taxi. Their vote goes to **North Sea Fish Restaurant,** 7–8 Leigh St., WC1 (✆ **020/7387-5892**), for the national dish, fish and chips. See p. 144.
- **Best Pub Grub:** The beef-and-ale pie at the **Museum Tavern,** 49 Great Russell St., WC1 (✆ **020/7242-8987**), is a hearty bite. Or, if you want to go gastropub, check out **The Atlas,** 16 Seagrave Rd., SW6 (✆ **020/7385-9129**), where the chef likes to apply a Spanish or a North African twist to his Mediterranean cuisine. See p. 127.
- **Best for Sunday Lunch:** The three-course Sunday lunch at **Maggie Jones's,** 6 Old Court Place, off Kensington Church Street, W8 (✆ **020/7937-6462**), is like granny used to make, offering such national culinary treasures as roast beef with Yorkshire pudding and yum-scrum apple crumble. See p. 124.
- **Best Barbecues:** Enjoy the sizzle and smells of steaks, lamb, sausages, and corn-fed chicken cooked to order by the Hellbergs, who run **Arkansas Café,** Old Spitalfields Market, E1 (✆ **020/7377-6999**). Keir gets up at dawn to choose the best meat from Smithfield Market and posts the life story of each cut. See p. 152.
- **Best for Vegetarians:** Amid the fleshpots of Soho, **Mildred's,** 45 Lexington St., W1 (✆ **020/7494-1634**), can do magical things with a pinto bean and organic wine. See p. 136.
- **Best for Nonsmokers:** You can't light up at **Wagamama,** 4a Streatham St.

(off Coptic St.), WC1 (© **020/7323-9223**), which is fun and frantically busy anyway. See p. 144. Nor is nicotine allowed to yellow the shelves at top shopping and lunch spot, **Books for Cooks,** 4 Blenheim Crescent, W11 (© **020/7221-1992**). See p. 130.

- **Best for a Romantic Dinner:** No restaurant can rival the cozy candlelit charm of **Andrew Edmunds,** 46 Lexington St., W1 (© **020/7437-5708**), where young locals whispering sweet nothings make up the bulk of the clientele. Afterward, wander the buzzing streets of Soho hand in hand. See p. 133.
- **Best View:** Raise yourself above the hoi polloi in Covent Garden Piazza at **Chez Gerard at the Opera Terrace,** First Floor, Covent Garden Central Market, WC2 (© **020/7379-0666**). Even the stilt-walkers won't be able to interrupt your meal. See p. 148.
- **Best for the Morning After: The Star Café,** 22 Great Chapel St., W1 (© **020/7437-8778**), does a fantastic all-day breakfast. And if the situation is grave enough, you can get a Bloody Mary from the pub downstairs. See p. 137.
- **Best Gory Story:** The 17th-century It-girl Lady Elizabeth Hatton was murdered in Bleeding Heart Yard in the middle of her annual winter ball. Now some say she's a see-through regular at **Bleeding Heart Bistro & Tavern,** off Greville Street, EC1 (© **020/7404-0333**), which you'll find in the yard today. This restored 1746 tavern serves earthy regional English cuisine and robust real ale. See p. 152.

2

Planning an Affordable Trip to London

Planning an affordable trip to one of the most expensive cities in the world is a challenge, but it's certainly not impossible, especially if you make arrangements in advance. Your trip will be much more fun—and certainly a lot smoother—if you plan it properly. This chapter is designed to help you do that, step by step.

1 The $95-a-Day Premise

Our premise is that two people traveling together can have a great time in London for about $95 a day per person. That will cover the price of a decent double room, a lunchtime refueling stop at a pub or sandwich shop, and dinner in the evening. It's likely that you'll get a free, full breakfast at your hotel.

After searching the streets of London, I've come up with the best of the budget deals. And don't worry—this doesn't mean you'll have to stay at dingy dives or eat nasty food. Keep in mind that London is now the most expensive city in the world after Tokyo. You may be able to vacation here for less than $95 a day, but it would be difficult. Of course you can definitely do it for a lot more. Included in the book are recommendations on how to do both.

We've found some gem hotels in great locations. Bloomsbury, for example, is a real hot spot for typically English guesthouses catering to travelers of modest means. We've even found a couple of great deals in hotels just off Oxford Street in Marylebone, in Soho, and off the Strand. If you're on a very strict budget, check out both the YHA hostels and the funky commercial ones for the snowboarding generation. I've also reviewed the best student halls.

The biggest revolution for savvy travelers, though, has taken place on the eating scene. New cuisines and revamped old ones—Thai one year, sushi the next, and now new-wave Indian—are storming through budget eateries. Healthy food, from freshly squeezed this to organic that, is converting the meat-and-two-veg crowd all across the city. Even pubs tend to offer much better fare, replacing congealed, pre-packed sludge with hearty homemade dishes. Some have even turned into understated but stylish restaurants known as *gastropubs.* The selections in this book are designed to guide you to the best value options and point out some of the locals' favorites. Take a break from sightseeing on at least 1 day because it's at lunchtime that some of the celebrity chefs lower their prices enough to let in the rest of us.

As for sightseeing, you can't get around the fact that some of the stock-in-trade sights are grossly overpriced—the Tower of London, Madame Tussaud's, and Buckingham Palace, in particular. The good news is that London's major and once pricey national museums have now introduced free admission, and many other exhibitions and galleries are free as well. So you can enjoy a splendidly rich vacation by enjoying these and the street and antiques markets, the rituals and ceremonies that make up London life, and just by strolling through this perennially fascinating city.

2 Fifty Money-Saving Tips

PRETRIP PLANNING & TRANSPORTATION SAVINGS

1. Information pays. Read as much as you can about London before you go. Talk to people who've been there recently. Check in with the **VisitBritain** offices in New York (see "Visitor Information," later in this chapter) for a wealth of free information, including brochures and details about several discount deals: the **London Pass,** a 1-, 2-, 3-, or 6-day saver pass to major museums and galleries (see tip 8, below), and **Great British Heritage Pass** (see tip 9, below). You'll also be able to get maps and helpful booklets like *London Planner, Where to Stay—Budget,* and more.
2. Make a note of the London fun that requires months of forethought. For instance, you'll need to write in for tickets to see the Ceremony of the Keys at the Tower of London (p. 175), or Trooping the Colour (see "London Calendar of Events," later in this chapter). The ballot for Wimbledon tickets closes in December.
3. Travel off season. Airfares and B&B rates are cheaper and easier to get if you travel from late fall through early spring. Winter 2004 saw round-trip New York to London airfares drop as low as $280 (keep in mind, though, that add-on airport taxes for international flights now average about $100). Hotel/flight package prices plummet by hundreds of dollars off season. And, unlikely as it sounds, London is great in the winter. Cultural life is at full throttle, and sightseeing is more rewarding without the summer hordes. You don't have to go in darkest January—in March or October, you'll still reap financial benefits.
4. Reserve and pay in advance, especially if you plan to rent a car. If you book with an agency like **Europe by Car** (© **800/223-1516** in the U.S., or 212/581-3040 in New York; www.europebycar.com), the broker **Kemwel** (© **800/576-1590** in the U.S.; www.kemwel.com), or **Holiday Autos** (© **0870/400-4447** in the U.K.; www.holidayautos.com), you'll pay much less than with a local hire company. Car-rental rates fluctuate based on demand at the online **www.easyRentacar.com**, from £18 ($34) weekdays, transaction fees and insurance included, if you book several weeks ahead, plus 20p (32¢) for every mile over 75 miles. This is a great value for day trips into the English countryside.
5. Fly during the week and early in the morning and save big money. Shop around for your airfare. This will probably be the most expensive part of your trip, so it pays to do some legwork. Surfing the Internet will turn up some great bargains. Alternatively, scour the newspaper for consolidators like **Cheap Tickets** (© **800/377-1000** or 212/570-1179; www.cheaptickets.com), which sells airline seats at a substantial—as much as 60%—discount. Certainly consult your travel agent, who will often be privy to special deals and package rates. Air carriers want to fill every seat on every flight, so they're constantly adjusting the pricing. Also investigate charter

flights on scheduled airlines offered by reliable operators in "Getting There," later in this chapter.

6. Consider buying a **vacation package:** one low price that includes airfare, transfers, accommodations, and some sightseeing discounts. For example, in 2005, Monograms, a division of **Cosmos** (✆ **800/556-5454;** www.globusandcosmos.com) is offering a week in a smartish hotel in London for $1,337 (per person, peak season). Many of the airlines have bargain packages, too. (See "Money-Saving Package Deals," later in this chapter for more information.)
7. Pack light. You won't need a porter, and you're less likely to succumb to the desire for a taxi. But pack small, too, so you don't have spaces just aching to be filled with shopping. ***Note:*** Luggage carts are free in London's airports.
8. If you're planning to visit several high-admission-price attractions, such as the Tower of London, Hampton Court, Kensington Palace, and Windsor Castle, consider buying a **London Pass,** valid for 1, 2, 3, or 6 days ($49, $77, $96, or $135 respectively, with discounts for children). It buys you admission to dozens of attractions, free canal-boat trips and Thames cruises, and discounts on theater and concert tickets, in restaurants and shops, on tours, and free foreign currency exchanges. To buy before you leave home, visit the website **www.londonpass.com**, or call or visit the **British Travel Shop,** 551 Fifth Ave., 7th floor, New York, NY 10176 (✆ **212/557-2170**), next to the VisitBritain office.
9. The **Great British Heritage Pass** is great if you're planning any day trips. You get free entry into 550 public and private historic properties owned by the National Trust, English Heritage, and Historic Royal Palaces. That means Hampton Court Palace, Kensington Palace State Apartments, and Windsor Castle, plus half-price at the Tower of London. Passes are valid for 4 days ($50), 7 days ($75), 15 days ($95), or a month ($130), and there are no discounts for children. In the U.S. call or visit the **British Travel Shop,** 551 Fifth Ave., 7th floor, New York, NY 10176 (✆ **212/557-2170**), next to the VisitBritain office. To obtain the pass in London, take your passport to the Britain & London Visitor Centre, 1 Regent St., SW1, or any tourist information center. At press time, however, the exchange rate did not favor that approach.
10. Before you leave, also get a 3-, 4-, or 7-day **London Visitor Travelcard,** which offers unlimited travel on public transport and is not available in the United Kingdom. Contact your travel agent or the **British Travel Shop** (✆ **212/557-2170**), or buy online from BritRail (www.britrail.com). Visitor Travelcards come with a bunch of discount vouchers, and you can travel at any time (in London, many passes only work after 9:30am: see "Getting Around," in chapter 3). You can choose all zones or just Central London, which will cover most of what you need, even stretching as far as Greenwich. Central zone (zones 1 and 2) adult passes cost $24 for 3 days, $29 for 4 days, and $36 for 7 days; children (ages 5–15) pay $11, $12, and $15 respectively (children under 5 travel free). All-zone cards are $35, $46, and $69 for adults, $16, $19, and $29 for children.
11. International phone calls are exorbitant. Although using a calling card overseas usually carries a surcharge, it's worth checking it out before leaving home: American Express cardholders should ask about the charges

using the company's "Connections" plan. Also see what AT&T, MCI, and Sprint have to offer.

Much less hassle is **eKit** (www.ekit.com)—both the Youth Hostel Association and Council Travel offer their own branded versions. Join for free on the Web, and you'll get free e-mail, cheap access to voice mail and to a "travel vault"—a secure place online to store passport and credit card details, medical records, and so on—and super-cheap international calling rates. The lowest British Telecom (BT) charges are only available on weekends. eKit has one rate 24 hours a day, but you will have to pay for a local call to access the cheapest discount price. Assuming you'll probably be using a pay phone, here's an approximate per-minute comparison calling after 6pm and before 6am: 9p (BT) and 4p (eKit) to the U.S., 9p (BT) and 4p (eKit) to Canada, 9p (BT) and 5p (eKit) to Australia, and 9p (BT), and 5p (eKit) to New Zealand.

ONCE YOU ARRIVE

12. Take public transportation from the airport into the city. The Piccadilly Line on the Underground runs directly from Heathrow to Central London and costs only £3.80 ($7), instead of the £40 ($74) or more that a taxi would cost.
13. Don't use traveler's checks or moneychangers like American Express and other bureaux de change. Instead, go to an overseas ATM and withdraw money from your account at home. You'll get a much better deal on the exchange rate. Do check with your bank first to find out what kind of fee you'll be charged for this service. Above all, don't draw cash on a credit card; you'll pay exorbitant interest rates. Though many of us now rely on credit cards for nearly every purchase we make, in England and elsewhere in Europe this convenience will cost you an additional 3% on average. That's the "conversion fee" many credit card companies and banks now tack on to purchases in a foreign currency.

ACCOMMODATIONS

14. When you're looking for a hotel, try a university area like Bloomsbury first. Other London neighborhoods worth investigating for a good supply of budget hotels are Paddington, Bayswater, Victoria, and Earl's Court. Many options in these and other budget neighborhoods are listed in the free publication, *Where to Stay—Budget,* available from the VisitBritain office in New York (see "Visitor Information," below).
15. Think about what you really want in a hotel room. If a private bathroom isn't crucial to you, you can save anywhere from £10 to £15 ($18–$28) a night.
16. Negotiate the price. Check if the management will give you a discount for staying 3 nights or more. Suggest trade-offs—a lower price for a smaller room or a room minus TV, and so on. Ask for an old-style per-person (not room) rate: On a tight budget, a couple may be able to downgrade to a 4-foot-wide bed normally used as a single; with a bit more cash, you could get a good rate on a triple. If you're on a hotel-lined street like Sussex Gardens in Paddington or Ebury Street near Victoria, keep checking out rooms until you find one you like for your price.
17. Consider alternatives to hotels and guesthouses. Many Londoners offer bed-and-breakfast in their homes, a cozy option that costs as little as £55 ($102) a night for two people (without a private bathroom) in Central London through **Host and Guest**

Service (✆ 020/7385-9922; www.host-guest.co.uk). Other similar services include **At Home in London** (✆ 020/8748-1943; www.athomeinlondon.co.uk), which offers rooms in Central London from £67 ($124) for a double and £50 ($92) for a single, and **Uptown Reservations** (✆ 020/7351-3445; www.uptownres.co.uk), with single rooms from £72 ($133) and doubles from £95 ($176) in Central London.

18. Or be even braver and do a house swap, which costs nothing once you've paid the yearly $49.95 matchmaking fee through U.S.-based **HomeExchange.com** (✆ **800/877-8723;** www.homeexchange.com).
19. Depending on your threshold of pain, consider staying at a youth hostel, or at one of the dozens of university dorms. **High Holborn Residence** charges £66 ($122) for a twin, and provides a continental breakfast, two TV lounges, a bar with two pool tables, table tennis, 24-hour laundromat, and a computer room.
20. If you want to splurge on a hotel in London, go on a weekend. Many of London's fancy business-class hotels offer special weekend rates.
21. Don't call home from a hotel phone unless you can access USA Direct or a similar company, and even then, check to see if there's a charge for the connection. Similarly, don't call directly from a pay phone, which may connect to carriers charging super-high prices.

DINING

22. Stay at a hotel providing a full breakfast, not the continental one that some hotels are switching to. I've noted which still serve the traditional cereals, bread, fruit, bacon, eggs, sausage, mushrooms, and tomatoes. That would cost you at least £6 ($11) a head outside the hotel.
23. Bring a knife, fork, plate, and corkscrew so that you can feast on delights from the splendid food halls at Harrods, Fortnum & Mason, and Selfridges; on simpler fare from Tesco Metro and Marks & Spencer; or the super-fresh produce from the city's farmers' markets.
24. If spreading your own butter is not your style, then check out the ever-expanding range of budget eating options, such as one of the many Soup Opera branches around Soho and Covent Garden, where prices start at £2.95 ($5.50) a cup and include bread and fruit.
25. At many a London restaurant, you'll find fixed-price and pretheater menus. Depending on the neighborhood, a two-course meal could cost as little as £6 ($11), and many are £10 to £15 ($18–$28). Note, though, that most of these menus offer a limited choice—that's why they're the price they are.
26. At many restaurants, service is included—don't make the mistake of tipping twice.

GETTING AROUND TOWN

27. Walk—it's the best way to explore the city and meet the locals. London is big, but it only takes a little forethought to schedule sights, shops, and meals by neighborhood. That way, you can explore on foot and save on Tube costs, as well as on wasted downtime.
28. If walking is not for you, take advantage of any discounts on public transport. Travelcards (see tip 10, above, and "Getting Around," in chapter 3) allow you to ride the buses and Underground throughout the two zones of Central London for £4.70 ($7) a day and £15 ($28) for 3 days (off-peak fares). They make sightseeing so much more spontaneous, too.

29. For London's cheapest tour, ride the no. 11 bus from Liverpool Street to Fulham Broadway, or the new **R1 Riverbus** service from Covent Garden to the British Airways London Eye, Tate Modern, the Globe, and over Tower Bridge to the Tower of London. Or any other route, for that matter. With a Travelcard, you can go wherever you please inside the zones to which it applies.

SIGHTSEEING & ENTERTAINMENT

30. Surf **www.londonfreelist.com**. It lists 1,500 permanently good deals and daily specials, most of which are free, and none costing more than £3 ($5.50), from famous London attractions to local neighborhood events—jumble and car boot sales (the British equivalent of rummage sales and flea markets); fetes and festivals; and so on.
31. All the national museums have now ditched their admission charges, for everyone! In addition, many museums and galleries put on tours, talks, hands-on workshops, and other entertainment to engage the public's interest, and much of it is free.
32. Make creative sightseeing choices. Some of the best things in life are free. A walk down any street in London is bound to turn up several buildings marked with blue plaques, showing that someone famous once lived there. No one can charge you for looking, so enjoy the architecture. And do make sure to walk across the marvelous Millennium Bridge between St. Paul's and Tate Modern.
33. If you go to a park, opt for the classic iron bench, not a deck chair which costs money.
34. Enjoy London's feast of festivals and ceremonial events: the Changing of the Guard at Buckingham Palace, St. James's Palace, and Whitehall; the Lord Mayor's Show; the Notting Hill Carnival; and a year-long list of many more (see "London Calendar of Events," later in this chapter, for details). You can enjoy the entertainment in the Piazza at Covent Garden any day—fire-eaters, mimes, a jazz trio, who knows what.
35. Take a seat in the galleries at the Old Bailey in the City, the Royal Courts of Justice in the Strand, and of course, the Houses of Parliament. They're all free and will give you a glimpse both into the past and into the institutions and social issues of contemporary London.
36. Visit a legion of long-dead celebrities at London's cemeteries. And not just Highgate—try Brompton Cemetery on Old Brompton Road, Hampstead Cemetery on Fortune Green Road, and the Dissenters' Graveyard at Bunhill Fields in the City. The Pet Cemetery in Kensington Gardens was the fashionable place to bury noble and not-so-noble cats and dogs, from Victorian times until 1967. Call ahead for permission to visit (✆ **020/7298-2117**).

NIGHTLIFE

37. Go to nightclubs early or very late to get a discount. For instance, **Bar Rumba** has a happy hour Monday to Thursday, 5 to 9pm, and there's no cover charge then. Also clip out the Privilege Pass, printed weekly in the listings magazine *Time Out.* And check Tower Records in Piccadilly Circus for cheap-deal flyers, which some of the clubs also post on their websites.
38. Queue at the tickets kiosk in Leicester Square for half-price West End theater tickets. Or pop into an Internet cafe and surf **www.lastminute.com** for right-now discounts. There are 11 handy branches of **easyEverything** (see "Surf 'n' Slurp @ the Best Internet Cafes," in chapter 6).

39. Go to matinees instead of evening performances. A top-price matinee will cost about £5 ($9) less than a top-price evening ticket.
40. On Monday nights, when all tickets are only £7.50 ($14), go to the **Royal Court Theatre,** Sloane Square, SW1 (✆ **020/7565-5000;** www.royalcourttheatre.com), which offers some of the city's most exhilarating and controversial contemporary drama.
41. Think literally about what constitutes an entertainment venue! **Borders** (p. 217) stages live music, readings, and talks usually at 6:30pm. Events at **Waterstone's** bookstore (p. 218) tend to start around 7pm and most are free, too.
42. Hunt down those free concerts. You'll find them in churches at lunchtime, in the foyers of Royal Festival Hall, at the Royal Opera House, and at London's many drama and music schools. For example, students of Trinity College give free concerts in Hinde Street Church on most Thursday lunchtimes during term. Call these places for information: the **Guildhall School of Music and Drama,** the Barbican, EC1 (✆ **020/7628-2571;** www.gsmd.ac.uk); **Royal Academy of Music,** Marylebone Rd., NW1 (✆ **020/7873-7373;** www.ram.ac.uk); or **Trinity College of Music,** 11–13 Mandeville Place, W1 (✆ **020/7935-5773;** www.tcm.ac.uk).
43. At many a jazz or other music club, sitting at the bar instead of at a table can save you anywhere from £6 to £12 ($11–$22) cover charge.
44. London has developed a happy-hour culture. Many bars offer discounted drinks—cocktails are the hip tipple these days—usually between 5:30 and 7:30pm, with prices slashed by 30% to 50%.

SHOPPING

45. Hang out at the outdoor markets: Camden Town on the weekends for a youth-oriented experience; Bermondsey and Portobello for antiques; and Borough Market and the city's new farmers' markets for mouthwatering fresh produce.
46. Come to London in January and shop the sales. Virtually every store of every description knocks down its prices, and Londoners indulge in a frenzy of post-Christmas spending.
47. Check if there's one of the grab-and-shop designer sales on during your stay. Mens- and womenswear is 40% to 80% off during these warehouse-style jamborees, put on by one company at a photographic studio near King's Cross and another at the Old Truman Brewery in Brick Lane (see "Regular Sales" under "Fashion," in chapter 8).
48. Check out Debenhams department store (p. 219), as well as High Street fashion chains like Top Shop (p. 221): They've invited big name designers to create exclusive collections for them, at unexclusive prices.
49. Trek a few extra Tube stops to find 25% to 80% discount on ends of lines at the Burberry factory shop (p. 221), or, for china and glass, Villeroy & Boch (p. 218).
50. Get your VAT refund—a whopping 17.5%. Fill out the appropriate forms in the shop; get the form and your receipt stamped at customs; and mail them back to the retailer.

3 Visitor Information

Information about London and traveling elsewhere in the country can be obtained from the New York office of **VisitBritain** (formerly called the British Tourist Authority), 551 Fifth Ave. (at 45th St.), 7th floor, New York, NY 10176 (© **800/462-2748** or 212/986-2266). The office is open for walk-in customers Monday to Friday from 9am to 6pm. The VisitBritain website (**www.visitbritain.com**) has sections tailored to each visitor's nationality, plus special deals on airfare and hotels.

At the **British Travel Shop** (© **212/557-2170**) next to the Manhattan VisitBritain office, you can buy **BritRail passes** (see chapter 10); the **London Pass,** good for discounts on a variety of London attractions (see tip 8); and the **Great British Heritage Pass** (see tip 9), which gives you free entry into some 550 historic properties across the country. At this office you can also buy **London Visitor Travelcards** (or call BritRail, © **866/BRITRAIL;** www.britrail.com) and order tickets for London plays. If you are traveling to the Continent from London, this office can also assist you with European train tickets and passes.

VisitBritain also has walk-in offices in **Australia,** at Level 2, 15 Blue St., North Sydney, NSW 2060 (© **02/9021-4400**); in **Ireland,** at 18–19 College Green, Dublin 2 (© **01/670-8000**); and in **New Zealand,** at Level 17, NZI House, 151 Queen St., Auckland 1 (© **09/303-1446**). VisitBritain's Canadian office closed in 2005.

In London, the main tourist information office is in the **Britain & London Visitor Centre,** 1 Regent St., SW1 (no phone). It's open Monday to Friday 9:30am to 6:30pm, Saturday and Sunday 10am to 4pm (Sat 9am–5pm, June–Oct). In addition to providing general tourist information, this office has a Globaltickets booking service for theater, sightseeing, and events; a bureau de change; and a Thomas Cook hotel and travel reservations office.

4 Entry Requirements & Customs

DOCUMENTS

Citizens of the United States, Canada, Australia, and New Zealand need only a valid passport to enter Great Britain.

CUSTOMS

WHAT YOU CAN BRING INTO THE U.K.

Overseas visitors are allowed to import duty-free either 200 cigarettes, or 100 cigarillos, or 50 cigars, or 250 grams of tobacco; 2 liters of still table wine plus 1 liter of alcoholic drinks over 22% volume, or 2 liters of alcoholic drinks under 22%; 60cc of perfume and 250cc of eau de cologne. Other items can be imported free of tax, provided they're for personal use or, in the case of gifts, do not exceed £145 ($232) in value. Live animals, plants, and produce are forbidden. So are counterfeit and copied goods and anything made from an endangered species: Leave your fake Rolex and your ivory jewelry at home.

WHAT YOU CAN BRING HOME FROM THE U.K.

Returning **U.S. citizens** who have been away for at least 48 hours are allowed to bring back, once every 30 days, $800 worth of merchandise duty-free. You'll be charged a flat rate of 4% duty on the next $1,000 worth of purchases. Be sure to have your receipts handy. On mailed gifts, the duty-free limit is $200. With some exceptions, you cannot bring fresh fruits and vegetables into the United States. For specifics on what you can bring back, download the invaluable free pamphlet *Know Before You Go* online at **www.customs.gov**. (Click on "Travel," and then click on "Know Before You Go Online Brochure.") Or contact the **U.S. Customs Service,** 1300 Pennsylvania Ave., NW, Washington, DC 20229 (✆ **877/287-8867**) and request the pamphlet.

For a clear summary of **Canadian** rules, write for the booklet *I Declare,* issued by the **Canada Customs and Revenue Agency** (✆ **800/461-9999** in Canada, or 204/983-3500; www.ccra-adrc.gc.ca). Canada allows its citizens a C$750 exemption, and you're allowed to bring back duty-free 1 carton of cigarettes, 1 can of tobacco, 40 imperial ounces of liquor, and 50 cigars. In addition, you're allowed to mail gifts to Canada valued at less than C$60 a day, provided they're unsolicited and don't contain alcohol or tobacco (write on the package "Unsolicited gift, under $60 value"). All valuables should be declared on the Y-38 form before departure from Canada, including serial numbers of valuables you already own, such as expensive foreign cameras. *Note:* The $750 exemption can only be used once a year and only after an absence of 7 days.

The duty-free allowance in **Australia** is A$400 or, for those under 18, A$200. Citizens can bring in 250 cigarettes or 250 grams of loose tobacco, and 1,125 milliliters of alcohol. If you're returning with valuables you already own, such as foreign-made cameras, you should file form B263. A helpful brochure available from Australian consulates or Customs offices is *Know Before You Go.* For more information, call the **Australian Customs Service** at ✆ **1300/363-263,** or log on to www.customs.gov.au.

The duty-free allowance for **New Zealand** is NZ$700. Citizens over 17 can bring in 200 cigarettes, 50 cigars, or 250 grams of tobacco (or a mixture of all three if their combined weight doesn't exceed 250g); plus 4.5 liters of wine and beer, or 1.125 liters of liquor. New Zealand currency does not carry import or export restrictions. Fill out a certificate of export, listing the valuables you are taking out of the country; that way, you can bring them back without paying duty. Most questions are answered in a free pamphlet available at New Zealand consulates and Customs offices: *New Zealand Customs Guide for Travellers, Notice no. 4.* For more information, contact **New Zealand Customs,** The Customhouse, 17–21 Whitmore St., Box 2218, Wellington (✆ **04/473-6099** or 0800/428-786; www.customs.govt.nz).

5 Money

CURRENCY

POUNDS & PENCE On January 1, 2002, the first 12 countries to make up the European Union launched the euro as legal tender. The U.K., however, still uses pounds and pence. Some posh London shops and hotels accept the new European currency. Otherwise, nothing is changing currency-wise, at least for the time being. The British pound (£), a small, thick, pale-yellow coin, is divided into 100 pence (pennies). These come in 1p and 2p

Tips No Commission, Thank You!

One benefit of the London Pass is free currency swapping at any branch of Exchange International, of which there are 17 in Central London, and 1 each at Gatwick and Heathrow.

The British Pound & the U.S. Dollar

At the time of writing, $1 = approximately 70p (or $1.85 = £1), and this was the rate used to calculate the dollar values in this book (rounded to the nearest dime if the amount is under $5, rounded to the nearest dollar if the amount is over $5). Exchange rates are volatile. If you have access to the Web, you can get the current equivalents at **www.xe.net/currency**.

U.K.£	U.S.$	U.K.£	U.S.$
.05	.09	6.00	11.10
.10	.18	7.00	12.95
.25	.46	8.00	14.80
.50	.92	9.00	16.65
.75	1.39	10.00	18.50
1.00	1.85	15.00	27.75
2.00	3.70	20.00	37.00
3.00	5.55	25.00	46.25
4.00	7.40	30.00	55.50
5.00	9.25	35.00	64.75

copper coins, and the silvery 5p, 10p, and 7-sided 20p and 50p coins. There are also large two-tone £2 coins. Notes are issued in £5, £10, £20, and £50 denominations.

CREDIT CARDS/ATMs

All major credit cards are widely accepted in London, but be aware that some budget B&Bs and restaurants do not accept any credit cards at all (this is one way they keep their costs down). Also be aware that many budget hotels and restaurants refuse American Express and Diners Club because of the merchant charges. In England, MasterCard is also called Access. Using plastic is certainly convenient, but it's not as economical as it once was because credit card companies and the banks that issue the cards now routinely tack on a 3% "conversion fee" for transactions made in foreign countries.

You'll save money if you use an ATM rather than convert your home currency at a traditional bureau de change. The fees are generally lower and the exchange rate is the "wholesale" rate, which is better. Check with your bank before you leave about any charges, daily withdrawal limit, and whether you need a new PIN. Your bank or its website can also supply a list of overseas ATMs. To find out which overseas banks belong to the **CIRRUS** network, call ✆ **800/424-7787** (www.mastercard.com). For **Visa Plus,** call ✆ **800/843-7587** (www.visa.com).

TRAVELER'S CHECKS

Traveler's checks are something of an anachronism from the days before the ATM made cash accessible at any time, though they used to be the only sound alternative to traveling with dangerously large amounts of cash.

These days, traveler's checks are less necessary because most cities have 24-hour ATMs that allow you to withdraw small amounts of cash as needed. However, keep in mind that you will likely be charged an ATM withdrawal fee if the bank is not your own, so if you're withdrawing money every day, you might be

What Things Cost in London	U.S.$
Taxi from Heathrow Airport to London	75.00
Underground from Heathrow to Central London	7.00
Local telephone call	.55
Double room at Hart House (splurge)	194.00
Double room at Luna Simone Hotel	148.00
Twin room at Bankside House	117.00
Dorm bed at Astor's Museum Inn	44.00
Fish and chips for one, at The Rock & Sole Plaice	12.00
Lunch for one at most pubs	12.00
Set lunch for one, at Criterion Grill	28.00
Sandwich at Pret a Manger	5.50
Double latte at Starbucks	3.60
Pint of beer	3.50
Coca-Cola in a can	1.00
Roll of ASA 400 film, 24 exposures	9.00
Admission to Tate Modern	Free
Adult admission to Tower of London	27.00
Walking tour	12.00
Movie ticket	12.50
Cheapest evening seat at *Mamma Mia!* in the West End	27.00

better off with traveler's checks—provided that you don't mind showing identification every time you want to cash one. Traveler's checks are easily exchanged in London, with banks and companies like American Express and Thomas Cook offering the best rates. ***Beware:*** Private currency-exchange businesses that stay open late charge high commissions.

Traveler's checks in pounds sterling are accepted at all but the smallest shops, restaurants, hotels, theaters, and attractions. But there are two drawbacks to carrying them. First, you'll have to exchange your money into pounds at home, where the transaction usually proves more expensive than it would in London. Second, you'll have to re-exchange unused pounds after the trip and pay again.

You can get traveler's checks at almost any bank. **American Express** offers denominations of $20, $50, $100, $500, and (for cardholders only) $1,000. You'll pay a service charge ranging from 1% to 4%. You can also get American Express traveler's checks over the phone by calling ✆ **800/221-7282;** Amex gold and platinum cardholders who use this number are exempt from the 1% fee.

Visa offers traveler's checks at Citibank locations nationwide, as well as at several other banks. The service charge ranges between 1.5% and 2%; checks come in denominations of $20, $50, $100, $500, and $1,000. Call ✆ **800/732-1322** for information. AAA members can obtain Visa checks without a fee at most AAA offices or by calling ✆ **866/339-3378.** **MasterCard** also offers traveler's checks.

Call ✆ **800/223-9920** for a location near you.

If you choose to carry traveler's checks, be sure to keep a record of their serial numbers separate from your checks in the event that they are stolen or lost. You'll get a refund faster if you know the numbers.

6 When to Go

Spring and fall are the best seasons for avoiding the hordes that descend on the major sights in summer. In winter, the weather in London can be pretty dreary—January and February are particularly grim—but the cultural calendar is rich, and the attractions much more peaceful.

If you're traveling with kids, it's a good idea to aim for English school holidays, including the 1-week minibreak in the middle of each of the three terms, as museums, galleries, and attractions put on extra fun. And there are lots of fairs, festivals, and special events. Not every school operates to exactly the same calendar but these dates cover the spread of options: spring half-term, February 18 to February 22; Easter holidays, March 25 to April 5; summer half-term, May 27 to June 7; summer holidays, July 19 to September 4; winter half-term, October 21 to November 1; and the Christmas holiday starts on December 20.

THE CLIMATE

London's infamous fogs were created by the exhaust from coal fires. Air-pollution controls put into place in the 1950s made it an offense to use anything but smokeless fuel, so "fog" is no longer in the forecast. Rain, drizzle, and showers are, of course. A typical weather forecast any time of year predicts "scattered clouds with sunny periods and showers, possibly heavy at times." Temperatures are mild and rarely go below freezing in winter or above 75° Fahrenheit (24°C) in summer—although there've been some major heat waves recently.

London's Average Monthly Daytime Temperature & Rainfall

	Jan	Feb	Mar	Apr	May	June	July	Aug	Sept	Oct	Nov	Dec
Temp. (°F/°C)	40/4	40/4	44/7	49/9	55/13	61/16	64/18	64/18	59/15	52/11	46/8	42/6
Rainfall (inches)	2.1	1.6	1.5	1.5	1.8	1.8	2.2	2.3	1.9	2.2	2.5	1.9

PUBLIC HOLIDAYS

Businesses are closed on Christmas Day, Boxing Day (Dec 26), and on New Year's Day. If any of these dates fall on a Saturday and/or Sunday, then the following Monday and/or Tuesday becomes a public holiday. A high proportion of offices, though not stores, actually close for the whole week between Christmas and New Year's. In Britain, Good Friday is a public holiday as well as Easter Monday. There are also three bank holidays, on the first and (usually) last Mondays in May, and the last Monday in August. In London, there's no fixed policy regarding the closing of shops, restaurants, museums, and other attractions on bank holidays, so call to check.

LONDON CALENDAR OF EVENTS

Please note that the dates for many of these events vary from year to year. Call or check the event website to verify the exact date.

January

New Year's Day Parade. Starting at noon, 10,000 musicians, dancers, acrobats, cheerleaders, clowns, and carnival floats set off from Parliament Square. January 1.

Charles I Commemoration. Banqueting House, Whitehall. Hundreds of men march through Central London, starting at 11:30am at St. James's Palace, dressed as cavaliers to mark the anniversary of the 1649 execution of King Charles I. January 27.

February

Great Spitalfields Pancake Day Race. Teams of four run in relays, and toss a pancake from one team member to the next. (Yes, really.) Why not join in? Noon on Shrove Tuesday (40 days before Easter) at Old Spitalfields Market, Brushfield St., E1 (✆ **020/7375-0441**).

Chinese New Year Parade. Chinatown, at Gerrard and Lisle streets. Festive crowds line the streets of Soho to watch the famous Lion Dancers and browse stalls crammed with crafts and delicacies. Mid-February.

March

BADA Antiques & Fair Art Fair. Duke of York Square on King's Road in Chelsea is the scene of this famous 6-day antiques fair (formerly known as the Chelsea Antiques Fair) (✆ **020/7589-6108;** www.bada-antique-fair.co.uk). Mid-March.

April

The Oxford & Cambridge Boat Race. The dark and light blues compete over a 4-mile course along the Thames from Putney to Mortlake. The race has been held since 1829, and crowds line the towpaths for the 3pm start to cheer the teams on (✆ **020/7611-3500;** www.theboatrace.org). Late March or early April.

Flora London Marathon. Over 45,000 serious athletes run 26 miles, from Greenwich to The Mall, SW1. The start is staggered from 9am (✆ **020/7902-0199;** www.london-marathon.co.uk). Mid-April.

May

Museums & Galleries Month. Thousands of attractions all over Britain put on special exhibitions and events linked to common guiding themes (**www.24hourmuseum.org.uk**). All month.

May Fayre & Puppet Festival. Procession at 10am; service at St. Paul's Covent Garden at 11:30am; then Punch & Judy until 6pm at this church where Samuel Pepys watched England's first show in 1662 (✆ **020/7375-0441**). Usually second Sunday in May.

Chelsea Flower Show. This international spectacular features the best of British gardening, with displays of plants and flowers for all seasons, set in the beautiful grounds of the Chelsea Royal Hospital. For ticket information, contact the Royal Horticultural Society (✆ **020/7834-4333;** www.rhs.org.uk) or buy tickets online at www.keithprowse.co.uk. Tickets go on sale in late November. Late May.

June

Royal Academy Summer Exhibition. This is the world's largest open-competition art exhibition and a great time to hear the critics at their bitchy best. Call ✆ **020/7300-8000** for info (www.royalacademy.org.uk). June through July.

The Derby. Pronounced "darby," and now called The Vodafone Derby, this is one of the highlights of the racing season at Epsom Racecourse in Surrey. Posh fashions, corporate suits, and much too much champagne, darling (✆ **01372/470047;** www.epsomderby.co.uk). Early June.

Meltdown. The Royal Festival Hall on the South Bank invites a celebrity artistic director to host his or her dream festival, pulling together any art forms and performers they choose (✆ **020/7960-4242;** www.sbc.org.uk). Usually the last 3 weeks of June.

Spitalfields Festival. Hawksmoor's Christ Church, Spitalfields, is the principal venue for a 3-week festival of medieval and early chamber music, new choral commissions, and much more, including walks and talks, some of which are free (✆ **020/7377-1362;** www.spitalfieldsfestival.org.uk). Usually starts second week of June.

Trooping the Colour. Horse Guards Parade, Whitehall. On the Saturday closest to her official birthday, Elizabeth II inspects her regiments from an open carriage and receives the salute as they parade their colors before her. It's quintessential English pageantry that still draws big crowds. Tickets are free and are allocated by ballot. Apply in writing between January and the end of February, enclosing an International Reply Coupon (available at most post offices) to: Brigade Major, Horseguards Whitehall, London SW1A 2AX. Canadians should apply to Royal Events Secretary, Canada House, Trafalgar Square, London SW1Y 5BJ. You can also see the event outside, from The Mall. For information call ✆ **020/7414-2479.** Mid-June.

Royal Ascot. This 4-day midweek event is held at Ascot Racecourse in Berkshire. It's *the* glamorous event of the racing season, as renowned for its fashion extravaganzas as for its high racing standards. The royal family attends (✆ **01344/876456;** www.ascot.co.uk). Mid- to late June. *Note:* Royal Ascot closed in 2004 for a complete overhaul of the track; until 2007 this event will be held in York.

City of London Festival. A 3-week extravaganza of over 100 events, covering the whole musical spectrum, at venues from St. Paul's Cathedral to City livery company halls not normally open to the public (✆ **020/7377-0540;** www.colf.org). From the third week of June.

Wimbledon Lawn Tennis Championships. This is a thrilling event where the posh and the plebs rub shoulders, and you can get right up close to the world's top tennis players. For full admission details, see "Spectator Sports," in chapter 7. Late June to early July.

Greenwich & Docklands International Festival. Ten days packed with music, dance, and theater in historic buildings by the Thames (✆ **020/8305-1188;** www.festival.org). Usually starts in late June.

July

Henley Royal Regatta. A serious international rowing competition—the course covers more than a mile, against the current—with serious champagne socializing on the side. Held at Henley-on-Thames, Oxfordshire (✆ **01491/572153;** www.hrr.co.uk). Early July.

Henry Wood Promenade Concerts. Famous summer musical season at Royal Albert Hall. Dating back to 1895, it runs the gamut from ancient to modern classics, and jazz, too. It's only £4 ($7.40) to rough it with the promenaders on the floor of the hall (✆ **020/7765-5575;** www.royalalberthall.com or www.bbc.co.uk/proms). Mid-July to mid-September.

Pride in the Park. A huge gay and lesbian march and parade from Hyde Park to Parliament Square is followed by live music, dancing, and fun. For more information, visit www.prideinthepark.com. First Saturday in July.

August

Great British Beer Festival. Organized by the Campaign for Real Ale, this festival fills Olympia Exhibition Centre to overflowing with over 500 different ales, beers, ciders, and perries, brewed the traditional way (✆ **01727/867201;** www.gbbf.org). Usually first week of August.

The Notting Hill Carnival. One of the largest street festivals in the world, this carnival attracts more than half a million people. Expect live reggae, steel bands, soul music, great Caribbean food, and a charged atmosphere—sometimes overcharged because it is much too big a crowd crammed into too small a space. Check the listings magazines for details (✆ **020/8964-0544**). Late August.

September

Mayor's Thames Festival. This festival features fireworks, theatrical shows, sculpture, art exhibitions, bankside entertainment, a river pageant, and a torch-lit procession (✆ **020/7928-8998;** www.thamesfestival.org). Mid-September.

London Open House Weekend. This event showcases centuries of British architecture, as over 400 London buildings usually closed to visitors throw open their doors for the weekend, for free! Call ✆ **090/0160-0061** (www.londonopenhouse.org). Usually third weekend in September.

October

Pearlies Harvest Festival. London's famous Pearly Kings and Queens, with their fabulous coats encrusted with shiny buttons, celebrate Harvest Festival at St. Martin-in-the-Fields, in Trafalgar Square, SW1 (✆ **020/7766-1100**). Usually first Sunday in October.

Chelsea Crafts Fair. This is the largest such fair in Europe: contact the Crafts Council for details (✆ **020/7806-2512;** www.craftscouncil.org.uk). Takes place during the last 2 weeks of October.

London Film Festival. This 2-week festival features movies from all over the world, including big name premieres, at the National Film Theatre on South Bank and in West End cinemas (✆ **020/7815-1433;** www.lff.org.uk). From late October to early November.

November

State Opening of Parliament, Whitehall and Parliament Square. Although the ceremony itself is not open to the public, crowds pack the parade route to see the queen make her way to Parliament in a gilded coach (✆ **020/7291-4272;** www.parliament.uk). Late October or early November.

London to Brighton Veteran Car Run. More than 300 veteran cars compete in this 57-mile run from London's Hyde Park to Brighton. Staggered start from 7:30 to 9am (✆ **01753/681736**). First week in November.

Guy Fawkes Fireworks Night. Hyde Park, Battersea Park, and other public spaces in London. Commemorates the "Gunpowder Plot," a Roman Catholic conspiracy to blow up King James I and his parliament in 1605. Huge bonfires are lit to burn effigies of the most famous conspirator, Guy Fawkes. Free. November 5 and closest Saturday.

The Lord Mayor's Procession and Show. Over 100 floats follow the new Lord Mayor in his gilded coach from Guildhall, in the City, to his inauguration at the Royal Courts of Justice in the Strand (✆ **020/7606-3030;** www.lordmayorsshow.org). Mid-November.

December

Tree Lighting Ceremony. Every year a giant Norwegian spruce, a gift from Norway, is lit in Trafalgar Square to signal the start of the Christmas holiday season. First Thursday in December.

Spitalfields Festival. This is a little Christmas festival adjunct to the main 3-week festival in June, with magical music by candlelight in Christ Church, Spitalfields (✆ **020/7377-1362;** www.spitalfieldsfestival.org.uk). Usually the week before Christmas.

Harrods' After-Christmas Sale, Knightsbridge. You'll find the store's best bargains of the year during this sale. Call ✆ **020/7730-1234** (www.harrods.com) for exact dates and hours. Late December.

New Year's Eve. Drunken lemmings party at Trafalgar Square, where the fountains are switched off to prevent drowning and hypothermia. And there's lots more fun across the city. To find the hottest hotspots, contact VisitBritain (see "Visitor Information," earlier in this chapter). December 31.

Greenwich & Docklands First Night. This is a fiesta of street theater, fireworks, music, and fun, from the afternoon right up to the big moment (✆ **020/8305-1818;** www.festival.org). December 31.

7 Travel Insurance

Check your existing insurance policies and credit card coverage before you buy travel insurance. You may already be covered for lost luggage, canceled tickets, or medical expenses. The cost of travel insurance varies widely, depending on the cost and length of your trip, your age, health, and the type of trip you're taking.

TRIP-CANCELLATION INSURANCE Trip-cancellation insurance helps you get your money back if you have to back out of a trip, if you have to go home early, or if your travel supplier goes bankrupt. Allowed reasons for cancellation can range from sickness to natural disasters to the State Department declaring your destination unsafe for travel. In this unstable world, trip-cancellation insurance is a good buy if you're getting tickets well in advance—who knows what the state of the world, or of your airline, will be in 9 months? Insurance policy details vary, so read the fine print—and especially make sure that your airline or cruise line is on the list of carriers covered in case of bankruptcy. For information, contact one of the following insurers: **Access America** (✆ 866/807-3982; www.accessamerica.com); **Travel Guard International** (✆ 800/826-4919; www.travelguard.com); **Travel Insured International** (✆ 800/243-3174; www.travelinsured.com); and **Travelex Insurance Services** (✆ 888/457-4602; www.travelex-insurance.com).

HEALTH INSURANCE Citizens and residents of Australia and New Zealand are entitled to free medical treatment and subsidized dental care while in Britain. Americans and other nationals will usually have to pay upfront, except in accident and emergency departments (until referral). Most health insurance policies cover you if you get sick away from home—but check, particularly if you're insured by an HMO. With the exception of certain HMOs and Medicare/Medicaid, your medical insurance should reimburse you for the cost of medical treatment—even hospital care—overseas. If you require additional medical insurance, try **MEDEX International** (✆ **800/527-0218** or 410/453-6300; www.medexassist.com) or **Travel Assistance International** (✆ **800/821-2828;** www.travelassistance.com; for general information on services, call the company's Worldwide Assistance Services, Inc., at ✆ **800/777-8710**). In addition, some credit card companies offer free, automatic travel-accident insurance, up to $100,000, when you buy tickets on their cards.

LOST-LUGGAGE INSURANCE On international flights (including U.S. portions of international trips), lost baggage coverage is limited to approximately $9.07 per pound, up to approximately $635 per checked bag. If you plan to check items more valuable than the standard liability, see if your valuables are covered by your homeowner's policy, get baggage insurance as part of your comprehensive travel-insurance package, or buy Travel Guard's "BagTrak" product. Don't buy insurance at the airport, as it's usually overpriced.

If your luggage is lost, immediately file a lost-luggage claim at the airport, detailing the luggage contents. For most airlines, you must report delayed, damaged, or lost baggage within 4 hours of arrival. The airlines are required to deliver luggage, once found, directly to your house or destination free of charge.

8 Specialized Travel Resources

FOR TRAVELERS WITH DISABILITIES

Most disabilities shouldn't stop anyone from traveling. There are more options and resources out there than ever before.

For information on traveling in Britain, contact **Holiday Care Services,** 7th floor, Sunley House, 4 Bedford Park, Croyden, Surrey CR0 2A (✆ **0845/124-9971** in the U.K., or 020/8760-0072 outside the U.K.; www.holidaycare.org.uk), between 9am and 5pm on weekdays. The organization publishes 120 information sheets on different topics and regions, for which it charges 50p (90¢) per sheet. Pay £19 ($34) to become a U.K. member, £38 ($69) if you live overseas, and you'll receive a newsletter and holiday discounts. **Tripscope** (✆ **0845/758-5641,** or 01179/397782 from outside the U.K.; www.tripscope.org.uk) is a very helpful transport-information service for people with disabilities, open Monday to Friday 9am to 4:45pm.

London's major museums and tourist attractions are fitted with wheelchair ramps, but call **Artsline** (✆ **020/7388-2227;** www.artsline.org.uk) for free advice on accessibility to theaters, galleries, and events around the city—including youth-oriented info. The phone line is open Monday to Friday from 9:30am to 5:30pm. It's common for theaters, nightclubs, and attractions to offer discounts, called "concessions," to people with disabilities. Ask for these before paying full price.

Many travel agencies offer customized tours and itineraries for travelers with disabilities. **Flying Wheels Travel** (✆ **507/451-5005;** www.flyingwheelstravel.com) offers escorted tours and cruises that emphasize sports and private tours in minivans with lifts. **Accessible Journeys** (✆ **800/846-4537** or 610/521-0339; www.disabilitytravel.com) caters specifically to slow walkers and wheelchair travelers and their families and friends.

Organizations that offer assistance to disabled travelers include the **MossRehab Hospital** (www.mossresourcenet.org), which provides a library of accessible-travel resources online; the **Society for Accessible Travel and Hospitality** (✆ **212/447-7284;** www.sath.org; annual membership fees: $45 adults, $30 seniors and students), which offers a wealth of travel resources for all types of disabilities and informed recommendations on destinations, access guides, travel agents, tour operators, vehicle rentals, and companion services; and the **American Foundation for the Blind** (✆ **800/232-5463;** www.afb.org), which provides information on traveling with Seeing Eye dogs.

For more information specifically targeted to travelers with disabilities, the community website **iCan** (www.icanonline.net/channels/travel/index.cfm) has destination guides and several regular columns on accessible travel. Also check out the quarterly magazine **Emerging Horizons** ($14.95 per year, $19.95 outside the U.S.; www.emerginghorizons.com).

FOR GAY & LESBIAN TRAVELERS

VisitBritain, the official U.K. tourism agency, has a gay and lesbian section on its website **www.visitbritain.com**. Their New York office (see "Visitor Information," earlier in this chapter) offers the free *Official Gay and Lesbian Guide* to London, packed with helpful information.

When you get to London, head for Old Compton Street in Soho and look for the free *Pink Paper* at gay bars, bookstores, and cafes. *Boyz* and *QX* are excellent for city listings, gossip, and scenes. *Time Out* (www.timeout.com) has a good gay listings section. And lastly, for advice on pretty much anything, including accommodations, call the 24-hour **Lesbian & Gay Switchboard** (© **020/7837-7324**; www.llgs.org.uk).

The International Gay & Lesbian Travel Association (IGLTA) (© **800/448-8550** or 954/776-2626; www.iglta.org) is the trade association for the gay and lesbian travel industry, and offers an online directory of gay- and lesbian-friendly travel businesses; go to their website and click on "Members." The purely online www.gaytoz.com, www.rainbownetwork.com, www.queercompany.com, www.gingerbeer.co.uk, www.outuk.com, www.lounge.uk.net, and http://uk.gay.com are also good resources.

Many agencies offer tours and travel itineraries specifically for gay and lesbian travelers. **Above and Beyond Tours** (© **800/397-2681**; www.abovebeyondtours.com) is the exclusive gay and lesbian tour operator for United Airlines. **Now, Voyager** (© **800/255-6951**; www.nowvoyager.com) is a well-known San Francisco–based gay-owned and operated travel service. **Olivia Cruises & Resorts** (© **800/631-6277** or 510/655-0364; www.olivia.com) charters entire resorts and ships for exclusive lesbian vacations and offers smaller group experiences for both gay and lesbian travelers.

The following travel guides are available at most travel bookstores and gay and lesbian bookstores, or you can order them from **Giovanni's Room** bookstore, 1145 Pine St., Philadelphia, PA 19107 (© **215/923-2960**; www.giovannisroom.com): ***Frommer's Gay & Lesbian Europe,*** an excellent travel resource; ***Out and About*** (© **800/929-2268** or 415-644-8044; www.outandabout.com), which offers guidebooks and a newsletter 10 times a year packed with solid information on the global gay and lesbian scene; ***Spartacus International Gay Guide*** and ***Odysseus,*** two annual English-language guidebooks focused on gay men; the ***Damron*** guides, with separate, annual books for gay men and lesbians; and ***Gay Travel A to Z: The World of Gay & Lesbian Travel Options at Your Fingertips*** by Marianne Ferrari (Ferrari Publications; Box 35575, Phoenix, AZ 85069), a good gay and lesbian guidebook series.

See also the "Gay & Lesbian London" section in chapter 9.

FOR SENIORS

In Britain, "senior citizen" usually means a woman at least 60 years old and a man at least 65. Seniors often receive the same discounts as students (both are categorized as "concessions" or "concs" for short). Some discounts are restricted to British citizens only, but check at all attractions, theaters, and other venues.

Members of **AARP** (formerly known as the American Association of Retired Persons), 601 E St. NW, Washington, DC 20049 (© **888/687-2277**; www.aarp.org), get discounts on hotels, airfares, and car rentals. AARP offers members a wide range of benefits, including *AARP: The Magazine* and a monthly newsletter. Anyone over 50 can join. If you're 55 or older, check out the educational programs sponsored by **Elderhostel,** 11 Ave. de Lafayette, Boston, MA 02111 (© **877/426-8056**; www.elderhostel.org). It has classes and programs galore in London and throughout Europe. Courses on literature, art, music, and many other topics last 1 to 4 weeks. Package prices include airfare, meals, lodging, daily instruction, and admission fees. For instance, in 2005 a 12-day trip called London in Depth cost $3,220 in peak season.

Recommended publications offering travel resources and discounts for seniors include: the quarterly magazine ***Travel 50 & Beyond*** (www.travel50andbeyond.com); ***Travel Unlimited: Uncommon Adventures for the Mature Traveler*** (Avalon); ***101 Tips for Mature Travelers,*** available from Grand Circle Travel (✆ **800/958-0405;** www.gct.com); ***The 50+ Traveler's Guidebook*** (St. Martin's Press); and ***Unbelievably Good Deals and Great Adventures That You Absolutely Can't Get Unless You're Over 50*** (McGraw-Hill).

FAMILY TRAVEL

If you have enough trouble getting your kids out of the house in the morning, dragging them thousands of miles away may seem like an insurmountable challenge. But family travel can be immensely rewarding, giving you new ways of seeing the world through smaller pairs of eyes.

When you're in London, remember that kids under 5 years of age can get into almost any attraction for free, and kids under 15 get in at lower children's rates. Many attractions sell "family tickets" which reduce the cost for two adults and two children. London's parks, especially Kensington Gardens, are favorite places for kids to run and explore. Kids under 15 can get reduced rates on public transportation. And though I'm not one to recommend fast-food chains or junk food, keep in mind that everything from McDonalds to KFC and Pizza Hut is easily available in London.

Familyhostel (✆ **800/733-9753;** www.learn.unh.edu/familyhostel) takes the whole family, including kids ages 8 to 15, on moderately priced domestic and international learning vacations. Lectures, field trips, and sightseeing are guided by a team of academics.

You can find good family-oriented vacation advice on the Internet from sites like the **Family Travel Network** (www.familytravelnetwork.com); **Traveling Internationally with Your Kids** (www.travelwithyourkids.com), a comprehensive site offering sound advice for long-distance and international travel with children; and **Family Travel Files** (www.thefamilytravelfiles.com), which offers an online magazine and a directory of off-the-beaten-path tours and tour operators for families.

For more tips, look for the soon-to-be-published ***Frommer's London with Kids*** (Wiley Publishing, Inc.). In addition, ***How to Take Great Trips with Your Kids*** (The Harvard Common Press) is full of good general advice that can apply to travel anywhere.

FOR STUDENTS

The **American Institute for Foreign Study,** River Plaza, 9 West Broad St., Stamford, CT 06902 (✆ **800/727-2437;** www.aifsabroad.com), offers 3- and 6-month academic programs in London, costing from $14,095 to $28,290, including meals and housing. The **Institute for International Education,** 809 United Nations Plaza, New York, NY 10017 (✆ **212/883-8200;** www.iie.org), also administers student grants and applications for study-abroad programs in England and other European countries. The **Council on International Educational Exchange (CIEE),** International Study Programs, 7 Custom House Street, 3rd Floor, Portland, ME 04101 (✆ **800/40-STUDY;** www.ciee.org), can offer a term or a whole year at its London study center, which combines Goldsmith College and Imperial College, both parts of the University of London, and the University of Westminster. It is also possible to enroll in summer courses at **Oxford University** (✆ **01865/270708;** www.ox.ac.uk), and **Cambridge** (✆ **01223/337733;** www.cam.ac.uk).

The **International Student Identity Card (ISIC)** is the only officially acceptable form of student identification, good for discounts on rail passes, plane tickets, theaters, museums, and so on. It has a partnership with eKit (see tip 11, earlier in this chapter) to offer a "communications solution" called ISIConnect for cheap phone calls and free e-mail. You also get basic health and life insurance and a 24-hour help line. If you're no longer a student but are still under 25, you can buy an **International Youth Travel Card,** which will get you the insurance and some of the discounts (but not student admission prices in museums). Professional full-time teachers can obtain similar discounts and benefits with the **International Teacher Identity Card (ITIC)**. All three passes cost $22 and are available from **STA Travel** (✆ **800/781-4040;** www.statravel.com). Ask for a list of offices in major cities so that you can keep the discounts flowing (and aid lines open) as you travel.

The **International Student Travel Confederation** website (www.istc.org) is a useful source of advice and directions to member organizations all over the world.

The **University of London Student Union** (**ULU**), Malet Street, WC1 (✆ **020/7664-2000;** http://www.uclu.org), caters to more than 70,000 students and may be the largest of its kind in the world. In addition to a gym and fitness center with squash and badminton courts, the Malet Street building houses several shops, bars, restaurants, a bank, a ticket-booking agency, and an STA travel office. And there's an action-packed schedule of gigs and club nights. Stop by or phone for information on university activities. The student union building is open Monday to Thursday from 8:30am to 11pm, Friday 8:30am to 1am, Saturday 9am to 1am, Sunday 9am to 10:30pm. It is sometimes closed on August weekends. Take the Tube to Goodge Street.

London's youth hostels are not only some of the cheapest sleeps, they're also great spots to meet other student travelers and pick up discounts to local attractions. You have to be a member of **Hostelling International (International Youth Hostel Federation),** which you can join at any hostel for $28 adults, $18 for seniors (55-plus), or free if you're under 18. To apply in the United States and make advance international bookings, contact **Hostelling International (AYH),** 8401 Colesville Rd., Silver Spring, MD 20910 (✆ **301/495-1240;** www.hiayh.org). You can also book dorm beds online and e-mail hostels about other options through the English website (www.yha.org.uk).

9 Planning Your Trip Online

SURFING FOR AIRFARES

The "big three" online travel agencies, **Expedia.com, Travelocity.com,** and **Orbitz.com,** sell most of the air tickets bought on the Internet. (Canadian travelers should try expedia.ca and Travelocity.ca; U.K. residents can go for expedia.co.uk and opodo.co.uk.) Each has different business deals with the airlines and may offer different fares on the same flights, so it's wise to shop around. Expedia and Travelocity will also send you **e-mail notification** when a cheap fare becomes available to your favorite destination. Of the smaller travel agency websites, **SideStep** (www.sidestep.com) has gotten the best reviews from Frommer's authors. It's a browser add-on that purports to "search 140 sites at once," but in reality only beats competitors' fares as often as other sites do.

Also remember to check **airline websites,** especially those for low-fare carriers

Frommers.com: The Complete Travel Resource

For an excellent travel-planning resource, we highly recommend **Frommers.com** (www.frommers.com). We're a little biased, of course, but we guarantee that you'll find the travel tips, reviews, monthly vacation giveaways, and online-booking capabilities thoroughly indispensable. Among the special features are our popular **Message Boards,** where Frommer's readers post queries and share advice (sometimes even our authors show up to answer questions); **Frommers.com Newsletter,** for the latest travel bargains and insider travel secrets; and **Frommer's Destinations Section,** where you'll get expert travel tips, hotel and dining recommendations, and advice on the sights to see for more than 3,000 destinations around the globe. When your research is done, the **Online Reservations System** (www.frommers.com/book_a_trip) takes you to Frommer's preferred online partners for booking your vacation at affordable prices.

such as Ryanair, whose fares are often misreported or simply missing from travel agency websites. Even with major airlines, you can often shave a few bucks from a fare by booking directly through the airline and avoiding a travel agency's transaction fee. But you'll get these discounts only by **booking online:** Most airlines now offer online-only fares that even their phone agents know nothing about.

Great **last-minute deals** are available through free weekly e-mail services provided directly by the airlines. Most of these are announced on Tuesday or Wednesday and must be purchased online. Most are only valid for travel that weekend, but some can be booked weeks or months in advance. Sign up for weekly e-mail alerts at airline websites or check mega-sites that compile comprehensive lists of last-minute specials, such as **Smarter Travel** (smartertravel.com). For last-minute trips, **site59.com** in the U.S. and **lastminute.com** in Europe often have better deals than the major-label sites.

If you're willing to give up some control over your flight details, use an **opaque fare service** like **Priceline** (www.priceline.com; www.priceline.co.uk for Europeans) or **Hotwire** (www.hotwire.com). Both offer rock-bottom prices in exchange for travel on a "mystery airline" at a mysterious time of day, often with a mysterious change of planes en route. The mystery airlines are all major, well-known carriers—and the possibility of being sent from Philadelphia to Chicago via Tampa is remote; the airlines' routing computers have gotten a lot better than they used to be. But your chances of getting a 6am or 11pm flight are pretty high. Hotwire tells you flight prices before you buy; Priceline usually has better deals than Hotwire, but you have to play their "name our price" game. If you're new at this, the helpful folks at **BiddingForTravel** (www.biddingfortravel.com) do a good job of demystifying Priceline's prices. Priceline and Hotwire are great for flights within North America and between the U.S. and Europe. But for flights to other parts of the world, consolidators will almost always beat their fares.

For much more about airfares and savvy air-travel tips and advice, pick up a copy of *Frommer's Fly Safe, Fly Smart* (Wiley Publishing, Inc.).

SURFING FOR HOTELS

Shopping online for hotels is much easier in the U.S., Canada, and certain parts of Europe than it is in the rest of the world. If you try to book a Chinese hotel online, for instance, you'll probably overpay. Also, many smaller hotels and B&Bs—especially outside the U.S.—don't show up on websites at all. Of the "big three" sites, **Expedia** may be the best choice, thanks to its long list of special deals. **Travelocity** runs a close second. Hotel specialist sites **hotels.com** and **hotel discounts.com** are also reliable. An excellent free program, **TravelAxe** (www.travel axe.net), can help you search multiple hotel sites at once, even ones you may never have heard of.

Priceline and Hotwire are even better for hotels than for airfares; with both, you're allowed to pick the neighborhood and quality level of your hotel before offering up your money. Priceline's hotel product even covers Europe and Asia, though it's much better at getting five-star lodging for three-star prices than at finding anything at the bottom of the scale. ***Note:*** Hotwire overrates its hotels by one star—what Hotwire calls a four-star is a three-star anywhere else.

SURFING FOR RENTAL CARS

For booking rental cars online, the best deals are usually found at rental-car company websites, although all the major online travel agencies also offer rental-car reservations services. Priceline and Hotwire work well for rental cars, too; the only "mystery" is which major rental company you get, and for most travelers the difference between Hertz, Avis, and Budget is negligible.

10 The 21st-Century Traveler

INTERNET ACCESS AWAY FROM HOME

Travelers have any number of ways to check their e-mail and access the Internet on the road. Of course, using your own laptop—or even a PDA or electronic organizer with a modem—gives you the most flexibility. But even if you don't have a computer, you can still access your e-mail and even your office computer from cybercafes.

WITHOUT YOUR OWN COMPUTER

It's hard nowadays to find a city that *doesn't* have a few cybercafes. Although there's no definitive directory for cybercafes, three places to start looking are at **www.cybercaptive.com**, **www.netcafe guide.com**, and **www.cybercafe.com**.

Aside from formal cybercafes, most **youth hostels** nowadays have at least one computer on which you can access the Internet. And most **public libraries** across the world offer Internet access free or for a small charge. Avoid **hotel business centers,** which often charge exorbitant rates.

Internet kiosks, which you'll see in airports, shopping malls, hotel lobbies, and tourist information offices, give you basic Web access for a per-minute fee that's usually higher than cybercafe prices. The kiosks' clunkiness and high price means they should be avoided whenever possible.

To retrieve your e-mail, ask your **Internet Service Provider (ISP)** if it has a Web-based interface tied to your existing e-mail account. If your ISP doesn't have such an interface, you can use the free **mail2web** service (www.mail2web.com) to view and reply to your home e-mail. For more flexibility, you may want to open a free, Web-based e-mail account with **Yahoo! Mail** (http://mail.yahoo.com). Microsoft's Hotmail is another popular option, but Hotmail has severe spam problems. Your home ISP may be able to forward your e-mail to the Web-based account automatically.

If you need to access files on your office computer, look into a service called **GoToMyPC** (www.gotomypc.com). The service provides a Web-based interface for you to access and manipulate a distant PC from anywhere—even a cybercafe—provided your "target" PC is on and has an always-on connection to the Internet (such as with Road Runner cable). The service offers top-quality security, but if you're worried about hackers, use your own laptop rather than a cybercafe to access the GoToMyPC system.

WITH YOUR OWN COMPUTER

Major Internet Service Providers (ISPs) have **local access numbers** around the world, allowing you to go online by simply placing a local call. Check your ISP's website or call its toll-free number and ask how you can use your current account away from home, and how much it will cost.

If you're traveling outside the reach of your ISP, the **iPass** network has dial-up numbers in most of the world's countries. You'll have to sign up with an iPass provider, who will then tell you how to set up your computer for your destination(s). For a list of iPass providers, go to www.ipass.com and click on "Reseller Locator." Under "Select a Country" pick the country that you're coming from, and under "Who is this service for?" pick "Individual." One solid provider is **i2roam** (www.i2roam.com; ✆ **866/811-6209** or 920/235-0475).

Wherever you go, bring a **connection kit** of the right power (British appliances operate on the E.U. standard of 240 volts) and phone adapters, a spare phone cord, and a spare Ethernet network cable.

Most business-class hotels throughout the world offer dataports for laptop modems, and a few thousand hotels in the U.S. and Europe now offer high-speed Internet access using an Ethernet network cable. You'll have to bring your own cables either way, so **call your hotel in advance** to find out what the options are.

If you have an 802.11b/**Wi-fi** card for your computer, several commercial companies have made wireless service available in airports, hotel lobbies, and coffee shops, primarily in the U.S. Community-minded individuals have also set up **free wireless networks** in major cities around the world. These networks are spotty, but you get what you (don't) pay for. Each network has a home page explaining how to set up your computer for their particular system; start your explorations at www.personaltelco.net/index.cgi/WirelessCommunities.

USING A CELLPHONE

The three letters that define much of the world's **wireless capabilities** are GSM (Global System for Mobiles), a big, seamless network that makes for easy cross-border cellphone use throughout Europe and dozens of other countries worldwide. In the U.S., T-Mobile, AT&T Wireless, and Cingular use this quasi-universal system; in Canada, Microcell and some Rogers customers are GSM, and all Europeans and most Australians use GSM.

If your cellphone is on a GSM system, and you have a world-capable phone such as many (but not all) Sony Ericsson, Motorola, or Samsung models, you can make and receive calls across civilized areas on much of the globe, from Andorra to Uganda. Just call your wireless operator and ask for "international roaming" to be activated on your account. Unfortunately, per-minute charges can be high—usually $1 to $1.50 in Western Europe and up to $5 in places like Russia and Indonesia.

Worldphone owners can bring down their per-minute charges with a bit of trickery. Call up your cellular operator and say you'll be going abroad for several months and want to "unlock" your phone to use it with a local provider. Usually, they'll oblige. Then, in your destination country, pick up a cheap, prepaid phone chip at a mobile phone store and slip it into your phone. (Show your phone to the salesperson, as not all phones work on all networks.) You'll get a local phone number in your destination country—and much, much lower calling rates.

Otherwise, **renting** a phone is a good idea. (Even worldphone owners will have to rent new phones if they're traveling to non-GSM regions, such as Japan or Korea.) While you can rent a phone from any number of overseas sites, including kiosks at airports and at car-rental agencies, we suggest renting the phone before you leave home. That way you can give loved ones your new number, make sure the phone works, and take the phone wherever you go—especially helpful when you rent overseas, where phone-rental agencies bill in local currency and may not let you take the phone to another country.

Phone rental isn't cheap. You'll usually pay $40 to $50 per week, plus airtime fees of at least a dollar a minute. If you're traveling to Europe, though, local rental companies often offer free incoming calls within their home country, which can save you big bucks. The bottom line: Shop around.

Two good wireless rental companies are **InTouch USA** (✆ **800/872-7626;** www.intouchglobal.com) and **RoadPost** (✆ **888/290-1606** or 905/272-5665; www.roadpost.com). Give them your itinerary, and they'll tell you what wireless products you need. InTouch will also, for free, advise you on whether your existing phone will work overseas; simply call ✆ **703/222-7161** between 9am and 4pm EST, or go to http://intouchglobal.com/travel.htm.

For trips of more than a few weeks spent in one country, **buying a phone** becomes economically attractive, as many nations have cheap, no-questions-asked prepaid phone systems. Stop by a local cellphone shop and get the cheapest package; you'll probably pay less than $100 for a phone and a starter calling card. Local calls may be as low as 10¢ per minute, and in many countries incoming calls are free.

True wilderness adventurers, or those heading to less-developed countries, should consider renting a **satellite phone** (see InTouch USA or RoadPost, above). Per-minute call charges can be even cheaper than roaming charges with a regular cellphone, but the phone itself is more expensive (up to $150 a week), and depending on the service you choose, people calling you may incur high long-distance charges.

11 Getting There

BY PLANE

More than 90 scheduled airlines serve London, more if you count Gatwick as well as Heathrow. They include these major North American carriers: **American Airlines** (✆ **800/433-7300;** www.aa.com), **Continental** (✆ **800/231-0856;** www.continental.com), **Delta** (✆ **800/241-4141;** www.delta.com), **Northwest Airlines** (✆ **800/447-4747;** www.nwa.com), **United Airlines** (✆ **800/538-2929;** www.ual.com), and **Air Canada** (✆ **888/247-2262;** www.aircanada.com).

British Airways (✆ **800/AIRWAYS** in North America, 300/134011 in Australia, 800/BRITISH in New Zealand; www.britishairways.com) is the largest U.K. airline and flies to London from the U.S., Australia, and New Zealand. **Virgin Atlantic Airways** (✆ **800/862-8621;** www.virgin-atlantic.com) flies from New York and Newark, New Jersey, as well as from Chicago, Boston, Las Vegas, Los Angeles, San Francisco, Orlando, Miami, and Washington, D.C. **Qantas** (✆ **1300/131313** in Australia; www.qantas.com) is the national Australian carrier, also serving New Zealand, and it code-shares with many foreign carriers. **Air New Zealand** (✆ **0800/737000** in New Zealand; www.airnz.com) flies daily to Heathrow.

FINDING THE BEST AIRFARE

London's popularity and the number of airlines flying there mean heavy competition for customers. So check local and national newspapers for special promotions and always shop around to find the cheapest seat.

The lowest-priced standard economy-class fare usually carries some restrictions like advance-purchase, minimum stay, or a Saturday stopover, as well as penalties for altering dates and itineraries. Note, too, that weekday flights are slightly cheaper than weekends, and early mornings are cheapest of all.

Make sure to check alternative ticket sources before buying direct from the airline. For instance, consolidators buy blocks of seats and sell them at a discount. Tickets are restrictive, valid only for a particular date or flight, nontransferable, and nonrefundable except directly from the consolidator, and they may not earn frequent flier miles. There are rarely set advance-purchase requirements; if space is available, you can buy just before you fly. Always pay with a credit card, though, to protect yourself in case the consolidator goes belly up.

The lowest-priced bucket shops are usually local backroom operations with low profiles and overheads. Look for their tiny ads jam-packed with cities and prices in the travel or classified section of your local newspaper. Those that advertise nationally are rarely as competitive, but they often have toll-free telephone numbers and may be more reliable. In 2005, with a reliable consolidator, you could get a high-season, midweek, round-trip ticket to London for **$520,** including taxes. Some to try are **Arrow Travel** (✆ **212/889-2550**); **Cheap Tickets** (✆ **800/377-1000** or 212/570-1179; www.cheaptickets.com); **TFI Tours International** (✆ **800/745-8000,** or 212/736-1140 in New York state; www.lowestairprice.com); **Travel Land International Inc.** (✆ **212/268-6464**); and **Up & Away Travel** (✆ **212/889-2345**).

Tips Make the Airline Pricing System Work for You

Increasingly sophisticated reservations software allows the airlines to practice yield management. They juggle twin priorities: filling the plane and making as much profit as possible from each flight. So, airlines constantly adjust the pricing of each seat on a particular flight according to the immediate demand. Save big money either by trawling the Internet, or by talking to a reliable travel agent or one of the companies that specialize in searching out low airfares. When we called, the best these guys could do in 2005 for a high-season, midweek, round-trip ticket from Newark to London was **$385: Fly 4 Less** (✆ 800/359-4537; www.fly4less.com); **Fare Busters International** (✆ 800/618-0571); and **1-800 Fly Cheap** (✆ 800/359-2432; www.flycheap.com).

For more information, consult "Planning Your Trip Online," earlier in this chapter.

Note: In this wonderful new electronic world, it's tempting to dispense with human contact altogether. But do call these guys, because their instant verbal quotes often undercut rates on their websites.

CHARTERS Another cheap way to cross the Atlantic is on a charter flight. Most operators advertise and sell their seats through travel agents, making them your best source of current information on the deals available.

FLYING INTO HEATHROW

Heathrow is a self-contained, self-sufficient microtown about 13 miles due west of Central London. The airport has shops, restaurants, and every kind of visitor service. The vast majority of flights from North America, Australia, and New Zealand arrive at terminals 3 and 4. Call **Heathrow** (✆ **020/8759-4321;** www.baa.co.uk) for any additional information. ***Note:*** Terminal 5, a massive new terminal to handle most of Heathrow's flights, is currently under construction and scheduled to open in 2011.

VISITOR INFORMATION The **Airport Information** desks are located at: **Terminal 3 Arrivals,** open daily from 5:30am to 10:30pm; **Terminal 3 Departures,** open daily from 7am to 9:30pm; and **Terminal 4 Arrivals,** open daily from 5:30am to 10:30pm. **London Travel Information Centres,** located in all the terminals, are open daily from 8am to 6pm (to 7pm, Mon–Sat, June–Sept).

HOTEL RESERVATIONS There are **British Hotel Reservation Centre** desks in the arrivals area of every terminal, open daily from 6am to midnight. The booth in the Terminal 4 Tube station opens daily 7am to 10:30pm. In the main Tube station concourse, the hours are 6:30am to 11:30pm. BHRC will book you into any accommodations anywhere, usually scoring big discounts. The nationwide 24-hour number is ✆ **020/7340-1616** (www.bhrc.co.uk).

CURRENCY EXCHANGE American Express, Terminal 4, Tube station concourse (✆ **020/8754-7057**), is open daily from 7am to 7pm. At all other bureaux de change, **British Airports Authority,** which runs Heathrow, guarantees charges will match or beat at least one of Britain's big-four High Street banks: for information on special deals, call ✆ **0800/844844.** These companies have numerous branches, open daily at both terminals: **Thomas Cook** (✆ **020/8272-8073** T3 or 020/8272-8100 T4) is open in T3 Arrivals from 5am to 10:30pm, and from 5:30am in T4; and in Departures from 5:30am to 10pm; **Travelex** (✆ **020/8897-3501,** T3 and T4) never closes in Arrivals, and from 5:30am to 10pm in Departures. There are ATMs throughout the airport.

CAR RENTALS Renting a car for a vacation in London is unwise (see "Getting Around," in chapter 3). If you must, however, airport pick-ups are very convenient. The big rental agencies all have branches at Heathrow: **Avis** (✆ **020/8899-1000**); **Budget Rent-a-Car** (✆ **020/8750-2511**); **Europcar** (✆ **020/8897-0811**); and **Hertz** (✆ **020/8897-2072**).

GETTING FROM THE AIRPORT TO TOWN There are lots of ways to get into London from Heathrow. Children under 5 travel free on most services.

The **Underground** is the best value. There are two airport Tube stations on the Piccadilly Line: one for terminals 1, 2, and 3, and one for Terminal 4. (***Note:*** The station for Terminal 4 will be closed until Sept 2006, and a replacement bus will take passengers to and from the Hatton Cross station.) The journey into Central London takes 40 to 50 minutes. Trains leave the airport from 5:13am to 11:50pm and arrive there from 6:29am to 1:07am (shorter hours on Sun). Heathrow is in zone 6 and therefore is not covered by most travel cards. One-way fares to or from zone 1, or Central

Tips Smaller Airports

If you're flying to London on a no-frills flight, you may land at **Stansted** (✆ **0870/000-0303;** www.baa.co.uk). The quickest way to get into London is the 42-minute train trip on the **Stansted Express** direct from the airport to Liverpool Street station. It runs from 4:30am to 11pm, every 15 minutes at peak times, otherwise half-hourly, and costs £15 ($27) one way (✆ **0845/600-7245;** www.stanstedexpress.com). The National Express **Airbus** (see above) makes the journey to Victoria Station in about 1 hour and 40 minutes and costs £8 ($15) one-way. Charters and cheapie airlines also fly into **Luton Airport** (✆ **01582/405100;** www.london-luton.com). The Greenline 757 bus leaves for London once an hour, takes 70 minutes, and charges £8 ($15) one-way (✆ **0870/608-7261;** www.greenline.co.uk). The **Thameslink CityFlier** takes about half an hour from the new Luton Airport Parkway station to King's Cross. There are eight trains an hour from 7am to 6pm Monday to Saturday, then four until 10pm. On Sundays trains run every 10 minutes from 9am to 5pm, then every 15 minutes until 8pm. One-way tickets cost £9.50 ($17). Call National Rail Enquiries for further information (✆ **0845/748-4950**). **London City Airport** (✆ **020/764-6000;** www.londoncityairport.com), only (10 miles) from the West End, handles flights to and from Europe. A **shuttle-bus** service takes passengers from the airport to Liverpool Street Station for £5 ($9).

London (see "Getting Around," in chapter 3), are £3.80 ($7) for adults and £1.60 ($3) for children ages 5 to 15. In the unlikely event that you miss the last Tube, the **N97 night bus** leaves at 20 minutes past the hour and 10 minutes before the top of the hour, from the Central Bus Station, and costs £1.50 ($2.40) for adults and children. Call **London Transport Travel Hotline** (✆ **020/7222-1234;** www.tfl.gov.uk) for more information.

Heathrow Express (✆ **0845/600-1515;** www.heathrowexpress.co.uk), the luxury nonstop rail service to and from Paddington Station, takes 15 minutes from terminals 1, 2, and 3, and 20 to 25 minutes from Terminal 4. Trains leave Heathrow from 5:07am to 12:08am and arrive there from 5:30am to midnight. All major airlines offer full check-in at Paddington—get there at least 2 hours before your flight, 1 hour if you've only got hand luggage. Standard-class one-way tickets cost £14 ($26), with discounts for online booking.

National Express (✆ **0870/574-7777** info, or 0870/580-8080 bookings; www.nationalexpress.com) runs two airport bus services and accepts online bookings. The **Airbus** leaves twice an hour from just outside every Heathrow terminal and goes to 23 stops in Central London. Ask your hotel or B&B if there's one close by because this may be the most convenient option. The service runs from Heathrow between 5:30am and 10:08pm, and from King's Cross (the last, or first, stop at the London end) between 4am and 8pm. One-way tickets cost £8 ($15) for adults and £4 ($7) for children ages 5 to 15. The **Hotel Hoppa** runs between each terminal and the main Heathrow hotels from 5:30am to 11:30pm. One-way tickets cost £2.50 ($4.60). One child ages 5 to 15 travels free with each adult. Both the Airbus and Hotel Hoppa take about 45 minutes door-to-door.

Hotelink (✆ **01293/552251;** www.hotelink.co.uk) is a door-to-door minibus service with desks at terminals 3 and 4

Arrivals. It runs every 30 minutes from 6am to 2pm daily, then hourly to 10pm, stopping at its passengers' hotels only, and costs £16 ($27) for a one-way ticket.

Black taxis (see "Getting Around," in chapter 3) are always available at Heathrow. The approximate fare to London is £45 ($83), which is a good value, door-to-door cost if you can fill the cab with the maximum five passengers and still have room for luggage. The taxi desk numbers are: **Terminal 3** (✆ **020/8745-4655**); **Terminal 4** (✆ **020/8745-7302**). To skip the tedious taxi line, book ahead with **Black Cab London** (✆ **877/405-7622** in the U.S., 020/8663-6400 from elsewhere overseas, or 0800/169-5296 in the U.K.; http://www.londonblackcabs.co.uk). The driver will meet you in arrivals and help carry that jumbo Samsonite. Such convenience comes at luxury prices, of course, but bear in mind that up to 5 passengers can also share this service. The ride from Heathrow into Central London will cost £55 ($102), instead of £45 ($83).

SPECIAL NEEDS There are **Help Points** throughout Heathrow. Use the green telephone to ask for a Help Bus (✆ **020/8745-5185**) to drive you around the airport, for a wheelchair, or just for general assistance. Travelers with disabilities can call the following numbers, in addition to those listed above, for advice or to make prearrangements: to prebook the assistance of a **Skycap porter** (✆ **020/8745-6011**); **Heathrow Travel-Care** (✆ **020/8745-7495**); and **TfL Access & Mobility** (✆ **020/7222-1234**).

FLYING INTO GATWICK

There are four ways of making the 25-mile trek into London (✆ **0870/000-2468;** www.baa.co.uk). The most popular is the **Gatwick Express** train, which takes around 30 minutes to reach Victoria, and costs £12 ($22) one-way. The station is below the airport, and trains depart every 15 minutes from 4:35am to 1:35am. The slightly cheaper option is **South Central Trains,** which charges £8.20 ($15) one-way and takes 35 to 45 minutes, depending how often it stops between Victoria station and the airport. For information on both, call National Rail Enquiries (✆ **0845/748-4950**), or prebook through **www.thetrainline.com**.

Hotelink (✆ **01293/552251;** www.hotelink.co.uk) runs the same minibus service here as it does at Heathrow but charges £20 ($37) to take you directly to your hotel, on the half-hour in the summer, on the hour in winter. **Checker Cars** (✆ **01923/502808** from South Terminal, or 01923/569790 from North Terminal) provides 24-hour taxi service between Gatwick and Central London; expect to pay about £65 ($120) for the 90-minute journey.

BY TRAIN

Each of London's train stations is connected to a vast bus and Underground network, and there are phones, restaurants, pubs, luggage-storage areas, shops,

---

Onward! Short Hops Around Britain & Across the Channel

If you want to fly to Europe, or even up to Scotland or across to Ireland, check out the no-frills **easyJet** (✆ **0870/600-0000;** www.easyjet.com), which flies from Stansted and Gatwick; and **Ryanair** (✆ **08701/569569;** www.ryanair.com), which flies from Stansted, Luton, and Gatwick. **Virgin Express** (✆ **020/7744-0004;** www.virgin-express.com) only flies from Heathrow. Keep an eye out for promotional deals in newspaper ads as lower prices are posted practically every day.

---

and London Transport Information Centres at all of them.

If you're **arriving from France,** the fastest way to get to London is by taking the hoverspeed connection between Calais and Dover (see "By Ferry & Hovercraft," below), where you can pick up a train into the city. If you prefer the ease of one-stop travel, you can take the Eurostar train (see below) directly from Paris—or go there and back in a day for a very swanky excursion.

VIA THE CHUNNEL The **Eurostar** (✆ **877/257-2887** from North America, or **08/705186186** in the U.K.; www.eurostar.com) direct train service runs from Paris Gare Du Nord and Brussels Central Station to Waterloo International in London. There are many fares to choose from, but I've found the cheapest seats at **Rail Europe** (✆ **888/382-7245** in the U.S. and Canada; www.raileurope.com). In 2005, RailEurope offered an amazingly low $45 one-way ticket (you had to purchase a return, too, so the cost was actually $90) that required advance purchase and a 1-night stay, and a Youth Flexi ticket for $75 one-way. Note that not all fares are available at all times.

FROM ELSEWHERE IN THE U.K. If you're traveling to London from elsewhere in the United Kingdom, consider buying a **BritRail Flexipass.** This allows unlimited rail travel in the U.K. for a certain number of days within a 2-month time period (**Eurailpasses** aren't accepted in Britain, although they are in Ireland). Buying through RailEurope (✆ **888/382-7245** in the U.S. and Canada; www.raileurope.com), a second-class Flexipass costs $265 for 4 days, $385 for 8 days, $585 for 15 days. Children under 5 travel free. One child ages 5 to 15 can travel free with each adult pass. All additional children pay half price. Travelers between 16 and 25 can purchase a **BritRail Youth Flexipass,** which allows unlimited second-class travel: $199 for 4 days, $285 for 8 days. For those over 60, the **BritRail Senior Flexipass** costs $336 for 4 days, $493 for 8 days. There are also passes for three or four people traveling in a group, and various day-trip specials for people who are only going to roam close to London.

You must purchase all special passes before you leave home: in the United States, at **RailEurope** (see above), the **British Travel Shop** next to the Manhattan Visit Britain office, or **BritRail** (✆ **866/BRITRAIL;** www.britrail.com).

BY BUS

Whether you're coming from the Continent or from another part of the country, London-bound buses almost always go to (and leave from) **Victoria Coach Station,** Buckingham Palace Road, which is 1 block from Victoria train station.

The **Brit Xplorer Pass**, available to non-U.K. residents only, is ideal for serious day-trippers and round-Britain tourers: a 7-day pass is £79 ($146). Under-25s can buy a discount card for £9 ($17), which cuts pass and individual ticket prices by 30%. If you're over 60, all bus trips are 50% off. You can buy all passes with a credit card, online, or by phone, direct from **National Express** (✆ **0870/580-8080;** www.nationalexpress.com); or, in person, at the Heathrow Central Bus Station and Victoria Coach Station, at National Express offices in St. Pancras station and Earl's Court Tube station, or at any travel agent displaying the National Express logo. Be sure to check the National Express website: in 2005, special £1 ($1.85) fares were available for those booking online. The U.S. agent for National Express is **British Travel International** (✆ **800/327-6097;** www.britishtravel.com).

Bus connections to Britain from the Continent are not so much uncomfortable as time-consuming, but it is very cheap compared to the train and plane, except for the no-frills carriers (see above). National Express is part of the **Eurolines** network of 31 companies in 25 countries. Buses leave Victoria for more than 460 destinations in Ireland and mainland Europe. For a serious pilgrimage around Europe, check out the 15-, 30-, and 60-day Eurolines Passes, which link you to 46 cities. A 30-day pass during the low season costs £136 ($252) for over-60s and under-26s, £167 ($309) for adults; high-season prices are £186 ($344) and £224 ($414).

BY FERRY & HOVERCRAFT

The shortest ferry crossings are also the closest to London: Dover to Calais, and Folkestone to Boulogne. Note that here, too, you pay less traveling out of season, on weekdays, and at unsociable hours, and if you prebuy tickets rather than just turn up. To have any hope of squeezing on board in the summer and during public holidays, you must book ahead anyway.

Check with VisitBritain (see "Visitor Information," earlier in this chapter) for a full listing of ferries to the Channel Islands, Ireland, the Isle of Man, and around the Scottish islands. All the companies below put together stopover packages if you fancy a Continental break from your London holiday. You can also get day-trip deals. And there are discounts for booking online.

CAR & PASSENGER FERRIES **P&O Stena Line** (✆ **0870/598-0333,** or 01304/864003 from outside the U.K.; www.poferries.com) operates car and passenger ferries between Dover and Calais, 35 departures a day, with a journey time of 1 hour 25 minutes. Summer one-way tickets cost from £70 ($129) for car and driver, and from £15 ($28) for an adult foot passenger. **Sea France** (✆ **0870/571-1711;** www.seafrance.com) runs 15 departures a day, with a journey time of 1½ hours. In 2005, round-trip peak-season tickets cost as little as £20 ($37) for an advance purchase fare for an adult foot passenger.

HOVERCRAFT & SEACATS Traveling by Hovercraft or SeaCat takes about half the time that a ferry does. For example, a hovercraft crossing from Calais to Dover with **hoverspeed** (✆ **0870/240-8070;** www.hoverspeed.co.uk) takes 35 minutes; they have 6 to 12 crossings per day. Their SeaCat crossings take a little longer, about 50 minutes, and there are five departures a day. One-way tickets on both in the high season cost £49 to £189 ($91–$165) for car and driver, and adult foot passengers pay £15 ($28).

BY CAR

If you plan to take a rented car across or under the Channel, check with the rental company about license and insurance requirements before you leave. Hertz runs a scheme called **Le Swap** for passengers taking Le Shuttle, which allows you to switch cars at Calais and change to the local steering-wheel position (right side in the U.K., left side in Europe).

LE SHUTTLE Le Shuttle (✆ **0870/535-3535;** www.eurotunnel.com) is the Channel Tunnel drive-on train service. Cars, charter buses, taxis, and motorcycles all do just that—drive on at Calais or Folkestone and off at the other end. It operates 24 hours a day, 365 days a year, running every 15 minutes during peak times and at least once an hour at night. The total travel time between the French and English highway system is about 1 hour (35 min. from platform to platform).

In summer especially, it's wise to book rather than just turn up, because stand-by queues can be very long and slow. Prices vary according to the season, the day of the week, and the time of day. A standard round-trip summer fare costs £223 ($413) but depending on your flexibility, round-trip fares can be as low as £98 ($181).

12 Money-Saving Package Deals

Package deals sometimes undercut what you'd pay by hunting down the deepest discounts for each separate component of your holiday. They also save you from spending hours doing all the planning work yourself. The discounts that tour operators and airlines can get with their buying power means you'll be staying in at least a 3- or 4-star hotel rather than a B&B. So check the ads in your newspaper's travel section.

Fully shepherded tours—where a group travels together and shares the same preplanned activities—are not only unnecessary for a holiday based mainly in London, but will probably make it harder for you to get the best out of this vibrant city. Packages don't have to be that regimented. In 2003, "budget" tour operator **Globus** (✆ **800/556-5454;** www.globusandcosmos.com) was offering a Week in London deal, including flights from New York, 6 nights accommodations, a ticket for the British Airways London Eye observation wheel, discount vouchers, a London Visitor Travelcard giving a day's free travel on buses and Tubes, and a helpful "host service." It cost from $1,487 to $1,647 per person, depending on season.

Airline packages can be very competitively priced if you avoid the plushest partner hotels. And airline packages are flexible as to the day and time you can travel and what's included in the deal. You decide whether to buy from the menu of extras, such as tours, sightseeing, theater tickets, and so on. The packages below are representative per person (sharing a double room) prices quoted at press time for summer season—the two-person price drops considerably between October and March—with midweek flights from JFK or Newark, airport transfers, taxes, and 6 nights in a hotel with breakfast: **Virgin Atlantic Vacations** (✆ **888/YESVIRGIN;** www.virgin.com/vacations) had a no-frills $849 "London Fling" deal for airfare and hotel only; **United Airlines Vacations** (✆ **800/377-1816;** www.unitedvacations.com) offered a good bare-bones air and London hotel package for $1,050; **British Airways Holidays** (✆ **800/428-2228;** www.baholidays.com) was charging about $1,200; **Continental Airlines Vacations** (✆ **800/301-3800;** www.coolvacations.com) was offering a package at $1,150; **American Airlines Vacations** (✆ **800/321-2121;** www.aavacations.com) was a little more expensive at $1,214. **Qantas**

Tips E-Package Deals

Lots of Frommer's surfers have reported good holiday experiences and good deals from **go-today.com**. So we thought we'd check out how the online holiday company compared to its "regular" terrestrial rivals. Pretty well, is the answer. A 2005 London special, including flights from New York and 3 nights in a London hotel started at $429 per person (double occupancy). The site pitches itself at folks who want to drop everything and go, but you can book well in advance. And you should, as the price clearly rises with demand (or waning supply, perhaps).

For more information about online travel bargains, consult "Planning Your Trip Online," earlier in this chapter.

sells Jetabout Holidays through travel agents or online (www.qantas.com).

British Travel International (✆ **800/327-6097;** www.britishtravel.com) can build you a package of discount deals and passes on planes, trains, automobiles, and buses, as well as accommodations. The excellent U.K. travel agent **Trailfinders** (✆ **0845/058-5858;** www.trailfinders.com) also has five Australian offices (✆ **1300/780-212;** www.trailfinders.com.au) and claims to be able to offer up to 75% discount on standard prices when it tailor-makes a vacation.

13 Recommended Books & Films

BOOKS

Why not set the scene with a little background reading about the country as a whole? The very funny *Notes from a Small Island* tells the tale of Bill Bryson's final walking tour around Britain, where he lived for 20 years, before moving home to the U.S. *The English: A Portrait of a People* is the mirror opposite—an exploration of the national quirks, without the humor, by arch-tiger BBC journalist Jeremy Paxman.

GENERAL Peter Ackroyd's 800-page *London: The Biography* treats the city as an organism, an entity with a life of its own, whose current state of health is inextricably linked to its past. John Russell's *London* is a very personal portrait filled with anecdotes, observations, color photographs, and illustrations. Novelist and literary critic V. S. Pritchett's *London Perceived* is another favorite.

Coming right up to date with a rapier-sharp eye on recent events, particularly Thatcherism, read novelist Julian Barnes' *Letters from London,* a set of essays originally printed in the *New Yorker.*

Then there are a couple of great books to take with you. *Americans in London,* by Brian N. Morton, is a great street-by-street guide to the clubs, homes, and favorite pubs of more than 250 famous Americans. *Looking Up in London,* by Jane Peyton, takes a fresh look at some of London's many architectural gems.

FICTION Of all the arts, England is probably richest in literature. Chronologically, start with Chaucer's bawdy portrait of medieval London in his *Canterbury Tales.* Follow with Shakespeare and Ben Jonson. Pepys and Evelyn are wonderful friends with whom to explore 17th-century London. For the 18th century, take Fielding, Swift, and Defoe. Anything by Dickens or Thackeray will unlock Victorian London for you. The period from the turn of the 20th century to the 1920s and 1930s is best captured in the works of Virginia Woolf, Henry Green, Evelyn Waugh, P. G. Wodehouse, and Elizabeth Bowen. Contemporary authors who provide insight into London society are, particularly, Muriel Spark, Iris Murdoch, Angus Wilson, V. S. Naipaul, Martin Amis, Angela Carter, Ian McEwan, Jeanette Winterson, Graham Swift, Anita Brookner, Kazuo Ishiguro, Hanif Kureishi, Nick Hornby, and a legion of others. One of the most entertaining novels about London, covering some 2,000 years of its history, is Edward Rutherfurd's *London.*

Michael Moorcock's novel *Mother London* was short listed for the U.K.'s prestigious Whitbread Prize. It's a magical epic, interweaving the stories of three outpatients from a mental hospital from the Blitz to the present day. Moorcock's *King of the City* and *London Bone* (short stories) come highly recommended too.

Zadie Smith was still at university when she wrote the hugely successful *White Teeth,* about tangled immigrant lives in North London from World War II to now.

BIOGRAPHY Amanda Foreman's *Georgiana, Duchess of Devonshire,* the

Impressions

It was a great way to get straight to where you were going in a cab, and not go by Harrods four times. At first, I was like, "So there are three Harrods in London?"

—Renée Zellweger, on speaking with an English accent while living in London to prepare for being *Bridget Jones,* March 2001

story of an 18th-century political and social siren, fashion icon, and chronic gambler, propelled the 30-something blonde to media stardom. *Bosie, A Life of Lord Alfred Douglas* is by another just-ex student, Douglas Murray—a companion read to Richard Ellman's *Oscar Wilde* (Knopf, 1988).

And there are so many others to choose from. Among the greats are Jackson Bate's study of Samuel Johnson, the many royal portraits written by Antonia Fraser, as well as her book on Oliver Cromwell, and Blake's *Disraeli.* For a portrait of Disraeli's opponent Gladstone, see those written by Richard Shannon or H. C. Matthews. Lytton Strachey's *Eminent Victorians* is a scintillating look at several famous figures from the Victorian era. When it comes to Winston Churchill, you can read his autobiography, or turn to Martin Gilbert's *Churchill: A Life* (St. Martin's, 1991). Also rated as a good read are the stories of Tory infighting and the substantial ghost of Maggie in John Major's *The Autobiography* (pretentious or what?), and the roaring indiscretions in the *Diaries* of Alan Clark, a minister for two terms under the Iron Lady.

As for the tabloid-harried royals, several books dredge up all the lurid details—Anthony Holden's *The Tarnished Crown,* A. N. Wilson's *The Rise and Fall of the House of Windsor,* and the very sleazy *Elizabeth: Behind Palace Doors,* by investigative hack Nicholas Davies. For Diana's perspective on the whole family and her role in it, read *Diana: Her True Story* by Andrew Morton. Trevor Rees-Jones tells of paparazzi-dodging on the dreadful day of the crash in *The Bodyguard's Story.* And Fergie sets the record straight, as far as she sees it, in *My Story, Duchess of York,* by Sarah Mountbatten-Windsor and Jeff Coplon.

FILMS

Get out the popcorn, take the phone off the hook, and settle down for a big preview night of London at the movies. It'll be like a scene out of *Bridget Jones,* the spot-on exposé of single life in London.

The most recent movies featuring London in a starring role were the alienating and irritating *Closer* and the heartfelt *Vera Drake.* Pierce Brosnan takes a rather speedy river cruise past some of the city's major landmarks to Docklands and on to Greenwich as James Bond in *The World is Not Enough.* The film goes perfectly back-to-back with the classic gangster movie *The Long Good Friday,* with Bob Hoskins. Or, for a superb drama set in London starring Glenda Jackson and Peter Finch, check out John Schlesinger's *Sunday Bloody Sunday.*

Merchant Ivory chose Mansion House for their adaptation of Henry James's *The Golden Bowl,* starring Nick Nolte and Uma Thurman. *Patriot Games* showcased the Royal Naval College at Greenwich.

To tread in Gwyneth Paltrow's footsteps, head for the Church of St. Bartholemew's the Great in Spitalfields, where much of *Shakespeare in Love* was made. *Sliding Doors* sent the lovely Gwyneth and John Hannah all over London, but the rainy shot in the boat took place just by Hammersmith Bridge; and most of the cafe scenes were shot at Mas Café in All Saints Road, at the bottom of Portobello. *Notting Hill* really put this neighborhood on the map.

Spotty-dog fans will recognize Burlington Arcade, in Piccadilly, as the location of several scenes in *101 Dalmatians.* Movie director Neil Jordan had to wheel out the smoke machines to create just the right grimly gloomy London day outside the Savoy for *The End of The Affair.*

Don't just restrict your preview pleasures to London-specific movies. Think of the following as British Culture 101. Start with the 1997 hit *The Full Monty.* Then add *Secrets and Lies, Naked, Trainspotting, Four Weddings and a Funeral, The Crying Game, Mona Lisa, My Beautiful Laundrette, Educating Rita,* and *A Clockwork Orange.* Oh, and the full Merchant Ivory backlist!

3

Getting to Know London

London is one of the most exciting cities in the world, and arriving there can be a bit of a shock for bleary-eyed and jet-lagged visitors. Almost seven and a half million people live in a sprawl of 600 square miles. Everything will probably seem too noisy, too fast, or too crowded. But it will also feel wonderfully familiar and exciting. The red buses and black taxis you've seen in hundreds of movies are suddenly driving past right in front of you. Despite the bustle, the city is very visitor-friendly: It's laid out in distinct, manageable areas, and traveling between them is easy on public transport.

This chapter will help you get your bearings. It provides a brief orientation and a preview of the city's most important neighborhoods. It also answers questions about how to use those double-decker buses, as well as the Tube. The "Fast Facts: London" section, later in this chapter, covers all the essentials from navigating the phone system to where to get a cheap and chic haircut.

1 Orientation

VISITOR INFORMATION

The **Britain & London Visitor Centre,** 1 Regent St., SW1 (no phone; www.visitbritain.com and www.visitlondon.com), is open Monday 9:30am to 6:30pm, Tuesday to Friday 9am to 6:30pm, Saturday and Sunday 10am to 4pm (10am–5pm, June–Oct). It brings together the English, London, Welsh, Scottish, and Irish Tourist Boards. There's a **Globaltickets** booking service for theater, sightseeing, and events; a bureau de change; and a **Thomas Cook** hotel and travel-reservations office.

Visit London (www.visitlondon.com) runs several **Tourist Information Centres (TICs)** offering a variety of services, including information, hotel booking, and maps. You'll find TICs at **Waterloo International arrivals hall,** SE1 (walk-in visitors only), open daily 8:30am to 10:30pm; in the **City of London** at St. Paul's Churchyard, EC4 (✆ **020/7332-1456**), open weekdays from 9:30am to 5pm and Saturday from 9:30am to 12:30pm; in **Greenwich** at Pepys House, 2 Cutty Sark Gardens, SE10 (✆ **0870/608-2000**), open daily from 10am to 5pm; and in **Southwark** at Vinopolis, Bank End, SE1 (✆ **020/7357-9168**).

There's also a convenient **information window** within the **TKTS** half-price ticket booth in **Leicester Square,** which opens from 10am to 6pm every day.

As you wander around the city, also look out for **i-plus** electronic booths, which provide touch-screen access to sightseeing information, theater bookings, and so on. You can even send short e-mails for free, though the process is laborious. You'll find one by Jubilee Place on King's Road (Chelsea), in Ossington Street in Notting Hill Gate, and near Kensington High Street, Bayswater, Pimlico, and Bond Street Tube

Fun Fact Name That Street

The weird and wonderful street names in the City aren't really weird at all, but an intricate guide to centuries of history. The "bury" of Bucklersbury and Lothbury comes from *burh,* the word for the stone mansions built by Norman barons. Ludgate, Aldgate, and Cripplegate really were gates, the original ones to the city. In the Middle Ages, *cheaps* were markets: hence modern street names like Eastcheap and Cheapside. As the city began to thrive as a commercial center, artisans and merchants gathered in particular streets. Today, you'll find Milk Street, Bread Street, and Friday Street, where fish was sold (England was Roman Catholic at the time and eating meat on Fri was forbidden). South of the river in Southwark is Clink Street. There used to be a prison there, hence the expression "in the clink."

stations. The budget hotel chains Travel Inn and Ibis have them, as do the London Transport Museum, Madame Tussaud's, Natural History Museum, Theatre Museum, and the Victoria & Albert Museum.

CITY LAYOUT

Central London is like the jam in a doughnut, an amorphous blob rather than an official definition. Ask a local, and they'd probably tell you it means anything falling within the Circle Line on the Underground: the **City,** the **West End,** and **West London** about as far as Earl's Court. Zone 2 of the Tube map loosely conforms to the broader definition of **Inner London. Greater London** includes the vast sprawling mass of suburbs.

The City is the oldest part of London. It covers the original 1-square-mile of the Roman settlement of Londinium. "Square Mile" and "The City" (always capitalized) are shorthand terms for London's financial district, akin to New York's Wall Street. The villages that sprang up around the original square-mile settlement—**Bloomsbury, Holborn, Kensington,** and so on—gradually melded together and became absorbed into the city proper. But each one still has its own heart and character.

The West End is harder to pin down because it's so much more than a geographical term. Locals use it as shorthand meaning razzle-dazzle—the special streets where they shop by day and play by night. **Marble Arch** and **Hyde Park Corner,** with **Park Lane** running between them, mark the westernmost points of the West End. **Westminster** and **Victoria** stand by themselves, outside any catchall description, except that Westminster, where the Houses of Parliament are located, is the center of government. Then, west of the West End, where homes finally outnumber offices, you come to **Bayswater, Notting Hill, Knightsbridge, Kensington, South Kensington,** and **Chelsea.**

This is the prime stomping ground for visitors. If you add on the best bits of Inner London—the cultural highlights close to the Thames at **South Bank, Bankside,** and **Southwark,** stretching as far east as **Greenwich,** as well as the markets of **Islington** and **Camden,** and pretty **Hampstead** village, to the north—that makes an area of around 65 sq. km (25 sq. miles).

FINDING YOUR WAY AROUND

Those inveterate organizers, the Victorians, introduced the postcode system to show where a neighborhood was located in relation to the original post office in the City, EC1 (for East Central). Moving west, the codes change from EC to WC (West Central) to W (West), and so on. But as London expanded, boroughs began to be labeled alphabetically. Now all you can be sure of is the general direction: W4 is Chiswick, at least ¾ of an hour west of the West End.

Where the Neighborhoods Are

Flip to the map, "Central London," on p. 8 for a clear picture of how all the neighborhoods described here actually fit together.

Street names are completely random. And house numbers can work in several different ways: odd on one side of the street, even on the other; or in the right order, but up one side and back down the other.

STREET MAPS Check the detailed foldout street map included with this book; you may find it's all you need to get around.

Otherwise, serious explorers should buy the one and only ***London A to Z*** immediately upon arrival, which is used by residents and visitors alike. These indispensable guides come in a wide range of sizes, formats, and prices. Just ask for an "A to Zed."

NEIGHBORHOODS IN BRIEF

KNIGHTSBRIDGE Posh Knightsbridge is the first area you come to west of the West End and south of Hyde Park. It's very wealthy and very fashionable in a way that is both solid establishment and gossip-column glitz. At **Harrods,** the main attraction in Knightsbridge, green-liveried doormen turn people away for having grubby clothing, ripped jeans, high-cut or cycling shorts, and bare midriffs or feet. The chic Harvey Nichols is 100 yards up the road toward Hyde Park Corner. The Lanesborough Hotel's covered central courtyard (what used to be St. George's Hospital) is a delightful place to splurge on afternoon tea. Knightsbridge Barracks, on the edge of the park, is where the Household Cavalry lives—they're the ones you see in the Changing of the Guard.

BELGRAVIA Located south of Knightsbridge, Belgravia reached the peak of its prestige in the reign of Queen Victoria, but for the *nouveau riche* and for those aristocrats whose forebears didn't blow all the family heirlooms, it's still a very fashionable address. The duke of Westminster, who owns vast tracts of Belgravia and Chelsea, lives at Eaton Square. Architecture buffs will love the town houses, especially in the area's centerpiece, Belgrave Square. Budget travelers can hover on the verge of a smart address at the B&Bs in Ebury Street, though that is really Victoria.

CHELSEA One end of this stylish district is defined by the north bank of the Thames, west of Victoria. The action really starts at **Sloane Square,** with Gilbert Ledward's Venus fountain at its center, and moves east down that dangerously captivating shopping heaven, the **King's Road**. Some large chain stores moved in a few years ago, but it's still more chic than cheap, and retains a funky fashionable feel begun in the 1960s by Mary Quant, who started the miniskirt revolution, and built on by that doyenne of tarty punk,

Vivienne Westwood. Chelsea has always been a favorite of writers and artists, including Oscar Wilde, Henry James, and Thomas Carlyle, whose home you can visit. Residents today include aging rock stars (Mick Jagger), aging politicians (Margaret Thatcher), wealthy young Euromigrant families, and former "Sloane Rangers" of the 1980s. Temporary residents won't find many cheap places to stay, but there are a handful of good values and a mix of cheap pop-in eats and restaurants with excellent set meals.

KENSINGTON This is the heart of the Royal Borough of Kensington & Chelsea. The asthmatic William III started the royal thing in 1689 when he fled Whitehall in search of cleaner air (long gone). Queen Victoria was born in **Kensington Palace,** which the royals now call "KP." The late Princess Diana lived there, and it's still home to a gang of family members. You can visit the palace (but not the royals, who inhabit their own wing). Beautiful **Kensington Gardens,** adjacent to the palace, is a great spot to stroll and hang out on a sunny day. Kensington lies between Notting Hill, to the north, and South Kensington. There are a couple of great bathless budget sleeps just off Kensington Church Street, which is lined with by-appointment-only antiques shops. **Kensington High Street** is a good mix of mainstream brands and bargains.

South Kensington is best known as the home of London's major museums, which stand along Cromwell Road: the **Natural History Museum, Victoria & Albert Museum,** and the **Science Museum.** They're all built on land bought with the proceeds of Prince Albert's Great Exhibition of 1851. He gave his name to two spectacular landmarks here: the **Royal Albert Hall,** where the famous promenade concerts are held every year, and the **Albert Memorial,** commissioned by his grief-stricken wife Queen Victoria and completed with garish Victorian splendor in 1872. South Ken, as it's often called, is stuffed to the gunwales with surprisingly good-value B&Bs and self-catering accommodations.

EARL'S COURT This neighborhood west of South Kensington has gone through many incarnations. Between the wars it was regarded as a staid residential district full of genteel ladies. It then became a haven for poor newcomers to Britain and young Brits buying an affordable first apartment. There are whole streets of budget hotels that really are dives and whole streets of lovely Victorian terraces. Things are changing overall, and an up-market sensibility is creeping in. You can see it on the main street, Earl's Court Road, where the smarter cafe chains are starting to join the late-night fast-food joints. The huge Earl's Court Exhibition Centre brings in a lot of convention-size business. Some hotels are upgrading to cater for it, providing good-value budget sleeps. London's first gay enclave, Earl's Court has gay bars, pubs, and a gay hotel.

NOTTING HILL Notting Hill is in the process of becoming a victim of its own hype. When house prices began to rise in the mid-1990s, the press climbed on the bandwagon and hip media, music, and fashion types moved in to what had been a decent and sometimes grotty neighborhood. The popular film *Notting Hill,* with Hugh Grant and Julia Roberts, provided a final rocket-blast to the real-estate boom. Richard Curtis, who wrote the movie, sold his Notting Hill house in 1999 for a rumored £1.4 million ($2.24 million). Now you might pay that much for a flat. Bye-bye boho scruffiness, hello Starbucks. Visitors flock here in hordes to visit the great **Portobello Market,** as you'll see if you stay at either of the good-value sleeps we've found for you on this winding street. **Holland Park,** the next stop west, is a chi-chi residential neighborhood for fat wallets only. Richard Branson runs his Virgin empire from here. Budget travelers can get a fantastic cheap sleep at the youth hostel located in the middle of the park itself.

PADDINGTON & BAYSWATER Since 1836, Paddington has been the terminus for trains coming into London from the west and southwest. The presence of the station eventually transformed the area's once-genteel Georgian and Victorian terraces into scruffy sleeps for people just passing through. The area is about to enjoy a massive redevelopment around the canal basin, north of the station—4.5 hectares (11 acres) of offices, overpriced apartments, shops, and eateries. But there are still good B&B deals to be had here, just west of the West End.

Bayswater is a generalization rather than a definable area, arising from Bayswater Road, the main road running across the top of **Hyde Park.** Walk 5 minutes from Paddington, and you'll come to it. The buzziest bit is **Queensway,** a street of cheap ethnic restaurants, often tacky shops, and an ice-skating rink, with the old Whiteley's department store, now a shopping mall, at the northern end. That is also where Westbourne Grove starts, an increasingly funky street that links up with Notting Hill.

MAYFAIR Bounded by Piccadilly, Hyde Park, Oxford Street, and Regent Street, Mayfair is filled with luxury hotels and grand shops. The Georgian town houses are beautiful, but many of them are offices now—real people can't afford to live in Mayfair anymore. **Grosvenor** (*Grove*-nur) **Square** is nicknamed "Little America" because it's home to the U.S. Embassy and a statue of Franklin D. Roosevelt. You must visit **Shepherd Market,** a tiny, rather raffish village of pubs and popular eateries: Sofra Bistro is a good and very reasonable Turkish restaurant. The old market was shut down for "fornication and lewdness," among other things, but up-market prostitutes reputedly still cater to loose-trousered politicians in the vicinity.

MARYLEBONE Most visitors head to Marylebone (*Mar*-lee-bone) to visit **Madame Tussaud's** waxworks, trudge up **Baker Street** in the fantasy footsteps of Sherlock Holmes, or explore lovely **Regent's Park,** home of the **London Zoo.** But overall, this is a somewhat anonymous area, with most of the action in a strip running just north of Oxford Street. Robert Adam finished Portland Place, a very typical square, in 1780. Horatio Nelson's wife waited in Cavendish Square for the admiral to return from the arms of Lady Hamilton. The one must-visit attraction is in Manchester Square: the mini–French château called Hertford House, which houses the **Wallace Collection,** one of London's loveliest free attractions. St. Christopher's Place is a pretty pedestrian street with some reasonable restaurants and unreasonable boutiques close to Bond Street Tube. Marylebone High Street now has a gaggle of posh shops. While budget hotels are as rare as hen's teeth here, you will find good-value, big-roomed splurges in Gloucester Place.

ST. JAMES'S Often called "Royal London," St. James's basks in its associations with everybody from the "merrie monarch" Charles II to Elizabeth II, who lives at its most famous address, **Buckingham Palace.** English gentlemen retreat to their St. James's clubs, those traditional bastions of male-only social superiority. St. James's starts at Piccadilly Circus and moves southwest, incorporating **Pall Mall, The Mall, St. James's Park,** and **Green Park.** Budget travelers must day-trip here to sample the lingering pomp and pompousness. Cheap eats are hard to find, except close to Piccadilly Circus, but the parks are prime picnic territory. You can get the necessities, or stop for tea, at the world's most luxurious grocery store, **Fortnum & Mason.** It has kept royals, explorers, empire-builders, and the warrior classes supplied with food parcels for over 200 years.

SOHO Cities are rarely sleaze-free, but few have their strip joints and red lights right next door to fancy restaurants, delis, thriving media companies, and a traditional fruit and veg market (Berwick St.). The council is enforcing ever more stringent controls on the sex trade by forcibly buying flats used as unlicensed brothels and selling them to charities that in turn develop social housing. Of all London's neighborhoods, Soho's narrow streets are the most densely thronged, especially on weekends, when it can be difficult to walk.

Soho is a wedge-shaped neighborhood. Its boundaries are **Regent Street, Oxford Street** (a mecca for mass-market shopping), **Charing Cross Road,** which is stuffed with bookshops, and the theater-lined **Shaftesbury Avenue.** Urban streetwear stores are finally starting to push back the tide of tourist schlock on **Carnaby Street,** where the 1960s swung the hardest. In the middle of Soho, **Old Compton Street** is the heart of gay London, with scores of gay bars, pubs, and cafes. Cross Shaftesbury Avenue and you come to **Chinatown,** which is small, yet authentic, and packed with excellent restaurants.

London's best-located youth hostel is on Noel Street in Soho, and there are good deals at the Regent Palace near Piccadilly Circus. But that's it.

PICCADILLY CIRCUS & LEICESTER SQUARE Piccadilly Circus was named after the "picadil," a ruffled collar created by the 17th-century tailor, Robert Baker. It's packed with crowds morning, noon, and way past midnight, grazing on fast food, gawking at the bright lights, and shopping at the megastores. There's a fast-food, commercial flavor to the area. Teenybopper delights abound at the **Trocadero,** where floor after floor is filled with video games and noisy attractions kids love. Its huge signs are part of a whole gallery of neon that illuminates the statue of Eros in the center of Piccadilly Circus. **Leicester** (*Les*-ter) **Square** is wall-to-wall neon, too. Once a posh address, it changed forever when the Victorians opened four giant entertainment halls, which today are megacinemas. At one end you'll find the **tkts** half-price tickets booth, an essential stop for theater-lovers. Crowds mill about the square until the early morning. (Keep a tight hold on your wallet, as pickpockets cruise for careless tourists.) Both Piccadilly Circus and Leicester Square are hubs for London's **West End theater** scene.

BLOOMSBURY Northeast of Piccadilly Circus, beyond Soho, is Bloomsbury, the academic heart of London. Much of the University of London, as well as several other colleges, are based here. It's quite a staid neighborhood, even boring, but writers such as Virginia Woolf, who lived here and put Bloomsbury into her book *Jacob's Room,* have fanned its reputation. Virginia and her husband Leonard Woolf were the unofficial leaders of a bohemian clique of artists and writers known as "the Bloomsbury

Group." **Russell Square** is the area's main hub, and the streets around it are crammed with excellent-value B&Bs. Most visitors come to see the treasures in the **British Museum,** and there are a few really good and good-value restaurants in the area.

Nearby is **Fitzrovia,** bounded by Great Portland Street, Oxford Street, and Gower Streets (lots of B&Bs there). Goodge Street is the main Tube stop and the village-like heart, with many shops and restaurants. It was the stomping ground of Ezra Pound, Wyndham Lewis, and George Orwell. Broadcasting House, in Portland Place, is an area landmark. It's the old BBC HQ, and you can get inside if you get tickets to a radio show.

HOLBORN This is the heart of legal London, where the ancient **Inns of Court** and **Royal Courts of Justice** lie. Dickens was a solicitor's clerk here when he was 14 and used the experience to good effect in *Little Dorrit.* Once you're off the traffic-laden High Holborn, time rolls back. The Viaduct Tavern, 126 Newgate St., was built over the notorious Newgate Prison. Holborn Viaduct was the world's first overpass. This is too business-like to be a hotel zone, stuck between the West End and the City, and northeast of Covent Garden. But you'll get a great cheap sleep at the Holborn Residence student dorm.

COVENT GARDEN & THE STRAND The fruit and flower market moved to an unromantic modern shed south of the river in 1970, and Professor Henry Higgins would find today's young women in Covent Garden far too fashionable for Eliza Doolittle–style experiments. This is a very fashion-oriented neighborhood, with more shopping and general razzle-dazzle than Soho, and certainly more tourists. It's quite pricey, too. The restored market hall is in the middle of **The Piazza,** a pedestrian square filled with boutiques, with the intriguing **Transport Museum** on one end. The character of Covent Garden owes a lot to its long theatrical history, which is why there are so many great pretheater deals at the restaurants. The Theatre Royal Drury Lane was where Charles II's mistress Nell Gwynne made her debut in 1665. And the actors' church designed by Inigo Jones, St. Paul's Covent Garden, holds memorials to many famous names from Ellen Terry to Boris Karloff to Vivien Leigh. The revamped **Royal Opera House** is a glorious place to stop for coffee—or a performance, if you like opera and ballet. Stay with visiting performers and fans at the eccentric Fielding hotel, just around the corner.

The **Strand** is a windy thoroughfare lined with theaters and hotels, including the Savoy, where the art of cocktail mixology was born and still flourishes in the American Bar. For a cheaper concoction, go next door to the newly restored **Somerset House.** The riverside Palladian mansion has three worthwhile museums, a wonderful riverside cafe, and a 50-jet courtyard fountain. The Strand runs northeast out of Trafalgar Square toward the City and marks the southern border of Covent Garden. **Trafalgar Square** is a visitor must-see all by itself. Nelson's Column—the triumphal memorial to England's victory over Napoleon in 1805—stands in the center, and the **National Gallery,** with the **National Portrait Gallery** just behind it, demarcates the northern side.

WESTMINSTER Edward the Confessor launched Westminster's rise to political power when he moved out of London to build his royal palace there in the 11th century. Dominated by the **Houses of Parliament** and Gothic

Westminster Abbey, Westminster runs along the Thames east of St. James's Park. **Whitehall,** which has long been synonymous with the armies of civil servants who really wield the power, is the main thoroughfare from Trafalgar Square to **Parliament Square.** Visit Churchill's **Cabinet War Rooms,** then peer through the gates guarding **Downing Street.** The Blairs actually live at no. 11 because the family wouldn't fit into no. 10.

Westminster also takes in **Victoria**, a strange area that is both businessy and, because it's dominated by the station, full of cheap (and sometimes nasty) hotels. The classiest ones are in Ebury Street on the fringes of Belgravia. Art lovers come here to visit **Tate Britain.**

THE CITY The City is where London began. Now it's one of the world's leading financial centers. The Bank of England (or the Old Lady of Threadneedle Street), the London Stock Exchange, and Lloyds of London are all located here. Much of the City was destroyed in the Great Fire of London, the Blitz, and later in the 1990s with some help from the IRA. Nowadays, it's a patchwork of the ancient and the very modern. You'll see some of the most god-awful modern architecture here, alongside such treasures as **St. Paul's Cathedral.** The **Museum of London** is home to 2000 years of history, including objects found during work on the Underground's new Jubilee Line extension. If you go to the **Barbican** cultural center, take a ball of string with you—following the painted directional lines is hopeless in this horribly planned concrete jungle. The biggest draw in this neck of the woods is the **Tower of London,** which should be at the top of every visitor's must-see list.

CLERKENWELL London's first hospital was here, and then Clerkenwell evolved into a muck-filled 18th-century cattle yard, home to cheap gin distilleries. In the 1870s, it became the center of the new socialist movement: John Stuart Mill's London Patriotic Club was in Clerkenwell, as was William Morris's socialist press later in the 1890s. Lenin lived here while he edited *Iskra.* Neither West End nor City proper, its fortunes then dwindled, but they're on the up and up again today as old commercial buildings turn into chic lofts and new restaurants open. Art galleries and shops run by small designers line Clerkenwell Green. Gritty working life goes on as meat lorries rumble into Smithfield Market. London's oldest church is here, too, the Norman St. Bartholomew-the-Great.

DOCKLANDS Since the London Docklands Development Corporation was set up in 1981, billions of pounds have gone into the most ambitious regeneration scheme of its kind in Europe. **Canary Wharf** is the focal point of this new river city, which runs east from Tower Bridge. Canary Wharf's 800-foot tower, designed by Cesar Pelli, is in the center of a covered piazza filled with shops with new skyscrapers sprouting up around it. It has taken 2 decades, but the once-bleak and isolated Canary Wharf is finally full, and developers are moving on to the World Trade Centre, five more skyscrapers in a gang of eight planned for Millennium Wharf nearby.

To see this area you might want to take a trip on the **Docklands Light Railway** (**DLR**). Up on elevated rails, it snakes past historic buildings, grotty empty spaces, and 21st-century shrines to big business. Or take the Jubilee Line: Canary Wharf station is one of the most striking of all the high-design stops on the new extension.

THE EAST END This collection of boroughs, east of the City, has long been one of the poorest areas of London. Now, though, it's hoped that the construction of a big Channel Tunnel rail interchange at Stratford will drag development eastwards. The Huguenots, fleeing religious persecution in France during the 16th century, were the first of the area's successive waves of immigrants right up to the large Bengali population today. Yet it's also home to the ultimate Londoner, the Cockney born within the sound of Bow Bells. This referred to the bells of St. Mary-le-Bow church, which rang the city curfew until the 19th century. Close to the docks, the East End was bombed to smithereens during the Blitz. Nudging Clerkenwell on the western edge is **Hoxton,** the hottest hotbed of young British artists and the entrepreneurs who know how to hype them. Otherwise, the few draws for visitors include the amazing Columbia Road flower market.

SOUTH BANK This is a loose definition, devised by Londoners on the north bank of the Thames, to define the only bit south of the river they're really interested in. As more and more redevelopment takes place, the definition widens. The core is the **South Bank Centre,** the largest cultural complex in Europe, which is now planning a big expansion and redevelopment. It houses the **National Theatre, Royal Festival Hall, Hayward Gallery,** and **National Film Theatre,** as well as several eateries. There's a browsable secondhand book market on the riverside walk near the National Theatre. Upriver, facing the Houses of Parliament, is the landmark observation wheel, the **British Airways London Eye.** Beside it is County Hall, once home to the Greater London Council, now part upscale Marriott hotel and part budget Travel Inn, with the **London Aquarium** in the basement and the new Saatchi Gallery and Dalí Universe upstairs. Go downriver (east), and you come to **Tate Modern** and the new **Millennium Bridge,** linking **Bankside** with St. Paul's and the City. With **Shakespeare's Globe Theatre** only a stone's throw away, this is a really exciting neighborhood. The London School of Economics student dorm, Bankside House, offers good-quality, cheap accommodations.

Still farther east, you come to London Bridge and **Southwark.** Known as the outlaw borough, it was the city's medieval hotspot for prostitutes, theaters, drinking dens, and crime. Pilgrims rested here, too, on their way to Thomas à Becket's shrine, as recorded in Chaucer's *Canterbury Tales.* There's a feast of history to revisit in this once-run-down area that has started to revive in a big way. Stop in **Southwark Cathedral,** and have a look at the new (opened in 2002) glass-walled **London City Hall,** HQ for the London Mayor and the Assembly; it's located right next to **Tower Bridge.**

ISLINGTON Islington is just north of Clerkenwell. It's always had a hint of raffishness. The Almeida theater, which has attracted such illustrious names as Ralph Fiennes, Kevin Spacey, and Rachel Weisz, has its home here. Gentrification is fairly recent, though, and still patchy despite the much-publicized influx of the New Labour "chattering classes." Or the outflux of residents such as Tony and Cherie Blair (who went straight to 11 Downing St.). Visitors should head for the antiques market at Camden Passage to look even if they can't afford to buy.

CAMDEN The Victorian slums that grew up around the canal have now been transformed into a hip, if still patchily seedy, neighborhood, first attracting artists such as Lucien Freud and Frank Auerbach, and later the burgeoning indie music industry. The biggest draw, and it is very big, is **Camden Market.** This isn't just a couple of stalls selling fruit and vegetables but a whole village of offbeat streets, covered areas, and old buildings, specializing in everything from new-age crystals to cheap clothes, bootleg tapes, and artsy-craftsy bits and bobs. Come early on a Sunday to beat the crowds.

HAMPSTEAD & HIGHGATE People who live in Hampstead live in Hampstead, not in London. This delightful village-style almost-burb northwest of Regent's Park has its own 800-acre patch of countryside, Hampstead Heath. Everybody from Sigmund Freud to D. H. Lawrence to Anna Pavlova to John Le Carré has lived here, and Glenda Jackson is the local MP. The wealthy residents still number a host of A-list celebs, who joined the less famous locals a few years ago to fight off a certain well-known U.S. burger chain. Hampstead makes a delightful day trip and isn't that far by Tube.

Highgate is on the northeastern edge of the Heath and is almost as villagey. It's worth a visit, if only to go to the famous **Highgate Cemetery,** where Karl Marx and George Eliot are buried. There are marvelous and morbid Victorian mausoleums.

PUTNEY & HAMMERSMITH It's a bit of a stretch to lump these boroughs together, but they're both found along the best sections of riverbank in London. There are boathouses all along this stretch of the Thames. The leafy path going westward along the south bank from Putney takes you past a bird sanctuary called **WWT Wetland Centre,** and it could be in the middle of the countryside. The famous Harrods Depository, a huge Victorian warehouse turned into chi-chi apartments, is just by Hammersmith Bridge. Cross over there, and continue along the north bank, with its succession of hugely popular pubs.

GREENWICH This charming port village is just about as far as you can go east along the south bank of the river without leaving London. It's the starting point for the reckoning of terrestrial longitudes and is a UNESCO World Heritage Site. Greenwich is used to fame, having enjoyed its first heyday in Tudor days. You can spend a whole day visiting the many historic delights of Greenwich, which include the 1869 tea clipper ***Cutty Sark,*** the **National Maritime Museum,** the **Old Royal Observatory,** and the Queen's House–all of them free.

2 Getting Around

BY PUBLIC TRANSPORTATION

The London Underground operates on a system of six fare zones. These radiate out in concentric rings from the central zone 1, which is where visitors spend most of their time. Zone 1 covers an area from the Tower in the east to Notting Hill in the west, and from Waterloo in the south to Baker Street, Euston, and King's Cross in the north. You will need a zone 2 ticket, though, for a trip to Camden, Hampstead, and Greenwich. The city's buses used to share the same zone system but **Transport for London** (TfL) simplified the bus system: now, for ticket-buying purposes, there's just zone 1, and then the rest of London; there are four fare zones for bus passes, though.

Tube, bus, and river service maps are available at all Underground stations, or you can download them from Transport for London's website, **www.tfl.gov.uk**. This also

Tube Update

The Tube is the oldest underground system in the world and also one of the deepest. Station escalators need millions of pounds' worth of upgrading. They are frequently closed for repair or have one side turned off forcing passengers to walk down to the platform. The Transport for London hotline (✆ **020/7222-1234;** www.thetube.com) provides up-to-the-minute recorded information as well as the option to speak to a live human being for detailed queries. Call if you have **restricted mobility** of any kind. The website also carries daily Tube travel information.

has an A-to-B journey planner. You can also call the 24-hour **travel hotline** ✆ **020/7222-1234.** There are Transport for London **Information Centres** at several major Tube stations: Euston, King's Cross, Liverpool Street, Piccadilly Circus, Victoria, St. James's Park, and Oxford Circus. They're all open daily—except for the last two, which close on Sundays—from at least 9am to 5pm.

FARES Kids up to age 4 travel free on the Tube and kids under 11 travel free on buses. From 12 to 15, they qualify for children's fares, generally around 40% less than adults. Fourteen- and 15-year-olds need a Photocard for discounts, so parents should bring recent pictures plus proof of their age to the nearest Tube station (just in case, most have photo booths).

Transport for London generally puts up its fares once a year in early January. At press time, prices were as follows:

Single (one-way) tickets within zone 1 on the Underground cost £2 ($3.70) for adults and 60p ($1.10) for children. Simply double that for a return (round-trip) fare. The price of a book of 10 single tickets, a **Carnet,** is £17 ($31). Adult bus fares are £1.20 ($2.20) anywhere within London. The flat daytime rate for children is 40p (70¢). A **Bus Saver** gives you six journeys for £6 ($11).

TRANSPORTATION DISCOUNTS Anyone planning to use public transport should check out the range of passes that are available for all public transportation: the Underground, buses, and the Docklands Light Railway. These make travel much cheaper, and also get you **a third off all river service tickets.**

Day Travelcards can be used for unlimited trips after 9:30am (off-peak) Monday to Friday, and all day on Saturday, Sunday, and holidays. Adults traveling within zones 1 and 2 pay £4.70 ($8.70). Children pay £2 ($3.70).

3-Day Travelcards are valid for any three consecutive days. For off-peak travel, these cost £15 ($28) for adults and £7.50 ($14) for children.

7-Day Travelcards are good for any number of trips on the Underground, any hour of the day. The card for zone 1 costs adults £19 ($34) and £7.30 ($13) for a child.

Family Travelcards, good for one day, are available to groups that include up to two adults, plus up to four children, and are only valid when they travel together. These can be used only after 9:30am during the week but all day on Saturday and Sunday. They cost £3.10 ($5.75) per adult in the group, and 80p ($1.85) per child, for zones 1 and 2.

Bus passes, valid for travel on citywide buses, are available for all zones for 1 day at £3 ($5.50) per adult and £1 ($1.85) per child, and for 1 week at £11 and £4 ($20 and $7.40).

You can buy all these, as well as monthly and yearly passes, at Tube stations, tobacconists, and newsagents with a **Pass Agent** sticker in their window.

THE UNDERGROUND

The Tube map is very easy to use. Every line has a different color: navy blue for the Piccadilly Line (the one that runs in from Heathrow), red for the Central Line, and so on. Station signs in the subway tunnels and on the different platforms clearly direct you to eastbound and westbound, or northbound and southbound trains. A sign at the front of the train and electronic notice boards on the platforms tell you the final destination of that line, so get to know the names of stations at the ends of the lines you use most often. The **Docklands Light Railway (DLR)** is an extension to the main Tube system. Its driverless trains run east on elevated tracks from Bank Tube station and Tower Gateway, close to Tower Hill. It operates daily at similar hours.

Except for Christmas Day, Tube trains run every few minutes from about 5:30am Monday to Saturday and 7am or so on Sunday. The Underground winds down between 11:30pm and 1am, as trains head back to home base, with stations closing behind them. The time of the last train is usually written on a board in each ticket hall, but assume that service on nearly all lines stops at 11:45pm. Assuming that the system is running smoothly, you can calculate how long a Tube journey will take by allowing 3 minutes per stop, adding in a bit extra if you have to change lines. But the system does have problems that often slow you down or stop trains completely.

Tube Tales

The genius behind **www.goingunderground.net**, "Annie Mole," posts irreverent observations on everything from Tube etiquette to celebrity-spotting on her site. The site has drawn an audience keen to participate and escalate the grumbling about the service.

This is a must-visit site for a passenger-eye view of the Underground. And, by the time your holiday is over, you may have tales to tell, too—perhaps some more nutty, but oh-so everyday, driver announcements to add to this selection.

- On the Hammersmith & City Line "I apologize for the delay but the computer controlling the signaling at Aldgate and Whitechapel has the Monday morning blues!"
- On the Waterloo & City Line "Good evening ladies and gents, and welcome to the Waterloo & City line. Sights to observe on the journey are, to your right, black walls and to your left, black walls. See the lovely black walls as we make our way to Waterloo. We will shortly be arriving at Waterloo where this train will terminate. We would like to offer you a glass of champagne on arrival and you will notice the platform will be lined with lap-dancers for your entertainment. Have a good weekend."
- On a Central Line "Mind the doors. Yes you, the woman in the long brown coat, love. I suggest you should shave your legs in future: it'll stop the hairs getting caught in the doors. Look at her everyone, mingin'! . . . Anyway, have a safe journey. Please, mind the doors. The doors are closing."

Tips Buy a Travelcard Before You Fly to Save Pounds

If you plan to use public transport a lot, think about buying a **London Visitor Travelcard** before you leave home. This special tourist deal, which includes discount vouchers for some major attractions, isn't available in the United Kingdom, and it includes travel on the Underground and buses with no time restrictions. All-zone adult passes cost $36 for 3 days and $78 for 7 days; child equivalents cost $12 and $34. Central Zone passes cost $30 and $42 for adults, $15 and $17 for kids. You can buy Visitor Travelcards online from BritRail (www.britrail.com).

There are two ways to buy tickets: at the station ticket window or using one of the push-button machines. Queuing at the window can be phenomenally time-consuming, particularly at West End stations during the summer. Elsewhere, the rush hour clogs things up, especially on a Monday when lots of people renew weekly travel passes. You will have to go to the window, though, if you want to buy a pass valid for longer than 2 days.

There are two kinds of machines: The first takes only coins and has buttons marked with little more than the price. (There should be a poster next to it that lists fares to every station.) The other machine has a button for each station and type of ticket, and will tell you the price of your choice. It accepts credit and debit cards, coins, and notes up to £10. The machines make change until they run out of spare coins, which tends to happen at busy times.

Hold onto your ticket throughout your ride because you'll need it to exit, and London Transport inspectors make random checks. No excuse, however imaginative or heartrending, will get you out of the rigidly imposed £10 ($18) penalty fare.

LONDON BUSES

London's comprehensive bus system makes for a very bewildering map. Most locals know only 2 of the 500-plus routes: from home to work and to the West End, and often that's the same thing. If you find the map completely incomprehensible, call the Transport for London Travel Line (see above), and they'll tell you how to get from A to B. And ask the driver or conductor to let you know when the bus has reached your destination.

To stop a bus when you're on it, press the bell (or tug the wire running the length of the ceiling in an old bus). Without any signal, the driver won't stop unless passengers are waiting to get on the bus. If you're the one waiting, make sure to note whether it is a compulsory (white background on the sign) or a request stop (red background). At the latter, give a big wave or the bus won't stop.

Traveling by bus is a great way to see London, but it can be frustratingly slow, particularly in rush hour and along Oxford Street and King's Road. Normal buses run until around midnight when night buses, with an N in front of the number, take over for the next 6 hours. On most routes, there's a night bus every half-hour or hour, and those to, from, and through the West End all go via Trafalgar Square, so if in doubt, head there.

You buy single-trip bus tickets on the bus itself. On older buses, a conductor comes around, but most new buses are now driver-only, so you pay when you board. In either case, you need exact change, so always carry some £1 coins and smaller change. If inspectors find you without a ticket, the on-the-spot fine is £5 ($9).

BY BOAT

Tony Blair and his government tried to use the millennium as the spur to regenerate the Thames and restore regular public transport services. But grand plans for an all-day Central London Fast Ferry ran aground. The building of new piers and tarting up of old ones has continued apace, though, so there are now 25 of them between Hampton Court and Gravesend. Westminster got an amazing £5 million ($8 million) pier, linked by a walkway to the Tube station, and Millbank Pier, near Tate Britain, was completed in 2003. "Tate to Tate" shuttle service is now available between Tate Modern and Tate Britain, with a stop at the London Eye, for £3.40 ($6.30) adults, £7.60 ($14) families. You can pick up tickets at either museum, or call ✆ **020/7887-8888** to book in advance. Transport bosses are hoping all the piers will act as a spur to regular river services. It would be a pleasant alternative to buses and the Tube.

Like buses and Tubes, boat operators now come under London mayor Ken Livingstone's control. He has already persuaded them to take part in an excellent deal, giving passengers with any Travelcard a third off fares. You will find river service booklets at most Tube stations. There are maps, timetables, and fare details on **www.tfl.gov.uk**. Or call the travel hotline ✆ **020/7222-1234.**

The most popular river cruises take you downriver to Greenwich or upriver to Kew Gardens and Hampton Court (see chapter 7 for details on all three). The Greenwich-bound boats are operated by **Thames River Services,** Westminster Pier, Victoria Embankment (✆ **020/7930-4091;** www.thamesriverservices.co.uk). The boats to Kew Gardens and Hampton Court, operated by **WPSA (Upriver) Ltd.** (✆ **020/7930-2062;** www.wpsa.co.uk), also leave from Westminster Pier.

BY CAR

Please don't rent a car for your holiday in Central London. The fact that London just instituted a new "Congestion Charge" in 2003 for cars coming into the city should tell you all you need to know about the traffic situation. Parking is an expensive nightmare. Gas (*petrol* in the U.K.) is stratospherically expensive—around 80p ($1.50) a liter, or $5.60 a gallon. It takes a while to get to know the city well enough to drive from A to B without going via Z, even with a navigator in the car. It takes more than a while to get anywhere as the average speed is 10 mph. And London drivers are a combative, aggressive lot. By comparison, even the most hellish public transport experience looks like nirvana. The only reason to rent a car is for a day trip into the countryside (not a city) or an around-Britain tour.

RENTING A CAR

Most car-rental companies in Britain will accept U.S., Canadian, Australian, and New Zealand driver's licenses, provided you've held it for more than a year. You'll also need

---

Fun Fact A Record-Setting Tube Ride

In 2000, a scout leader set a new record by visiting all 282 Tube stations in 19 hours, 59 minutes, and 37 seconds. Even more amazing, he only suffered a 30-minute delay.

---

a passport. Many companies have a minimum age requirement, of either 23 or 25. Anyone with a record for drunk driving will have a problem renting a car.

You can save money by booking a car in your home country before you travel, usually at least 48 weekday hours ahead, and for periods of a week or more. But try to reserve more than 2 weeks in advance because some rental companies will then guarantee a home-currency rate. Obviously, you must call around to find the best quote. In each case, check if the price includes the 17.5% value-added tax (VAT), personal accident insurance, and collision-damage waiver (CDW). Also remember to specify an automatic if that's what you're used to because most Brits drive stick-shifts.

Some of the big companies have North American toll-free numbers, and they're listed here, followed by the London equivalents: **Avis** (✆ **800/230-4898,** 0870/606-0100; www.avis.com); **Budget Rent-a-Car** (✆ **800/527-0700,** 0800/181-1881; www.budget.com); and **Hertz** (✆ **800/654-3001,** 0870/844-8844; www.hertz.com). But make sure to check out **Europe by Car** (✆ **800/223-1516** nationwide, 212/581-3040 in New York; www.europebycar.com) because it often undercuts the majors. So does British broker **Holiday Autos** (✆ **800/576-1590** in the U.S., or 0870/400-0099 in the U.K.; www.holidayautos.com), especially with discounts for online booking. It has offices all over the world.

easyRentacar (www.easyrentacar.com) rents cars from depots at London Bridge, off King's Road, Chelsea, and near Edgware Road Tube station. You can only book online. Rates fluctuate according to demand, so the deal is always better if you book ahead: 1 day costs £9 to £28 ($17–$52), plus a £10 ($18) car-cleaning fee (waived if you bring the car back clean). The downsides are that you only get 121km (75 miles) free, above which the charge is 20p (37¢) a mile, and every car has easy's orange logo glowing on its side.

PARKING

On-street parking is heavily regulated. Some areas are for residents with permits only. Some are for general use, either paid for at a meter next to the parking space or at an automatic Pay and Display ticket machine that covers a small length of street. Each local council makes different rules even for different areas within its own area. Check the streetside notices and information on meters. Never park on single or double yellow lines, zigzag white lines at the edge of the road, or in bus lanes. And never stop for even a second where there are red lines.

Penalties are harsh, and any one of the following can apply whenever and wherever you break the rules. Council parking tickets/fines range from £40 to £80 ($74–$148) and police fines are currently around £40 ($74). ***Warning:*** All unpaid tickets eventually end up back at the rental company, which will send you a bill. If you still do not pay up, this will go on a central record and may prevent your re-entry into the United Kingdom.

Wheel clamps are called Denver Boots in London. It generally takes an hour from the time you call the number on the clamping sticker to get it off. You have to pay £60 ($111). It costs up to £135 ($250) to get a towed car out of the pound. If you come back and find that your car's been towed, call the 24-hour **Vehicle Trace Hotline** (✆ **020/7747-4747**) to find out which pound it's gone to.

Blue signs point the way to **National Car Parks (NCP)**, which are spread throughout the city. Prices vary, and most set a minimum stay of 2 hours. That costs upwards of £7.50 ($12) in the West End. To find the closest, call NCP (✆ **020/7499-7050;** www.ncp.co.uk).

DRIVING RULES

Buy a copy of the *British Highway Code,* available at most newsagents and bookstores. Otherwise, there are a few basic things to remember, apart from driving on the left side of the road. Except where indicated, the speed limit in Central London, as in any built-up area, is 48kmph (30 mph). In Britain, everyone in the car must wear a seatbelt, even passengers in the back. You may not turn right on a red light. Cars must stop as soon as a pedestrian steps onto a zebra crossing—the black-and-white-striped crosswalk. These are in the middle of the block, not at the corner, and are well-lit.

BY TAXI

Black cabs carry up to five people and can make sound economic sense for group jaunts. All the drivers are licensed and have to pass a test called The Knowledge first, so they know London very well. Look for the yellow FOR HIRE sign lit up on the roof and wave wildly. Before you get in, tell the driver where you want to go. Except in the West End, many drivers go home at midnight. You can order a black cab, but you'll have to pay an extra charge for the time it takes the taxi to get to you—up to £3.80 ($7). Two companies dispatch cabs around the clock: **Dial a Cab** (✆ **020/7253-5000**) and **Radio Taxis** (✆ **020/7272-0272**).

The average cost of a taxi ride is said to be £8 ($13)—but that means daytime, within Central London, and with no unusual traffic jams. The minimum charge is £1.40 ($2.60), and the meter goes up in increments of 20p (37¢). Ken Livingstone has talked about changing the surcharge system but, at the moment, you'll pay 60p to 90p ($1.10–$1.70) depending on the time of day (generally after 8pm and between midnight and 6am on weekdays, and slightly different times at weekends, or public holidays). Other extras on the basic fare include 40p (75¢) for every passenger after the first one and 10p (18¢) for every piece of luggage over .6m (2 ft.) long or that has to go in front with the driver. If you have any complaints, call the **Public Carriage Office** (✆ **020/7230-1631**).

Minicabs are generally cheaper than black cabs, but drivers don't have to have a special license, and some won't know their way around any better than you do. Technically, they must operate from a sidewalk office or through phone bookings and are not allowed to cruise for fares. But some do, of course, particularly at main railway stations and late night in the West End. With minicabs there are none of the guarantees you get with a black cab. Minicabs don't have meters. Always negotiate the fare with the office, and confirm it with the driver. Most firms are open round the clock, and you can prebook for later, or for the next morning if you've got an early start. They tend to be locally based, so ask your hotel or B&B to recommend a reputable one. **Addison Lee** (✆ **020/7387-8888**) operates citywide.

BY BICYCLE

Serious cyclists should check out the **London Cycling Campaign,** Unit 228, 30 Great Guildford St., SE1 OHS (✆ **020/7928-7220;** www.lcc.org.uk), for information, maps, and advice on city two-wheeling. I've also suggested a place to rent bicycles in the section on "Organized Tours," in chapter 7.

Telephone Dialing Info at a Glance

- To call London from home, dial the international access code: ✆ **011** from the **United States** and **Canada,** ✆ **0011** from **Australia,** and ✆ **00** from **New Zealand.** Follow that with **44,** and then the area code minus its initial zero, and finally the number.
- To call home from London, the international codes are ✆ **001** for the **United States** and **Canada,** ✆ **0061** for **Australia,** and ✆ **0064** for **New Zealand.** Then add the area code minus any initial zero, and the number. Or, you can use these **long-distance access codes:** AT&T USA Direct (✆ **0800/890-011**), MCI Worldphone (✆ **0800/890-222**), USA Sprint Global (✆ **0800/890-877**), Canada Direct (✆ **0800/890-016**), Telstra Direct for Australia (✆ **0800/890-061**), and New Zealand Direct (✆ **0800/890-064**).
- When you're in London, dial ✆ **100** for the U.K. national operator, ✆ **155** for the international operator, ✆ **192** for Directory Enquiries to find out a U.K. telephone number, and ✆ **153** for International Directory Enquiries.
- Free dial-a-directory **Scoot** (✆ **0800/192-192**) can give you the name, address, and phone number of any service you might need in London.

FAST FACTS: London

Airport See "Getting There," in chapter 2.

American Express American Express (✆ **01273/696933** for general U.K. information; www.americanexpress.com) has over a dozen city center offices. The branch at 30–31 Haymarket, SW1 (✆ **020/7484-9610;** www.americanexpress.co.uk; Tube: Piccadilly Circus), is open Monday to Friday 9am to 6pm, Saturday 9am to 6:30pm, and Sunday 10am to 5pm. Cardholders and anyone with American Express traveler's checks can receive mail there, but weekends are currency-exchange only. The company has a 24-hour toll-free line to report lost or stolen cards (✆ **0800/550-011**) and traveler's checks (✆ **0800/521-313**).

Babysitters Many hotels and B&Bs can arrange babysitting for you (see the reviews in chapter 5). **Universal Aunts** (✆ **020/7386-5900;** www.universal aunts.co.uk) has been up and running for 17 years. It charges £6.50 ($12) per daytime hour and £5 ($9) after 6pm. The minimum booking is 4 hours, and the agency fee is £3.50 ($6.50) for up to 5 hours and £6.50 ($12) thereafter. You will also pay the sitter's travel both ways.

Business Hours Bank opening hours are Monday to Friday 9:30am to 3:30 or 4:30pm. Some are also open Saturday 9:30am to noon. Business offices are generally open Monday to Friday from 9am until 5 or 5:30pm. By law, pubs can open Monday to Saturday 11am to 11pm, and noon to 10:30pm on Sunday; most London pubs keep these hours. Some bars in the city center have late licenses that let them close up to 4 hours later, and some dance clubs stay open until 4 or 5am. Restaurants, other than cafes and really cheap eats, serve lunch from noon to 2:30pm and dinner 6 to 10:30pm (see chapter 6). A few go on later. Stores are generally open Monday to Saturday from 10am to 6pm. Many stay open for at least 1 extra hour on a Wednesday or Thursday, depending on the neighborhood (see chapter 8). Some shops around touristy Covent Garden don't close until 7 or 8pm nightly. Supermarkets and many of the stores in busy shopping areas are also open on Sundays, usually starting at 11am.

Car Rentals See "Getting Around," earlier in this chapter.

Climate See "When to Go," in chapter 2.

Credit Card Hotlines For lost or stolen cards in the U.K., call Mastercard ✆ **0800/964-767;** Visa ✆ **0800/895-082;** or Diners Club ✆ **0800/460-800.** Also see "American Express," above.

Currency See "Money," in chapter 2.

Dentists Try the **Dental Emergency Care Service,** Guy's Hospital, St. Thomas's St., SE1 (✆ **020/7955-5000**), a first-come, first-served clinic on the 23rd floor, Monday to Friday 8:45am to 3pm. On Saturday and Sunday, emergency dental service is available from 9am to 4pm at **Kings College,** Denmark Hill, Camberwell SE5 (✆ **020/7345-3591**). You can also call **Eastman Dental Hospital,** 256 Gray's Inn Rd., WC1 (✆ **020/7915-1000**).

Doctors The National Health Service now runs a telephone help line, **NHS Direct** (✆ **020/0845-4647**), which is a useful first port of call for noncritical illnesses. Otherwise, London has five private walk-in **Medicentres,** offering the same services as a GP. Those at Victoria Station and the Plaza mall at Bond Street Tube station are open every day; call for times and directions (✆ **0870/600-0870**). **Medcall,** 2 Harley St., W1 (✆ **0800/136106**), operates a late-night practice and 24-hour call-out. **Medical Express,** 117A Harley St., W1 (✆ **020/7499-1991;** www.medicalexpressclinic.com), is a private clinic with walk-in medical service (no appointment necessary) Monday through Friday 9am to 6pm and Saturday 9:30am to 2:30pm.

Documents See "Entry Requirements & Customs" in chapter 2.

Driving Rules See "Getting Around," earlier in this chapter.

Drugstores The Brits call them chemists. **Bliss Chemist,** 5 Marble Arch, W1 (✆ **020/7723-6116**), is open daily 9am to midnight. **Zarfash Pharmacy,** 233–235 Old Brompton Rd., SW5 (✆ **020/7373-2798**), never closes. In daytime hours, there are branches of **Boots** and **Superdrug** everywhere.

Electricity British appliances operate on the E.U. standard of 240 volts. If you're bringing a hair dryer, travel iron, shaver, and so on, you need a transformer. British sockets take different three-pronged plugs than those in the U.S. London department stores and most branches of **Boots** sell adapters, in case you arrive without one. Hotels and B&Bs sometimes have one you can borrow.

Embassies & High Commissions This list will help you out if you lose your passport or have some other emergency:

- **Australia** The **High Commission** is at Australia House, Strand, WC2 (✆ **020/7379-4334;** www.australia.org.uk), and is open Monday to Friday from 9am to 5pm. Tube: Holborn or Temple.

- **Canada** The **High Commission** is at Macdonald House, 1 Grosvenor St., W1 (✆ **020/7258-6600;** www.canada.org.uk), and is open Monday to Friday from 8am to 11am. Tube: Bond St.
- **Ireland** The Embassy is at 17 Grosvenor Pl., SW1 (✆ **020/7235-2171**).
- **New Zealand** The **High Commission** is at **New Zealand House,** Haymarket, SW1 (✆ **020/7930-8422;** www.newzealandhc.org.uk), and is open Monday to Friday from 10am to noon and 2 to 4pm. Tube: Piccadilly Circus.
- **The United States** The embassy at 24 Grosvenor Sq., W1 (✆ **020/7499-9000;** www.usembassy.org.uk), is open for walk-in enquiries 8:30am to 12:30pm, 2 to 5pm (to 5:30pm for phone calls). Calls to the 24-hour visa hotline (✆ 09068-200-290), available in the U.K. only, cost £.60 per minute. Tube: Marble Arch or Bond Street.

Emergencies Dial ✆ **999** free from any phone for police, fire, and ambulance.

Holidays See "When to Go," in chapter 2.

Hospitals Around a dozen city hospitals offer 24-hour walk-in emergency care. The most central is **University College Hospital,** Grafton Way, WC1 (✆ **020/7387-9300**). The two best alternatives are **Chelsea & Westminster Hospital,** 369 Fulham Rd., SW10 (✆ **020/8746-8000**), on the Chelsea/Fulham border; and **St. Mary's Hospital,** Praed St., W2 (✆ **020/7886-6666**), in Paddington.

Hotlines Anyone who is distressed about anything can call the **Samaritans** (✆ **0845/790-9090;** www.samaritans.org.uk) at any time to hear a friendly voice. **Alcoholics Anonymous** runs a help line from 10am to 10pm every day (✆ **020/7833-0022;** www.alcoholics-anonymous.org.uk), and **Narcotics Anonymous** does the same (✆ **020/7730-0009;** www.ukna.org).

Information See "Visitor Information," earlier in this chapter.

Internet Access There are cybercafes all over London, one of the most common being **EasyInternetcafe** (www.easyinternetcafe.com). A few budget hotels will send and receive e-mails for you, and access is available in all hostels (see chapter 5). You can also send short e-mails for free from the many **i-plus** information booths around the city (see "Visitor Information," earlier in this chapter).

Liquor Laws The government has promised to update the antiquated English and Welsh licensing laws, but it hasn't happened yet. In the meantime, no one under 18 can buy or consume alcohol, with one exception: 16- and 17-year-olds may purchase "beer, porter, or cider," with a table meal. Under-14s may enter some pubs but only when accompanied by an adult. Adults can buy beer, wine, and spirits in supermarkets, liquor stores (called "off-licenses"), and many local grocery stores, during the same opening hours as pubs (see "Business Hours," above). Admission-charging nightclubs are allowed to serve alcohol to patrons until 3am or so. After 11pm, hotel bars may serve drinks to registered guests only. Do not drink and drive because the police are eagle-eyed and the penalties very stiff.

Lost Property If you lose something on the bus or Tube, wait 3 working days before going to the **Transport for London Lost Property Office,** 200 Baker St., NW1 (✆ **020/7486-2496** recorded information), open Monday to Friday 9:30am to 2pm. For buses, you need to call and find out which depots are at either end of that particular line (✆ **020/7222-1234**). There are also lost-property offices at all train stations and at Victoria Coach Station. **Taxi Lost Property** (✆ **020/7918-2000**) at Baker Street is open weekdays 9am to 4pm, but only for things left in black cabs.

Mail Stamps for postcards and airmail letters up to 10 grams to anywhere outside Europe cost 47p (87¢). For more information, call the **Post Office Helpline** (✆ **0845/722-3344;** www.postoffice.co.uk or www.royalmail.co.uk). See "Post Office," below.

Maps See "City Layout," earlier in this chapter.

Newspapers & Magazines All of London's newspapers are fighting for increased circulation by downsizing size and content, so more and more of them are starting to look like tabloids. The *Guardian, Independent,* the *Times,* and *Daily Telegraph* are the so-called quality national daily newspapers, listed here from left to right across the political spectrum. The *Daily Mail* and *Express* are supposedly middle-of-the-road, but very right-wing, tabloids. All have Sunday editions. (The *Guardian* has a sister paper, *The Observer.*) The *Evening Standard* is the only paid-for citywide local paper—it has a freebie sister, *Metro,* carried on Tube trains in the morning—and publishes updated editions from 10am to around 5pm. On Thursdays, it has a what's-on supplement, *Hot Tickets.* Most Sunday broadsheets produce entertainment guides, too. But the listings bible is the weekly *Time Out* magazine (www.timeout.com).

Post Office The **Trafalgar Square Post Office,** 24–28 William IV St., Trafalgar Square, WC2, is open Monday to Friday from 8am to 8pm, opening at 9am on Saturday. Travelers can receive mail, marked "Poste Restante," here and must bring identification to collect it. Most other post offices are open Monday to Friday from 9am to 5:30pm, and Saturday 9am to noon. Look for the red Royal Mail signs. To contact the Trafalgar Square Post office or find the nearest local one, call the **Post Office Helpline** (✆ **0845/722-3344;** www.postoffice.co.uk or www.royalmail.co.uk).

Restrooms The Brits have three printable words for restrooms: toilet, lavatory (the lav), and loo. Some "Public Toilets" are free—St. Christopher's Place, near Bond Street, and the uninviting but well-maintained subway facilities at Tottenham Court Tube station—but keep a few 20p coins handy for the many paid-for ones. There are top shop loos (no charge) at John Lewis (Oxford Street), Waterstone's (Piccadilly), Harvey Nichols (Knightsbridge), and Peter Jones (Sloane Square, Chelsea). You'll get a glare and often a lecture if you use a pub restroom without buying a drink, so be discreet and act natural. The same goes for nonguests popping into loos at posh hotels.

Safety Violent crime is no more common in Central London than in any other big city, and less common than in many. But don't take risks—keep wallets and purses hidden, bags held tight to your side, backpacks zipped, and never leave possessions unattended, even on the floor between your feet. And don't flash your cash, credit cards, or jewelry.

Salon A really great budget deal is the **Vidal Sassoon School,** 53 Davies Mews, W1 (✆ **020/7318-5205**), which trains recently qualified hairdressers. Men and women can get a classic or creative cut for about £10 ($18), a fraction of the cost of one at Vidal Sassoon's world-famous salons. The academy is open Monday to Friday, with appointments at 10am and 3pm.

Smoking You can't light up anywhere on the Underground or on buses. Many restaurants have nonsmoking sections, and some ban it completely. Things are also starting to change in budget hotels and B&Bs. A few don't allow smoking at all. More are now keeping some rooms as nonsmoking.

Taxes There are no separate county or city sales taxes in Britain. The national 17.5% value-added tax (VAT) is levied on most goods and services and is included in the price. Takeaway food is exempt, hence the two price lists at those eateries that offer both. Except for the luxury ones, hotels usually include VAT in quoted prices (all rates in this book include tax). Foreign visitors can reclaim the VAT on goods they're taking out of the U.K. Ask for a form from the sales clerk at those stores participating in the Tax-Free Shopping scheme. Then show it and the goods at the VAT desk at the airport. Refunds cannot be processed at the airport. For more information, see chapter 8.

Taxis See "By Taxi," above.

Telephones Several companies operate London phone boxes, each branded differently, but BT (British Telecom) is still the largest. There are also pay phones in most large public buildings. Most accept any coin upward of 10p. Others take credit cards and prepaid BT phonecards, which are available in post offices and newsagents.

Pay-phone **call rates** are the same every day, all day. The minimum cost is 20p (37¢) for the first 67 seconds of a local call and 43 seconds of all other calls. Pay phones accept up to four coins at a time. They don't make change so, unless you're calling long-distance, use small denominations.

Private businesses, such as pubs and B&Bs, can calibrate their pay-phones to charge any rate they want—it's an accepted money-spinner—but they must advertise that rate on the phone. Also check the rates before using the **in-room phone** in your hotel because these will often include massive surcharges.

In Britain, the main **toll-free** code is **0800** or **0500,** but not all customer-service, information, or central-reservations lines use it. There are dozens of other special codes, which may be charged at the local rate (the 0845 numbers you'll see throughout the book), regional, or national rate (0870). Calls to premium-rate 090-prefixed lines cost at least 60p ($1) a minute—by law, the operator must warn you about the charges at the start of the call. You can check any code with the operator (✆ **100**) to avoid nasty shocks.

Time Zone London's clocks are set on Greenwich Mean Time—5 hours ahead of U.S. Eastern Standard Time, 10 hours behind much of Australia, and 12 hours behind New Zealand. To find out the time, dial **Timeline** (✆ **123**). Daylight saving time is used in Britain, too. The clocks move 1 hour back, to British Summer Time, on the last weekend of March, and forward to GMT again on the last weekend of October.

Tipping The more expensive restaurants tend to add a service charge of 12.5% to the bill. Cheaper ones sometimes do, too, but more often only if you're a big group. The tipping policy should be written on the menu. If in doubt, ask. And make sure to check the bill before filling in the gap for a gratuity. In Britain, it is usual practice to tip cab drivers, staff in restaurants, hairdressers, some bars with table service, and hotels, but never pubs. Budget hotels and B&Bs will rarely add a percentage to the bill, so it's up to you. The usual amount on any occasion is 10%.

Weather Surf **www.bbc.co.uk/weather** for 5-day forecasts. Weathercall charges 60p ($1.10) a minute for 7-day forecasts (© **090/6654-3268**). Temperatures are always given in centigrade, not Fahrenheit (see inside front cover for conversion formula).

4

Suggested London Itineraries

Londoners often poke fun at the hectic pace of Americans, Canadians, Australians, and New Zealanders trying to squeeze in as many of the "greatest London hits" as their brief vacations allow. Pay no mind. Familiarity makes the locals blasé toward their national treasures. And London abounds in treasures of all kinds. The following three itineraries are designed for visitors with a reasonable amount of stamina and a desire to see the most famous sights. High cab fares put London taxis out of reach for budget travelers, so in these day-by-day plans you'll be walking and using the Tube (or Underground), London's subway system. You'll save a lot of money by using a special one- or multi-day Travelcard pass (see "Getting Around," in chapter 3).

1 The Best of London in One Day

To see the highlights in one day requires an early start. This tour is meant to show off the A-list of must-see London sights in a way that makes the most sense for walking and using public transportation. *Start: Tube to Leicester Square or Charing Cross.*

---

❶ Trafalgar Square ★★

From the Tube stop, make your way to busy Trafalgar Square, London's unofficial hub and scene of public gatherings and demonstrations. It's also the spot where the commercial West End meets The Mall, the regal avenue that leads to Buckingham Palace, and Whitehall, the governmental quarter. Nelson's Column rises in the center of the square, with the National Gallery facing it on the north and the Church of St. Martin-in-the-Fields east at about 2 o'clock. See p. 174.

❷ Buckingham Palace ★★★, the Changing of the Guard ★★★, Royal Mews ★★

Walk down The Mall, through St. James's Park, to Buckingham Palace, making sure that you're in front of the Palace by 11:15am to watch the colorful Changing of the Guard (for important scheduling information, see p. 161). The palace itself is hardly thrilling, except that you've heard about it all your life and it's the official London residence of the queen. You can visit the State Rooms when the palace is open to the public in August and September. If you're not visiting the palace, spend a few minutes checking out the horses and carriages in the Royal Mews. See p. 164.

❸ Houses of Parliament ★★★

From Buckingham Palace, you can walk to the Houses of Parliament or take the Tube one stop from St. James's Park to Westminster. The splendidly ornate Houses of Parliament—where sit the House of Commons and the House of Lords—face Parliament Square and are flanked on one side by the world-famous clock tower called Big Ben (actually, Big Ben is one of the bells that chimes within the clock tower) and by ancient Westminster Abbey on the other. For anyone on a schedule, it's a pain to get inside the Houses of Parliament except in August and September when excellent 1-hour tours are given. See p. 167.

❹ Westminster Abbey ★★★

From the Houses of Parliament you can walk the equivalent of 1 block to reach Westminster Abbey—one the oldest, most hallowed, and crowded sights in England. Kings and queens are crowned here, some are buried in elaborate chapels, and British literary greats are honored in Poets' Corner. It's an 800-year-old time capsule of English and royal history. See p. 175.

❺ British Airways London Eye ★★★

Walk across Westminster Bridge to the impossible-to-miss British Airways London Eye, a giant observation wheel put up for the millennium celebrations and so continuously popular that no one wants to take it down. You'll save time by buying a specific entry-time ticket in advance, but you can also get one at the box office on-site. A 30-minute "flight" on the giant wheel will give you a 25-mile bird's-eye view of the London landmarks you don't have time to visit. See p. 160.

❻ Tower of London ★★★

From Westminster you can take the Tube east to Tower Hill or, more fun, take a boat from Westminster Pier down to Tower Pier. Your destination is the Tower of London, as famous a spot as any in the Western world. Within these history-soaked walls there is enough to see—including the Crown Jewels—to keep you happily engrossed for hours. For maximum enjoyment, however, join one of the free tours led throughout the day by the Beefeaters. See p. 173.

❼ St. Paul's Cathedral ★

There's one last biggie on today's itinerary, and to get there you can take the Tube from Tower Hill to St. Paul's. Everyone wants to see St. Paul's, but frankly, it's expensive and I don't think you're missing much if you don't get inside (open until 4pm Mon–Sat). It doesn't have the history of Westminster Abbey, and the interior is rather bare. However, the famous dome is one of those quintessential London sights. See p. 170.

2 The Best of London in 2 Days

If you've already hit all the megamusts on "The Best of London in 1 Day," above, you're ready to experience more of this fascinating city. On your second day, savor a couple of truly great museums and the excitement of the West End. ***Start:*** *Tube to Russell Square.*

---

❶ British Museum ★★★

The British Museum, with its new Great Court, is a must, and it's a good idea to get there early before the crowds appear. Taking a tour will help you hone in on the museum's most famous holdings, but this is also a place to wander and ponder; whatever you do, don't miss the Parthenon Marbles (formerly called the Elgin Marbles), a magnificent group of Greek sculptures. There's so much to see that you need to do some advance planning and give yourself at least 2 hours. See p. 161.

❷ Covent Garden

It's time for some street life and maybe a bit of shopping. Take the Tube to Covent Garden, and you'll exit close to the Piazza—a nonstop people-watching show. This is one of London's great shopping areas, so just wander around and have fun until you're ready for lunch. For more, see the Covent Garden dining section in chapter 6, and "The Shopping Scene," on p. 213.

3 WAGAMAMA ★
Cross Charing Cross Road and you're in Soho, a warren of streets packed with cafes, clubs, and restaurants. At Wagamama you'll dine at long communal tables and order from a menu you'd find in a Japanese noodle bar. It's delicious and, for London, inexpensive. 10a Lexington St., W1. ✆ **020/7292-0990.** See p. 144.

4 National Gallery ★★ or National Portrait Gallery ★★

Do you want to look at masterpieces of painting or portraits of every famous Brit you've ever heard of? If the former, head for the National Gallery, an easy walk from Wagamama or anywhere in Soho or Covent Garden. The National Portrait Gallery, right behind it, is the museum equivalent of *People* magazine, only the celebs on view come from every segment of English life, from the Middle Ages to the present, including royalty, writers, film stars, politicians, and sports heroes. You need at least a couple of hours in either museum.

5 Leicester Square, Piccadilly Circus, and Regent Street

You can't say you've been to London if you haven't seen Piccadilly Circus. On your way there, walk through Leicester Square to see what half-price theater tickets are available for that evening at the tickets booth (p. 233). Then continue on to Piccadilly Circus. Truth to tell, this isn't the most attractive part of the city; it's the neon-clad equivalent of Times Square, full of superstores and lots of tat. But on one side of Piccadilly Circus you'll find the curved elegance of Regent Street, perfect for a short shopping stroll. For more information, see "Piccadilly Circus & Leicester Square" in chapter 3, p. 53, and "The Shopping Scene" in chapter 8, p. 213.

6 Dinner and a Show

You're in the heart of the West End, within walking distance of restaurants in Covent Garden, Soho, and Chinatown. Choose one that appeals from chapter 6, and then, half-price ticket in hand, head for the theater and the evening's entertainment. See "London's Theater Scene" and "The Performing Arts" sections in chapter 9 for more suggestions.

3 The Best of London in 3 Days

If you've hit the highlights listed in "The Best of London in 1 Day" and "The Best of London in 2 Days," above, it's time to expand your London horizons with a visit to a palace, a stroll in a couple of London's world-famous parks, and a visit to another fabulous museum. ***Start:*** *Tube to High St. Kensington or Queensway.*

1 Kensington Palace ★★

From the Tube station, make your way into Kensington Gardens; the Broad Walk will bring you to this late-17th-century palace where Queen Victoria was born and where Princess Diana made her home after the divorce from Charles. Inside, on a self-guided audio tour, you'll visit an impressive series of state rooms and a fascinating collection of royal gowns and haberdashery. See p. 168.

2 THE ORANGERY ★★
Have lunch or tea in this lovely 18th-century conservatory right outside Kensington Palace; it's not quite as expensive as its royal connection might lead you to expect. Kensington Palace Gardens, W8. ✆ **020/7376-0239.**

❸ Kensington Gardens & Hyde Park

The "personality" of London is definitely enhanced by its remarkable parks, where a calming green peace offsets urban grit and growl. When you come out of Kensington Palace you'll be in Kensington Gardens, which has a host of differently landscaped areas to admire, including the Albert Memorial erected by Queen Victoria for her prince of a husband. Walking east along the pretty Serpentine lake, you'll enter adjoining Hyde Park with its famous Speaker's Corner at its northeast corner. For more on both Kensington Gardens and Hyde Park, see "Parks & Gardens" in chapter 7, p. 201.

❹ A Museum of Your Choice

I don't want to steer you towards a museum you have no interest in seeing, so this one is up to you. All the choices are free, so you might want to squeeze in a couple of them. In South Kensington, within walking distance of Kensington Gardens, you'll find the **Natural History Museum** ★★, famed for its robotic dinosaurs and breathtaking gems (p. 169); the **Science Museum** ★★, chockablock with amazing scientific artifacts and exhibits (p. 170); and the gargantuan **Victoria & Albert** ★★, one of the world's great historic and decorative art collections (p. 174). Farther away, in Pimlico, is the **Tate Britain** ★★, a must for fans of British painting (p. 172). In Bankside on the South Bank of the Thames, is the fabulous **Tate Modern** ★★★, a world-class modern art collection housed in a former power plant and open until 10pm on Friday and Saturday (p. 172).

❺ A Pub, a Play, or a Concert

How do you want to celebrate your last night in London? There are plenty of pubs where you can raise a pint with the locals (see "The Drinking Game: Pubs & Wine Bars," chapter 9, p. 249). If it's summer, you might want to consider seeing a play at Shakespeare's Globe Theatre, a replica of the original Elizabethan theater on the South Bank of the Thames (see "London's Theater Scene," chapter 9, p. 233). Music lovers always have plenty to choose from, including symphony concerts and two opera houses that offer a year-round program of opera and dance (see "The Performing Arts," chapter 9, p. 237). Or you might just want to wander—the streets of London provide priceless entertainment that doesn't cost a penny.

5

Accommodations You Can Afford

Spend the night in a cupboard. Wash in a cup, then dry yourself with a handkerchief. Practice climbing and build your endurance on the Stairmaster. Whatever it is, do something to prepare yourself for the budget accommodations you'll find in London. It's unlikely that you'll be staying in a new hotel with an elevator (called a "lift" in England) and spacious rooms with marble bathrooms. Instead, if you opt for a B&B, you'll more likely be in an historic building, either Georgian or Victorian, with a certain amount of charm (hopefully) but few luxuries. Authorities are strict about what can and cannot be altered in historic buildings, both inside and out. Bedrooms are small, and private bathrooms (called "en suite facilities") are mainly an afterthought and as tiny as the toilet in an airplane. In many budget B&Bs the bathrooms are prefab shower/sink/toilet units that have been fit into the rooms. And there's rarely an elevator to bypass the precipitous stairs in these old buildings. Even if the stairs don't take your breath away, the room rates might.

We don't mean to paint too bleak a picture because there are plenty of good, small, even charming B&Bs where you'll be perfectly comfortable. We just want you to be prepared.

But facts must be faced, and one fact that can't be overlooked is that London is among the most expensive cities in the world. The problem isn't that hotels have drastically raised their rates, because they haven't. In many hotels listed below, the rates haven't changed in three or more years. The problem, at least for visitors from the U.S., is that the dollar is currently so weak against the British pound. As a result, prices for U.S. visitors have risen considerably since our last edition, in some cases by almost 20%! As things now stand, visitors from the U.S. will be hard-pressed to find a decent double room in a London B&B or hotel for under £80 ($150) a night for a double. It is possible, of course, and in the following pages I list some great budget options such as university residence halls and youth hostels.

Every hotel with a website told me that readers should check the hotel's website for special offers. Using the Web, you might find a lower rate than the nondiscounted rack rates I list below.

In this guide, the top price for a double, in the splurge category, is about £150 ($278). Even at that price you won't have attained much in the way of luxury, so I've limited my splurge choices mainly to budget neighborhoods where you get more for spending more. Otherwise, you'd do better to try out the hot tips below and score a properly posh room at a discount, either through Web surfing or going with an airline/hotel package.

As always, it's a good idea to book ahead. Most places guard against no-shows by charging 1-night's stay as a nonrefundable deposit. Some ask for full payment on arrival. A very few charge for accepting credit cards. And even fewer, the really sneaky ones, quote rates without VAT (the value-added tax of 17.5%). Check all this out when you call. Ask if the hotel has any special offers. You could also ask if they have earned any quality awards. The English Tourist Board, Automobile Association (AA), and Royal Automobile Club (RAC) now adhere to a common set of standards and award stars or diamonds. To qualify, the hotel must have a restaurant, liquor license, lounge, and private bathrooms in 75% of its rooms. Guesthouses, B&Bs, and self-catering accommodations—most of the places reviewed in this book—are rated with up to five diamonds.

1 How to Save on Sleeping

If you know where to look and what to ask for, you can find bargains in London. If you are not booking accommodations as part of a package deal (see "Money-Saving Package Deals," in chapter 2), read on. And don't forget to check "Fifty Money-Saving Tips," in chapter 2 for more ideas on how to save.

- **Play the supply-and-demand game.** Avoid high season. Most hotels make their annual rate increase in April and drop down again in October.
- **Go native.** Many Londoners offer bed-and-breakfast in their homes. The Bed & Breakfast and Hosts Association sets quality standards and the following three members are all well established. Rates are per night and for two people sharing a room: **At Home in London** (✆ **020/8748-1943;** www.athomeinlondon.co.uk) from £79 ($146) in West London; **Host and Guest Service** (✆ **020/7385-9922;** www.host-guest.co.uk) from £60 ($111) in Central London; and **Uptown Reservations** (✆ **020/7351-3445;** www.uptownres.co.uk) from £95 ($176) in Central London.
- **Consider apartment hotels or rooms with kitchens.** Staying in self-catering accommodations can cut down on expensive restaurant bills. Agencies to try include **Emperors Gate Short Stay Apartments,** SW5 (✆ **020/7244-8409;** www.apartment-hotels.com); **The Independent Traveller** (✆ **01392/860807;** www.gowithIT.co.uk), run by the very friendly and experienced Mary and Simon Ette; **Residence Apartments** (✆ **020/7727-0352;** www.residence-apartments.com); and the superbudget **Acorn Management Services** (✆ **020/8202-3311;** www.acorn-london.co.uk).
- **Go back to school.** During the summer and sometimes at Easter, you can find accommodations starting at around £23 ($43) per person at the dozens of university dorms in London. I've reviewed a handful of the top options. For fuller details of

Tips A Tip for the Bedless

If you arrive in London without a bed for the night, you can call the **British Hotel Reservation Centre** accommodations hotline (✆ **010/7340-1616**) and book a room using a credit card. There is no charge for their service, and the rates offered are always less than the rack rate you'd pay if you contacted the hotel yourself. They operate a reservation desk at the Underground station of Heathrow airport.

Index of London Hotel Maps

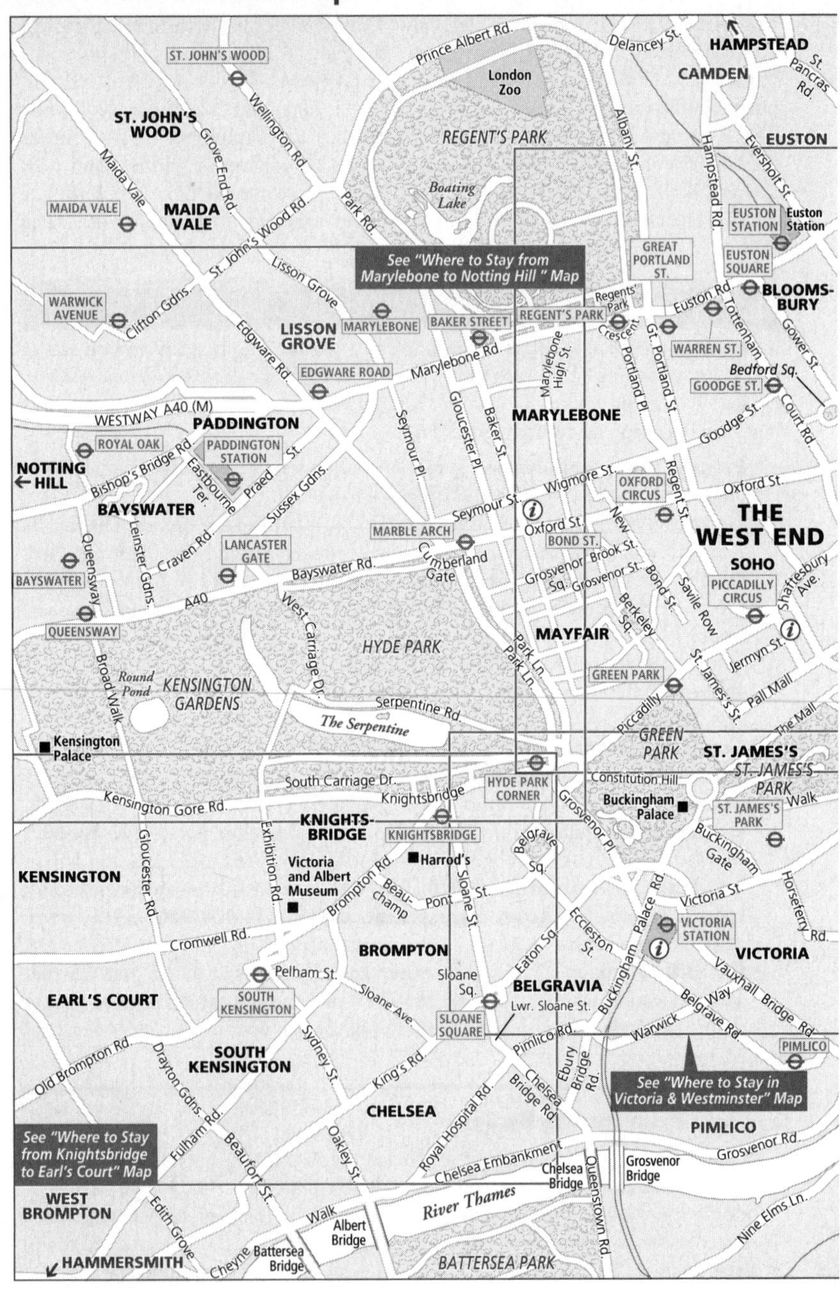

See "Where to Stay from Marylebone to Notting Hill" Map
See "Where to Stay in Victoria & Westminster" Map
See "Where to Stay from Knightsbridge to Earl's Court" Map
HAMPSTEAD
CAMDEN
EUSTON
ST. JOHN'S WOOD
MAIDA VALE
LISSON GROVE
PADDINGTON
NOTTING HILL
BAYSWATER
MARYLEBONE
BLOOMSBURY
THE WEST END
SOHO
MAYFAIR
ST. JAMES'S
KNIGHTSBRIDGE
KENSINGTON
BROMPTON
BELGRAVIA
VICTORIA
EARL'S COURT
SOUTH KENSINGTON
CHELSEA
PIMLICO
WEST BROMPTON
HAMMERSMITH
London Zoo
REGENT'S PARK
Boating Lake
HYDE PARK
KENSINGTON GARDENS
Round Pond
The Serpentine
GREEN PARK
ST. JAMES'S PARK
Kensington Palace
Buckingham Palace
Victoria and Albert Museum
Harrod's
Euston Station
River Thames
BATTERSEA PARK
Albert Bridge
Battersea Bridge
Chelsea Bridge
Grosvenor Bridge

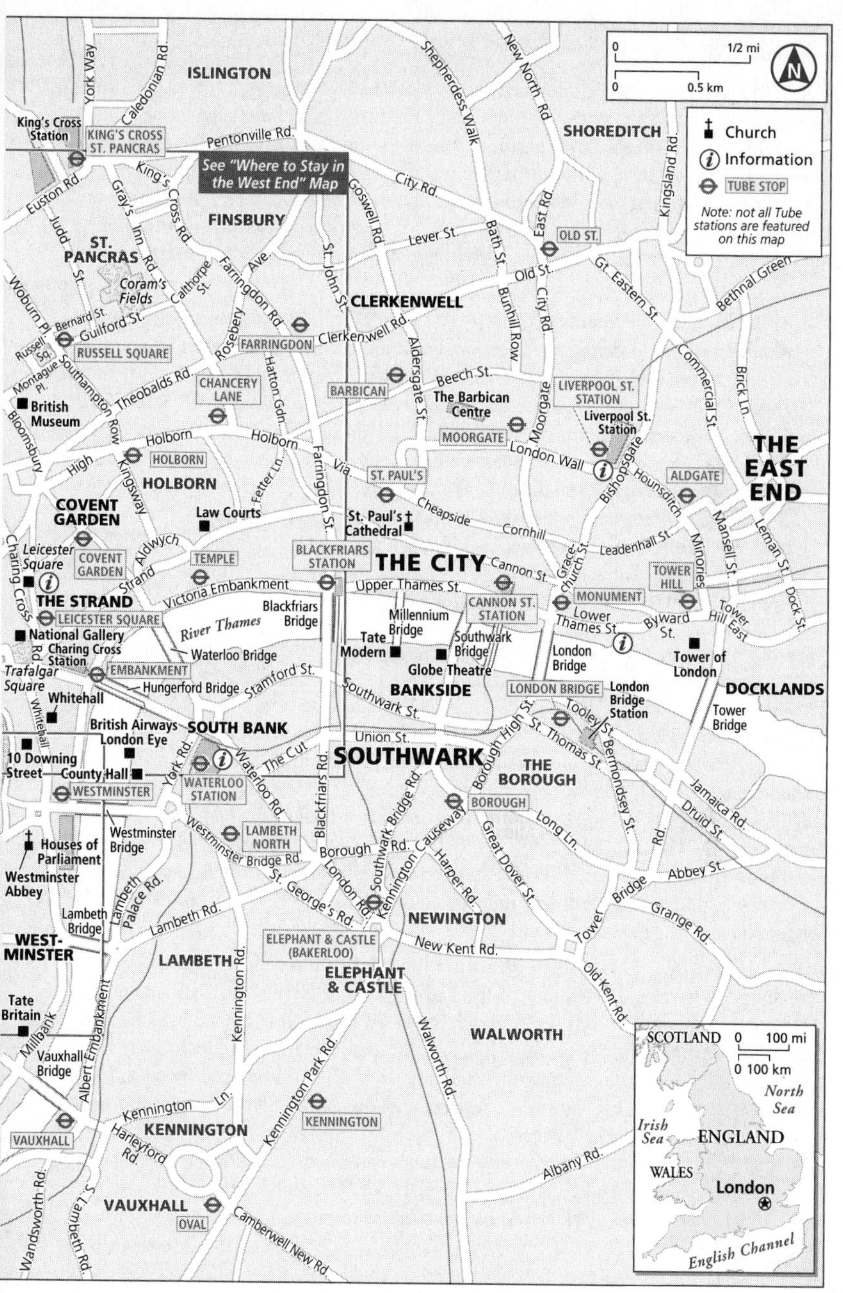
ISLINGTON
SHOREDITCH
FINSBURY
ST. PANCRAS
CLERKENWELL
HOLBORN
COVENT GARDEN
THE STRAND
THE CITY
THE EAST END
BANKSIDE
SOUTH BANK
SOUTHWARK
THE BOROUGH
DOCKLANDS
NEWINGTON
WEST-MINSTER
LAMBETH
ELEPHANT & CASTLE
WALWORTH
KENNINGTON
VAUXHALL
See "Where to Stay in the West End" Map
Church
Information
TUBE STOP
Note: not all Tube stations are featured on this map
0 1/2 mi
0 0.5 km
N
King's Cross Station
KING'S CROSS ST. PANCRAS
FARRINGDON
RUSSELL SQUARE
CHANCERY LANE
BARBICAN
LIVERPOOL ST. STATION
Liverpool St. Station
MOORGATE
OLD ST.
HOLBORN
ST. PAUL'S
ALDGATE
COVENT GARDEN
TEMPLE
BLACKFRIARS STATION
TOWER HILL
MONUMENT
CANNON ST. STATION
LEICESTER SQUARE
EMBANKMENT
LONDON BRIDGE
London Bridge Station
WATERLOO STATION
WESTMINSTER
BOROUGH
LAMBETH NORTH
ELEPHANT & CASTLE (BAKERLOO)
KENNINGTON
VAUXHALL
OVAL
British Museum
Coram's Fields
The Barbican Centre
Law Courts
St. Paul's Cathedral
Leicester Square
National Gallery
Charing Cross Station
Trafalgar Square
Whitehall
British Airways London Eye
10 Downing Street
County Hall
Houses of Parliament
Westminster Abbey
Westminster Bridge
Lambeth Bridge
Tate Britain
Vauxhall Bridge
River Thames
Blackfriars Bridge
Waterloo Bridge
Hungerford Bridge
Millennium Bridge
Tate Modern
Southwark Bridge
Globe Theatre
London Bridge
Tower of London
Tower Bridge
York Way
Caledonian Rd.
Pentonville Rd.
King's Cross Rd.
Euston Rd.
Gray's Inn Rd.
Judd St.
Woburn Pl.
Bernard St.
Guilford St.
Russell Sq.
Montague Pl.
Southampton Row
Bloomsbury
Theobalds Rd.
Calthorpe St.
Farringdon Rd.
Rosebery Ave.
Hatton Gdn.
St. John St.
Goswell Rd.
City Rd.
Shepherdess Walk
New North Rd
Bath St.
East Rd.
Kingsland Rd.
Lever St.
Old St.
Bunhill Row
Gt. Eastern St.
Bethnal Green
Clerkenwell Rd.
Aldersgate St.
Beech St.
Commercial St.
Brick Ln.
Holborn
High
Kingsway
Fetter Ln.
Farringdon St.
Holborn Via.
London Wall
Moorgate
Bishopsgate
Houndsditch
Cheapside
Cornhill
Leadenhall St.
Gracechurch St.
Minories
Mansell St.
Leman St.
Cannon St.
Aldwych
Strand
Charing Cross Rd.
Victoria Embankment
Upper Thames St.
Lower Thames St.
Byward St.
Tower Hill East
Dock St.
Stamford St.
Southwark St.
Union St.
Tooley St.
Borough High St.
St. Thomas St.
Bermondsey St.
Jamaica Rd.
Druid St.
The Cut
York Rd.
Waterloo Rd.
Blackfriars Rd.
Southwark Bridge Rd.
Westminster Bridge Rd.
Borough Rd.
London Rd.
St. George's Rd.
Kennington Causeway
Harper Rd.
Great Dover St.
Long Ln.
Tower Bridge Rd.
Abbey St.
Grange Rd.
Lambeth Palace Rd.
Lambeth Rd.
New Kent Rd.
Old Kent Rd.
Kennington Rd.
Albert Embankment
Millbank
Kennington Park Rd.
Walworth Rd.
Kennington Ln.
Harleyford Rd.
Albany Rd.
Camberwell New Rd.
Wandsworth Rd.
S. Lambeth Rd.
SCOTLAND
0 100 mi
0 100 km
North Sea
Irish Sea
ENGLAND
WALES
London
English Channel

Tips Net Savings

The **British Hotel Reservation Centre** (✆ **020/7340-1616;** www.bhrc.co.uk) site is simple to navigate, with the BHRC price next to the rack rate for more than 120 hotels and B&Bs all over London. There are big savings to be had through **www.laterooms.com**, which publishes comparable prices, for bookings up to 3 weeks in advance. It does self-catering accommodations, too. If you can bear the tension, wait until a few days before you fly and then scan **www.lastminute.com**.

what's on offer, try **Venuemasters** (✆ **0114/249-3090;** www.venuemasters.co.uk), which promotes academic conference and vacation facilities all over the U.K. Or contact the three Central London universities directly: **University of London** (✆ **020/7862-8880;** www.lon.ac.uk/accom); **University of Westminster** (✆ **020/7911-5796;** www.westminster.ac.uk/comserv/halls.htm); or **City University** (✆ **020/7477-8037;** www.city.ac.uk/ems/accomm/accomm.html).

- **Sleep super-cheap.** Hostel dorm beds cost from £16 to £25 ($30–$46) per night, and many of them have cheap twin rooms, too. There are also seven **Youth Hostel Association** sites (✆ **020/7373-3400;** www.yha.org.uk), the best of which are reviewed below. For a full list of British YMCAs, call the **National Council of YMCAs** (✆ **020/8520-5599;** www.ymca.org.uk).

2 Kensington & Chelsea

In addition to the Trafalgar Square location (see later in this chapter), **Citadines** (✆ **0800/376-3898;** www.citadines.com) also has an apartment hotel on Gloucester Road near the Tube station, another in Holborn near Covent Garden, and a fourth in the Barbican. Special-offer studios start as low as £83 ($133) a night off season if you stay 1 week. Meanwhile, you'll get an even better deal at **Nell Gwynn House** ★, Sloane Avenue, SW3 3AX (✆ **020/7589-1105;** fax 020/7589-9433; www.nghapartments.co.uk), where rates start at £470 ($870) per week for a small two-person studio. The downside is that reservations are only taken for whole weeks, the upside that the longer you stay the lower the price.

Abbey House ★ There are no private bathrooms at Abbey House, which is why it can charge these rates in such a posh part of town. It's only a short walk up to Notting Hill, or downhill to Kensington High Street. Abbey House, owned by Albert and Carol Nayach, is a gem set in a gracious Victorian square. The bright hallway has a checkerboard floor and wrought-iron staircase lined with lithographs of glum-faced royals. The bedrooms are simple, attractive, and big for London. The second-floor room at the front gets the balcony above the front door. The bathrooms are Laura Ashley style and impeccable; there's one for every three bedrooms. And there's a kitchenette, where you can make tea and coffee for free. The staff treat you terribly well here, whether you need a hair dryer, babysitting, or restaurant advice.

11 Vicarage Gate, London W8 4AG. ✆ **020/7727-2594.** Fax 020/7727-1873. www.abbeyhousekensington.com. 16 units, none w/bathroom. £45 ($83) single; £74 ($137) double/twin; £90 ($166) triple; £100 ($185) quad. Rates include full English breakfast. Discount available off season. No credit cards. Tube: High St. Kensington or Notting Hill Gate. **Amenities:** Babysitting arranged. *In room:* TV, no phone.

Prince's Gardens Halls, Imperial College ★ Prince's Gardens is like a holiday camp. The maze of rooms is decorated in the usual student style, and most are singles, so book early if you want a twin. There are no private bathrooms, but only four rooms share each public facility. Because Prince's Gardens is part of the campus at Imperial College, you get to use all the on-site amenities. There's a bank as well as a bureau de change, a tourist information desk and travel agency, even a medical center. Guests also get a discount rate at the sports center. The Basics restaurant does pizza for half the price you'll pay anywhere else, and you can do a bar crawl without even leaving the complex. You'll want to leave, though, because this is a fantastic location. Harrods, the Victoria & Albert Museum, the Natural History Museum, Kensington Gardens, Hyde Park, and the Royal Albert Hall are all within a short walk.

Watts Way, Prince's Gardens, London SW7 1LU. ✆ **020/7594-9507.** Fax 020/7594-9504. www.imperial-accommodationlink.com. 608 units, none w/bathroom. £42 ($77) single; £63 ($117) twin. Rates include full English breakfast. MC, V. Open Easter and summer vacations. Tube: South Kensington. No children under 10. **Amenities:** Restaurant; bar; sports center with pool; game room; tour desk; salon; coin-op washers and dryers. *In room:* No phone.

Swiss House Hotel ★ This is a lovely place with decent-size double rooms and lots of greenery—plants hang from every window ledge, railing, and balcony. Inside, chintz, dried flowers, and original fireplaces create a homey, country-style atmosphere. Traffic noise can be a problem on Old Brompton Road, so try to get a room at the back looking over the peaceful communal garden (you'll have to be content with looking, though; it's not open to guests). The proprietor is an extremely welcoming and helpful host, providing room service of soups and "monster" sandwiches from midday until 9pm. You can also pay a £6 ($10) supplement for a full English breakfast. Someone will carry your bags up and buy your favorite newspaper. Swiss House is popular with families, but around 80% of its guests are middle-aged U.S. tourists.

171 Old Brompton Rd., London SW5 0AN. ✆ **020/7373-2769.** Fax 020/7373-4983. www.swisshousehotel.com. 16 units, 15 w/bathroom (most w/shower only). £56 ($104) single w/o bathroom; £80 ($148) single w/bathroom; £95–£120 ($176–$222) double/twin w/bathroom; £135 ($222) triple w/bathroom; £145 ($268) quad w/bathroom. Rates include continental breakfast. Discount of 5% for 1-week stay and cash payment (U.S. $ accepted). AE, DC, MC, V. Tube: Gloucester Rd. **Amenities:** Secretarial services; limited room service; babysitting arranged; laundry service; nonsmoking rooms. *In room:* TV, hair dryer.

SUPER-CHEAP SLEEPS

Holland House Youth Hostel ★ This hostel is located right in the middle of a leafy public park that used to be the grounds for Holland House (1607), a redbrick and white-stone Jacobean mansion that was partially destroyed by bombs in World War II. The youth hostel splits its accommodations between what's left of the house and a second building from the 1950s. In the summer, open-air opera is staged in the ruins of Holland House (see "Performers in the Park," p. 238). Residents can sit in the courtyard and enjoy the music for free. The hostel has all the normal useful stuff like a kitchen, TV room, quiet room, and Internet access. The cafeteria has a liquor license and serves cheap meals from 5 to 8pm. The only drawback is that a lot of school groups stay here. Some dorms sleep 6 to 8, but most sleep 12 to 20 people. There are

---

The Difference Between Singles, Twins & Doubles

In British English, a **single** is a room with one bed for one person. A **twin** has two beds, each for one person. A **double** has one bed big enough for two.

Where to Stay from Knightsbridge to Earl's Court

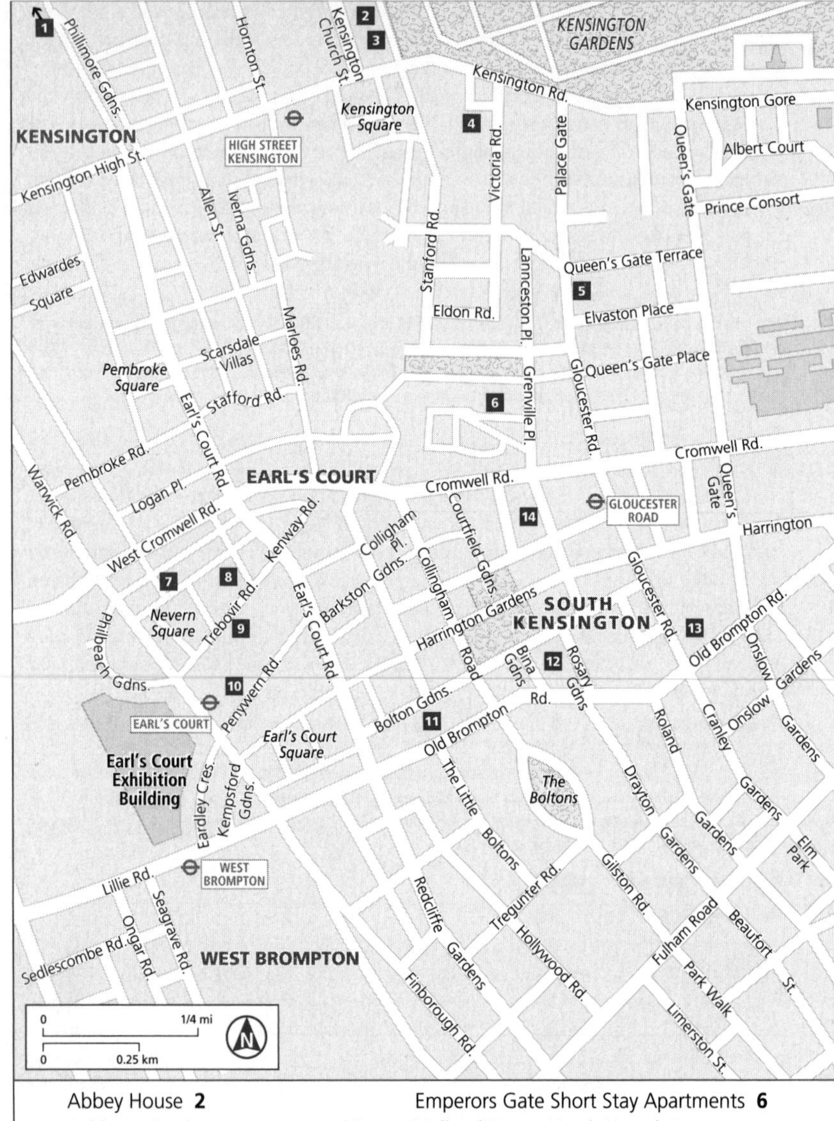

Abbey House **2**
Ashburn Gardens Apartments **14**
Astons Apartments **12**
Citadines, South Kensington **5**
Clearlake Hotel **4**
Earl's Court Youth Hostel **11**
Emperors Gate Short Stay Apartments **6**
Holland House Youth Hostel **1**
Kensington International Inn **7**
Mayflower Hotel **9**
Mowbray Court Hotel **10**
Nell Gwynn House **16**

Prince's Gardens Halls, Imperial College **15**

Rushmore Hotel **8**

Swiss House Hotel **13**

Vicarage Private Hotel **3**

The Willett Hotel **17**

no family bunkrooms. But you're only a 10-minute walk from a Tube station and a quick ride into the middle of town.

Holland Walk, Holland Park, London W8 7QU. ✆ **020/7937-0748.** Fax 020/7376-0667. www.yha.org.uk. 201 units, none w/bathroom. £22 ($40) per adult; £20 ($36) per person under 18. Rates include full English breakfast. AE, MC, V. Tube: Holland Park or High St. Kensington. **Amenities:** Restaurant; coin-op washers and dryers; communal kitchen; Internet access; garden. *In room:* No phone.

DO-IT-YOURSELF DEALS

Ashburn Gardens Apartments ★ *Kids* Staying here off-season is one of the best deals in London. One-bedroom apartments with kitchens undercut the B&Bs in tony South Kensington. And the bigger ones beat rates in budget neighborhoods. Using the sofa bed, you can fit four people in a one-bedroom and six people in a two-bedroom. The rooms are generous in size, if a bit drab in their furnishings and color schemes. Ashburn Gardens is a small street that joins Cromwell Road midway between a big Sainsbury supermarket and London's museum row. Though it isn't busy itself, anyone sensitive to traffic noise should ask to be at the back and above the first floor to get more of a view. Mr. Aresti and his family have owned the business since 1974. Behind the Georgian facade and entrance hall, you'll find that everything has been refurbished and modernized. The beds were all new in 1998, and the bathrooms and open-plan kitchens with electric stoves and microwaves were redone in 1999 and 2000. Maid service is part of the deal, and it's more frequent than at a Citadines. They'll clean up every weekday, and change the linen once a week and the towels on alternate days. These apartments are popular with families, so there's a whole cupboard of cribs, high chairs, and strollers at the reception desk. You'll get a discount if you book online.

3 Ashburn Gardens, London SW7 4DG. ✆ **020/7370-2663.** Fax 020/7370-6743. www.ashburngardens.co.uk. 24 units. £665 ($1,230) per week 1-bedroom apt; from £1,050 ($1,942) per week 2-bedroom apt. Minimum stay 1 week. MC, V. Tube: Gloucester Rd. *In room:* TV, kitchen, fridge, coffeemaker, hair dryer, iron.

Astons Apartments ★★ Behind the redbrick facades of three Victorian town houses you'll find the very model of a modern apartment hotel. Maids swoop through every day. You can see your face in the lovely, polished, wood handrail on the stairs. The reception desk—where you can send a fax, drop off your dry cleaning or have someone order a theater or tour ticket—is manned until 9pm. Prices verge on being a splurge for budget travelers, but you get good value for your money and the website often has hot deals. If money is tight, forget the singles and the great family room in the basement with its proper open-plan kitchen and sofa bed for the kids. You can do better elsewhere. But the rest of the studios should impress even the most exacting guests. A dozen were recently refurbed, with more in the works. The Executive doubles and quads are larger and have some extra amenities, including larger bathrooms. Bathrooms throughout are tiled and have showers. All the studios have fully equipped kitchenettes, hidden behind foldaway doors, and there's a big supermarket nearby. All in all, Astons is a nice place to come home to in the evening, and it's so centrally located that you can walk to the South Ken museums and get into the West End or just about anywhere in Central London in about 10 minutes.

31 Rosary Gardens, London SW7 4NH. ✆ **800/525-2810** in the U.S., or 020/7590-6000. Fax 020/7590-6060. www.astons-apartments.com. 54 units. Standard studios: £65 ($120) single; £90 ($166) double; £125 ($231) triple. Executive studios: £125 ($231) double; £165 ($305) quad. Rates do not include 17.5% VAT. Discount available for Frommer's readers; inquire when booking. Children stay free in parent's room. AE, DISC, MC, V. Tube: Gloucester Rd. **Amenities:** Business center; nonsmoking rooms. *In room:* TV, dataport, wi-fi, fully equipped kitchenette, coffeemaker, hair dryer, trouser press.

Clearlake Hotel ★ *Kids* This splendidly unglamorous hotel, owned and managed for nearly 50 years by Andrew Asherskovic, offers a range of fantastic-value, self-catering options in an upscale, unbeatable location. It's located on a quiet street opposite Kensington Gardens at the eastern end of Kensington High Street. What really sells the Clearlake is the huge amount of space you get, except where modern partitions cut into the gracious proportions to make single rooms or toe-to-toe twins. Despite some recent redecoration, many of the apartments resemble student digs—a jumble of fancy gilt mirrors, next to a host of 1970s horrors, and even theater props left over from plays the owner puts on. Idiosyncratic is the best word to describe the place. It's ideal for families. Staff can lend you cribs, strollers, and high chairs, as well as arrange babysitting. For maximum space, stay in the building next door, where every floor is a huge, old-fashioned flat. For an extra £4 ($6) you can have continental breakfast served in your room.

18–19 Prince of Wales Terrace, London W8 5PQ. ✆ **020/7937-3274.** Fax 020/7376-0604. www.clearlakehotel.co.uk. 25 units, all w/bathroom (some w/shower only). £53 ($99) double; £65 ($120) double/twin studio; £80 ($148) triple studio; £98–£110 ($181–$203) 1-bedroom apt; £115–£125 ($213–$231) 2-bedroom apt; £197 ($364) 3-bedroom apt. Weekly rates and long-stay discounts available. AE, DC, MC, V. Tube: High St. Kensington or Gloucester Rd. **Amenities:** Babysitting arranged; laundry and dry cleaning service; nonsmoking rooms. *In room:* TV, kitchen, coffeemaker, hair dryer.

WORTH A SPLURGE

Vicarage Private Hotel ★ Eileen Diviney, who runs Vicarage Private Hotel, recently added en suite bathrooms to the first and second floors and redecorated the rooms. An en suite ground-floor twin at the back, no. 3, is a splurge but marvelous—high-ceilinged and furnished with pretty painted tables and old-fashioned metal bedsteads. But you really don't have to splash out here. Most of the rooms are big, the ceilings are high up to the fourth floor, and all are done in a Victorian country style. Four bedrooms share each public bathroom, and there are separate toilets. If you're trying to weigh this B&B up against Abbey House right next door, then there are other things to consider apart from the fancier decor here and marginally higher price. Instead of putting TV sets in the rooms, Vicarage Private Hotel has a TV lounge. Hair dryers are standard, instead of at the reception desk. And you don't have to leave your room to make tea or coffee. Also there are kippers (smoked herring) and porridge on a breakfast menu fit for warriors.

10 Vicarage Gate, London W8 4AG. ✆ **020/7229-4030.** Fax 020/7792-5989. www.londonvicaragehotel.com. 17 units, 8 w/bathroom. £46 ($85) single w/o bathroom; £78 ($144) double/twin w/o bathroom; £102 ($189) double/twin w/bathroom; £95 ($167) triple w/o bathroom; £102 ($189) family room w/o bathroom. Rates include full English breakfast. No credit cards. Personal checks from U.S. banks accepted if received at least 2 months ahead of visit. Tube: High St. Kensington or Notting Hill Gate. **Amenities:** Babysitting arranged. *In room:* Coffeemaker, hair dryer, no phone.

The Willett Hotel ★★ Part of a quiet redbrick terrace, The Willett is noteworthy for its mansard roof, bay windows, and a host of the other Victorian architectural details. This is a dream location for shopaholics, just off Sloane Square and a 5-minute walk to Chelsea's King's Road. The Willett has been refurbished throughout in a heavily traditional style to match the building. All the rooms are different; standards are very high. Deluxe rooms have canopies over the beds, voluptuous swagged curtains, matching armchairs, and nice but not terribly large bathrooms. You'll probably want to avoid the tiny standard twins where you sleep head to head along one wall, but the small double is a fantastic value for this swanky area. The porter will stagger upstairs with your bags. Reception can order your favorite newspaper. And, best of all, guests can relax in the secluded communal garden. It's all just so civilized.

32 Sloane Gardens, London SW1 8DJ. ✆ **800/270-9206** in the U.S., or 020/7824-8415. Fax 020/7730-4830. www.eeh.co.uk. 19 units, all w/bathroom (most w/shower only). £130 ($240) small double/twin; £160 ($296) standard double/twin; £170 ($306) triple. Rates do not include 17.5% VAT. Full English breakfast included. AE, DC, MC, V. Tube: Sloane Sq. **Amenities:** Limited room service; laundry service; dry cleaning. *In room:* TV, fridge, coffeemaker, hair dryer.

3 Earl's Court

Mayflower Hotel ★ With its black pillars and showy window boxes, this hotel is determined to look a cut above its cut-price competitors in Earl's Court. Fortunately, the inside lives up to the promise. The owners have just refurbished every bedroom and bathroom, giving the rooms (all decorated differently) a subdued, minimal elegance with wood floors, sumptuous fabrics, and gorgeous marble showers. Generally, the rooms aren't a bad size for London. There's a great second-floor family room that leads onto the front porch, and there's even an elevator. The staff here have always been solicitous, lending out irons, hair dryers, and adapter plugs, and making life easy for their guests. Now the owners are aiming for even smoother service, "like the Holiday Inn." Mmm, it sounds like a good deal all round, especially at this budget price. Lower rates below are for weekends.

The Mayflower also has 35 attractive self-catering accommodations, the **Court Apartments,** on busy Warwick Way. Studios start at £85 ($157) per night.

26–28 Trebovir Rd., London SW5 9NJ. ✆ **020/7370-0991.** Fax 020/7370-0994. www.mayflowerhotel.co.uk. 48 units, all w/bathroom (some w/tub only). £65–£89 ($120–$165) single; £82–£125 ($152–$231) double/twin; £105–£145 ($194–$268) triple; £130–£169 ($240–$313) family room. Rates include continental breakfast. AE, MC, V. Tube: Earl's Court. **Amenities:** Secretarial services; limited room service; dry cleaning; nonsmoking rooms. *In room:* TV, coffeemaker.

Mowbray Court Hotel ★★ *Kids* Brothers Tony and Peter Dooley run this spotlessly clean hotel, which their parents opened 41 years ago. Mowbray Court is a very friendly, very good value, old-fashioned budget hotel. It's comfortable without being glamorous and even has a bar and a lounge with Internet service. The rooms tend to be basic, most with prefab bathroom units with shower, basin, and toilet. Otherwise, four bedrooms share every public bathroom. There's a family room with seven beds in the basement of the main building and a triple with a little kitchen in the annex. Rooms at the back face the overground Tube line, but double-glazing keeps out the noise. The party-wall paneling in the breakfast room is a bit grim. The hotel will arrange shuttle-bus service to and from Heathrow for £15 ($24) and £22 ($35) to Gatwick. There's even a Vidal Sassoon–trained visiting hairdresser. Present your Frommer's guide, and they'll give you a 5% discount.

28–32 Penywern Rd., London SW5 9SU. ✆ **020/7373-8285.** Fax 020/7370-5693. www.m-c-hotel.mcmail.com. 82 units, 70 w/bathroom (most w/shower only). £45 ($83) single w/o bathroom; £52 ($96) single w/bathroom; £56 ($104) double w/o bathroom; £67 ($124) double w/bathroom; £69 ($128) triple w/o bathroom; £80 ($148) triple w/bathroom; £84 ($155) quad w/o bathroom; £95 ($176) quad w/bathroom; £100 ($185) family room w/o bathroom; £115–£125 ($213–$231) family room w/bathroom; £145 ($268) 7-bed room w/bathroom. Rates include continental breakfast. AE, DC, MC, V. Tube: Earl's Court. **Amenities:** Bar; babysitting arranged; laundry service; dry cleaning; 15 nonsmoking rooms; airport shuttle. *In room:* TV, hair dryer, safe, trouser press.

Rushmore Hotel ★★ This gracious town-house hotel makes art directors at interiors magazines go weak in the knees. Italianate classical scenes decorate the hallway and ceilings. The breakfast room is in a limestone-paved conservatory with wrought-iron furniture and potted orchids. Every bedroom is a different exuberant stage set. One has Gothic looping curtains and a canopy over the bed. In another, you'll find a chandelier and Louis XIV pale-blue walls, with panels sketched out in gold. There's a marvelous family room under the eaves, and a porter will carry up your bags. The Rushmore will take bookings for specific rooms (there are five for nonsmokers), and you can preview some of them on the website (which features seasonal specials). All the rooms had new carpet a couple of years ago, and the bathrooms were given a tiled makeover in 2003. The welcoming staff will let you send a fax and pick up e-mail. There are irons at reception and safety deposit boxes. If the Rushmore were anyplace other than in Earl's Court, it would certainly bust the budget.

11 Trebovir Rd., London SW5 9LS. ✆ **020/7370-3839.** Fax 020/7370-0274. www.rushmore-hotel.co.uk. 22 units, all w/bathroom (most w/shower only). £59 ($109) single; £79 ($146) double/twin; £89 ($165) triple; £99 ($183) family room. Rates include continental breakfast. Discount available for 1-week stays. 10% discount for seniors. Children under 12 stay free in parent's room. AE, DC, MC, V. Tube: Earl's Court. **Amenities:** Laundry services; dry cleaning; nonsmoking rooms. *In room:* TV, coffeemaker, hair dryer.

SUPER-CHEAP SLEEPS

Earl's Court Youth Hostel If you're going to stay somewhere cheap in Earl's Court, you're far better off going to the youth hostel than one of the dozens of super-budget hotels. At least you know what you're getting, and the location is great. This garden square is just north of Old Brompton Road. On the other side of the street, the millionaires' mansions in the Boltons mark the beginning of posh South Kensington. Earl's Court is backpacker central, and they flock to this very lively international hostel. The big, half-stuccoed Victorian building has a good mix of pretty basic dorms, from a few twins up to some with nine beds or more. There are kitchen facilities so you can always supplement the shockingly meager, packed continental breakfast (in fine weather you can take your plate out to the hostel's courtyard garden). When it comes to an evening chow-down, Earl's Court is packed with cheap but often unappetizing restaurants. There are lots of late-night shops, too. If the pennies aren't too tight, head for the more up-market Gloucester Road, which is almost as close.

38 Bolton Gardens, London SW5 0AQ. ✆ **020/7373-7083.** Fax 020/7835-2034. www.yha.org.uk. 159 units, none w/bathroom. £20 ($37) per adult; £17 ($32) per person under 18. Rates include bed linen and continental breakfast. MC, V. Tube: Earl's Court. **Amenities:** Game room; travel desk; coin-op washers and dryers; communal kitchen; Internet access; garden. *In room:* No phone.

WORTH A SPLURGE

Kensington International Inn ★ *Finds* This polished and professionally run establishment on an elegant 1860s street reopened in 2003 after a half-million-pound overhaul. It's high in style and low in price. The rooms are small to medium in size, but the contemporary decor is surprisingly chic, utilizing pale wheaty colors and sleek wooden headboards and furnishings. Bathrooms are also small, with glass-walled showers. There's a hip little bar, a conservatory lounge, and a high standard of service. You may find a lower price on their website than the rack rates listed below.

4 Templeton Place, London SW5 9LZ. ✆ **020/7370-4333.** Fax 020/7244-7873. www.kensingtoninternationalinn.com. 60 units, all w/bathroom (shower only). £110 ($203) single; £130 ($240) twin/double; £145 ($268) triple. Rates include continental breakfast. AE, DC, MC, V. Tube: Earl's Court. **Amenities:** Bar; nonsmoking rooms. *In room:* TV, coffeemaker, hair dryer, safe, trouser press.

4 Notting Hill

Imperial College charges the same rates at the spartan **Pembridge Gardens Halls** (✆ **020/7594-9407;** www.imperial-accommodationlink.com) as at its main Prince's Gardens campus. That's because the gracious houses on this quiet side street sell for multimillions and the location, between Portobello Market and Kensington Gardens, is fantastic. Singles cost £41 ($76) or £50 ($92) with a bathroom; twins are £63 ($117) or £72 ($133) with a bathroom. Guests can use all the campus facilities, which are located three Tube stops away from Notting Hill Gate at South Kensington.

Comfort Inn Notting Hill ★ *Value* This is rather a sneaky good deal. Comfort Inn is a franchise, but the owners of this hotel actively urge you to book directly with them and not through central reservations. And so do we because it gets you a lower rate. The hotel will make deals based on occupancy levels, so the quoted offer can change every day. Located on a quiet, pretty street off Notting Hill Gate, the Comfort Inn stretches across five terrace houses. The rooms are on the three upper floors (there is an elevator) and are a fair size for London. Rear windows look across fire escapes and rooftops, while second-floor rooms on the front have access to an east-facing balcony. Rooms have been redecorated with a nice business feel and equipped with firm new beds. The bathrooms are also newly renovated. There are a few newly redone and fairly charming rooms on a little internal courtyard. The Comfort Inn is a practical choice in a superb location. Breakfast is a self-service buffet, or you can pay £5.95 ($10) for full English.

6–14 Pembridge Gardens, London W2 4DU. ✆ **020/7221-3433.** Fax 020/7229-4808. www.lth-hotels.com. 64 units, all w/bathroom. £75 ($139) single; £100 ($185) double/twin; £125 ($231) triple; £145 ($268) quad. Rates include continental breakfast. AE, DC, MC, V. Tube: Notting Hill Gate. **Amenities:** Bar; babysitting arranged; laundry service; dry cleaning; Internet access; nonsmoking rooms. *In room:* TV, dataport, coffeemaker, hair dryer, safe, radio.

The Gate Hotel ★ Portobello Road is a hot tourist spot because of its market and antiques shops—which makes The Gate a fun place to stay if you don't mind crowds of people marching past. Look for a tiny, brick, curved-front, late-Georgian house with hanging baskets and a parrot (named Sargeant Bilko) living in a caged-in area in front. Guests eat breakfast in their rooms, which have all been refurbished. The look is attractive—with paneled furniture, blue carpet, linen, and ceiling fans. The bigger rooms each have a small sofa bed for an extra person. Hair dryers are available at reception. If you pay with a credit card, an additional 3% "processing" charge is tacked on.

6 Portobello Rd., London W11 3DG. ✆ **020/7221-0707.** Fax 020/7221-9128. www.gatehotel.com. 6 units, 5 w/private bathroom (most w/shower only). £55–£60 ($102–$111) single; £80–£99 ($148–$183) double. Rates include continental breakfast. MC, V. Tube: Notting Hill Gate. *In room:* TV, fridge, radio.

InterneSt@Portobello Gold ★ *Finds* Whatever you do, do not try to make it to InterneSt until at least 6pm if you're arriving on Saturday. The road closes during the day for Portobello Market, and there's zero chance of forcing luggage through the crowds and past the antique stalls set up in front of the building. The conservatory restaurant, with its romantic dining platform, is a local institution and a great deal: two courses could cost you as little as £15 ($28). The bar menu is almost as long, and dishes rarely top £7 ($13). Guests have unlimited Web access in the second-floor cybercafe and in their room. The rooms are almost comically tiny but freshly decorated. All the rooms have a shower but only three have a toilet; the rest share the facility in the hallway. If you have long legs, ask for the 7-foot-long Captain's bed. For a very special treat, rent the two-story apartment with private roof terrace, then make like a movie star and tour London in Portobello Gold's 1952 Buick convertible (£60/$111 for up to five people).

97 Portobello Rd., London W11 2QB. ✆ **020/7460-4910.** Fax 020/7460-4911. www.portobellogold.com. 6 units, 3 w/bathroom, 1 apt. £35–£60 ($65–$92) single w/o bathroom; £75 ($120) single w/bathroom; £75–£80 ($139–$148) double w/o bathroom; £85 ($157) double w/bathroom; £180 ($333) apt. Rates include continental breakfast. Lower price Sun–Thurs. Discount for 1-week stays. MC, V. Tube: Notting Hill Gate. **Amenities:** Restaurant; bar; free Internet access. *In room:* TV, wireless Internet access.

Manor Court Hotel Clanricarde Gardens is a quiet cul-de-sac just off Notting Hill Gate where it turns into Bayswater Road. The gated enclave known as Embassy Row occupies the other, tonier, side of the main road. Neighborhood gentrification is only just reaching Clanricarde Gardens, but Manor Court, frankly a bit down at the heels, is popular with families on holiday from the Continent. The decor is basic, but most of the rooms are a fair size for London. Check out the huge second-floor double room, which has deep ceiling moldings and access to the balcony through floor-to-ceiling windows. My choice would be one of the triples—a bargain for two people, and you'll get a tub/shower, too. The bathrooms are clean, though some of the tiling shows signs of patching. There are hair dryers at the reception desk. The dining room smelled stuffy and not very appetizing when we last visited. This wouldn't be anyone's first choice, but it's only a 10-minute walk from the funky Portobello Road.

7 Clanricarde Gardens, London W2 4JJ. ✆ **020/7792-3361.** Fax 020/7229-2875. 20 units, 16 w/bathroom (shower only). £30 ($55) single w/o bathroom; £40–£50 ($74–$92) single w/bathroom; £50–£65 ($92–$120) double/twin w/bathroom; £60–£75 ($111–$139) triple w/bathroom; £85 ($157) family room w/bathroom. Rates include continental breakfast. Discount of 10% for 1-week stays. AE, DC, MC, V. Tube: Notting Hill Gate. *In room:* TV.

5 Paddington & Bayswater

Ashley Hotel ★ A sign on the front door announces that "this is a highly respectable establishment" and won't let you in if you're "untidy" or don't have luggage. It sounds grimly Victorian, but it does keep out the riff-raff and means that guests feel safe and secure. The Davies brothers started this place in 1967 when many British still didn't holiday abroad, and it remains a very old-fashioned sort of place with creaky floors, no elevator, and a prim, quiet air. Most guests are still British, and many come with church groups. Single women would feel safe staying here. Refurbished in 2000, the bedrooms are comfortable and traditional, with washbasins in the rooms because the bathrooms are so tiny. Rooms on the front, six of which have balconies, face Norfolk Square's pretty public garden, an oasis of calm in the often noisy purlieus of Paddington. At the back, ask to be above the second floor to avoid looking out on a wall (the hotel does not have a lift). Kids will enjoy the unusual bunks in the basement family room, a single above a double. And reception can lend you hair dryers, irons, and adapter plugs.

15–17 Norfolk Sq., London W2 1RU. ✆ **020/7723-3375.** Fax 020/7723-0173. www.ashleyhotels.com. 53 units, 43 w/bathroom (shower only). £30–£40 ($55–$79) single w/o bathroom; £40–£55 ($79–$102) single w/bathroom; £60–£85 ($111–$157) double/twin w/bathroom; £89–£99 ($165–$183) triple w/bathroom; £80–£105 ($148–$194) family room. Rates include full English breakfast. £1 ($1.85) surcharge for 1-night stays. DISC, MC, V. Tube: Paddington. *In room:* TV, coffeemaker, radio.

Dolphin Hotel ★ Mr. and Mrs. Moros have run the Dolphin for over 20 years. It's a nice place, though the lobby smelled of stale cigarette smoke when we visited, and it vies with Norfolk Court (see below) as the best deal in Norfolk Square. The hotel occupies what were once Victorian houses, so the bedrooms vary widely in size. But

Where to Stay from Marylebone to Notting Hill

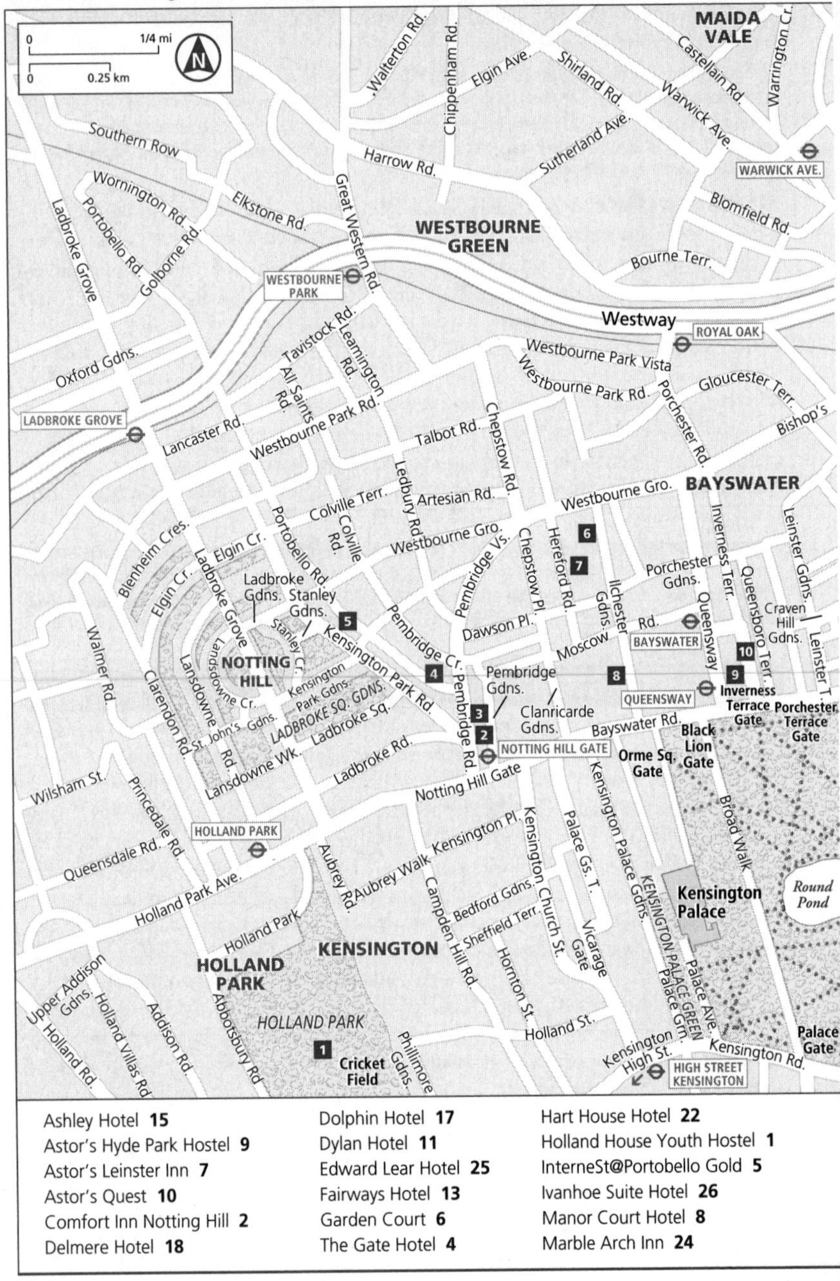

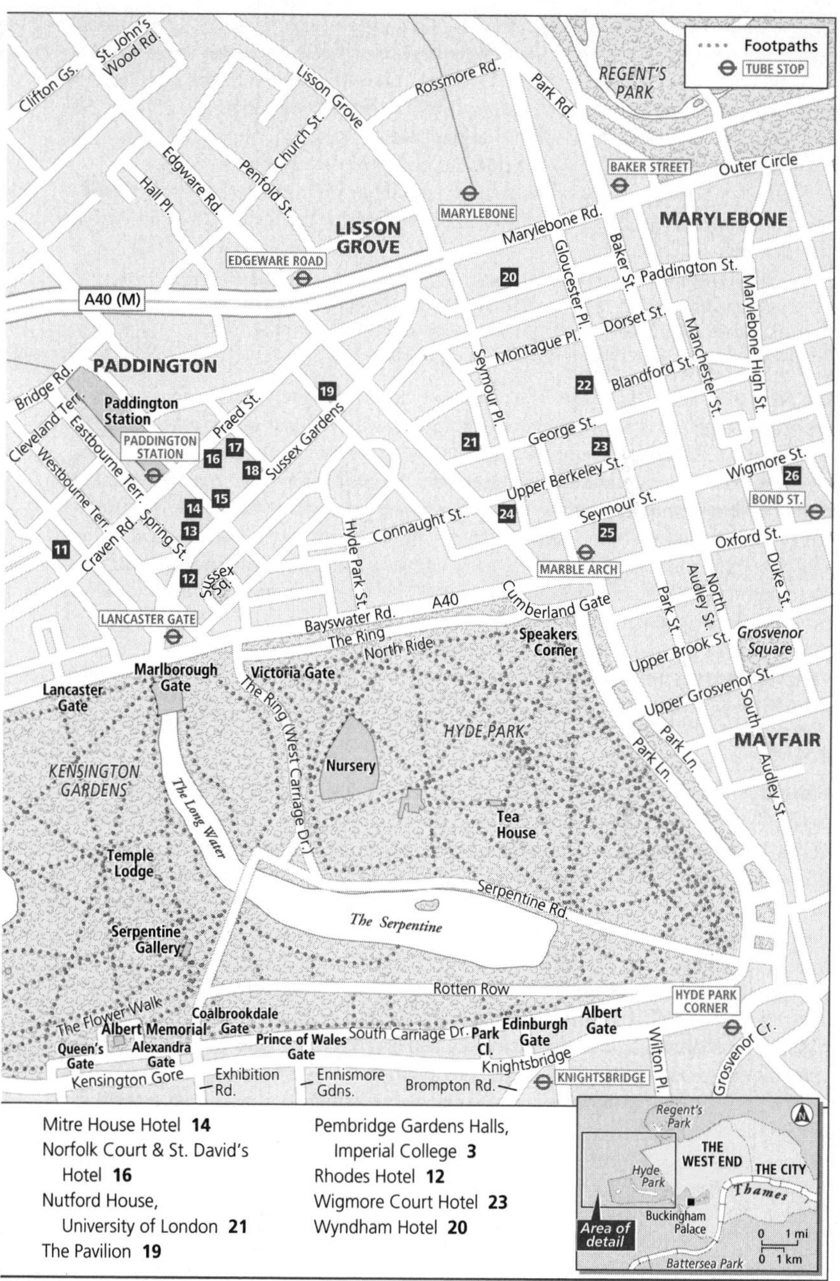

Mitre House Hotel **14**
Norfolk Court & St. David's Hotel **16**
Nutford House, University of London **21**
The Pavilion **19**
Pembridge Gardens Halls, Imperial College **3**
Rhodes Hotel **12**
Wigmore Court Hotel **23**
Wyndham Hotel **20**

all are comfortably decorated, with a table and chairs, tiled bathrooms, a fridge, and some with safes, trouser presses, and lovely moldings. The continental breakfast buffet is actually quite an extravaganza, with cheese, cakes, yogurt and honey, eggs cooked any way, and more. If that isn't enough, it will only cost you £2.50 ($4.60) for full English (I was told that the English breakfast would be free to Frommer's readers, so flash this guidebook). Lower rates below are for bathroomless rooms.

If there's no room at this particular inn, ask about their place next door: **Shakespeare Hotel,** 22–28 Norfolk Sq. (✆ **020/7402-4646;** fax 020/7723-7233; www.shakespearehotel.co.uk).

34 Norfolk Sq., London W2 1RP. ✆ **020/7402-4943.** Fax 020/7723-8184. www.dolphinhotel.co.uk. 34 units, 22 w/bathroom (most w/shower). £38–£56 ($70–$104) single; £52–£76 ($96–$141) double/twin; £69–£86 ($128–$154) triple; £80–£98 ($148–$181) quad. Rates include continental breakfast. AE, DC, MC, V. Tube: Paddington. *In room:* TV, fridge, coffeemaker, hair dryer.

Dylan Hotel ★ The recent redecoration of the Dylan resulted in an exuberant decor that mixes dark red, fake-damask wallpaper with red-and-gold flock and paint. The style fits the date of the house but may not be to everyone's taste. The bedrooms are bright and more restrained. All the en suite rooms have a fridge (relatively rare in this price range and very handy for keeping picnic provisions fresh). No bathroom worries here—they really do sparkle. Try to avoid the top of the house because the stairs go on forever. All in all, the Dylan is a great value. One of the cheaper B&Bs in Paddington, it's off the main drag facing a quiet public square and still only 5 minutes from the Tube station.

14 Devonshire Terrace, London W2 3DW. ✆ **020/7723-3280.** Fax 020/7402-2443. www.dylan-hotel.com. 18 units, 9 w/bathroom (some w/shower only). £38–£45 ($70–$83) single w/o bathroom; £52–£66 ($96–$104) double w/o bathroom; £65–£76 ($120–$141) double w/bathroom; £80–£98 ($148–$181) family room. Rates include full English breakfast. Discount for 3-night stays. AE, MC, V. Tube: Paddington or Lancaster Gate. *In room:* TV, coffeemaker, hair dryer, fan.

Fairways Hotel ★ This is a large, late-Georgian house designed in the 1820s in the style of John Nash. The inside exudes a truly charming English ambience. Stephen James Adams, who took over the management from his parents (they ran the hotel for 25 years), made several improvements in 2002, laying new carpeting and redoing all the communal toilets and showers. The strong personal touch throughout Fairways makes it a home away from home. All the rooms are different, the ones in back much quieter. There's a lovely first-floor double at the back, which has the biggest closet in London, brass fittings in the bathroom, and two boudoir chairs flanking a little lace-covered table. The basic twin is a good deal. The decor is a bit more mix 'n' match, but it's a nice-size room and only shares the bathroom with a single. Since our last edition, they've lowered their prices by not offering breakfast—the savings are significant. Guests with a car can park for free in the front. The Mitre Hotel next door is the only other place to offer that.

186 Sussex Gardens, London W2 1TU. ✆ **020/7723-4871.** Fax 020/7723-4871. www.fairways-hotel.co.uk. 17 units, 10 w/bathroom (some w/shower only). £40 ($74) single w/o bathroom; £50 ($92) single w/bathroom; £60 ($111) twin w/o bathroom; £70 ($129) double/twin w/bathroom; £80 ($148) triple w/bathroom; £90 ($166) family room w/bathroom. MC, V. Tube: Paddington. **Amenities:** Nonsmoking rooms. *In room:* TV, coffeemaker, hair dryer, safe, no phone.

Garden Court ★ There are cheaper B&Bs in Bayswater, but what you won't find elsewhere is such out-and-out appeal, such high standards, or such a genuinely warm welcome. Edward Connolly's grandfather opened Garden Court in 1954 in a pair of pretty Victorian town houses. Inside, it's not luxe—except for the swanky new entrance hall—it's more like a much-loved home. The main lounge has some fine old furniture, ancestral portraits, fat novels to borrow, and free hot drinks. The best values are the rooms without private bathrooms (they all have washbasins) because only two rooms share each public facility. Otherwise, the prices are a little high for Queensway. The rooms are all different: One has pretty yellow wallpaper and white painted furniture, another broad blue stripes. Second-floor, front bedrooms lead out onto balconies. The hotel has a small private terrace at the back and access to the public garden square opposite. Breakfast is called "continental," but you can get eggs and bacon if you want. The lower prices below are for rooms without private bathrooms.

30–31 Kensington Gardens Sq., London W2 4BG. ✆ **020/7229-2553.** Fax 020/7727-2749. www.gardencourthotel.co.uk. 32 units, 16 w/bathroom (some w/shower only). £39–£58 ($72–$107) single; £58–£88 ($107–$163) double/twin; £72–£99 ($133–$183) triple; £82–£120 ($152–$222) family room. Rates include continental breakfast. MC, V. Tube: Bayswater or Queensway. **Amenities:** Garden. *In room:* TV, hair dryer.

Mitre House Hotel ★★ *Kids* This fine hotel stretches across four Georgian town houses and is kept in tiptop shape by the Chris brothers, who took over management when their parents retired. It's a great family hotel because of the assortment of accommodations. There are rooms with a double bed and two singles, 2-bedroom family suites with a private bathroom, and superior family suites that face quiet, leafy Talbot Square and have a toilet and tub/shower off a little private corridor. Junior suites, with lots of extra amenities and a Jacuzzi in the bathroom, make a good splurge choice. All the rooms are above-average size for London; those at the back are quieter, though the view north across back alleys to Paddington isn't very inspiring. Mitre House may not be the cheapest deal around, but it's a good value. Hair dryers and tea/coffeemakers are available at the reception desk. There's a big and very pleasant lounge and bar, and even an elevator.

178–184 Sussex Gardens, London W2 1TU. ✆ **020/7723-8040.** Fax 020/7402-0990. www.mitrehousehotel.com. 69 rooms, all w/bathroom (some w/shower only). £70 ($129) single; £80 ($148) double/twin; £90 ($166) triple; £100 ($185) family room; £110 ($203) junior suite. Rates include full English breakfast. AE, DC, MC, V. Tube: Paddington. **Amenities:** Bar; babysitting arranged; laundry service; dry cleaning. *In room:* TV, radio.

Norfolk Court & St. David's Hotel ★ In early 2002, George and Foulla Neokleos finished the mammoth job of refurbishing all four of their buildings. The new look is unusual but appealing, with vanilla-colored walls and moldings and original fireplaces highlighted with yellow. Norfolk Court & St. David's is a treasure trove of architectural details. One room has a domed ceiling, and there's a lovely, stained-glass window on the stairs of no. 20. These Victorian houses have balconies across the front from which guests on the second floor can admire the pretty communal gardens. In the basement, there's a truly enormous and a very good-value family room that can fit five people and has a proper built-in shower. The others are drop-in units that vary in size depending on what each bedroom can cope with. Irons and hair dryers are available at reception. When they say "full English breakfast" here, it really does mean full, with mushrooms, tomatoes, and baked beans on top of all the rest. All in all, this is a very good-value choice. Lower prices listed below are for rooms without bathrooms.

14–20 Norfolk Sq., London W2 1RS. ✆ **020/7723-4963.** Fax 020/7402-9061. www.stdavidshotels.com. 70 units, 60 w/bathroom (most w/shower only). £35–£49 ($65–$91) single; £59–£69 ($109–$128) double; £80 ($148) triple; £100 ($185) quad. All rates include full English breakfast. AE, DC, MC, V. Tube: Paddington. *In room:* TV, coffeemaker.

Rhodes Hotel ★★ *Kids* Chris Crias, the owner of the Rhodes since 1978, recently spruced up the entire hotel. The velvet-curtained lounge and the downstairs dining room now boast handpainted Greek-inspired murals, and painted angels gaze down from the ceiling on the way to the second floor. Other recent improvements include air-conditioning in the main part of the hotel (though not in the annex, which is why the rooms are cheaper there) and dataports for Internet access (free except for phone charges) in all the rooms. The bedroom decor is quite simple and comfortable. No. 220 has its own little private roof terrace, complete with table and chairs. The bunks in the family room are the nicest I've seen, dark wood and 3 feet wide. The continental breakfast includes ham and cheese; you can order an English breakfast for £3 ($4.80).

195 Sussex Gardens, London W2 2RJ. ✆ **020/7262-0537.** Fax 020/7723-4054. www.rhodeshotel.com. 18 units, all w/bathroom (most w/shower only). £50–£60 ($92–$111) single; £70–£85 ($129–$157) double/twin; £85–£95 ($157–$176) triple; £95–£110 ($176–$203) quad. Discount available for weekday and 3-day stays. Rates include continental breakfast. MC, V. Tube: Paddington. *In room:* TV, dataport, fridge, coffeemaker, hair dryer.

SUPER-CHEAP SLEEPS

Astor's Hyde Park Hostel ★ These three Georgian terrace houses have survived through years as a bargain sleep with their gracious internal spaces and beautiful moldings unmolested. Astor's even decreed that the crazy murals, a hallmark of its hostels, be painted on removable boards here at Hyde Park. The company has turned this into its London flagship. The dorms have anything from 4 to 10 bunks, hence the wide price range, and there are great discounts to be had in winter. But the changes have been much bigger than a lick of paint and new carpet. As well as replacing the bathrooms, Astor's has taken advantage of the existing commercial kitchen to open the ITA (International Travellers Association) club, bar, and canteen-style cafe. Different DJs guest each night—guests get to DJ themselves on Wednesdays. Meals rarely cost more than £3 ($5.50). And beer starts at £1 ($1.85) during happy hour. If you check out the other amenities, you'll see these guys have thought of everything necessary to create a community for travelers. The 18-to-35 age restriction, unique in the London hostels reviewed, reinforces that spirit. Astor's has two other hostels in Queensway: **Leinster Inn,** 7–12 Leinster Sq., London, W2 4PR (✆ **020/7229-9641;** fax 020/7221-5255), famed for its weekend club nights, and the smaller, more laid-back **Quest,** 45 Queensborough Terrace, London, W2 8SY (✆ **020/7229-7782;** fax 020/7727-8106). There is a fourth hostel in **Victoria** (p. 107) and the long-established **Museum Inn** in Bloomsbury (p. 104).

2–6 Inverness Terrace, London W2 3HY. ✆ **020/7229-5101.** Fax 020/7229-3170. www.astorhostels.com. 200 units, none w/bathroom. £11–£18 ($20–$33) per person in a dorm; £50 ($92) twin. Rates include bed linen and continental breakfast. Discount available for 1-week stays off season. MC, V. Tube: Queensway or Bayswater. 18–35 age restriction. **Amenities:** Club; bar; cafe; game room; coin-op washers and dryers; Internet access; communal kitchen; safe. *In room:* No phone.

WORTH A SPLURGE

Delmere Hotel ★★ Keep an eye on the Delmere's website because there's usually a promotion that makes the cost comparable to the local B&Bs. The Delmere calls itself a "boutique town house hotel," hence the gold nameplates and charming window boxes along the top of the late-Georgian porch, and the real-flame fire in the lounge. It caters to a mix of business and pleasure travelers. The rooms, all recently refurbished and with new bathrooms, are very comfortable, but the decor is a bit too safe for real elegance except for the more expensive Crown Room up under the eaves, which has a Jacuzzi in the bathroom, a canopied bed, frilled tablecloth, and ruched blind that gives it the air of a rich widow's cabin on a cruise liner. Check out the bedrooms in the annex, which feel like you're in your own place. The windows look onto a small courtyard, though, so you may be able to hear the music from the hotel's jazz bar. Avoid the lower floor, which is a real hole in the ground. The La Perla restaurant does three-course meals for around £24 ($44).

130 Sussex Gardens, London W2 1UB. ✆ **020/7706-3344.** Fax 020/7262-1863. www.delmerehotels.com. 36 units, all w/bathroom (most w/shower only). £69–£98 ($128–$191) single; £95–£121 ($176–$224) double/twin. Rates include continental breakfast. AE, DC, DISC, MC, V. Tube: Paddington. **Amenities:** Restaurant; bar; limited room service; dry cleaning. *In room:* TV, dataport, coffeemaker, hair dryer, safe, radio.

The Pavilion ★ Splurging here won't get you room service except when someone brings your continental breakfast (there's no dining room). It won't get you a grand-size bedroom, or even a luxurious bathroom (the showers are small and rather dated, though they are well maintained). No, what you're paying for is the glam va-va-va-voom that makes you want to raid the costume cupboard and party with rock stars. Ex-model Danny Karne and his sister Noshi took over The Pavilion a over decade ago and turned it into London's grooviest affordable town-house hotel. Every room is decorated with billowing fabrics, antiques, and recycled junkshop finds, sometimes with more dash than polish. "Honky Tonk Afro" pays homage to 1970s kitsch, with sequins and disco glitter, while "Highland Fling" has dark paneling, portraits, and acres of tartan. "White Day Soul Nights" on the top floor is a light, bright, cream-on-cream confection. The only downside is the general scarcity of closet space. A new sitting room, with doors out to a little courtyard, is called the Purple Parlour. The Pavilion is for people who want something memorable—something more than a place to sleep, wash, and change clothes between adventures. It's an adventure itself. You might even bump into a future rock star on the stairs, as this is a favorite music business sleep—which is probably why it can smell kind of smoky.

34–36 Sussex Gardens, London W2 1UL. ✆ **020/7262-0905.** Fax 020/7262-1324. www.msi.com.mt/pavilion/. 27 units, all w/bathroom (most w/shower only, 2 w/tub only). £60–£85 ($111–$151) single; £100 ($185) double/twin; £120 ($222) triple. Rates include continental breakfast. AE, DC, MC, V (4% surcharge for paying by credit card). Tube: Edgware Rd. *In room:* TV, coffeemaker.

6 Marylebone

Edward Lear Hotel Previous reviews of this hotel always mentioned the pretty Georgian houses with their gold-tipped railings and luxuriant window boxes; the excellent location, just behind Marble Arch; the nice people working there; and the charming lounge and big-windowed breakfast room. Then came the "but . . . ," because the standards upstairs—up five narrow flights in one house and four in the other—never matched up to the rest. Long-time owner Peter Evans finally began a renovation program in 2001, and some of the bedrooms have now been redecorated. The new look is drab but clean, and the rooms aren't a bad size for London, with decent storage provided by the quirky built-in furniture. Try for room no. 18, a double overlooking a mews in back with its bathroom down a little flight of stairs. There's no double-glazing at the Edward Lear, so rooms in the front bear the brunt of traffic noise along busy Seymour Street. Some rooms have a cupboard-size shower but no toilet, and the rest share bathrooms that are adequate but dated. So there are good deals here, depending on how laid-back you are about weird and/or shared plumbing.

28–30 Seymour St., London W1H 5WD. ✆ **020/7402-5401.** Fax 020/7706-3766. www.edlear.com. 31 units, 4 w/bathroom (8 w/shower only). £38–£4 ($70–$88) single w/o bathroom; £48–£60 ($89–$111) single w/bathroom; £55–£67 ($98–$123) double w/o bathroom; £60–£89 ($110–$165) double/twin w/bathroom; £63–£79 ($117–$146) triple w/o bathroom; £84–£105 ($155–$194) family room w/bathroom. Rates include full English breakfast. Children under 2 stay free in parent's room; £9.50 ($18) for extra child's bed. MC, V. Tube: Marble Arch. **Amenities:** Lounge; Internet access. *In room:* TV, coffeemaker, hair dryer, radio.

Marble Arch Inn The plus side of this B&B is that it's very reasonably priced for its location, just behind Marble Arch. The minus side is that it has a reception area and hallways painted a sickly shade of lavender and small, fairly dreary (but clean) rooms. The showers are all drop-in units. Anyone on a tight budget should consider foregoing a private shower because only two rooms share each public facility. There's no dining room, so you get breakfast in your room. There's a fridge and satellite TV in every room, which is quite rare in this price range.

The owner, Mr. Kassam, has another B&B in Victoria: **Dover Hotel,** 42–44 Belgrave Rd., SW1 (✆ **020/7821-9085;** fax 020/7834-6425; www.dover-hotel.co.uk). The rates there are even lower: A double room with private shower costs £50 to £69 ($92–$128).

49–50 Upper Berkeley St., London W1H 7PN. ✆ **020/7723-7888.** Fax 020/7723-6060. www.marblearch-inn.co.uk. 29 units, 23 w/bathroom (shower only). £45–£55 ($83–$102) single/double w/o bathroom; £70–£75 ($129–$139) single/double/twin w/bathroom; £70–£80 ($129–$148) triple w/bathroom; £100–£120 ($185–$222) family room w/bathroom. Rates include continental breakfast. Lower rates apply Jan–Feb. Discount of 5% for 4-night stays, 10% for 7-night stays, 15% for 14-night stays. AE, DC, DISC, MC, V. Tube: Marble Arch. **Amenities:** Nonsmoking rooms. *In room:* TV, fridge, coffeemaker, hair dryer, safe.

Nutford House, University of London ★ *Finds* If you don't mind classic student sleeping arrangements, then this is an absolutely fantastic deal. It's hugely popular with 20-somethings and retired travelers. You get to stay in a quiet side street, just north of Marble Arch, for half the price of anywhere else in the neighborhood. Nutford House is a marvelous redbrick building put up during World War I as a hostel for "distressed gentlewomen." All the rooms are basic singles in good, clean condition. There are kitchenettes for making snacks on all four floors—there is an elevator—and five people share each public shower or tub. The twin rooms, which also have kitchenettes, are in three terrace houses across the road. Dining in the canteen is a great deal, too; dinner is practically given away at £5 ($8) for two courses. An army could march for days on the breakfast menu, which changes daily. And both meals include vegetarian options. Nutford House is nonsmoking throughout, and it has a blissfully peaceful walled garden at the back. Don't forget to pack a bath towel.

Brown St., London W1H 6AH. ✆ **0870/147-9031.** Fax 020/7258-1781. www.lon.ac.uk/accom. 180 units, none w/bathroom. £25 ($46) single; £30 ($55) single w/evening meal; £40 ($74) twin; £50 ($92) twin w/evening meal. Rates include bed linen, hand towel, and full English breakfast. Minimum stay 2 nights. No credit cards. Open mid-June to Aug 25. Tube: Marble Arch. **Amenities:** Restaurant; coin-op washers and dryers; nonsmoking rooms; communal kitchens; garden. *In room:* No phone.

Wyndham Hotel ★ *Value* *Finds* Gordon Hammé used to be the world's biggest bullion dealer, based in London's Hatton Garden. In 1999 he sold out, decided to buy a B&B, and took over and completely restored the Wyndham, an early-19th-century Georgian building on a pretty little terrace just off the busy Marylebone Road. The place has already won some quality awards. The rooms are attractive but very small. There are showers in all rooms, but the toilets are shared. A basket of fruit is there to welcome arriving guests. You can call down to reception for sandwiches and salads, pick up your e-mail there, or borrow an iron or hair dryer. The breakfast room leads out into the beautiful little terraced garden. If other guests beat you to a seat in the sun, you can always look down on them from the roof terrace. You don't often find this kind of charm at these low prices.

30 Wyndham St., London W1H 1DD. ✆ **020/7723-7204.** Fax 020/7723-2893. www.lhghotels.co.uk. 10 units, none w/toilet, all w/shower. £39–£49 ($72–$91) single; £59–£67 ($109–$123) double/twin. Rates include continental breakfast. Discount of 10% for 1-week stays. MC, V. Tube: Marylebone, or Baker St. **Amenities:** Garden. *In room:* TV, minibar, coffeemaker, radio.

WORTH A SPLURGE

Hart House Hotel ★★ Andrew Bowden, who took over the management of Hart House from his parents, has one of the most welcoming and professionally run B&Bs in London. This Georgian town house, built in 1782, was used by members of the French nobility during the French Revolution. It has retained its dignified entrance hall (with a huge fragrant bouquet of white lilies when we visited) and polished paneling that gives way to pretty floral wallpaper. The rooms (all nonsmoking) are attractive and comfortable with small but immaculate bathrooms. Double-glazing screens out the traffic roar on Gloucester Place, the busy road from Oxford Street to Baker Street. The top floor double is a peaceful high-up hideaway, but there's no elevator to reach it. Room no. 6, a huge twin at the back with a marvelous leaded-glass bay window and its bathroom up a little flight of stairs, is another sought-after room. Reception has cots to lend out.

51 Gloucester Place, London W1H 3PE. ✆ **020/7935-2288.** Fax 020/7935-8516. www.harthouse.co.uk. 15 units, all w/bathroom (some w/shower only). £75 ($139) single; £105 ($194) double/twin; £130 ($240) triple; £150 ($277) quad. Rates include full English breakfast. Discounts for 6 nights or more. AE, MC, V. Tube: Marble Arch or Baker St. **Amenities:** Babysitting arranged; laundry service; dry cleaning; nonsmoking rooms. *In room:* TV, coffeemaker, hair dryer.

Ivanhoe Suite Hotel St. Christopher's Place is a pretty piazza, just off Oxford Street, filled with designer boutiques and restaurants with tables outside. The hotel, located above a restaurant, doesn't actually offer suites, but the rooms are big enough for a table and chairs, where you eat breakfast brought up to you in the morning. Each room has its own front-door bell, and guests can check on callers via the closed-circuit TV camera linked to their television. The rooms were recently redecorated but not everyone will like the cantaloupe-and-blue color scheme; bathrooms are off a small lobby as you walk in. Some rooms face a narrow street, others have a view over the piazza fountain. Unfortunately, after being meticulously run by the same person for 29 years, this hotel was recently sold and the personal touch that was once a hallmark seems to be lost. Some of the rooms looked a bit forlorn when we visited. Still, the location is great.

1 St. Christopher's Place, Barrett St. Piazza, London W1M 5HB. ✆ **020/7935-1047.** Fax 020/7224-0563. 7 units, all w/bathroom (some w/shower only). £75 ($139) single; £95 ($176) double; £120 ($222) triple. Rates include continental breakfast. AE, DC, MC, V. Tube: Bond St. **Amenities:** Limited room service. *In room:* TV, fridge, coffeemaker, hair dryer, trouser press.

Wigmore Court Hotel ★★ *Finds* The owner of this rather appealing Georgian-era B&B, Najma Jinnah, knows the long climb to the fifth floor is a turnoff for a lot of guests, even though they get help with their bags, so she has introduced a reward system. Anyone who does make it to the top can sink into a four-poster bed to recover. There are two more, one each on the second and third floors. Budget travelers can get a very good deal here. There's a small fourth-floor double which shares a bathroom, one floor up, with a single and costs £13 ($21) less than the others. Though it faces the front, there is double-glazing throughout. The rooms at the back look over a mews. The decor is a pleasant mix of traditional styles. Guests can use the kitchen and laundry facilities.

23 Gloucester Place, London W1H 3PB. ✆ **020/7935-0928.** Fax 020/7487-4254. www.wigmore-hotel.co.uk. 18 units, 16 w/bathroom (some w/shower only). £52–£67 ($96–$124) single; £78–£98 ($144–$181) double; £120 ($222) triple; £130 ($240) quad. Rates include full English breakfast. Discount of 10% for 1-week stays. MC, V. Tube: Marble Arch. **Amenities:** Laundry facilities; use of kitchen. *In room:* TV, coffeemaker, hair dryer.

7 Soho & Oxford Circus

SUPER-CHEAP SLEEPS

Oxford Street Youth Hostel This excellent cheap sleep is above some offices, in a location most people would kill for—the northern border of Soho. The legendary Carnaby Street, where London first took off as cult fashion capital in the swinging 1960s, is just around the corner, and hip new fashion shops are finally pushing back the trashy tourist traps. All the rooms are the same size—small. So, if you've got the cash, ask to share with one other person because the four-bedders feel like a cabin on a sleeper train. The bunks are nice sturdy wooden ones, with crisp cotton sheets. There are soft drinks and snack machines, as well as Internet access, in the lounge. The hostel is too small to have a restaurant, so this place is entirely self-catering. The communal kitchen is a great excuse for a 5-minute walk to Berwick Street market. The hostel also changes money.

14–18 Noel St., London W1. ✆ **020/7734-1618.** Fax 020/7734-1657. www.yha.org.uk. 75 units, none w/bathroom. £23 ($42) adult; £18 ($34) children under 18. Rates include bed linen. MC, V. Tube: Oxford Circus. No children under 6. **Amenities:** Lounge, coin-op washers and dryers; communal kitchen; Internet access. *In room:* No phone.

WORTH A SPLURGE

Regent Palace Hotel ★ *Value* This London behemoth, located smack dab in the center of the West End just off Piccadilly Circus, was built in 1915, long before travelers expected private bathrooms in their rooms. In recent years it's been gradually upgrading by installing pre-fab shower/toilet/basin units in some of the rooms, sprucing up room decor, and making the endless hallways more welcoming. The rooms without "en suite facilities" are actually preferable because they have a bit more space (they're also cheaper). The public bathrooms are kept locked to make sure they're spotless; if you need to use a shower, the housekeeper will ride the elevator up at any time with the key and fresh towels. That's quite a deal at a weekday price that knocks socks off many B&Bs. The decor is comfortable if plain, and some of the beds aren't as firm as Americans like them; the spruced-up lobby looks like an air terminal, right down to the weekend check-in queues. Breakfast is extra, but we recommend that you skip it and find some charming cafe in nearby Soho instead. That's really the selling point of the Regent Palace—its fabulous location right in the heart of everything. This hotel has a history of offering cheap rates through a host of accommodations sites, so plug the name into a search engine and see what you come up with. The higher prices listed below are for weekends.

Glasshouse St., Piccadilly Circus, London W1A 4BZ. ✆ **020/7734-0716.** Fax 020/7734-6435. www.regentpalacehotel.co.uk. 887 units, 383 w/bathroom (shower only). £69–£79 ($128–$146) single w/o bathroom; £79–£89 ($146–$165) double/twin w/o bathroom; £129–£139 ($239–$257) double/twin w/bathroom; £95–£105 ($152–$168) triple w/o bathroom. 32 units adapted for travelers w/disabilities. Lower rates apply Sun–Thurs. Discount available for long stays. AE, DC, MC, V. Tube: Piccadilly Circus. **Amenities:** Pub and coffee bar; concierge; limited room service; laundry service; dry cleaning; nonsmoking rooms. *In room:* TV, coffeemaker, radio.

8 Bloomsbury

Arran House Hotel ★ *Kids* It's hard to get excited by something as ordinary as a kitchen, but most B&Bs don't let guests use theirs, and apart from Wigmore Court in Marylebone, none of the others that do are as welcoming or as nice as this one. Heat up your own supper—great for budget travelers and parents with kids—and dine in style in the pleasant breakfast room. Proprietor John Richards has started a round of refurbishments to spruce up the place. The bedrooms are simple, light, and homey. If you go for one with a shower but no toilet you'll get one of the best deals on Gower Street. The public bathrooms and showers are perfectly clean, though a bit worn. Avoid the tiny basic twins where the beds are head to head along one wall. The front rooms are double-glazed, which cuts out the traffic hum. The coin-operated Internet terminal in the comfy lounge lets you pick up your e-mails and there are self-service laundry facilities. Arran House is very family-friendly; cribs are free. And you won't find a more beautiful garden in London. The lower prices below are for rooms without en suite bathrooms or showers.

77 Gower St., London WC1E 6HJ. ✆ **020/7636-2186** or 020/7637-1140. Fax 020/7436-5328. www.arranhotel-london.com. 28 units, 13 w/bathroom (shower only). £45–£55 ($83–$102) single; £72–£85 ($133–$157) double; £90–£113 ($166–$209) triple; £96–£117 ($178–$216) quad; £105–£130 ($199–$240) quint. Rates include full English breakfast. MC, V. Tube: Goodge St. or Russell Sq. **Amenities:** Lounge; use of kitchen; babysitting arranged; laundry facilities; Internet access; garden. *In room:* TV, hair dryer.

La Brasserie Townhouse ★ *Finds* If you're up for something out of the ordinary, this is one of those secret London places that make for a truly memorable stay. Only a tiny handful of hotels so centrally located can match the twin-room price—most are at least £10 ($18) a night more expensive. The singles are even more of a steal, a few pounds more than what you'd pay to sleep at a youth hostel. That's because the rooms really are one-person big. The other *quid pro quo* for the low price is that there is only one public bathroom for what could be six guests. But so what? There's a real charm in this place, which is above the small La Brasserie Townhouse restaurant and run by the same team. The rooms are pleasantly minimalist, the furniture white and the decor vanilla. Room no. 201 is definitely the best choice. You'll pay more for a room with breakfast, but it's a full English breakfast and you can have it served anytime between 9:30am and noon. You do have to wait until 4pm to check in, though. Presumably, that's when there's a lull in the brasserie, where Chef Raoul Duclos from Lyon presides over operations. The cuisine is classic French with a nouvelle twist and prices for a fixed-price meal are low enough to make dining here as affordable as staying here. Did I mention that the location, a 2-minute walk from the British Museum, is outstanding?

24 Coptic St., London WC1A 1NT. ✆ **020/7636-2731.** labrasserietownhouse@hotmail.com. 4 units, none w/bathroom. £28 ($45) single w/o breakfast; £32 ($51) single w/breakfast; £50 ($80) double w/o breakfast; £60 ($96) double w/breakfast. AE, DC, MC, V. Tube: Holborn or Tottenham Court Rd. **Amenities:** Restaurant; bar; limited room service; nonsmoking rooms. *In room:* TV, hair dryer, iron, no phone.

Euro Hotel ★ *Kids* The kids' drawings that festoon the walls behind reception are a pretty heavy clue as to where the hotel's strength lies—as a favorite of families on holiday. Generally, prices are high-ish for Cartwright Gardens, a Georgian crescent in north Bloomsbury that is more expensive than Gower Street but has more of a neighborhood feel to it. However, the Euro does do a good-value rate for children under 16 who share a room with their parents. You pay the normal single or double price, depending on the number of adults, plus £10 ($18) per child. Toddlers under 2½ stay

Where to Stay in the West End

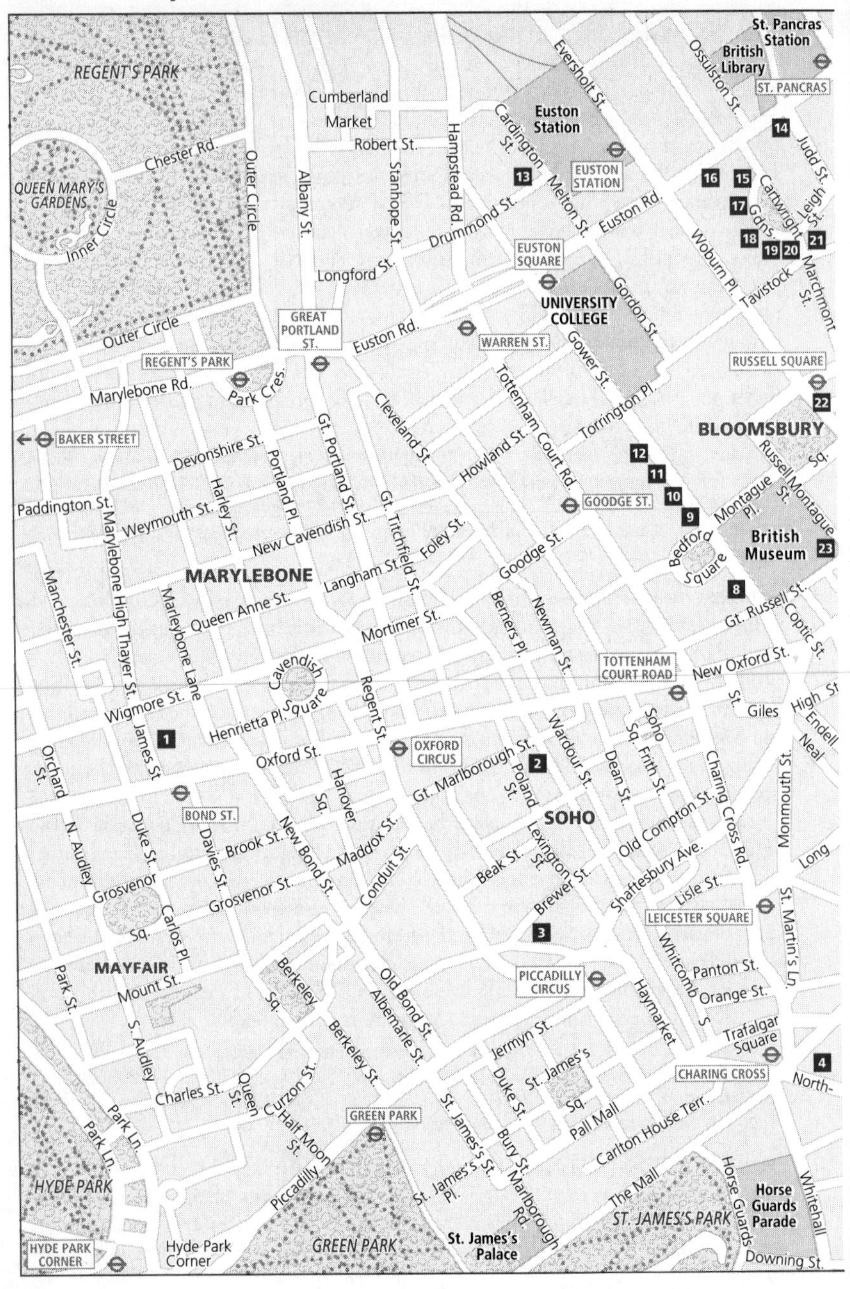

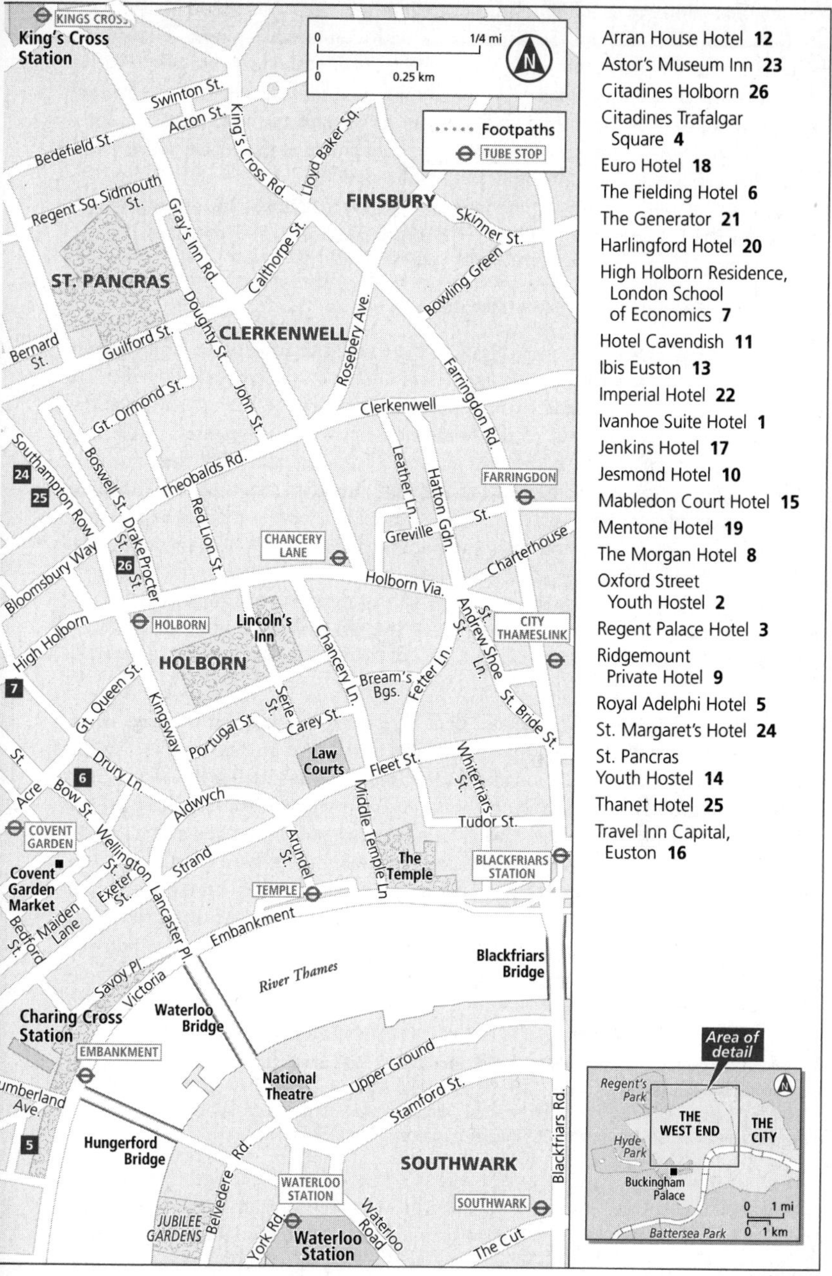
Arran House Hotel 12
Astor's Museum Inn 23
Citadines Holborn 26
Citadines Trafalgar Square 4
Euro Hotel 18
The Fielding Hotel 6
The Generator 21
Harlingford Hotel 20
High Holborn Residence, London School of Economics 7
Hotel Cavendish 11
Ibis Euston 13
Imperial Hotel 22
Ivanhoe Suite Hotel 1
Jenkins Hotel 17
Jesmond Hotel 10
Mabledon Court Hotel 15
Mentone Hotel 19
The Morgan Hotel 8
Oxford Street Youth Hostel 2
Regent Palace Hotel 3
Ridgemount Private Hotel 9
Royal Adelphi Hotel 5
St. Margaret's Hotel 24
St. Pancras Youth Hostel 14
Thanet Hotel 25
Travel Inn Capital, Euston 16
0
1/4 mi
0
0.25 km
N
Footpaths
TUBE STOP
KINGS CROSS
King's Cross Station
FINSBURY
ST. PANCRAS
CLERKENWELL
HOLBORN
SOUTHWARK
FARRINGDON
CHANCERY LANE
HOLBORN
CITY THAMESLINK
COVENT GARDEN
TEMPLE
BLACKFRIARS STATION
EMBANKMENT
WATERLOO STATION
SOUTHWARK
Lincoln's Inn
Law Courts
The Temple
Covent Garden Market
Charing Cross Station
Waterloo Bridge
Blackfriars Bridge
River Thames
National Theatre
Hungerford Bridge
JUBILEE GARDENS
Waterloo Station
Swinton St.
Acton St.
Bedefield St.
King's Cross Rd.
Lloyd Baker Sq.
Regent Sq.
Sidmouth St.
Gray's Inn Rd.
Calthorpe St.
Skinner St.
Bowling Green
Rosebery Ave.
Doughty St.
Bernard St.
Guilford St.
Gt. Ormond St.
John St.
Clerkenwell
Farringdon Rd.
Southampton Row
Boswell St.
Theobalds Rd.
Red Lion St.
Leather Ln.
Hatton Gdn.
Greville St.
Charterhouse
Bloomsbury Way
Drake St.
Procter St.
Holborn Via.
St. Andrew St.
Shoe Ln.
High Holborn
Chancery Ln.
Fetter Ln.
Bream's Bgs.
St. Bride St.
Gt. Queen St.
Kingsway
Serle St.
Portugal St.
Carey St.
Whitefriars St.
St.
Acre
Drury Ln.
Bow St.
Fleet St.
Aldwych
Middle Temple Ln
Tudor St.
Wellington St.
Arundel St.
Strand
Exeter St.
Maiden Lane
Bedford St.
Lancaster Pl.
Embankment
Savoy Pl.
Victoria
Upper Ground
Stamford St.
umberland Ave.
Rd.
Belvedere
York Rd
Waterloo Road
The Cut
Blackfriars Rd.
24
25
26
7
6
5
Area of detail
Regent's Park
THE WEST END
THE CITY
Hyde Park
Buckingham Palace
Battersea Park
0 1 mi
0 1 km

free, and you can borrow a high chair and crib at the reception desk. The Euro is a clean, pleasant, friendly, and attractive place with comfortable rooms. The shared bathrooms were recently renovated. The hotel offers guests videos, use of the office safe and fax machine, and e-mail pick-up, all for free. And if the kids still need wearing out after a day on the tourist trail, you can play tennis in the gardens opposite. The Euro can lend you rackets and balls. The only potential drawback: no elevator. The higher prices below are for rooms with bathrooms.

53 Cartwright Gardens, London WC1H 9EL. ✆ **020/7387-4321**. Fax 020/7383-5044. www.eurohotel.co.uk. 35 units, 10 w/bathroom (some w/shower only). £49–£70 ($91–$129) single; £69–£89 ($128–$147) double/twin; £85–£105 ($157–$194) triple; £95–£115 ($176–$213) family room. Rates include full English breakfast. Special rates for children under 16. Discount of 10% for 1-week stays off season. AE, MC, V. Tube: Euston or Russell Sq. **Amenities:** Lounge; tennis court; garden. *In room:* TV, coffeemaker, radio.

Harlingford Hotel ★★ Andrew Davies is the third generation of his family to run this B&B, a dignified, dove-gray, Georgian-era building on the corner of Marchmont Street and Cartwright Gardens. A perfectionist by nature, he recently oversaw the smart, designer-aided overhaul of the hotel interiors, which use neutral colors and bright splashes of color. The bathrooms are small but adequate. With their gracious arched windows and high ceilings, the lounge and breakfast rooms on either side of the white, airy entrance hall are a real asset. The breakfast room is modern and cheery. As a guest, you can get a key and enjoy the communal gardens opposite the hotel. The only downside: no elevator.

61–63 Cartwright Gardens, London WC1H 9EL. ✆ **020/7387-1551**. Fax 020/7387-4616. www.harlingfordhotel.com. 44 units, all w/bathroom (shower only). £75 ($139) single; £95 ($176) double/twin; £105 ($204) triple; £110 ($203) quad. Rates include full English breakfast. AE, DC, MC, V. Tube: Euston or Russell Sq. **Amenities:** Lounge. *In room:* TV, coffeemaker.

Hotel Cavendish *Value* The Beatles slept here. That was back in the days when there were five of them, and the record label EMI used to book rooms at the Cavendish for try-out bands. Eluned Edwards' mother was running this clean, cozy, and welcoming B&B back then. None of the rooms in Hotel Cavendish have private bathrooms; there are new power showers in all the shared facilities and a small washbasin in every room. No two bedrooms are the same, but all have candlewick bedspreads and nice furniture you'd find in a home cleverly decorated on a budget. And it's a haven for the budget traveler who doesn't care so much about frills or room size but wants cleanliness and a bit of charm. The £48 ($89) double is very small but why spend more if you're going to be out all day and partying half the night? The pinnacle of desirability is the spacious £70 ($125) double at the back. Hair dryers are available at reception. Guests can sit out in the back garden in the summer.

75 Gower St., London WC1E 6HJ. ✆ **020/7636-9079**. Fax 020/7580-3609. www.hotelcavendish.com. 20 units, none w/bathroom. £42–£45 ($78–$83) single; £48–£70 ($89–$125) double; £75–£84 ($140–$155) triple; £90–£100 ($166–$185) quad. Rates include full English breakfast. Discount available for groups. AE, MC, V. Tube: Goodge St. or Russell Sq. **Amenities:** Garden. *In room:* Coffeemaker, no phone.

Ibis Euston ★ This chain of budget hotels, owned by the French group Accor, has cloned itself all over the country (see "Near the Airport," later in this chapter). It's a good deal for travelers who prefer up-to-date identikit accommodations and are willing (or want) to forego the quirks and homier pleasures of a B&B. Room rates compete with those on Gower Street, though breakfast is not included. You'd never choose the Ibis for the beauty of its location. The "wrong" side of Euston Road is a bit bleak and businessy, but the Ibis has made its modern redbrick building very welcoming with hanging baskets and striped awnings. The inside is blandly appealing, too: the first floor has the open feel of a food court at a shopping mall. There's a railway-themed bar and a restaurant. Supper is very reasonably priced both there and at Tracks, though I wouldn't recommend eating at either. Upstairs, the rooms are medium-size, all with small but adequate bathrooms. This hotel has an elevator, and you can send e-mail for free via the i-plus electronic information booth in the foyer. The lower rate quoted below is for weekends only.

3 Cardington St., London NW1 2LW. ✆ **020/7388-7777.** Fax 020/7388-0001. www.ibishotel.com. 380 units, all w/bathroom (shower only). £75–£80 ($139–$148) double/twin. 8 units adapted for travelers w/disabilities. Rates do not include breakfast. Children under 12 stay free in parent's room. AE, DC, MC, V. Tube: Euston. **Amenities:** Restaurant; bar; room service; Internet access. *In room:* TV.

Jenkins Hotel ★ Jenkins has been a hotel since the 1920s and appeared in the PBS mystery series *Poirot.* Today the style is trad-lite, very English but relaxed about it. Sam Bellingham and his partner Felicity Langley-Hunt recently refurbished the entire hotel, putting en suite bathrooms in all but one of the rooms. A double with private bathroom is still a few pounds cheaper here than elsewhere in Cartwright Gardens. Rivals score points for having lounges, but Jenkins offers better in-room amenities. There's one nice double room (no. 10) on the fourth floor (no elevator), but the top choice is the second-floor room no. 5, where two rooms on the front, with floor-to-ceiling windows, have been knocked into one. The room to avoid is the pretty but cavelike basement double. Sam's two friendly Labradors, Tiggy and George, hang out in the kitchen which, with its huge pine table, doubles as reception. There are rackets and balls to borrow if you want to play tennis in communal gardens opposite. Jenkins is completely nonsmoking.

45 Cartwright Gardens, London WC1H 9EH. ✆ **020/7387-2067.** Fax 020/7383-3139. www.jenkinshotel.demon.co.uk. 13 units, 12 w/bathroom (most w/shower only). £52–£72 ($96–$133) single; £85 ($157) double/twin; £105 ($194) triple. Rates include full English breakfast. MC, V. Tube: Euston or Russell Sq. **Amenities:** Nonsmoking rooms; garden. *In room:* TV, fridge, coffeemaker, hair dryer, safe.

Jesmond Hotel The Jesmond's proprietors, Mr. and Mrs. Beynon, have been running this small B&B in a listed building in Central London for nearly 25 years. A lot of the rooms are small, though the choice of blonde-wood furniture helps to counteract feelings of claustrophobia, and the cabinets around the in-room sinks provide extra storage. Only a few rooms have private bathrooms. Those that do are competitively priced, and those that don't are positively cheap. And the Beynons make sure the atmosphere and welcome are top-notch. The rooms at the front have double-glazing, which makes them pretty quiet. There's a pleasantly homey lounge with a cold-drink machine and free tea and coffee, plus free Internet access. This is one of the few places that still puts a fruit bowl out in the morning.

63 Gower St., London WC1 6HJ. ✆ **020/7636-3199.** Fax 020/7323-4373. www.jesmondhotel.org.uk. 16 units, 5 w/bathroom (shower only). £36 ($67) single w/o bathroom; £46 ($85) single w/bathroom; £54 ($100) double/twin w/o bathroom; £68 ($126) double/twin w/bathroom; £70 ($129) triple w/o bathroom; £80 ($148) triple w/bathroom; £82 ($152) quad w/o bathroom; £90 ($166) quad w/bathroom; £95 ($176) five-bed w/o bathroom. Rates include full English breakfast. MC, V. Tube: Goodge St. or Russell Sq. *In room:* TV, coffeemaker, hair dryer, radio, no phone.

Mabledon Court Hotel ★ Dating from the 1950s, this is a modern building by local standards, but it fits in well with its Georgian and Victorian neighbors. It's popular with academics and conference-goers visiting nearby London University. In 2002 the bedrooms were given a fresh coat of paint, new carpets, beds, curtains, and bedspreads. The rooms are all small but functional. The bathrooms have sparkling white tiles and wooden floors. There's an elevator and a nice breakfast room downstairs with a skylight. The hotel was on the market when we visited, so it may or may not still exist when you read this.

10–11 Mabledon Place, London WC1H 9BA. ✆ **020/7388-3866.** Fax 020/7387-5686. www.mabledonhotel.com. 32 units, all w/bathroom (shower only). £75 ($139) single; £85 ($157) double. Rates include full English breakfast. AE, DC, MC, V. Tube: Euston or Russell Sq. *In room:* TV, coffeemaker, hair dryer.

Mentone Hotel ★ This is the second B&B along the south end of Cartwright Gardens. It's a bit cheaper than the neighboring Jenkins Hotel, and although the welcome is friendly and the decor newish, it doesn't have quite the same charm. The Mentone stretches across three houses and has been run by the same family for over 25 years. Simon Tyner took over from his mother in 1997. He's refurbished the bedrooms with nice matching quilt covers and curtains. The family has resisted chopping up the original Georgian rooms, so the only funny shapes come from the private bathrooms. You do get a big room here, which is not something you can say about many London B&Bs. There's enough space in some for a small sofa, and though the ceilings are lower on the top floor (originally the servants' quarters), the rooms don't feel cramped. You can borrow a hair dryer at the reception desk, as well as a key to get into the gardens opposite. The lower rates below are for off-season stays.

54 Cartwright Gardens, London WC1H 9EL. ✆ **020/7387-3927.** Fax 020/7388-4671. www.mentonehotel.com. 42 units, all w/bathroom (shower only). £55–£60 ($102–$111) single; £75–£83 ($139–$154) double/twin; £85–£95 ($157–$176) triple; £95–£105 ($170–$194) quad. Rates include full English breakfast. AE, DC, MC, V. Tube: Euston or Russell Sq. **Amenities:** Garden. *In room:* TV, coffeemaker.

The Morgan Hotel ★★ It's a real treat to find a B&B with air-conditioning and double-glazing, particularly in an elegant 18th-century terrace house. It makes staying at The Morgan Hotel a pleasure. It's more expensive than other local B&Bs (still cheaper than Cartwright Gardens), but then, period-style decoration does tend to bump the price up. There are pretty floral bedspreads and decorative borders on the walls, and every room is different. If there are two of you, go for the first-floor room that opens onto the garden at the back, which no one else gets to use. The basic single room is absolutely tiny, and there are much better single rooms elsewhere. Otherwise, it's almost worth staying here just to see the oak-paneled breakfast room with its wooden booths. A few doors away, The Morgan has four wonderful one-bedroom apartments, which go for £125 ($200) a night including breakfast, or £175 ($280) if you want to have a foldaway bed and sleep three.

24 Bloomsbury St., London WC1B 3QJ. ✆ **020/7636-3735.** Fax 020/7636-3045. www.morganhotel.co.uk. 15 units, all w/bathroom (most w/shower only). £65–£80 ($120–$148) single; £95–£105 ($176–$194) double/twin; £130 ($240) triple. Rates include full English breakfast. MC, V. Tube: Goodge St. or Tottenham Court Rd. *In room:* A/C, TV, hair dryer.

Ridgemount Private Hotel *Value* Royden and Gwen Rees, the charming Welsh proprietors who've run this B&B for 38 years, have a reputation for providing a warm-hearted welcome and get lots of returning customers as a result. One U.S. college has been sending its exchange students to stay here every January for 14 years. The Ridgemount stretches across two buildings, one of which still has all the original fireplaces and cornices. The decor is simple, old-fashioned, and comfortably dowdy. Some of the rooms are quite small, particularly the basic twins. But if you're looking for a double room with a private bathroom—several of which are brand new—you're unlikely to find a cheaper rate anywhere else on Gower Street. All the rooms on the front are double-glazed against the traffic noise. Free coffee and tea are available in the lounge, and you can borrow an electric fan at reception. Mr. and Mrs. Rees will even do laundry. And like most of the B&Bs on Gower Street, you can use the garden in the summer. The lower prices below are for rooms without bathrooms.

65–67 Gower St., London WC1E 6HJ. © **020/7636-1141.** Fax 020/7636-2558. www.ridgemounthotel.co.uk. 32 units, 13 w/bathroom (shower only). £37–£48 ($68–$89) single; £52–£68 ($96–$126) double/twin; £69–£81 ($128–$145) triple; £82–£92 ($152–$170) quad; £90–£95 ($166–$176) quint w/o bathroom. Rates include full English breakfast. MC, V. Tube: Goodge St. or Russell Sq. **Amenities:** Lounge; laundry facilities. *In room:* TV, no phone.

St. Margaret's Hotel ★★ The welcome here inspires devoted loyalty. One guest stayed for 28 years, then asked to have her ashes buried in the back garden! Mrs. Marazzi is the second generation of her family to run this nonsmoking B&B, which rambles over four houses. The rooms are simple, and no two are alike. Budget travelers should go for the cheap double, which has the toilet just outside. The Marazzis recently created some beautiful extra public bathrooms, so it's easy to survive the sharing experience. If you can afford it, room no. 53 is a marvelous first-floor triple, which normally costs £125 ($200) but which two people can take for £100 ($160). It has a king-size bed, a single bed, and a gray-tiled, private bathroom with a corner tub. And off it is a small private conservatory, looking onto the quiet communal garden that all the guests can use. St. Margaret's has two lounges, one with a TV and the other for guests who prefer peace and quiet. Newspapers are delivered. You'll pay an extra £1 ($1.85) if you stay only 1 night.

26 Bedford Place, London WC1B 5JL. © **020/7636-4277.** Fax 020/7323-3066. www.stmargaretshotel.co.uk. 64 units, 10 w/bathroom (most w/shower only). £52 ($95) single w/o bathroom; £64 ($117) double w/o bathroom; £92–£98 ($170–$180) double w/bathroom. Rates include full English breakfast. MC, V. Tube: Russell Sq. or Holborn. **Amenities:** Lounge; babysitting arranged; nonsmoking rooms; garden. *In room:* TV.

Thanet Hotel This quiet, 200-year-old Georgian terrace links busy Russell Square with the more peaceful Bloomsbury Square and is very close to Covent Garden and the rest of the West End. The Orchard family, the third-generation hoteliers that run the Thanet, began to refurbish the hotel in 2002. The bedrooms were repainted and have new carpet, curtains, and bedcovers. Room no. 5 has French doors and its own balcony. The Orchards have also redone the bathrooms with bright white tiles. This guesthouse, with its blue awning, exuberant window boxes, and lovely blue-toned breakfast room, has long won plaudits as a good budget bet. It's a bit more expensive than St. Margaret's Hotel, across the way, which has two lounges and offers guests the use of the garden.

The Orchards recently took over the former University of Iowa student hostel next door and began to tidy it up. **Pickwick Hall** (© **020/7323-4958;** www.pickwickhall.co.uk) is a friendly place, with no age restrictions and space for 35 people. It costs £25 ($46) for a single, £44 ($81) for a twin.

8 Bedford Place, London WC1B 5JA. © **020/7636-2869.** Fax 020/7323-6676. www.thanethotel.co.uk. 16 units, all w/bathroom (shower only). £74 ($137) single; £98 ($181) double/twin; £108 ($200) triple; £118 ($218) quad. Rates include full English breakfast. AE, MC, V. Tube: Russell Sq. or Holborn. *In room:* TV, coffeemaker, hair dryer, radio.

SUPER-CHEAP SLEEPS

Travel Inn Capital (© **020/7554-3400;** fax 020/7554-3419; www.travelinn.co.uk), reviewed under "Just South of the River," later in this chapter, has another great value hotel at 1 Dukes Rd., WC1H 9PJ. It has similar rates, decor, and amenities as its hotel in South Bank (for this one, take the Tube to Euston). For a super-cheap sleep opposite the British Library, check out the modern **St. Pancras Youth Hostel** (✆ **020/7388-9998;** fax 020/7388-6766; www.yha.org.uk) at 79–81 Euston Rd., NW1 2QS. It costs £25 ($46) per night for adults, £21 ($38) for children under 18. Children under 3 are welcome, and cots are available. Take the Tube to Euston or King's Cross. **Astor's Museum Inn,** 27 Montague St., London WC1B 5BH (✆ **020/7580-5360;** fax 020/7636-7948; www.astorhostels.com), is the company's longest-established hostel, up and running for 20 years. Dorm beds cost £15 to £24 ($28–$44) per night. Because it is next to the British Museum and in a listed Georgian terrace, the Museum Inn is quieter than the Hyde Park HQ (see "Paddington & Bayswater," earlier in this chapter). Age restriction 18 to 35. Take the Tube to Russell Square or Holborn.

The Generator ★ Hidden away in Tavistock Place, this new-style hostel opened in 1995 in what used to be a police section house. Inside, it's like a cross between the set of *Alien* and a hip Soho coffee bar. Aluminum pipes and blue neon lights snake across the ceiling in reception. The different floors are called Level 01, 02, and so on. And all the signage, including room numbers, is spray-stenciled, packing-crate-style. The spartan bedrooms, all nonsmoking and with bunks, are equipped with funky metal basins, and it's about eight people to every shower. The 800-bed Generator is more expensive than its private sector rivals, except in the biggest dorms. Breakfast is self-service in the Fuel Stop canteen. There is no self-catering, which can be a bind when you're traveling on this kind of budget. The bar is very Soho, but prices are lower than even a local pub's, and it stays open until 2am. In fact, the only real drawback to The Generator is that it caters for a lot of groups, so be prepared for hordes of kids on tour.

Compton Place, off 37 Tavistock Place, London WC1H 9SD. ✆ **020/7388-7666.** Fax 020/7388-7644. www.the-generator.co.uk. 217 units, none w/bathroom. £35–£37 ($65–$68) single; £50–£53 ($92–$98) twin; £60–£65 ($111–$120) triple. Rates include bed linen, towels, and continental breakfast. Discount available for 5-night stays and for groups. MC, V. Tube: Russell Sq. **Amenities:** Bar; game room; nonsmoking rooms; Internet access. *In room:* No phone.

WORTH A SPLURGE

Imperial Hotel ★ *Value* A few pounds more expensive than Bloomsbury's toniest B&Bs, the Imperial is both a splurge and a good deal. The decor isn't particularly plush. In fact, it's rather dated. What you do get, though, is an affordable, full-service hotel just a stone's throw from Covent Garden and Soho. From the outside it looks like a huge, corrugated, concrete box taking up half the eastern side of Russell Square with a row of shops at street level. There are nine floors of bedrooms, and the third is nonsmoking. The hotel does a lot of tour-group business, but the rooms have stood up well to the traffic. They're all a decent size, have unusual triangular-shaped bay windows, and excellent storage space. In most of the doubles and twins, the en suite toilet and tub/shower are handily separate. The Imperial has a vineyard to make its Bordeaux house wine and a farm just outside London, which delivers produce every day to be served up in the rather grim Elizabethan Restaurant. Otherwise, the Day & Night Bar, an oasis of up-to-the-minute style with Internet sites, is open for light food and drinks until 2am. If you'd rather forego the amenities and pay a few pounds less, check out the website because the company owns five other Bloomsbury hotels, all a few pounds cheaper than the Imperial.

Russell Sq., London WC1B 5BB. ✆ **020/7278-7871.** Fax 020/7837-4653. www.imperialhotels.co.uk. 448 units, all w/bathroom. £73 ($117) single; £98 ($157) double/twin. Rates include full English breakfast. AE, DC, DISC, MC, V. Tube: Russell Sq. **Amenities:** Restaurant; cafe/bar; access to nearby health club; concierge; limited room service; babysitting; laundry service; dry cleaning; nonsmoking rooms. *In room:* TV, coffeemaker, trouser press, radio.

9 Covent Garden, the Strand & Holborn

High Holborn Residence, London School of Economics ★ *Kids* This is a tiptop student residence in a tiptop location, with double-glazed windows to cut down on the traffic noise of High Holborn. It's right in the middle of Theatreland and a 5-minute walk to Covent Garden, which is why it can charge B&B hotel rates. That, and the fact that the beds have the fattest, most civilized mattresses I've ever seen in a student hall. It's very popular with moms and pops, who pay £5 ($7.25) a night for a foldaway bed plus the same again for an extra breakfast, making this one of the cheapest family rooms in town. Blocks of six rooms share a toilet, shower, and kitchen (bring your own utensils). Every second floor has two extra shared tubs, and everything is in very good shape. Downstairs, there's a huge breakfast room–cum–lounge with vending machines for snacks. For a modest fee you can use the open-air pool at the Oasis Sports Centre next door. The hall is open from early July to the end of September.

178 High Holborn, London WC1. ✆ **020/7955-7575.** Fax 020/7955-7676. www.lsevacations.co.uk. 428 units, 24 w/bathroom (shower only). £31 ($57) single w/o bathroom; £49 ($91) twin w/o bathroom, £66 ($122) twin w/bathroom; £70 ($129) triple. 4 units adapted for travelers w/disabilities. Rates include continental breakfast. MC, V. Open summer vacation. Tube: Holborn. **Amenities:** Game room; coin-op washers and dryers; communal kitchen; Internet access. *In room:* No phone.

Royal Adelphi Hotel *Finds* We like this unassuming hotel for its in-the-thick-of-it location, behind Trafalgar Square on the lively pedestrian walk that leads from the Strand to Embankment and Hungerford Bridge, and for the friendliness of the management. It's a favorite with London Marathon runners, so you'll have to book early if you want to stay here in April. The rooms are modest and can get hot in summer because there's no air-conditioning. The decor is respectable rather than plush, and the lounge and hotel bar (open 24 hr.) show signs of wear and tear. But refurbishment is in the works. Room no. 504 is a cozy triple with a good-size white-tiled bathroom with a tub and shower. There's double glazing on the windows, but ask for a room in back if you're particularly noise-sensitive. The breakfast is not included (full English is £8/$15 and continental £4/$7).

21 Villiers St., London WC2N 6ND. ✆ **020/7930-8764.** Fax 020/7930-8735. www.royaladelphi.co.uk. 47 units, 34 w/bathroom (some w/shower only). £50 ($92) single w/o bathroom; £68 ($126) single w/bathroom; £68 ($126) double/twin w/o bathroom; £90 ($166) double/twin w/bathroom; £120 ($222) triple w/bathroom. AE, DC, MC, V. Tube: Embankment or Charing Cross. **Amenities:** Bar. *In room:* TV, coffeemaker, hair dryer, radio.

DO-IT-YOURSELF DEALS

Citadines Trafalgar Square ★ The French company Citadines pioneered the "aparthotel" concept in London. It opened its Trafalgar Square flagship in a 1930s building in 1998, then totally refurbished the premises in 2001. Unfortunately, the prices have shot up quite a bit since our last edition, pushing this property into the splurge category, but four people sharing a one-bedroom apartment still make the rate competitive for the area. Fill a bigger duplex and you'll get a bargain. The inside is all marble-tiled and corporate looking, with a 24-hour welcome. The studios sleep two on a deluxe sofa bed and have fully equipped kitchenettes. The apartments have the same arrangement, with the tub/shower and toilet separate to cut down on awkward traffic jams. Every unit controls its own heating and air-conditioning, and the phones have handy voice mail. Reception can lend you a crib, bottle warmer, and changing mat. It will also organize extra maid services, otherwise it's one towel change a week. Citadines has a breakfast room where you can have an expensive continental breakfast

The Bargain Business

Business hotel chains need to fill their beds when lucrative corporate customers go home so they offer special rates (often called Leisure Breaks, or Super Savers). These put city-center 3- and even 4-star sleeps on a par with a pricey B&B and may even make posher hotels an affordable splurge. What you'll actually pay will fluctuate according to seasonal demand, so always ask for the best deal. Some special deals are available only by booking on the Web. **Choice Hotels** (✆ **0800/444444;** www.choicehotels.com) claimed to have a myriad of offers running all the time at its Comfort Inns rather than offering a vacation package. But, in fact, there's generally a so-called "promotional rate" available all year-round as a rebuttal offer to any caller whose reaction to the rack rate is: "Oh, that's too expensive." Sneaky! Many chains also do special-interest packages including theater tickets or admissions to attractions (for out-of-town options, see chapter 10). And savvy bargain hounds know it's always worth surfing hotel chain websites for e-deals. The rates below are for two people sharing a room and bed-and-breakfast. These were some of the specials available as of press time.

- **Best Western** (✆ **08457/747474;** www.bestwestern.co.uk): Getaway Breaks any day; from £68 ($125). The best value Best Western hotel is Raglan Hall in Highgate. Only 15 minutes by Tube from the West End, it's in a quiet residential area and has a delightful garden and terrace.
- **Hilton** (✆ **08705/909090;** www.hilton.com): Leisure Breaks; from £129 ($239) for 2 nights. Several of the hotels do great 1-night Sunday Specials all year-round: and there's a 2-night Winter Break for £179 ($331), with dinner, at the fab four-star Hilton Hyde Park, which has Nintendo consoles in every room if the notorious British weather turns against you.
- **Holiday Inn** (✆ **0800/897121;** www.basshotels.com/holiday-inn): Offers various advance purchase and discounted AAA- and AARP-membership specials from £90 ($166) in the Holiday Inn Express Southwark; prices go up to £105 ($194) for the swanky and centrally located Crowne Plaza.
- **Jarvis Hotels** (✆ **01494/436256;** www.jarvis.co.uk): Leisure Breaks any day; from £66 ($107) for a 1-night stay at the centrally located Ramada Jarvis Hyde Park.
- **Radisson Hotels** (✆ **0800/374411;** www.radisson.com): Special Web offers from £105 ($194) for a double. This hotel group aims for classic English style and has several good-value Radisson Edwardians right in the thick of things. And ask about theater packages—oddly, they are sometimes cheaper than a basic bed-booking.
- **Thistle Hotels** (✆ **0800/181716;** www.thistlehotels.com): Leisure Breaks any day; minimum 2 nights; and Weekend Breaks from £100 ($185) per night for a double, breakfast included. For the best deal but scant aesthetic stimulation, go for the modern London Ryan Hotel in King's Cross. For a few pounds more, though, you can buy a more traditional sleep at the brilliantly located Bloomsbury Park (between Russell Square and Holborn).

for £8 ($13) if you don't want to cook yourself. For a cheaper central sleep, try the clone: **Citadines Holborn,** 94–99 High Holborn, London, WC1V 6LF (✆ **020/7395-8800;** fax 020/7395-8789; Tube: Holborn). Studios cost from £97 ($179) a night if you stay 1 week; special offers sometimes bring the weeklong price down as low as £81 ($145) per night.

18–21 Northumberland Ave., London WC2N 5BJ. ✆ **0800/376-3898** or 020/7766-3700. Fax 020/7766-3766. www.citadines.com. 187 units. £120–£145 ($222–$268) studio; £172–£210 ($318–$386) 1-bedroom apt; £232–£255 ($429–$472) 2-bedroom apt. Lower rates apply to 1-week stays. 16 studios and a 1-bedroom apt suitable for travelers w/disabilities. AE, DC, MC, V. Tube: Charing Cross or Embankment. **Amenities:** Coin-op washers and dryers; dry cleaning; nonsmoking rooms. *In room:* A/C, TV, kitchenette, fridge, iron, safe.

WORTH A SPLURGE

The Fielding Hotel ★ Just an aria away from the Royal Opera House in Covent Garden, this famous hotel is a clean, tidy, and regularly renovated 1970s time warp. The very narrow hallways and stairs are brown and orange, and metallic glam-rock pictures and chocolate-box alpine scenes cover the walls. Other than that, the bedrooms are attractive with comfortable new beds and faded coverlets and curtains. The Fielding has finally upgraded its famously antiquated electrics and plumbing, so there are nice new bathrooms throughout. Breakfast is not included. The hotel doesn't score marks for extra bits-and-bobs, but for London picturesque and convenience to the West End it can't be beat. It sits in a pretty, pedestrian street just minutes from the action at Covent Garden. And it really is one of a kind.

4 Broad Court, Bow St., London WC2B 5QZ. ✆ **020/7836-8305.** Fax 020/7497-0064. www.the-fielding-hotel.co.uk. 24 units, all w/bathroom (shower only). £76 ($141) single; £100–£130 ($185–$240) double/twin. No 1-night bookings on Sat. AE, DC, MC, V. Tube: Covent Garden. No children under 13. *In room:* TV, coffeemaker.

10 Victoria & Westminster

Astor's, the hostel people, has a small hostel here, the **Victoria Hotel** on Belgrave Road, SW1 (✆ **020/7834-3077;** fax 020/7932-0693; www.astorhostels.com), where it costs £16 to £19 ($30–$35) per night to sleep in a 4- to 8-bed dorm. For more information on Astor's, see "Paddington & Bayswater," earlier in this chapter.

Collin House ★ *Value* You could easily walk straight past the discreet slate nameplate announcing Collin House. That would be a shame because it's one of the best B&Bs on Ebury Street. For a start, it's well worth foregoing a private bathroom, even though all the showers are new, because there are never more than two bedrooms sharing each public facility. You'll also get a room at the back, which is blissfully quiet. All the rooms with private bathrooms look out onto Ebury Street, and there is no soundproofing. Most of the rooms have been redecorated within the past couple of years and there is new carpeting on the stairs. Last year the first-floor bedroom at the front was converted into an attractive lounge. None of the other Ebury Street B&Bs listed here have got one, as the buildings are quite small. The small basement breakfast room has bench seating and a skylight. The look is half-canteen, half-chapel. Collin House is nonsmoking throughout.

104 Ebury St., London SW1W 9QD. ✆/fax **020/7730-8031.** www.collinhouse.co.uk. 12 units, 8 w/bathroom (shower only). £55 ($102) single w/bathroom; £68 ($126) double/twin w/o bathroom; £82 ($152) double/twin w/bathroom; £95 ($176) triple w/o bathroom. Rates include full English breakfast. MC, V. Tube: Victoria. **Amenities:** Lounge; nonsmoking rooms. *In room:* TV, no phone.

Harcourt House *Value* This early Victorian town house served as gentlemen's lodgings in the late 1880s, and the proprietors, David and Glesni Wood, spent years lovingly redecorating the whole place to recapture the original style and atmosphere. Heritage junkies will love it so long as they're not too finicky about details, but other guests may find the preponderance of winey colors rather dark. The two-tone maroon and rich yellow rooms have reproduction brass bedsteads. The only place where modern decoration is allowed to intrude is in the bright-tiled bathrooms. The Woods are clearly avid antiques hunters. The hall and stairs are lit with crystal chandeliers and decorated with junk-shop finds like the framed montage of *Titanic* memorabilia. The breakfast room has a real-flame fire and a restored wood-and-slate floor. Harcourt House is a bit cheaper than the other Ebury Street B&Bs; the lower prices are for November through March.

50 Ebury St., London SW1W 0LU. ✆ **020/7730-2722.** Fax 020/7730-3998. www.harcourthousehotel.co.uk. 10 units, all w/bathroom (shower only). £50–£60 ($93–$111) single; £70–£85 ($129–$157) double/twin. Rates include full English breakfast. Discount available off season. AE, MC, V. Tube: Victoria. *In room:* TV, coffeemaker, hair dryer, no phone.

James & Cartref House ★ Ebury Street calls itself Belgravia, but this is no hushed tycoon's enclave. There are dozens of places to stay on either side of the junction with Elizabeth Street. James House and Cartref House are separate B&Bs on opposite sides of the road, both run by the very welcoming Derek and Sharon James. The main difference between the two B&Bs is in the number of private bathrooms. All 10 rooms in James House have one, but they're very small, so you might be better off without, especially since only three rooms share each immaculately kept bathroom at Cartref house. All the bedrooms are nicely decorated—nothing fancy, but comfortable. Fans have been installed in all the rooms, a boon during summer heat waves. There's a delightful conservatory dining room. Two things to note: Breakfast stops at 8:30am, and kids have to be over 12 to stay in the top bunk in the James House family room. Both houses are totally nonsmoking. Lower rates below are for rooms that share bathrooms.

108–129 Ebury St., London SW1W 9DU. ✆ **020/7730-7338** or 020/7730-6176. Fax 020/7730-7338. www.jamesandcartref.co.uk. 19 units, 13 w/bathroom (shower only). £52–£62 ($96–$115) single; £70–£85 ($129–$157) double/twin; £95–£110 ($175–$203) triple; £135 ($249) family room w/bathroom. Rates include full English breakfast. AE, MC, V. Tube: Victoria. **Amenities:** Nonsmoking rooms. *In room:* TV, coffeemaker, hair dryer, fan, no phone.

Luna Simone Hotel ★★ *Finds* This family-run hotel stands out by a mile on this scruffy terrace. The outside of the big stucco-fronted house gleams bright white and has glass panels etched with the hotel name around the entrance porch. The Desiras have worked wonders on the inside, too. They've renovated all the bedrooms and put private bathrooms in all but two singles. The rooms vary widely in size, but with their blue carpeting, cream-colored walls, and newly tiled bathrooms, they beat all the dowdy, badly designed hotels and B&Bs for miles around. The beechwood and marble-clad reception area is all new, too, as is the smart-looking breakfast room, now totally nonsmoking. The look throughout is light, simple, and modern, a refreshing change from the drab, shabby interiors of so many Victorian buildings.

47–49 Belgrave Rd., London SW1V 2BB. ✆ **020/7834-5897.** Fax 020/7828-2474. www.lunasimonehotel.com. 36 units, 34 w/bathroom (shower only). £35–£40 ($65–$74) single; £60–£80 ($111–$148) double/twin; £80–£100 ($148–$185) triple. Rates include full English breakfast. MC, V. Tube: Victoria or Pimlico. **Amenities:** Lounge; Internet access. *In room:* TV, coffeemaker, hair dryer, safe.

Where to Stay in Victoria & Westminster

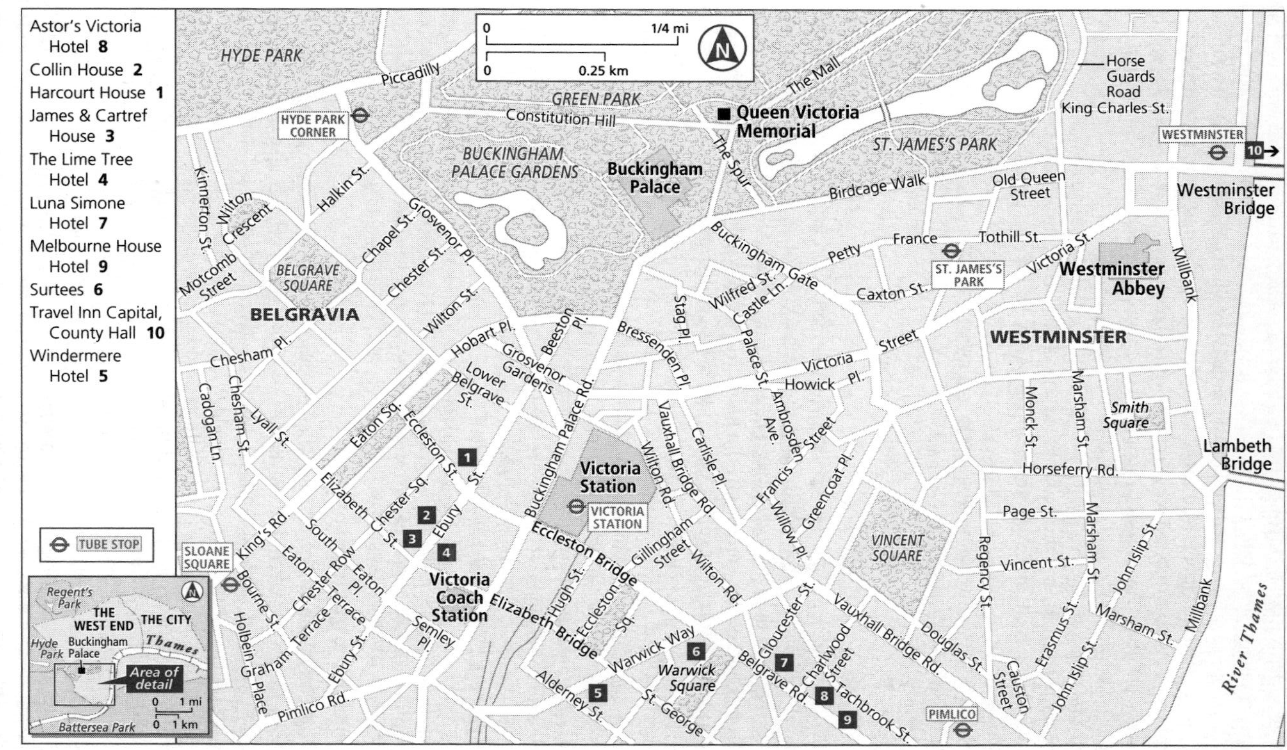

Melbourne House Hotel Hotel bathrooms are expensive and hard work to maintain, so many small budget hotels really let guests down. Not so Melbourne House, where the tiles gleam and the shower units were all replaced in 1999. John Desira (cousin of Peter Desira, who owns Luna Simone up the road) and his wife have run this spotless, nonsmoking B&B for 30 years. Don't come here if you're looking for snazzy frills and fancy fabrics, though. The rooms are a decent size for Central London, but the decor is very simple with a pinky-coral color scheme that won't be everyone's cup of tea. Carpets, beds, and furniture (a desk and ample storage space) were recently replaced, and the lounge given a facelift. There's a family room that combines a double, a twin, and a private bathroom, good for parents traveling with two older children.

79 Belgrave Rd., London SW1V 2BG. ✆ **020/7828-3516.** Fax 020/7828-7120. www.melbournehousehotel.co.uk. 17 units, 15 w/bathroom (most w/shower only). £35–£60 ($65–$111) single; £75 ($139) double/twin; £95 ($170) triple; £110 ($203) family room. Rates include continental breakfast. MC, V. Tube: Pimlico or Victoria. **Amenities:** Nonsmoking rooms. *In room:* TV, coffeemaker, hair dryer.

Surtees *Value* Warwick Avenue is a rather pretty street of small Victorian terrace houses, so it's a bit of a shame that traffic thunders down it from early morning until nearly midnight. That's partly why the B&Bs here are around £10 ($18) a night cheaper than those in posher (and quieter) Ebury Street. Ahmed Akoudad has owned Surtees for 18 years and runs it with his wife. The B&B stands out from its sometimes grotty neighbors because it is one of the few buildings on the block festooned with hanging baskets. Inside, too, it's very clean and well cared for. Mr. Akoudad does much of the decorating work himself and has spruced up most of the rooms, each one in a different style, and the bathrooms. The basic triple is a good choice for friends traveling together: The only other room sharing the shower and two toilets is a single. There are also good deals to be had in the basement family rooms, as long as you don't mind looking out onto an internal courtyard. There's one that combines a single room with a triple. There are cribs and VCRs to borrow at reception. Lower rates below are for basic rooms with shared bathrooms.

94 Warwick Way, London SW1V 1SB. ✆ **020/7834-7163** or 020/7834-7394. Fax 020/7460-8747. www.surtees-hotel.co.uk. 10 units, 8 w/bathroom (shower only). £40–£50 ($79–$93) single; £55–£65 ($102–$120) double/twin; £70–£80 ($129–$148) triple; £90–£120 ($166–$222) family room. Rates include full English breakfast. AE, DC, DISC, MC, V. Tube: Victoria or Pimlico. *In room:* TV, coffeemaker, hair dryer, iron, radio.

WORTH A SPLURGE

The Lime Tree Hotel ★ David and Marilyn Davies ran Ebury House, across the road, until 1994 when they moved to The Lime Tree Hotel. Mr. Davies is something of a champion when it comes to award-winning window boxes; there are twice as many at The Lime Tree than on any other hotel in the street. The hotel is just as attractive inside, with deep cornices in the hall and statues and flowers in the alcoves up the stairs. The more expensive rooms are quite luxurious, with swagged curtains, canopied beds, and pretty furniture. There is one on the first floor that leads out to a table and chairs on its own little terrace. The lower price applies to doubles and twins on the upper floors, which are more restrained but still very attractive. Don't expect a lift as part of your splurge, though. The authorities are very stringent about what they'll let people do to historic Victorian houses. The bathrooms are spotlessly clean with glass-doored showers. The dining room is on the first floor, and in the summer, many guests take their breakfast out into the rose garden.

135–137 Ebury St., London SW1W 9RA. ✆ **020/7730-8191.** Fax 020/7730-7856. www.limetreehotel.co.uk. 26 units, all w/bathroom (most w/shower only). £70–£80 ($129–$148) single; £105–£125 ($144–$231) double/twin; £145–£160 ($286–$296) triple; £165–£180 ($305–$333) quad. Rates include full English breakfast. AE, DC, MC, V. Tube: Victoria. No children under 5. **Amenities:** Garden. *In room:* TV, coffeemaker, hair dryer, safe.

Windermere Hotel ★ *Kids* *Finds* One of the nicest places to stay in Victoria is a pair of wedge-shaped rooms at the top of this house, with windows on two sides so it feels like you're in a lighthouse with an urban view. The Windermere dates from 1857, and it became one of the first-ever B&Bs in the area 24 years later. You can spot it today by the pale-blue porch and pillars, a much grander architecture than the cluster of rivals down the street. Owner Nicholas Hambi and his wife have completely refurbished it over the past few years. The big top-price double on the second floor is more like a minisuite—that's why it's the same price as a triple—with a sofa, armchairs, and a canopied bed. A toned-down version of the same look extends into the rest of the hotel. Budget travelers get a fair deal at the Windermere, too: The so-called basic double comes with a key to a hallway bathroom that only keyholders can use. Every room is double-glazed, and eight are nonsmoking, as are all the public areas. The quad with a double and two singles is popular with parents traveling with two small kids. The Hambis run an evening restaurant, called the Pimlico Room after the original B&B's name, serving modern British and European food; two courses cost from £14 ($26), more than reasonable for London dining. Lower rates below are for rooms that share bathrooms.

142–144 Warwick Way, London SW1V 4JE. ✆ **020/7834-5163.** Fax 020/7630-8831. www.windermere-hotel.co.uk. 22 units, 20 w/bathroom (some w/shower only). £69–£99 ($128–$183) single; £89–£149 ($165–$183) double; £145 ($268) triple; £149 ($270) quad w/bathroom. Rates include full English breakfast. AE, MC, V. Tube: Victoria. **Amenities:** Restaurant; bar; limited room service; nonsmoking rooms. *In room:* TV, dataport, coffeemaker, hair dryer, safe.

11 Just South of the River

Bankside House, London School of Economics ★ *Kids* Culture buffs fall over themselves to stay at this student hall, so make sure to call as far ahead as you can. Imagine finding somewhere to stay right behind the new Tate Modern at Bankside and Shakespeare's Globe Theatre. It's just a 5-minute walk to the new Southwark Tube station on the Jubilee line, which links the maritime village of Greenwich (a UNESCO World Heritage Site) to Bond Street and shopping heaven. Like High Holborn Residence, this isn't a super-cheap sleep, but then you do get rather more than a souped-up camp bed and a pin-board. Bankside House is a new building and more like a hotel (the mattresses, for instance, are thick and comfortable). There are even four rooms especially designed for families, with cribs and high chairs available at the reception desk. Although Bankside House does not have the usual student kitchenettes, staying there will help people on tight budgets to keep their food bills down: three courses at the cheap and cheerful restaurant can cost as little as £10 ($18).

24 Sumner St., London SE1 9JA. ✆ **020/7955-7575.** Fax 020/7955-7676. www.lse.ac.uk/vacations. 564 units, 306 w/bathroom (shower only). £33 ($61) single w/o bathroom; £45 ($85) single w/bathroom; £63 ($117) twin w/bathroom; £81 ($150) triple w/bathroom; £96 ($178) family room w/bathroom. 32 units adapted for travelers w/disabilities. Rates include full English breakfast. MC, V. Open summer vacation only. Tube: Southwark. **Amenities:** Restaurant; bar; game room; coin-op washers and dryers. *In room:* Coffeemaker.

Travel Inn Capital, County Hall ★★ *Kids* No budget hotel ever had a better location. County Hall is a mammoth 1920s monument to civic pride, across the Thames from the Houses of Parliament. It used to be home to the Greater London Council until Margaret Thatcher abolished it in 1986. Now millionaires at the Marriott, which occupies the plum parts of County Hall, enjoy *the* London view. Guests at the Travel Inn, sadly, do not. Some rooms look downriver, but you can't see much because the 135-foot-high British Airways London Eye observation wheel is located right next door. Most rooms face into a big central courtyard or out at luxury apartments behind. Inside there are six floors (five nonsmoking) of bland identical corridors, but that's what budget chains do. The rooms are of a decent size, the decor good quality, and the price is an absolute steal. All rooms are standard doubles and the rate is the same even if the room is made into a twin, triple, or quad. In the family rooms, maximum capacity is two kids under 16 on the sofa bed, one toddler under 2 in a crib, and two grown-ups. There are no adult-only triples or quads. Breakfast is not included. If you're traveling with kids, the restaurant serves a children's dinner menu and there's a McDonald's and a YO! Sushi down below in County Hall, as well as the London Aquarium, the Dalí Universe exhibition, and the new Saatchi Gallery of contemporary art.

There are several other Travel Inn Capitals, of which the best located is **Euston. Putney Bridge** is near the river in quite a chi-chi bit of West London. **Tower Bridge** is less sexy than it sounds, too far into no man's land south of the river to be convenient.

Belvedere Rd., London SE1 7PB. ✆ **0870/242-8000.** Fax 020/7902-1619. www.travelinn.co.uk. 313 units, all w/bathroom. £85–£87 ($157–$161) single, double/twin, and family room; lower rates are for weekends. Units adapted for travelers w/disabilities. Rates do not include breakfast. AE, DC, MC, V. Tube: Waterloo or Westminster. **Amenities:** Restaurant; bar; nonsmoking rooms; Internet access. *In room:* TV, coffeemaker, hair dryer, radio.

SUPER-CHEAP SLEEPS

St. Christopher's Village ★★ Only Astor's is cheaper, but even its swanky Hyde Park hostel can't boast a hot tub as part of the deal. In 1999, St. Christopher's gutted some marvelous old buildings on busy Borough High Street and turned them into what it calls a "hostel with attitude." The American diner-style bar called Belushi's puts on endless low-rent alcohol-fueled entertainment, from guest DJs to quiz nights. The hostel lounge has a dance floor, too. Or you can chill out on the rooftop deck where the hot tub and sauna are located. Instead of the usual self-catering arrangements, St. Christopher's subsidizes the food (£1.50/$2.20 for cooked breakfast) and drink. The company has two other hostels on Borough High Street. The first is above the historic St. Christopher's Inn (no. 121) where the floors are lopsided, the rooms are clean, and the showers are all new. (Don't stay here for the weekend if you're an early-bedder, because the pub goes ballistic and the floors are paper-thin.) The second is above the Orient Espresso coffee bar just up the road (no. 59). This is much quieter and suits post–Generation X-ers and families with children. Southwark is still a bit grotty but it's on the rise, with the Tate Modern, Shakespeare's Globe, and the mouth-watering Borough Market only a few minutes away.

St. Christopher's also has hostels in **Camden, Greenwich,** and **Shepherds Bush.** You can book them all through the telephone number and website below.

165 Borough High St., London SE1 1NP. ✆ **020/7407-1856.** Fax 020/7403-7715. www.st-christophers.co.uk. 164 units, none w/bathroom. £16–£24 ($30–$44) per person in a 2-to-14-bed dorm. Full facilities for travelers w/disabilities. Rates include linen and continental breakfast. Discount available off season and for 1-week stays. MC, V. Tube: London Bridge or Borough. **Amenities:** 2 bars; hot tub; sauna; coin-op washers and dryers; Internet access. *In room:* No phone.

12 Near the Airport

Ibis London Heathrow Airport Located at the end of a long row of more expensive suburban-looking hotel chains, this recently refurbished Ibis basically offers the same amenities and decor as the Ibis Euston (see "Bloomsbury," earlier in this chapter), without the railway theme. The weekend rate for an en suite double/twin is a steal at £50 ($92), but you certainly wouldn't want to be stuck out in this no man's land for long. Breakfast is £4.50 ($8) extra, but not particularly appetizing.

112–114 Bath Rd., Hayes, Middlesex, UB3 5AL. ✆ **020/8759-4888.** Fax: 020/8564-7894. www.ibishotels.com. 150 units. £70 ($129) double; £50 ($92) double on weekends. AE, MC, V. Bus: Hotel Hoppa H3 from Heathrow terminals 1–3, H13 from Terminal 4. **Amenities:** Restaurant; lounge. *In room:* TV, hair dryer.

Harmondsworth Hall ★★ *Finds* Harmondsworth is the perfect place to get over jet lag or catch a last glimpse of picture-book England before you go. This pretty little village has two pubs, an old-fashioned post office, and an 800-year-old church mentioned in the Domesday Book. It takes only 15 minutes to get to one of the world's busiest airports, yet the village isn't even under the flight path. Harmondsworth Hall is a rambling, 17th-century, redbrick house, with wrought-iron gates leading into a lovely country garden where there's even a Tudor cannon. The inside is beautiful, with a checkerboard floor in the hall, coffered ceiling in the wood-paneled breakfast room, an elegant drawing room, and Turkish carpets everywhere. It may sound like a museum, but it feels more like a cherished home. The rooms have lovely old furniture, and each one is decorated differently. No. 6 is a huge double with a polished wood floor. Rooms in what was originally a separate cottage are relatively modern and have less character. Elaine Burke will organize your transport to and from Heathrow if you give her enough warning. She has a lot of loyal regulars, and it's easy to see why.

Summerhouse Lane, West Drayton, Middlesex, UB7 0BG. ✆ **020/8759-1824.** Fax 020/8897-6385. www.harmondsworthhall.com. 10 units, 7 w/bathroom (shower only). £55 ($102) single w/bathroom; £70 ($130) double/twin w/bathroom; £75 ($139) family room w/bathroom. Rates include full English breakfast. Discount available for longer stays. V. Bus: U3 from Heathrow terminals 1–3 or West Drayton train station. **Amenities:** Lounge; garden. *In room:* TV, coffeemaker, hair dryer.

6

Great Deals on Dining

The Brits get really bored by the constant slurs cast on their cooking. It can even cause them to forget their manners. And rightly so. That old cliché is about as accurate as the one that says the city is permanently enveloped in a pea-soup fog. The last 2 decades have seen an explosion of new eateries, new tastes, and new celebrities in the kitchen. Today, London is one of the great food capitals of the world. The only problem is, eating out at the best restaurants costs a small fortune.

But don't despair, because it's still possible to eat out, eat creatively, and eat well, without breaking the bank. Indian entrepreneurs have been hatching the hottest ideas: Mela and Masala Zone are pioneering a new trend toward cheap authentic street food. It's a far cry from the chicken tikka masala, hailed by one electioneering politician as Britain's true national dish. Ironically, this concoction was unknown on the subcontinent until British tourists started asking for it. Legend has it that a London chef whipped it up in the early 1970s from some spices, cream, and a can of Campbell's tomato soup to satisfy a difficult customer who was demanding gravy.

The curry houses are not the only places undergoing makeovers. Great institutions all over the city are ditching institutional grub long past its sell-by date. First came the transformation of nicotine-stained "boozers" into innovative bare-boards restaurants called "gastropubs." And now most of London's major museums and prime attractions are also serving posh contemporary nosh.

Many cheap eats and fancier restaurants are now turning into homogenized chains. Sometimes it works, especially in the faster cheaper versions of highly-regarded eateries, as you'll see in the reviews. Sometimes it doesn't, which is why you won't see any Conran establishments. As a matter of fact, some of those mega-eateries pioneered by Terence Conran in the booming 1990s are now looking kind of empty in the downsized 21st century.

MEALTIMES AND RESERVATIONS

Restaurant hours vary, but lunch is usually noon to 2:30pm and dinner 6 to 10:30pm. Some eateries shut down on Sundays or, if not, for one weekday meal. You'll never go hungry, though, because the city is stuffed with all-day cafes and diners. Except for these supercheapies, most restaurants accept reservations, and it is always wise to call ahead, especially from Thursday night through the weekend.

It may be quaintly old-fashioned, but I still pick up the phone to book a table—you get a quick yes or no, with no fiddling about. But there's one website that comes close to changing my mind. The chatty and user-friendly **www.toptable.co.uk** has overcome the fierce independence natural to restaurateurs, and persuaded over 1,000 of them to accept it as a reservations middleman. Its searchable database is much more comprehensive than just listing the usual e-friendly suspects—those expensive restaurants that are adept at marketing and local restaurants of dubious quality. Even if you don't use it to book, Toptable is a top information source, not only publishing menus but also giving a 360-degree photographic view inside many of the restaurants so that you can check the place out before you go.

1 How to Eat Without Losing £s

Seasoned bargain-hunters will recognize many of these dining tips, but it never hurts to have a checklist, especially as a meal for two with wine in a good Central London restaurant is now reckoned to cost around £100 ($185)!

- **Net Savings.** The reservations site mentioned above, **www.toptable.co.uk**, is a good source of special offers. Also surf **www.5pm.co.uk**.
- **Sign Up for Discount Deals.** The **London Pass** has a handful of offers at London eateries, from free appetizers to discounts on meals. For information, see "Fifty Money-Saving Tips," in chapter 2.
- **Check the Charges.** Left to their own devices, Brits tip 10%, and so should you. However, some restaurants automatically add an "optional" 12% to 15% service charge. Knock it off if you're at all dissatisfied.
- **Bring Your Own Booze.** There are still a few unlicensed eateries left in London. You can take your own drink, saving pounds on inflated restaurant prices. Some charge a small fee per bottle, known as "corkage." Here's a BYOB directory: Mandola (p. 127), Patogh (p. 132), Centrale (p. 137), Diwana Bhel Poori House (p. 145), and Food for Thought (p. 147).

2 Restaurants by Cuisine

AFTERNOON TEA

Dorchester ★ (Mayfair, p. 157)
St. James's Restaurant at Fortnum & Mason (St. James, p. 158)
The Orangery ★★ (Kensington, p. 157)
Richoux (St. James, p. 140)

AMERICAN

Arkansas Café ★★ (The City, p. 152)
Hard Rock Café (Chain, p. 157)
Joe Allen (Covent Garden & the Strand, p. 149)
Planet Hollywood (Chain, p. 157)

BELGIAN

Belgo Centraal (Covent Garden & the Strand, p. 147)

BRITISH DINER

Café in the Crypt (Covent Garden & the Strand, p. 147)
Café Grove (Notting Hill, p. 130)
Chelsea Kitchen (Kensington & Chelsea, p. 125)
Quiet Revolution (Marylebone, p. 133)
The Star Café ★ (Soho & Chinatown, p. 137)

BRITISH/MODERN

Andrew Edmunds ★ (Soho & Chinatown, p. 133)
Bleeding Heart Bistro & Tavern ★★ (Clerkenwell, p. 152)
Boxwood Café ★★ (Knightsbridge, p. 121)
The Engineer ★ (Camden, p. 156)
Vingt-Quatre ★ (Kensington & Chelsea, p. 125)

BRITISH/TRADITIONAL

Browns (Mayfair, p. 140)
Criterion Grill ★ (Soho & Chinatown, p. 139)
Maggie Jones's ★ (Kensington & Chelsea, p. 124)
Richoux (St. James, p. 140)

Index of London Restaurant Maps

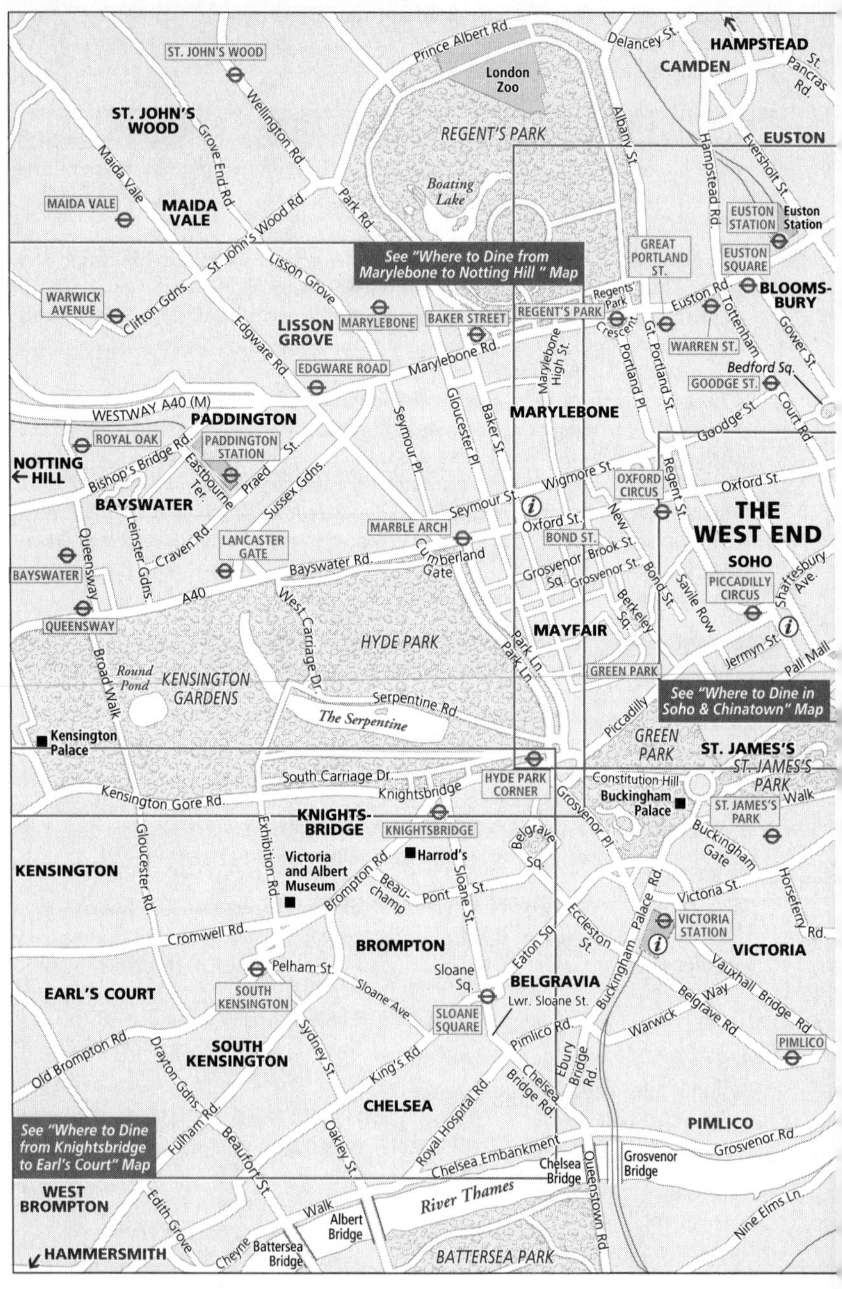

ST. JOHN'S WOOD
ST. JOHN'S WOOD
MAIDA VALE
MAIDA VALE
Wellington Rd.
Grove End Rd.
Maida Vale
St. John's Wood Rd.
Park Rd.
Prince Albert Rd.
London Zoo
REGENT'S PARK
Boating Lake
Delancey St.
HAMPSTEAD
CAMDEN
St. Pancras Rd.
EUSTON
Albany St.
Hampstead Rd.
Eversholt St.
EUSTON STATION
Euston Station
GREAT PORTLAND ST.
EUSTON SQUARE
See "Where to Dine from Marylebone to Notting Hill" Map
WARWICK AVENUE
Clifton Gdns.
Lisson Grove
LISSON GROVE
MARYLEBONE
BAKER STREET
REGENT'S PARK
Regents' Park Crescent
Euston Rd.
BLOOMSBURY
Tottenham
Gower St.
WARREN ST.
Edgware Rd.
EDGWARE ROAD
Marylebone Rd.
Marylebone High St.
Portland Pl.
Gt. Portland St.
Bedford Sq.
GOODGE ST.
WESTWAY A40 (M)
PADDINGTON
Seymour Pl.
Gloucester Pl.
Baker St.
MARYLEBONE
Goodge St.
Court Rd.
ROYAL OAK
PADDINGTON STATION
NOTTING HILL
Bishop's Bridge Rd.
Eastbourne Ter.
Praed St.
Sussex Gdns.
Wigmore St.
OXFORD CIRCUS
Regent St.
Oxford St.
BAYSWATER
Seymour St.
THE WEST END
Queensway
Leinster Gdns.
Craven Rd.
LANCASTER GATE
MARBLE ARCH
Cumberland Gate
Oxford St.
BOND ST.
New Bond St.
Brook St.
SOHO
BAYSWATER
Bayswater Rd.
Grosvenor Sq.
Grosvenor St.
Savile Row
PICCADILLY CIRCUS
Shaftesbury Ave.
A40
West Carriage Dr.
Berkeley Sq.
QUEENSWAY
HYDE PARK
MAYFAIR
Jermyn St.
Pall Mall
Broad Walk
Round Pond
KENSINGTON GARDENS
Park Ln.
Park Ln.
GREEN PARK
Serpentine Rd.
The Serpentine
See "Where to Dine in Soho & Chinatown" Map
Kensington Palace
Piccadilly
GREEN PARK
ST. JAMES'S
ST. JAMES'S PARK
South Carriage Dr.
HYDE PARK CORNER
Constitution Hill
Kensington Gore Rd.
Knightsbridge
Buckingham Palace
Walk
ST. JAMES'S PARK
KNIGHTSBRIDGE
KNIGHTSBRIDGE
Grosvenor Pl.
Gloucester Rd.
Exhibition Rd.
Victoria and Albert Museum
Brompton Rd.
Harrod's
Belgrave Sq.
Buckingham Gate
KENSINGTON
Beauchamp
Pont St.
Sloane St.
Palace Rd.
Victoria St.
Horseferry Rd.
Cromwell Rd.
Eaton Sq.
Eccleston St.
VICTORIA STATION
BROMPTON
VICTORIA
Buckingham
Pelham St.
Sloane Sq.
BELGRAVIA
Vauxhall Bridge Rd.
EARL'S COURT
SOUTH KENSINGTON
Sloane Ave.
Lwr. Sloane St.
Belgrave Rd.
Warwick Way
SLOANE SQUARE
Pimlico Rd.
PIMLICO
Old Brompton Rd.
Drayton Gdns.
SOUTH KENSINGTON
Sydney St.
King's Rd.
Ebury Bridge Rd.
Royal Hospital Rd.
Chelsea Bridge Rd.
CHELSEA
PIMLICO
See "Where to Dine from Knightsbridge to Earl's Court" Map
Fulham Rd.
Beaufort St.
Oakley St.
Chelsea Embankment
Chelsea Bridge
Queenstown Rd.
Grosvenor Bridge
Grosvenor Rd.
WEST BROMPTON
Edith Grove
Walk
Albert Bridge
River Thames
Nine Elms Ln.
HAMMERSMITH
Cheyne
Battersea Bridge
BATTERSEA PARK

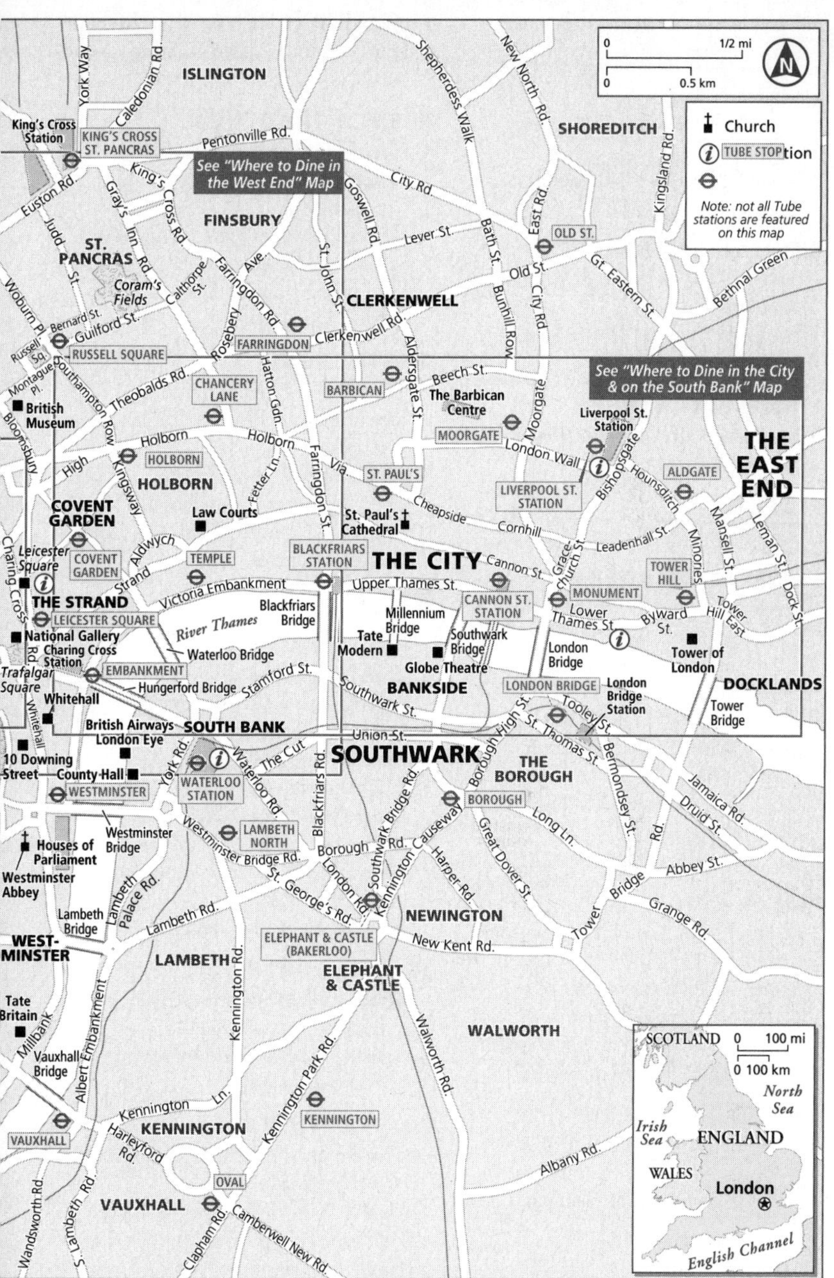

ISLINGTON
SHOREDITCH
FINSBURY
ST. PANCRAS
CLERKENWELL
HOLBORN
COVENT GARDEN
THE CITY
THE EAST END
THE STRAND
SOUTH BANK
BANKSIDE
DOCKLANDS
SOUTHWARK
THE BOROUGH
NEWINGTON
LAMBETH
WEST-MINSTER
ELEPHANT & CASTLE
WALWORTH
KENNINGTON
VAUXHALL
See "Where to Dine in the West End" Map
See "Where to Dine in the City & on the South Bank" Map
Church
Information
Tube stop
Note: not all Tube stations are featured on this map
0 1/2 mi
0 0.5 km
King's Cross Station
KING'S CROSS ST. PANCRAS
FARRINGDON
RUSSELL SQUARE
CHANCERY LANE
BARBICAN
MOORGATE
ST. PAUL'S
OLD ST.
LIVERPOOL ST. STATION
Liverpool St. Station
ALDGATE
HOLBORN
TEMPLE
COVENT GARDEN
BLACKFRIARS STATION
CANNON ST. STATION
MONUMENT
TOWER HILL
LEICESTER SQUARE
EMBANKMENT
LONDON BRIDGE
London Bridge Station
WATERLOO STATION
WESTMINSTER
LAMBETH NORTH
BOROUGH
ELEPHANT & CASTLE (BAKERLOO)
KENNINGTON
OVAL
VAUXHALL
British Museum
Coram's Fields
The Barbican Centre
Law Courts
St. Paul's Cathedral
Leicester Square
Charing Cross
National Gallery
Charing Cross Station
Trafalgar Square
Whitehall
10 Downing Street
British Airways London Eye
County Hall
Houses of Parliament
Westminster Abbey
Westminster Bridge
Lambeth Bridge
Tate Britain
Vauxhall Bridge
River Thames
Waterloo Bridge
Hungerford Bridge
Blackfriars Bridge
Millennium Bridge
Tate Modern
Globe Theatre
Southwark Bridge
London Bridge
Tower of London
Tower Bridge
York Way
Caledonian Rd.
Pentonville Rd.
King's Cross Rd.
Euston Rd.
Gray's Inn Rd.
Judd St.
Woburn Pl.
Bernard St.
Guilford St.
Russell Sq.
Montague Pl.
Southampton Row
Bloomsbury
Theobalds Rd.
Calthorpe St.
Farringdon Rd.
Rosebery Ave.
St. John St.
Goswell Rd.
Shepherdess Walk
New North Rd.
City Rd.
Lever St.
Bath St.
East Rd.
Kingsland Rd.
Old St.
Gt. Eastern St.
Bethnal Green
Bunhill Row
Clerkenwell Rd.
Aldersgate St.
Beech St.
Moorgate
Hatton Gdn.
Holborn
High Holborn
Kingsway
Fetter Ln.
Farringdon St.
Holborn Via.
London Wall
Bishopsgate
Houndsditch
Cheapside
Cornhill
Leadenhall St.
Minories
Mansell St.
Leman St.
Aldwych
Strand
Victoria Embankment
Upper Thames St.
Cannon St.
Gracechurch St.
Lower Thames St.
Byward St.
Tower Hill East
Dock St.
Stamford St.
Southwark St.
Union St.
Borough High St.
St. Thomas St.
Tooley St.
Bermondsey St.
Jamaica Rd.
Druid St.
The Cut
York Rd.
Waterloo Rd.
Blackfriars Rd.
Southwark Bridge Rd.
Westminster Bridge Rd.
Borough Rd.
Kennington Causeway
Harper Rd.
Great Dover St.
Long Ln.
Abbey St.
Tower Bridge Rd.
Grange Rd.
St. George's Rd.
London Rd.
Lambeth Palace Rd.
Lambeth Rd.
New Kent Rd.
Kennington Rd.
Albert Embankment
Millbank
Kennington Park Rd.
Walworth Rd.
Kennington Ln.
Harleyford Rd.
Albany Rd.
Wandsworth Rd.
S. Lambeth Rd.
Clapham Rd.
Camberwell New Rd.
SCOTLAND
0 100 mi
0 100 km
North Sea
Irish Sea
ENGLAND
WALES
London
English Channel

Rules ★★★ (Covent Garden & the Strand, p. 150)

CHINESE

Jenny Lo's Teahouse ★ (Victoria, p. 150)
Royal China ★★ (Paddington & Bayswater, p. 131)

CHINESE/CANTONESE

Golden Dragon (Soho & Chinatown, p. 134)
Mr Kong (Soho & Chinatown, p. 136)

CHINESE/NORTHERN

YMing ★ (Soho & Chinatown, p. 139)

ECLECTIC

Rainforest Café (Chain, p. 157)

EUROPEAN/MODERN

Bank Aldwych ★ (Covent Garden & the Strand, p. 148)
Bright Light Café ★ (Just South of the River, p. 154)
The Chapel ★ (Marylebone, p. 132)
Ebury Wine Bar & Restaurant (Victoria, p. 151)
Mash ★ (Bloomsbury & Fitzrovia, p. 146)
Mirabelle ★★ (Mayfair, p. 141)

FISH & CHIPS

Costas Fish Restaurant ★ (Notting Hill, p. 131)
North Sea Fish Restaurant ★ (Bloomsbury & Fitzrovia, p. 144)
The Rock & Sole Plaice ★ (Covent Garden & the Strand, p. 147)

FRENCH BRASSERIE

Brasserie St. Quentin ★ (Knightsbridge, p. 120)
Oriel (Kensington & Chelsea, p. 125)

FRENCH/MODERN

Criterion Grill ★ (Soho & Chinatown, p. 139)
Incognico ★★ (Soho & Chinatown, p. 134)

FRENCH/PROVENCAL

Lou Pescadou ★ (Earl's Court, p. 127)

FRENCH/TRADITIONAL

Chez Gerard at the Opera Terrace (Covent Garden & the Strand, p. 148)
L'Escargot Marco Pierre White ★★ (Soho & Chinatown, p. 139)
Mon Plaisir (Covent Garden & the Strand, p. 149)

GASTROPUBS

The Atlas ★★ (Earl's Court, p. 127)
Bleeding Heart Bistro & Tavern ★★ (Clerkenwell, p. 152)
The Chapel ★ (Marylebone, p. 132)
The Engineer ★ (Camden, p. 156)
Pan-Asian Canteen @ Paxton's Head (Knightsbridge, p. 120)

GREEK

Lemonia ★ (Camden, p. 155)

INDIAN

Café Lazeez ★ (Kensington & Chelsea, p. 126)
Masala Zone ★★ (Soho & Chinatown, p. 138)
Mela ★★ (Covent Garden & The Strand, p. 148)
Soho Spice ★ (Soho & Chinatown, p. 138)
Veeraswamy ★ (Mayfair, p. 141)

INDIAN/SOUTH

Diwana Bhel Poori House (Bloomsbury & Fitzrovia, p. 145)
Malabar Junction ★ (Bloomsbury & Fitzrovia, p. 146)

INTERNATIONAL

The Bar at Villandry ★ (Bloomsbury & Fitzrovia, p. 141)
Cork & Bottle Wine Bar (Soho & Chinatown, p. 138)
Giraffe ★ (Marylebone, p. 132)
Portobello Gold (Notting Hill, p. 130)

IRANIAN
Patogh (Marylebone, p. 132)

ITALIAN
Aperitivo ★ (Soho & Chinatown, p. 134)
Carluccio's Caffè ★ (Bloomsbury & Fitzrovia, p. 144)
Centrale (Soho & Chinatown, p. 137)
Vasco & Piero's Pavilion ★ (Soho & Chinatown, p. 138)

JAPANESE
Tokyo Diner ★ (Soho & Chinatown, p. 136)

JAPANESE NOODLES
Wagamama ★ (Bloomsbury & Soho, p. 144)

LEBANESE
Al Waha ★ (Paddington & Bayswater, p. 131)

MEDITERRANEAN
The Atlas ★★ (Earl's Court, p. 127)
Mosaique ★ (Holborn, p. 144)

NORTH AFRICAN
Mô Tearoom (Mayfair, p. 140)
Moro ★★★ (Clerkenwell, p. 154)

PACIFIC RIM
Suze in Mayfair ★ (Mayfair, p. 140)

PAN-ASIAN
Itsu ★★ (Kensington & Chelsea, p. 124)
Pan-Asian Canteen @ Paxton's Head (Knightsbridge, p. 120)

PIZZA & PASTA
ASK (Chain, p. 156)
La Spighetta ★★ (Marylebone, p. 132)
Oliveto ★ (Victoria, p. 151)
Pizza Express (Chain, p. 156)
Pizza on the Park ★ (Knightsbridge, p. 120)

POLISH
Wódka ★ (Kensington & Chelsea, p. 126)

PUBS/TRADITIONAL
George Inn (South Bank, p. 133)
Museum Tavern (Bloomsbury, p. 133)
Nag's Head (Knightsbridge, p. 133)
Salisbury (West End, p. 133)

SANDWICHES
EAT (Chain, p. 157)
Pret a Manger (Chain, p. 157)

SCOTTISH
Boisdale ★ (Victoria, p. 151)

SEAFOOD
Back to Basics ★★ (Bloomsbury & Fitzrovia, p. 146)
Fish! ★★ (Just South of the River, p. 155)
Livebait ★ (Covent Garden & the Strand, p. 149)
Lou Pescadou (Earl's Court, p. 127)

SOUP
EAT (Chain, p. 157)
Quiet Revolution (Marylebone, p. 133)
Soup Opera (Chain, p. 157)

SPANISH
Cambio de Tercio ★★ (Kensington & Chelsea, p. 126)
Moro ★★★ (Clerkenwell, p. 154)

SUDANESE
Mandola ★ (Notting Hill, p. 127)

SUSHI
Itsu ★★ (Kensington & Chelsea, p. 124)
YO! Sushi (Soho & Chinatown, p. 136)

THAI
Bangkok (Kensington & Chelsea, p. 124)
Tawana ★ (Paddington & Bayswater, p. 131)

TURKISH
Sofra (Covent Garden & the Strand, p. 150)
Tas ★ (Just South of the River, p. 154)

VEGETARIAN

Food for Thought (Covent Garden & the Strand, p. 147)
Mildred's ★ (Soho & Chinatown, p. 136)
The Place Below ★ (The City, p. 152)

WINE BARS

Cork & Bottle Wine Bar (Soho & Chinatown, p. 138)
Ebury Wine Bar & Restaurant (Victoria, p. 151)

3 Knightsbridge

Pan-Asian Canteen @ Paxton's Head *Finds* GASTROPUB/PAN-ASIAN There's been a pub on this spot since 1632, but the present one dates from the turn of the last century. Every inch of it, inside and out, is paneled in polished mahogany. So the Pan-Asian Canteen upstairs comes as a bit of a surprise. The cool, modern, Bangkok-green dining room has three big teak tables, which can seat 12 people each, eating communal style. Depending on the day and time, you could have one to yourself or be elbow-to-elbow with businessmen, backpackers, and babes on a shopping break. The fixed-price dinners are a great value, and the prices make this a perfect light meal break. Quality can be dicey, though, and some dishes definitely fare better than others. The menu is strong on seafood, but there's a lot to tempt vegetarians and carnivores, too. When in doubt, go for a chicken curry. The pub has several real ales on tap.

153 Knightsbridge, SW1. ✆ **020/7589-6627.** Reservations not accepted. Main courses £6–£8 ($11–$15); fixed-price dinners £17–£20 ($21–$37). MC, V. Mon–Sat noon–10:30pm; Sun noon–9pm. Tube: Knightsbridge.

Pizza on the Park ★ PIZZA & PASTA This is one of the most popular jazz venues in London and pulls in all the big names. Unfortunately, you have to pay extra for the basement gigs—from £16 ($30) depending on who's playing—and you must book ahead. But come here Sunday lunchtime, and there's live background music (not usually jazz) upstairs as well. This is a very classy pizza joint, with high ceilings, dramatic pillars, and tables set with fresh flowers. The pizzas have lots of tomato on the base and interesting toppings. The *Quattro Formaggi (*four cheeses) is great. Pastas aren't always so successful. Pizza on the Park also does breakfast until 11:30am. The best view is from the inside looking out at the park. Pavement tables are a bit too close to traffic.

11 Knightsbridge, SW1. ✆ **020/7235-5273.** Reservations required for music room. Breakfast £4.95 ($9); main courses £8–£14 ($15–$26). AE, DC, MC, V. Daily 8:30am–midnight. Tube: Hyde Park Corner.

GREAT DEALS ON FIXED-PRICE MEALS

Brasserie St. Quentin ★ FRENCH BRASSERIE This attractive brasserie with chandeliers, etched mirrors, and well-starched tablecloths is right on the border between Knightsbridge and South Kensington and caters to a pretty affluent clientele (there's a reassuringly high number of French patrons, too). But the brasserie has excellent value fixed-price meals, two or three courses, both at lunch and pretheater. These offer a blend of classic and updated French fare, from shoulder of lamb with root vegetables to roast monkfish. Vegetarian options include artichoke fondant with seasonal vegetables.

243 Brompton Rd., SW3. ✆ **020/7589-8005.** Reservations recommended. Main courses £11–£24 ($19–$43); fixed-price lunch/pretheater menus £15–£17 ($27–$31). AE, DC, MC, V. Daily noon–3pm; Mon–Sat 6–11:30pm; Sun 6:30–10:30pm. Tube: Knightsbridge or South Kensington.

Moveable Feasts

There's nothing more blissful on a sunny summer's day than dining alfresco. London is full of green spaces that are great for picnics. Get there early at lunchtime and find your patch, because the locals grab any chance to leave their desks. At the weekend, the parks look just like flesh-toned penguin colonies, with barely an inch of lawn visible.

That's particularly true of Soho Square, a grassy oasis right in the heart of the West End (Tube: Tottenham Court Rd.). There are lots of nearby places to pick up the necessary stuff. The **Marks & Spencer Food Hall,** 458 Oxford St., W1 (✆ **020/7935-7954**), has deli fare, including sandwiches and pre-chopped veggies and salads for busy yuppies. I'd also recommend **I Camisa & Son,** 61 Old Compton St., W1 (✆ **020/7437-7610**), which is a scented heaven of Italian sausages, cheeses, and olives. Then pop around the corner to **Berwick Street market** for salad ingredients and great bread.

Bloomsbury Cheeses, 61b Judd St., WC1 (✆ **020/7387-7645**), carries a mammoth range of cheeses, as well as wine, olives, and delicious bread. **Alara Wholefoods,** 58–60 Marchmont St., WC1 (✆ **020/7837-1172**), is great for salads and sandwiches. A little farther west, stock up for a lazy day in Regents Park at the **Villandry Foodstore,** which is part of the restaurant The Bar at Villandry (p. 141)

Fortnum & Mason, 181 Piccadilly, W1 (✆ **020/7734-8040**), is the only place to go before setting off to Green Park (Tube: Green Park or Hyde Park Corner). Its food halls will demand iron self-control. The obvious supply store for a picnic by the Serpentine in Hyde Park or, if you don't mind the walk, the Round Pond in Kensington Gardens, is another famous food hall: **Harrods,** 87–135 Brompton Rd., SW1 (✆ **020/7730-1234**).

Walking to Kensington Gardens from Notting Hill Gate, pop in and buy a cheap takeaway bite at **Café Diana,** 5 Wellington Terrace, Bayswater Rd., W2 (✆ **020/7792-9606**). It's like a shrine to the princess, with barely an inch of wall not covered by photographs. Diana brought one in herself, with her signature scrawled across the bottom.

If you pick **Holland Park** as your picnic spot, take the Tube to Holland Park and shop for lunch at one of the two French patisseries, the deli, or the pricey grocery store that are all in a row right by the station.

Note: You can also take a picnic if you go to the **Royal Botanic Garden Kew** (p. 203) or **Hampton Court Palace** (p. 166) on the banks of the Thames.

WORTH A SPLURGE

Boxwood Café ★★ *Kids* MODERN BRITISH This may be the most stylish kid-friendly restaurant in London, but grownups will find plenty of comforting delights on the menu. Created by Gordon Ramsay, Boxwood Café is chic without being fussy, and the same goes for the food, which emphasizes fresh and healthy dishes. For the fixed-price lunch you might choose a starter of cold smoked knuckle of pork with piccalilli and thyme toast or pan-fried duck's egg, grilled asparagus, and roasted tomatoes,

Where to Dine from Knightsbridge to Earl's Court

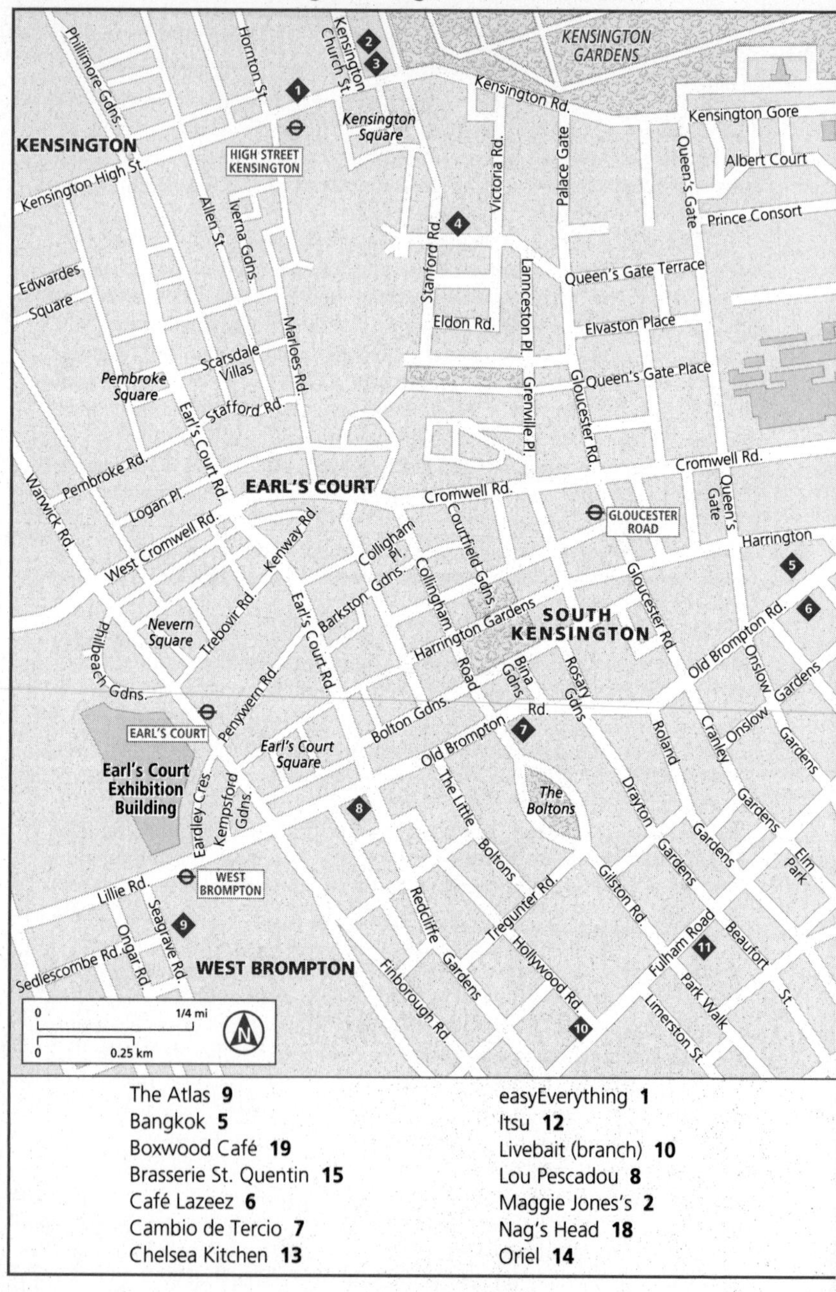

The Atlas **9**	easyEverything **1**
Bangkok **5**	Itsu **12**
Boxwood Café **19**	Livebait (branch) **10**
Brasserie St. Quentin **15**	Lou Pescadou **8**
Café Lazeez **6**	Maggie Jones's **2**
Cambio de Tercio **7**	Nag's Head **18**
Chelsea Kitchen **13**	Oriel **14**

KENSINGTON GARDENS
HYDE PARK CORNER
KNIGHTSBRIDGE
KNIGHTSBRIDGE
Kensington Rd.
Knightsbridge
Rutland Gate
Enismore Gardens
Montpelier St.
Sloane St.
Square
Lowndes
Kinnerton St.
Wilton Cres.
Halkin St.
Rd.
Prince's Gardens
Gardens
Garden Mews
Exhibition Rd.
Brompton Square
Cheval Pl.
Brompton Rd.
Hans Cr.
Hans Rd.
Basil St.
Pavilion Road
Belgrave Square
Beauchamp Place
Walton St.
Pont Street
Chesham Pl.
Belgrave Pl.
Victoria & Albert Museum
Cromwell Rd.
Egerton Gdns
Brompton Rd.
Thurloe Place
Square
Thurloe
Sloane St.
Cadogan Place
Cadogan Lane
Chesham St.
Lyall St.
Cadogan Square
Pavilion Rd.
Hasker St.
Milner St.
King's Rd.
Ellis St.
SOUTH KENSINGTON
Pelham St.
Cadogan Gdns.
Cadogan St.
Eaton Terrace
Bourne
SLOANE SQUARE
Pelham Crescent
Onslow Square
Draycott Avenue
Sloane Avenue
Draycott Place
BELGRAVIA
Sumner Pl.
Fulham Rd.
Ixworth Place
Elystan St.
King's Rd.
Lower Sloane
Pimlico Rd.
Elystan Place
Cale St.
Astell St.
King's Rd.
Smith St.
Chelsea Bridge Rd.
Chelsea Square
Dovehouse St.
Sydney St.
CHELSEA
Radnor Walk
Tedworth Square
Old Church St.
Chelsea Manor St.
Flood St.
Christchurch St.
Royal Hospital Rd.
West St.
Tite St.
RANELAGH GARDENS
King's Rd.
Glebe Place
Oakley St.
Information
TUBE STOP
CHELSEA PHYSIC GARDENS
Chelsea Embankment
Thames
Pan-Asian Canteen @ Paxton's Head 16
Pizza on the Park 20
Vingt-Quatre 11
Wagamama (branch) 3
Wódka 4
YO! Sushi, at Harvey Nichols 17
Regent's Park
THE WEST END
THE CITY
Hyde Park
Buckingham Palace
Thames
Area of detail
0 1 mi
0 1 km
Battersea Park

then move on to poached breast of chicken or a warm salad of seared marinated salmon with baby artichokes. A la carte main choices range from a baked macaroni of wild mushrooms and Parmesan to fresh steamed fish, grilled calves' liver, roast chicken salad, veal, and steaks. The entire restaurant is nonsmoking.

Berkeley Hotel, Wilton Place, SW1. ✆ **020/7235-1010.** Reservations recommended. Main courses £14–£25 ($25–$46); fixed-price lunch £21 ($39); children's menu £7.50 ($14). AE, DISC, MC, V. Mon–Fri noon–3pm; Sat–Sun noon–4pm; daily 6–11pm. Tube: Hyde Park Corner or Knightsbridge.

4 Kensington & Chelsea

Bangkok THAI This is a veteran neighborhood restaurant just off the busy Old Brompton Road. It's tiny, cafelike, and only has about 10 dishes on the menu, but the food is good and the service very friendly, which is why it has such a fiercely loyal clientele. The staff will describe each dish in English to Thai-food novices. Spicy beef with basil and chili is delicious, and the noodle dishes are good, but the prawns may be too hot for most tongues to handle. Bangkok isn't in anywhere near the same league as Tawana in Bayswater, but it is a great budget choice in this very tony neighborhood—not to mention a great way to meet the tony neighbors.

9 Bute St., SW7. ✆ **020/7584-8529.** Reservations recommended. Main courses £7.75–£13 ($14–$23). MC, V. Daily 12:15–2:30pm; Mon–Sat 6:45–11pm. Tube: South Kensington.

Itsu ★★ PAN-ASIAN/SUSHI This is the brainchild of Julian Metcalfe, who created Pret a Manger, the chain of hip and healthy sandwich shops that revolutionized the British lunch market. Itsu has the superfashionable conveyor belt, with 35 menu items circling on white, red, black, and gold plates to show the different prices. The menu subverts tradition with Pan-Asian and Western influences. On the cheapest white plates you'll find salmon sushi and a sweet omelet roll with chives. Salmon plays a big part on the menu, from the smoked variety with avocado and flying-fish eggs, to some marinated with chives, or turned into sashimi. The gold plates include tasty grilled chicken with green soba noodles. Itsu is evangelically healthy, except for the oddball crème brûlée on the black-plate list, and is nonsmoking. There's sometimes a £1 ($1.85) per-plate special between 4 and 6pm and 10:30 and 11:30pm. A new Soho branch opened at 103 Wardour St., W1 (✆ **020/7479-4794;** Tube: Leicester Square or Piccadilly Circus).

118 Draycott Ave., SW3. ✆ **020/7590-2401.** Colored plate selections £1.95–£5.95 ($3.60–$11). AE, MC, V. Mon–Thurs noon–11pm; Fri–Sat noon–midnight; Sun 1–10:30pm. Tube: South Kensington.

Maggie Jones's ★ TRADITIONAL BRITISH This veteran bistro has a charming staff and a quirkily cozy atmosphere that pulls in a diverse clientele. Maggie Jones's is like a junkshop crammed with farmhouse kitchen ephemera—copper warming pans, toddlers' rocking horses, and sheaves of dried corn hang down from the ceiling. The food is hearty farmhouse-style, too—big portions, not much finesse—from slices of eggy quiche to wild boar sausages and mash, as well as duck, venison, guinea fowl, and rabbit. And the menu tosses avocado about with 1970s abandon. The three-course Sunday lunch is a classic, offering such national culinary treasures as roast beef with Yorkshire pudding and apple crumble. There's a cover charge in the evening, and the bill includes a 12.5% service charge, so watch for the total left blank on your credit card slip.

6 Old Court Place, off Kensington Church St., W8. ✆ **020/7937-6462.** Reservations essential at dinner and for Sun lunch. Main courses £5.50–£20 ($10–$36); fixed-price Sun lunch £16 ($29). Cover charge at dinner £1 ($1.85). AE, DC, MC, V. Daily 12:30–2:30pm; Mon–Sat 6:30–11pm; Sun 6:30–10:30pm. Tube: Kensington High St.

Oriel *Kids* FRENCH BRASSERIE Oriel is in a fantastic location, right on the corner of Sloane Square, and everyone knows it. It's always hopping, so if you're planning to eat rather than grab a coffee or a quick drink (wine by the glass is very reasonably priced), try to arrive a little ahead of normal mealtimes. The upstairs is classic brasserie, with big mirrors, square-topped tables, and high ceilings. There are a few pavement tables for people-watching. Downstairs, marshmallow-soft sofas make you never want to leave. The food is a good value, from *moules marinières* (mussels) to salads or sausage and mash. Oriel has vegetarian dishes and will provide reduced-price portions for the kids. The only problem is that the service can sometimes be rushed or snooty or both.

50–51 Sloane Sq., SW1. ✆ **020/7730-2804.** Main courses £8.50–£14 ($16–$26). AE, DC, MC, V. Mon–Sat 8:30am–10:45pm; Sun 9am–10pm. Tube: Sloane Sq.

Vingt-Quatre ★ MODERN BRITISH This is a proper restaurant that serves proper food 24 hours a day. It's a West London institution and pretty unique across the whole city. Bedraggled partygoers roll in here to finish off the night with steak and fries or a rip-roaring English breakfast. Vingt-Quatre recently had a refurb, smartening up its diner image and adding healthy options to the menu. Of course, you don't have to stay up all night to eat here. It's a great spot for a standard supper that isn't standard at all. The menu changes regularly but might include the delicious Caesar salad, grilled tuna, or tortellini with mascarpone. If you do come for a session in the wee small hours, Fulham Road is one of the more reliable places for finding a taxi.

325 Fulham Rd., SW10. ✆ **020/7376-7224.** Main courses £5.75–£14 ($11–$26). Cover charge £1 ($1.85) 10:30pm–7am. AE, MC, V. Open 24 hr. Tube: Gloucester Rd. or South Kensington. Bus: 14 or N14.

SUPER-CHEAP EATS

Chelsea Kitchen BRITISH DINER This is a sister to the Stockpot chain, which also has a diner on King's Road. The Chelsea Kitchen is a lot more convenient, and the food is a little better. The cuisine is not remotely haute by any stretch of the imagination, but it's a fantastically good deal. The menu never changes. It runs from

---

Tips Where to Go for a 24-Hour Munchie Fix

However cosmopolitan London gets, it still can't grasp the round-the-clock thing. There are only a few places to assuage the munchies if they strike at an inconvenient hour. The top spot is the legendary Soho diner, **Bar Italia,** 22 Frith St., W1 (✆ **020/7437-4520;** Tube: Tottenham Court Rd.). The simple food ranges from hot panini specials to mouthwatering pastries and cakes. Another Soho never-closer is **1997,** 19 Wardour St., W1 (✆ **020/7734-2868**), a friendly Chinese restaurant, cheekily decked out with posters of Mao and Deng Xiaoping. The mainly gay **Balans Soho,** 60 Old Compton St., W1 (✆ **020/7439-2183;** Tube: Leicester Sq.), which stays open until 5am Monday through Thursday, and until 6am on Friday and Saturday, is good for sandwiches, light meals, and drinks. Otherwise, there's the omelet and shake place, Clerkenwell's **Tinseltown,** 44–46 St. John St., EC1 (✆ **020/7689-2424;** Tube: Barbican or Farringdon); the **Brick Lane Beigel Bake,** 159 Brick Lane, E1 (✆ **020/7729-0616;** Tube: Shoreditch); and **Vingt-Quatre** (reviewed above).

---

omelets and burgers to salads and more substantial hot dishes, such as goulash, spaghetti Bolognese, and braised lamb chops. Chelsea Kitchen is no-frills on the decor side, too, with polished wooden tables and bum-numbing booths. The service sometimes sorely lacks a smile. But the prices are so "Old World" that it gets screamingly busy, particularly in the evening.

98 King's Rd., SW3. ✆ **020/7589-1330.** Main courses £3–£6.50 ($5.50–$12); fixed-priced meal £6–£7 ($11–$13). No credit cards. Mon–Sat 7:30am–11:45pm. Tube: Sloane Sq.

GREAT DEALS ON FIXED-PRICE MEALS

Café Lazeez ★ INDIAN A two-time winner of Carlton TV's Best Indian Restaurant award, this is another place that has ditched flocked wallpaper and canned ethnic music for a cool modern approach, evolving new dishes but losing nothing of its authenticity in the kitchen. There's a bar/brasserie on the ground floor with the dining room upstairs. In summer, diners hang out on a terrace framed with flower boxes. There's so much good stuff to choose from and at such a range of prices that you'd have to go back several times to work out which is the best deal. The £16 ($29) House Feast—a host of different meats cooked in the tandoor oven—could easily feed two people. Just ask for extra cutlery. There are two other branches: at 88 St. John St., EC1 (✆ **020/7253-2224;** Tube: Barbican or Farringdon), and at the Soho Theatre, 21 Dean St., W1 (✆ **020/7434-9393;** Tube: Tottenham Court Rd.).

93–95 Old Brompton Rd., SW7. ✆ **020/7581-9993.** Reservations recommended. Main courses £8–£18 ($15–$33); fixed-price meals £11–£17 ($20–$31). AE, DC, MC, V. Mon–Sat 11am–1am; Sun 11am–10:30pm. Tube: South Kensington.

Wódka ★ POLISH This friendly Kensington restaurant takes a new look at classic Polish dishes, served amid simple modern decor. The two- and three-course fixed-price lunches are a great value. You might start with a meal-in-itself, such as *zur* (sausage and sour rye soup), or light fluffy blinis with aubergine mousse. The main courses are likely to include at least one Western European dish, like the delicious fishcakes. If you've got a bit of spare cash, come in the evening instead. It's a much better time to enjoy Wódka's real specialty: the mile-long menu of vodkas, served by the shot or carafe. There's every flavor under the sun, from bison grass to rose petal, or a honey one that's served hot. Wódka is a firm favorite with locals and not-so-locals who want to kick up their heels.

12 St. Alban's Grove, W8. ✆ **020/7937-6513.** Reservations recommended. Main courses £11–£15 ($20–$27); fixed-price lunch £11–£15 ($21–$27). AE, DC, MC, V. Mon–Fri 12:30–2:30pm; daily 7–11:15pm. Tube: High St. Kensington or Gloucester Rd.

WORTH A SPLURGE

Cambio de Tercio ★★ SPANISH Several changes of chef have done nothing to dent the standards or popularity of the stylish Cambio de Tercio. The dramatic interior is decorated in a rich yellow with damask-spread tables and chairs swathed in burgundy cloth. The walls are hung with pictures of bullfights and a matador's cloak and swords. The charming Spanish staff guides you through a menu of regional delights. Ham is the house specialty—from the expensive plate of ham Jabugo, made from acorn-fed black pig, to the suckling pig Segovia style. But you could also get dishes like poached eggs with grilled asparagus, Basque wine mousseline, and sautéed foie gras. You should dress up a bit for this place and starve yourself beforehand.

163 Old Brompton Rd., SW5. ✆ **020/7244-8970.** Reservations required for dinner. Main courses £14–£16 ($25–$30). AE, MC, V. Daily 12:30–2:30pm; Mon–Sat 7–11:30pm; Sun 7–11pm. Tube: Gloucester Rd. or South Kensington.

5 Earl's Court

The Atlas ★★ GASTROPUB/MEDITERRANEAN The doors open for drinkers at noon here, and that's when you should come if you want to get a table (especially one outside). The Atlas is incredibly popular, and rightly so: the food is delicious, the ambience laid-back, and it has a real neighborhood feel. The Manners brothers run the place, with George as the chef and grand creator of grilled Tuscan sausages with Puy lentils, or pan-fried calves' liver. While he is big on balsamic vinegar, pancetta, and Parmesan, the rich flavors characteristic of Spanish and North African cooking spice up both starters and main courses made from the freshest of whatever's in season. And do leave space for dessert because George's are some of the best in town. Choose from the menu chalked up on the board and order at the bar. The Atlas has several ales on tap and around 10 wines available by the glass.

16 Seagrave Rd., SW6. ✆ **020/7385-9129.** Main courses £8–£12 ($15–$22). MC, V. Food served daily 12:30–3pm; Mon–Sat 7–10:30pm; Sun 7–10pm. Tube: West Brompton.

GREAT DEALS ON FIXED-PRICE MEALS

Lou Pescadou ★ SEAFOOD/FRENCH PROVENCAL You can't miss Lou Pescadou's porthole front window. The fishy theme carries over inside, with scallop ashtrays, marine-blue oilcloths on the tables, and boat pictures hanging on the walls. Service is enthusiastic but often chaotic. Food standards can be patchy, but overall the cooking here is reliable, fresh, and tasty, which is why the restaurant has a loyal local clientele. You can sit out on the sidewalk during the summer. Going a la carte gets expensive, but the weekend three-course fixed-price menu is a good value. If you get a shellfish option, make sure it comes with Lou Pescadou's velvety mayonnaise. Main courses are sturdy and old-fashioned, from whole sea bass grilled with fennel to smoked haddock with juniper butter. We'd actually go for one of the meat dishes, also classically French—the chef really knows how to cook a steak, with shallot sauce, *saignant.*

241 Old Brompton Rd., SW5. ✆ **020/7370-1057.** Reservations essential. Main courses £8–£14 ($15–$26); weekday fixed-price lunch £11 ($20); weekend fixed-price meal £15 ($27). AE, DC, MC, V. Daily noon–3pm; Mon–Fri 7pm–midnight; Sat–Sun 6:30pm–midnight. Tube: Earl's Court.

6 Notting Hill

Mandola ★ SUDANESE This little local restaurant started out as the half-hearted annex to the takeout joint next door. Now it has grown into an attractive and mildly eccentric restaurant with very good food but unbelievably slow service. The best deal is the £12 ($22) starter, which gives two diners free run at everything the salad bar has to offer—though to call it just a "salad bar" doesn't do it justice. Options include white cabbage and onions in peanut sauce, aubergine *salata aswad,* and Sudanese

---

Moments **Heavenly Smells**

The simplest pleasures are often the greatest—like the mouthwatering aromas of really good street food. At Notting Hill Farmers' Market, the gourmet-mushroom man sautés his wares, with herbs and garlic, right there on a little camping stove. His ciabatta sandwiches cost £2 ($3.70). Stand there a moment and inhale before sampling the food.

Where to Dine from Marylebone to Notting Hill

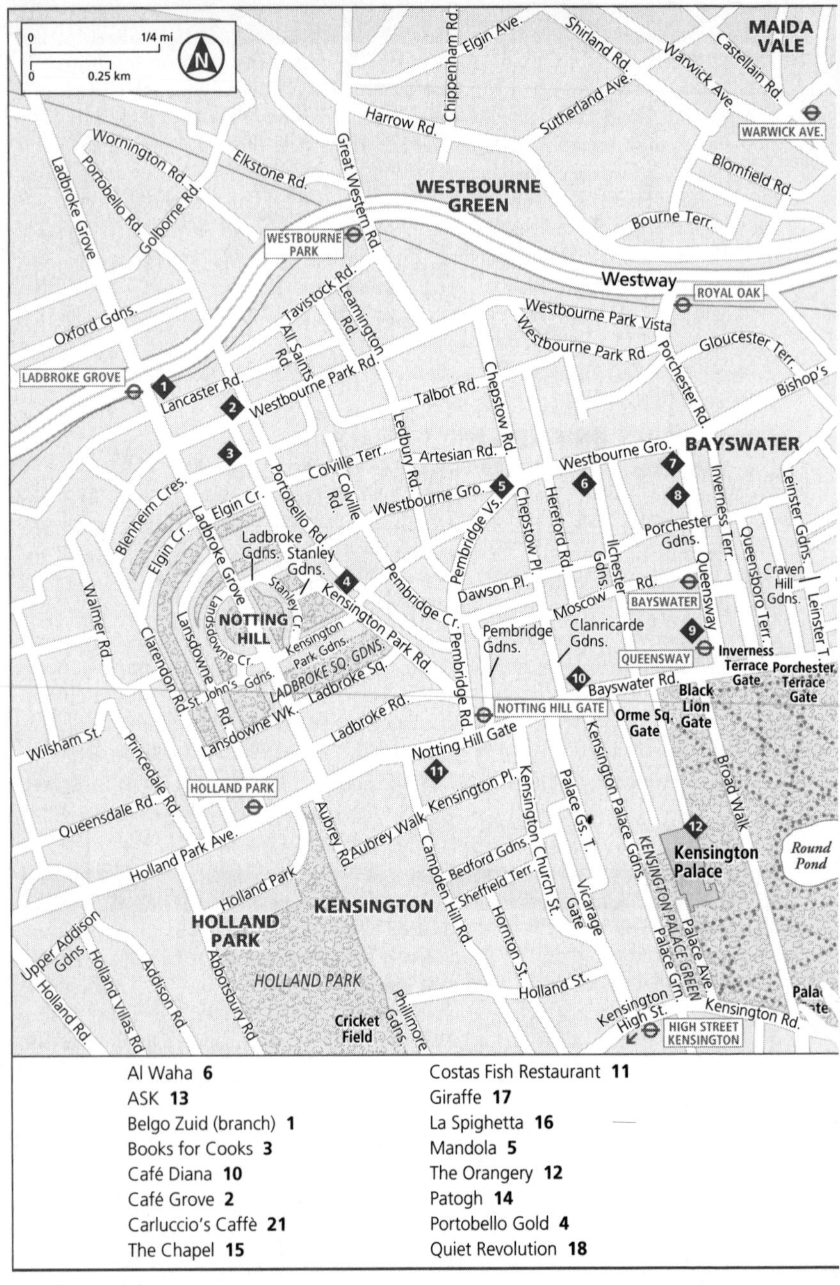

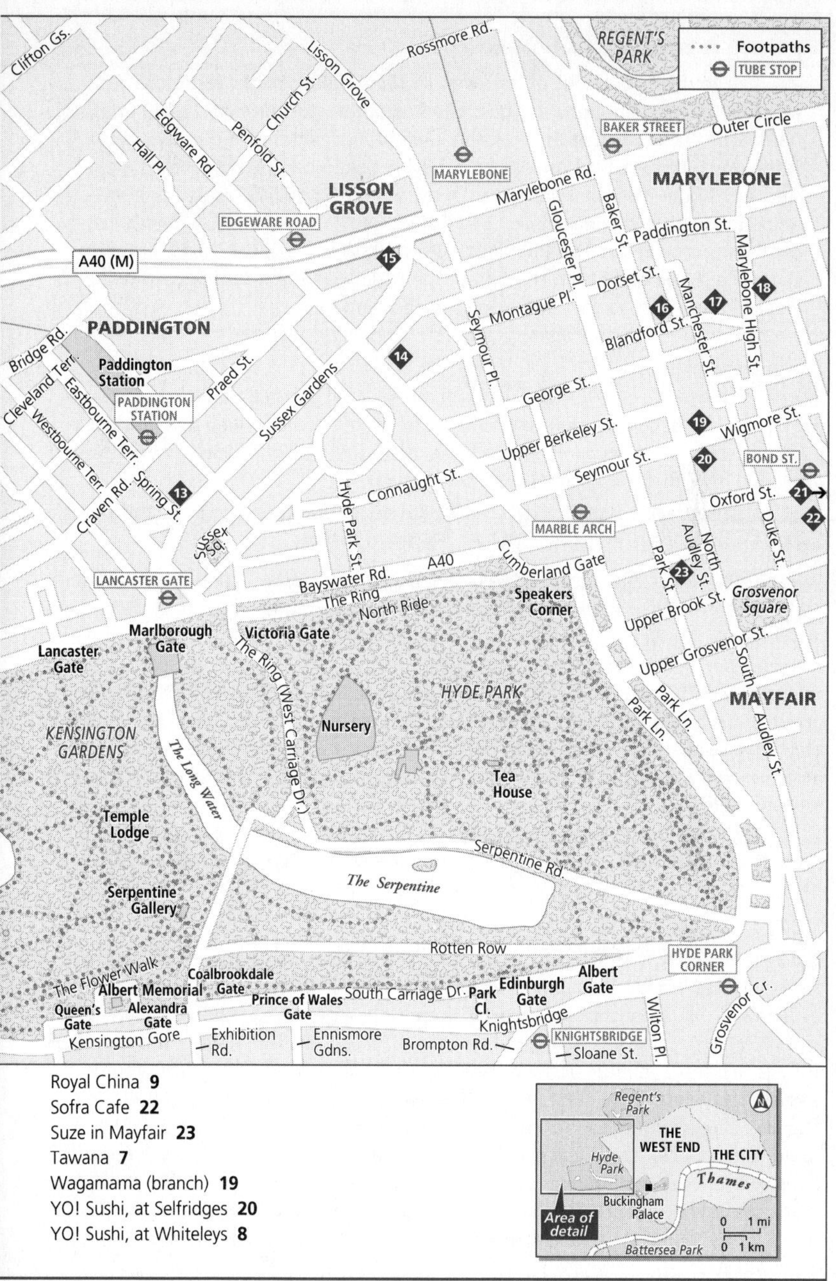
Footpaths
TUBE STOP
Regent's Park
Clifton Gs.
Rossmore Rd.
Lisson Grove
Church St.
Edgware Rd.
Penfold St.
Hall Pl.
BAKER STREET
Outer Circle
MARYLEBONE
MARYLEBONE
LISSON GROVE
Marylebone Rd.
EDGEWARE ROAD
Gloucester Pl.
Baker St.
Paddington St.
A40 (M)
Dorset St.
Marylebone High St.
Manchester St.
Montague Pl.
Seymour Pl.
Blandford St.
PADDINGTON
Bridge Rd.
Paddington Station
Cleveland Terr.
Eastbourne Terr.
PADDINGTON STATION
Praed St.
Sussex Gardens
George St.
Westbourne Terr.
Wigmore St.
Upper Berkeley St.
Seymour St.
BOND ST.
Craven Rd.
Spring St.
Hyde Park St.
Connaught St.
Oxford St.
Sussex Sq.
MARBLE ARCH
North Audley St.
Duke St.
LANCASTER GATE
Bayswater Rd.
A40
Cumberland Gate
Park St.
The Ring
Speakers Corner
Grosvenor Square
North Ride
Upper Brook St.
Marlborough Gate
Victoria Gate
Lancaster Gate
The Ring (West Carriage Dr.)
Upper Grosvenor St.
HYDE PARK
South Audley St.
MAYFAIR
Park Ln.
KENSINGTON GARDENS
Nursery
The Long Water
Tea House
Temple Lodge
Serpentine Rd.
The Serpentine
Serpentine Gallery
Rotten Row
HYDE PARK CORNER
The Flower Walk
Coalbrookdale Gate
Albert Gate
Albert Memorial
Edinburgh Gate
Prince of Wales Gate
South Carriage Dr.
Park Cl.
Queen's Gate
Alexandra Gate
Grosvenor Cr.
Knightsbridge
Wilton Pl.
Kensington Gore
Exhibition Rd.
Ennismore Gdns.
Brompton Rd.
KNIGHTSBRIDGE
Sloane St.
13
14
15
16
17
18
19
20
21
22
23
Regent's Park
THE WEST END
THE CITY
Hyde Park
Thames
Buckingham Palace
Area of detail
Battersea Park
0 1 mi
0 1 km
N

Royal China **9**
Sofra Cafe **22**
Suze in Mayfair **23**
Tawana **7**
Wagamama (branch) **19**
YO! Sushi, at Selfridges **20**
YO! Sushi, at Whiteleys **8**

Finds A Bookshop Cookshop

The first muffins come out of the oven at 10am, filling **Books for Cooks** with heavenly smells. This mecca for gastronomes, which stocks nearly 12,000 titles, has a little test kitchen at the rear and a handful of tables where browsers can settle down for a cup of coffee and a freshly baked cake. Light lunches are a steal at £5 ($9)—hot soup and bread in the winter (£3/$5.50), a salad or homemade savory tart in the summer (£4/$7.40), three courses for £7 ($13). It's just off the Portobello Road at 4 Blenheim Crescent, W11 (✆ **020/7221-1992;** Tube: Ladbroke Grove or Notting Hill Gate). Open Tues–Sat 10am–6pm; closed last 3 weeks in Aug and 10 days between Christmas and New Year's.

falafel. Each would cost over £2 ($3.20) on its own, and you get pita bread to accompany them. Main courses are just as simple, from super-tender lamb and chicken in pungent sauces to the vegetarian stews. Mandola is unlicensed, so you can bring your own wine for a £1 ($1.60) corkage fee per bottle.

139–143 Westbourne Grove, W11. ✆ **020/7229-4734.** Reservations recommended for dinner. Main courses £6.50–£11 ($12–$19). MC, V. Mon–Sat noon–midnight. Tube: Notting Hill Gate.

Portobello Gold *Finds* INTERNATIONAL In December 2000, Bill Clinton popped into this little local pub-restaurant while Hillary did her Christmas shopping in Portobello Market. That's not necessarily a recommendation, but it does tell you that this popular restaurant draws a varied clientele. The evening set-price menu might start with oysters on the half-shell, haddock fish cakes, or chicken liver and pecan pâté, then move on to seabream baked in cider or lamb ragout. On Sundays they serve classic roasts (beef, lamb, pork). Vegetarians will always find several dishes on the menu. Portobello Gold also has an Internet cafe and a handful of B&B bedrooms (p. 86).

95–97 Portobello Rd., W11. ✆ **020/7460-4900.** Reservations recommended for dinner and Sunday lunch. Main courses £7–£13 ($13–$25); set lunch £10–£13 ($18–$25); set dinner £20 ($37). DC, MC, V. Mon–Sat noon–5pm and 7:30–11:15pm; Sun 1–5pm and 7:30–9:30pm. Tube: Notting Hill Gate.

SUPER-CHEAP EATS

Café Grove BRITISH DINER This is the perfect refueling spot after a morning at Portobello Market. In the summer, diners sit out on the roof terrace, enjoying the bustle below. It naturally gets a lot quieter during the week and in winter. Café Grove looks like a scruffy campus hangout from the 1970s, despite the freshly painted walls, and the menu is a mixture of the worthy and the wicked. You can breakfast your way around the world here—on huevos rancheros, perhaps, or pancakes. The very ungreasy English breakfast, served all day in winter and until 12:30pm in summer, could stop a truck: it's a huge plate of bacon, sausages (vegetarian or "carnivorous"), tomato, fried eggs, mushrooms, baked beans, potatoes, and toast. For lunch, there are salads, build-your-own sandwiches, melts, Mexican wraps, and homemade cakes. Café Grove serves Victorian lemonade, wine, and beer (including organic brands), but not Coke or Pepsi.

253a Portobello Rd., W11. ✆ **020/7243-1094.** Sandwiches and light meals £5.50–£10 ($10–$18). No credit cards. Winter 9:30am–5pm; summer Mon 8:30am–6pm, Tues–Sat 8:30am–11pm. Tube: Ladbroke Grove.

Costas Fish Restaurant ★ FISH & CHIPS Costas is a tiny, time-warp Cypriot restaurant that serves up some of the best fish and chips in town. The battered haddock is delicious, even if the portion is smaller than some rivals dish out (it's cheaper, too), and the chips are good and crunchy. The Greek influence is evident in the side orders, which include hummus and desserts such as baklava. We prefer this place to another local institution, Geales, round the corner, which has ideas above its chippie station and often fails to live up to them. Don't confuse this place with Costas Grill, which is at nos. 12 to 14 Hillgate sts.

18 Hillgate St., W8. ✆ **020/7727-4310.** Reservations recommended for dinner. Main courses £4.70–£7.90 ($9–$15). No credit cards. Daily noon–2:30pm; Tues–Sat 5:30–10:30pm. Tube: Notting Hill Gate.

7 Paddington & Bayswater

Al Waha ★ LEBANESE Al Waha, considered one of the best Lebanese restaurants in London, delivers spectacularly and elegantly, with dishes that taste as fresh as their ingredients. Mix and match the starters, which include miniature lamb sausages and grilled halloumi cheese, or go straight to a main course. There are lots of grills and daily specials such as chicken stuffed with prune and pine nuts, and there's always fish on Fridays.

75 Westbourne Grove, W2. ✆ **020/7229-0806.** Reservations recommended. Main courses £9–£18 ($17–$33); fixed-price lunch £13 ($23), fixed-price dinner £21–£25 ($34–$46). Cover charge £1.50 ($2.80). MC, V. Daily noon–midnight. Tube: Bayswater or Queensway.

Royal China ★★ CHINESE Royal China's dim sum is reckoned by many to be the best in London. The decor is marvelously over-ornate, with Hong Kong casino-style black-and-gold paneling. But you don't have to be a high roller to dine here: A dim sum extravaganza is unlikely to set you back much more than £15 ($28). The most popular dish, and deservedly so, is the roast pork puff. The touch is always light as air, whether on the standard menu dumplings or daily specials, such as a delicate *mange tout* (snowpeas) combination. No wonder Sundays here are as big a scrum as the Harrods sale. Come during the week when it's a lot more peaceful, and the staff are more likely to have their happy faces on.

13 Queensway, W2. ✆ **020/7221-2535.** Reservations recommended. Main courses £5.50–£40 ($10–$74); dim sum £1.80–£5 ($3.30–$9); fixed-price dinner £23–£35 ($43–$65). AE, DC, MC, V. Mon–Thurs noon–11pm; Fri–Sat noon–11:30pm; Sun 11am–10pm; dim sum to 5pm daily. Tube: Bayswater or Queensway.

GREAT DEALS ON FIXED-PRICE MEALS

Tawana ★ THAI Elbow room is at a premium during the weekend crush at this very popular restaurant. Yet Tawana maintains a certain cool charm that sets it apart from the string of garish cheap joints on Queensway. And the food is the real thing. The hot and sour chicken soup, made with coconut milk, is so filling that you may not find room for curry. Tawana has none of the namby-pamby Western attitude to chile, so some dishes may render you temporarily speechless. With other dishes the flavors are subtle and delicious. As at many Thai restaurants, desserts are pretty missable, unless you need a sorbet to cool down your taste buds. There's a £10 ($18) minimum charge.

3 Westbourne Grove, W2. ✆ **020/7229-3785.** Reservations recommended. Main courses £5.50–£18 ($10–$33). Fixed-price meal £16 ($29). AE, DC, MC, V. Mon–Sat noon–3pm and 6–11pm; Sun noon–10pm. Tube: Bayswater or Queensway.

8 Marylebone

The Chapel ★ GASTROPUB/MODERN EUROPEAN The Chapel is one place that deserves to be called a gastropub. The food is ambitious, beautifully executed, and primarily modern European. The blackboard lists a handful of daily starters, from brie en croute to parma ham and Tuscan bean salad in a phyllo basket. Main courses that sound traditional (many don't) have a very modern twist, like the pork with caramelized apples and fluffy fishcakes. Don't graze too enthusiastically at the complimentary basket of delicious breads because the desserts are extremely wicked and deserve close attention. The interior is bright and spacious, but the bare-board floor makes it rather noisy. In the summer, head out to the garden where you can escape the cigarette smoke and sip a glass of wine (25 are available by the glass) or a pint of London Pride.

48 Chapel St., NW1. ✆ **020/7402-9220.** Main courses £8.50–£13 ($16–$25). AE, DC, MC, V. Daily noon–2:30pm and 7–10pm. Tube: Edgware Rd.

Giraffe ★ INTERNATIONAL The first thing staff see when they turn up at this hard-working restaurant is a queue of eager eaters, and that's at 8 o'clock in the morning! I defy anyone not to leave Giraffe in a warm glow of contentment, not only because of the delicious food, but also because of the friendly atmosphere (completely nonsmoking). Go with a group, and you could all be eating in a different country—from English herby sausages to Moroccan-spiced meat dishes to something with enough garlic to win you honorary French citizenship. Try a delicious fruit smoothie with your meal or a glass of wine. There's a kids' menu and lots of daily specials. The fixed-price evening meal is a great deal. Giraffe also has several other locations, including 46 Rosslyn Hill, NW3 (✆ **020/7435-0343;** Tube: Hampstead); 29 Essex Rd., N1 (✆ **020/7359-5999;** Tube: Angel), and a brand-new one in Royal Festival Hall.

6–8 Blandford St., W1. ✆ **020/7935-2333.** Reservations recommended, not accepted for weekend lunch. Main courses £4.95–£9.95 ($9–$18); fixed-price dinner Mon–Fri £6.95–£8.95 ($13–$17). AE, MC, V. Mon–Fri 8am–11pm; Sat 9am–11pm; Sun 9am–10:30pm. Tube: Baker St. or Regent's Park.

La Spighetta ★★ PIZZA & PASTA This little basement eatery is the better-value sister of Spiga in Covent Garden. It was "created," as the higher echelons of the restaurant world say, by Giorgio Locatelli, who is chef and part owner of Knightsbridge's illustrious and molto pricey Zafferano. The menu is as authentic and uncomplicated as the decor, using an Italian wood-fired oven for the pizzas. The ingredients are simple: mozzarella, artichoke, spicy salami, pecorino cheese, and so on, all melting together on superbly crispy bases. There are several pasta dishes and lots of meat and fish main courses to choose from, plus daily specials. The menu changes every week, but maybe you'll find the marvelous wind-dried tuna starter, one of several dishes that show La Spighetta's posh pedigree. Cheaper children's portions are available on request, though I doubt the kids would thank you for sparing them even one mouthful of the homemade ice cream. This place is justly popular for working lunches and for R&R after the day is done.

43 Blandford St., W1. ✆ **020/7486-7340.** Reservations recommended. Main courses £7–£13 ($13–$24). AE, MC, V. Mon–Sat noon–2:30pm; Sun–Thurs 6:30–10:30pm; Fri–Sat 6:30–11pm. Tube: Baker St.

SUPER-CHEAP EATS

Patogh IRANIAN If you like simple Persian cooking, you'll love Patogh. The kebabs are legendary. Left to marinate overnight, the organic lamb or chicken practically melts in the mouth. The skewers come on a huge circle of seeded bread, with yogurt dips and

Tips Good Old-fashioned Pub Grub

Swapping nicotine-stained wallpaper for chi-chi minimalist restaurant walls makes gastropub cuisine a lot pricier than honest no-frills pub grub. But budget travelers and traditionalists needn't despair. There are still lots of old-fashioned British boozers serving up great pub grub.

For a really hearty homemade meat pie, for about £6.50 ($12), try the **Salisbury,** 90 St. Martin's Lane, WC2 (✆ **020/7836-5863**). You can get hot food from 11am until 11pm (Sunday noon–10pm). Farther north, in Bloomsbury, there's a great place to stop after a visit to the British Museum. The **Museum Tavern,** 49 Great Russell St., WC1 (✆ **020/7242-8987**), can fix you up with a very decent beef-and-ale pie, or a ploughman's lunch for £5 to £9 ($9–$17) at any time of the day. Built as a jail in 1780, the **Nag's Head,** 53 Kinnerton St., SW1 (✆ **020/7235-1135**), is supposed to be the smallest pub in London. Wash down the shepherd's pie or sausages with one of the big range of on-tap real ales. The food will cost you £5 to £8 ($9–$15), a bargain in Belgravia. Meanwhile bar food really is pub grub at the **George Inn,** a 17th-century coaching inn owned by the National Trust at 77 Borough High St., SE1 (✆ **020/7407-2056**). Sausage and mash or a ploughman's lunch will set you back about £6 ($11), and there's an excellent range of real ales. Head south from London Bridge Tube station and it's on the left down a little alley.

Note: For more Great British Boozers, check out "The Drinking Game: Pubs & Wine Bars," in chapter 9, "London After Dark."

Middle-Eastern salad. If kebabs ain't your thing, there are plenty of other choices, from chicken pieces to a whole host of ready-prepared salads and starters. There's hummus, marinated tomato, and other *meze* (small entrees). You could stack a plate high without coming close to busting the budget. Patogh is unlicensed, too, so you can bring your own bottle of wine or beer, and you won't even be charged any corkage.

8 Crawford Place, W1. ✆ **020/7262-4015.** Reservations recommended. Main courses £6–£12 ($11–$22). No credit cards. Daily 1pm–midnight. Tube: Edgware Rd.

Quiet Revolution BRITISH DINER/SOUP Originally a soup manufacturer, Quiet Revolution has won awards for its certified organic concoctions like the Polska Tomato soup—suitable for vegans, 35 calories per 100 grams, 5 grams of carbohydrate, 1.3 grams of fat. It branched out into a daytime cafe-diner in 2000 to serve its super-healthy food direct to the public. No meat is served, but there are always good fish and veggie options such as ratatouille.

28 Weymouth St., off Marylebone High St., W1. ✆ **020/7487-5683.** Main courses £5.95–£9.95 ($11–$18); soups £3–£5.50 ($5.50–$10). MC, V. Mon–Fri 9am–7pm; Sat 9am–6pm. Tube: Baker St.

9 Soho & Chinatown

Andrew Edmunds ★ *Finds* MODERN BRITISH This charming Soho restaurant started life as a wine bar and is attached to the print gallery next door. Popular for business lunches by day, at night it becomes the haunt of romantic young couples eating dinner by candlelight. They have to whisper their sweet nothings because the tables are pretty close together. The handwritten menu changes frequently but always offers modern European cuisine in healthy portions. Menu offerings might include grilled sardines with balsamic vinegar, duck and lentil stew, white bean and lemon soup, or black pudding and caramelized apples with watercress salad and chive crème fraîche. The desserts are delicious classics, from tiramisu to almond tart.

46 Lexington St., W1. ✆ **020/7437-5708.** Reservations recommended. Main courses £7.95–£14 ($15–$25). MC, V. Mon–Fri 12:30–3pm and 6–10:45pm; Sat 1–3pm and 6–10:45pm; Sun 1–3pm and 6–10:30pm. Tube: Oxford Circus or Piccadilly Circus.

Aperitivo ★ ITALIAN This restaurant is the baby sister of the much-lauded Assaggi in Notting Hill, which I haven't included because it's so overpriced. Aperitivo certainly isn't that, and the quality is consistently high. The menu works like Spanish tapas, only here you accumulate small dishes of multiregional Italian cuisine—meat, fish, vegetables, and salads. It's a budget heaven in the form of a rather stylish restaurant. You can drop in at any time of day and spend as much or as little as you like. The idea is to order up lots of dishes and share them, reckoning on about two per person. The most unusual is poached egg and tomato baked in a parcel of Sardinian bread called *carta da musica*. Finish off with panna cotta, which is delicious. There's a new branch of Aperitivo in Camden at 30 Hawley Crescent, NW1 (✆ **020/7267-7755;** Tube: Camden Town).

41–45 Beak St., W1. ✆ **020/7287-2057.** Main courses £3.95–£9.50 ($7–$18). MC, V. Daily noon–11pm. Tube: Oxford Circus or Piccadilly Circus.

Golden Dragon CANTONESE The crowds of local Chinese diners who come here back up the claim that the Golden Dragon serves up some of the best dim sum in town—and dim sum is what you should stick to because the other dishes don't always live up to their promise. If you decide on dim sum, make sure to try the steamed scallop dumplings and prawn cheung fen. A real blowout shouldn't cost you more than £15 ($24), but you'll have to get here before 5pm. And reserve in advance, especially on Sundays when the place is packed. The service is variable because the staff is usually so busy.

28–29 Gerrard St., W1. ✆ **020/7734-2763.** Reservations recommended. Main courses £6.50–£25 ($12–$46); dim sum £1.80–£3.90 ($3.50–$7.25); fixed-price menus £13–£35 ($23–$65). AE, DC, MC, V. Mon–Thurs noon–11:30pm; Fri–Sat noon–midnight; Sun 11am–11pm. Tube: Leicester Sq.

Incognico ★★ MODERN FRENCH The quality of cooking at this restaurant has unfortunately dropped a notch, which is a real shame, but it's still worth visiting at lunchtime for the super-value £13 ($23) set menu. Incognico opened to showcase the superlative French cooking style of Michelin-star-winning Nico Ladenis, who's still the owner but now retired. Ladenis' signature dish, pan-fried foie gras with brioche and caramelized orange, is on the a la carte menu here as an expensive starter. Otherwise, Incognico prices compare favorably with other mid-range London restaurants. With its heavy paneling and starched white tablecloths, it looks like an international bourgeois brasserie. There are fish and vegetarian choices, such as Parmesan risotto with mushrooms.

117 Shaftesbury Ave., WC2 ✆ **020/7836-8866.** Reservations essential. Main courses £12–£25 ($13–$46); fixed-price lunch and pretheater meal £13 ($23). Cover £1.50 ($2.80). AE, DC, MC, V. Daily noon–3pm and 5:30–11:30pm. Tube: Leicester Sq. or Tottenham Court Rd.

Where to Dine in Soho & Chinatown

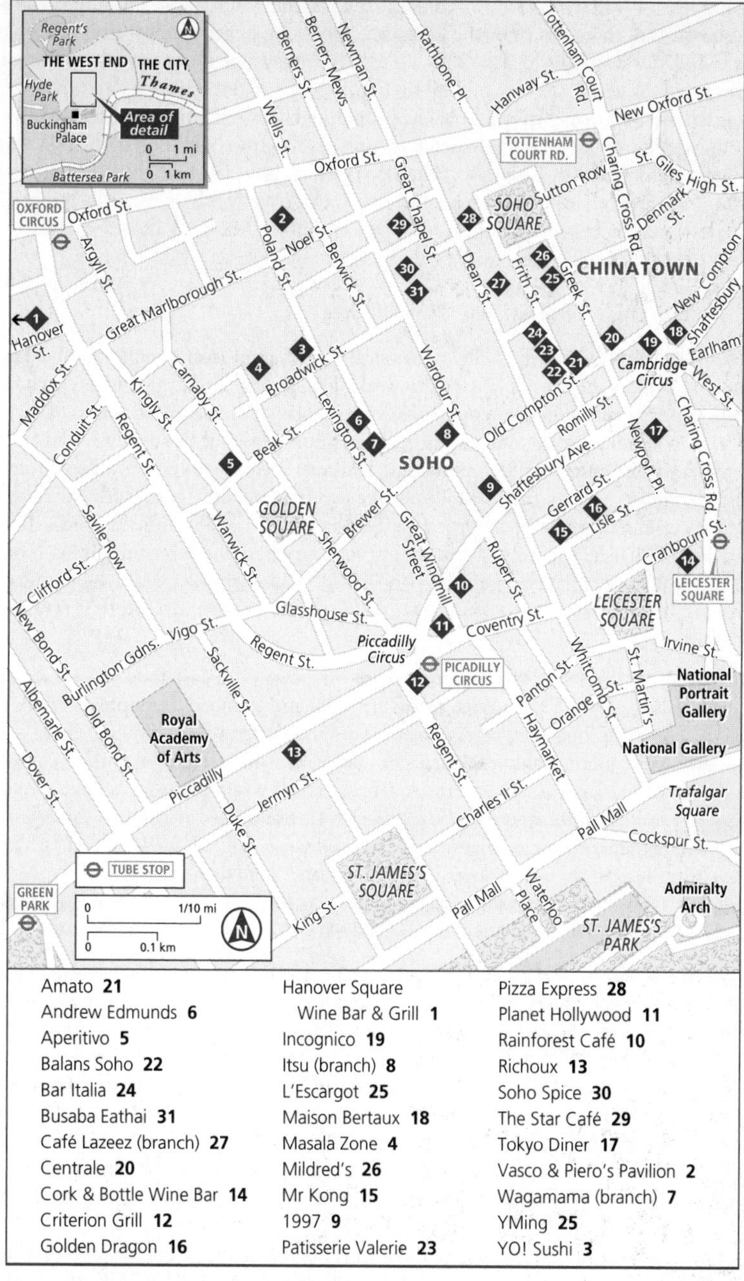

Mildred's ★ VEGETARIAN Mildred's is a smashing lunch spot that's open in the evenings, too, though it's not the best place for a long lingering meal (this is a small cafe, and you may have to share a table). Mildred's may look like a product of the current trend for healthy eating in London, but it's been around since the days when vegetarian meant lunatic fringe to most people and few restaurants offered meatless options. All the vegetarian ingredients are organically grown and used in the right season whenever possible. Legumes cooked every which way are a firm fixture, as are stir-fries. The menu changes every week but may include winners like pistachio and goat's cheese risotto or a broccoli, poppyseed, and lime burger. Mildred's also serves delicious desserts and organic wines. And it's completely nonsmoking.

45 Lexington St., W1. ✆ **020/7494-1634.** Reservations not accepted. Main courses £6.25–£7.95 ($13–$15). Mon–Sat noon–11pm. No credit cards. Tube: Tottenham Court Rd.

Mr Kong CANTONESE This rather shabby restaurant is so popular that it's busy long past midnight every night of the week. The cheaper fixed-price menu includes soup, a choice of three main courses—beef with black-bean sauce, for instance—and rice. The more expensive one covers four courses and is a lot better value. Over 150 dishes are listed on three different menus. The daily specials are generally a bit cheaper and less exotic. Or you can choose from the regular selection: Sliced pork, salted egg, and vegetable soup is a house specialty. The service is friendly, and the menu translated into English. The only caveat: try not to be seated in the basement dining room.

21 Lisle St., WC2. ✆ **020/7437-7341.** Reservations required for weekend dinners. Main courses £5.90–£26 ($11–$48); fixed-price dinner £10–£22 ($18–$41). AE, DC, MC, V. Daily noon–2:30am. Tube: Leicester Sq. or Piccadilly Circus.

Tokyo Diner ★ JAPANESE Come here for great value fast food in traditional, Japanese-diner style. The wooden tables are small and cramped, but nobody seems to mind. The bento boxes are a great value at around £10 ($16), and they include rice, noodle salad, salmon sashimi salad, and a main dish, which might be pork or chicken *tonkatsu,* or chicken, salmon, or mackerel teriyaki. If you really want to save money, make a meal from the *donburi*—boxes filled with rice topped with seasoned egg and chicken, perhaps, or chicken flambéed in teriyaki sauce. You can get sushi and sashimi, too. Tea is free, and Japanese beer is slightly cheaper here than at pubs.

2 Newport Place, WC2. ✆ **020/7434-1414.** Reservations only accepted on weekdays and for more than 6 people. Main courses £3.90–£13 ($7–$24); set lunch £4.90–£7.90 ($9–$15). MC, V. Daily noon–midnight. Tube: Leicester Sq.

YO! Sushi *Kids* SUSHI The relentless self-congratulation of this fast-expanding chain has become something of a turnoff, and the staff doesn't know much about the food that's being sold. But you can still enjoy this original Soho sushi bar with its blitz of brand messages because it remains a novel experience. Talking drink trolleys circle the restaurant like R2D2, and diners pick out what they want. Sushi-making robots turn out 1,200 pieces an hour, which circle around on a conveyor belt. The different-colored plates indicate the price. Do keep a running tally, or this could turn out to be a budget-buster. At the branches other than this one, kids eat for free from Monday to Friday, and they'll love it. There are scaled down and toned-down dishes for them, from chicken nuggets to fish fingers.

Other good lunchtime deals are the £5 ($9) bento box and a beer at **YO! Below,** the Japanese beer and sake hall downstairs at Poland Street (✆ **020/7439-3660**), and below the new YO! Sushi at 95 Farringdon Rd., EC1 (✆ **020/7841-0785** restaurant, or 020/7841-0790; Tube: Farringdon). This latter is now the biggest YO!, and it has a kids' eating zone. So does the one at the Harvey Nichols store in Knightsbridge, SW1 (✆ **020/7235-6114**). Others useful to know about are at Selfridges on Oxford Street, W1 (✆ **020/7318-3944**); the Whitelys shopping center in Queensway (✆ **020/7727-9293**); at Bloomsbury's Myhotel, 11–13 Bayley St., WC1 (✆ **020/ 7667-6000;** Tube: Goodge St. or Tottenham Court Rd.); and at County Hall on the South Bank by the London Eye (✆ **020/7928-8871;** Tube: Waterloo or Westminster), which is the only one that accepts reservations.

52 Poland St., W1. ✆ **020/7287-0443.** Sushi selections from £1.50–£5 ($2.80–$9) per plate. AE, DC, MC, V. Mon–Thurs noon–11pm; Fri–Sat noon–midnight; Sun noon–10:30pm. Tube: Oxford Circus. No smoking.

SUPER-CHEAP EATS

Centrale ITALIAN This ought to be the ideal choice for diners who've splurged on theater tickets and want a cheap eat. But beware: The portions at Centrale are so huge that a tired traveler might fall asleep halfway through the first act. This isn't a spot for a romantic assignation, or for people who don't like people, but the old-fashioned no-frills restaurant has a great deal of charm and a very loyal clientele. People in their night-out finery mix with students on a shoestring and business people snatching a bite, all crammed together on black vinyl banquettes at narrow, red Formica-topped tables. The starters are traditional budget menu items like minestrone soup. You can eat meat for the main course. But forget all that, and do what everyone else does and fill up on pasta. Often you'll get more pasta than whatever's supposed to go with it; the cheaper the ingredients, the cheaper the cost (mushroom is a good choice). And don't forget to bring a bottle of wine with you (corkage is 50p/90¢).

16 Moor St., W1. ✆ **020/7437-5513.** Main courses £3.75–£7.50 ($7–$14). No credit cards. Mon–Sat noon–10:30pm. Tube: Leicester Sq. or Tottenham Court Rd.

The Star Café ★ BRITISH DINER This ex-pub has been run by the same family for 70 years and is proud to boast being the oldest cafe in Soho. The walls of the main floor are hung with old enamel shop signs and radio sets. The no-frills menu includes

Sinful Soho: Dens of Delicious Iniquity

Whoever said the Brits are poker-faced in public and only sin behind closed doors had obviously never been to Soho. I'm not talking about sleazy strip joints, but the wicked delights of the neighborhood's famous patisseries. The French had to show them how to do it, but supposedly stodgy Londoners have taken to sweet flaky pastries, tarts, and cakes with a vengeance. Just watch the shameless hordes that flock here on a Sunday.

The most venerable patisserie is **Maison Bertaux,** 28 Greek St., W1 (✆ **020/7437-6007**), and I defy you to pass by its delectable window without wanting to dunk a brioche in a cup of coffee. **Patisserie Valerie,** 44 Old Compton St., W1 (✆ **020/7437-3466**), is *the* place to gawk at film and theater types who've fallen for its chocolate truffle cake. The crowds are smaller at **Amato,** 14 Old Compton St., W1 (✆ **020/7734-5733**), but its alcoholic chocolate-and-coffee mousse cake is to die for.

staples like jacket potatoes, toasted sandwiches, and pasta, with daily luncheon specials such as roast chicken with crispy bacon stuffing, steak and onion pie, or salmon filet with broccoli. Most people come for the all-day, full English breakfast, including vegetarians, who get a very superior spread with peppers and diced roast potatoes. Unfortunately, The Star Café closes after lunch and at the weekends.

22 Great Chapel St., W1. ✆ **020/7437-8778.** Main courses £4.95–£7.25 ($9–$13). MC, V. Mon–Fri 7am–4pm. Tube: Tottenham Court Rd.

GREAT DEALS ON FIXED-PRICE MEALS

Cork & Bottle Wine Bar INTERNATIONAL/WINE BAR This very unusual wine bar is in a cozy basement bar in the heart of London's theater district—don't go until after 8pm if you want a seat. There are about 25 wine selections available by the glass. The menu spans Pacific Rim, Afro-Caribbean, with some good British and European staples, too. It's a good value in the evening, as well as with the fixed-price lunch. The owner's other West End wine bar is closed on the weekends: **The Hanover Square Wine Bar & Grill,** 25 Hanover Sq., W1 (✆ **020/7408-0935;** Tube: Oxford Circus).

44–46 Cranbourn St., WC2. ✆ **020/7734-7807.** Main courses £4.50–£13 ($8–$24); bistro lunches £10–£12 ($18–$22). AE, DC, MC, V Mon–Sat 11am–11:30pm; Sun noon–10:30pm. Tube: Leicester Sq.

Masala Zone ★★ Kids INDIAN Like Mela in Shaftesbury Avenue, Masala Zone reacts against the determined upward mobility of London's Indian restaurants (never mind that its owners run Veeraswamy, one of the poshest of the lot). Masala Zone was one of the first restaurants that attempted to introduce Britain to the way India really eats at home—off *thalis* and at the roadside chaat stall. A thali is a fixed-price meal on a tray, including a curry, bowls of vegetables, dal, yogurt curry, rice, poppadums, chapattis, chutneys, and raita. The street food is often anglo-influenced comfort food, like *gosht dabalroti,* a lamb curry with white bread mixed in and topped by crispy fried noodles. Masala Zone is in the bottom of a concrete block near Carnaby Street. Two Indian tribal artists came all the way from Maharashtra to decorate the inside. Long teak tables invite shared eating. There's also a takeaway counter. Another plus: it's smoke free.

9 Marshall St., W1. ✆ **020/7287-9966.** Reservations not accepted. Main courses £5.50–£11 ($10–$20); fixed-price meals £6–£12 ($11–$21); children's meal, available at weekends, £4 ($7.50). MC, V. Mon–Fri noon–3pm and 5:30–11pm; Sat 12:30–11pm; Sun 12:30–3:30pm and 6–10:30pm. Tube: Oxford Circus.

Soho Spice ★ INDIAN The food at this successful modern 100-seat restaurant is as stylish as the decor. Antique spice jars and brilliantly colored powders line the window, and waiters wearing brightly colored kurtas serve diners seated at wood tables. The menu, strong on kebabs and curries, is supplemented by dishes focusing on a particular Indian regional cuisine. Punjabi, for example, means such dishes as *rara gosht,* lamb cooked in the tandoor and then stir-fried with cardamom and dried ground ginger masala. There's a new bar and a DJ on Friday and Saturday nights.

Amin Ali is also a partner in a cheap eat, **Busabai Eathai,** 106–110 Wardour St., W1 (✆ **020/7255-8686;** Tube: Piccadilly Circus, Tottenham Court Rd.), where tasty bowls of Thai noodle soup cost around £5 ($9).

124–6 Wardour St., W1. ✆ **020/7434-0808.** Main courses £9–£12 ($17–$21). AE, DC, MC, V. Mon–Tues noon–midnight; Wed–Sat noon–3am; Sun noon–10:30pm. Tube: Leicester Sq. or Tottenham Court Rd.

Vasco & Piero's Pavilion ★ ITALIAN This cozy, comfortable restaurant attracts a business and sophisticated older crowd who consider it their secret favorite hideaway. Unfortunately, so many of them have written glowingly about it in newspaper columns that you must book ahead. The Matteucci family has run the restaurant for 35 years, and the welcome is one of the warmest around. Vasco still does much of the cooking. The unpretentious cuisine is light on butter and cream, with flavors clear as a bell, whether marinated anchovies or asparagus perfectly cooked al dente. Many of its ingredients come from local producers in Umbria, except for the pasta, which they make themselves. The fixed-price menus change daily, and you can choose either two or three courses from a fantastic selection of seven or eight of each. Ask what's best that day, and order it. Calves' liver, allegedly the best in London, is a house specialty.

15 Poland St., W1. ✆ **020/7437-8774.** Reservations recommended. Main courses £9.50–£16 ($17–$29); fixed-price lunch £15 ($27); fixed-price dinners £21–£25 ($39–$46). AE, MC, V. Mon–Fri noon–3pm and 6–11pm; Sat 6–11pm. Tube: Oxford Circus.

PRETHEATER BARGAINS

L'Escargot Marco Pierre White ★★ TRADITIONAL FRENCH Dining in a Michelin one-star restaurant for £15 ($28) is a fantastic value. This is serious food, in seriously elegant surroundings, and you ought to dress up and make a real occasion of it. The walls are hung with works by Marc Chagall, Joan Miró, and David Hockney. The first-floor restaurant's 2- or 3-course fixed-price menu changes every week. Diners get to choose from three starters, main courses, and desserts, all classic French dishes perfectly executed. For example, you could have tartare of red mullet, followed by ravioli langoustine; or swap one of those for chocolate tart with praline ice cream. Choices are limited for vegetarians. Prices are higher in the upstairs Picasso Room, but the service is uniformly impeccable.

48 Greek St., W1. ✆ **020/7437-2679.** Reservations recommended. Main courses £13–£15 ($24–$28); fixed-price lunch and pretheater menu £15–£18 ($28–$33). AE, DC, MC, V. Mon–Fri 12:15–2:15pm; Mon–Sat 6–11:30pm; pretheater dinner served 6–7pm. Tube: Leicester Sq. or Tottenham Court Rd.

YMing ★ NORTHERN CHINESE Light and airy YMing is a tranquil antidote to more in-your-face local eateries. The large tables are prettily set, the service is smooth and unobtrusive, and the food is superb northern Chinese cuisine. Even though a la carte prices aren't outrageous, we recommend the three-course pretheater menu. The dishes change regularly but will include a choice of appetizer (crispy won ton, spring roll, tofu, or aubergine in spiced salt, for example), followed by a main course like fish slices in Chinese wine sauce or braised tofu. If duck, prawn, or lamb are on the list, go for those. The sizzling dishes are very popular: prawns with fresh mango, or lamb with fresh leek or with ginger and spring onion. You can sip YMing's excellent tea all the way through.

35–36 Greek St., W1. ✆ **020/7734-2721.** Main courses £5–£10 ($9–$18); fixed-price menu (served noon–6pm) £10 ($18). AE, DC, DISC, MC, V. Mon–Sat noon–11:45pm. Tube: Leicester Sq.

WORTH A SPLURGE

Criterion Grill ★ MODERN FRENCH/BRITISH It's almost worth coming to the Criterion just to see its Byzantine palace interior with a gold vaulted ceiling. The food—a mixture of modern French and British standards—doesn't quite match the grandeur of the decor, but it's generally quite good. You can order Brit faves like haddock or sausages or French faves like slow-roast duck with apple sauce or steak au poivre. This place is smack-dab on Piccadilly Circus, frequently jammed, and the staff is often pressed for time. The fixed-price lunches and dinners are a great deal.

224 Piccadilly, W1. ✆ **020/7930-0488.** Reservations essential. Main courses £11–£23 ($19–$42); fixed-price lunch and pretheater dinner 5:30–7pm £15–£18 ($28–$33). AE, DC, MC, V. Daily noon–2:30pm; Mon–Sat 5:30–11:30pm. Tube: Piccadilly Circus.

10 Mayfair & St. James's

Browns TRADITIONAL BRITISH Browns takes the brasserie idea and makes it terribly English. The food is pretty predictable and not terribly inspired, but it's reasonably priced, which is rare in Mayfair, where restaurants tend to cater to the super-affluent and child-free. Browns is divided into two sections, filled with wood paneling and mirrors. The restaurant is at the back beyond the bar, which is a popular after-work meeting point. The food ranges from pastas, salads, and sandwiches to main courses such as steak, mushroom, and Guinness pie. There are lighter, more modern dishes, too, like chargrilled chicken breast with tarragon butter. There are six other branches: the most central is located at 82 St. Martins Lane, WC2 (✆ **020/7497-5050;** Tube: Leicester Sq.).

47 Maddox St., W1. ✆ **020/7491-4565.** Hot sandwiches and main courses £7.95–£17 ($15–$31). AE, DC, MC, V. Mon–Sat noon–11:30pm; Sun noon–10:30pm. Tube: Oxford Circus.

Richoux *Kids* AFTERNOON TEA/TRADITIONAL BRITISH Richoux is an old-fashioned tearoom and restaurant, a place that won't win any cooking awards but will always have loyal clients who like its pleasant, non-fussy atmosphere and welcoming attitude towards children. The menu is loaded with old school favorites such as fish cakes, Welsh rarebit, fish and chips, and shepherds pie, but also makes a bow to France, Italy, and Asia. You can also get an all-day breakfast or a traditional afternoon tea.

172 Piccadilly, W1. ✆ **020/7493-2204.** Main courses £5.95–£19 ($11–$34); fixed-price lunch and dinner £16–£18 ($29–$33); afternoon teas £7.95–£15 ($15–$28). AE, DC, MC, V. Mon–Fri 7am–7pm; Sat 7:30am–9pm; Sun 8am–6pm. Tube: Piccadilly Circus.

Suze in Mayfair ★ PACIFIC RIM You won't find a friendlier restaurant (or wine bar) in Mayfair, and the New Zealand–inspired cooking may surprise and inspire you. For starters, sample the succulent green-tipped mussels from New Zealand, a house specialty. Then you can either choose a sharing platter (vegetarian, seafood, antipasti, or cheese), something simple from the light menu (like a New Zealand "pokeno" pie with lamb, or go for something more substantial like fresh Australasian fish with chips and salad. For dessert you are compelled to try the Pavlova, another New Zealand house specialty, made with meringue and topped with fresh fruit.

41 N. Audley St., W1. ✆ **020/7491-3237.** Main courses £6.95–£15 ($12–$28); platters to share £4.95–£13 ($9–$23); light menu £4.95–£11 ($9–$20). AE, DC, MC, V. Mon–Sat 11am–11pm. Tube: Marble Arch.

SUPER-CHEAP EATS

Mô Tearoom NORTH AFRICAN You'll still marvel at the exuberantly Moorish decor, crammed with jewel-colored glass lights and copper urns, but I'm sorry to report that the food just ain't what it used to be. It's a real pity because the Tearoom was such a delightful spot to dine. It still straddles the gap between daytime cafe and evening restaurant, serving alcohol and staying open late. The food is still a relatively good value, especially for Mayfair, with Moroccan staples such as hummus, goat's cheese, and meat-filled pancakes. The teas are a bit sweet but fragrantly minty.

If you want really good Moroccan cooking, you'll have to try the more expensive **Momo,** next door at 25 Heddon St.; it's the "parent" of the Tearoom. Beaded curtains and sensual swathes of fabrics add a tantalizing casbah mystique, and the food is much better than at the Tearoom. Main courses cost £15 to £20 ($27–$36), while the fixed-price lunch is £17 ($32). You must book ahead, at the number below. The restaurant is open Monday through Saturday from noon to 2:30pm and 7 to 11pm, Sundays 7 to 10:30pm.

23 Heddon St., W1. ✆ **020/7434-4040.** Reservations not accepted. Main courses £3.50–£5 ($6.50–$9). AE, DC, MC, V. Mon–Wed noon–10:15pm; Thurs–Sat noon–midnight. Tube: Piccadilly Circus.

GREAT DEALS ON FIXED-PRICE MEALS

Veeraswamy ★ INDIAN This will probably be the most extraordinary Indian restaurant you'll ever encounter. Established in 1926 by a general and an Indian princess, Veeraswamy claims to be the oldest Indian restaurant in London. Over the years, it's been the haunt of princes and potentates, from the Prince of Wales to King Hussein and Indira Gandhi. Nowadays it's very hip, painted in vibrant colors, with frosted-glass panels dividing up the sections and ultramodern furniture. For starters, the stir-fried mussels with coconut and Kerala spices are sublime. For an exotic and only mildly hot choice, try the shanks of lamb curried in bone stock and spices. Unless you're in the mood to splurge, this isn't the place to sample lots of different dishes. Go for a great-value fixed-price menu and enjoy the best of new Indian cuisine. **Masala Zone,** its new sister restaurant in Soho, is much cheaper and much praised (p. 138).

99–101 Regent St., off Swallow St., W1. ✆ **020/7734-1401.** Reservations recommended. Main courses £10–£18 ($18–$33); lunch and pre-/posttheater menu £14–£16 ($25–$29); Sun menu £16 ($30). AE, DC, MC, V. Mon–Sat noon–2:30pm and 5:30–11:30pm; Sun 12:30–3pm and 5:30–10:30pm. Tube: Piccadilly Circus.

WORTH A SPLURGE

Mirabelle ★★ MODERN EUROPEAN As long as you don't indulge your urge to wash down your meal with a £30,000 ($48,000) bottle of 1847 Chateau d'Yquem, this is the best-value mouthful of Marco Pierre White's cooking you will ever eat. The lower-priced, two-course, fixed-price lunch may be a splurge, but it costs less than most of his main courses. And the food is sensational, made with tricky ingredients timed perfectly. The entrance to Mirabelle is pretty nondescript but behind it lies a lounge decorated with tongue-in-cheek murals, then the long bar, and finally the brasserie-style restaurant. Diners are a little cramped but don't seem to care. On sunny days, you can sit out on the terrace. The menu changes seasonally but includes MPW classics. The two courses could be terrine of duck with foie gras and potatoes in a beetroot dressing, and then ballotine of salmon or caramelized wing of skate with winkles (mollusks) and *jus* a la Parisienne. A few extra pounds will get you a dessert or a selection of creamy French cheeses. This offer is only on at lunchtime.

56 Curzon St., W1. ✆ **020/7499-4636.** Reservations essential. Main courses £15–£25 ($27–$46); fixed-price lunch £17–£20 ($31–$36). AE, MC, V. Daily noon–2:30pm and 6–11:30pm. Tube: Green Park.

11 Bloomsbury, Holborn & Fitzrovia

The Bar at Villandry ★ INTERNATIONAL This new offshoot of the famous gourmet hotspot is a godsend for budget travelers. You can swing by any time of day, without a reservation. The menu changes every week and picks the best of everything in season. In the early evening, the bar raids the Villandry food store for produce to make its snacks. The typically English ploughman's lunch with farmhouse Stilton and onion marmalade is pricier than the average pub version, but the cheese is creamy and moist. Tiger prawns with chile-and-lemon dipping sauce could use a little more oomph. All in all, The Bar at Villandry is an exuberant place where you can feel wicked and wholesome at the same time.

The restaurant with its big glass windows serves Modern British cuisine at lunch every day and dinner from Monday to Saturday. It is totally nonsmoking and it's pretty expensive but the food is wonderful. The restaurant is open for lunch and dinner Monday

Where to Dine in the West End

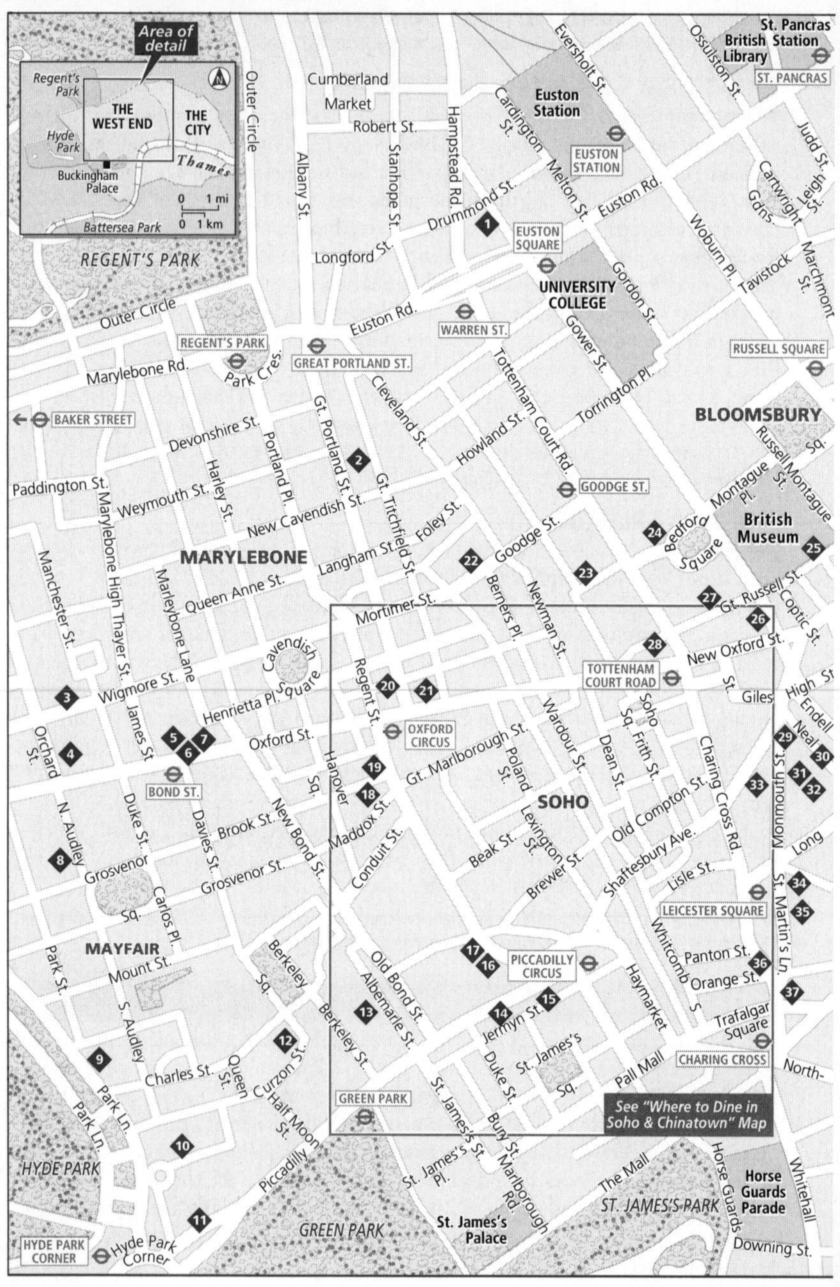

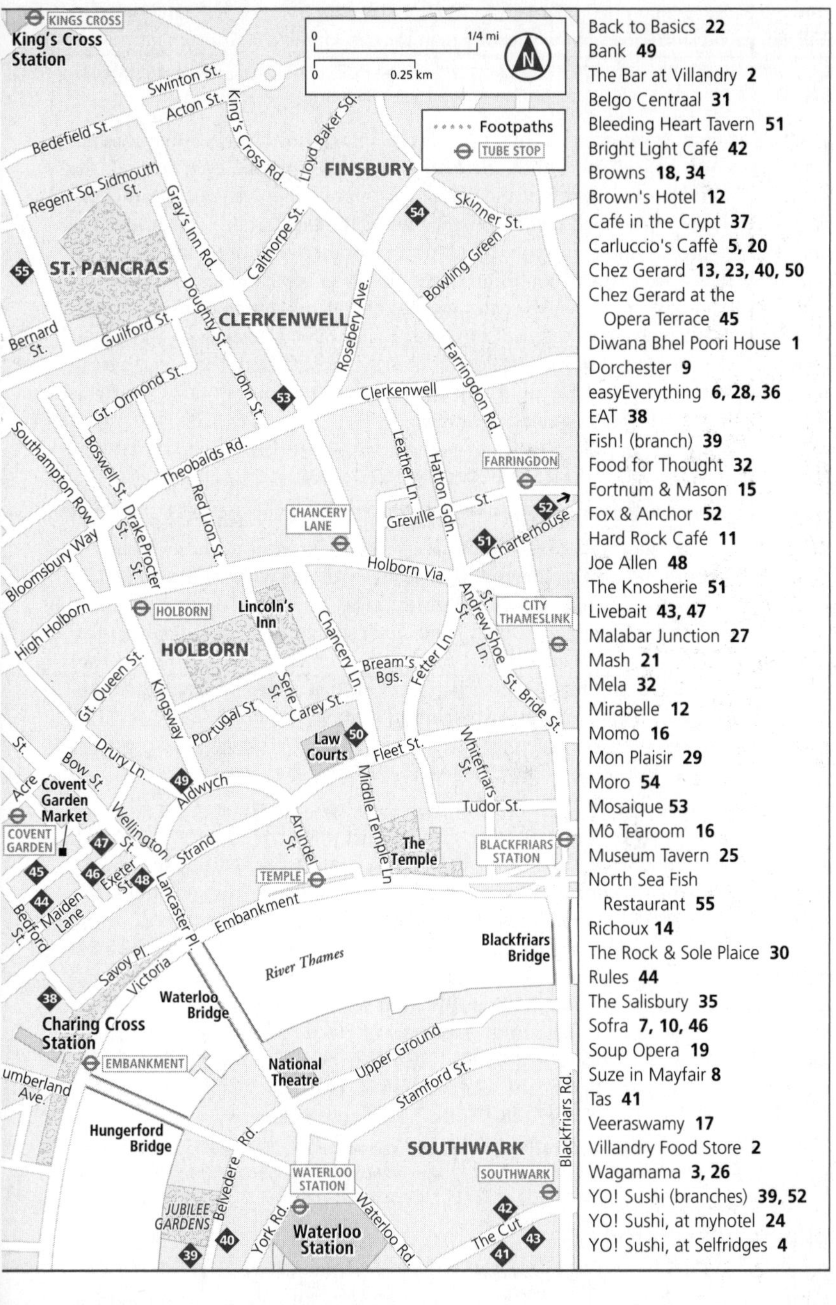
KINGS CROSS
King's Cross Station
0
1/4 mi
0
0.25 km
N
Footpaths
TUBE STOP
Swinton St.
Acton St.
Bedefield St.
King's Cross Rd.
Lloyd Baker Sq.
FINSBURY
Regent Sq.
Sidmouth St.
Gray's Inn Rd.
Calthorpe St.
Skinner St.
Bowling Green
ST. PANCRAS
Doughty St.
Rosebery Ave.
CLERKENWELL
Bernard St.
Guilford St.
Farringdon Rd.
Gt. Ormond St.
John St.
Clerkenwell
Southampton Row
Boswell St.
Theobalds Rd.
Leather Ln.
Hatton Gdn.
FARRINGDON
Red Lion St.
CHANCERY LANE
Greville St.
Charterhouse St.
Bloomsbury Way
Drake St.
Procter St.
Holborn Via.
St. Andrew St.
HOLBORN
Lincoln's Inn
CITY THAMESLINK
High Holborn
HOLBORN
Chancery Ln.
Shoe Ln.
Gt. Queen St.
Kingsway
Bream's Bgs.
Fetter Ln.
St. Bride St.
Serle St.
Carey St.
Portugal St
Law Courts
Whitefriars St.
Acre St.
Bow St.
Drury Ln.
Fleet St.
Covent Garden Market
Aldwych
Middle Temple Ln
Tudor St.
COVENT GARDEN
Wellington St.
Strand
Arundel St.
The Temple
BLACKFRIARS STATION
Exeter St.
TEMPLE
Lancaster Pl.
Bedford St.
Maiden Lane
Embankment
Blackfriars Bridge
Savoy Pl.
Victoria
River Thames
Waterloo Bridge
Charing Cross Station
EMBANKMENT
National Theatre
Upper Ground
Cumberland Ave.
Stamford St.
Blackfriars Rd.
Hungerford Bridge
Rd.
SOUTHWARK
Belvedere
WATERLOO STATION
SOUTHWARK
JUBILEE GARDENS
York Rd.
Waterloo Station
Waterloo Rd.
The Cut
Back to Basics 22
Bank 49
The Bar at Villandry 2
Belgo Centraal 31
Bleeding Heart Tavern 51
Bright Light Café 42
Browns 18, 34
Brown's Hotel 12
Café in the Crypt 37
Carluccio's Caffè 5, 20
Chez Gerard 13, 23, 40, 50
Chez Gerard at the Opera Terrace 45
Diwana Bhel Poori House 1
Dorchester 9
easyEverything 6, 28, 36
EAT 38
Fish! (branch) 39
Food for Thought 32
Fortnum & Mason 15
Fox & Anchor 52
Hard Rock Café 11
Joe Allen 48
The Knosherie 51
Livebait 43, 47
Malabar Junction 27
Mash 21
Mela 32
Mirabelle 12
Momo 16
Mon Plaisir 29
Moro 54
Mosaique 53
Mô Tearoom 16
Museum Tavern 25
North Sea Fish Restaurant 55
Richoux 14
The Rock & Sole Plaice 30
Rules 44
The Salisbury 35
Sofra 7, 10, 46
Soup Opera 19
Suze in Mayfair 8
Tas 41
Veeraswamy 17
Villandry Food Store 2
Wagamama 3, 26
YO! Sushi (branches) 39, 52
YO! Sushi, at myhotel 24
YO! Sushi, at Selfridges 4

through Saturday noon to 3pm and 6 to 10:30pm, Sunday from 11:30am to 4pm. The Villandry food store closes an hour earlier than the bar.

170 Great Portland St., W1. ✆ **020/7631-3131.** Main courses in bar £5.50–£10 ($10–$18); main courses in restaurant £11–£22 ($19–$41). AE, MC, V. Mon–Sat 8am–11:30pm; Sun 4–9:30pm. Tube: Great Portland St.

North Sea Fish Restaurant ★ FISH & CHIPS Locals love North Sea's version of what is, of course, the national dish. Here the look is country-cozy, even down to the stuffed fish on the walls. Diners at the rear of the chippie sit on velvet-covered chairs at wooden tables. You'll find a good mix of cabbies on a tea break, local academics, and tourists here. Dining in, you could do two starters—smoked mackerel and scampi, perhaps—or one and a portion of deliciously crispy fat chips, for under £9 ($17). The best deal, though, is the enormous seafood platter, which comes with bite-size, battered pieces of lots of different sorts of fish and seafood. You can go for straight cod, of course, or skate, haddock, plaice, all brought in fresh from Billingsgate every morning. And after all that I'll salute any diner who's got room for one of the traditional desserts. North Sea also does takeaway.

7–8 Leigh St., WC1. ✆ **020/7387-5892.** Reservations recommended for dinner. Main courses £7.90–£17 ($15–$31). AE, DC, MC, V. Mon–Sat noon–2:30pm and 5:30–10:30pm. Tube: Russell Sq. or King's Cross.

Mosaique ★ MEDITERRANEAN Tourists staying on the beaten track never find this wonderful restaurant in Holborn, but the people who work in the area know it well. The interior is bright and cheerful, with yellow walls and white tablecloths glowing under skylights. The menu choices feature dishes from all across the Mediterranean region, prepared with an assured hand. You can dine here on the mezes, such as grilled halloumi or tabbouleh, or feast on a lamb or chicken "shish" (shish kebab) served with vegetables and rice. Vegetarian choices include risotto primavera and vegetable moussaka. At night a jazz pianist adds to the ambience.

73 Gray's Inn Rd., WC1. ✆ **020/7404-7553.** Main courses £7.50–£15 ($14–$28); mezes £2.95–£3.95 ($5.50–$7.50). AE, MC, V. Mon–Fri noon–midnight; Sat 5pm–midnight. Tube: Chancery Lane.

Wagamama ★ *Kids* JAPANESE NOODLES I eat at one or more of the Wagamamas every time I'm in London and crave the yaki soba when I'm away. At this branch and the one in Soho, stairs lead down to a dining room set up with ranks of long shared tables like a traditional Japanese noodle bar; it's easy on kids and adults, but expect to queue at peak hours. The thread noodles come in soups, pan-fried, or else served with various toppings. The menu actually tells you to slurp because the extra oxygen adds to the taste. There's a special fixed-price menu that includes a drink and an inexpensive kids' menu, too. You probably won't want to linger too long in the bus-station bustle. Wagamama is also in the basement of Harvey Nichols (p. 219); at 10a Lexington St., W1 (✆ **020/7292-0990**); 101a Wigmore St., W1 (✆ **020/7409-0111**); 26a Kensington High St., W8 (✆ **020/7376-1717**); and 11 Jamestown Rd., Camden Town, NW1 (✆ **020/7428-0800**). All are nonsmoking.

4a Streatham St. (off Coptic St.), WC1. ✆ **020/7323-9223.** Main courses £5.50–£9.25 ($10–$17); fixed-price meals £11–£12 ($20–$21); kids' menu £3.50 ($6.50). AE, MC, V. Mon–Sat noon–11pm; Sun noon–10pm. Tube: Tottenham Court Rd.

SUPER-CHEAP EATS

Carluccio's Caffè ★ *Kids* ITALIAN Antonio Carluccio was one of the first celebrity chefs in Britain. That the locals no longer think of Italian cuisine simply as pizza and soggy lasagna is largely due to him. The cafe uses many imported ingredients and still manages to be a megacheap eat. Make a quick lunch stop for soup and antipasti, or come for an evening reviver. Even if you choose the most expensive items for each course—a huge plate of antipasti, followed by moist grilled swordfish, then a culinary tour of regional Italian cheeses—and have the most expensive aperitif, glass of wine with the meal, and coffee, you'd still spend under £35 ($64). Choose the cheapest, and it would be under £18 ($33), including drinks. There are cheaper dishes for kids, and the deli can provide top picnic pickings. There are eight branches scattered all over London.

8 Market Place, W1. ✆ **020/7636-2228.** Main courses £4.95–£11 ($10–$20). AE, MC, V. Mon–Fri 7:30am–11pm; Sat 10am–11pm; Sun 10am–10pm. Tube: Oxford Circus.

Diwana Bhel Poori House SOUTH INDIAN It's hardly worth pulling out your credit card to pay for a meal at Diwana Bhel Poori House. The buffet lunch is still under a fiver and surprisingly good if you avoid the oilier dishes. At other times, you'll be hard pressed to spend more than £10 ($18) a head and can set up your own buffet of South Indian vegetarian dishes for everyone to share. The *dosas*—semolina pancakes filled with spicy potato and vegetables—are a delight. If you go for the fixed-price *thali,* hold back from ordering anything else because it's a bonanza of breads, bhajees, dal, rice, vegetables, and pickles. Diwana Bhel Poori House has a sister restaurant across the road, Chutney's, but it's more expensive. And this one is unlicensed: you can bring wine, and there's no corkage fee.

121 Drummond St., NW1. ✆ **020/7387-5556.** Main courses £4.95–£6.50 ($9–$12); buffet lunch £4.50 ($8); fixed-price menu £6.50 ($12). AE, DC, MC, V. Daily noon–11:30pm. Tube: Euston or Warren St.

GREAT DEALS ON FIXED-PRICE MEALS

Malabar Junction ★ SOUTH INDIAN After a bar meal here I can almost guarantee that you'll want to come back. Okay, so the choice is limited—chicken, lamb, or vegetarian curry—but a bumper plate of curry for just £3.50 ($6.50)? This attractive restaurant serves South Indian cuisine, specifically from Kerala. Behind an unprepossessing entrance, the domed dining room is furnished with potted palms, and exudes a languid tropical air. In addition to curry, the four-page menu features a long list of mix-and-match house specialties: masala *dosa,* a traditional Kerala pancake, filled with potato masala and served with *sambar* and chutney; and *rasa vada,* a lentil doughnut in a hot spicy tomato and tamarind broth. Fish is another specialty, cooked in combinations of coconut, turmeric, ginger, chile, garlic, cumin and curry leaves. Every dish is a taste sensation: Try the green bananas flavored with spices and onions. After 7pm, the minimum check is £10 ($18).

107 Great Russell St., WC1. ✆ **020/7580-5230.** Reservations essential. Main courses £7.50–£11 ($14–$19); fixed-price bar meal (served noon–5pm) £3.50 ($6.50). AE, MC, V. Daily noon–3pm and 6–11:30pm (until 11pm Sun). Tube: Tottenham Court Rd.

WORTH A SPLURGE

Back to Basics ★★ SEAFOOD You don't have to splurge to eat here, but that means forgoing a fishy main course because these start at £13 ($24). The daily-changing menu, chalked up on the blackboard, always lists at least 12 dishes created from whatever was freshest that day at the market. The flavors are modern European, from pesto and sun-dried tomatoes, to chili, saffron, ginger, melted goat cheese, or honey mustard. The vegetable of the day is included with the sausage platters, lamb, chicken, and beef (but not with fish), making these a very good value. If it's warm, you can sit outside.

Surf 'n' Slurp @ the Best Internet Cafes

The handy **www.netcafeguide.com** has a pretty good London listing, including the **easyInternetCafe** chain. There are 18 of these giant Internet cafes in the capital—simple sandwiches (£3–£5/$5.50–$9.25) and drinks are available (the Subway sandwich chain has moved into some locations, and in others, the cafe has moved into McDonald's). But cafe is really a misnomer, as the hundreds of screens in the largest locations make them look like telemarketing sweatshops, and you don't hear any conversation, just the clicking of keyboards. The charging system is radical because surfers buy credit, not minutes. The minimum spend is £2 ($3.70), and the amount of time you get for that is in inverse proportion to how busy the branch is. The rate is adjusted every 5 minutes and posted on video screens, a bit like a stock exchange. Your ticket has a user ID, which notes the current rate when you first log on. That becomes your rate. You'll never pay more, but if things quiet down your credit will buy more time—a pound could be worth up to 6 hours, or so they claim. easyEverything never closes so avoid afternoons and early evenings, and surf with the creatures of the night and early morning. Check www.easyeverything.com for new branches to add to this list: 358 Oxford St., W1 (Tube: Bond St.); 9–16 Tottenham Court Rd., W1 (Tube: Tottenham Court Rd.); 160–166 Kensington High St. (Tube: Kensington High St.); 456–459 Strand, WC2 (Tube: Charing Cross); and 9–13 Wilton Rd., SW1 (Tube: Victoria). As befitting a large chain, the telephone number for all locations is ✆ **020/7241-9000.**

Note: You can send short e-mails up to about 90 words for **free** from any **i-plus** electronic information kiosk, and you don't need to have your own e-address. But this is one-way communication, only, and the touch-screen is irritating if you're used to typing on a keyboard. To find out where the nearest kiosk is, see "Visitor Information," in chapter 3.

21a Foley St., W1. ✆ **020/7436-2181.** Reservations essential for lunch. Main courses £13–£16 ($24–$29). AE, DC, MC, V. Daily noon–3pm; Mon–Sat 6–10:30pm. Tube: Goodge St.

Mash ★ MODERN EUROPEAN You splurge here for the buzz rather than for ambrosial food. Oliver Peyton opened this sleek and gargantuan resto-deli in 1998. It was one of London's first microbreweries, with huge tanks visible at the back of the first-floor cafe. Couches invite customers to linger. The cuisine is modern Mediterranean-Italian, of sorts: Paper-thin pizzas, with non-trad toppings such as crispy duck, cucumber, Asian greens, and hoisin sauce, appear from a wood-fired grill. Main courses include standards such as whole sea bass with mussels and bean cassoulet, and a lamb burger with apple, mango, and mint relish. This is a great place to come for a full-works brunch on the weekend: Your choice of Mash menu, American, or vegetarian costs £10 ($18). In the evening you can also dine unsplurgily on bar snacks.

19–21 Great Portland St., W1. ✆ **020/7637-5555.** Main courses £9.50–£17 ($18–$32); bar snacks 6–11pm £2–£6 ($3.70–$11); brunch £10 ($18). AE, DC, MC, V. Restaurant: Mon–Fri noon–3:30pm; Sat–Sun noon–4pm; Mon–Sat 6–11pm. Bar: Mon–Sat 11am–2am; Sun noon–4pm. Tube: Oxford Circus.

12 Covent Garden & the Strand

The Rock & Sole Plaice ★ FISH & CHIPS Endell Street is a peaceful oasis only one block away from Covent Garden's unrelenting crowds. But it's best to avoid The Rock & Sole Plaice in the early evenings, when it's crowded with theatergoers. It opened in 1871 and claims to be London's oldest surviving fish-and-chips shop. The decor is very Covent Garden, with theatrical posters and pavement tables. The Dover sole certainly has to be the cheapest in town at £11 ($18), and the other fish are half that price. Choose from halibut, mackerel, tuna, haddock, plaice, or cod. If you've never tried skate, then do so here–it's a moist, flaky fish with a wonderful flavor. The chips are thick and wedge-shaped, and you can add on mushy peas and pickled onions. For non-fish-eaters, there's steak-and-kidney and several other pies, plus sausage in batter.

47 Endell St., WC2. ✆ **020/7836-3785.** Reservations recommended for dinner. Fish and chips: eat in £8 ($15); takeout £6 ($11). Main courses £8–£14 ($15–$25). MC, V. Mon–Sat 11:30am–11pm (11:45pm for takeout); Sun noon–10pm. Tube: Covent Garden.

SUPER-CHEAP EATS

Café in the Crypt BRITISH DINER Right on Trafalgar Square, this is a great place to grab a bite to eat between a visit to the National Gallery and marching off down The Mall to Buckingham Palace. Or pop in with the kids after a session at the church's brass-rubbing center. Simple healthy food costs a lot less here than at more commercial places, and the subterranean ambience is sublime. It's a self-service cafeteria, where diners choose from a big salad bar and a choice of two traditional main courses—one might be shepherd's pie. The other light-lunch options include filled rolls and delicious cups of soup. The menu changes daily, but one fixture is that most traditional of British desserts, bread-and-butter pudding (bread soaked in eggs and milk with currants or sultanas and then oven-baked). The door to the crypt is on the right-hand side of the church.

St. Martin-in-the-Fields, Duncannon St., WC2. ✆ **020/7839-4342.** Rolls and sandwiches £2.50–£3.50 ($4.60–$6.50); main courses £5.95–£7.50 ($11–$14); fixed-price meal £5.25 ($10). No credit cards. Mon–Wed 10am–7:30pm; Thurs–Sat 10am–10:15pm. Tube: Charing Cross.

Food for Thought VEGETARIAN An enduring stalwart of the vegetarian movement, Food for Thought manages to lure in a broad clientele because of its unpreachy wholesome food and very cheap prices. It's a pop-in kind of a place, and you're best off popping in for brunch or maybe a strawberry scone for tea because it's mobbed both at lunchtime when all dishes are £3.80 ($7) and for the £6 ($11) evening special. The decor is simple with pine tables, fresh flowers, and original art on the walls. The menu always features a quiche and a vegetable stir-fry. Otherwise, it will have a few salads, stews, and hot dishes, always with vegan and gluten-free options. The desserts look irresistible and in the eating, most manage to disguise their healthy virtuousness. The cafe is unlicensed, so bring your own bottle: There's no corkage fee.

31 Neal St., WC2. ✆ **020/7836-0239.** Main courses £3–£6.50 ($5.50–$12). No credit cards. Mon–Sat 9:30am–8:30pm; Sun noon–5pm. Tube: Covent Garden. No smoking.

GREAT DEALS ON FIXED-PRICE MEALS

Belgo Centraal BELGIAN Blatant concept restaurants often have a very short life span, but the Belgian national dish of *moules, frites,* and *bière* (mussels, fries, and beer), served at long refectory tables by staff dressed as monks, has become a London dining staple. The place became famous because it served a good kilo pot of mussels, prepared any one of three ways. Nonseafood dishes are featured on the fixed-price lunch menu. Unfortunately, the food quality here has dropped. The best thing about Belgo Centraal now is the great Belgian beer—you might want to skip the food entirely.

Opening times and meal deals vary from branch to branch, so call ahead to check: **Belgo Noord,** 71 Chalk Farm Rd., NW1 (© **020/7681-8182;** Tube: Chalk Farm); **Belgo Zuid,** 124 Ladbroke Grove, W10 (© **020/8982-8400;** Tube: Ladbroke Grove); and the **Bierdrome,** 173 Upper St., NW1 (© **020/7226-5835;** Tube: Highbury, Islington, or Angel).

50 Earlham St., WC2. © **020/7813-2233.** Reservations recommended. Main courses £8.75–£18 ($16–$33); lunch £5.95 ($11). AE, DC, MC, V. Mon–Thurs noon–11pm; Fri–Sat noon–11:30pm; Sun noon–10:30pm. Tube: Covent Garden.

Chez Gerard at the Opera Terrace TRADITIONAL FRENCH From a conservatory on top of the old market, diners look down at the throngs of people in Covent Garden Piazza. The clientele has a definite air of affluence, especially in the evening, yet the fixed-price brasserie lunch menu is a remarkable value. The only problem is the cuisine, which is traditional French with little and sometimes no finesse. For the budgetarily challenged, the bar has a short but decent menu of hot dishes, platters, and salads. It also has tables outside, but they're hard to nab and you can't make reservations.

There are eight other branches in London, including a very useful one near the London Eye and County Hall on the South Bank, at 9 Belvedere Rd., SE1 (© **020/7202-8470;** Tube: Waterloo). Otherwise, try: 31 Dover St., W1 (© **020/7499-8171;** Tube: Green Park); 119 Chancery Lane, WC2 (© **020/7405-0290;** Tube: Chancery Lane); or 8 Charlotte St., W1 (© **020/7636-4975;** Tube: Tottenham Court Rd., Goodge St.).

45 East Terrace, The Market, The Piazza, Covent Garden, WC2. © **020/7379-0666.** Reservations recommended. Main courses £10–£15 ($18–$28); fixed-price brasserie lunch 11am–5pm £8 ($15); fixed-price restaurant meals 5:30–7pm £13–£17 ($25–$31). Cover charge £1.50 ($2.20). AE, DC, MC, V. Mon–Sat 11am–11:30pm; Sun noon–10:30pm. Tube: Covent Garden.

Mela ★★ INDIAN In 2001 this place won the Moet & Chandon award as best Indian restaurant in London. It claims to take its inspiration from Wali Gali, where Delhi's workers go to refuel at midday from a food stall on the street. Lunch here is a fantastic deal: curry or dal of the day, with bread, pickle, and chutney for under £2 ($3.20). That's less than you'd pay for a sandwich in this neck of the woods. Pay a little more and you can build your own version, from lots of different breads and toppings, culminating in the bargain-for-under-a-fiver, which has rice and salad thrown in, too. This is a great way for curry novices to have a cheap taster—and to see it being made in the open kitchen. But do come back in the evening for a proper go at the innovative Indian country cuisine. Early birds can get a three-course pretheater menu. The word *mela* means fair, and Mela the restaurant is energetic in its efforts to create a festive atmosphere.

152–156 Shaftesbury Ave., WC2. © **020/7836-8635.** Main courses £4.95–£19 ($10–$35); light lunches £1.95–£4.95 ($3.60–$9); pretheater menu £11 ($20). AE, MC, V. Mon–Sat noon–11:30pm; Sun noon–10:30pm. Tube: Leicester Sq.

PRE- & POSTTHEATER BARGAINS

Bank Aldwych ★ MODERN EUROPEAN The chefs are part of the noisy frenetic performance here, rushing around in the kitchen behind a big glass window. Bank Aldwych *was* a bank until an extremely hip conversion stripped bare the structure, put in a suspended, armor-plated ceiling, and turned it into London's most stylish brasserie. You could come here for the weekend brunch, but it's better to feast early or late on the set menu. A great value for either two or three courses, the seasonal cuisine brings together Continental and Southeast Asian influences, from seared rare spiced tuna with mango salad to roast rabbit with couscous and spiced crab. The only quibbles are that the service can be too quick and the tables are close together. Bank Aldwych recently replicated itself in Victoria: 45 Buckingham Gate, SW1 (same phone).

1 Kingsway, WC2. ✆ **020/7379-9797.** Reservations recommended. Main courses £11–£21 ($20–$39); fixed-price lunch and pre-/posttheater dinner £13–£15 ($23–$28). AE, DC, MC, V. Mon–Sat 11:30am–11pm; Sun 11:30am–9pm. Tube: Covent Garden, Holborn, or Temple.

Joe Allen AMERICAN This dark wood-paneled basement, with its ridiculously discreet entrance, is a Theatreland institution where Londoners dining late rub shoulders with the cream of West End talent. You'll have to splurge to join them or stick to starters and salads where the portions are pretty generous. Joe Allen does have good value pretheater deals, though, for two or three courses. The menu changes daily, except for the perennial bowl of chili, and the cuisine is a mix of classic down-home dishes and others that look suspiciously like modern British cooking and should be avoided (stick to the basics here). The service is sometimes perfunctory, and the tables are too close together, but the lively atmosphere and live jazz on Sunday nights compensate.

13 Exeter St., WC2. ✆ **020/7836-0651.** Reservations essential at weekends. Main courses £9–£15 ($17–$28); fixed-price lunch and pretheater menu £14–£16 ($26–$30); weekend brunch menu £18–£20 ($32–$36). AE, MC, V. Mon–Fri noon–12:45am; Sat 11:30am–12:45am; Sun 11:30am–11:15pm. Tube: Covent Garden.

Livebait ★ SEAFOOD If you like fish so fresh that it still looks surprised, then you'll love this very friendly, white-tiled place. There's a cheap way to enjoy it, too: Settle down in the bar for a bowl of cockles and a mixed-green salad, and it'll only cost you about £7.50 ($14). In the restaurant, you have to have a main course. The fixed-price menus are all a steal, and early booking is essential. You get two or three courses, and two dishes to choose from in each. Fish soup with aioli is a good way to start. Seafood haters should stay away because Livebait makes absolutely no concessions to meat eaters. It has also been spawning new branches: 43 The Cut, SE1 (✆ **020/7928-7211;** Tube: Waterloo or Southwark); 175 Westbourne Grove, W11 (✆ **020/7727-4321;** Tube: Bayswater or Queensway); and in Chelsea at 2 Hollywood Rd., SW10 (✆ **020/7349-5500;** Tube: Earl's Court).

21 Wellington St., WC2. ✆ **020/7836-7161.** Reservations recommended. Main courses £9.75–£29 ($18–$54); fixed-price lunch and pre-/posttheater menu £15–£19 ($27–$34). AE, DC, MC, V. Mon–Sat noon–11:30pm; Sun 12:30–9pm. Tube: Covent Garden.

Mon Plaisir TRADITIONAL FRENCH This *grande dame* of French restaurants opened in the 1940s. Behind the narrow glass front lies a warren of charming rooms, hung with pans and posters, where diners are packed in like sardines. Things have changed just a fraction in the past few years since chef Patrick Smith, a veteran of several well-known London restaurants, came in. He hasn't ditched the classics so you'll still find good old-fashioned coq au vin, snails, perfectly grilled entrecote, and so on. But new dishes have crept onto the menu, such as roast duck breast with Szechuan pepper and beet-root and onion marmalade. The pretheater menus are either two courses or three if you fancy finishing with something like profiteroles and chocolate sauce. Service is sometimes a bit snooty and it can get a little touristy because Mon Plaisir is such an institution.

21 Monmouth St., WC2. ✆ **020/7836-7243.** Main courses £14–£22 ($26–$41); fixed-price lunch £13–£16 ($24–$29); pretheater menu £14–£16 ($26–$29); fixed-price dinner plus glass of wine £16 ($29). AE, DC, MC, V. Mon–Fri noon–2:15pm; Mon–Sat 6–11:15pm. Tube: Covent Garden or Leicester Sq.

Sofra TURKISH At this very modern Turkish eating house the cuisine is completely authentic, although the food is not as spicy as some chile fans would like, nor are the portions as generous at Sofra as they are at more basic ethnic restaurants. But the ingredients are super-fresh and so is the way they're treated. The chef goes light on the oil, chargrilling instead. The fixed-price meals are a fantastic value, comprising 11 mezes and meat dishes—super-tender diced lamb, velvety hummus, the classic Middle Eastern eggplant dish, *Imam Bayildi,* and so on. This place has two little sisters: The best for stopping off mid-shopping in Oxford Street, or for dining outside, is **Sofra Cafe,** 1 St. Christopher's Place, W1 (✆ **020/7224-4080;** Tube: Bond St.). For Sunday lunch, head for **Sofra Bistro,** 18 Shepherd Market, W1 (✆ **020/7493-3320;** Tube: Green Park or Hyde Park Corner).

36 Tavistock St., WC2. ✆ **020/7240-3773.** Mixed meze £6.95 ($13); main courses £7.95–£15 ($15–$27); fixed-price lunch £8.95 ($17); pre- and posttheater menu £12 ($22). AE, DC, MC, V. Daily noon–midnight. Tube: Covent Garden.

WORTH A SPLURGE

Rules ★★★ TRADITIONAL BRITISH This ultra-British restaurant has been around for 200 years and seems likely to survive another 200. Lily Langtry and Edward VII used to tryst here, and it's about the only place in London where you'll still see a bowler hat. But despite the old-fashioned quaintness, Rules is a very modern restaurant operation. It markets the house specialty, "feathered and furred game," as healthy, free range, additive-free, and low in fat, and it has added vegetarian dishes. The fixed-price posttheater meal is a splurge, but it's still a great deal if you can wait until 10pm to eat. On the menu you might find lobster and asparagus salad with mango dressing, followed by fallow deer with spiced red cabbage, blueberries, and bitter chocolate sauce. The food is delicious: traditional yet innovative, until you get to the puddings (desserts), which are a mix of nursery and dinner-dance classics. The wine list is pricey, but Rules does have three brown ales, so try one of those instead.

35 Maiden Lane, WC2. ✆ **020/7836-5314.** Reservations essential. Main courses £16–£21 ($29–$38); fixed-price posttheater menu Mon–Thurs 10pm–closing £18 ($33). AE, DC, MC, V. Mon–Sat noon–11:30pm; Sun noon–10:30pm. Tube: Charing Cross or Covent Garden.

13 Victoria

Jenny Lo's Teahouse ★ CHINESE Jenny Lo's father was Britain's best-known Chinese chef, and this is where he had his cookery school. His restaurant, Ken Lo's Memories of China, is still going strong in nearby Ebury Street, but it's very pricey. This teahouse, however, is quite affordable. The decor is simple but stylish, utilizing long shared tables, wooden chairs, and bright splashes of color. There's a short menu, mainly rice, soup noodles, and wok noodles, including ones with a southeast Asian twist (hot coconut). Try the luxurious black-bean seafood noodles. Side dishes include such street-food classics as onion cakes. The staff is extremely friendly and helpful, which helps soothe any irritation you may feel if you have to wait for a table. Jenny Lo has also commissioned her own tonic teas from Chinese herbalist Dr. Xu. Long life and happiness are on the menu here.

14 Eccleston St., SW1. ✆ **020/7259-0399.** Reservations not accepted. Main courses £5.50–£8 ($10–$15). No credit cards. Mon–Fri 11:30am–3pm; Sat noon–3pm; Mon–Sat 6–10pm. Tube: Victoria.

Oliveto ★ PIZZA & PASTA This is a cheaper offshoot spawned by Olivo, the successful Italian restaurant just 'round the corner. Oliveto offers the same quality but simpler, faster food, with the focus on pizza (which is also the cheapest main course). There are 15 different and deliciously crisp pizzas to choose from. One fave is the *quattro stagioni*, a revitalized old favorite made with mozzarella, tomato, sausages, prosciutto, mushroom, and squash; another is made with Gorgonzola, arugula, tomato, and mozzarella. There are always a few pasta dishes—a delicious *linguine al granchio* made with fresh crabmeat, garlic, and chile, for example. The daily specials, tuna or swordfish perhaps, top the price list. Oliveto has a very mixed clientele, from platinum credit-carded families who live in Belgravia to young Pimlico singles out for a relaxed supper. If you're feeling a little more flush, try **Olivo,** 21 Eccleston St., SW1 (✆ **020/7730-2505**). Main courses cost £14 to £15 ($25–$28), and the cuisine is robust, modern Italian.

49 Elizabeth St., SW1. ✆ **020/7730-0074.** Main courses £9.50–£13 ($18–$24). AE, MC, V. Mon–Fri noon–2:30pm; Mon–Sat 7–11pm; Sun 7–10:30pm. Tube: Victoria.

GREAT DEALS ON FIXED-PRICE MEALS

Boisdale ★ SCOTTISH This is clan territory. Owned by Ranald Macdonald, the very model of a modern chieftain-in-waiting, the Boisdale bar boasts London's biggest range of hard-to-find single-malt whiskies and a tartan menu to match. The cheaper fixed-price lunch is a cultural treat you'll want to boast about at home: a hearty fish soup, then haggis made by the world famous McSween in Edinburgh, neeps (mashed swede, or rutabaga), and tatties (mashed potato). This is the dinner that Robert Burns wrote his famous ode in praise of and which guests salute as it's brought to the table at the annual celebration of his birthday on January 25th. If centuries of tradition can't persuade you to try oatmeal and sheep's innards, you can choose from the more expensive fixed-price meal with a wide choice of starters and main courses, which are bound to include venison, salmon, and Scottish beef. You might not want to dine here if you have a strong aversion to smoke: What else would a fat cat want to go with the single malt other than a big fat Cuban cigar?

15 Eccleston St., SW1. ✆ **020/7730-6922.** Reservations recommended. Main courses £15–£24 ($28–$49); fixed-price menu £14–£17 ($25–$32). AE, DC, MC, V. Bistro Mon–Fri noon–2:30pm; Mon–Sat 7–11pm. Bar Mon–Sat to 1am. Tube: Victoria.

Ebury Wine Bar & Restaurant MODERN EUROPEAN/WINE BAR The food here won't win any grand dining prizes, but it's a friendly, welcoming place to eat and convenient if you're staying in Victoria. The main courses should make it a splurge (especially when you add in the annoying £2/$3.70 cover charge), but you can have a good meal for the price of a single dish if you stick to the two-course fixed-price lunch or pretheater dinner. On the changing menu you might find chicken-and-bacon terrine with red-onion marmalade or rich mushroomy sausages with mash and onion gravy. Accompany your meal with a glass of one of the carefully selected and reasonably priced wines.

139 Ebury St., SW1. ✆ **020/7730-5447.** Reservations recommended. Main courses £10–£20 ($18–$36); fixed-price lunch and pretheater dinner £13 ($23). Cover £2 ($3.70). AE, DC, MC, V. Daily noon–2:45pm; 6-10:15pm Sun noon–2:30pm and 6–9:15pm. Tube: Victoria.

14 The City & Clerkenwell

THE CITY

Arkansas Café AMERICAN The U.S. Embassy swears by the barbecuing skills of Keir and Sarah Hellberg. If you're important enough to get onto the Independence Day guest list there, you'll probably find them catering the party. And this is *the* place to come on Thanksgiving (the only time it's open in the evening except for parties of 25 people or more). Arkansas Café is at Old Spitalfields Market, and diners sit out in the covered central space and enjoy the sizzle and delicious smells while the Hellbergs cook steaks, lamb, sausages, ribs, and corn-fed chicken to order. Mr. Hellberg personally selects the best cuts of meat from Smithfield market. Go for a jumbo sandwich as a cheaper option or take the meat on its own. The beef brisket and ribs are home-smoked, the desserts fabulous.

Unit 12, Old Spitalfields Market, E1. ✆ **020/7377-6999.** Main courses £5–£15 ($9–$27). MC, V. Mon–Fri noon–2:30pm; Sun noon–4pm. Tube: Liverpool Street.

The Place Below VEGETARIAN St. Mary-le-Bow is a beautiful Christopher Wren church built on the site of a much-earlier one. Today, the arched Norman vaults are home to one of the most atmospheric and delicious cheap eateries in The City. The menu changes daily, but you'll always find a hot dish of the day, two salads (one dairy-free), and a quiche. Because The Place Below gets so busy at lunchtime, it offers £2 ($3.70) off all main-course prices between 11:30am and noon. You'll save about the same amount on most dishes if you take out rather than eat in. Soup is a dynamite deal at £3.10 ($6). The Place Below has just had a tart up, introducing a new espresso and sandwich bar, and extending its hours to 3:30pm. So you could just come for a rich chocolate brownie and a cappuccino (good Illy coffee is a steal at 80p/$1.50). There is seating for 50 outside in Bow Churchyard.

St. Mary-le-Bow, Cheapside, EC2. ✆ **020/7329-0789.** Main courses £5.50–£7.50 ($10–$14). MC, V. Mon–Fri 7:30am–3:30pm. Tube: St. Paul's or Bank.

CLERKENWELL

Bleeding Heart Bistro & Tavern GASTROPUB/MODERN BRITISH Beautiful 17th-century it-girl Lady Elizabeth Hatton was murdered in Bleeding Heart Yard while strolling with the European ambassador during her annual winter ball. Today, there's a remarkable gastropub on the site. The restored 1746 tavern is the London flagship of regional brewery and wine merchant Southwold Adnams. It is *the* place to quaff real ale (from £2.50/$4.60 a pint) while enjoying earthy dishes such as spit-roasted suckling pig or casserole of Lincolnshire rabbit with mash and cider onion gravy.

There are two other parts to this place, with successively higher prices. At the bistro, tucked around the corner and across a courtyard, similar-style cuisine generally costs a couple of pounds more than in the tavern. For a real splurge, head for the expensive and ever-so-French restaurant below the tavern. You'll enjoy the atmosphere as much as the food.

Bleeding Heart Yard, off Greville St., EC1. ✆ **020/7404-0333.** Reservations essential in restaurant. Main courses in tavern £7.95–£13 ($15–$24), bistro £7.95–£15 ($15–$28), restaurant £12–£22 ($22–$42). AE, DC, MC, V. Tavern Mon–Fri 7:30am–11pm; bistro Mon–Fri noon–3pm and 6–10:30pm; restaurant Mon–Fri noon–2:30pm and 6–10:30pm. Tube: Chancery Lane or Farringdon.

Where to Dine in the City & on the South Bank

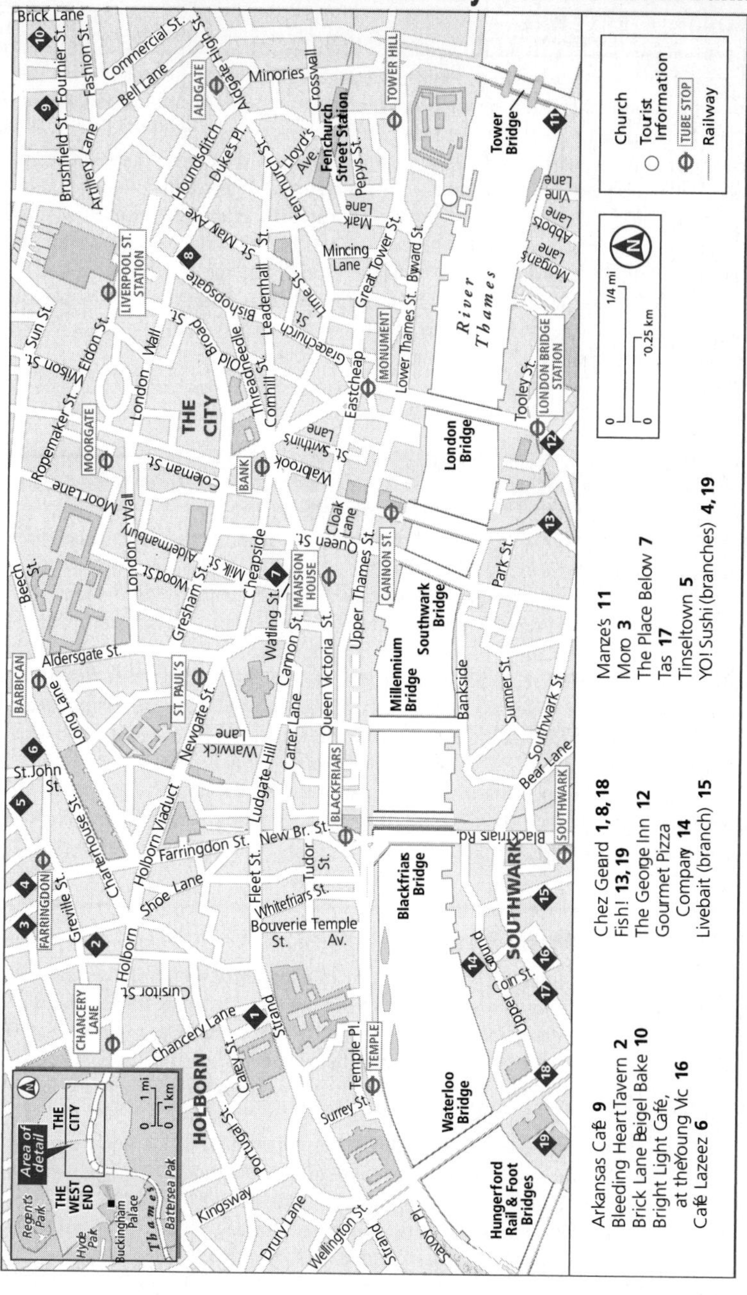

WORTH A SPLURGE

Moro ★★★ NORTH AFRICAN/SPANISH Clerkenwell, on the run-down fringes of the City, has become a very hip neighborhood in recent years. If you didn't know that, then an evening at Moro will quickly put you in the picture. It opened in 1997, has amassed a pot full of awards, and gets better every day. The decor is modern and minimalist with bare walls and stripped wood and a quieter conservatory corner. The Spanish and North African cuisine is earthy and powerful. You can dine very reasonably on delicious tapas, but splurge, if you can, because the kitchen uses only the best ingredients, organic whenever possible, in its daily-changing menu. The charming staff will explain any of the menu's exotic mysteries. Highly recommended are the quail baked in flatbread with pistachio sauce and the tender wood-roasted pork, marinated in sherry. For dessert, try one of the yummy house-specialty desserts: yogurt cake with pistachios or rosewater and cardamom ice cream.

34–36 Exmouth Market, EC1. ✆ **020/7833-8336.** Reservations recommended. Main courses £14–£18 ($25–$32); tapas £3–£5 ($5.50–$9). Mon–Fri 12:30–2:30pm; Mon–Sat 7–10:30pm. AE, DC, MC, V. Tube: Angel or Farringdon.

15 Just South of the River

GREAT DEALS ON FIXED-PRICE MEALS

Tas ★ TURKISH This bright bustling restaurant lists more than 100 dishes, which is ridiculous even for a meze-style meal. So go for one of the set menus. Even the cheapest will bring you three courses and for well under a tenner. And the food is very good, from the complimentary appetizer, cheese and herb dip, to the homemade pita bread, and eggplant in any number of different incarnations. A "tas" is a Turkish cooking pot, and casseroles are a main-course specialty—chicken and almond, for instance, with a side of apricot rice. Tas stocks Turkish wine, as well. The great value and the fact that the area (SE1) has hitherto been a culinary wasteland mean large crowds at lunch and in the evening. So if you hate noise, it probably isn't for you.

Tas has become something of a minichain, with another convenient branch at 72 Borough High St. (✆ **020/7403-7200**; Tube: London Bridge) and elsewhere throughout the city.

Finds **Pie & Mash: History on a Plate**

It's a curious taste, but visitors who want to experience working-class London as it scarcely exists any more have got to put pie & mash on the menu. This dish is edible social history, dating back to when eels were two-a-penny in the Thames. But minced beef has long since taken their place as a cheaper substitute under the flaky pastry. That's what you get today, served with mash, liquor (a kind of green parsley gravy), and maybe eels on the side.

Most of London's pie & mash shops are an inconvenient bus ride from East End Tube stations—but they're the real deal, not packaged heritage. One of the more convenient is **Manze's,** 87 Tower Bridge Rd., SE1 (✆ **020/7407-2985;** Bus: 1, 42, or 188), open from 11am to 2pm on Monday, 10:30am to 2pm Tuesday to Thursday, 10am to 2:15pm Friday, and 10am to 2:45pm Saturday. No credit cards.

---

33 The Cut, SE1. ✆ **020/7928-2111.** Reservations recommended. Main courses £4.95–£14 ($9–$26); fixed-price menu £7.95–£9.95 ($15–$18); 10 meze sampler £19 ($34) per person. AE, MC, V. Mon–Sat noon–11:30pm; Sun noon–10:30pm. Tube: Southwark.

SUPER-CHEAP EATS

Bright Light Café ★ *Finds* MODERN EUROPEAN If dreary weather has dogged your London vacation, it might be worth your while to spend a couple of hours under the fake-sunshine lighting, the kind designed to combat Seasonal Affective Disorder, at this permanently sunny cafe. If that doesn't work, the food will. Local deli Konditor & Cook runs this brasserie, which stretches all the way across the front of the Young Vic theater. It dishes up scrumptious quick bites, from soup to sandwiches, and good-value light meals. You might find warm potato cakes with smoked salmon or a delicious spinach-ricotta tortellini. The bright lights switch off a little earlier in the evening if there's no performance, so call ahead to check.

Young Vic, 66 The Cut, SE1. ✆ **020/7620-2700.** Main courses £5.50–£9.50 ($10–$18). MC, V. Mon–Fri 8:30am–11pm; Sat 10:30am–11pm (closes 8pm if no performance). Tube: Waterloo or Southwark.

WORTH A SPLURGE

Fish! ★★ *Kids* SEAFOOD Tate Modern is turning Southwark into one of the hippest neighborhoods in London. Another draw is the Borough Market, the foodie mecca where you'll find Fish! This futuristic diner is all glass and steel, and very noisy, especially when it's full of families at weekend lunchtimes. The restaurant has high chairs, toys, and a two-course children's menu with things like tuna Bolognese. For the grown-ups, evangelical notes on the place mats detail why fish is good for you and how it should be caught. The choose-your-own menu lists 20 fish with ticks against those that are available that day, to be grilled or steamed as you like, with a choice of five accompanying sauces. Big thumbs up for the tender halibut and scallops. Chips cost extra but are perfectly cooked and well worth it. There are several new branches, including one a couple of miles upriver at **County Hall;** call the central reservations number below.

Cathedral St., Borough Market, SE1. ✆ **020/7407-3803.** Reservations recommended. Main courses £8.95–£18 ($17–$33); fixed-price children's meal £6.95 ($13). AE, MC, V. Mon–Fri 11:30am–11pm; Sat noon–11pm; Sun noon–10pm. Tube: London Bridge or Borough.

16 Farther Afield

CAMDEN

Camden is packed with hole-in-the-wall cafes and stalls selling cheap street food. Cruise any section of Camden Market to find an array of kebabs, hot dogs, falafel, and pizza, starting at around £2.50 ($4.60) a pop.

GREAT DEALS ON FIXED-PRICE MEALS

Lemonia ★ GREEK This long-established restaurant, with its classic Greek menu, is a real favorite with the locals. It's a charming place, more than living up to its name: Lemons are absolutely everywhere. The mix of polished wood and marble-topped tables cluster near the fully open front window, up on a dais, and in the conservatory. There are even a few out on the pavement. If you don't want to come this way for lunch, then the meze, which gets you a mixed bag of starters and main courses, is a fantastic deal—look around and you'll see that's what most diners are having.

Otherwise, top recommendations include the moussaka, which is a triumph of eggplant, zucchini, potatoes, tomatoes, and ground beef in a creamy sauce, and the subtly flavored *afelia* (cubes of pork marinated in wine, coriander seeds, and spices), all washed down with Greek wine. Lemonia is especially crowded at the weekends when the ritual is to walk off the feast on Primrose Hill, which has one of the best views across London.

89 Regent's Park Rd., NW1. © **020/7586-7454.** Reservations essential. Main courses £7.75–£13 ($14–$24); fixed-price lunch £7.25–£8.50 ($13–$16); meze £15 ($28) per person. MC, V. Sun–Fri noon–3pm; Mon–Sat 6–11:30pm. Tube: Chalk Farm.

WORTH A SPLURGE

The Engineer ★ GASTROPUB/MODERN BRITISH With its huge glass windows and scrubbed tables in the bar, restaurant, and garden, this was one of the gastropub pioneers. It's pricey, but skinny wallets can fill their stomachs with simple but delicious meals in a bowl, while the less restricted can have something like lemon-scented risotto with yellow-pepper puree, Gorgonzola, and walnuts. And splurgers can enjoy seared swordfish with vanilla-scented sweet-potato mash and tropical fruit, or chargrilled squid with green papaya, cucumber, and mint salad. Lunchtime main courses are much lighter than the evening fare. The menu changes every two weeks, and the meat is all organic. This is a delightful place and screamingly busy, particularly at the weekends as a popular local stop before or after a visit to Camden Market. Book ahead.

65 Gloucester Ave., NW1. © **020/7722-0950.** Reservations recommended. Main courses £11–£17 ($20–$31). MC, V. Daily 9am–11pm. Tube: Camden Town or Chalk Farm.

17 Best of the Budget Chains

The past two decades have brought a massive explosion in restaurant chains to Britain. It began with bland *faux*-French cafes. Now no high concept eatery seems to be without a business plan to clone itself in as many places as possible. London's sushi and noodle bars are a prime example, as you'll see from the reviews. Apart from them, the best budget spots are a mix of fast-ish food clichés and snack-stops riding the health fad.

Pizza Express introduced the Italian staple to Britain when even metropolitan Londoners dismissed it as filthy foreign muck. It's still the quality benchmark, and a pizza will cost you about £5 to £9 ($9–$17). There are over 60 branches across London, most of them in very upscale-looking premises. One of the liveliest is in Soho: 10 Dean St., W1 (© **020/7437-9595;** Tube: Tottenham Court Rd. or Leicester Sq). Surf the website for a full list (www.pizzaexpress.co.uk). Newcomer **ASK** is putting up a very worthy challenge. It uses fancy ingredients familiar in up-market cuisine—goat cheese, sun-dried tomatoes, and so on. It's a restaurant, not a joint, with cool modern decor and smooth service. Yet pizza prices are very reasonable at £5 to £7.50 ($9–$14). There are about 20 ASKs—look for the blue neon signs. Two are extra handy for budget hotels: in Paddington, at 41–43 Spring St., W2 (© **020/7706-0707**); and Victoria, at 160–162 Victoria St., SW1 (© **020/7630-8228**).

Otherwise, there are several friendly faces for U.S. travelers—not counting the epidemic of coffee bars such as Starbucks (you'll find them all over, with one of the biggest and busiest right on Leicester Sq.). Burgers cost from £7.75 ($14) at the original **Hard Rock Café,** 150 Old Park Lane, W1 (© **020/7629-0382;** Tube: Hyde Park

Corner); they're even pricier, starting at £8.50 ($16), at **Planet Hollywood,** Trocadero, 13 Coventry St., W1 (✆ **020/7287-1000;** Tube: Piccadilly Circus). Both are noisy tourist traps and attract megaqueues. The third, and possibly the worst in terms of culinary standards, is the **Rainforest Café,** 20 Shaftesbury Ave., W1 (✆ **020/7434-3111**). Kids seem to love this themed dining among fake jungle vegetation, rocks and waterfalls, tropical birds and wailing animatronic animals, thunderclaps and sudden storms (as if London needed pretend ones). There's a children's menu, and grown-ups can choose between standard fast food and more exotic Asian concoctions for £8 to £15 ($15–$29). Be forewarned: The food, which some consider the worst in London, tastes like cardboard.

Healthy meals-in-a-cup are definitely big in London. Prices at **Soup Opera** include a piece of bread and fruit, and start at £2.95 ($5.50) for a 12-ounce carton. There are 10 branches; I'd try the one near Oxford Circus at 6 Market Place, W1 (✆ **020/7631-0777;** www.soupopera.co.uk).

A big cup of soup costs £1.95 to £2.95 ($3.60–$5.45) at **EAT,** a healthy cafe chain that has blossomed into 25 Central London branches from the original Embankment branch at 39–41 Villiers St., WC2 (✆ **020/7839-2282**). It has won prizes for its hot sandwiches and yummy tortilla wraps (£1–£3/$1.85–$5.50), and does sushi, too. Although West End branches stay open until 7pm, this is mostly a daytime snack stop, as is **Pret a Manger,** a top-notch chain of sandwich shops which use good breads and fresh ingredients; sandwiches range in price from £1.95 to £4.50 ($3.60–$8). Besides sandwiches you can grab a cappuccino, sushi box, or a piece of cake. There are nearly 70 branches in London, and they're a godsend for travelers on a tight budget.

18 Afternoon Tea

The ladies at the **Chelsea Physic Garden** are demon bakers in true Women's Institute style, so it's well worth making a special trip to sample their wares. The garden is open on Wednesday and Sunday afternoons, from April through October: See "Parks & Gardens," in chapter 7, for more information.

KENSINGTON

The Orangery ★★ *Kids* AFTERNOON TEA The cakes here are homemade English treats, from Victoria sponge on the cheapest set menu to the Belgian chocolate on the priciest. There are three teatime blowouts to choose from: Level one gets you sandwich, shortbread, and the aforementioned cake; add £1 to swap the sandwich for a scone with cream and jam; and the top treat assembles all of the above, plus a glass of bubbly. The atmosphere is lovely in this elegant 18th-century conservatory by Kensington Palace. Yet the prices make most tea spots look like a real rip-off.

Kensington Palace, Kensington Gardens, W8. ✆ **020/7376-0239.** Fixed-price teas £6.95–£15 ($13–$28). MC, V. Daily 10am–6pm (5pm Nov–Feb); tea served from 3pm. Tube: Kensington High St. or Queensway. No smoking.

MAYFAIR

Dorchester ★ AFTERNOON TEA The Promenade may not have quite the limitless luxury of the Ritz's Palm Court, but it comes pretty close. Gold decoration and marble floors and pillars make this a very posh corridor in which to take afternoon tea. The Dorchester is famed for its pastries: The fluffy scones that follow the sandwich first course and the strawberry tart, white chocolate parcel, coffee éclair, and the host of other cakes will send you out into the Mayfair early evening with a real sugar

Finds The Best Baddest Breakfast in Town

Playing hooky from your B&B breakfast may mean doubling up the bacon bill, but you've gotta be wicked at least once while you're in London. The best budget breakfast is the £6.50 ($11) special at the **Brew House,** at Kenwood House on Hampstead Heath (p. 198). The ingredients are top-notch: free-range scrambled eggs and pork sausages, bacon, mushrooms, tomatoes, and toast. And you can tuck in from 9am every day. Make it a weekend treat, as the locals do, and bring your newspaper. During the week, head east to the **Fox & Anchor,** 115 Charterhouse St., EC1 (✆ **020/7253-5075;** Tube: Barbican or Farringdon). The pub opens at 7am and the £7 ($13) death-by-breakfast is fittingly carnivorous for the location, just round the corner from Smithfield Market: black pudding as well as sausages, bacon, eggs, fried bread, tomatoes, and baked beans. Two other top breakfast spots are **Star Café** in Soho (p. 137) and **Café Grove** in Portobello Road (p. 130).

rush. The higher priced tea includes a glass of champagne. Don't wear jeans or tennis shoes; the dress code is "smart casual."

54 Park Lane, W1. ✆ **020/7629-8888.** Reservations recommended. Fixed-price tea £24–£30 ($43–$55). Daily 3–6pm. AE, DC, MC, V. Tube: Hyde Park Corner.

ST. JAMES'S

St. James's Restaurant at Fortnum & Mason AFTERNOON TEA This store is world famous, and so are its eateries, which are always mobbed with tourists. Unfortunately, the downstairs Fountain restaurant has discontinued its famous ice-cream tea, which was a favorite of kids everywhere. Now you must have your traditional tea upstairs in the St. James's restaurant. You'll get a nice spread that includes freshly baked scones with clotted cream and strawberry jam and a slice of cake.

181 Piccadilly, W1. ✆ **020/7734-8040.** Afternoon tea £20–£22 ($36–$40). AE, DC, MC, V. Tues–Sat tea 3–5:30pm; Sun noon–5pm; Mon 10am–5pm. Tube: Green Park or Piccadilly.

7

Exploring London

It was nothing short of amazing. In 2001, after months of wheeler-dealering and changes to the tax regulations, London's major national museums dropped their admission charges. Each one used to charge as much as £8 ($15) to enter. Now you can indulge in sci-fi fantasy at the Science Museum for free. At the Natural History Museum, you can experience an earthquake and see a fabulous dinosaur collection for free. Without shelling out a pence, you can visit, but not bounce on, the Great Bed of Ware in the Victoria & Albert's remodeled British Galleries. You can inhale the aroma of cheesy socks and closely confined unwashed bodies in the Imperial War Museum's submarine simulator, or wander through the superb galleries at the National Gallery, the National Portrait Gallery, the Tate Modern, and the Tate Britain for free. And for nothing more than the cost of your transportation to Greenwich, you can see the original model for Nelson's Column and the Admiral's bullet-pierced coat at the National Maritime Museum.

All those great, now-free museums make visiting London on a budget possible. But be forewarned: Other essential London attractions such as the Tower of London cost a small fortune. For suggested 1-, 2-, and 3-day London itineraries, see chapter 4.

HOW TO PLAN YOUR SIGHTSEEING

The **Visit Britain & London Visitor Centre** in London at 1 Regent St. (✆ **020/8846-9000;** www.visitlondon.com) and the **Visit Britain & London** office in New York at 551 Fifth Ave. (✆ **800/462-2748**) provide helpful information and have walk-in information centers. (For more details on where to find the capital's tourist offices, see "Visitor Information," at the start of chapter 3.)

If you're planning to visit several top attractions—not the free museums, but expensive tourist sites such as the Tower of London, Kensington Palace, Hampton Palace, and Windsor Palace—check out the potential savings of the **London Pass** (www.londonpass.com).

While you're online, you can check out the one-stop **www.24hourmuseum.org.uk**, a gateway to virtually every museum in the country. The *Evening Standard* website is useful (**www.thisislondon.com**), as is the always-essential *Time Out,* both for the right-now listings in the magazine and for its electronic city guide (**www.timeout.com**).

There is always something going on in the capital—anniversaries, historic pageants, festivals, and carnivals. The really big stuff is listed in the "London Calendar of Events," in chapter 2, and you'll find lots more dates, particularly for art, craft, and antiques events, in "Top Tips for Bargain Hounds," in chapter 8. Otherwise, surf **www.artsfestivals.co.uk** and **www.londontown.com/events**, which has a very forward-looking events calendar.

Knowing the dates of the school year is also vital. Museums, galleries, and attractions put on lots of extra fun at half-term—the 1-week minibreak in the middle of each semester—and during the holidays. This is a great time for families to come to London. Look at the bumper issues of the listings magazines, and you'll see that the tours, talks, walks, exhibitions, and festivals are not just for kids. (See "When to Go," chapter 2.)

Note: A family ticket usually covers two adults and two children, but sometimes you can take an extra offspring. Children under 5 get free admission to most attractions, while the age limit to qualify as a child varies widely, from 15 to 18.

1 How to Spend Less and See More

London will never be a cheap thrill, but fortunately, in addition to the top-dollar tourist draws there are now scads of free museums, galleries, and historic buildings. We've reviewed more than 40 in our listings, enough to keep even repeat London tourists happy. And remember, London's major national museums are now free.

There are lots more ways to have fun on the cheap. Take a look at the suggestions below and at "Frommer's Favorite London Moments," in chapter 1.

- **Net Savings.** A top site for budget travelers is **www.londonfreelist.com**. It has details of 1,500 permanently good deals and special offers, most of which are free, and none costing more than £3 ($5.50).
- **Check out the Discount Deals.** Special cards and passes are best for energetic travelers because you have to cram a lot into each day to get your money's worth. Check out details on the **London Pass** and the **Great British Heritage Pass** under "Fifty Money-Saving Tips," in chapter 2.
- **Look for Two-Fors.** If the discount passes don't fit your holiday needs, you can still save money by grabbing any joint ticket offers: **Tower of London** and **Hampton Court,** for instance (see "London's Top Attractions," below); **London Zoo** and a **boat trip** with the London Waterbus Company on the Regent Canal (see "Especially for Kids," later in this chapter); **The Monument** and **The Tower Bridge Experience;** or a big **Bus Tour** package with entry to popular attractions like Madame Tussaud's.

2 London's Top Attractions

British Airways London Eye ★★★ *Kids* "Passengers" on the Eye can see straight into the Buckingham Palace garden, much to the Queen's annoyance. And both the Ministry of Defense and Shell have spent thousands spy-proofing their offices after discovering that someone with the right gadgetry could look in and pinch their secrets. At 443 feet high, this is the world's tallest observation wheel (don't say "Ferris;" it's a dirty word to these guys). On the south bank, next to County Hall, the half-hour, very slow-mo "flight" gives a stunning 25-mile view over the capital. It's better when the sun isn't shining, as the glare makes it difficult to see out. And the pod should have a map of the landmarks running round the inside—instead you have to pay £4.50 ($8) for a guide book. Book your "boarding ticket" in advance to avoid too much hanging about; if you book online, you'll save 10%. Though it was supposed to close in 2002, the Eye has proven to be so popular that it will keep revolving for some time to come.

Jubilee Gardens, SE1. ✆ **0870/500-0600.** www.ba-londoneye.com. Admission £13 ($23) adults, £10 ($18) seniors, £6.50 ($12) children 5–15. Open daily 9:30am; last admission varies seasonally (May–June and Sept 9pm; July–Aug 10pm; Oct–Dec 8pm; Feb–Apr 8pm). Closed Jan–Feb 9. Tube: Waterloo or Westminster. River services: Festival Pier.

Kids Changing of the Guard ★★★

Looking more like toy soldiers than honed fighting machines, these men somehow do their duty, oblivious to kids pulling silly faces and the clicking of holiday snaps. **Changing of the Guard** takes place at **Buckingham Palace** daily from April through August at 11:15am, and on alternate days September through March; at **St. James's Palace,** St. James's Street, W1 (Tube: Green Park) at 11:15am, same dates; and at **Horse Guards** (Tube: Charing Cross) Monday through Saturday at 11am, and 10am on Sunday.

Appropriately, it's the Household Cavalry that mounts the guard at Horse Guards. The soldiers ride across town every day from Knightsbridge Barracks, on the edge of Hyde Park, in their shiny breastplates and plumed helmets. The smartest men at the morning inspection get the plum position, on horseback in the sentry boxes, and get to go home at 4pm. Those on foot have to stay until 8pm.

Very bad weather and state events disrupt the schedules.

British Museum ★★★ To get the maximum visual kerpow from your first sight of the **Great Court,** use the main south entrance into the museum—the one with the too-white portico made of the wrong kind of stone. Except for that embarrassing blunder, the recent redevelopment of the British Museum, designed by Lord Norman Foster, has won high praise. The 2-acre Great Court used to serve as a giant store cupboard. Now covered by a stunning steel-and-glass roof, it has become the light-filled hub of the Bloomsbury complex, staying open after the galleries close, with an education center, restaurants where you can have supper Thursday through Saturday, and coffee shops.

But the real excitement is that for the first time, visitors can enter the copper-domed **British Library Reading Room.** The giant drum in the middle of the Great Court is clad in the same too-white stone, while the interior has been restored to its Victorian blue, cream, and gold glory. Designed by Robert Smirke and completed in 1857, it inspired Thomas Carlyle, Virginia Woolf, Mahatma Gandhi, Lenin, George Bernard Shaw, Karl Marx (who wrote *Das Kapital* here), and a host of other great names. It houses the museum's books on the upper floors, with a public reference library and media center down below (the rare books, maps, manuscripts, and historic documents that were once in the Reading Room and museum vaults are now at the British Library Exhibition Centre, described later in this chapter).

From a collection purchased from Sir Hans Sloane in 1753, the British Museum has grown into one of the richest storehouses of antiquities, prints, drawings, manuscripts, and objets d'art in the world, rivaled only by the Smithsonian in Washington, D.C. There are 2½ miles of galleries, so you'll need to weed out what really interests you and make a plan of attack. The £2.50 ($5) *Visit Guide* will help. Otherwise, let the museum take the stress out of deciding: The 90-minute highlight tour takes place daily at 10:30am, 1pm, and 3pm and costs £8 ($15) for adults, £5 ($9) concessions (seniors, people with disabilities) and children under 11. There are also free single-gallery tours, EyeOpeners, which last 50 minutes and take place from 11am to 3:30pm. You can also rent audio guides for £3.50 ($6).

Central London Sights

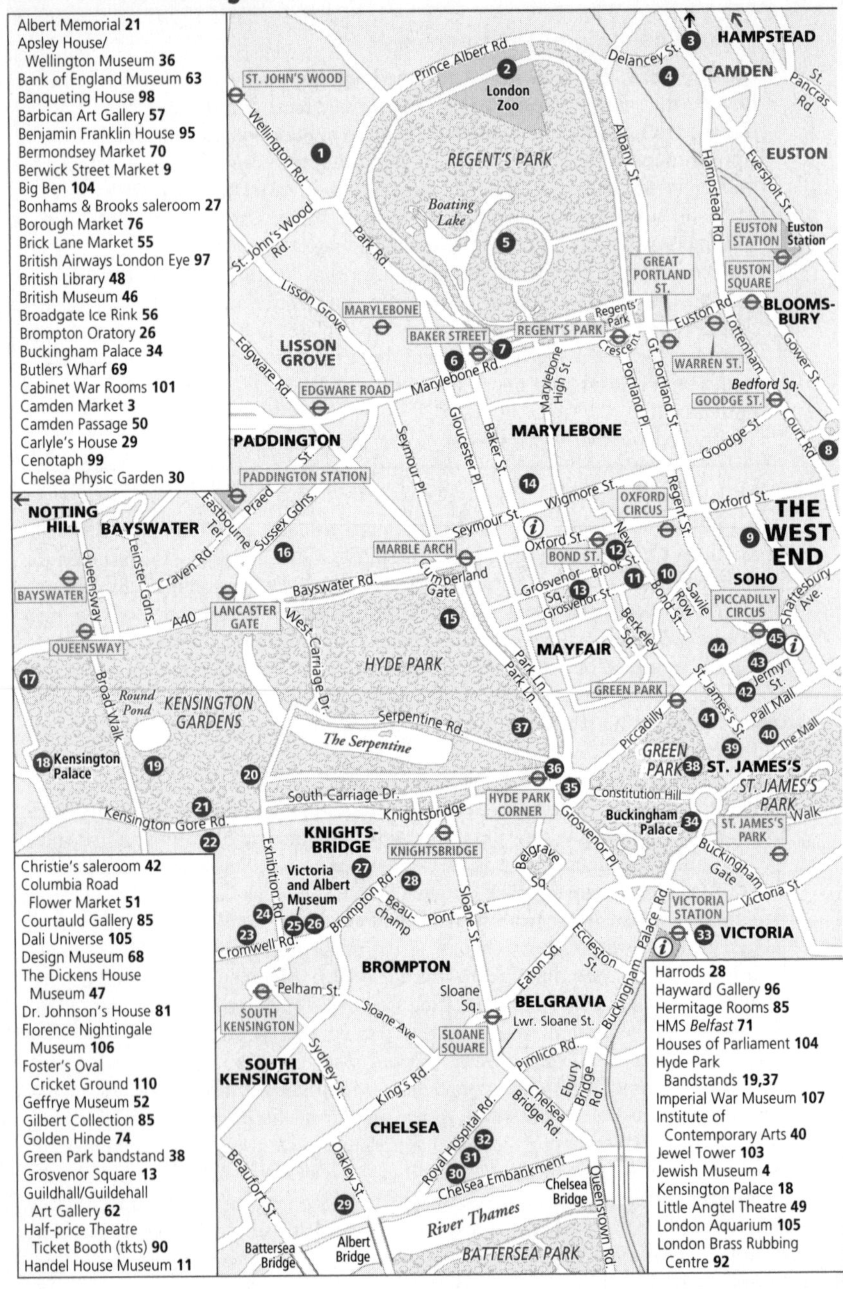

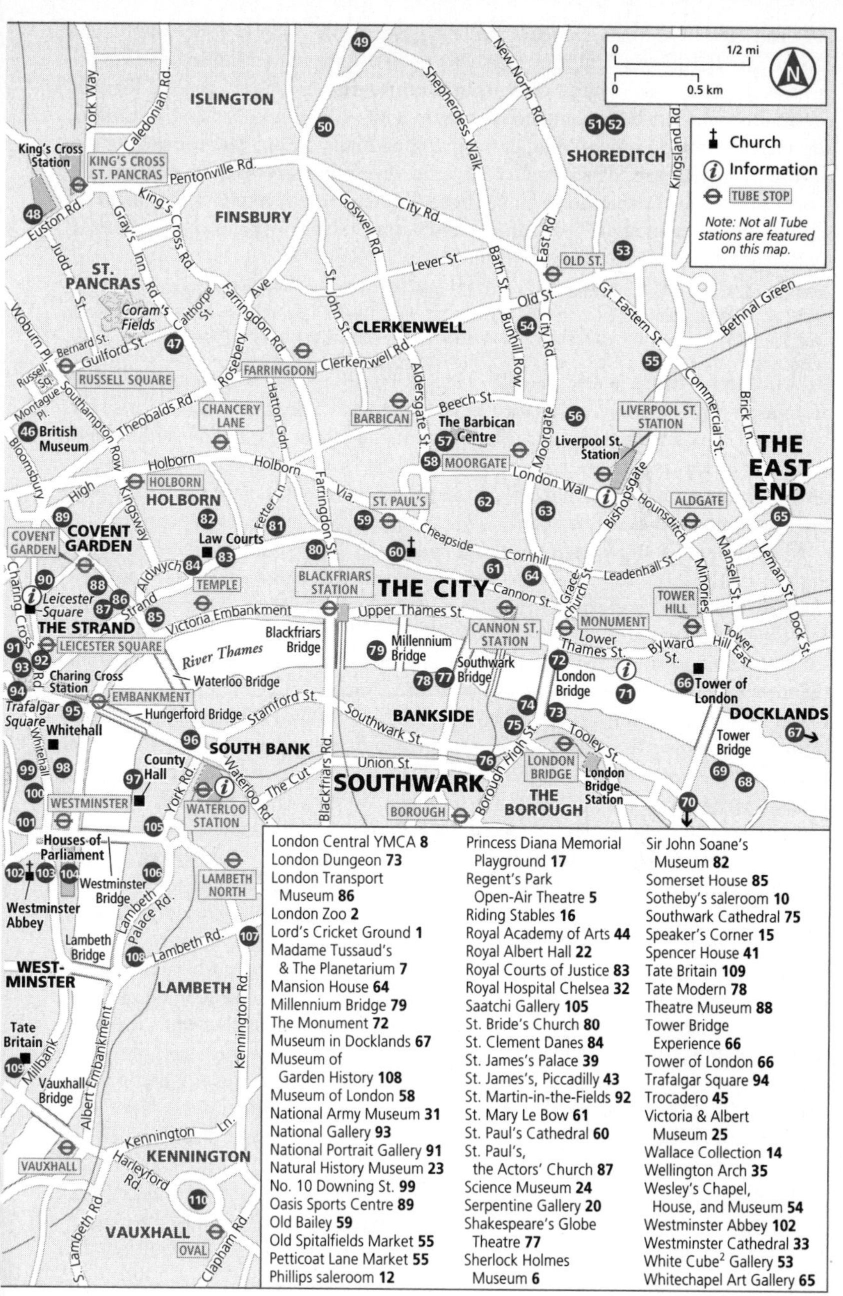
0
1/2 mi
0
0.5 km
N
Church
Information
TUBE STOP
Note: Not all Tube stations are featured on this map.
ISLINGTON
SHOREDITCH
FINSBURY
ST. PANCRAS
CLERKENWELL
HOLBORN
COVENT GARDEN
THE STRAND
THE CITY
THE EAST END
BANKSIDE
SOUTH BANK
SOUTHWARK
THE BOROUGH
DOCKLANDS
WEST-MINSTER
LAMBETH
KENNINGTON
VAUXHALL
King's Cross Station
KING'S CROSS ST. PANCRAS
York Way
Caledonian Rd.
Pentonville Rd.
Euston Rd.
King's Cross Rd.
Gray's Inn Rd.
Judd St.
Coram's Fields
Calthorpe St.
Farringdon Rd.
Ave.
Rosebery
Woburn Pl.
Bernard St.
Guilford St.
Russell Sq.
RUSSELL SQUARE
Montague Pl.
Southampton Row
Theobalds Rd.
British Museum
Bloomsbury
High
Kingsway
HOLBORN
Holborn
Holborn Via.
CHANCERY LANE
Hatton Gdn.
Fetter Ln.
Farringdon St.
FARRINGDON
Clerkenwell Rd.
Goswell Rd.
St. John St.
Shepherdess Walk
New North Rd.
City Rd.
Lever St.
Bath St.
East Rd.
OLD ST.
Old St.
Gt. Eastern St.
Bethnal Green
Kingsland Rd.
Bunhill Row
City Rd.
Aldersgate St.
BARBICAN
Beech St.
The Barbican Centre
MOORGATE
Moorgate
London Wall
Liverpool St. Station
LIVERPOOL ST. STATION
Commercial St.
Brick Ln.
Bishopsgate
Houndsditch
ALDGATE
ST. PAUL'S
Cheapside
Cornhill
Leadenhall St.
Minories
Mansell St.
Leman St.
Law Courts
Aldwych
TEMPLE
Strand
COVENT GARDEN
Leicester Square
LEICESTER SQUARE
Charing Cross Rd.
BLACKFRIARS STATION
Victoria Embankment
Upper Thames St.
Cannon St.
CANNON ST. STATION
Gracechurch St.
MONUMENT
TOWER HILL
Lower Thames St.
Byward St.
Tower Hill East
Dock St.
Tower of London
River Thames
Blackfriars Bridge
Millennium Bridge
Southwark Bridge
London Bridge
Waterloo Bridge
Charing Cross Station
EMBANKMENT
Hungerford Bridge
Stamford St.
Southwark St.
Tooley St.
Trafalgar Square
Whitehall
County Hall
York Rd.
Waterloo Rd.
The Cut
Union St.
Blackfriars Rd.
Borough High St.
LONDON BRIDGE
London Bridge Station
Tower Bridge
BOROUGH
WESTMINSTER
WATERLOO STATION
Houses of Parliament
Westminster Bridge
Westminster Abbey
LAMBETH NORTH
Lambeth Palace Rd.
Lambeth Bridge
Lambeth Rd.
Kennington Rd.
Tate Britain
Millbank
Albert Embankment
Vauxhall Bridge
VAUXHALL
Kennington Ln.
Harleyford Rd.
S. Lambeth Rd
OVAL
Clapham Rd.
London Central YMCA 8
London Dungeon 73
London Transport Museum 86
London Zoo 2
Lord's Cricket Ground 1
Madame Tussaud's & The Planetarium 7
Mansion House 64
Millennium Bridge 79
The Monument 72
Museum in Docklands 67
Museum of Garden History 108
Museum of London 58
National Army Museum 31
National Gallery 93
National Portrait Gallery 91
Natural History Museum 23
No. 10 Downing St. 99
Oasis Sports Centre 89
Old Bailey 59
Old Spitalfields Market 55
Petticoat Lane Market 55
Phillips saleroom 12
Princess Diana Memorial Playground 17
Regent's Park Open-Air Theatre 5
Riding Stables 16
Royal Academy of Arts 44
Royal Albert Hall 22
Royal Courts of Justice 83
Royal Hospital Chelsea 32
Saatchi Gallery 105
St. Bride's Church 80
St. Clement Danes 84
St. James's Palace 39
St. James's, Piccadilly 43
St. Martin-in-the-Fields 92
St. Mary Le Bow 61
St. Paul's Cathedral 60
St. Paul's, the Actors' Church 87
Science Museum 24
Serpentine Gallery 20
Shakespeare's Globe Theatre 77
Sherlock Holmes Museum 6
Sir John Soane's Museum 82
Somerset House 85
Sotheby's saleroom 10
Southwark Cathedral 75
Speaker's Corner 15
Spencer House 41
Tate Britain 109
Tate Modern 78
Theatre Museum 88
Tower Bridge Experience 66
Tower of London 66
Trafalgar Square 94
Trocadero 45
Victoria & Albert Museum 25
Wallace Collection 14
Wellington Arch 35
Wesley's Chapel, House, and Museum 54
Westminster Abbey 102
Westminster Cathedral 33
White Cube² Gallery 53
Whitechapel Art Gallery 65

If you only have time or interest for "the greatest hits," pop in to see the much-fought-over **Parthenon Sculptures** formerly known as the Elgin Marbles. The Egyptian antiquities are also a must—they include **mummies,** sarcophagi, and the **Rosetta Stone.** It would also be a shame not to take in a bit of local history, like the leathery remains of garroted **Lindow Man,** or the glittering Anglo-Saxon silver and gold of the **Sutton Hoo treasure.** Then wander into the new **Sainsbury African Galleries,** a modern imaginative exhibition a far cry from the dusty trophy rooms of Empire days. Check out the fabulous 1950s fantasy coffins from Ghana: My favorite is one that looks like a white Mercedes, with the number plate RIP2000.

Great Russell St., WC1. ✆ **020/7323-8000,** or 020/7323-8299 info desk. www.thebritishmuseum.ac.uk. Main galleries free. Special exhibitions £2–£8 ($4–$15). Galleries Sat–Wed 10am–5:30pm; Thurs–Fri 10am–8:30pm. Great Court Sun–Wed 9am–6pm; Thurs–Sat 9am–11pm. Tube: Russell Sq., Holborn, or Tottenham Court Rd.

Buckingham Palace ★★★ *Overrated* This is Her Maj's official London residence and supposedly the one she likes least of all her palatial homes. It gets three stars for star-power, not for anything intrinsically interesting about the building itself. You know the queen is there when the royal standard is flying. Liz and her husband, the duke of Edinburgh, occupy only 12 of the palace's 600 rooms. The rest are used by the royal household as offices and for royal functions, banquets, and investitures.

King George III and Queen Charlotte bought the house from the duke of Buckingham in 1762, but it was George IV who converted it into a palace. He commissioned John Nash to pump up the grandeur, which he did by adding wings at the front and extending those at the back, all for £700,000 ($1,295,000). Neither George nor his brother William IV actually lived here, and by the time Queen Victoria came to the throne, doors wouldn't close, windows wouldn't open, bells wouldn't ring, and the drains were clogged. Victoria sent Nash packing, and Edward Blore completed the repairs. But it quickly became too small for an official residence. So, in 1847, the queen had the East Front built, facing The Mall, and moved Marble Arch from the palace forecourt to the top of Park Lane. Sir Aston Webb designed the facade in 1913.

The queen first opened the 18 formal **State Rooms,** including the **Throne Room,** in 1993 to help raise money to repair Windsor Castle after a fire. Overlooking the 45-acre gardens, where she gives her famous summer parties, they contain priceless pictures, tapestries, and a few pieces of furniture from the royal collections. Queen Victoria's vast ballroom—the ceilings are 45 feet high and there's room to park 35 double-decker buses—is part of the self-guided tour. Although you have to pay an exorbitant price to get in the palace, don't expect a fly-on-the-wall glimpse of royal home life. For a start, you can only visit during August and September when the family is on holiday. And these rooms are not where the royals put their feet up with a reviving cup of tea—it could be almost any unlived-in stately home or grand private collection. Tickets can be purchased in person, from 9am to 4pm on the day: Eager tourists start queuing at sunrise, and an hour-long wait is the rule. Booking a fixed-time ticket by phone or online is less hassle.

A much better value is the **Royal Mews** ★★ (entrance in Buckingham Palace Rd.). These superb working stables house the royal carriages, including the gold state coach used at every coronation since 1831, and the horses that draw them. By tradition, the queen always has grays.

The newly revamped **Queen's Gallery** ★ displays hundreds of items from the royal art collection in changing exhibitions. The £10-million ($18-million) refurbishment, which the queen unveiled in 2002 as part of her Golden Jubilee gig, was the biggest

Sights from Knightsbridge to Earl's Court

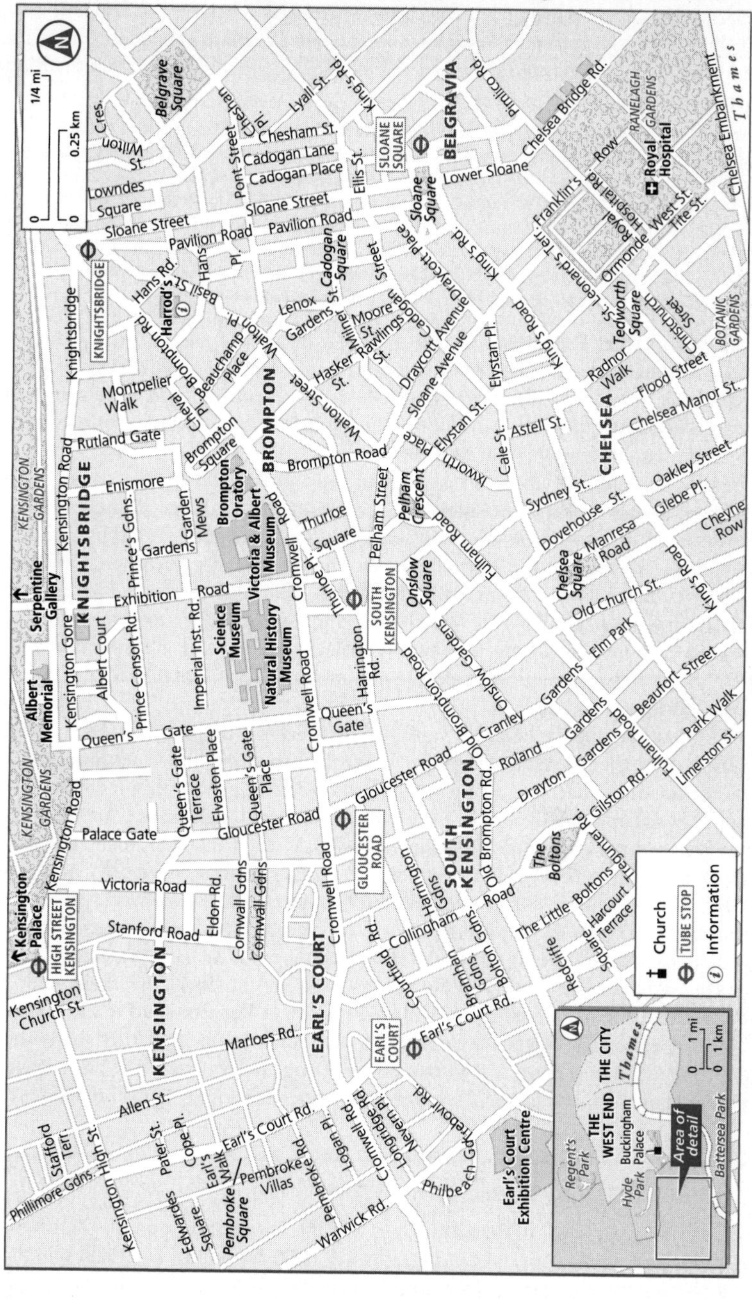

building project at Buckingham Palace since George V stuck on the Portland stone facade in 1913. An imposing new Doric portico now leads into a series of modern galleries and a much-expanded range of exhibits, including photographs from the Royal Archives at Windsor.

The Mall, SW1. © **020/7839-1377,** 020/7799-2331 recorded info, 020/7766-7300 credit card bookings, or 020/7766-7324 for visitors with disabilities. www.royalresidences.com. State Rooms £14 ($25) adults, £12 ($21) seniors, £7 ($13) children under 17, £34 ($63) family ticket. July 30–Sept 27 daily 9:30am–6:30pm (last admittance 4:15pm). Royal Mews £6 ($11) adults, £5 ($9) seniors, £3.50 ($6) children under 17, £14 ($25) family ticket. Mar–July and Oct Sat–Thurs 11am–4pm (last admission 3:15pm); July 25–Sept daily 10am–5pm (last admission 4:15pm). Queen's Gallery £7.50 ($14) adults, £6 ($11) over 60 and student, £4 ($7) under 17. Daily 9:30am–5:30pm (last admittance 4:30pm). Closed Jan 10–Feb 10 and Dec 25–26. Combined ticket for palace, Queen's Gallery, Royal Mews £23 ($43) adults, £20 ($36) senior, £13 ($23) under 17. Tube: Victoria, St. James's Park, or Green Park.

Hampton Court Palace ★★★ *Kids* Bring a picnic because a visit to Hampton Court makes a splendid day out. You'll need 2 to 3 hours to look round the palace itself, plus time to wander through the 60 acres of gardens. And then there's the famous **maze,** with its half a mile of twisting paths—most people take 20 minutes or so to extricate themselves from its green clutches.

Hampton Court is about 15 miles southwest of London on the banks of the Thames. Henry VIII's pleasure-loving Lord Chancellor, Cardinal Wolsey, took the house in 1515 as a retreat from the city's poisonous air and water. His grandiose remodeling plan called for 280 rooms, new courtyards and gardens, and 500 staff. When the cardinal fell into disfavor in 1528, the greedy king confiscated his property. Henry spent a whopping £18 million ($29 million) in today's money and turned Hampton Court into a very sophisticated palace with bowling alleys, tennis courts (yes, really), a chapel, pleasure gardens, a hunting park, The Great Hall for dining, and a 36,000-square-foot kitchen.

His daughter, Queen Elizabeth I, planted the gardens with new discoveries, such as tobacco and potatoes brought back by Sir Francis Drake and Sir Walter Raleigh from South America. Under the Stuarts, the palace collections grew with hundreds of new paintings and other lavish objets d'art. Charles II banished the gloom of Cromwell's brief stay here with his lively court and many mistresses. William and Mary found the palace apartments old-fashioned and uncomfortable, so they commissioned Sir Christopher Wren to make improvements and asked such artists as Grinling Gibbons, Jean Tijou, and Antonio Verrio to decorate the rooms. George III ended royal occupation—his grandfather used to box his ears in the State Apartments, so he hated the place.

The highlights for visitors to Hampton Court are the **Tudor Kitchens** and the **King's Apartments,** as well as the **Wolsey Rooms** and **Renaissance Picture Gallery.** One of Henry VIII's wives, the hapless (and ultimately headless) Catherine Howard, has reputedly been sighted several times in the **Long Gallery,** where she ran, terrified, to pound on the king's locked door and plead desperately for her life. Throughout the

---

Tips A Money-Saving Joint Ticket

Buying a joint ticket to **Hampton Court** and the **Tower of London** (p. 173) saves around £6.50 ($12) per person. It costs £20 ($37) for adults, £15 ($28) seniors and students, £13 ($24) children under 16, or £58 ($107) for a family ticket, and must be used within 24 hours.

---

palace, costumed guides bring the centuries of history to life, as does the full calendar of special events and festivals. You'll save £1 ($1.85) on your admission price if you book in advance online or via phone.

East Molesey, Surrey. ✆ **0870/752-7777,** or 0870/753-7777 tickets by phone. www.hrp.org.uk. Admission £12 ($22) adults, £8.70 ($16) students and seniors, £7.70 ($14) children under 16, £35 ($65) family ticket. Apr–Oct daily 10am–6pm (last admission 5:15pm); Nov–Feb Mon 10:15am–4:30pm, Tues–Sun 9:30am–4:30pm (last admission 3:15pm); Mar daily 10am–4:30pm (last admission 3:30pm). Park daily 7am–dusk. Closed Dec 24–26. Train: Waterloo to Hampton Court, 30-min. journey time. River services from Westminster pier (✆ **020/7930-2062;** www.wpsa.co.uk), 3- to 4-hr. journey time; £20 ($36) standard adult return fare; schedules vary seasonally.

Houses of Parliament ★★★ This neo-Gothic extravaganza, with its trademark clock tower, is the ultimate symbol of London. Edward the Confessor built the first palace here, and the site was home to the monarchy and court until Henry VIII's time. In 1834 a fire lit to burn the Exchequer's tally sticks got out of control, sparing only Westminster Hall (1097), which is not open to the public, and the **Jewel Tower** (p. 182). Charles Barry designed the Houses of Parliament (1840) you see today. Augustus Welby Pugin created the paneled ceilings, tiled floors, stained glass, clocks, fireplaces, umbrella stands, and even inkwells. There are more than 1,000 rooms, 100 staircases, and 2 miles of corridors. Big Ben, by the way, is not the clock tower itself, as many people think, but the largest bell (14 tons) in the chime.

The parliamentary session runs from mid-October to the end of July, with breaks at Christmas and Easter. Visitors can watch debates from the **Strangers' Galleries** in both houses. Most visitors are struck by how small the **Commons chamber** is. It was rebuilt in precise detail in 1950 after being destroyed during the Blitz of 1941. Only 437 of the 651 MPs can sit at any one time; on the rare occasions when most of them turn up, the rest crowd noisily around the door and the Speaker's chair. The ruling party and opposition sit facing one another, two sword lengths apart, though from the volume of the arguments you'd think it was more like 2 miles. The Mace, on the table in the middle, is the symbol of Parliament's authority. The queue for the **House of Lords** is usually shorter, as debates here are less crucial (some might say inconsequential) and a lot more polite. The Lords' chamber is fantastically opulent, decorated with mosaics and frescoes. The Lord Chancellor presides over proceedings from his seat on the Woolsack, a reminder of the days when wool was the source of Britain's wealth. You'd think such tradition would make the place sacrosanct. Yet, in 2000, New Labour made all the hereditary peers prove their worth to keep their privileges and ousted 600 of them. And in 2001 it appointed the promised "people's peers," though the prominent professionals chosen seemed scarcely more representative of the general population than the aristocracy.

During the recess (Aug to early Oct, 9:15am–4:30), you can take a fascinating 75-minute **tour of the Houses of Parliament** ★★★ for £7 ($13). It isn't really suitable for young children as rest stops are limited. You must be there 10 minutes before your timed-entry tour starts. Call ✆ **0870/906-3773** or visit www.firstcalltickets.com for tickets and information. In August, tours are available on Monday, Tuesday, Friday, and Saturday; in September and October, you can tour on Monday, Friday, and Saturday.

Bridge St. and Parliament Sq., SW1. ✆ **020/7219-4272** House of Commons or ✆ **020/7219-3107** House of Lords. www.parliament.uk. Free admission to Strangers' Galleries, subject to recess and sitting times. House of Commons: Mon 2:30–10:30pm; Tues–Wed 11:30am–7:30pm; Thurs 11:30am–6:30pm; Fri (when sitting) 9:30am–3pm. House of Lords: Mon–Wed from 2:30pm; Thurs and occasionally Fri from 11am. Queue for both at St. Stephen's entrance, near the statue of Oliver Cromwell. Tube: Westminster. River services: Westminster Pier.

Kensington Palace State Apartments and Royal Ceremonial Dress Collection ★★ The palace has been a pilgrimage site ever since Princess Diana died in August 1997, when people flocked to the gates and carpeted the ground with floral tributes. Several of her best-known designer frocks are now on permanent display here, as are dozens of the dowdy dresses, shoes, and hats worn by the queen over the past 50 years.

The asthmatic William and his wife Mary bought this house from the Earl of Nottingham in 1689 to escape from the putrid air enveloping Whitehall. Then they commissioned Sir Christopher Wren to remodel the modest Jacobean mansion. Queen Anne, who came to the throne in 1702, laid out the gardens in English style, had the Orangery built after designs by Nicholas Hawksmoor, and died here in 1714 from apoplexy brought on by overeating. The first two Georges lived at Kensington Palace. George III abandoned it in favor of Buckingham House (now Palace). But his fourth son, Edward Duke of Kent, did have apartments here. Queen Victoria was his daughter. The Archbishop of Canterbury and the Lord Chamberlain roused her from sleep here on June 27, 1837, with news of the death of her uncle, William IV, and her succession to the throne. That night was the first she had ever slept outside her mother's room. Three weeks later, aged 18, she moved into Buckingham Palace.

Princess Margaret lived at Kensington Palace until her death in 2002. Today, the duke and duchess of Gloucester and Princess Michael of Kent have apartments there. Only the **State Apartments,** filled with art treasures from the Royal Collection, and the display of court fashions and uniforms from 1760 in the **Royal Ceremonial Dress Collection** are open to the public. See the Cupola Room, where Queen Victoria was baptized, and marvel at William Kent's magnificent *trompe l'oeils* and paintings in the King's Drawing Room, Presence Chamber, and on the King's Staircase. The audioguide that comes with your ticket is a good way to self-guide yourself through the palace. And you can have lunch or tea in The Orangery (described in chapter 6).

Kensington Gardens. ✆ **0870/751-5170.** www.hrp.org.uk. Admission £11 ($20) adults, £8 ($15) seniors and students, £7 ($13) children under 16, £32 ($59) family ticket. Nov–Feb daily 10am–5pm; Mar–Oct daily 10am–6pm. Tube: Queensway or High St. Kensington.

Madame Tussaud's & the Planetarium *Overrated* Madame Tussaud had an extraordinary life. Born Marie Grosholtz, she learnt her craft from her mother's doctor employer, who had a talent for wax modeling. Such was her renown that Louis XIV and Marie Antoinette appointed her as their children's art tutor. In an ironic turn of events, in order to prove her loyalty to the revolution and get out of Laforce Prison, Marie had to make the royal couple's death masks after their executions in 1793. You can see several casts from her original molds—a spooky Voltaire, for instance—at this "museum." But most of its space is devoted to modern celebrities, some of them royal, some with a shelf life of about a nanosecond, and superstars like Nicholas Cage, Julia Roberts, and Mel Gibson (the staff once found a pair of ladies underpants in his pocket). Craftsmen take more than 200 measurements from each star sitter. And stars know they're on the wane when Tussaud's boils their figure down and uses the wax to make someone else. The Spirit of London ride is fun, but the dungeon-level Chamber of Horrors is the stuff tourist traps are made of. It "honors" psychopathic murderers like Charles Manson and Jack the Ripper, offers a rendition of Joan of Arc burning at the stake, and shows the grisly unmentionables done to Gunpowder Plotter Guy Fawkes. Madame Tussaud's is incredibly expensive and overrated, but it attracts more than 2.5 million visitors a year. So it has introduced a fast-track system whereby you pre-book time slots. Use it, or you may end up queuing for longer than the 2 hours or so it takes to go round.

If you're into stars of the celestial variety, it's worth spending the extra couple of pounds for a combined ticket to Madame Tussaud's and the **London Planetarium** next door. This copper-domed London landmark is the largest planetarium in Europe. Its state-of-the-art Digistar II projection system re-creates an earth-based view of 9,000 stars and planets scattered across the night sky, and takes you on a journey past exploding nebulae right to the edge of the universe.

Marylebone Rd., NW1. ✆ **020/7935-6861**, or 0870/400-3000 advance reservations. www.madame-tussauds.com. Madame Tussaud's £20 ($37) adults, £17 ($31) seniors, £16 ($30) children under 16. Combined ticket with planetarium £22 ($41) adults, £19 ($35) seniors, £18 ($33) children under 16. Planetarium only £8.75 ($16) adults, £5.75 ($11) children under 16. Madame Tussaud's Mon–Fri 9:30am–5:30pm; Sat–Sun 9am–6pm. Planetarium daily 10am–5:30pm. Shows run every 40 min., 12:20–5pm; weekends/holidays from 10:20am. Closed Dec 25. Tube: Baker St.

National Gallery ★★ Britain's national art collection comprises more than 2,300 paintings dating from 1260 to 1900, supplemented by masterpieces on loan from private collectors. The gallery is arranged in four time bands. The **Sainsbury Wing** shows work from 1260 to 1510 by such artists as Giotto, Botticelli, Leonardo da Vinci, Piero della Francesca, and Raphael. The **West Wing** takes on the next 90 years, with El Greco, Holbein, Bruegel, Michelangelo, Titian, and Veronese. The **North Wing** holds the 17th-century masters, Rubens, Poussin, Velázquez, Rembrandt, and Vermeer. Van Dyck's *The Abbé Scaglia* entered the collection in 1999, given by a private owner in lieu of inheritance tax. Works by Stubbs, Gainsborough, Constable, Turner, Canaletto, van Gogh, Corot, Monet, Manet, Renoir, and Cézanne are all in the **East Wing.** From May to September, the National Gallery lets natural daylight illuminate many of the paintings, particularly in the Sainsbury Wing, to magical effect—the colors are truer, and it cuts down on glare and shadow from the frames. You'll need to choose a sunny day for your visit, though, because artificial help steps in if it gets too gloomy. Weekday mornings and late on Wednesday are the quietest times.

There's a free (donation invited) audioguide to every painting on the main floor, and free guided tours start at 11:30am and 2:30pm every day, plus 6 and 6:30pm on Wednesday evenings, and at 12:30 and 3:30pm on Saturdays. Most of the gallery talks are also free. There are two eateries: the Crivelli's Garden Restaurant and Italian Bar (✆ **020/7747-2869**) on the first floor of the Sainsbury Wing, and the Gallery Cafe in the basement of the main building.

Trafalgar Sq., WC2. ✆ **020/7747-2885.** www.nationalgallery.org.uk. Main galleries free; Sainsbury wing £3–£7 ($6–$13) for some special exhibitions. Daily 10am–6pm (Wed until 9pm). Closed Jan 1 and Dec 24–26. Tube: Charing Cross or Leicester Sq.

Natural History Museum ★★ Kids It roars. It opens its jaws and moves its head. And it's the biggest hit the museum has ever had: a **robotic Tyrannosaurus Rex** hovering over a fresh dino-kill. It's worth a trip just to watch the 12-foot-tall toothy beast (not suitable for young kids). Before you see "T" you'll encounter two cunning-looking animatronic raptors eyeing you from atop a perch. All this takes place in a Victorian hall full of **dinosaur skeletons** and exhibitions about the life of the 'saurs. Head to the **Earth Galleries** for earthquake and volcano simulations that hint at the terror of the real thing. Kids also love the slithery and slimy critters in the **Creepie-Crawlies** exhibit.

Sir Hans Sloane was such a prolific collector that his treasures overflowed the British Museum. Hence the decision to build this palatial building (1881), with its towers, spires, and nave-like hall, fit "for housing the works of the Creator." Yet it, too, can display only a fraction of its specimens—animal, vegetable, and mineral. An exciting project is set to revolutionize all that, opening both the storerooms and the science labs, with their 300 white-coated experts, to public view. The £28-million ($52-million) first phase of the Darwin Centre opened in summer 2002. The museum already has the new Clore Education Centre, where kids can use video microscopes and bug-hunting magnifying glasses, build their own websites, and take part in regular events. Highlight and themed tours start near the entrance to the Life Galleries.

Cromwell Rd., SW7. ✆ **020/7942-5000.** www.nhm.ac.uk. Free admission. Free tours of the Darwin Centre offered throughout the day; book upon arrival. Mon–Sat 10am–5:50pm; Sun 11am–5:50pm. Closed Dec 23–26. Tube: South Kensington.

St. Paul's Cathedral ★ No one who saw the wedding of Prince Charles and Lady Diana in 1981 will ever forget the image of the royal carriages approaching St. Paul's. In 2002, the queen had a ceremony of thanksgiving here to celebrate her Golden Jubilee. This magnificent cathedral is 515 feet long and 360 feet high to the cross on the famous dome, which dominated the skyline until ugly office buildings rose around it after World War II. To thwart interference from his paymasters, who harassed him constantly over the 35 years it took to complete the building (1675–1710), Christopher Wren laid out the whole base first, so that the church walls would have to rise on the shape and size he wanted. Wren was buried in the crypt; his epitaph reads: *"Lector, si monumentum requiris, circumspice"* ("Reader, if you seek his monument, look around you"). Many artists worked on the decoration, most notably Grinling Gibbons, who carved the choir screens and stalls. Frescoes depicting the life of St. Paul line the inner dome. You can see them best from the **Whispering Gallery,** famous for its amazing acoustics, which can project a murmur right across the void. A second steep climb leads to the Stone Gallery, and a third to the highest Inner Golden Gallery. In all, it's 530 steps to the top, with the views ever more awe-inspiring.

Ninety-minute "Supertours" of the cathedral and crypt take place at 11, 11:30am, 1:30, and 2pm, and cost £2.50 ($5) for adults, £2 ($3.70) concessions, £1 ($1.85) children, plus admission. Audioguides are available in five languages until 3pm: £3.50 ($6.50) for adults, £3 ($6) seniors and students. "Triforium" tours take in the library, geometric staircase, the West End gallery, and Trophy Room where Wren's Great Model is on display. Tickets are £12 ($22), including admission. Call Monday to Friday, 9am to 4pm, to book. There are often organ recitals at 5pm on Sunday, at no charge. Fuel up at the Crypt Café first.

St. Paul's Churchyard, EC4. ✆ **020/7246-8348** or 020/7246-8319. www.stpauls.co.uk. Admission £8 ($15) adults, £7 ($13) students and seniors, £3.50 ($6) children under 16, £20 ($36) family ticket. Mon–Sat 8:30am–4pm; Sun for worship only. Tube: St. Paul's or Mansion House.

Science Museum ★★ *Kids* This is one of the best science museums in the world. The striking new £45-million ($83-million) **Wellcome Wing** houses new exhibitions presenting the latest developments in science, medicine, and technology. Find out what the kids might look like in 30 years in the ***Who am I?*** gallery. For a more intimate portrait, check out the gory digital cross-sections in ***The Visible Human Project.*** This is fantasyland for gadget geeks, who'll love all the interactivity. There's a 450-seat IMAX cinema on the first floor and another huge new gallery, **Making the Modern World,** links the Wellcome Wing to the old museum. Using some of the most iconic treasures of the permanent collection—the Apollo 10 space capsule, an early train known as Stephenson's Rocket, and a fleece from famous Scottish clone Dolly the Sheep—it charts 250 years of technological discoveries and their effects on our culture.

Moments **Water Magic**

Time your visit right and you can see the fountains in the Somerset House courtyard doing their balletic synchronized spouting: there's a quick 4-minute session every half-hour from 10am to 11pm, with bumper 11-minute performances at 1, 6, and 10pm. The fountains are turned off from December through February. For a few weeks over Christmas, the courtyard transforms into an outdoor ice rink.

The new galleries are stunning, but don't let them dazzle you into forgetting the rest of this marvelous museum. It is home to many pioneering machines: Arkwright's spinning machine, for instance, and the Vickers "Vimy" aircraft, which made the first Atlantic crossing in 1919. The basement is dedicated to children with water, construction, sound and light shows, and games for 3- to 6-year-olds in the **garden,** and the **Launch Pad** for 7- to 15-year-olds. Of course, the Wellcome Wing is even more ambitious: its first-floor **Pattern Pod** aims to convert kids to science from the age of 3 months! For info about museum sleepovers, see "Unforgettable Overnights," on p. 192.

Although the museum introduced free admission in December 2001, it charges for shows at the IMAX and rides on its two simulators.

Exhibition Rd., SW7. ✆ **020/7942-4000,** or 0870/870-4771. www.sciencemuseum.org.uk. Free admission. IMAX £7.50 ($14) adults, £6 ($11) seniors and children. Daily 10am–6pm. Closed Dec 24–26. Tube: South Kensington.

Somerset House ★★ The late Queen Mother once remarked how sad it was that the courtyard at Somerset House had become a parking lot for the Inland Revenue office. It was just the spur needed by the long-running campaign to open up the 1,000-room civil service palace, designed by Sir William Chambers (1724–96), to the public. The government moved its workers out, and the Heritage Lottery Fund coughed up the millions needed to restore the buildings, the courtyard with its new fountains, and the river terrace, where there's now a summer cafe (it's cheaper than the new restaurant indoors). A heady mix of high culture and street entertainment, the "new" Somerset House contains three major museums and hosts a program of open-air performances, talks, and workshops (✆ **020/7845-4670** box office). The restoration is proceeding in phases, and you can already visit the **Seamen's Waiting Hall,** where naval officers came to collect their commissions. On the first Saturday of every month there are free 45-minute tours at 11:30am, 2:30pm, and 3:45pm.

The **Courtauld Gallery** ★ (✆ **020/7848-2526;** www.courtauld.ac.uk) has been in Somerset House since 1989. Its chief benefactor, textile mogul Samuel Courtauld, collected Impressionist and post-Impressionist paintings, which are still the gallery's main strength—Manet's *Bar at the Folies Bergères;* Monet's *Banks of the Seine at Argenteuil; Lady with Parasol* by Degas; *La Loge* by Renoir; van Gogh's *Self-Portrait with Bandaged Ear;* and several Cézannes, including *The Card Players.* But you'll find work by most great names (lots of Rubens), right up to modern greats Ben Nicholson, Graham Sutherland, and Larry Rivers.

The **Gilbert Collection** ★★ (✆ **020/7420-9400;** www.gilbert-collection.org.uk) is also in the South Building, as well as in the vaults beneath the river terrace. The glittering gold, silver, and mosaics were valued at £75 million ($120 million) when Arthur Gilbert donated the 800-piece collection to the nation in 1996. There are objects here from Princess Diana's old home, Althorp.

The last and most extraordinary of the treasures of Somerset House are the **Hermitage Rooms** ★ (✆ **020/7845-4630;** www.hermitagerooms.com). This offshoot of the State Hermitage Museum in St. Petersburg exhibits pieces from the Russian Imperial collections in changing shows.

Strand, WC2. ✆ **020/7845-4600.** www.somerset-house.org.uk. Somerset House free. Courtauld Gallery, Gilbert Collection, Hermitage Rooms each £5 ($9) adults, £4 ($7) seniors, free for children under 18; Courtauld Collection free Mon 10am–2pm. Same-day admission to 2 collections, save £2 ($3.70); all 3, save £3 ($5). Courtyard 7:30am–11pm (7pm in winter). Galleries and exhibitions daily 10am–6pm (last admittance 45 min.–1 hr. earlier). Closed Jan 1 and Dec 24–26. Tube: Temple, Covent Garden, or Charing Cross.

Tate Britain ★★ The new Tate Modern at Bankside hogs most of the limelight, but the shifting around of the Tate collections has also seen a huge overhaul at the original gallery, founded in 1897. The refurbished Tate Britain reopened in November 2001 with more exhibition space and a suite of airy new galleries. Having handed international modernism over to Bankside, Tate Britain now concentrates on British work dating back to 1500. It ditched the chronological displays for a thematic approach. **Art Now** focuses on new media and experimental work by foreign artists living in London and Brits based here and abroad; **Private and Public** includes portraits and scenes of daily life; **Artists and Models** explores nudes and self-portraiture; **Literature and Fantasy** is for visionary artists such as William Blake and Stanley Spencer; and **Home and Abroad** looks at the landscape artist at home and abroad. Important artists like Gainsborough, Constable, Hogarth, and Hockney get their own rooms, which should pacify the traditionalists.

Guided tours (Mon–Fri 11am, noon, 1:15, 2, and 3pm; Sat–Sun noon, 2:30, and 3pm), lectures, and films are mostly free. Tate Britain also has shops, a good cafe and espresso bar, and a well-regarded but pricey restaurant.

Millbank, SW1. ✆ **020/7887-8000,** or 020/7887-8888 for events. www.tate.org.uk. Permanent collection free; temporary exhibitions £6.50–£8.50 ($12–$16). Daily 10am–5:50pm. Closed Dec 24–26. Tube: Pimlico. River services: Millbank Pier.

Tate Modern ★★★ The Tate Modern, London's new and wildly popular cathedral of modern art, occupies the defunct Bankside Power Station on the South Bank of the Thames opposite St. Paul's Cathedral. Except for a two-story glass addition on the roof, the vast bunker-like facade looks much as it ever did, right down to the London grime. Then you enter the building, down a ramp into the huge old turbine hall, and three floors of ultra-plain white galleries. The work is arranged thematically rather than chronologically: **Landscape/Matter/Environment, Still Life/Object/Real Life, History/Memory/Society,** and **Nude/Action/Body.** In some rooms, paintings are next to sculptures next to installations. Others are devoted to a single artist—like the

---

Finds Picnic on Top of the World

If you're not in the mood to wait in the long queue for a table at Café Level 7 at Tate Modern, smuggle in your own sandwiches and sodas, ride the elevator to the seventh floor, and then walk along the viewing corridor to the opposite side of the old power station. There's a bizarrely empty room there with a stupendous three-way panorama. Nobody will bat an eyelid if you hunker down and tuck in. In fact, they'll be horribly envious.

---

marvelous Joseph Beuys sculptures. The display concept is certainly challenging, but the themes often seem spurious, lacking the quirky spirit of a mixed private collection where one person's taste is the guide.

Set aside half a day for your visit. Free guided tours start daily at 11am, noon, and 1, 2, and 3pm, each focusing on one of the four themes. There's also a busy talks program (usually £6/$11; free talks weekdays at 1pm); music; and children's workshops and storytelling sessions. An audio tour costs £2 ($3.70). But if you only do one thing at Tate Modern, go up to the glass-roofed level seven to see the spectacular views across the Thames. The cafe there is often mobbed, so time your visit for early mealtimes and during the week. It is also open for dinner until 9:30pm on Friday and Saturday but doesn't take reservations.

Bankside, SE1. ✆ **020/7887-8000,** or 020/7887-8888 for events. www.tate.org.uk. Permanent collection free; temporary exhibitions £5.50–£8.50 ($10–$16). Sun–Thurs 10am–6pm; Fri–Sat 10am–10pm; galleries open at 10:15am. Closed Dec 24–26. Tube: Southwark, Mansion House, or St. Paul's (cross over Millennium Bridge). River services: Bankside Pier.

Tower of London ★★★ *Kids* This is the most perfectly preserved medieval fortress in Britain, and you'll need at least 2 or 3 hours for your visit, especially since the restored New Armouries building has opened as a delicious and good-value cafe.

Over the centuries, the Tower has served as a palace and royal refuge; a prison, military base, and supplies depot; home to the Royal Mint and the Royal Observatory; and finally, a national monument. It has only twice come into practical use since the late 19th century: in World War I, 11 spies were executed here; then, in World War II, Rudolph Hess was a prisoner here for 4 days, and another spy was executed. The oldest part is the massive **White Tower,** built in 1078 by the Norman king, William the Conqueror, to protect London and discourage rebellion among his new Saxon subjects. Every king after him added to the main structure, so that when Edward I completed the outer walls in the late 13th century, they enclosed an 18-acre square. Walk round the top of them for a bird's-eye view of how the Tower of London would have looked in its heyday.

The **Crown Jewels,** glittering in the Jewel House in Waterloo Barracks, are the real must-see. No words can do justice to the Imperial State Crown, encrusted with 3,200 precious stones, including a 317-carat diamond. A moving walkway is meant to keep visitors flowing through, but it can still be a long wait. The **Martin Tower** exhibition tells the stories of two of the world's most famous diamonds, the Koh-i-Noor and Cullinan II, as well as of a botched attempt to steal the State regalia in the late 17th century.

Visitors with a more ghoulish bent should start at **The Chapel Royal of St. Peter ad Vincula,** which contains the graves of all the unfortunates executed at the Tower. The Scaffold Site, where the axeman dispatched seven of the highest-ranking victims, including Henry VIII's wives, Anne Boleyn and Catherine Howard, is just outside. Everyone else met his or her end on **Tower Green.** Imagine their terror as they arrived by boat at the dread **Traitors' Gate.** The **Bloody Tower** was where Richard of Gloucester locked up his young nephews while he usurped his crusading brother Edward IV. The princes' bodies were later mysteriously found by the White Tower. Today, an exhibit re-creates how Sir Walter Raleigh might have lived during his 13-year imprisonment after the Gunpowder Plot against James I.

The royal menagerie moved out in 1834 to form the new London Zoo—all except the **ravens.** Legend has it Charles II was told that if they ever left the Tower the monarchy would fall. Ever since, a few birds with clipped wings have been kept in a lodging next to Wakefield Tower, looked after by a yeoman warder. The **yeoman warders,** or Beefeaters, have guarded the Tower for centuries. They lead tours every half-hour from 9:30am to 3:30pm and give vivid talks at 9:30, 10:15, 11:30am, 2:15, 4:30, and 5:15pm (the first one on Sun is at 10:30am). Costumed guides also re-create historic happenings.

As well as the daily **Ceremony of the Keys** (see box, below), there's a schedule of state events and gun salutes. Call for info. **Beating the Bounds** takes place every third year on Ascension Day, the Thursday 40 days after Easter. The Chief Yeoman Warder leads 31 choirboys around the 31 parish boundary marks in the surrounding streets, beating each one with willow wands, to signal the Tower's independence from the jurisdiction of the city. Now *that's* tradition.

Tower Hill, EC3. ✆ **0870/756-6060,** or 0870/756-7070 box office. www.hrp.org.uk. Admission £15 ($27) adults, £11 ($20) students and seniors, £9.50 ($18) children under 16, £42 ($78) family ticket. Save £1 ($1.85) booking in advance by phone or online. Mar–Oct Tues–Sat 9am–6pm, Sun–Mon 10am–6pm; Nov–Feb Tues–Sat 9am–5pm, Sun–Mon 10am–5pm. Last tickets sold 1 hr. before closing. Last entry to buildings 30 min. before closing. Closed Jan 1 and Dec 24–26. Tube: Tower Hill. DLR: Tower Gateway. River services: Tower Pier.

Trafalgar Square ★★ Tourists have been flocking to Trafalgar Square (along with pigeons) since it opened in 1845. It used to be an island in the middle of a roaringly busy traffic circle, but after a major redesign, it reopened in 2003 with one side attached to the steps of the National Gallery, so visitors can easily reach it. Besides being a major tourist attraction, the square is the site of many large gatherings, such as political demonstrations and holiday celebrations. The square honors military hero Horatio Viscount Nelson (1758–1805), who lost his life at the Battle of Trafalgar against the French. Nelson's Column, with fountains and four bronze lions at its base, rises 145 feet above the square. At the top, a 14-foot-high statue of Nelson (who stood at 5 ft. 4 in. in real life) looks commandingly toward Admiralty Arch, passed through by state and royal processions between Buckingham Palace and St. Paul's Cathedral.

Bounded on the north by Trafalgar, on the west by Cockspur St., and on the east by Whitehall. Tube: Charing Cross.

Victoria & Albert Museum ★★ Even the staff drop bread crumbs to find their way around this labyrinthine treasure house. Recent plans to extend the 7 miles of galleries devoted to the decorative and fine arts with an ultramodern, and ultracontroversial, new building by Daniel Libeskind had to be scaled down, but the **British Galleries** reopened in late 2001 after a £31-million ($50-million) overhaul. The revamped galleries reflect a new, interactive approach: there are pieces to handle, video re-creations of how they were used, and commentaries on taste by historical figures and today's top designers. Iconic objects, such as the Great Bed of Ware, which Shakespeare mentions in *Twelfth Night,* tell the story of Britain's 400-year rise (1500–1900) to world power and cultural authority.

Once you've "done" the British Galleries, you'll want to cherry-pick the highlights from the rest of the V&A's collections: the designer dresses in the **Costume Gallery,** textiles, sculpture, furniture, prints, paintings, photographs, silver, glass, ceramics, and jewelry, from Britain and all over the world. Not only is the museum worth a good long visit, but there are so many regular activities you'll want to keep coming back. Free guided tours take place daily every hour, 10:30am to 3:30pm, plus 4:30pm on Wednesday.

Cromwell Rd., SW7. ✆ **020/7942-2000,** or 020/7942-2209 events. www.vam.ac.uk. Free admission. Daily 10am–5:45pm; Wed and last Fri each month 10am–10pm. Closed Dec 24–26. Tube: South Kensington.

The Ceremony of the Keys

Every night for 700 years, the guards have secured the Tower of London with the **Ceremony of the Keys.** The chief yeoman warder marches out across the causeway at 10 o'clock precisely to lock the entrance gate, then returns with the guard to do the same at the Byward Tower. As the pair approaches the Bloody Tower, the sentry cries, "Halt, who goes there?" and the chief yeoman warder replies "The Keys." "Whose keys?" comes the demand. "Queen Elizabeth's keys." The sentry presents arms, and the chief warder raises his Tudor bonnet, yelling, "God preserve Queen Elizabeth." The ritual ends with a rousing "amen" from the whole guard. Tickets to see it are free. Write at least 2 months in advance, enclosing two International Reply Coupons (or a self-addressed envelope with British postage), to: Ceremony of the Keys, HM Tower of London, London EC3N 4AB, England.

Westminster Abbey ★★★ This ancient building is neither a cathedral nor a parish church, but a "royal peculiar," under the jurisdiction of the dean and chapter, and subject only to the sovereign. It's also one of the most popular tourist attractions in London and tends to be packed in the summer months.

Largely dating from the 13th to 16th centuries, Westminster Abbey has played a prominent part in British history—most recently with the funeral of Princess Diana and, in 2002, of the Queen Mother. All but two coronations since 1066 have taken place here. The oak **Coronation Chair,** made in 1308 for Edward I, can be seen in the **Chapel of Edward the Confessor.** From 1266 when the English seized it until 1998 when it was finally returned to St. Giles Cathedral in Edinburgh, the coronation chair held the ancient Stone of Scone, on which the kings of Scotland were crowned. Visit the **Norman Undercroft** to see the replica coronation regalia.

Five kings and four queens, including half-sisters Queen Elizabeth I and Mary Tudor and Elizabeth's rival for the throne, Mary Queen of Scots, are buried in the beautiful, fan-vaulted **Chapel of Henry VII.**

In 1400, Geoffrey Chaucer became the first literary celebrity to be buried in **Poets' Corner**. Ben Jonson is there, as well as Dryden, Samuel Johnson, Sheridan, Browning, and Tennyson. The practice of putting up literary memorials began in earnest in the 18th century with a full-length figure of Shakespeare, but the sinner Oscar Wilde didn't get a memorial window until 1995.

The **Tomb of the Unknown Soldier** honors the fallen of World War I. The nameless man lies under Belgian stone in soil brought back from the battlefields of France. Above the West Door, on the outside, you'll see **statues of 20th-century martyrs** such as Martin Luther King and Maximilian Kolbe, the Catholic priest who died at Auschwitz.

Guided tours of the abbey, lead by the vergers, cost £4 ($7). These start at 10, 10:30, 11am, 2, 2:30, and 3pm during the week April through October; at 10, 11am, 2, and 3pm on winter weekdays; and at 10, 10:30, and 11am on Saturday year-round. It's best to reserve ahead. Audioguides are £3 ($5). Call to find out if any concerts are scheduled; hearing music in this space is a memorable experience.

Dean's Yard, SW1. ✆ **020/7222-5152.** www.westminster-abbey.org. Admission £8 ($15) adults; £6 ($11) seniors, students, children under 16; £18 ($33) family ticket. Cloisters, College Garden, St. Margaret's Church free. Abbey Mon–Fri 9:30am–3:45pm (Wed until 7pm); Sat 9:30am–1:45pm; Sun for worship only. Abbey Museum daily

10:30am–4pm. Cloisters 8am–6pm. College Garden Apr–Sept 10am–6pm; Oct–Mar 10am–4pm. St. Margaret's Church Mon–Fri 9:30am–3:45pm; Sat 9:30am–1:45pm; Sun 2–5pm. Tube: Westminster.

3 Churches, Cathedrals & a Cemetery

Many of the churches listed below put on lunchtime concerts. Tickets are usually free, although it's customary to leave a small donation. The **City Information Centre,** St. Paul's Churchyard, EC4 (✆ **020/7332-1456**), can give you a full list. It's open from 9:30am to 5pm, daily April through September and weekdays October through March, and 9:30am to 12:30pm on winter Saturdays.

Brompton Oratory ★ The priests of the Institute of the Oratory, founded by St. Philip Neri, serve this amazing church, which architect Herbert Gribble modeled after the Chiesa Nuova in Rome. Completed in 1884, its baroque extravagance marked a revival of English Catholicism. The marble statues of the apostles are by Mazzuoli and were originally in Siena Cathedral. The Oratory is famous for its beautiful musical services—the organ has nearly 4,000 pipes—and for the Latin Mass, sung at 11am on Sunday.

Thurloe Place, Brompton Rd., SW7. ✆ **020/7808-0900.** Free admission. Daily 6:30am–8pm. Tube: South Kensington.

Highgate Cemetery Serpentine pathways wind through this beautiful cemetery, which opened in 1829 and quickly became the fashionable place to be buried. You have to take a tour to visit the old western part of the cemetery; the eastern section was added 3 decades later. Victorian funerary rituals were extraordinarily elaborate—witness the tomb-lined Egyptian Avenue, which leads up to the catacombs in the Circle of Lebanon. Scientist Michael Faraday, poet Christina Rossetti, and many other famous figures are buried here in an atmosphere that is part fright-night movie, part woodsy wildlife sanctuary. The grave of Karl Marx, marked by a gargantuan bust, lies in the eastern cemetery, as does that of novelist George Eliot, whose real name was Mary Anne Evans. The cemetery is still very much in use. No children under 8 can enter the western side, and you have to buy a permit to use a camera (no video allowed).

Swain's Lane, N6. ✆ **020/8340-1834.** East Cemetery £2 ($3.70); West Cemetery £3 ($6); £1 ($1.85) to bring a small camera. East Cemetery Apr–Oct Mon–Fri 10am–4:30pm, Sat–Sun 11am–4:30pm; Nov–Mar last admission 3:30pm. West Cemetery tours Mar–Nov Mon–Fri 2pm, Sat–Sun 11am, noon, 1, 2, and 3pm. Tube: Archway. No children under 8 in the West Cemetery.

St. Bride's Church St. Bride's is in Fleet Street, once the heart of Britain's newspaper industry, which is why it is known as the "journalists' and printers' church." An archaeological dig, carried out after the 1940 bombing, discovered a Roman house preserved in the crypt—there's a museum there now. St. Brigit of Ireland founded the first Christian church here, and the present one is the eighth on the site. After the Great Fire, Sir Christopher Wren supervised the rebuilding. The spire was added later. This "madrigal in stone"—four octagonal tiers capped by an obelisk, itself topped off with a ball and vane—is 234 feet tall and supposedly inspired the wedding cakes of a 17th-century Fleet Street pastry cook. St. Bride's has had many famous parishioners, including writers John Dryden, John Milton, and the diarist Samuel Pepys, who was baptized here. There are half-hour concerts every Tuesday and Friday.

Fleet St., EC4. ✆ **020/7427-0133.** Free admission. Mon–Fri 8am–4:45pm; Sat 10am–3:30pm; Sun 10am–12:30pm and 5:30–7:30pm. Concerts at 1:05 or 1:15pm on Tues and Fri. Tube: Blackfriars.

St. Clement Danes No one knows for certain where the "Danes" comes from, but there was once a wooden Saxon church on this site. Rebuilt in stone in the late 10th century, it survived the Great Fire but was declared unsafe. Sir Christopher Wren (him again!) was commissioned to rebuild it, though James Gibbs designed the spire. Samuel Johnson attended services regularly, and the wife of poet John Donne is buried here. Gutted in the Blitz, St. Clement's was rebuilt in the late 1950s and underwent another big renovation in 1999. This is the RAF's church and contains memorials to the British, Commonwealth, and American airmen who flew in World War II.

Strand, WC2. ✆ **020/7242-8282.** Free admission. Daily 8:30am–4:30pm. Tube: Temple (closed Sun), Charing Cross, or Blackfriars.

St. James's Church, Piccadilly ★ In the late 17th century, the thriving city expanded its western borders into a new aristocratic enclave known as St. James's. Its patrons naturally commissioned Sir Christopher Wren to build their parish church, while Grinling Gibbons carved the reredos, organ case, and font. As might be expected, this church has rich historical associations. William Blake, the poet and artist, and William Pitt, who became England's youngest prime minister at age 24, were both baptized at St. James's. The church has seen some colorful weddings in its time—like that of explorer Sir Samuel Baker to a woman he bought at a Turkish slave auction. St. James's holds lunchtime recitals on Monday, Wednesday, and Friday and has an irregular program of inexpensive evening concerts and talks. The courtyard market is worth a look for odd little gifts amid the crafty kitsch.

197 Piccadilly, W1. ✆ **020/7734-4511.** Free admission. Daily 8am–7pm. Free recitals Mon, Wed, and Fri at 1:10pm. Courtyard market: antiques Tues, crafts and souvenirs Wed–Sat. Tube: Piccadilly Circus or Green Park.

St. Martin-in-the-Fields ★ This church is one of the best loved in London. The current building dates from 1726. Designed by James Gibbs, the intricate plasterwork ceiling enhances the simple nave. Curiously, the parish boundary passes through the middle of Buckingham Palace, and the names of many royal children appear on the baptismal registry. St. Martin's is famous for its music: Handel played the organ here, though not the current 3,637-pipe instrument, which was installed in 1990. There are free concerts at 1pm on Monday, Tuesday, and Friday. Evening recitals take place from Thursday to Saturday. Many are by candlelight, and the program leans heavily toward the baroque. The choral music during the three Sunday services is sublime. Evensong is the most quintessentially Anglican, usually at 5pm, but call ahead for specific times.

In the crypt of St. Martin's is the **London Brass Rubbing Centre,** which has replicas of about 100 medieval and Tudor church brasses as well as unusual Celtic patterns and early woodcuts of the zodiac. Materials and instruction are provided, and it's great fun. If you have time, take a break for tea or a delicious meal at the **Café in the Crypt** (see chapter 6).

Trafalgar Sq., WC2. ✆ **020/7766-1100** for church info, 020/7839-8362 for box office, or 020/7930-9306 London Brass Rubbing Centre. www.stmartin-in-the-fields.org. Free admission to church and lunchtime recitals, evening concerts £6–£17 ($11–$31). Brass rubbings £3–£15 ($6–$28) based on the size and complexity of brass. Church daily 9am–6pm (except during services); London Brass Rubbing Centre Mon–Sat 10am–6pm; Sun noon–6pm. Tube: Charing Cross or Leicester Sq.

St. Mary Le Bow Traditionally, to be a true Cockney, you have to be born within the sound of Bow bells—the ones that ring at this church. St. Mary's colorful history has been marked by a series of bizarre incidents. The first happened in 1091, when a storm ripped off the roof. Then, in 1271, the church tower collapsed, killing 20 people. In

1331, Queen Philippa and her ladies-in-waiting plummeted to the ground when a wooden balcony collapsed during a joust to celebrate the birth of the Black Prince. The Great Fire destroyed the church, and it was rebuilt by the great architect Wren and rededicated in 1964 after a big restoration. As well as the Thursday lunchtime concerts, the rector holds discussions with an intriguing range of guests, from museum curators to movie directors and representatives of other faiths, every Tuesday during school terms.

Cheapside, EC2. ✆ **020/7248-5139.** Free admission. Mon–Thurs 6:30am–6pm; Fri 6:30am–4pm. Lunchtime concerts Thurs 1:05pm. Dialogues Tues 1:05pm during school terms. Closed major holidays and the week after Christmas and Easter. Tube: St. Paul's, Bank, or Mansion House.

St. Paul's, The Actors' Church The Drury Lane Theatre, the Theatre Royal, and the Royal Opera House are all within the parish of St. Paul's, so it's little wonder that it has become known as the actors' church. Inside, you'll find dozens of memorial plaques dedicated to such thespian luminaries as Vivien Leigh, Boris Karloff, and Noel Coward, to name but a few. It is also the last resting place of wood-carver Grinling Gibbons, writer Samuel Butler, and the doctor's daughter Margaret Ponteous, who was the first victim of the Great Plague in 1665. Famous baptisms here have included that of landscape painter J. M. W. Turner and librettist W. S. Gilbert. Despite substantial and repeated restoration work over the years, particularly after a fire in 1795, the church is still largely how Inigo Jones designed it for the earl of Bedford in the 17th century, with its quiet garden piazza in the rear. St. Paul's celebrates the Eucharist at 11am on Sunday. Every second Sunday of the month, there is choral evensong at 4pm.

Bedford St., WC2. ✆ **020/7836-5221.** Free admission. Mon–Fri 8:30am–4:30pm; Sun 9:30am–12:30pm. Tube: Covent Garden.

Southwark Cathedral ★ Archaeological evidence proves this to have been a place of worship for more than 1,000 years. The present church dates from the 15th century, though it was partially rebuilt in 1890. And it has just had a £10-million ($18.5-million) makeover: The stonework is clean of London grime and floodlit; the riverside courtyard has been cleared of the modern offices; and a new visitor center has opened to teach people about the history of Southwark. In medieval times, this was a raucous borough where theaters flourished, prostitutes plied their trade, and people enjoyed the cruel sport of bear-baiting. It was also the first stop on the pilgrimage to Canterbury, as immortalized by Chaucer's Tales. Chaucer and Shakespeare both worshipped here—don't miss the Bard's carved memorial. Southwark Cathedral has a notable choir, so it's worth attending a service here just for the music. Otherwise, there are free concerts every Monday and Tuesday at 1pm and a program of other events. In the summer, tables are put out in the courtyard, which makes a very nice pit-stop on a day out on the south bank of the Thames.

Montague Close, London Bridge, SE1. ✆ **020/7367-6700.** www.dswark.org. Free admission, suggested donation £4–£6.50 ($7–$12). Mon–Fri 7:30am–6pm; Sat–Sun 8:30am–6pm. Tube: London Bridge. River services: London Bridge City.

Wesley's Chapel, House & Museum John Wesley, the founder of Methodism, established this chapel in 1778 as his London base. There's a daylong service every year on November 1 to celebrate the occasion and another on May 24 to mark his full conversion. This simple man, who traveled around England on horseback and preached in the open air, is buried in a grave behind the chapel. The building somehow survived the Blitz but later fell into serious disrepair, until a major restoration in the 1970s. The museum in the crypt traces the history of Methodism. Look out for Wesley's bizarre experimental machine for electric shock treatment. Come here for one of the Tuesday lunchtime music recitals. Across the road in **Bunhill Fields** is the Dissenters Graveyard where Daniel Defoe, William Blake, and John Bunyan are buried.

49 City Rd., EC1. ✆ **020/7253-2262.** Free admission. House and museum Mon–Sat 10am–4pm (closed Thurs 12:45–1:30pm, worshippers welcome); Sun noon–1:45pm. Music recital every Tues at 1:05pm. Tube: Old St. or Moorgate.

Westminster Cathedral ★ The land this cathedral stands on once belonged to the monks of Westminster Abbey, who used it for a market and feast-day fairs. After the dissolution of the monasteries under Henry VIII, it changed hands several times until 1882, when Cardinal Henry Edward Manning bought the land for what was to become the premier Roman Catholic church in Britain. John Francis Bentley designed the massive brick-and-stone edifice (1903)—360 feet long and 156 feet wide—in spectacular Byzantine style. The richly decorated interior uses 100 different kinds of marble, and mosaics emblazon the chapels and the vaulting of the sanctuary. The controversial Stations of the Cross are the work of famous sculptor Eric Gill. You can take an elevator to the gallery at the top of the 273-foot-tall **campanile** ★ for a fantastic panoramic view over London. Music is an extremely important part of cathedral life and has been since composer Sir Edward Elgar premiered his celebrated choral work *The Dream of Gerontius* at its opening. On Sundays you can attend a free organ recital or sung mass. Call for information on the concert program.

Ashley Place, SW1. ✆ **020/7798-9055.** www.westminstercathedral.org.uk. Cathedral and Sun organ recitals free; tower £2 ($3.70) adults, £1 ($1.85) children under 16. Cathedral daily 7am–7pm; Campanile lift Apr–Nov daily 9am–5pm, Dec–Mar Thurs–Sun 9am–5pm. Tube: Victoria.

4 Memorials & Monuments

Since ancient times, nations have honored their heroes with imposing public memorials. And there can be few more imposing than **Nelson's Column** in Trafalgar Square (the original model for the column is on display at the National Maritime Museum, p. 194). The admiral's victory at the Battle of Trafalgar in 1805 staved off the French invasion and cost him his life. It took almost 40 years to complete the 185-foot Corinthian column, a copy of one in the temple of Mars Ultor (the Avenger) in Rome. Bronze reliefs on the sides of the pedestal commemorate Nelson's most famous battles. By the time Landseer's lions were added in 1867, their four empty plinths had become a standing joke, as is the one that has now been empty for 161 years while city grandees debate which famous person deserves such high-profile immortalization. It may be Nelson Mandela.

Fun Fact Size Matters

Nelson's Column may be the most famous in the world, but **The Monument** is nearly 20 feet taller. Christopher Wren and Robert Hooke built it in 1677 to commemorate the Great Fire of London: The Doric column is 202 feet high, which matches the distance from Monument Street to the famous baker's shop in Pudding Lane where the fire started. It's a grueling 311-step climb to the viewing gallery at the top—well worth it for the view over the City of London. Open 10am to 5:40pm daily; £2 ($3.70) adults, £1 ($1.85) seniors, students, and children. For info, call ✆ **020/7626-2717;** the Tube stop is Monument.

Thanks to a new pedestrian-friendly scheme, you can now walk directly into Trafalgar Square to marvel at Nelson's Column from the National Gallery without bumper-to-bumper buses spoiling the view and forcing you to dodge traffic. This is the first phase of an urban renaissance project due to extend down to Parliament Square, sprucing up Whitehall on the way. Whitehall is where you'll find the **Cenotaph,** a very simple, but eloquent, memorial to the fallen of World Wars I and II. Designed by Sir Edwin Lutyens, it is the center of Remembrance Day ceremonies on November 11.

The **Wellington Arch** is a Hyde Park Corner landmark. Originally commissioned as a posh gateway to Buckingham Palace, it was later recycled into a memorial to Wellington's victory over Napoleon. Wellington's statue on top was too big and was sent off to army headquarters in 1882 when the arch was moved to ease a traffic bottleneck. A sculpture called *Peace Descending on the Quadriga of War* by Adrian Jones replaced it and looks spectacular with the bronze relieved of its wartime black paint. The arch was a police station for a while, but now the public can go inside and see the view from the top down Constitution Hill. There is also an exhibition about London's memorials and monuments. The arch is open Wednesday to Sunday from 10am to 5pm, closing at 4pm in winter, and tickets cost £3 ($5.50) adults, £2.30 ($4.25) seniors and students, and £1.50 ($2.75) for children (✆ **020/7930-2726;** www.english-heritage.org.uk).

London's most extraordinary monument is the **Albert Memorial** in Kensington Gardens. Queen Victoria was so devastated by Albert's premature death from typhoid fever in 1861 that she withdrew from public life for more than a decade and wore her trademark black until she died in 1901. Unveiled in 1998 after a 10-year restoration, this ostentatious Gothic icon is in better condition than when it was built to designs by Sir George Gilbert Scott. Gilding removed in World War I glows once more, and missing statuary and mosaics have been replaced.

Dedicated to Princess Diana, the **Peter Pan playground** in Kensington Gardens, not far from the Albert Memorial, is a wonderland with a pirate galleon for children to scramble about on. This replaced the idea for a memorial garden, which locals feared would be besieged by hordes of pilgrims. **Westminster Abbey** and **St. Paul's Cathedral** both hold memorials to many famous people and events, as do the sacred places listed in the section above.

5 Lots More Sights to See

HISTORIC BUILDINGS

London is filled with historic buildings, but most visitors have a hard enough time just visiting the city's major attractions without seeking out these secondary sites. Part of the fun of visiting London, though, is discovering its lesser-known treasures.

Banqueting House This is all that remains of the great Palace of Whitehall after the fire of 1698. A masterpiece of English Renaissance architecture (1619–22), it was designed by Inigo Jones for James I. The main hall was used for posh banqueting (as it still is today), hence the nine magnificent ceiling paintings by Rubens, depicting the Divine Right of Kings (evidently one of their divine rights was to eat as much as possible). You can also visit the undercroft (crypt), where the king could get drunk with his mates. The bust of Charles I above the entrance reminds visitors that, king by "divine right" or not, he was beheaded in front of the building. Combine a visit with watching the Changing of the Guard, at Horse Guards opposite (p. 61).

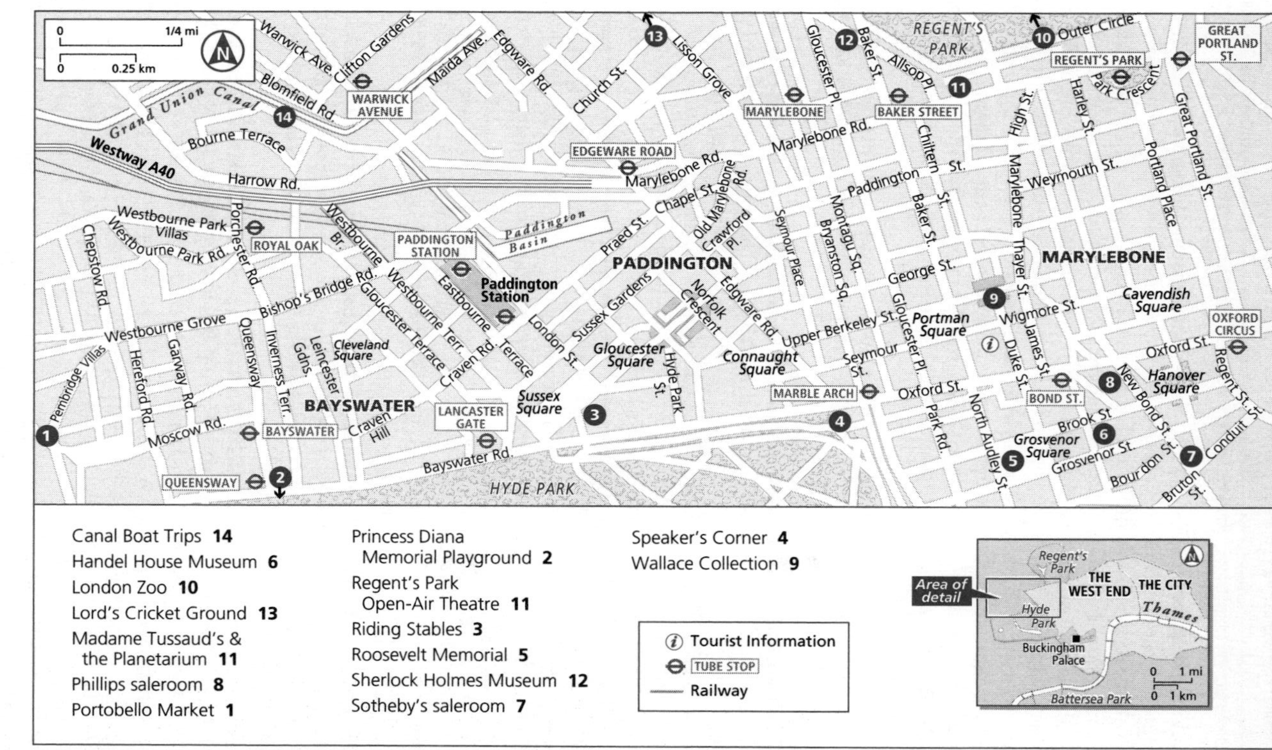
Canal Boat Trips 14
Handel House Museum 6
London Zoo 10
Lord's Cricket Ground 13
Madame Tussaud's & the Planetarium 11
Phillips saleroom 8
Portobello Market 1
Princess Diana Memorial Playground 2
Regent's Park Open-Air Theatre 11
Riding Stables 3
Roosevelt Memorial 5
Sherlock Holmes Museum 12
Sotheby's saleroom 7
Speaker's Corner 4
Wallace Collection 9
Tourist Information
TUBE STOP
Railway
Area of detail
Regent's Park
THE WEST END
THE CITY
Thames
Hyde Park
Buckingham Palace
Battersea Park
0 1 mi
0 1 km
0 1/4 mi
0 0.25 km
MARYLEBONE
PADDINGTON
BAYSWATER
HYDE PARK
REGENT'S PARK
Paddington Station
Paddington Basin
Grand Union Canal
Westway A40
GREAT PORTLAND ST.
OXFORD CIRCUS
REGENT'S PARK
BAKER STREET
MARYLEBONE
EDGEWARE ROAD
PADDINGTON STATION
WARWICK AVENUE
ROYAL OAK
BAYSWATER
QUEENSWAY
LANCASTER GATE
MARBLE ARCH
BOND ST.
Great Portland St.
Portland Place
Regent St.
Oxford St.
Cavendish Square
Hanover Square
New Bond St.
Conduit St.
Bruton St.
Bourdon St.
Grosvenor St.
Brook St.
Grosvenor Square
North Audley St.
Duke St.
James St.
Wigmore St.
Thayer St.
Marylebone High St.
Weymouth St.
Harley St.
Park Crescent
Outer Circle
Baker St.
Allsop Pl.
Chiltern St.
Paddington St.
George St.
Portman Square
Gloucester Pl.
Park Rd.
Montagu Sq.
Bryanston Sq.
Seymour Place
Upper Berkeley St.
Seymour St.
Connaught Square
Edgware Rd.
Marylebone Rd.
Old Marylebone Rd.
Crawford Pl.
Chapel St.
Lisson Grove
Church St.
Praed St.
Norfolk Crescent
Hyde Park St.
Gloucester Square
Sussex Gardens
London St.
Sussex Square
Eastbourne Terrace
Craven Rd.
Westbourne Terr.
Gloucester Terrace
Craven Hill
Bayswater Rd.
Westbourne Br.
Bishop's Bridge Rd.
Cleveland Square
Leincester Gdns.
Inverness Terr.
Queensway
Porchester Rd.
Maida Ave.
Clifton Gardens
Warwick Ave.
Blomfield Rd.
Bourne Terrace
Harrow Rd.
Westbourne Park Villas
Westbourne Park Rd.
Westbourne Grove
Garway Rd.
Hereford Rd.
Moscow Rd.
Chepstow Rd.
Pembridge Villas

Opposite Horse Guards Parade, Whitehall, SW1. ✆ **0870/751-5178.** www.hrp.org.uk. Admission £4 ($7) adults, £3 ($6) seniors and students, £2.60 ($4.80) children 5–16. Mon–Sat 10am–5pm. Last admission 4pm. Closed Dec 24–Jan 1, Good Friday, and for government functions. Tube: Charing Cross, Embankment, or Westminster.

Cabinet War Rooms ★★ This warren of underground rooms served as Prime Minister Winston Churchill's nerve center and the secret HQ of the British government during World War II. It is preserved exactly as it was back then: the Cabinet Room, where the PM, his ministers, and military men made their crucial decisions; the Map Room, where they plotted out the progress of the war; the Telephone Room, where so many calls were placed to and received from FDR; even the PM's Emergency Bedroom. In 1995, the Heritage Lottery Fund bought the Churchill Papers for the nation. The core of the collection is held in Cambridge, but there are always pieces on display here. It is eerie and oddly exciting imagining the great man and his staff living their tense subterranean life. Unfortunately, the admission price has almost doubled since our last edition.

Clive Steps, King Charles St., SW1. ✆ **020/7930-6961.** www.iwm.org.uk. Admission £10 ($18) adults, £8 ($15) students and seniors, free for children under 16. Daily 9:30am–6pm; last admission 5pm. Closed Dec 24–26. Tube: Westminster or St. James's Park.

Guildhall & Guildhall Art Gallery The Guildhall has been the seat of government for the City of London for more than 800 years. The building dates from 1411 and has the largest medieval crypt in a capital crawling with crypts. What you see doesn't look particularly ancient, though, because the Guildhall has been restored on several occasions, notably after the Great Fire and the Blitz. Among the decorations are the banners of the 100 livery companies and inscriptions in the windows recording the names of all the lord mayors since 1189. Some of them also merit a monument, as do Churchill, Wellington, and Nelson. Statues of the legendary giants Gog and Magog guard the institution. The recently reopened Guildhall Art Gallery displays mostly 19th-century paintings by the likes of Millais and Landseer.

Off Gresham St., EC2. ✆ **020/7606-3030,** or 020/7332-3700 Art Gallery. www.corpoflondon.gov.uk. Free admission to Guildhall; Art Gallery £2.50 ($4.60) adults, £1 ($1.85) seniors, free for children under 16, free on Fri and from 3:30pm. Guildhall Apr–Sept daily; Oct–Mar Mon–Fri 9:30am–5pm, Sat 9:30am–12:30pm. Art Gallery Mon–Sat 10am–5pm, Sun noon–4pm. Closed Jan 1, Good Friday, Easter Monday, Dec 24–26, and for ceremonial occasions. Tube: Bank.

Jewel Tower Opposite the Houses of Parliament, this is one of only two surviving buildings from the medieval Palace of Westminster. It was built around 1365 so that Edward III had somewhere to stash his treasures. The exhibition explains how Parliament works and runs a virtual-reality tour of both houses.

Abingdon St., Westminster, SW1. ✆ **020/7222-2219.** www.english-heritage.org.uk. Admission £2.20 ($4.10) adults, £1.70 ($3.15) seniors, £1.10 ($2) children under 16. Apr–Oct daily 10am–6pm; Nov–Mar daily 10am–4pm. Closed Dec 24–26 and Jan 1. Tube: Westminster.

Royal Hospital Chelsea Inspired by the Hôtel des Invalides in Paris, Charles II founded this dignified home for veteran soldiers in 1682. Hence the statue of the king, by Grinling Gibbons, in the courtyard. Sir Christopher Wren completed the buildings in 1692, and there's been little change since, except for minor work done by Robert Adam in the 18th century and the addition of Sir John Soane's stables in 1814. In the main block, you can look around the museum, chapel, and Great Hall, where the duke of Wellington lay in state for a week in 1852. The east and west wings are dormitories for around 400 ex-servicemen pensioners, in blue uniforms for everyday,

Moments **Your Day in Court**

You can witness mainly civil cases at the **Royal Courts of Justice,** in the Strand, WC2. Designed by G. E. Street, the neo-Gothic court buildings (1874–82) contain more than 1,000 rooms. Sessions run from 10:30am to 1pm, and 2 to 4pm, Monday to Friday, except during August and September (✆ **020/7947-6000;** www.courtservice.gov.uk; Tube: Temple).

The nation's Central Criminal Court is in the City. Affectionately known as the **Old Bailey,** it has seen many famous trials, including those of Oscar Wilde, Lord Haw Haw, and the Yorkshire Ripper. Take a seat in one of the public viewing galleries to watch the bewigged barristers presenting their cases. The courts are on Newgate Street, EC4 (✆ **020/7248-3277;** Tube: St. Paul's). There's even a remnant of the original city walls down in the basement. Sessions keep the same hours as above; you can't take cameras, electronic equipment (mobile phone, pager, radio, and so on), large bags, food, or drink, and the court cannot look after anything for you, so leave all your gear at your hotel. No children under 14.

red on ceremonial occasions. The grounds play host to the annual Chelsea Flower Show (p. 26), and the buildings are close to the National Army Museum (p. 188) and the Chelsea Physic Garden (p. 201).

Royal Hospital Rd., SW3. ✆ **020/7881-5204.** www.chelsea-pensioners.org.uk. Free admission. Mon–Sat 10am–noon and 2–4pm; Sun 2–4pm (closed Sun Oct–Mar). Tube: Sloane Sq.

MUSEUMS & GALLERIES

If you are interested in England's sporting history, check out the museums of cricket, rugby, and tennis in "Spectator Sports," later in this chapter.

Bank of England Museum Housed in the old Stock Office, designed in 1793 by Sir John Soane, the museum traces the history of the "Old Lady of Threadneedle Street" from its foundation by Royal Charter in 1694 to its current role as the nation's central bank. Gold glitters in ancient ingots and the modern market bar, and you can feel how heavy they are. There are also displays of bank notes, coins, and the pikes and muskets used to defend the bank. The private financial papers of such famous clients as the duchess of Marlborough, George Washington, and Horatio Nelson are there for everyone to nose through. One interactive presentation gives an intriguing insight into the intricacies of bank note design and production. Another lets you risk it all on the Dollar/Sterling Exchange market.

Threadneedle St., EC2. ✆ **020/7601-5491.** www.bankofengland.co.uk. Free admission. Mon–Fri 10am–5pm. Closed bank holidays. Tube: Bank.

Barbican Art Gallery This is the Barbican's main exhibition space, where shows ranging from established artists to design, photography, and low-culture surprises are mounted. Shows in the Concourse Gallery on level "0" (rechristened **The Curve)** are free; admission is charged for the other shows. The Barbican complex, dating from the 1970s, is one of the ugliest urban renewal schemes in the world: a perfect example of Brutalism at its very worst.

Level 3, Barbican Centre, Silk St., EC2. ✆ **0845/121-6828.** www.barbican.org.uk. Admission £8 ($15) adults; £6 ($11) students, seniors, and children under 15. Daily 10am–8pm (closes 6pm Tues and Thurs). Tube: Barbican or Moorgate.

British Library ★★ If you love English literature, make it a point to visit the British Library, housed in a new building in St. Pancras designed by Colin St. John Wilson and opened in 1998. This is the national research library responsible for Britain's printed archive. Legally, publishers must send in one copy of everything they produce. The library has three exhibition spaces. The **John Ritblat Gallery** displays the permanent collection of treasures brought from the library's old home, the British Museum: the *Magna Carta,* Shakespeare's first folio, the handwritten manuscript of Charlotte Brontë's *Jane Eyre,* and dozens of others. Throughout, there are audio stations where visitors can listen to poets and writers reading from their works—James Joyce from *Finnegan's Wake,* for example, or Virginia Woolf giving a lecture on the BBC. Truly amazing, though, are the interactive exhibits that allow you to flip through an illuminated manuscript, such as Leonardo's *Notebooks.* A second gallery is used for temporary exhibitions, and the third, The Workshop of Words, Sounds & Images, traces the history of book production from the earliest written documents to the current digital revolution—and there are regular free book-craft demonstrations. Also in the busy events schedule are free Monday lunchtime talks and Friday lunchtime author visits and discussions. There's also an excellent shop and a very pleasant and reasonably priced cafeteria.

96 Euston Rd., NW1. ✆ **020/7412-7332.** www.bl.uk. Free admission. Galleries and public areas Mon and Wed–Fri 9:30am–6pm; Tues 9:30am–8pm; Sat 9:30am–5pm; Sun 11am–5pm. Tours of public areas: Mon, Wed, and Fri 3pm, Sat 10:30am and 3pm; tickets £6 ($11) adults, £4.50 ($8.30) seniors and students. Tours including a reading room: Sun 11:30am and 3pm; tickets £7 ($13), £5.50 ($10) seniors and students. Tube: Euston or King's Cross.

Dalí Universe This gallery, curated by Dalí's long-time friend and collector Benjamin Levi, is pretty underwhelming unless you're an avid Dalí fan who'll pay to see anything he created. The iconic pieces have a curiosity value—the voluptuous Mae West Lips sofa, now looking a little grubby, and the eyeball painting for the set of Hitchcock's *Spellbound.* Otherwise, you need to be an expert to appreciate the crowded ranks of illustrations, drawings, and paintings.

County Hall, Riverside Building, SE1. ✆ **0870/744-7485.** www.daliuniverse.com. Admission £9 ($17) adults, £8 ($15) seniors and students, £5.50 ($10) kids 8–16 years, £3.50 ($6.50) kids 4–7 years. Daily 10:30am–5:30pm. Tube: Waterloo or Westminster. River services: Festival Pier.

Design Museum It's a bit out of the way, about a 10-minute walk east of Tower Bridge on the South Bank side, but if you're a design enthusiast you'll want to check out this museum (and its gift shop). Everything from Corbusier chairs to the Coke bottle is chronicled here. Changing shows highlight the important role that commercial design plays in our everyday lives. Plus there are great river views, and the surrounding area of converted warehouses is fascinating to explore.

Butlers Wharf, Shad Thames, South Bank, SE1. ✆ **0870/833-9955.** www.designmuseum.org. Admission £6 ($11) adults, £4 ($7.40) seniors and students, £16 ($30) family ticket. Daily 10am–5:45pm. Tube: Tower Hill or London Bridge.

Dulwich Picture Gallery ★★ This is Britain's oldest public picture gallery, set up in 1817 to house a superb collection of European Old Masters—Canaletto, Gainsborough, Poussin, Rembrandt, Rubens, and Van Dyck—put together at the behest of the king of Poland for his national museum. Forced to abdicate before paying his English art dealer, he never took possession. Sir John Soane designed the beautiful original building, now linked by an airy glass cloister to a new wing, comprising extra exhibition space, a lecture hall, cafe, and working studio. Each year, three temporary exhibitions borrow important works from all over the world (contact the museum for details). Free gallery tours take place every Saturday and Sunday at 3pm. And there is a whole program of talks, concerts, evening events, and children's workshops.

Gallery Rd., Dulwich Village SE21. ✆ **020/8693-5254.** www.dulwichpicturegallery.org.uk. Admission £4 ($7.40) adults, £3 ($5.50) seniors, free for students and children under 16. Tues–Fri 10am–5pm; Sat–Sun (and bank holiday Mon) 11am–5pm. Closed Jan 1, Good Friday, and Dec 24–26. Tube: Brixton, then P4 bus. Train: Victoria Station to West Dulwich.

Florence Nightingale Museum The reconstruction of a ward in Scutari Hospital in war-torn Crimea shows exactly the ghastly scene that fired Florence Nightingale's reforming zeal. She founded her School of Nursing here in 1860, dedicating her life to improving hospital standards and public health. You can see Nightingale's copious notebooks, as well as a bracelet she wore that was woven from her mother's and sister's hair (there is more of her jewelry at the National Army Museum; see below). There are free guided tours every weekday, and entrance tickets are valid for a month.

St. Thomas' Hospital, 2 Lambeth Palace Rd., SE1. ✆ **020/7620-0374.** www.florence-nightingale.co.uk. Admission £5.80 ($11) adults, £4.20 ($8) children and seniors, £13 ($24) family. Mon–Fri 10am–5pm; Sat–Sun 11:30am–4:30pm; last admission 1 hr. before closing. Closed Good Friday, Easter Sunday, and Dec 25–Jan 2. Tube: Westminster or Waterloo.

Geffrye Museum ★ *Finds* Located in Shoreditch, this gem of a museum is devoted to the home life of the English urban middle classes from 1600 to 2000. Based in the old Ironmongers' almshouses (1715), separate rooms re-create each era down to the last detail, as though the occupant had just popped out. Time-travel past Elizabethan oak, refined Georgian aesthetics, and hideously ornate Victoriana, to the 20th-century snapshots in the new wing. There you'll find Art Deco, postwar utility, the 1960s plastics explosion, even a 1990s loft conversion. December is magical as the rooms sparkle with festive decorations, bringing to life 400 years of Christmas tradition. As well as the original walled herb garden, a series of garden rooms trace the evolution of that green-fingered English passion. There's also a shop, restaurant, and a space dedicated to showcasing contemporary designers.

Kingsland Rd., E2. ✆ **020/7739-9893.** www.geffrye-museum.org.uk. Free admission. Tues–Sat 10am–5pm; Sun and holidays noon–5pm. Closed Jan 1, Good Friday, and Dec 24–26. Herb garden and period garden rooms open Apr–Oct. Tube: Liverpool St., then no. 149 or 242 bus.

Hayward Gallery ★ This highly regarded modern art gallery is wedged between the Royal National Theatre and the Royal Festival Hall on the South Bank. Built in 1968 (the era of ugly "brutalist" architecture), it has one of the largest and most versatile spaces in Britain. Shows conform to one of four different formats: single artists, historical themes and artistic movements, other cultures, and contemporary. There are always linked events—talks, children's workshops, video-recorded interviews with the artist, and so on—and often live guides who are happy to chat about an exhibition. Come early on weekends because the queues can be staggering.

Belvedere Rd., SE1. ✆ **020/7960-5226.** www.hayward-gallery.org.uk. Admission varies but is usually around £7 ($13) adults, £5 ($9) seniors, £3 ($5.50) students, free for children under 17. Tues–Wed 10am–8pm; Thurs–Mon 10am–6pm. Tube: Waterloo or Embankment. River services: Festival Pier.

Imperial War Museum ★★ Kids The IWM excels in explaining and re-creating 20th-century conflicts, honoring those who fought in them, and making sure they never happen again. A clock in the basement keeps a grim tally of the human cost of war—over 100 million people now. The Holocaust Exhibition, opened in 2000, continues that tradition. Four years in the making, it uses historical material—a funeral cart from the Warsaw Ghetto, victims' diaries and photograph albums, part of a deportation railcar—to tell the story of Nazi persecution. Eighteen survivors have given their testimony, while other exhibits explain the spread of anti-Semitism across Europe after World War I. Life in the trenches during World War I is the subject of another exhibit, as is the Blitz of World War II, which dramatically re-enacts an air raid with special effects, sound, and scents—clinical disinfectant, dusty old buildings, burnt wood, and cooking at the tea stands serving the rescuers. The curators, who collect a lot of witness reminiscences, say that smells are often the strongest memories. So they often use them to heighten reality, like the cheesy feet and body odor in the simulated submarine, which kids will love. There are tales of espionage and dirty tricks in the Secret War section, plus a German Enigma machine, invisible ink, and a re-creation of the SAS operation to break the Iranian Embassy siege in 1980.

Lambeth Rd., SE1. ✆ **020/7416-5320.** www.iwm.org.uk. Free admission. Daily 10am–6pm. Closed Dec 24–26. Tube: Lambeth North or Waterloo.

Institute of Contemporary Arts (ICA) The ICA is a major forum for the avant-garde arts, with two galleries, a theater, cinema, media center, cafe, bar, bookshop, and lecture program. Since it opened in 1948, many artists have held their first solo shows here. Among the more recent are Damien Hirst, Helen Chadwick, Gary Hume, and Steve McQueen. The ICA also hosts Beck's Futures, the largest art prize in the U.K: the shortlist exhibition runs from March to May. The admission price covers a 1-day membership. If you are attending a movie or performance, you can take in the galleries at no extra cost.

The Mall, SW1. ✆ **020/7930-3647,** or 020/7930-6393 recorded info. www.ica.org.uk. Galleries Mon–Fri £1.50 ($2.75) adults, £1 ($1.85) seniors; Sat–Sun £2.50 ($4.60) adults, £2 ($3.70) seniors; free with cinema or show ticket. Daily noon–9:30pm. Tube: Piccadilly Circus or Charing Cross.

Jewish Museum This museum focuses on the history and traditions of Jewish life in Britain from the Norman Conquest (11th c.) to the present day. In the History Gallery you can see notched, wooden tax receipts from the medieval era and loving cups presented to the lord mayors of London by the Spanish and Portuguese synagogues. The exceptional Ceremonial Art Gallery displays ritual objects of great beauty, including a 16th-century Italian synagogue ark, Nathan Meyer Rothschild's *Book of Esther,* and silver Torah bells crafted in London. The museum is very big on talks, family history workshops, and children's events. In 1995 the museum moved to an elegant historic house not far from the Camden Underground station.

The sister Jewish Museum, **The Sternberg Centre,** 80 East End Rd., N3 (✆ **020/8349-1143**), in Finchley, traces the history of immigration and settlement in London, with displays like the reconstructions of East End tailoring and furniture workshops. A moving exhibition traces the life of one London-born Holocaust survivor. It is open 10:30am to 5pm Monday to Thursday and 10:30am to 4:30pm Sunday. Admission is £2 ($3.70) for adults, £1 ($1.85) seniors and students, and free for children. Also at the center is a shop, cafe, and a garden.

129 Albert St., NW1. ✆ **020/7284-1997.** www.jewishmuseum.org.uk. Admission £3.50 ($6) adults, £2.50 ($4.60) seniors, £1.50 ($2.75) students and children, £8 ($15) family ticket. Mon–Thurs 10am–4pm; Sun 10am–5pm. Closed Jewish and public holidays. Tube: Camden Town.

London Transport Museum ★★ *Kids* This enjoyable museum, in the old Covent Garden flower market, traces the 200-year history of public transport in London, from the days when cabs were horse-drawn. Like a Noah's Ark for machinery, it has examples of just about everything Londoners have used to get around, from omnibuses to trams to Tube trains, as well as paintings, posters, working models, and interactive exhibits. Kids love it. Actors play characters like a 1906 tunnel miner and a World War II clippie (bus conductor). There's a lot of stuff to pull and push. The museum even organizes guided London tours, with a focus on transportation, on the river, Tube, or bus (£10/$18). The shop is terrific, selling models, posters, and other original gifts.

The London Transport Museum can only display about 400 of the 370,000 items in its massive collection, so it has taken over a defunct Tube shed in West London for storage and as somewhere to work on conservation. On the last Friday of the month, there are guided tours of **The Depot,** 118 Gunnersbury Lane, W3 (Tube: Acton Town). Tickets cost £10 ($18), and you must book ahead. There are also a few open weekends each year, when you can explore the main shed and its vehicles, machinery, signs, and shelters, as well as enjoy the stalls and themed displays.

The Piazza, Covent Garden, WC2. ✆ **020/7565-7299** recorded info, or 020/7379-6344 booking tours. www.ltmuseum.co.uk. Admission £5.95 ($11) adults, £4.50 ($8) seniors and students, free for children under 16. Sat–Thurs 10am–6pm; Fri 11am–6pm (last admission 5:15pm). Closed Dec 24–26. Tube: Covent Garden or Charing Cross.

Museum of Garden History In an old church next to Lambeth Palace (the Archbishop of Canterbury's official residence), this museum is devoted to *the* quintessential British passion and the horticulturalists, botanists, and collectors who have nurtured it. Follow the lives of John Tradescant and his son (also John), the royal gardeners to Charles I and II, who are buried here. Learn more about noted English landscape designer Gertrude Jekyll (1843–1932), best known for her collaboration with architect Sir Edwin Lutyens. The museum's own patch is planted in a 17th-century Knot Garden design and contains many rare plants introduced into the country by the Tradescants. Captain Bligh of mutiny fame is buried here too, as is John Smith, who married Pocahontas. Gardening enthusiasts will enjoy the weekday and evening lectures, which cost £3 to £10 ($6–$18).

St. Mary-at-Lambeth, Lambeth Palace Rd., SE1. ✆ **020/7401-8865.** www.museumgardenhistory.org. Free admission, donation suggested £3 ($6) adults, £2.50 ($4.50) seniors and students. Daily 10:30am–5pm. Tube: Lambeth North.

Museum of London ★★ *Kids* If you love London, you will probably love this fascinating museum, which recently opened two new galleries as part of its ongoing redevelopment. **World City Gallery** traces London's development between 1789 and 1914 into the first great metropolis of the industrial age. **London Before London** rewinds history to look at life before the Romans, when hippos and elephants roamed Trafalgar Square.

Not only is this the biggest and most comprehensive city museum in the world, but it is genuinely engaging and creative. Among the highlights are a reconstruction of a Roman interior; a bedroom in a merchant's house from the Stuart period; the lord mayor's coach; a brilliant, audiovisual, dioramic presentation on the Great Fire with a voiceover reading diarist Samuel Pepys' account; a Victorian barber's shop; and the original elevators from Selfridges department store. The museum's archaeologists get called in at the start of most big building projects in London, and their finds generally go on display once the study and conservation process is completed. Many of the resident experts take part in the talks, museum tours, and workshops program (ranging in cost from free to £5/$9). There's a cafe and museum shop on the premises.

150 London Wall, EC2. ✆ **0870/444-3852.** www.museumoflondon.org.uk. Free admission. Mon–Sat 10am–5:50pm; Sun noon–5:50pm; last admission 5:30pm. Tube: St. Paul's, Moorgate, or Barbican.

National Army Museum This is the British Army's own museum and tells the soldier's story, starting in 1415. It's crammed with life-size models, medals, paintings of battle scenes by Gainsborough and Reynolds, weapons, and uniforms. Among the highlights are a 420-square-foot model of the Battle of Waterloo; the skeleton of Napoleon's horse, Marengo; and the saw that was used to amputate the leg of Lieutenant-General, the earl of Uxbridge, during the battle. Even weirder is the now-stuffed cat brought back from Sebastopol by a sentimental officer during the Crimean War. Each exhibit aims to let you inside the soldiers' everyday lives—Henry V's archers shivering at Agincourt, Wellington's troops standing shoulder to shoulder at Waterloo, and British Tommies scrambling over the top at the Somme. Visitors can experience what it was like in a World War I trench, as well as try on an excruciatingly uncomfortable civil war helmet, or test the crushing weight of a cannonball. One exhibition focuses on the contribution women have made to the army and armed conflict. The new Modern Army Gallery focuses on today's high-tech military force. Lunchtime talks take place most Thursdays at 1pm.

Royal Hospital Rd., Chelsea, SW3. ✆ **020/7730-0717.** www.national-army-museum.ac.uk. Free admission. Daily 10am–5:30pm. Closed Jan 1, Good Friday, May bank holiday, Dec 24–26, and public holidays. Tube: Sloane Sq.

National Portrait Gallery ★★ Celebrity vanity and the paparazzo spirit are clearly nothing new, evidenced by this gallery of 10,000 paintings and 250,000 photographs. The portrait gallery charts the history of the nation through its famous faces. The curators have consigned Helmut Newton's portrait of Margaret Thatcher, among others, to the historical section, to make room for such nanosecond icons as David Beckham (Posh Spice's footballer husband) and megabucks celeb J. K. Rowling, author of *Harry Potter.* The flow through the gallery is much improved by the bright-white Ondaatje Wing, built in a courtyard pinched from the neighboring National Gallery. The permanent collection is displayed chronologically. You'll find Henry VII, Henry VIII, and Sir Thomas More, all painted by Holbein; the only extant portrait of Shakespeare; and T. S. Eliot by Sir Jacob Epstein. There are endearing amateur daubs, too, including one of Jane Austen by her sister, and the three talented Brontë sisters painted by their untalented brother Branwell.

The NPG puts on free lectures and events, on a huge range of topics, on Tuesday and Thursday lunchtimes and weekend afternoons. Thursday-evening lectures mostly start at 7pm (free–£3/$6). On Friday at 6:30pm, there are free musical events. As well as the cafe, there is the stunning **Portrait Restaurant & Bar** (✆ **020/7312-2490**), looking out across the rooftops from under the Ondaatje Wing's glass roof.

St. Martin's Place, WC2. ✆ **020/7306-0055.** www.npg.org.uk. Free admission; special exhibitions £5 ($9) adults, £3 ($6) seniors and students. Sat–Wed 10am–6pm; Thurs–Fri 10am–9pm. Closed Jan 1, Good Friday, and Dec 24–26. Tube: Leicester Sq. or Charing Cross.

Planetarium See Madame Tussaud's & The Planetarium on p. 168.

Royal Academy of Arts Sir Joshua Reynolds and Thomas Gainsborough were founding members of The Royal Academy (1768), the nation's first art school and the first institution to hold an annual exhibition. In June and July, it hosts one of the world's biggest open shows of contemporary painting, sculpture, and drawing. The hanging panel's choices always excite frenzied media debate. The year-round stalwart is the Friends Room, which displays the recent work (often for sale) by Royal Academicians. In the last 2 weeks of June, you can see and maybe invest in pieces by hot young artists at the end of 3 postgraduate years at the Royal Academy schools.

Burlington House, Piccadilly, W1. ✆ **020/7300-8000.** www.royalacademy.org.uk. Ticket prices vary depending on the exhibition. Sat–Thurs 10am–6pm; Fri 10am–10pm. Closed Dec 24–25. Tube: Piccadilly Circus or Green Park.

Saatchi Gallery Charles Saatchi certainly knows how to create a sensation. He was the force behind the ultracontroversial show of the same name (Sensation) that was shown at the Brooklyn Museum and caused city officials to wet their pants in fury. In my opinion a lot of the Saatchi collection is vacuous, self-publicizing crap. But that doesn't mean you shouldn't have a look at the art trends of the second. The ex-adman Saatchi has amassed one of the largest independent collections of contemporary British and international art in the world. He is famous for launching new British artists and for creating brand trends (Neurotic Realism). In April 2003, after a predictable flurry of publicity, the Saatchi Gallery moved to County Hall (former home of the Greater London Council) on the south bank, right next to the British Airways London Eye observation wheel. It exhibits art from its own collections and also hosts exhibitions from other international collections and museums.

County Hall, Southbank, SE1. ✆ **020/7823-2363.** www.saatchi-gallery.co.uk. Admission £9 ($17) adults, £6.75 ($12) seniors and students. Sun–Thurs 10am–8pm; Fri–Sat 10am–10pm. Tube: Waterloo or Westminster.

Serpentine Gallery This delightful gallery opened over 30 years ago in a 1934 tea pavilion in Kensington Gardens, and it now attracts more than 400,000 people a year to see shows of modern and contemporary art, arranged by theme or single artist. In recent years, it's been on a mission to stimulate and provoke. The Architecture Commission is a new yearly event in which a celebrity architect is asked to create a pavilion on the front lawn; the pavilion becomes part of a June-to-September exhibition program and is used as a venue for talks and events.

Kensington Gardens (near Albert Memorial), W2. ✆ **020/7402-6075.** www.serpentinegallery.org. Free admission. Daily 10am–6pm. Tube: Knightsbridge, Lancaster Gate, or South Kensington.

Shakespeare's Globe ★★ For information on tours and the exhibition, see p. 236.

Sherlock Holmes Museum The quintessential English detective "resided" at this address from 1881 to 1904. It's not really a museum—there's nothing about Sir Arthur Conan Doyle, Sherlock Holmes's creator, for instance—it's a re-creation of the Victorian chambers as they *might* have been if the fictional Holmes had inhabited them. In the living room, you can pick up Sherlock Holmes's pipe, don a deerstalker, and take a photograph of yourself snooping around. Other "exhibits" include Dr. Mortimer's stick from *The Hound of the Baskervilles* and numerous letters written to Holmes asking him to solve individual mysteries and his "replies." But it's not worth the ticket unless you're an avid Holmes fan.

221b Baker St., NW1. ✆ **020/7935-8866.** www.sherlock-holmes.co.uk. Admission £6 ($11) adults, £4 ($7) children under 16. Daily 9:30am–6pm. Tube: Baker St.

Theatre Museum *Kids* The demonstrations and workshops are the best part of this otherwise surprisingly dull and untheatrical museum. Kids love learning how make-up artists create hideous scars and trying on costumes made in the style of famous designers—a Versace *School for Scandal,* perhaps—to find out how they help an actor create a character. Otherwise the displays are pretty static. An offshoot of the V&A, the Theatre Museum holds the national collections of everything relating to the performing arts—theater, ballet, opera, music hall, pantomime, puppetry, circus, and rock 'n' pop. It tells the story of the British stage, from Shakespeare to the present day, with models, posters, props, and souvenirs of such legendary British thespians as Garrick, Kean, and Irving. The museum also has a big Diaghilev archive, and it recently acquired the Tiller-Clowes marionettes, the last and most complete collection of Victorian puppets in Britain.

Russell St., WC2. ✆ **020/7943-4700.** theatremuseum.org. Free admission. Tues–Sun 10am–6pm. Daily guided tours at noon; makeup demonstrations at 11:30am, 1, 2:30, 3:30, and 4:30pm; costume workshops at 12:30 and 3pm. Closed all bank holidays. Tube: Covent Garden or Charing Cross.

Wallace Collection ★★ According to the terms of Lady Wallace's bequest, this collection must remain "unmixed with other objects of art." So the collection remains a perfect time capsule of 19th-century Anglo-French taste. Sir Richard Wallace was the illegitimate heir of the Marquis of Hertford, and the fifth generation to add to the acquisitions of exquisite furniture, armor, paintings, and decorative arts in the family's London home. There's much to delight the eye—Sèvres porcelain, Limoges enamels, 17th-century Dutch paintings, 18th-century French (Watteau, Fragonard, and Boucher) and British art, and Italian majolica. The new sculpture garden and cafe

Tips Backstage Tours

London is a wonderland for actors and lovers of the performing arts. There are several stages where you can step behind the footlights and see what life is like backstage. The first **Theatre Royal Drury Lane** was built in 1663, though the present one is 150 years younger. It was here that women (including Nell Gwynne) first appeared on stage—to a less than rapturous response from the critics, who thought boys in drag were better at playing the fairer sex. Professional actors bring the history of the theater to life in 1-hour tours. **Through the Stage Door** (✆ **020/7494-5091**) takes place on Sunday, Monday, Tuesday, Thursday, and Friday at 2:15 and 4:45pm; and on Wednesday and Saturday at 10:15am and noon. Tickets cost £11 ($20) adults, £8.50 ($16) children.

The **Royal National Theatre** and **Royal Opera House** also invite visitors behind the scenes (see chapter 9). So does the BBC. Its landmark West End HQ, designed by G. Val Myers in 1932, burst at the seams long ago, and the corporation has shifted many of its operations to the labyrinthine **BBC Television Centre,** Wood Lane, W12 (✆ **0870/603-0304;** www.bbc.co.uk; Tube: Wood Lane). You must prebook the 1½-hour tour. It sets off at 10:30am, 1:30, and 3:15pm, and costs £7.95 ($15) adults, £6.95 ($13) seniors, £5.95 ($11) students and over-9s. No children under 9. (See "Freebies," at the beginning of chapter 9, "London After Dark," for information on tickets to TV and radio shows.)

Finds Young & Hung in East London

The neighborhood around Hoxton Square has become a vibrant creative community, bursting with young British artists and hot new galleries in old industrial buildings. Entrepreneur Jay Jopling, who has a fine line in creating bankable art stars, has turned an old warehouse into a new gallery, **White Cube^2,** 48 Hoxton Sq., N1 (✆ **020/7930-5373;** www.whitecube.com). It is open Tuesday to Saturday 10am to 6pm. **Victoria Miro Gallery,** 16–18 Wharf Rd., N1 (✆ **020/7336-8109;** www.victoria-miro.com), is also open Tuesday to Saturday 10am to 6pm. Turner prizewinner Chris Ofili, of elephant dung fame, is one of her artists. To visit both of these, take the Tube to Old Street.

under a glass roof covering the internal courtyard is a real boon. For free tours, come at 1pm any weekday, 11:30am on Wednesday and Saturday, or 3pm on Sunday.

Hertford House, Manchester Sq., W1. ✆ **020/7563-9500.** www.the-wallace-collection.org.uk. Free admission. Daily 10am–5pm. Closed Dec 24–26. Tube: Bond St.

Whitechapel Art Gallery Canon Barnett of Toynbee Hall founded this gallery in 1901 to lighten and enlighten the lives of the poor of the East End. Though its fortunes have fluctuated ever since, largely due to the perennial shortage of cash, the Whitechapel has managed to maintain its independence from any stylistic or aesthetic pressures. The gallery presents an international program of contemporary and 20th-century art; check the local art listings to see what's currently on view. Exhibitions, which may be solo or group shows, or shows dedicated to an acknowledged master (such as the recent show on Mies van der Rohe), cover all forms of art, including paintings, sculpture, architecture, video, and photography. There's also a bookstore and a nice cafe.

80–82 Whitechapel High St., E1. ✆ **020/7522-7888.** www.whitechapel.org. Admission varies by show, generally £8.50 ($16) adults, £4.50 ($8) seniors and students. Tues–Sun 11am–6pm (Thurs until 9pm). Closed holidays. Tube: Aldgate East.

6 Maritime & Waterfront Sights

SOUTH BANK

The new twin foot-crossings flanking **Hungerford Bridge** have added a sleek contemporary look to what was for decades a cramped and pretty unattractive footbridge over the Thames. Suspended from steel pylons, the new pedestrian crossings link the West End (at Embankment Tube station) to the vibrant South Bank. On the upstream side you'll see the giant **British Airways London Eye** observation wheel (p. 160). Beside it is County Hall, home to the **London Aquarium** (p. 200), **Dalí Universe** (p. 189), the new **Saatchi Gallery** (p. 189), and a couple of cheap fast eats.

BANKSIDE

This once-scruffy neighborhood east of the officially designated South Bank area has it all, from the very ancient to the super-modern, and enough of it to keep you buzzing for days. Check out **Tate Modern** (p. 172), **Shakespeare's Globe** (p. 236), **Southwark Cathedral** (p. 178), and, nearby, **Borough Market** (p. 226) and the ancient **The George.**

The **Millennium Bridge** is the first new foot-crossing on the Thames since the 19th century and a photo opportunity to rival the best in the capital. Sir Norman Foster designed the £14-million ($26-million) streak of steel and light. From Bankside, it looks like a space-age causeway leading straight to St. Paul's Cathedral. The infamous wobble that closed the bridge the very weekend it opened has since been repaired.

Golden Hinde ★ *Kids* Purists may mutter "theme park," but this meticulous replica of the galleon in which Sir Francis Drake circumnavigated the globe (1577–80) is no cardboard sham. Since her 1973 launch, the *Golden Hinde* has sailed over 140,000 miles herself, even repeating Drake's historic feat. The ship is very hot on the educational stuff. During half-terms and holidays, you can drop the kids off for a 4-hour workshop where they'll learn to load cannons, sing Tudor sailing songs, and discover the horrors of Elizabethan surgical techniques. Prices vary, and you need to book ahead. Families and small groups can even stay overnight: see "Unforgettable Overnights," below. Prices below are for prebooking a guided tour; you save £1 ($1.85) by taking a self-guided tour.

St. Marie Overie Dock, Cathedral St., SE1. ✆ **0870/011-8700**. www.goldenhinde.co.uk. Admission £4.50 ($8) adults, £3.50 ($6) children under 16, £15 ($28) family ticket. Open daily, call for opening times. Tube: London Bridge. River services: Bankside.

TOWER BRIDGE

A walk across iconic **Tower Bridge,** just east of Bankside, is a must (a visit to Tower Bridge Experience, see below, lets you see the inner workings), as is the **Tower of London** (p. 173) on the north bank. Facing the Tower across the river is the stunning new **London City Hall,** The Queen's Walk SE1 (✆ **020/7983-4000**), housing the mayor and the London Assembly. Designed by Foster and Partners (that is, Lord Norman Foster, who designed the acclaimed Great Hall in the British Museum and the Millennium Bridge) and completed in 2002, the City Hall's unusual spherical shape comes from a "green" approach to design, making use of natural ventilation and daylight. Located next to Tower Bridge, the city's newest landmark is open to visitors Monday through Friday from 8am to 8pm. Admission is free. You can visit the lower, first, and second floors after a bag search and metal-detector scan. Architecture buffs won't want to miss this. The **Design Museum** (p. 184) is about a 10-minute walk east of Tower Bridge on the river's south bank.

Kids Unforgettable Overnights

One Saturday a month, February through November, families can zip back 400 years and stay on a replica of Sir Francis Drake's galleon, the **Golden Hinde** (✆ **0870/011-8700;** www.goldenhinde.co.uk; Tube: London Bridge). Actors play the officers and crew preparing for a voyage, while the parents and kids (6–12) join the work dressed in Tudor clothes, eat rather better food than the sailors would have, and sleep on the lower decks. At £40 ($73) per person, it costs about the same as a bed-and-breakfast. Kids ages 8 to 11 can also camp out for the night with their parents at the **Science Museum** (p. 170). The galleries become a private playground, where they learn to make slime or how to drop an egg without breaking it. A sleepover costs £25 ($46) for adults and £30 ($55) for kids. To find out more, call ✆ **020/7942-4749** or visit www.sciencemuseum.org.uk.

HMS *Belfast* ★ *Kids* This 11,500-ton, 32-gun battle cruiser played a vital role in World War II—during the Normandy landings, the sinking of the *Scharnhorst* in the Battle of the North Cape, and on the terrible Arctic convoy route to North Russia. HMS *Belfast* has nine decks to explore, from the Bridge to the boiler and engine rooms. Along the way visitors can operate anti-aircraft guns and imagine what life was like for the sailors in the mess decks. Cramped but pretty boozy is the answer: From 1950 to 1952, when the ship served in the Far East, the crew consumed 56,000 pints of navy rum, along with 134 tons of meat and 625 tons of potatoes. Was that a gun or burp?

Morgan's Lane, Tooley St., SE1. ✆ **020/7940-6300.** www.iwm.org.uk/belfast. Admission £7 ($13) adults, £5 ($9) seniors and students, free for children under 16. Mar–Oct daily 10am–6pm; Nov–Feb daily 10am–5pm. Closed Dec 24–26. Tube: London Bridge or Tower Hill. River services: London Bridge City.

Tower Bridge Experience ★ *Kids* Tower Bridge is a London landmark, and possibly the most celebrated and photographed bridge in the world. A certain American tried to buy it, but asked for London Bridge by mistake, as he discovered when he unpacked his enormous parcel to find nary a tower in sight. Neo-Gothicky Tower Bridge dates from 1894, and the twin towers are made of steel clad in stone. Inside, interactive exhibits trace its history and construction and, in the south tower, you can see the old (pre-1976) hydraulics used to raise and lower the bridge—not that big a thrill unless you're an engineer. It uses electrical power now, and about five ships a day pass through in the summer months. The views from the pedestrian walkways are glorious to St. Paul's, the Tower, and the distant Houses of Parliament.

London SE1. ✆ **020/7403-3761.** www.towerbridge.org.uk. Admission £5.50 ($10) adults, £4.25 ($8) seniors and students, £3 ($4.70) ages 5–16 (you can walk across the bridge for free). Apr–Oct daily 10am–6:30pm; Nov–Mar daily 9:30am–6pm (last entry 5pm). Closed Dec 25–26. Tube: Tower Hill or London Bridge. River services: Tower Pier.

DOCKLANDS

This riverside area east of Tower Bridge along the north bank of the Thames was once London's hustling and bustling port area, where ships unloaded cargoes from around the world. In recent years it has become part of a massive revitalization scheme. If you want to check it out, you can get there via the Docklands Light Rail (see "Getting Around," in chapter 3). Canary Wharf, with one of Europe's tallest buildings, is the most visibly redeveloped area.

Museum in Docklands *Kids* Housed in an early-19th-century warehouse at East India Quay, London's newest museum (it opened in May 2003) unlocks the history of London's river, port, and people. Originally used to house imports of exotic spices, rum, and cotton, the warehouse-turned-museum now holds a wealth of objects, from enormous whale bones to World War II gas masks, which provide glimpses of the people that have come and gone from the Docks over the last 2,000 years, from the Roman founders to Viking invaders and from gentleman pirates to today's city workers. The state-of-the-art galleries include a fully interactive play and learning area that introduces kids between 5 and 12 to the history of Docklands. They can winch and weigh cargoes, get a diver's eye view of work under water, balance the cargo in the hold of a 19th-century clipper, and discover archaeological finds in the foreshore discovery box. There's a regular program of storytelling events, gallery tours, and walks.

No. 1 Warehouse, West India Quay, Hertsmere Rd., E14. ✆ **0870/444-3856.** www.museumindocklands.org.uk. Admission £5 ($9) adults, £3 ($5.50) seniors, free for students and children under 16. DLR: West India Quay.

GREENWICH

A town and borough of Greater London, Greenwich is located about 4 miles east of the City. The world's clocks are set according to Greenwich Mean Time, and visitors from around the globe flock here to stand on the Prime Meridian, the line from which the world's longitude is measured (see Royal Observatory Greenwich, below). There are several attractions in Greenwich that make for a great day trip. The easiest way to get there is by the Jubilee Underground line to Greenwich. You can also take **Docklands Light Rail** (see "Getting Around" in chapter 3) from Tower Gateway near the Tower of London to Island Gardens, the last stop, and then walk through the Victorian foot tunnel beneath the Thames. You'll come out next to the Cutty Sark. You can also reach Greenwich by boat. Vessels operated by **Thames River Services,** Westminster Pier, Victoria Embankment (✆ **020/7930-4097;** www.thamesriverservices.co.uk; Tube: Westminster), depart from Westminster Pier throughout the year for the 1-hour trip to Greenwich. A return (round-trip) fare is £8.20 ($15) for adults, £6.70 ($12) for seniors, £4.10 ($7.60) for children, and £22 ($41) for a family ticket.

Cutty Sark ★ This 19th-century sailing clipper is one of the most famous to have survived its era. Built in Dumbarton, Scotland, it launched in 1869, too late to succeed in the tea trade, which had been taken over by steamers after the opening of the Suez Canal. Instead, it carried Australian wool, circling the globe round the Cape of Good Hope on the outward journey and Cape Horn on its return. Designed for speed, the *Cutty Sark* could cover almost 400 sea miles a day. It was restored in 1922 and has been in dry dock since 1954. On board, you'll see how tough life was for the Victorian crew and officers. The Long John Silver Collection of merchant ship figureheads is the biggest in the country.

King William Walk, SE10. ✆ **020/8858-3445.** www.cuttysark.org.uk. Admission £4.50 ($8) adults, £3.75 ($7) seniors and students, £3.30 ($6) children, £9.80 ($16) family. Daily 10am–5pm. Closed Dec 24–26. DLR: Cutty Sark. River services: Greenwich Pier.

National Maritime Museum We found this museum pretty boring until they opened a new gallery called Maritime London. In it are displayed things like the 7-foot-tall stone model for Nelson's Column, wreckage from a Zeppelin shot down in 1915 as it bombed the docks, and a 2-ton remnant salvaged from the Baltic Exchange after the 1992 IRA bomb. The museum is one of the largest of its kind in the world—the ceremonial opening in 1937 was the first duty of the new King George VI after the abdication crisis. Now, with 12 new galleries, modern interactive technology looks at modern maritime issues: how pollution threatens the sea, new ways of exploring its ultimate depths, pleasure-cruising, and more. But you have to be way more nautical than I am to appreciate the museum's collection of 2,500 ship models, 50,000 charts, and 750,000 ship plans, plus its hundreds of scientific and navigational instruments. The National Maritime Museum also runs two additional nearby attractions: the Royal Observatory and Queen's House.

All time is measured from the Prime Meridian Line at the **Royal Observatory Greenwich** ★, which Charles II founded in 1675 as part of his quest to determine longitude at sea. Clockmaker John Harrison eventually solved the problem in 1763 and received £20,000 ($37,000) for his pains. You can stand astride the meridian (with a foot in each hemisphere) and set your watch precisely by the falling time-ball, which is how shipmasters set their chronometers from 1833 on. Set high on a hill above the Thames in Greenwich Park, the observatory has a collection of historic timekeepers and astronomical instruments, and Britain's largest refracting telescope. Planetarium shows happen every weekday afternoon and on Saturdays from Easter through August.

The innovative Inigo Jones designed the **Queen's House** (1616) for Anne of Denmark, wife of James I. She died before it was completed, so Charles I gave it to his new queen, Henrietta Maria. The house's cantilevered tulip staircase was the first of its kind. The Queen's House has now become an art gallery, where the museum can show revolving exhibitions from its collection of 4,000 paintings.

Romney Rd., SE10. ✆ **020/8858-4422** or 020/8312-6565. www.nmm.ac.uk. Free admission. Daily 10am–5pm; last entrance 30 min. before closing. Closed Dec 24–26. DLR: Cutty Sark or Greenwich. River services: Greenwich Pier.

Old Royal Naval College ★ Sir Christopher Wren designed this complex as a naval hospital in 1696. Its 4 blocks, named after King Charles, Queen Anne, King William, and Queen Mary, are split into two sections so as not to block the view of the river from the Queen's House. UNESCO recognized the architectural and historic importance of the college and the other historic buildings in Greenwich by naming them a World Heritage Site. If you're in the neighborhood, do stop in to see Thornhill's magnificent Painted Hall where Nelson lay in state in 1805. You can also visit the Georgian Chapel of St. Peter and St. Paul, or come at 11am on Sunday for the choral Eucharist. The navy moved out of the college in 1998, and it is now home to departments of the University of Greenwich and other public organizations.

King William Walk, off Romney Rd., SE10. ✆ **0800/389-3341,** or 020/8269-4747. www.greenwichfoundation.org.uk. Free admission. Daily 10am–5pm. Closed Dec 24–26. Rail: Charing Cross to Maze Hill. DLR: Cutty Sark or Greenwich. River services: Greenwich Pier.

WOOLWICH

Firepower, The Museum of the Royal Artillery This museum, which caters to those who have an interest in weapons and warfare, opened in 2001 at the Royal Arsenal in Woolwich. From the 17th century, this vast and well-guarded complex was the home base of the Royal Regiment of Artillery. Firepower will eventually fill four buildings, first the ordnance laboratories and former ammunition factories, and then the Hawksmoor military academy once it is restored. The main Field of Fire gallery simulates being in combat. Visitors can learn how to point and fire the big guns in the interactive Real Weapon gallery. Its unique collection of big guns spans nearly 300 years.

Royal Arsenal, Woolwich, SE18. ✆ **020/8855-7755.** www.firepower.org.uk. £5 ($9) adults, £4.50 ($8) seniors and students, £2.50 ($4.60) children. Apr–Oct Wed–Sun; Nov–Mar Fri–Sun 10am–5pm. Tube: North Greenwich, then bus no. 161, 422, or 472. Train: Woolwich Arsenal.

Thames Barrier This giant feat of engineering opened in 1982 to protect London from flooding. The barrier has four 3,000-ton gates, each as tall as a five-story building, and six smaller ones. They take 1½ hours to raise—which has happened around 60 times so far. Now, global warming is raising water levels and threatening to halve the barrier's projected life to 50 years. The Visitor Centre on the south bank shows how it works—and even re-creates the Great Stench, which wafted up from the river before pollution control in the 19th century (be prepared to hold your nose, or your breath). Take a boat because it's a pain to get to any other way.

Unity Way, Woolwich, SE18. ✆ **020/8305-4188.** Admission £1 ($1.85) adults, 50p (90¢) children 5–17. Mon–Fri 10am–5pm; Sat–Sun 10:30am–5:30pm. Train: Charlton. River services: Barrier Gardens Pier.

HAMMERSMITH

The path along the south bank of the Thames, between Putney and Hammersmith bridges, is one of the loveliest walks in London. The urban clatter seems miles away in the green-lit tunnel of trees—even the rowers glide by almost noiselessly on the river below. The only downside is the stream of arrogant cyclists who assume that you'll jump out of their way.

WWT The Wetland Centre *Kids* This 105-acre network of lakes, lagoons, and marshes is the first created on such a scale in any capital city anywhere. The Wildfowl & Wetland Trust shifted thousands of tons of concrete and recycled 500,000 cubic meters of soil to turn the old reservoirs into a Site of Special Scientific Interest. Paths loop out in two directions from the Discovery Center, across little bridges and past observation hides. Turn one way for World Wetlands, where some of the world's rarest ducks, geese, and swans live in 14 mocked-up habitats, and for life in a native pond (Wildside). Turn the other for three eco-friendly designer gardens, a children's farmyard full of ducks, and wetland crafts in Waterlife. A great place to take a break, whether you're a bird-spotter or not. The view from the observatory is breathtaking. You can watch the wardens feed the birds at noon and 3:30pm, or take a tour at 11am and 2:30pm.

Queen Elizabeth's Walk, SW13. ✆ **020/8409-4400.** www.wetlandcentre.org.uk. Admission £6.75 ($12) adults, £5.50 ($10) seniors, £4 ($7) children, £18 ($32) family ticket. Summer daily 9:30am–6pm; winter daily 9:30am–5pm. Tube: Hammersmith, then bus no. 283, 33, 72, or 209.

7 At Home with History's A-List

London has nurtured (and aggravated) so many famous heroes, aristocrats, artists, writers, musicians, scientists, and all-round superstars that every other street boasts somebody's former home. English Heritage (✆ **020/7973-3000;** www.english-heritage.org.uk) marks significant spots with a blue plaque, and there are now almost 800 stuck up on walls all over the city: at Jimi Hendrix's Mayfair lair; at Mahatma Gandhi's student digs in Fulham; in Noel Road, Islington, where playwright Joe Orton lived until his murder in 1967; at 173 Cromwell Rd., SE5, where composer Benjamin Britten had his student digs while he was at the Royal College of Music (1931–33). Usually, a blue plaque is all that's left to mark the past, but there are a few exceptions.

Apsley House, The Wellington Museum ★ Once known as "No. 1 London" because it was the first house outside the tollgate, Apsley House has been the magnificent city residence of the dukes of Wellington since 1817. (The name comes from its first owner, the earl of Bathurst, Baron Apsley.) Wellington moved in on his return from a triumphant military career in India, Spain, and Portugal, culminating in the victory at Waterloo. He entertained extravagantly, dining off the gorgeous Sèvres Egyptian Service that Napoleon had commissioned for Josephine, and a vast silver Portuguese service with a 26-foot-long centerpiece. Wellington's heroic military success earned him lavish gifts as well as royal respect. No wonder the original Robert Adam house (1771–78) had to be enlarged to house the duke's treasures. Today, it is crammed with silver, porcelain, sculpture (note the nude glamorized statue of Napoleon by Canova on the main staircase), furniture, medals, and hundreds of paintings by Velázquez, Goya, Rubens, Bruegel, and other masters. It's one of the few great London town houses where such collections remain intact and the family is still in residence: The eighth duke of Wellington and his son have private apartments.

Tips Benjamin Franklin Holds Open House

St. Paul's Cathedral was the first public building in the world to get one of Benjamin Franklin's new-fangled lightning conductors. The American scientist, philosopher, printer, writer, inventor, statesman, and creator of perfect sound bites lived in London between 1757 and 1775. His "genteel lodgings" at **36 Craven St.,** near Charing Cross, served as the first de facto American embassy after independence. The Friends of Franklin House formed a trust over 25 years ago to rescue the great man's home; it's the only Franklin home remaining in the world today. The first floor of the **Benjamin Franklin House** is due to open to the public early in January 2006. To find out more, call ✆ **020/7930-9121;** www.rsa.org.uk/franklin.

149 Piccadilly, Hyde Park Corner, W1. ✆ **020/7499-5676.** Admission (includes audioguide) £4.50 ($8) adults, £3 ($5.50) seniors, free for children under 18. Tues–Sun 11am–5pm. Closed Jan 1, Good Friday, May 1, and Dec 24–26. Tube: Hyde Park Corner (exit 3).

Carlyle's House ★ The bearded gent on the front wall plaque is writer and historian Thomas Carlyle, who lived in this Queen Anne terrace house from 1834 until he died in 1881. Many famous friends visited the "Sage of Chelsea" here, including Chopin, Dickens, Tennyson, and George Eliot, whose house was around the corner on Cheyne Walk. Virtually unaltered, the house has the original furniture and many books, portraits, and mementos from his day. The walled Victorian garden has been restored and is a delight.

24 Cheyne Row, SW3. ✆ **020/7352-7087.** www.nationaltrust.org.uk. Admission £3.70 ($7) adults, £1.80 ($3.30) children under 17. Apr–Oct Wed–Fri 2–5pm, Sat–Sun 11am–5pm. Tube: Sloane Sq.

The Dickens House Museum This terraced house on the edge of Bloomsbury was home to Victorian London's quintessential chronicler for only 2 years (1837–39). In that time, though, the prolific Dickens produced some of his best-loved works, including a portion of *The Pickwick Papers, Nicholas Nickleby,* and *Oliver Twist.* His letters, furniture, and first editions are on display in rooms restored to their original appearance.

48 Doughty St., WC1. ✆ **020/7405-2127.** www.dickensmuseum.com. Admission £5 ($9) adults, £4 ($7) students and seniors, £3 ($5.50) children, £14 ($25) families. Mon–Sat 10am–5pm; Sun 11am–5pm. Tube: Russell Sq. or Chancery Lane.

Dr. Johnson's House The house is tucked away behind Fleet Street, on a little square at the end of an ancient labyrinth of alleys and passages. Samuel Johnson lived here from 1748 to 1759, while he compiled the first comprehensive English dictionary. In the top garret, six copyists transcribed the entries. Johnson sat elsewhere reading and making lists of words from the best literature of the time. You can actually see the original dictionary, published in 1755, as well as letters, prints, portraits, and other memorabilia.

17 Gough Sq., Fleet St., EC4. ✆ **020/7353-3745.** www.drjh.dircon.co.uk. Admission £4 ($7) adults, £3 ($5.50) students and seniors, £1 ($1.85) children 10–16, free for children under 10, £9 ($17) family ticket. May–Sept Mon–Sat 11am–5:30pm; Oct–Apr Mon–Sat 11am–5pm. Tube: Blackfriars or Chancery Lane.

Fenton House ★ This lovely Hampstead house, built in 1693, belonged to a merchant named Fenton (what a surprise!) in the 18th century. In the 1950s, then-owner

Lady Binning handed it over to the National Trust with her fine collection of Oriental and European porcelain, needlework, and furniture. Now it is also home to the Benton Fletcher collection of early keyboard instruments, all in working order, including a 1612 harpsichord that Handel probably played. You'll feel as if you've stepped back into a much more gracious time.

Hampstead Grove, NW3. ✆ **020/7435-3471.** www.nationaltrust.org.uk. Admission £4.40 ($8) adults, £2.20 ($4) children, £11 ($20) family ticket. Apr–Oct Sat–Sun 11am–5pm, Wed–Fri 2–5pm. Closed Nov–Feb. Tube: Hampstead.

Handel House Museum This museum opened in November 2001. Brook Street was new when composer George Frideric Handel moved here in 1723. Although he had come to England a decade earlier, this was his first proper home. It was in this house that he composed some of his most famous and oft-played works, including *Messiah* and *Music for the Royal Fireworks.* Using his will and an inventory taken after he died in 1759, the Handel House Trust painstakingly restored the interior, even commissioning a particular crimson fabric to swathe a magnificent full-tester bed lent by English Heritage, and building a harpsichord to Handel's original specifications (live music is part of the visit).

25 Brook St., W1. ✆ **020/7495-1685.** www.handelhouse.org. Admission £5 ($9) adults, £4.50 ($8) seniors and students, £2 ($3.70) children. Tues–Sat 10am–6pm (Thurs until 8pm); Sun noon–6pm. Tube: Oxford Circus.

Keats House The romantic poet John Keats fell in love with Fanny Brawne, his neighbor's daughter, when he lived in this charming Regency cottage in Hampstead (1818–20). Sadly, he had tuberculosis and left to winter in Italy, where he died the following year. While at the cottage, Keats penned "Ode to a Nightingale"—a first edition is on display with books, diaries, letters, memorabilia, and some original furnishings. There is always a full summer schedule of tours and events.

Keats Grove, NW3. ✆ **020/7435-2062.** Admission £3 ($5.50) adults, £1.50 ($2.75) seniors and students, free for children under 16. Free admission to garden. Tues–Sun noon–5pm (Nov–Mar until 4pm). Call to check times and winter closure. Tube: Hampstead or Belsize Park.

Kenwood House ★★ English Heritage recently gave the palatial Kenwood House a makeover, replacing the chilly blues and grays with deep, bold colors that are a perfect foil for the astounding art collection, left to the nation with the house by Lord Iveagh in 1927. It includes the Rembrandt self-portrait and Vermeer's *The Guitar Player,* among others. Remodeled to neoclassical perfection by Robert Adam in the late 18th century, Kenwood House sits high on Hampstead Heath, overlooking the lake, and is famous for

---

Moments A Bandstand with a View

A snowy walk on Hampstead Heath inspired C. S. Lewis to write *The Lion, the Witch and the Wardrobe*. They do feel like a parallel universe, these 800 acres of half-wild, half-manicured green in northwest London. Sundays are like a fiesta: Lay back and listen to the bandstand concerts on Parliament Hill, with its unparalleled view across the capital. People fly kites, play Frisbee, fish, swim, and race model boats in the ponds. The Heath & Hampstead Society organizes a 2-hour walk on the first Sunday afternoon of every month except January. Call Michael Welbank (✆ **020/7435-6553;** www.heathandhampsteadsociety.org.uk). Hampstead Heath has a very helpful information center (✆ **020/7482-7073**).

---

its summer open-air concerts (see chapter 9). The Brew House is a favorite pit stop, especially for a lazy breakfast in its walled garden (it opens at 9am year-round). And make sure to see the colorful Gypsy caravan in one of the outbuildings.

Hampstead Lane, NW3. ✆ **020/8348-1286.** www.english-heritage.org.uk. Free admission. Apr–Oct daily 10am–5pm; Oct daily 10am–5pm; Nov–Mar daily 10am–4pm (10:30am Wed and Fri). Tube: Archway, Golders Green, Hampstead, or Highgate, then no. 210 bus from outside all stations.

Sir John Soane's Museum ★★ The son of a bricklayer, Sir John Soane (1753–1837) apprenticed himself to George Dance the Younger and Henry Holland before opening an architectural practice of his own. He married into great wealth and began collecting the objects displayed in this house, which he both designed and lived in. It's a marvelous hodgepodge, stuffed full of architectural fragments, casts, bronzes, sculpture, and cork models. The sarcophagus of Seti I (Pharaoh 1303–1290 B.C.) is also here. Soane used colored glass and mirrors to create reflections of architectural details and other dramatic effects—magical during evening opening when the rooms are candlelit. The collection includes works by Turner, three Canalettos, and two series of paintings by Hogarth, *An Election* and *The Rake's Progress.* Others, including a wonderful group of Piranesi drawings, are ingeniously hung behind movable panels in the Picture Room. Meanwhile, the gallery displays changing exhibitions from Soane's collection of over 30,000 architectural drawings, which includes works by Dance, Sir Christopher Wren, Sir William Chambers, and Robert and James Adam. There's a tour every Saturday at 2:30pm. Tickets cost £3 ($5.50) and go on sale half an hour before. Be early—there are only 22 spaces.

13 Lincoln's Inn Fields, WC2. ✆ **020/7405-2107.** www.soane.org. Free admission (£1/$1.85 donation requested). Tues–Sat 10am–5pm; 1st Tues of each month also 6–9pm. Tube: Holborn.

Spencer House ★ The first Earl Spencer—an ancestor of Princess Diana—married his sweetheart Georgiana Poyntz secretly at Althorp and set about building this splendid house (1756–66) in St. James. Today, it is the only 18th-century private palace in London still intact. Quite an achievement since it stopped being a home in 1927 and was then rented out. The Spencers also took things like the fireplaces, doors, and moldings to safety at Althorp during the Blitz. Painstaking restoration began in 1987 and has returned the house to its original opulent splendor. The earl and countess were a very wealthy couple; the diamond buckles on John's honeymoon shoes alone were valued at £3,000 ($5,550). The eight staterooms were some of the first neoclassical interiors created in London by John Vardy and James Stuart. The Painted Room contains superb gold furniture set against a mural celebrating the Triumph of Love. There is no unsupervised wandering; you have to take the 1-hour tour. Come early because you can't prebook. On certain spring and summer Sundays, the garden is open too. Backing on to Green Park, it has recently been restocked with plants fashionable in the 18th and 19th centuries.

27 St. James's Place, SW1. ✆ **020/7499-8620.** www.spencerhouse.co.uk. Admission only on timed tour ticket: £9 ($17) adults, £7 ($13) seniors and children 10–16. Sun 10:30am–5:45pm (closed Jan and Aug). Tube: Green Park. No children under 10.

8 Especially for Kids

Pick up a copy of the invaluable ***Kids Out,*** the monthly listings magazine spawned by *Time Out.* We've tried to make life easier, too, by flagging the best-fun attractions in the reviews with the Kids icon.

Tips How to Bribe a Bored Teen

If your offspring are revolting against going to any more boring old museums and galleries, try bribing them with a session at the **Trocadero** in Piccadilly Circus. This trashy entertainment mall has virtual-reality arcade games, dodgems, a puke-inducing ride that whips you up 9 stories and then drops like a stone, junky souvenir shops, and junk eateries. Bring lots of £1 coins and a pair of earplugs. The Troc (✆ **09068/881100**) is open Sunday through Thursday 10am to midnight, closing at 1am on Friday and Saturday.

The top kid-picks are: touring the **Tower of London,** seeing the **Changing of the Guard** at Buckingham Palace, climbing to the top of **Tower Bridge,** taking a "flight" in the **British Airways London Eye,** shivering the timbers of the pirate galleon in **Peter Pan playground** in Kensington Gardens, or feeding the ducks at **WWT The Wetland Centre.** London's museums are shaking off their dusty image, not only with interactive exhibits, but fun workshops, especially during half-terms and holidays. Topping the hit list are the **Science Museum** (see "Unforgettable Overnights," p. 192), the **London Transport Museum,** the **Museum of London,** the **Theatre Museum,** the **British Museum,** and the **V&A.** Two more places offering sneakily educational role-playing are **Shakespeare's Globe** (p. 236) and the **Golden Hinde. Madame Tussaud's** is always a hit. You should also try the **London Brass Rubbing Centre** in the crypt at St. Martin-in-the-Fields (see p. 177).

Founded in 1948, **Unicorn** is London's oldest professional children's theater company. It stages old favorites and commissioned works for 4-to-12-year-olds. The company's new theatre in an area called More London (on the south bank of the Thames near Tower Bridge) is set to open in late 2005; call the office or go online to find out what's playing (✆ **020/7700-0702;** www.unicorntheatre.com).

Little Angel Theatre This magical theater is the only one like it in London. It puts on a huge variety of puppet shows from fairy tales to adaptations of children's books, by its own company and visiting masters of the art. Performances take place on weekends at 11am and 3pm, from July through August, and during half-terms and school holidays. It's not for children under 3, and every show is designated for a specific age group.

14 Dagmar Passage, Islington, N1. ✆ **020/7226-1787.** www.littleangeltheatre.com. Tickets £5.50–£8 ($10–$15). Box office Mon–Fri 11am–5pm; Sat–Sun 10am–4:30pm. Tube: Angel, Highbury, or Islington.

London Aquarium Down in the basement of County Hall is one of Europe's largest aquariums. If you've been to any really great aquariums, this one will probably disappoint you because it's not very imaginatively done. The two main tanks contain hundreds of varieties of marine life from the Atlantic and Pacific. Kids enjoy the shallow Beach Pier where they can stroke stingrays and other fish, while there are less alarming but equally yucky things in the Touchpool. Other zones whiz you through a rainforest, mangrove swamp, coral reef, and an English stream on a summer's day.

County Hall Riverside Building, Westminster Bridge Rd., SE1. ✆ **020/7667-8000.** www.londonaquarium.co.uk. Admission £9.75 ($18) adults, £7.50 ($14) seniors, £6.25 ($12) children ages 3–14, £29 ($54) family ticket. Daily 10am–6pm (last admission 5pm). Closed Dec 25. Tube: Westminster or Waterloo. River services: Festival Pier.

London Dungeon ★ This state-of-the-art horror chamber has huge appeal for kids with a taste for the gruesome and ghoulish, but it will frighten the little ones, so be careful. You have to deal with things like warty actors with wild hair leaping out at you in the dark. The dungeon re-enacts the goriest events from British history: one bloody night in the life of Jack the Ripper, the passing of a death sentence that sends you by barge through Traitors' Gate at the Tower of London, a medieval city ransacked by invaders, a roaring red tableau of the Great Fire of London, and so on. Rank smells and a smoke machine ratchet up the atmosphere. Much more fun than Madame Tussaud's, though just as ghoulishly expensive.

28–34 Tooley St., SE1. ✆ **09001/600-0666.** www.thedungeons.com. Admission £15 ($27) adults, £13 ($22) students 16–18, £12 ($21) children under 15 (must be accompanied by an adult). Apr–Sept daily 10am–6:30pm; Oct–Mar daily 10am–5:30pm; late openings July–Aug. Closed Dec 25. Tube: London Bridge. River services: London Bridge City Pier.

London Zoo London Zoo looks after more than a hundred endangered species. It also takes part in 146 breeding programs, so there are always cute baby animals to see, as well as the perennial favorites: penguins, lions, tigers, hippos, chimps, and so on. There's something going on every hour of the day, from chow-time to the elephants' bath-time, so pick up a copy of the daily guide. The newest attraction is Web of Life, a state-of-the-art education center promoting conservation and biodiversity. The zoo opened in 1827 and is like a 36-acre architectural theme park.

Regent's Park, NW1. ✆ **020/7722-3333.** www.londonzoo.co.uk. Admission £14 ($28) adults, £12 ($22) seniors and students, £11 ($20) children 3–15, £45 ($83) family. Mar–Oct daily 10am–5:30pm; Nov–Feb daily 10am–4pm. Closed Dec 25. Tube: Camden Town. London Waterbus: From Camden Lock or Little Venice; for joint boat trip/zoo entry tickets, see "Boat Trips," below.

9 Parks & Gardens

PRIVATE

From April through August, enthusiastic amateurs and the not-so-amateur open their private gardens to the public to raise money for charity, organized by the **National Gardens Scheme.** This is a chance to see the British at their most passionate, horticulturally speaking, for a nominal entry fee—a pound or two at the most. You can pick up an NGS handbook (called *The Yellow Book*), listing which garden is open on what day, from most bookstores. Or contact the NGS at Hatchlands Park, East Clandon, Guildford, Surrey, GU4 7RT (✆ **01483/211535;** www.ngs.org.uk).

Founded in 1673 by the Society of Apothecaries to teach apprentices how to identify medicinal plants, the **Chelsea Physic Garden,** at 66 Royal Hospital Rd. (enter from Swan Walk), SW3 (✆ **020/7352-5646;** www.chelseaphysicgarden.co.uk), is the second-oldest botanical garden in England. Behind its high walls is a rare collection of exotic perennials, shrubs, and trees, including those that gave us steroids, aspirin, and other common pills and potions. The rockery (1773) was restored in 2001—see if you can tell the Icelandic lava from the old stones "borrowed" from the Tower of London. Admission is £5 ($9) for adults, £3 ($5.50) for students and children. The garden is open April through October, on Wednesday noon to 5pm, and 2 to 6pm on Sunday. It's a lovely place to stop for tea and homemade cakes. The English Gardening School holds lectures throughout the summer. Take the Tube to Sloane Square.

PUBLIC

Behind Kensington High Street, **Holland Park** is a pretty oasis of woods and gardens set around the ruins of Holland House. That's where the open-air theater and opera (✆ **020/7602-7856;** see chapter 9) take place in the summer, ousting the noisy peacocks.

A former summer ballroom is now an upscale restaurant, and there's a cafe, too. You'll find an adventure playground for kids and lots of sports facilities (squash, tennis, cricket, golf nets, and football); call ✆ **020/7602-2226** for reservations. Also worth seeking out is the Japanese Kyoto Garden. Take the Tube to High Street Kensington or Holland Park.

Regent's Park, Hyde Park, Kensington Gardens, Green Park, and St. James's Park all come under the aegis of the **Royal Parks Agency** (✆ **020/7298-2000;** www.royalparks.gov.uk). Most organize guided walks around the monuments and hidden historical byways, as well as take part in a Summer Festival of music, theater, and children's events. Striped canvas deck chairs are ubiquitous in the parks, and fee collectors seem to appear from nowhere to startle visitors who didn't realize they had to pay to sit down—it costs £1 ($1.85) to crash out for 4 hours.

Hyde Park (✆ **020/7298-2100**) is the largest (350 acres) and most popular of all London's parks. The aptly named Serpentine Lake, created in the 1730s, is its most notable feature. Take a boat out, lounge by its side, or swim from the Lido—although the amount of bird droppings makes this a pretty unpleasant proposition. Or go horseback riding (see "Staying Active," below) along Rotten Row, a corruption of *route du roi,* laid out by King William III from the West End to Kensington Palace. On Sunday the park really comes alive. People flock to the contemporary Serpentine Gallery (✆ **020/7402-6075;** p. 189), while artists of dubious talent hang their works along the Bayswater Road railings. On Sundays, the northeast corner near Marble Arch becomes **Speaker's Corner.** Anyone can stand on a soapbox here and spout their opinions and grievances—anarchists, stand-up comics, religious fanatics, would-be politicians, and the deeply eccentric. This tradition is often touted as an example of Britain's tolerance of free speech. In fact, the ritual began several hundred years ago when condemned prisoners were allowed a few final words before they were hanged on Tyburn gallows, which stood on the very same spot. Take the Tube to Marble Arch.

Kensington Gardens (✆ **020/7298-2117**) abuts the western perimeter of Hyde Park, and it's almost impossible to spot the boundary. Laid out in the early 18th century, the trees, lawns, and crisscrossed paths stretch over to Kensington Palace (p. 168) on the opposite side. There, you can wander around the sunken gardens, enjoy a bite at The Orangery, and while away the time on a bench near the Round Pond, where enthusiasts make their model boats buzz between the ducks. Close to the northwestern entrance to the park is the Princess Diana Memorial Playground, where kids can clamber about on a mock pirate galleon. And do show them the Elfin Oak. In the 1930s, Ivor Innes carved hundreds of little gnomes, goblins, and fairies peering out of the nooks and crevices in a 10-foot-high tree stump. It really is enchanting. Near the Long Water, you'll find the famous bronze statue of Peter Pan with his rabbits. And, on the south side of the park, near Queen's Gate, is the overpoweringly neo-Gothic Albert Memorial. The Pet Cemetery in Kensington Gardens was the fashionable last resting place for cats and dogs, noble and mutt, from Victorian times until 1867; call the number above for permission to visit. Take the Tube to Queensway or Bayswater.

Regent's Park (✆ **020/7486-7905**) was once Henry VIII's private hunting ground—as were most of the royal parks—but it was formally laid out in 1811 by the Prince Regent and John Nash as part of an elaborate remodeling of London. Now, it's the people's playground. In summer, you'll see everyone and his brother walking their dogs; playing cricket, soccer, and baseball; doing gymnastics; and throwing Frisbees. Beside the zoo, Regent's Park is famous for the boating lake, summer open-air theater

(✆ **020/7486-2431;** see chapter 9), brass band concerts on Holme Green, and bat-watching walks. There are 30,000 blossoms and 400 different varieties in Queen Mary's Rose Garden. And don't miss the Italianate Avenue Gardens, the Japanese Gardens, and the wildflowers flanking the Regent's Canal. Get there by Tube to Regent's Park, Baker Street, or Camden Town.

Opposite Buckingham Palace, **St. James's Park,** The Mall (✆ **020/7930-1793**), is perhaps the most beautiful of all of London's parks. It was landscaped by Le Notre and John Nash. The famous lake and Duck Island are a waterfowl sanctuary for lots of species, including coots and white and Australian black swans, which give the park a romantic atmosphere. Come at 3pm to see the keepers feeding the pelicans, descendants of a feathered present given by a 17th-century Russian ambassador. You can get a great view of Buckingham Palace from the bridge. Lots of benches and plenty of grass and shade make this an ideal picnicking place. Take the Tube to St. James's Park.

Named for its absence of flowers (except for a short time in spring), **Green Park** (✆ **020/7930-1793**) provides ample shade from tall trees that make it an ideal picnic bower. For other places to *déjeuner sur l'herbe,* and where to buy supplies, see the box "Moveable Feasts" on p. 121.

Royal Botanic Gardens Kew ★★ Nine miles southwest of Central London near Richmond, Kew is home to the best-known botanic gardens in Europe, and **Kew Palace**, former residence of George III and Queen Charlotte. More than 240 years of plant collecting, cultivation, and scientific research have won Kew recognition as a UNESCO World Heritage Site. There are more than 35,000 different plants in this magnificent park, which covers 300 acres amassed from the royal Kew and Richmond estates. Its borders, arboretum, lakes, glasshouses, follies, museums, galleries, and working buildings are a lasting testament to countless famous names, from 18th-century gardener Capability Brown and architect John Nash to contemporary Shigeru Ban, who designed the eco-friendly Paper Forest Pavilion made out of recycled paper.

Look out for the oldest potted plant in the world—a Cycad brought back to Kew in the 1770s—in the 4-acre Victorian **Palm House** (1844–48). The **Princess of Wales Conservatory** (1987) is an exuberant Eden split into 10 climactic zones growing prickly cacti, elegant orchids, and mangrove swamps. The **Museum,** across the lake from the Palm House, is worth a visit for its wonderful oddities: a Pacific Islands newspaper printed on beaten bark, rubber dentures, and a shirt made from pineapple fiber. As for outside, the wonders are too numerous to list. Spring is magical as more than two million crocuses bloom into a sea of color, and then the bluebells take over. In summer, wheat and wildflowers flank the Broadwalk. The garden map is split into three different areas, each one keeping the visitor busy for 2 to 3 hours.

Kew Palace and **Queen Charlotte's Cottage** are set within the Royal Botanic Gardens. The palace was constructed in 1631; at its rear is the very formal Queen's Garden, filled with plants thought to have grown here in the 17th century. The palace, used as a home by George III, is reminiscent of an elegant country house. Queen Charlotte's Cottage was used by the royal family as a summer house. Unfortunately, the palace is closed for renovations, and the cottage is not open to the public except on special occasions.

Richmond, Surrey. ✆ **020/8332-5622.** www.rbgkew.org.uk. Admission £10 ($19) adults, £7 ($13) late entry 45 min. before buildings close, free for children under 16. Daily from 9:30am; closing times vary seasonally (3:45, 5, 5:30, 6pm), buildings close 1 hr. earlier. Tube: District Line to Kew Gardens. Train: Waterloo to Kew Gardens or Kew Bridge. River services: From Westminster Pier (✆ **020/7930-2062/4721;** www.wpsa.co.uk) to Kew Pier; £17 ($31) return adults, £11 ($20) seniors, £8.25 ($15) children, £41 ($76) family. Schedules from Westminster and return from Kew vary seasonally.

10 Organized Tours

Joining an organized tour can be a useful way both to orient yourself when you arrive and to make the most of limited time. And the guides are a mine of quirky tales, as well as historical facts and humor.

GUIDED WALKS

The best way to soak up the atmosphere of London's most interesting streets is to explore them on foot. The **Original London Walks** ★★, P.O. Box 1708, London NW6 4LW (✆ **020/7624-3978** or 020/7625-9255; www.walks.com), has been going since 1965. It boasts an unrivalled schedule of themed tours, from spies, to royalty, to rock-'n'-roll legends, all led by experts, actors, and top Blue Badge guides. You can even go on a historic Thames-side pub crawl. The famous "Jack the Ripper" walk leaves daily at 7:30pm from Tower Hill Tube station. Try to go when Donald Rumbelow, a retired city policeman and authority on the subject, is leading the tour—call, or get the info online. Tours cover up to 1½ miles and take around 2 hours: £5.50 ($10) adults, £4.50 ($8) seniors and students, free for children under 15 with parent. No need to book. It's an even better bargain if you buy a **Discount Walkabout Card** (£2/$3.70): every walk after the first one then costs £4.50 ($8). This company also does out-of-London Explorer Day tours every Saturday (see chapter 10).

Every night is fright night with historian, ghost researcher, and Magic Circle member **Richard Jones** (✆ **020/8530-8443;** www.london-ghost-walk.co.uk). His hauntingly good 2-hour London Ghost Walk tour starts at 7:30pm at Bank Tube station (Royal Exchange exit). Tickets cost £5.50 ($10). You must book ahead.

Tours of the royal parks are free: you just have to call and find out when they are (see "Parks & Gardens," above). **Shakespeare's Globe** also puts on Walkshops, a combined guided tour of Southwark, a hotbed of historical licentiousness, and a look round the theater itself (see chapter 9).

BICYCLE RIDES

For a faster pace, try the **London Bicycle Tour Company,** 1a Gabriel's Wharf, 56 Upper Ground, London SE1 9PP (✆ **020/7928-6838;** www.londonbicycle.com; Tube: Waterloo or Blackfriars). You'll cover 6 to 9 miles in around 3½ hours, with pauses for historical gossip and refreshment. It costs £15 ($28), including bike rental. If you want to go solo, the company rents out bikes for £2.50 ($4.60) an hour, or £12 ($22) for the first day and then £7 ($13) a day, or £40 ($74) a week, with discounts for kids. It also does 2- and 3-day weekend breaks.

BUS TOURS

If your time is more limited than your budget, then bagging all the big sites from the top of a double-decker bus may be the best bet. **The Big Bus Company** (✆ **020/7233-9533;** www.bigbus.co.uk) leaves from Green Park, Victoria, and Marble Arch daily, from 8:30am to 7pm (4:30pm in winter) on three different routes that take anywhere from 1½ to 2½ hours. Tickets include a river cruise and walking tours and cost £18 ($33) for adults and £8 ($15) children ages 5 to 15. Valid for 24 hours, they let you hop on and off at 54 locations. Big Bus often has special offers, too, throwing in cheap theater tickets, fast entry to popular attractions, and so on. The **Original London Sightseeing Tour** (✆ **020/8877-1722;** www.theoriginaltour.com) has been going since 1951. The 2-hour tour leaves from Piccadilly Circus, Victoria, Baker Street, or Marble Arch every 15 to 20 minutes, from 8:30am to 7pm. This one has 90 stops to hop on and off at during the day. It costs £16 ($30) for adults, £10 ($19) for children under 16, and £60 ($111) for a family. No need to book, and you can buy your tickets on board; though you'll save a bit by booking online.

BOAT TRIPS

The unique and fabulously entertaining **London Duck Tours** ★★ (✆ **020/7928-3132;** www.frogtours.co.uk) has adapted several World War II amphibious troop carriers, known as DUKWs, to civilian comfort levels, painted them screaming yellow, and now runs 80-minute road and river trips. Tours start behind County Hall (site of the British Airways London Eye giant observation wheel). You're picked up on Chicheley Street, then rumble through Westminster and up to Piccadilly, passing many of London's major tourist sites. Then the vehicle splashes into the Thames at Vauxhall for a 30-minute cruise up as far as the Houses of Parliament. The ticket price of £18 ($32) for adults, £15 ($28) seniors, £12 ($22) children, and £52 ($95) for families is worth it in vacation-snap value alone. The ongoing commentary is very funny.

You can now use your Travelcard to get a discount on most boat-trip tickets. The Thames has always served as the city's highway, and there are 23 piers along its London stretch, from Hampton Court to Gravesend in the estuary. The funky Millbank Pier, by Tate Britain, is the newest (2002) and fanciest. At last count, more than 10 companies were running cruises and rush-hour-only ferries. There's a full schedule on the London Transport website www.londontransport.co.uk/river; or pick up its **Thames River Services** booklet at Tube stations and tourist information offices.

The best value (even before the Travelcard discount) is the **Crown River Cruises** service (✆ **020/7936-2033**; www.crownriver.com) from Westminster to St. Katherine's Dock, stopping by the South Bank Centre and London Bridge, from 11am to 6:30pm (daily Mar–Nov, weekends only Dec–Feb). A return ticket costs £6.50 ($12) for adults, £5.50 ($10) seniors, and £3.50 ($6.50) children under 16. The round-trip takes 1 hour, but the ticket is valid all day, so you can hop on and off to sightsee.

Don't forget: You can go to Hampton Court (p. 166) and the Royal Botanic Gardens Kew (p. 203) by boat. Those trips are more expensive, and there are fewer headline sights on the way, but they do make for a great day out. See the individual reviews for more details.

You can also take a boat along the Regent's Canal. From April to October, **Jason's Trip** (✆ **020/7286-3428;** www.jasons.co.uk; Tube: Warwick Ave.) operates a 90-minute tour from the wharf opposite 60 Blomfield Rd. in Little Venice. The painted

---

Tips Seeing London by Bus

Buy a **Travelcard** or a 1-day **Bus Pass** (£3/$5.50 adults, £1/$1.85 children; see "Getting Around," in chapter 3), and you can tour all over London on the top of a red double-decker anytime you want. The no. 11 bus has one of the best routes—Liverpool Street Station to Fulham Broadway, via King's Road, Westminster Abbey, Whitehall, Horse Guards, Trafalgar Square, the National Gallery, the Strand, Law Courts, Fleet Street, and St. Paul's Cathedral. A new **Riverbus** service travels from Covent Garden to the British Airways London Eye, Tate Modern, the Globe, and the Tower of London. For more information call the London Transport hotline (✆ **020/7222-1234**) or check out www.londontransport.co.uk.

---

narrow boat leaves at 10:30am (except in Oct), 12:30, and 2:30pm and takes you past Brownings Island (so called because Robert Browning lived there), through the Maida Hill Tunnel and Regent's Park, to Camden Lock. The round-trip price is £7 ($13) for adults, £5.50 ($10) for children 14 and under, £22 ($41) for a round-trip family ticket. **London Waterbus Company** (✆ **020/7482-2660;** Tube: Warwick Ave. or Camden Town) travels the same stretch of canal, with departures between 10am to 4pm (weekends only in winter). One-way fares are £5.60 ($10) adults, £3.70 ($6.50) children (ages 3–15). At £11 to £11 ($20)for kids, and £14 to £15 ($27)for adults, their all-in-one ticket including admission to the London Zoo is a real bargain.

11 Staying Active

For information on cycling, check out "Bicycle Rides," above.

GOLF

You'll have to travel into the burbs if you want to tee off while you're here. Contact the **English Golf Union** (✆ **01526/354500;** www.uk-golfguide.com) to find out where.

HORSEBACK RIDING

Both these stables take groups out riding in Hyde Park every day except Monday. **Hyde Park Stables,** 63 Bathurst Mews, W2 (✆ **020/7723-2813;** www.hydeparkstables.com), charges £40 ($74) an hour for all ages. **Ross Nye Stables,** 8 Bathurst Mews, W2 (✆ **020/7262-3791**), also charges £40 ($74) an hour for adults, £35 ($65) for children. You can't gallop or jump, only amble rather sedately around the sandy track. Both get booked up early for weekends. Take the Tube to Lancaster Gate or Paddington.

ICE SKATING

Open-air ice skating is enjoying quite a revival. They turn off the fountains at **Somerset House** (p. 171) in December and for a few weeks the courtyard is transformed into a romantic ice rink. There's even talk of building two "pads"—for roller as well as ice skating—on the traffic island next to Marble Arch.

Broadgate Ice Rink ✪ This is London's only purpose-built open-air rink that operates all winter. It is tiny, surrounded by city wine bars and skyscrapers, and the state-of-the-art sound system will knock your skates off.

Broadgate Circus, Eldon St., EC2. ✆ **020/7505-4068.** Admission £6 ($11) adults, £4 ($7) seniors and students; skate rental £2 ($3.70) adults, £1 ($1.85) students and seniors. Late Oct to Apr Mon–Thurs noon–2:30pm and 3:30–6pm; Fri noon–2:30pm, 3:30–5:30pm, and 6–9pm; Sat–Sun 11am–1pm, 2–4pm, and 5–7pm (8pm on Sat). Tube: Liverpool St.

INLINE SKATING

The inline skating cult erupts in London's streets and parks as soon as there's the least sign of summer. Every Wednesday from mid-May, hundreds of people meet up at 8pm opposite the bandstand on Serpentine Road in Hyde Park for a 2½-hour marshaled skate. The route takes in the capital's most famous landmarks, from Big Ben to Buckingham Palace. The hardcore don't turn around until they reach Tower Bridge, while the lightweights stop for a drink on the river. Taking part in **London Skate** (✆ **0800/169-3889;** www.sweatybetty.com/bettyblade) is free, as is instruction if you're a little nervous about keeping up. Be warned, though—neither this event, nor the **Friday Night Skate (FNS),** which also starts at 8pm (same location), is for novices. The excellent **www.citiskate.com** organizes FNS and is a one-stop info shop

Tips **Where to Go for Sports Info**

Visit **www.sportal.com** for information on everything from football to Formula One motor-racing. Otherwise, **Sportsline** (✆ **020/7222-8000**) will answer any questions, on where to work out as well as where to catch a game, Monday through Friday from 10am to 6pm.

for everything about the sport, including where to rent skates. **Slick Willies,** 12 Gloucester Rd., W7 (✆ **020/7225-0004;** Tube: Gloucester Road), charges £10 a day ($18), and £15 overnight ($28). You can rent skates by the hour at **Urban Chaos,** 324 Old Brompton Rd. (✆ **020/7373-1193;** Tube: Earl's Court), where prices are £5 ($9) for 1 hour, £7.50 ($14) for 2 hours, £10 ($18) per day, or £15 ($28) all weekend. Both shops take a big deposit.

SWIMMING & FITNESS

London Central YMCA Super-snazzy for a Y, this West End health and fitness center has a pool, weight room, squash and badminton, short tennis, cardiovascular equipment, sauna, and solarium. It's membership only, so you pay a flat fee to do as much or as little as you want. There are also beauticians, plus massage and holistic therapists.

112 Great Russell St., WC1. ✆ **020/7637-8131.** Admission £15 ($28) per day, £39 ($72) per week. Mon–Fri 7am–10:30pm; Sat–Sun 10am–9pm. Tube: Tottenham Court Rd.

Oasis Sports Centre *Finds* This place has pretty much everything and at very reasonable prices for London. But the irresistible draw is the roof-top open-air pool. Come and tune out after a hard day's sightseeing.

32 Endell St., WC2. ✆ **020/7831-1804.** Swim £3 ($5.50) adults, £1.50 ($2.75) children under 16. Gym £6–8 ($11–$15). Sauna £7 ($13) peak times, £4 ($7.50) before noon and 2–4pm. Indoor pool Mon and Wed 6:30am–6:30pm; Tues 6.30am–5:30pm; Thurs–Fri 6:30am–7:15pm; Sat–Sun 9:30am–5pm. Outdoor pool Mon–Fri 7:30am–9pm (8:30pm Thurs); Sat–Sun 9:30am–5:30pm. Tube: Covent Garden or Holborn.

12 Spectator Sports

CRICKET

Lord's and the Oval are London's two cricket venues. Tickets to county games are the budget-friendliest at around £10 ($18), and you can just turn up on match day. Book ahead for international Test matches and 1-day games: For schedules (called fixtures), call the international hotline ✆ **0870/533-8833.** Tickets are pricey at £25 to £50 ($46–$92). The cricket season runs from April through September.

Foster's Oval Less stodgy and prettier than Lord's, except for the gasometer looming up behind it, the Oval is home to Surrey County Cricket Club. It also traditionally hosts the final game in the summer international Test series. The box office is open Monday to Friday 9:30am to 4pm.

The Oval, Kennington, SE11. ✆ **020/7582-6660,** or 020/7582-7764 box office. Tube: Oval.

Lord's This hallowed ground is the home of both the ancient Marylebone Cricket Club (which governs the game) and the Middlesex County Cricket Club, which plays league matches here. The international Tests have the aura of high society, or at least corporate hospitality, events. The box office is open Monday to Friday 9:30am to 5:30pm.

You don't have to endure a cricket match to make a pilgrimage to Lord's. There are **guided tours** at noon and 2pm from October to March, with an extra one at 10am in spring and summer. These include a visit to the **museum,** which has exhibits on legendary cricketers and houses the Ashes trophy, for which the English and Australians furiously compete. The Marylebone Cricket Club moved here in 1816. On the tour, you'll see the pavilion, where the dressing rooms are, the "real tennis" court, and the space-pod-style media center. Then watch bowling machines fire practice balls at 100 mph in the indoor school, before popping into Lord's Tavern for a pick-me-up.

St. John's Wood Rd., NW8. ✆ **020/7432-1066,** or 020/7616-8595 for tours. www.lords.org/mcc. Tours and museum £7 ($13) adults, £5.50 ($10) seniors and students, £4.50 ($8) children, £20 ($37) family ticket. Tube: St. John's Wood.

FOOTBALL (SOCCER)

Soccer attracts quasi-religious devotion here. The violent hooliganism that's marred the national game has declined with the building of all-seat stadiums, but it still happens and can be an ugly spectacle. The football season runs from August to April, and matches usually kick off at 3pm on Saturdays or 7:45pm on Wednesdays. The capital has more than a dozen clubs in different leagues. Tickets cost from £8 to £30 ($15–$55) and more for gold-dust Premiership games. London's glamour clubs are: **Arsenal,** Arsenal Stadium, Avenell Road, N5 (✆ **020/7704-4000,** or 020/7704-4040 for the box office; www.arsenal.co.uk; Tube: Arsenal); **Tottenham Hotspur** ("Spurs"), White Hart Lane, 748 High Rd., N17 (✆ **020/8365-5000,** or 020/8365-5050 for the box office; www.spurs.co.uk; Tube: Seven Sisters); and **Chelsea,** Stamford Bridge, Fulham Road, SW6 (✆ **020/7385-5545,** or 020/7386-7799 for tickets; www.chelsea fc.co.uk; Tube: Fulham Broadway).

GREYHOUND RACING

Wimbledon Stadium This people's sport is enjoying a big renaissance as *the* alternative night out. The minimum bet is £1 ($1.85), but the results are even less predictable than horse races. You can eat, drink, and make very merry at quasi-posh restaurants, bars, and fast-food stalls.

Plough Lane, SW19. ✆ **020/8946-8000.** Admission £5.50 ($10) adults, £2.75 ($5) children ages 7–15, free for children 6 and under. Races Tues and Fri–Sat 7:30–10:30pm (stadium open 6:30pm). Tube: Wimbledon Park.

HORSE RACING

Royal Windsor Racecourse ★★ Windsor does hold sporadic afternoon race meetings during the chillier months, but the festive summer Monday evenings are by far the best fun. The relaxed crowd is a mix of champagne Charlies and regular Joes, sampling the restaurants and bars (dress code demands a tie), or diving into a home-packed picnic. Even the journey is a delight. Turn right out of the train station, and

---

Tips Go Native with the Sporting Pub Crowd

Pay-per-view TV channels own the live-broadcast rights to most of the hottest fixtures, from football to rugby and cricket. Rather than pay to view at home, fans use this as an excuse to enjoy their two favorite things at the same time—sport and downing a pint with the lads. Find a local pub with a big-screen TV and you've got *the* authentic English experience!

---

follow the crowd to the Riverbus for the 35-minute trip up the Thames to the racecourse. It leaves on the hour, and at 20 and 40 minutes past, from an hour or so before the first race, to a half-hour after the last one. Buy your ticket on board.

Maidenhead Rd., Windsor, Berkshire, SL4 5JJ. ✆ **0870/220-0024** or 01753/865234. www.windsor-racecourse.co.uk. Admission £5–£16 ($9–$30), free for children under 16. Discount for online booking. Race meetings: Mar and Oct–Nov afternoons; May–Aug Mon evenings; start times vary, 5–6pm. Train: Windsor Riverside, then Riverbus (✆ **01753/851900**; www.boat-trips.co.uk) from nearby Barry Ave. Promenade, £2.50 ($4.60) each way.

RUGBY UNION

The capital's top clubs are the **London Wasps,** Loftus Road Stadium, South Africa Road, W12 7PZ (✆ **020/8743-0262;** www.wasps.co.uk) and the **Harlequins,** Stoop Memorial Ground, Langhorn Drive, Twickenham, Middlesex, TW2 7SX (✆ **020/8410-6000;** www.quins.co.uk). This ultramacho game can be very exciting, and dangerous, too, since more than one rugby player has died or been incapacitated as a result of "heading" the ball over the years. The season runs from August to May, with games on Saturday and Sunday afternoons. Tickets are relatively easy to obtain (though it is wise to book ahead) and cost £10 to £25 ($18–$46). For full fixtures listings, surf **www.rfu.com**.

Twickenham Stadium The Rugby Football Union HQ hosts international games (very hard to get tickets) and cup finals (a little easier). The annual Six Nations battle between Scotland, Ireland, Wales, England, France, and Italy takes place from January to March, whipping up a fever of patriotism.

Take the **Stadium Tour** to walk through the players' tunnel and see what they see on the big day, visit the dressing room to savor the lingering smell of sweaty socks, and hear lots of sporting stories. There's a scrum machine (a bit like a blocking sled in American football) in the **Museum of Rugby,** where you can test your own strength. You'll see lots of memorabilia, including the oldest jersey still in existence, and the best rugby moments of all time on film.

Rugby Rd., Twickenham, Middlesex, TW1 1DZ. ✆ **020/8892-8877,** -8892 for tours. www.rfu.com, then click on Twickenham Museum and/or tour £6 and £4 ($11 and $7) adults, £4 and £3 ($7 and $5.50) seniors and students, £19 ($35) family ticket. Stadium tours Tues–Sat 10:30am, noon, 1:30, and 3pm; Sun 3pm. Museum of Rugby Tues–Sat 10am–5pm; Sun 2–5pm; match and postmatch days from stadium opening to 1 hr. after final whistle. Train: From Waterloo to Twickenham, then bus no. 281.

TENNIS

Ever since players in flannels and bonnets took to the courts in 1877, the **Wimbledon Lawn Tennis Championships** have drawn a crowd. Save up and savor the extortionately priced strawberries and cream that are part of the experience. Show court seats are mostly sold by ticket ballot. The allocation is random, so you can't request a specific court or date. To be included, write between August 1 and December 31 of the preceding year for an application form, enclosing a self-addressed envelope with an International Reply Coupon, to **All England Lawn Tennis Club,** P.O. Box 98, Church Road, Wimbledon, SW19 5AE (✆ **020/8944-1066** or 020/8971-2473; www.wimbledon.org). For the first 8 days of the tournament, around 500 seats for each show court are sold on match day. People camp out in line on the pavement to get them; depending on the court and the day, prices range from £24 to £79 ($44–$146). If you have the dough, you can forego the ballot and get your Wimbledon tickets and a complete "entertainment package" through **Keith Prowse** ticket agency (✆ **800/669-8687;** www.keithprowse.com).

During the earlier rounds, you can watch lots of top-rankers playing on the outside courts if you just buy Ground Admission. Prices start at £16 ($30), winding down to £7 ($13) at the end of the 2 weeks when there's much less to see; or £10 ($18) falling to £4 ($7), if you come after 5pm to catch the tail-end of the day's play. There are two more great deals, too: People leaving the show courts are encouraged to turn in their tickets for cheap resale, with the proceeds going to charity; and on the middle Saturday of the tournament all prices are discounted, including 2,000 Centre Court tickets. The gates open every day at 10:30am, and play starts at noon on the outside courts, 1pm on Centre and No. 1 courts (except finals weekend when it's 2pm). Come early—and I mean any time from 7am—because there are 6,000 ground tickets and the gates close for the day when the crowd inside reaches capacity.

The **Wimbledon Lawn Tennis Museum** (© **020/8946-6131**) is open daily 10:30am to 5pm. Tickets cost £5 ($8) adults, £4.25 ($7) students and seniors, and £3.50 ($6) for children under 16. It has all sorts of memorabilia, from costumes and tennis kit to TV footage of famous matches. A visit includes a tour of Centre Court. The museum is closed Friday to Sunday before the championships, the middle Sunday, and the Monday after it finishes. During those 2 weeks, it is only open to tournament visitors. It is also closed December 24 to 26 and January 1. Take the Tube to Southfields, then a no. 39, 93, or 200 bus.

8

Shopping

The Brits still like to see, touch, scratch, and sniff what they're buying, so they're not into online shopping as much as Americans are. Shopping is a British buzz and, with around 30,000 stores, nowhere is buzzier or busier than London.

Stores are usually open from 10am to 6pm, and most add on an extra hour at least 1 night a week. There's "late-night shopping," as it's called, on Wednesday in Knightsbridge, Kensington, and Chelsea, and on Thursday in the West End. Around touristy Covent Garden, many doors don't close until 7 or 8pm every night. Shops can open for 6 hours on a Sunday, and many do, usually from 11am or noon.

TAXES & SHIPPING

In Britain, most goods and services, with the exception of books, newspapers, groceries, and children's clothing, carry 17.5% value-added tax (VAT), which is included in the price. Visitors from non-E.U. countries can reclaim the tax on some of the shopping they take home. In order to do so, you'll need to do your shopping at stores where you see the **GLOBAL REFUND TAX-FREE SHOPPING** sign. And although there is no official minimum purchase requirement, many stores set their own, usually around £75 ($139).

To make a claim, you must show identification at the store and fill out a VAT reclaim form then and there. Keep the receipt, form, and goods handy to show to the British Customs office at the airport (allowing a half-hour to stand in line). There are two ways to get the money. The easiest way is to go to the **Global Refunds** desk, where you will get an immediate cash refund (but lose money on the conversion rate if you take other than sterling). The second way is to mail the stamped form back to the store, choosing a credit card refund. For more info, call Customs' **Passenger Enquiry Point** (✆ **020/8910-3744**) or check out www. globalrefund.co.uk.

VAT is not charged on goods shipped directly out of the country by the supplier. Some stores will do that for you, but it's expensive and you may have to pay import duty at home. If you have overshopped and need to ship stuff yourself, contact **Excess Baggage,** which has branches in every Heathrow and Gatwick terminal, and at all of London's major rail stations (✆ **0800/783-1085;** www.excess-baggage.com).

1 Top Tips for Bargain Hounds

Britain is a pricey place. But never fear—we've unearthed plenty of money-saving strategies, budget-friendly stores, and ideas for affordable but quintessentially English souvenirs (see the "London's Best Buys" box, below).

- **Net Savings.** Journalist Noelle Walsh will make your mouth water with her tales of amazing savings at **www.gooddealdirectory.co.uk**.

London's Best Buys

Smart shoppers stock up on specialties found only in Britain or that are made better here than anywhere else. Here are just a few ideas.

- Unusual **pickles** and **preserves.** As well as the stores and markets reviewed below, **Indian Spice Shop,** 115–117 Drummond St., NW1 (© **020/7916-1831;** Tube: Euston, Warren St., or Great Portland St.), is a hot spot for authentic Indian chutneys. **Mr Christian's,** 11 Elgin Crescent, W11 (© **020/7229-0501;** Tube: Ladbroke Grove), has shelves full of unusual preserves, such as quince and rose-petal jelly.
- **Stationery** is another best buy. Try **John Lewis** (see "Department Stores," later in this chapter) for leather-bound address books, and **Paperchase,** 213 Tottenham Court Rd., W1 (© **020/7580-8496;** www.paperchase.co.uk; Tube: Charing Cross), for beautiful papers and notebooks. If you know anyone who still uses a Filofax, head straight for **The Filofax Centre,** 21 Conduit St., W1 (© **020/7499-0457;** Tube: Oxford Circus), the British HQ where you can pick up every insert made for every size of filer.
- **Wet weather gear.** Few things are more British than the umbrella, and **James Smith & Sons,** 53 New Oxford St., WC1 (© **020/7836-4731;** www.james-smith.co.uk; Tube: Holborn, Tottenham Court Rd.), has been making them since 1830. Traditional "brollies" come in nylon or silk, stretched over wood or metal frames, and prices start at about £35 ($65). Then head off to the **Burberry** factory shop for the classic trench coat at a discount (see "Discount" under "Fashion," later in this chapter).
- **Classic entertainment.** For suitcase-friendly gifts for Anglophiles of every age, try the **BBC World Service Shop,** Bush House, Strand, WC2 (© **020/7557-2576;** Tube: Temple). It stocks recordings of drama, comedy, and book readings from Radio 4, and lots of stuff for kids.

- **Traditional Sales.** January sales are as English as plum pudding—and that's one thing always reduced by 30% after the Christmas holiday. London's summer sell-offs are exciting, too, and start earlier every year—certainly by the end of June. ***Buyer beware:*** Many stores ship stuff in especially for sales, and it may be of lower quality.
- **Samples, Seconds, and Ends of Lines.** As well as the two established sale companies (see "Regular Sales" under "Fashion," later in this chapter), which put on bimonthly bargain fests, the individual fashion designers also mark down their own excess inventory. The last week of November and the first few weeks of December are packed with sample sales: check the listings magazines for details. Other labels operate sale stores (see "Discount" under "Fashion," later in this chapter). If you like fancy table settings, don't miss the Villeroy & Boch Factory Shop (see "China & Glass," later in this chapter).
- **High Fashion at Low Prices.** Many chain stores now commission top designers to create exclusive collections just for them. These include **Marks & Spencer** and

Debenhams (see "Department Stores," later in this chapter), as well as **Top Shop** (see "Contemporary" under "Fashion," later in this chapter).

- **Markets.** Knowledgeable locals and bargain-hunting visitors love to cruise London's outdoor markets (see "Markets," later in this chapter) for food, clothing, furniture, books, and crafts.

EVENTS

There are all sorts of annual fairs, festivals, and special events in London that provide a bumper crop of bargain-hunting. The only downside is that you may have to part with £5 to £10 ($9–$18) for admission. Check *Time Out* for details, particularly around Christmas when lots of charities raise money through craft fairs.

For instance, the art world may seem a scary and expensive place, but anyone can become a collector—it is largely a matter of timing. The **Art School degree shows** in May and June are great for hot talent at debut prices—you might spot Charles Saatchi shopping for his famous gallery. If you're in London in March or October (dates vary yearly), visit the **Affordable Art Fair** in Battersea Park. Over 100 stands display paintings, prints, and sculpture, all priced at under £3,000 ($5,550). Tickets cost £10 ($18) at the door: For details, call ✆ **020/7371-8787;** www.affordableartfair.co.uk.

New Designers is a super-degree show in July for 4,000 graduates from across Britain—jewelry, textile and glass-makers, ceramicists, and so on—at the Business Design Centre (✆ **020/7359-3535;** www.newdesigners.com). Canny collectors of decorative arts might also plan a trip to London at the end of the year. The **Chelsea Crafts Fair** is the largest in Europe and takes place at Chelsea Old Town Hall, King's Road SW3, during the last 2 weeks of October: Contact the Crafts Council for details (✆ **020/7278-7700;** www.craftscouncil.org.uk). The **Hidden Art** festival (✆ **020/7729-3301;** www.hiddenart.co.uk) runs over the last weekend in November and first in December. It mobilizes more than 300 members of East London's design community to open their studios and workshops, and sell directly to the public. There are also frequent rare and antiquarian book fairs at the Hotel Russell, Russell Square, WC1 (✆ **01763/248400;** www.pbfa.org).

2 The Shopping Scene

The **West End** is the heart of London shopping. Its main artery is **Oxford Street,** a mile of mass-market chains and department stores like John Lewis, Selfridges, and Marks & Spencer. At the eastern end, St. Giles High Street is the gateway into **Covent Garden,** a warren of narrow streets lined with stores selling quirky specialties and the hottest fashion trends. The old market is home to boutiques and craft stalls, while the piazza is a nonstop street festival of mime artists, singers, and entertainers.

Oxford Circus is the first big intersection walking west along Oxford Street, where it crosses the patchily elegant **Regent Street:** Turn south for Liberty, Aquascutum, Austin Reed, and Hamleys. Sixties' hot spot **Carnaby Street** is tucked in behind Liberty. After years as a gaudy tourist trap, it is now a hub of street and extreme-sports fashion.

The next landmark westwards is New Bond Street, which changes to Old Bond Street as it heads south through **Mayfair.** It's wonderful for designer window-shopping and for fine art and antiques. Both Regent Street and Old Bond Street run into Piccadilly, to the south of which is **St James's** and some seriously upper-crust shopping. Here you'll find Hatchards for books; Swaine, Adeney Brigg & Sons for fine leather goods and riding equipment; and the fabulous food halls of Fortnum & Mason. **Jermyn Street** is famous for shirtmakers; other fine shops include Paxton & Whitfield, a specialist cheesemonger, Taylor of Old Bond Street, for men's shaving and toiletry articles, and Floris, which has been blending perfume and soaps since 1730.

Continue west from Piccadilly and Hyde Park Corner, to posh **Knightsbridge** and the world-famous Harrods department store on Brompton Road. Off Knightsbridge (it's a street as well as a neighborhood), is **Sloane Street**, lined with the most rarified names in haute couture. This runs down to Sloane Square and King's Road in **Chelsea. King's Road** was the center of Swinging London in the 1960s and of the punk revolution a decade later. Mainstream boutiques have invaded now, but there's still a healthy dose of streetwise avant-garde.

Young fashion and outdoor sports gear flourishes on **Kensington High Street.** Nearby **Notting Hill** is crammed with funky boutiques of every kind, especially around **Portobello Market,** though budget-busters are pushing out the neighborhood bargains—**Westbourne Grove** and **Ledbury Road** are *Vogue*'s idea of heaven. You have to travel east to find a hip shopping scene still on the way up: creative **Clerkenwell,** or **Brick Lane** in the City, where you'll find a market and Dray Walk, an enclave of quirky studio-shops and galleries.

3 Shopping A to Z

ANTIQUES

There are thousands of antiques stores in London—hardly surprising because the place is ancient and the Brits never throw anything away. Gangs of dealers gravitate together like husbands at a barbecue, so there are several arcades on the must-visit list. Otherwise, **Kensington Church Street,** W8, offers superb browsing: The shops here are the sort where you have to ring the bell to get in. Also check out "Markets" and "Auction Houses," below.

Alfie's Antique Market With 150-plus dealers crammed into this old Edwardian department store, Alfie's would fox the most expert maze-builder. You name it, you'll find it here, from Art Deco lighting to 20th-century ceramics, and at prices below the West End. Closed Sunday and Monday. 13–25 Church St., NW8. ✆ **020/7723-6066.** www.alfiesantiques.com. Tube: Edgware Rd. or Marylebone.

Antiquarius More than 120 dealers have set up shop in this Arts and Crafts–style building. They sell everything from classic luggage to Art Nouveau sculpture and jewelry. Bargain-hunters head for the lower-priced basement hall. Closed Sundays. 131–141 King's Rd., SW3. ✆ **020/7351-5353.** Tube: Sloane Sq.

Finds **Mick the Trolley**

One man's junk is another man's nice little earner. The rag-and-bone men knew that. These wily traders used to drive their horses and carts around London, knocking on people's doors offering to take away any unwanted household items. Then they sold the best stuff. Mick the Trolley still trawls wealthy Chelsea. You can usually find him, as well as some impressive bargains, at the car boot sale that takes place every 3 weeks at Christchurch Church of England School, Caversham St., SW3 (✆ **020/7351-5597;** Tube: Sloane Sq.). Call for dates. Entry is 50p (90¢).

Camden Passage Bargains are hard to find, but there's wonderful browsing at the arcades, malls, and specialty stores lining this little enclave. The outdoor stalls are open on Wednesday and Saturday, bringing the dealer-count up to 250, and these are the best days to look for affordable jewelry, silverware, and trinkets. Off Upper St., N1. ✆ **020/7226-4474.** Tube: Angel.

Grays Antiques Market & Grays in the Mews The main antiques market is home to 85 dealers and is red hot on jewelry, but the Mews is a better bet for bargain hunters, especially if they're looking for something pocket-size, like a model car or music box. **Biblion** is an enormous hall especially for books, antiquarian and merely secondhand. Grays is closed on the weekends. Call for details on regular exhibitions. 58 and 1–7 Davies St., W1. ✆ **020/7629-7034.** www.egrays.com. Tube: Bond St.

London Silver Vaults This is a marvelous place to buy a wedding or christening present. Over 40 dealers trade in modern and antique silver, with prices starting at around £20 ($32). Closed Sundays. Chancery House, 53–64 Chancery Lane, WC2. ✆ **020/7242-3844.** www.thesilvervaults.com. Tube: Chancery Lane.

ART

Cork Street, Mayfair, is nose to tail with grand commercial galleries, while **Hoxton,** on the City's northern edge, has become the stalking ground of the brash new art entrepreneurs. Both are strictly for window-shopping. If you really want to get your wallet out, head for the **Alternative Art Market,** held Sundays at Old Spitalfields Market (p. 227).

Will's Art Warehouse Will Ramsay set up his warehouse in an old motorcycle garage in 1996 to debunk art-market snobbishness and offshore-bank-account prices. The 200 pictures on display change every 6 weeks. Customers can peruse the entire collection on a computer screen and choose which piece(s) they would like to see. Prices range from £50 ($92) to £3,000 ($5,550), and you can buy works on Will's website, too. The venture has spun off into the now biannual **Affordable Art Fair** in Battersea Park (see "Events," above). Unit 3, Heathmans Rd., SW6. ✆ **020/7371-8787.** www.wills-art.com. Tube: Parson's Green.

AUCTION HOUSES

A Monet sold for millions to a mystery bidder always grabs the headlines, but it's a tiny part of what passes through London's salerooms, from toys to fine wine, and Roman coins to rock stars' underpants. Emotions and prices run high, so it's a great spectator sport, and the lots go on view to the public for a few days beforehand. London's four biggest auction houses first banged their gavels in the 18th century. To find out what's on (little in August), contact their main salerooms: **Bonhams & Brooks,** Montpelier Street, SW7 (✆ **020/7393-3900;** www.bonhams.com; Tube: Knightsbridge); **Sotheby's,** 34–35 New Bond St., W1 (✆ **020/7293-5000;** www.sothebys.com; Tube: Bond St.); and **Christie's,** 8 King St., SW1 (✆ **020/7839-9060;** www.christies.com; Tube: Green Park).

Chiswick Auctions *Finds* This friendly local salesroom is a place where travelers on a budget can dare to raise their hands as prices start as low as £10 ($18). Loony lots often add to the party atmosphere: fake marble columns from a props company or 5-foot-high bronze parrots. But there's good stuff, too. Chiswick Auctions handles a lot of private libraries. Viewing runs from Sunday afternoon until the auction starts on Tuesday—small goods at 5pm, furniture from 7pm, every week. 1 Colville Rd., W3. ✆ **020/8992-4442;** www.chiswickauctions.co.uk. Tube: Acton Lane.

Moments Take Five

When you're all shopped out, nerve ends fraying and feet aflame, take five in the peaceful churchyard of St. Paul's in Covent Garden. Enclosed by buildings, it's a soothing place with benches and rambling roses. The garden is open from 8:30am to 4:30pm Monday to Friday; enter on Henrietta Street or King Street.

BATH & BODY

Lush You've probably never seen anything quite like Lush—it's a beauty shop that takes "organic" to a whole new level. Huge slabs of soap made with pineapple slices (good for the skin) or poppy seeds (a great exfoliator) sit on tables and counters like rounds of cheese at a deli. You can have the amount you want sliced off, or buy already-cut bars. The store whips up fresh facial masks and keeps them on ice. Just scoop some into a take-home container and keep refrigerated. Lush is a fabulous source for gifts. Their bestseller is the "bath bomb," which fizzes and scents the water. There are branches on King's Road, Chelsea, and Carnaby Street in Soho, as well as at Victoria railway station. Units 7 and 11, The Piazza, Covent Garden, WC2. ✆ **020/7240-4570.** www.lush.co.uk. Tube: Covent Garden.

Neal's Yard Remedies Founded in 1981, this is still the best shop in London for herbal toiletries, homeopathic hair remedies, and alternative medicines. Most of the products come in cobalt-blue glass bottles, and make attractive and reasonably priced gifts. Try Remedies-to-Roll, roll-on essential oils to fit in your handbag, including one for sleep. Or create your own potions, choosing oils and extracts to add to base lotions and creams. They also have the best lip balm we've ever used. The store is at the end of a short cul-de-sac off Short's Gardens. There is a second one at Chelsea Farmers Market in Sydney Street, SW3. 15 Neal's Yard, WC2. ✆ **020/7379-7222.** www.nealsyardremedies.com. Tube: Covent Garden.

Penhaligon's Barber William Penhaligon opened for business in 1841, and the scents are still made by hand according to his formulas. This lavish store sells soaps, eau de cologne, and shaving kits. It also has a fine selection of antique scent bottles and silver accessories, such as boxes, mirrors, and manicure sets. The most famous women's scents are Violetta and Bluebell. Love Potion No. 9 is irresistible. 41 Wellington St., WC2. ✆ **020/7836-2150.** www.penhaligons.co.uk. Tube: Covent Garden.

Taylor of Old Bond Street In business since 1854, this rather quaint emporium is devoted to the shaving and personal hygiene needs of men. Here's where you'll find the world's finest collection of shaving brushes, razors, and combs, plus soaps and hair lotions. 74 Jermyn St., SW1. ✆ **020/7930-5544.** Tube: Piccadilly Circus.

BOOKS

London is one of the best places in the world for avid readers and bibliophiles. The city has 1,000 or so booksellers, dealing in new, used, and antiquarian volumes. Look for entire shops devoted to art, science fiction, religion, medicine, crime, politics, sport, and travel. Browsers should start at Leicester Square Tube station and walk north along **Charing Cross Road,** the heart of London's bookselling community. And don't ignore side streets like St. Martin's Court and Cecil Court. Bloomsbury (**Museum Street** in particular) also has more than 30 secondhand book shops and scholarly antiquarian dealers. Or pop into the **Biblion** book hall at Grays (see "Antiques," above).

Books Etc. Books Etc., with a much more user-friendly layout than its U.S. parent, Borders, is very good on modern fiction and holds some backlist titles. And it regularly puts on readings and author signings, as does the branch at 26 James St., Covent Garden. There are branches everywhere. 421 Oxford St., W1. ✆ **020/7495-5850.** www.booksetc.co.uk. Tube: Bond St.

Books for Cooks This store in Notting Hill stocks nearly 12,000 cookbooks, everything from the classics to hot manifestos from celebrity chefs and recipes from virtually every ethnic cuisine. BFC has also compiled a series of little books of recipes tried out in its test kitchen—a great bargain buy. That's also where the chefs rustle up the soups, salads, and puddings that make this such a great pit-stop. 4 Blenheim Crescent, W11. ✆ **020/7221-1992.** www.booksforcooks.com. Tube: Ladbroke Grove or Notting Hill Gate.

Borders This U.S. import stocks almost 250,000 titles and, allegedly, the largest selection of newspapers and magazines in the country. The busy Café Express, where Borders holds readings and events, is on the second floor. There's a second branch in Charing Cross Road. 203–207 Oxford St., W1. ✆ **020/7292-1600.** www.bordersstores.com. Tube: Oxford Circus or Tottenham Court Rd.

Children's Book Centre A brilliant place for baby bookworms and their parents. There are more than 15,000 titles for every age group up to 15, from fiction to fun factual stuff. The shop is crammed with toys, CD-ROMs, and audiotapes, too. Some Saturdays, it arranges "personal appearances" by popular cartoon characters. 237 Kensington High St., W8. ✆ **020/7937-7497.** www.childrensbookcentre.co.uk. Tube: Kensington High St.

Foyles The famous, and famously old-fashioned, Foyles finally gave itself a partial makeover. It launched a website, started opening on Sundays, and at last stacks fiction alphabetically rather than having separate sections for each publisher. Reassuringly, the store still looks chaotic, crammed with books on virtually every topic under the sun. It's the place to come for titles other shops have stopped stocking, or never had in the first place. 113–119 Charing Cross Rd., WC2. ✆ **020/7440-5660.** www.foyles.co.uk. Tube: Leicester Sq. or Tottenham Court Rd.

Garden Books Gardening has never been more popular in Britain, in part because of the endless backyard makeovers featured on gardening shows on TV. This store opened in 1996 and now carries around 7,000 titles, including a section on interior design. If a book ain't here, then it's probably out of print. 11 Blenheim Crescent, W11. ✆ **020/7792-0777.** Tube: Ladbroke Grove or Notting Hill Gate.

Gay's the Word The amazingly comprehensive stock makes this Britain's biggest gay and lesbian bookshop. It has everything from literary fiction to detective novels and erotica, as well as issues-based titles, philosophy, and politics. 66 Marchmont St., WC1. ✆ **020/7278-7654.** www.gaystheword.co.uk. Tube: Russell Sq.

Hatchards A holder of Royal Warrants from the duke of Edinburgh and the Prince of Wales, Hatchards has been selling books since 1797. Oscar Wilde shopped here, and his wife Constance reputedly had an affair with the owner. It carries popular fiction and nonfiction titles and all the latest releases. Just climbing the creaking stairs and browsing the venerable wooden stacks makes one feel frightfully upper-crust. 187 Piccadilly, W1. ✆ **020/7439-9921.** www.hatchards.co.uk. Tube: Piccadilly Circus.

Stanfords Map & Travel Bookshop Stanford's is world-renowned for its exhaustive collection of travel literature, guidebooks, atlases, and maps of every kind, from maritime to historical, for biking or hiking, and covering every region of the world. It has a good selection of globes, too. Oddly enough, though, there are few guides to London—not exotic enough, obviously. 12–14 Long Acre, WC2. ✆ **020/7836-1321.** www.stanfords.co.uk. Tube: Covent Garden.

The Travel Bookshop This little gem is the last of the trio of specialist bookshops in Blenheim Crescent—you'll find the cooking and gardening ones in the list above. It carries a huge variety of travel literature and guidebooks, both old and new, mainstream and more adventurous. Remember that Hugh Grant/Julia Roberts movie, *Notting Hill?* This bookshop had a starring role. 13–15 Blenheim Crescent, W11. ✆ **020/7229-5260.** www.thetravelbookshop.co.uk. Tube: Ladbroke Grove.

Waterstone's It seems a bit insulting to call this a mere bookshop when it's the largest bookstore in Europe. Spread over seven floors in the building where posh store Simpson used to be, the Waterstone's flagship is the very model of a modern literary emporium. There are over 265,000 titles here, as well as Internet access, a juice bar, cafe, lounge bar, and the Red Room restaurant. It holds regular events and is a great place for a free wee if you get caught short sightseeing and need a bathroom. 203–206 Piccadilly, W1. ✆ **020/7851-2400.** www.waterstones.co.uk. Tube: Green Park or Piccadilly Circus.

CHINA & GLASS

Reject China Shop Most of the very wide range of English china sold here (including Portmeiron, Wedgwood, and Royal Doulton) is seconds or discontinued lines. This branch also stocks cutlery and Waterford crystal. Shoppers who know the going prices in the United States may pick up a bargain, but with the current exchange rate you may be better off shopping at home. The other shops are in Brompton Road, Knightsbridge, and Covent Garden Piazza. 134 Regent St., W1. ✆ **020/7734-2502.** www.chinacraft.co.uk. Tube: Piccadilly Circus.

Royal Doulton Founded over 200 years ago, Royal Doulton is one of the most famous names from the heart of English china production in Staffordshire. The company also produces Minton, Royal Albert, and Royal Crown Derby, all stocked here. 154 Regent St., W1. ✆ **020/7734-3184.** www.royal-doulton.com. Tube: Piccadilly Circus.

Villeroy & Boch Factory Shop This German company has been making high-quality tableware since 1748. You can find it in all the top London stores, from Harrods to Selfridges and Liberty. However, take the Tube to the wealthy suburb of Wimbledon, near the end of the District line, and you'll save a whopping 30% to 70% on seconds and discontinued ranges. 267 Merton Rd., SW18. ✆ **020/8875-6006.** www.villeroy.com. Tube: Southfields.

Waterford Wedgwood Waterford crystal and Wedgwood china share the same table at this upscale shop. Fine cut-glass vases, platters, and objets d'art come in a wide range of prices. You'll find complete sets of the famous powder-blue and white Jasper china, and lots of other styles and patterns, too. There's a smaller branch on Piccadilly. 158 Regent St., W1. ✆ **020/7734-7262.** www.waterfordwedgwood.co.uk. Tube: Piccadilly Circus.

CRAFTS

For years, popular prejudice lauded the noble artist and dissed the craftsman. Not anymore. Britain is in the grip of a passion for great design. Ceramicists, jewelry and textile-makers, glassworkers, and others command huge respect and all-too respectable prices. Check out **Contemporary Applied Arts,** 2 Percy St., W1 (✆ **020/7436-2344;** www.caa.org.uk; Tube: Tottenham Court Rd.): The organization represents more than 200 makers, with diverse skills, and exhibits their work in what is the largest specialist gallery in Britain. The independent but publicly funded **Crafts Council** has two shops—one is at the Victoria & Albert Museum (see chapter 7) and the other at its gallery, 44a Pentonville Rd., N1 (✆ **020/7806-2559;** www.craftscouncil.org.uk; Tube: Angel). Big pieces are expensive, but small ceramics, jewelry, or scarves shouldn't bust the budget. The Crafts Council can also give you a schedule of open-studio days, when individual designers welcome visitors to their workshops, and you can buy without paying the middleman's mark-up. Call ✆ **020/7278-7700.**

DEPARTMENT STORES

Debenhams Once-dowdy Debenhams shocked the fashion pack when it became one of the first chain stores to persuade big-name designers to descend to High Street level. Now the list of hot-name collaborators includes **Pearce II Fionda, Maria Grachvogel, Edina Ronay, John Rocha,** and undies queen **Janet Reger. Tristan Webber** is the latest addition. As well as her covetable womenswear, **Elspeth Gibson** has created the Sweet Pea range for girls ages 3 to 8. Debenhams is even roping some of these same designers into creating interiors. 334–348 Oxford St., W1. ✆ **020/7580-3000.** www.debenhams.co.uk. Tube: Bond St. or Oxford Circus.

Harrods Opened in 1849, Harrods claims it's the most famous department store in the world and that anything in the world can be bought (or ordered) here. The incredible ground-floor food halls are a feast for all the senses. And, for sheer theme-park excess, nothing beats the Egyptian escalator and the children's department with its cartoon cafe and specialty hairdresser. On the minus side, the store layout is frustrating and the fashions can be dowdy as opposed to cool. With around 35,000 visitors a day, Harrods can become a nightmare experience, like Disney World on the 4th of July. Harrods also has a snooty dress code: no dirty or unkempt clothing, ripped jeans, high-cut shorts, athletic tops, cycling shorts, or, horror of horrors, bare tummies or feet. Knightsbridge, SW1. ✆ **020/7730-1234.** www.harrods.com. Tube: Knightsbridge.

Harvey Nichols This elegant store is nicknamed Harvey Nics by its fashion-pack and It-Girl clientele, and it could hardly be more different from its brash Knightsbridge neighbor, Harrods. Whereas the latter is crammed to opulent bursting point with everything under the sun, and much of it in dubious taste, Harvey Nichols is a cool haven of chic. It pioneered the showcasing of designer collections from London, Paris, and Milan—from Chloe to Gaultier, Tocca to Joseph—and has a decent menswear department, too. And you won't go hungry here either: as well as the food hall and fifth-floor bar, cafe, and restaurant, Harvey Nics also has a YO! Sushi (p. 136) and a Wagamama (p. 144). 109–125 Knightsbridge, SW1. ✆ **020/7235-5000.** www.harveynichols.com. Tube: Knightsbridge.

Tips **Beware the Bathroom Rip-off**

Harrods makes shoppers pay an outrageous £1 ($1.85) to use its bathrooms. The only way to beat the charge is to say "yes" when the attendant asks if you've been to the cafe. Otherwise, nip up the road to Harvey Nichols (a 5-min. walk) where there's no charge and the queues to have a wee-wee are a good deal wee-er.

John Lewis This is one of the few remaining traditional department stores that really does stock everything, from fashions and fashion fabrics, to curtain fabrics and furniture, clothing, washing machines, and nice leather-bound daily planners. John Lewis makes a big promise—"Never Knowingly Undersold." If customers find the same goods locally at a better price, the store will refund the difference. (And it employs an army of undercover shoppers to check out the competition.) Sister store **Peter Jones,** Sloane Square, SW1 (✆ **020/7730-3434;** www.peterjones.co.uk; Tube: Sloane Sq.), is spiritual home to the Sloane Rangers—those Range-Rover driving upper-class aristocrats who live around Sloane Square. It's £80-million refurb was completed in 2004. 278–306 Oxford St., W1. ✆ **020/7629-7711.** www.johnlewis.com. Tube: Oxford Circus.

Liberty If Selfridges is all flash, cash, marble, and gold, then Liberty is baroque sensuality. London's prettiest department store may be olde worlde on the outside (neo-Tudor, in fact), but everything here is very, very stylish. As well as clothing with the famous Liberty imprint, it has a big array of women's fashions by well-known and up-and-coming designers. And don't miss the world-famous furnishing and dress fabrics. Liberty is far from cheap, but you're bound to find something to take home as a small gift on the bazaar-like first floor or among the housewares downstairs. 210–214 Regent St., W1. ✆ **020/7734-1234.** www.liberty-of-london.com. Tube: Oxford Circus.

Marks & Spencer When the French protested against closures of Marks & Spencer in Paris, the Brits wondered why on earth they were so upset. That's because the home crowd has lost all respect for the venerable M&S. Neither the new vampy undies range, Salon Rose, nor the Autograph label, designed by Katherine Hamnett, Betty Jackson, and others, managed to reverse its plummeting fortunes. If it hasn't gone bankrupt by the time you arrive, at least stop in at the food hall, which does yummy lunchtime sandwiches and salads. 458 Oxford St., W1. ✆ **020/7935-7954.** www.marksandspencer.com. Tube: Marble Arch.

Selfridges Chicago salesman Harry Selfridge opened this store in 1909, stunning Londoners with his marble halls and sheer variety of goods. An opulent revamp, just completed, is stunning them again. The ground-floor perfumery and cosmetics department is the biggest in Europe. Upstairs is crammed with covetable designer fashions and home accessories. And Miss Selfridge is several shops within a shop. It has its own teen-queen label—which you can also find in a chain of outlets around the country—and hosts High Street names, including Oasis and Warehouse, alongside some funky young designers. Selfridges also boasts one of London's finest food halls, and the biggest choice of restaurants and cafes of all the department stores. 400 Oxford St., W1. ✆ **020/7629-1234.** www.selfridges.co.uk. Tube: Bond St. or Marble Arch.

FASHION

CHILDREN

Womenswear designer Elspeth Gibson has turned to a younger clientele—girls ages 3 to 6—and created the Sweet Pea collection for **Debenhams** (see "Department Stores," above). The store also has a 0-to-3 range by **Jaspar Conran,** Junior J, and its own label. Also check out **H&M** (see below). It is virtually unique among the fashion chains in doing kids clothes—like Gap with a Euro-twist and almost half the price.

CONTEMPORARY

No one wants to look like a chain store clone, but the big stores compete so hard for quality and design nowadays, and change their stock so often, that it is easy to put together a chic and individual look, especially if you follow our advice for nabbing bargain designer pieces to mix in with your budget imitations. Start at Oxford Circus. Near H&M and Top Shop, you'll find another favorite, **Oasis,** 12–14 Argyll St., W1 (© **020/7434-1799**), where you can park the man in your life on a comfy sofa while you try on the clothes. Just opposite is **Warehouse,** 19–21 Argyll St., W1 (© **020/7437-7101**). For **Miss Selfridge,** check out Selfridges in "Department Stores," above.

Apart from M&S, Britain's clothing stores are still pretty hopeless at catering for women of other than average size (4–10 in the U.S., which is 8–14 in the U.K.). H&M and Top Shop are rare exceptions, as is **Dorothy Perkins,** West One Shopping Centre, 379 Oxford St., W1 (© **020/7495-6181;** www.dorothyperkins.co.uk; Tube: Bond St). It has both a petite range and one that goes up to size 20 (16 U.S.).

Accessorize This fabulous shop can help you turn any old dress into a knock-'em-dead dazzler, and prices are so reasonable you don't have to save up to buy its wares or save them just for special occasions. It also has sumptuous scarves, hats, and girly jewelry, in all the season's prettiest colors. You'll find branches all over, including Covent Garden, King's Road, Kensington High Street, and Brompton Road. 386 Oxford St., W1. © **020/7491-9424.** www.accessorize.co.uk. Tube: Bond St.

H&M This Swedish chain has its flagship store on the other side of Oxford Circus from Top Shop. It's been around a long time yet always seems to be of the moment, constantly refreshing its image. Like ice-cream flavors, different H&M labels cater to different tastes, from frontline fashion trends to clubbing skimpies, slouching streetwear to classics for work. And three cheers for a store that recognizes women are not all Hollywood lollipop-heads: the Big is Beautiful range goes up to size 30 (26 U.S.). H&M also does funky maternity wear, tough stuff for kids, and menswear too; guys, if you're looking for a men's skirt, this is where you'll find it. All at very good-value prices. 261–271 Regent St., W1. © **020/7493-4004.** www.hm.com. Tube: Oxford Circus.

Top Shop/Top Man The multi-floored, multi-everything Top Shop used to sell cheap togs for teenyboppers, but its funky styles have now become top wannabuys for would-be style junkies. Yet, it's still amazingly cheap. The TS Design label boasts an army of A-list names: **Clements Ribeiro, Hussein Chalayan, Tracey Boyd,** plus **Markus Lupfer.** Others who haven't quite become international names yet take guest spots at Bazaar, a section that apes the feel of Portobello or Camden market. Top Shop's Tall Girl label features women's jeans with a 36 inch leg! You can get your clothes customized, get a haircut, and get severe brain ache because this is the kind of noisy full-on place that turns even dedicated shopaholics into shopping-phobes. 214 Oxford St., W1. © **020/7636-7700.** www.tops.co.uk. Tube: Oxford Circus.

DISCOUNT

Browns Labels for Less Browns is the sort of name that wins star treatment from a designer when the buyer visits a collection. The main boutique at 23–27 Moulton St. showcases only the best names—from Chloe to Jill Sander—and can make a hot young newcomer. All unsold stock from last season is moved across to Browns Labels for Less, where it is discounted from 30% to 70%. You never know what you'll find: Issy Miyake, perhaps, or Comme des Garcons, Dries van Noten, and Prada accessories. 50 S. Molton St., W1. © **020/7514-0052.** www.brownsfashion.com. Tube: Bond St.

Burberry's Factory Outlet Burberry is back from the dead. Not long ago only tourists actually wore the famous plaid, but now Britain's best-known luxury marque is also one of the hippest and best loved. And that plaid is on everything—from trench coats to trench dresses, and even undies, eye masks, and bikinis. You have to take a local train to get to the factory shop, but savings of up to a third on samples and ends of lines will more than cover the cost of your ticket. (Burberry also has a very swanky new store at 21–23 New Bond St., W1.) 29–53 Chatham Place, E9. ✆ **020/8328-4320.** Train: Hackney Central BR station.

Central Park The clothes at Central Park may not be built to last a lifetime, but they'll look good while they last. Few things cost more than £25 ($46). 22 Kensington Church St., W8. ✆ **020/7937-3672.** Tube: High St. Kensington.

Paul Smith There are three floors stocking this hot British designer, mens and kidswear only, and mostly last season's. Discounts range from 30% to 70%. 23 Avery Row, W1. ✆ **020/7493-1287.** www.paulsmith.co.uk. Tube: Bond St.

REGULAR SALES

Vivienne Westwood, Valentino, Dolce & Gabana, Elspeth Gibson, Miu Miu, Prada, Gucci, Neisha Crosland, Paul Smith, John Smedley . . . the list goes on and on. Both the sales organizers below claim to have bagged all these hot designers and dozens more.

Designer Sale UK Registering online for free lets you in on the Wednesday preview day. This is hardly exclusive because anybody qualifies, but it might just give you an edge. Sales go on until Sunday and take place every couple of months. Discounts on the 150 rails of hot designer mens and womenswear and accessories sometimes go as high as 90%. Entry is £2 ($3.70). Atlantis Gallery, Old Truman Brewery, 146 Brick Lane, E1. ✆ **01273/470880,** or 020/7247-8595 on sale week. www.designersales.co.uk. Tube: Liverpool St. or Aldgate East.

Designer Warehouse Sales For 40% to 80% discounts on canceled orders, showroom and catwalk samples, and pre-*passé* styles from nearly 100 top fashion names, check out the bimonthly Designer Warehouse Sales. These run for 3 days—menswear usually the week after womenswear—starting on a Thursday, which is when you should go for the best pickings. Register online, for free, to get advance warning of sale dates. Entry is £2 ($3.70). The Worx, 45 Balfe St., N1. ✆ **020/7704-1064.** www.dwslondon.co.uk. Tube: King's Cross.

SHOES

London's shoe stores almost outnumber pubs and churches. **King's Road** in Chelsea, **Neal Street** in Covent Garden, and **South Molton Street** just by Bond Street Tube are the best for hot but affordable styles.

Clarks British kids have been growing up in Clarks' sensible shoes for over 175 years. Now this staid brand has blossomed, selling a small collection of great-value fashion shoes. Most are for well-scrubbed eco-hippies. Some are simple but smart. But none of them will give you bunions. 260 Oxford St., W1 ✆ **020/7499-0305.** www.clarks.co.uk. Tube: Oxford Circus.

Office This store sells the sort of shoes you drool over in glossy magazines—for men as well as women—but for very reasonable prices. There's a branch of the sister sports shoe shop, **Offspring,** nearby at 60 Neal St. The **Office Sale Shop** at 61 St. Martin's Lane, WC2, has ends of lines and last year's models at up to half price. 57 Neal St., WC2. ✆ **020/7379-1896.** www.office.co.uk. Tube: Covent Garden.

Fun Fact **Footwear Fables**

Doc Martens—those funky, clunky boots with the air-cushioned soles that are requisite street wear for cool kids the world over—were invented by Dr. Klaus Maertens in postwar Germany as a comfort shoe for old ladies. At **Dr. Marten's Department Store,** 1–4 King St., WC2 (✆ **020/7497-1460;** www.drmartens.com; Tube: Covent Garden), you can pick up a pair of the basic shoes for £50 to £60 ($92–$111). Camden Market has them at a discount.

VINTAGE & SECONDHAND

Fashion babes, covergirls, and even movie stars are now deep into thrift-shop chic. The stock can be very good quality. **Oxfam** (www.oxfam.org.uk) is Britain's fifth-biggest retailer, selling Fair Trade products, gifts, furnishings, and books, as well as second-hand clothes. **Oxfam Originals** stores concentrate solely on funky, retro fashions. There are three in Central London, at 123a King's Rd., Shawfield St., SW3 (✆ **020/7351-7979;** Tube: Sloane Sq.); 22 Earlham St., WC2 (✆ **020/7836-9666;** Tube: Covent Garden); and 26 Ganton St., W1 (✆ **020/7437-7338;** Tube: Oxford Circus).

Otherwise, **Monmouth Street** in Covent Garden is a hot spot for retread fashions. For great 1970s gear, head to **Pop Boutique** (no. 6; ✆ **020/7497-8344**). **The Loft** (no. 35) is a dress agency handling the city girl's favorite labels. **Cenci** (no. 31) has mostly secondhand Italian stuff, for boys and girls.

Blackout II This fun emporium has hidden depths—below the small store front is a basement crammed with old clothes. From the glamorous 1930s to the glam 1970s and 1980s, from crocodile handbags and feather boas to kitsch fake fur and bell bottoms, you'll find it here. You can rent for a wild London club night, as well as buy. 51 Endell St., WC2. ✆ **020/7240-5006.** www.blackout2.com. Tube: Covent Garden.

Cornucopia The stock is so huge that there are definitely bargains to be found here, it just takes a bit of rummaging to find them. But that's actually fun with this treasure trove of costumes from the 1920s on, all arranged by era. Women off to the hottest parties in town come here for entrance-making evening wear and the costume jewelry to go with it. 12 Upper Tachbrook St., SW1. ✆ **020/7828-5752.** Tube: Victoria.

Pandora Ladies who lunch don't throw last season's haute fashions away: They sell them through this Knightsbridge dress agency. Pandora is the grande dame of the secondhand scene, claiming to hold every famous designer from Armani to Zilkha (Ronit, that is). The stock is seasonally correct, and there are even sales: from July to August, and December to January. 16–22 Cheval Place, SW7. ✆ **020/7589-5289.** Tube: Knightsbridge.

Retro Man, Retro Woman, and Retro Home There are no guarantees with secondhand stores, but the stuff at these three is generally good quality, with a smattering of designer names and barely-worn bargains. Both clothing stores have £5 ($8) bargain basements. The handbags and shoes at no. 30 often include names such as Gucci. Part of the burgeoning Music & Video Exchange empire, these stores operate the same pricing policy: the longer an item hangs around, the further the price falls. And you can take your own stuff in to swap or sell. 30, 32, 34 Pembridge Rd., W11. ✆ **020/7792-1715** or 020/7727-4805. www.buy-sell-trade.co.uk. Tube: Notting Hill Gate.

WOOLENS

Westaway & Westaway The window mannequins at this old-fashioned store look like Hitchcock heroines frozen in time, but then the stock is very traditional, ranging from lambswool sweaters to Shetland knits with handmade fair isle yokes to miniature kilts for the kids. Prices are old-fashioned, too: £35 ($65) for a woven lambswool stole, for example. 64–65 Great Russell St., WC1. ✆ **020/7405-4479.** www.westaway.co.uk. Tube: Holborn.

FOOD & DRINK

FOOD HALLS

London's department-store food halls are a Bacchanalian feast of vibrant colors and exotic smells. Pick your treats wisely, though, or you could break the bank. **Harrods** is the king of food halls. There are close to 20 departments, of which the meat, fish, and poultry room—with its mosaics of peacocks and wheat sheaves, ceramic fish, scallop shells, boars, and more—is the most amazing. The best handbag-size buys are jams made with fruits rarely found at home, like gooseberries. Rows of food counters sell every kind of portable lunch, perfect for a picnic in Hyde Park across the road. Or try neighboring **Harvey Nichols,** lauded for its stylish branded goods. The **Selfridges** food hall is much more compact than Harrods, but it packs an awful lot in, and the wine and chocolate departments are separate.

Fortnum & Mason This may be a department store but few shoppers penetrate beyond the food hall—unless it's to have afternoon tea (see chapter 6). Mr. Fortnum and Mr. Mason opened their doors in 1707, and it is *the* place to find the aristocratic foods and Empire-building delicacies you've only seen in period movies—traditional hams and pies, for instance, as well as cheeses, handmade chocolates, and preserves. Fortnum knows everything there is to know about tea: The house range is pricey but includes more than 50 blends, and it's said that if you take along a sample of your tap water, they'll know which one to pair it with. 181 Piccadilly, W1. ✆ **020/7734-8040.** www.fortnumandmason.com. Tube: Green Park or Piccadilly Circus.

SPECIALITIES

A. Gold *Finds* Opposite Old Spitalfields Market, this store specializes in traditional British foods, from candy to liqueurs and clotted cream to tea cakes. And it is all totally authentic, unlike the many so-called traditional treats packaged and priced for the tourist market. 42 Brushfield St., E1. ✆ **020/7247-2487.** Tube: Liverpool St.

The Chocolate Society The Chocolate Society uses the venerated Valrhona in all its chocolates. This is 70% cocoa solids, more than three times a normal candy bar, so when you come into this little shop, stand and inhale the mouthwatering smell. Shelves groan with truffles, chocolate-dipped fruit, cakes, and more. 36 Elizabeth St., SW1. ✆ **020/7259-9222.** www.chocolate.co.uk. Tube: Victoria or Sloane Sq.

Condon Fishmongers *Finds* This place is truly scent-sational. Salmon, haddock, eels, cod's roe, and much more pass through the traditional smokehouse in the back of the store. Herrings turn into kippers here, creating the aroma of a traditional British breakfast. The store is closed after 1pm on Thursday, Sunday, and Monday. 363 Wandsworth Rd., SW8. ✆ **020/7622-2934.** Tube: Stockwell, then no. 77 bus.

Neal's Yard Dairy This is *the* place for British and Irish cheeses, from old favorites to delicious new ones developed by farmhouse cheese-makers. Staff are delighted for you to try before you buy. Then pop 'round the corner to **Neal's Yard Bakery,** 6 Neal's

Yard, WC2 (© **020/7836-5199**), for still-warm bread to go with your selection. There is a second dairy at Borough Market, SE1 (see "Markets," below). 17 Shorts Gardens, WC2. © **020/7379-7646.** Tube: Covent Garden.

Paxton & Whitefield London's most venerable cheese shop (est. 1797) concentrates on English and French farmhouse cheeses—about 200 in all—and matures each one itself. Prices are refreshingly reasonable despite the upper-crust location, and shelves groan with a big selection of wine and port, plus gourmet accessories such as olives and biscuits, to go with whichever cheese you choose. 93 Jermyn St., SW1. © **020/7930-0259.** www.cheesemongers.co.uk. Tube: Green Park.

TEA

The Tea House Besides teapots and tea balls, this wonderful-smelling shop sells more than 70 varieties of tea from India, China, Japan, and the rest of the world. Available loose or in bags, traditional English blends make excellent, light, and inexpensive gifts. 15 Neal St., WC2. © **020/7240-7539.** Tube: Covent Garden.

Whittard of Chelsea Whittard has everything you need to make a luvverly cuppa, even pure origin teas you can blend yourself. It sells a full range of coffees, too, and colorful ceramics. There are more than 20 branches in London. 38 Covent Garden Market, WC2. © **020/7379-6599.** www.whittard.com. Tube: Covent Garden.

WHISKY

Milroys of Soho Milroys has perhaps the longest whisky list in London, including the rare and collectable, from Ireland and Scotland, New Zealand, Czechoslovakia, and Japan. There are American bourbons, too, if you're feeling homesick. The store has moved into the cellar to make room for a tasting bar at street level, open Monday to Saturday, 11am to 11pm. 3 Greek St., W1. © **020/7437-9311.** www.milroys.co.uk. Tube: Leicester Sq.

The Vintage House This little store opened just after World War II and stocks over 750 whiskies, as well as rare old bottles of other spirits, champagne, fine wines, and Cuban cigars. It stays open until 11pm and is closed on Sundays. 42 Old Compton St., W1. © **020/7437-2592.** www.sohowhisky.com. Tube: Leicester Sq.

MARKETS

Farmers' markets may be old hat in the United States, but they're a new idea in London. The produce is all English, whatever's in season, and much of it chemical-free and non-genetically modified. Farmers sell only their own produce and also make the sausages, cheese, jams, and so on—even buffalo pastrami. You'll find the biggest range at **Islington Farmers' Market,** Essex Road opposite Islington Green, N1 (Tube: Angel), open Sundays 10am to 2pm. **Notting Hill Farmers' Market,** behind Waterstone's on Notting Hill Gate, W11 (Tube: Notting Hill Gate), Saturday 9am to 1pm; **Swiss Cottage Farmers' Market,** 02 Centre car park, near Finchley Road, NW3 (Tube: Finchley Rd.), Wednesday 10am to 4pm. For information, call © **020/7704-9659;** www.londonfarmersmarkets.com.

Bermondsey Market Forget Portobello Road, charming though it is. This is where serious antiques collectors and dealers come—burglary victims, too, tracking down stolen possessions. It starts at dawn with the serious business done by 9am and stalls closing from noon. The market is a bit of a trek from the Tube, but it's an adventure. Fri only 5am to 2pm. Bermondsey Sq., SE1. Tube: Bermondsey, London Bridge.

Berwick Street Market London's most-filmed stallholder works near the top end of this little Soho market—he still shouts out his wares, so he's God's gift to the BBC. It's mostly fruit and veg here, with lots of bargains towards the end of the day. The biggest variety of stalls, including bread, cheese, olives, and dried herbs, spices, and fruit, turn out on Friday and Saturday. Monday – Satruday, 8am-5pm. Berwick St., W1. Tube: Piccadilly Circus.

Borough Market Celebrity chefs are said to fill their shopping baskets at this covered food market next to Southwark Cathedral. Stalls laden with fruit and vegetables, meats (including bacon and venison), fish, olives, chocolates, bread, pies, organic beers, and much more are wickedly tempting. The third weekend of every month, twice as many producers turn out for "The Big One." Friday noon to 6pm, and Saturday 9am to 4pm. Borough Sq., SE1. Tube: London Bridge.

Brick Lane Market This is one of the last places you can try that oh-so English delicacy, jellied eels, yet one of the hippest markets in London. As well as fruit and veggies, cheap clothes, and lots of leather, there's the **Laden Market** at 103 Brick Lane—a covered space abuzz with young fashion and accessory designers, great for cheap unique gifts. Combine Brick Lane with a visit to neighboring Old Spitalfields Market (see below). General Market open Sunday 8am to 1pm; Laden Market is open Monday through Saturday 11am to 6pm and Sunday 10am to 4:30pm. Brick Lane, E1. Tube: Liverpool St., Aldgate East.

Brixton Market Brixton is the heart of Afro-Caribbean London, and Brixton Market is its soul. Electric Avenue (immortalized by Jamaican singer Eddie Grant) is lined with exotic fruit and vegetable stalls. Turn right at the end for a terrific selection of the cheapest secondhand clothes in London. Granville Arcade, off the avenue, is crammed with foods, African fabrics, and reggae records. Open Monday to Tuesday, Thursday through Saturday 8am to 6pm; Wednesday 8am to 3pm. Electric Ave., SW9. Tube: Brixton.

Camden Market This vast market fills the streets, arcades, and courtyards. Hundreds of stalls sell crafts, bric-a-brac, clothes, and furniture, with a big hippy-trippy contingent. The Stables concentrates on clothing, almost-junk, and 20th-century collectibles. The best vintage clothing can be found on Buck Street, Camden High Street, and in Electric Market (good for cheap Doc Martens). In an old timber yard by the canal, Camden Lock is crammed with craft workshops, stores, and cafes. It hosts a Producers' (Farmers') Market on Saturday and Sunday. Come to Camden early, particularly on Sundays, as this is one of London's biggest tourist attractions. Camden Market open Thursday to Sunday 9am to 5:30pm; Camden Lock daily 10am to 6pm; Stables Market Saturday to Sunday 8am to 6pm; Camden Canal Market Saturday to Sunday 10am to 6pm; Electric Market Sunday 9am to 5:30pm. Camden High St. and Chalk Farm Rd., NW1. Tube: Camden Town or Chalk Farm.

Columbia Road Flower Market It's pure torture for gardeners and plant-lovers coming here on a spring or summer Sunday morning. The sights and smells at this heavenly flower market are so tantalizing and the prices so reasonable you'll wish it wasn't illegal to take growing plants home. But if you're looking for souvenirs, you're bound to find a pretty pot or garden accessory. Columbia Rd., E2. Tube: Old St.

Greenwich Market The market is an essential part of a visit to this bustling and historic maritime borough. Greenwich is pretty chi-chi, which is reflected in the quality of stuff on sale: from upscale antiques to collectors' oddities, old and new. The Central Market, which is a treasure trove of vintage clothing and music stalls, and the

Food Market are on Stockwell Street, just off the high road. The Craft Market is in College Approach. Antiques Market open Saturday to Sunday 9am to 5pm; Central Market indoor Friday through Saturday 10am to 5pm, Sunday 10am to 6pm, outdoor Saturday 7am to 6pm, Sunday 7am to 5pm; Craft Market Thursday 7:30am to 5pm, Friday through Sunday 9:30am to 5:30pm; Food Market Saturday 10am–4pm. From Greenwich High Rd. (opposite St. Alfege's Church), SE10. DLR: Cutty Sark or Greenwich.

Old Spitalfields Market Like Brick Lane, this market has burgeoned under the wave of trendoids moving into the city fringes. It's mostly antiques and crafts during the week, with designer and retro fashion stalls setting up at the weekend. On Friday and Sunday, the market turns into a cornucopia of edible delights, too. Organic producers sell pickles, relishes, cakes, fruit, and vegetables. Sunday is the busiest and definitely the best day to go as, on top of everything else, that's when the Alternative Art Market happens. This is also where new young designers come for Alternative Fashion Week, a series of free events just after the official event: call © **020/7375-0441.** Organic Market Friday, Sunday 10am to 5pm; General Market Monday through Friday 11am to 3pm, Sunday 10am to 5pm. From Lamb St. to Brushfield St., E1. Tube: Liverpool St.

Petticoat Lane This ancient market is not what it used to be now that stores open on Sunday, and other events draw the crowds. But it almost feels like discovering the real London, if you can ignore the hordes of tourists. Batteries and cigarette lighters are sold in bulk. Shoes and clothes are cheap and rarely chic. And the jewelry glitters as though it were fake gold. Sunday 9am to 2pm. Middlesex St., E1. Tube: Liverpool St. or Aldgate.

Portobello Market Portobello Market is a lot of fun, despite the seething masses. Saturday is the full-on armoires-to-lava-lamps day. More than 2,000 antiques dealers set out their stalls at the southern, uphill, end: Head for Notting Hill Gate Tube station. For retro, street-hip, and club-chic clothing, secondhand music, and junkabilia, go to Ladbroke Grove instead. Cross the road out of the station to the passage left of the bridge. Weekdays, Portobello is an old-fashioned fruit and veg market, with organic food on Thursdays. Antiques Market Saturday 4am to 6pm; General Market Monday through Wednesday 8am to 6pm, Thursday 9am to 1pm, Friday through Saturday 7am to 7pm; Organic Market Thursday 11am to 6pm. Clothes & Bric-a-brac Market Friday 7am to 4pm, Saturday 8am to 5pm, Sunday 9am to 4pm. Portobello Rd., W10, W11. Tube: Notting Hill Gate, Ladbroke Grove.

MUSIC

Denmark Street is *the* musicians' hangout. This scruffy cut-through off Charing Cross Road is lined with shops selling everything you need to get a band on the road.

NEW RECORDS, CDS & TAPES

Check out the stores below, and especially Tower Records, for flyers offering cheap entry into London's hippest night clubs (see "Dance Clubs & Discos," in chapter 9).

HMV This HMV is a mega-megastore, so whatever you want it's probably got it. Dance music is a real strength, and the ground floor has all the new rock, soul, reggae, and pop releases. The range of world music and spoken-word recordings is huge. Last year, HMV opened a new super hi-tech branch at 360 Oxford St., W1 (© **020/7514-3600;** Tube: Bond St.). It's the first music store in the country where customers can create their own CDs with digital downloads. 150 Oxford St., W1. © **020/7631-3424.** www.hmv.co.uk. Tube: Oxford Circus.

Tower Records A warehouse of sound, Tower has four floors of records, tapes, and compact discs—pop, rock, classical, jazz, bluegrass, folk, country, soundtracks, and more, all in separate departments. Downstairs you'll find a fantastic selection of international music magazines. You can also buy tickets to gigs here, and there are in-store signings. This store is open until midnight every day except Sunday. 1 Piccadilly Circus, W1. ✆ **020/7439-2500.** www.towerrecords.co.uk. Tube: Piccadilly Circus.

Virgin Megastore The Virgin Megastore is a microcosm of Richard Branson's ever-expanding Virgin empire. You can buy a mobile phone, an airline ticket, or an hour on the Internet, as well as hardware and software for computer games, MP3 players . . . oh, and the usual albums and singles. And it holds regular live performances and signings. 14–16 Oxford St., W1. ✆ **020/7631-1234.** www.virginmega.co.uk. Tube: Tottenham Court Rd.

VINTAGE & SECONDHAND

Hanway Street, close to Tottenham Court Road, and **Berwick Street** in Soho both have lots of secondhand stores and are heaven for vinyl buffs.

Harold Moores Records & Video Classical heaven, this store is full of stock ranging from 78s to LPs—70,000 of them—and CDs, some rare and precious to the tune of thousands of pounds. But it has great sales and it will do part-exchange, so surf the website to find out what the store is interested in acquiring. 2 Great Marlborough St., W1. ✆ **020/7437-1576.** www.haroldmoores.com. Tube: Oxford Circus.

Mole Jazz Jazz fans come here for historic recordings, whether it be New Orleans traditional, swing, or modern. You can ring up or e-mail to ask for an auction list, too, if you're on the hunt for something really rare. 311 Gray's Inn Rd., WC1. ✆ **020/7278-0703.** www.molejazz.co.uk. Tube: King's Cross.

Music & Video Exchange There are four stores all in a row and each specializes in something different. Together they offer bargain buys and collectible rarities; CDs, tapes, and vinyl; the classics, jazz, folk, dance music; and more. And they have an excellent policy on prices, which keep on dropping the longer something stays on the shelf. 36–42 Notting Hill Gate, W11. ✆ **020/7243-8573.** www.buy-sell-trade.co.uk. Tube: Notting Hill Gate.

TOYS

Hamleys William Hamley founded Noah's Ark, as it was called in 1760, and it became one of the largest toy stores in the world. There are seven floors stuffed with more than 26,000 toys, games, models, dolls, cuddly animals, and electronic cars—even executive toys at very adult prices. Recently refurbished, the store is easier to get around, but you still have to navigate through the crowds watching toy demonstrations. 188–196 Regent St., W1. ✆ **020/7494-2000.** www.hamleys.com. Tube: Oxford Circus or Piccadilly Circus.

Tips **Video Warning**

Britain uses the PAL broadcast standard, which is incompatible with the U.S. standard NTSC. Even if a videotape says VHS, it won't play in an American VCR.

London Dolls House Company Girls little and big will love this store. Collectible dollhouses can fetch a breathtaking £5,500 ($8,800), but kits start at £65 ($104) and miniature furnishings at 50p (80¢). Just like the real-life property market, it's a matter of tailoring your aspirations to meet your budget. 29 Covent Garden Market, WC2. ✆ **020/7240-8681.** www.thedollshousecompany.co.uk. Tube: Covent Garden.

Science Museum This museum shop sells minirobots, oddball clocks and telescopes, books, high-tech games, puzzles, and other gimmickry, including glow-in-the-dark T-shirts and a miniature hot-air balloon. The museum also has a small concession at Selfridges. Exhibition Rd., SW7. ✆ **020/7942-4499.** www.sciencemuseum.org.uk/shop. Tube: South Kensington.

9

London After Dark

For many visitors, London is synonymous with great theater, and seeing a West End show is a must. But don't limit yourself only to the West End (the equivalent of Broadway in New York). True, it's in the West End that you'll find new megamusical hits like *Mary Poppins.* But for new plays and innovative productions, scout around the diverse off–West End scene. In recent years, millions of pounds from lottery funds have poured into venues all over the city, improving facilities and restructuring ticket prices.

The news coming out of the club scene is a weird mixed bag, as usual. On the one hand, intimate club bars are supposedly becoming trendier than gargantuan superclubs. But on the other hand, gigantic raves are still in, and what do you make of SchoolDisco.com, a Saturday-night event for which 2,000 allegedly cool dudes and dudettes dress up in *school uniforms* to re-create their teenage years but without the pimples. Only in London!

BUY BEFORE YOU FLY The hottest West End shows, opera, ballet, big festivals, rock concerts, and other spectaculars can sell out, so if getting in is more important to you than getting a great deal, just hand over the cash and book before you go. Ticket-agency fees vary according to the event and seat quality. There's usually a handling charge, too. **Globaltickets** (✆ **800/223-6108** in the U.S.; www.globaltickets.com) adds up to 20% to box office prices. The office is open from 9am to 8pm Monday through Saturday, and noon to 7pm on Sunday. In London, Globaltickets operates out of the Britain Visitor Centre, 1 Regent St., SW1 (✆ **020/7734-4555**). **Ticketmaster** (✆ **0870/606-9999;** www.ticketmaster.co.uk) takes phone and e-bookings around the clock for a fee of £1 to £5.50 ($1.85–$10), plus a variable handling charge. It has branches in Tower Records and HMV (both reviewed on p. 228). **Firstcall** (✆ **0870/906-3838;** www.firstcalltickets.com) charges £1 to £5.65 ($1.85–$10), plus a £1.50 ($2.75) handling charge, and never sleeps. Pop concert specialist **Stargreen** (✆ **020/7734-8932;** www.stargreen.co.uk) imposes a £2 to £5 ($3.70–$9) fee and takes calls Monday through Saturday 10:15am to 6pm.

WHERE TO GET YOUR CULTURE INFO Even if you have zero intention of actually buying a ticket from them, surf the ticket agencies' websites for advance notice of what's going on. You will find more useful e-directories at the start of each section of this chapter. Once you get to London, make sure to buy a copy of the listings bible *Time Out* (www.timeout.com), which comes out on Wednesdays. The *Evening Standard* (www.thisislondon.com) produces a supplement, *Hot Tickets,* on Thursdays. You'll also find good guides in the weekend newspapers.

1 Entertainment on a Shoestring

Having a blast is a lot more affordable here than in other swinging cities. If you put in the legwork, join a few queues, and time your foray just right, you can cruise around town on a wave of dynamite deals. Below are my favorite London freebies and cheapies, as well as some money-saving strategies.

FREEBIES

- **Holland Park Theatre** (p. 238) Don't buy a ticket; just sit on the grass outside and soak up the music for free.
- **Royal Festival Hall** (p. 242) Come for hot **Commuter Jazz** in the foyer on Fridays from 5:15 to 6:45pm.
- **Lamb & Flag** (p. 250) Fantastic free jazz at a fantastically traditional pub in Covent Garden every Sunday night.
- **Bar Rumba** (p. 245) Between 5 and 9pm, Monday through Thursday, drinks are two for the price of one *and* there's no cover charge, so come early and stay late for free clubbing.
- **Notting Hill Arts Club** (p. 247) Come before 8pm, or 6pm on Sundays, for some wicked live music and DJ nights at this tiny basement bar.
- **The Social** (p. 247) There's no cover charge at the downstairs dance-club bar, except for Wednesday nights when the two indie bands perform Acoustically Heavenly music. Then, it's a bargain at only £3 ($5.50).
- **Popstarz** (p. 248) At the Scala now, and still packing them in, the original gay indie club night is free before 11pm with a flyer or Web ad.
- **Heaven** (p. 248) London's most famous gay club is free with a flyer before 11:30pm on a Friday. Other nights that'll get you in for £1 ($1.85).
- **National Portrait Gallery** (p. 188) Many of the gallery's side events are free, but you never have to pay to listen to the early Friday evening concerts.
- **Summertime Inline Skate-athons** You'll need to hire the skates, but joining the crowd for Wednesday's London Skate and the Friday Night Skate is free. Both start at 7pm on the north side of the Serpentine in Hyde Park.
- **Borders** (p. 217) No reservations taken, so come early for live music, readings, and talks at this mammoth bookstore, usually at 6:30pm.
- **Waterstone's** (p. 218) This bookstore is so big there are even function rooms. Events tend to start around 7pm, and most are free (or £1–£2/$1.85–$3.70). Reservations recommended.
- **BBC TV and Radio Recordings** The Beeb is always looking for audiences for its radio and TV shows, and tickets are free. For more information, contact **BBC Audience Services** (✆ **020/8576-1227;** www.bbc.co.uk/tickets).
- **Street Entertainment** Fire-eaters, mime artists, and musicians playing Andean nose flutes all do their thing for the throngs at the Piazza, Covent Garden.

CHEAPIES

Below are the greatest entertainment deals, plus a few alternative nights out that you might not have thought of.

- **Royal Festival Hall** (p. 242) Top orchestras play at this concert hall, and seats in the balcony, where the sound is just as good, generally cost £10 ($18) or less.

- **Barbican Centre** (p. 240) Seats for concerts by the London Symphony Orchestra are practically given away at £5 ($9) at the concert hall box office; the top price is £20 ($38).
- **Royal Court Theatre** (p. 233) The cutting edge of contemporary theater for £7.50 ($14) a ticket every Monday night. Last-minute standbys at the Theatre Downstairs cost a token 10p (18¢).
- **Shakespeare's Globe** (p. 236) Just as the Bard did it, both the stage and production style. Stand in the raucous central yard for only £5 ($9).
- **Soho Theatre** (p. 237) Monday nights, all tickets are £5 ($9) at this recently relaunched hotbed of new writing and community theater.
- **The English National Opera** (p. 238) At the box office you can get a £5 ($9) day-of-performance ticket to see one of Britain's finest and most risk-taking opera companies.
- **Comedy Café** (p. 243) The cover is only £5 ($9) on Thursdays. You can go for free on Wednesday, when new acts try out.
- **Rumba Pa'Ti** (p. 245) On Tuesday nights, Elder Sanchez teaches uptight Brits to be sinuous Latinos and Latinas in a 2-hour salsa class (6:30–8:30pm) at Bar Rumba. Then the pa'ti really starts, with guest DJs and live bands. You don't need a partner, and it only costs £4 ($7.40).
- **G.A.Y. at the Astoria** (p. 248) Pick up a flyer to have fabulous fun at this club for just £1 ($1.85).
- **After-Dark Walking Tours** (p. 204) Discover Jack the Ripper's haunts or the city's most haunted streets on a £6 ($11) walking tour.
- **Windsor Racecourse** (p. 208) Take a boat up the Thames from the train station to see Monday-evening horse racing, summer only: Tickets start at £5 ($9).
- **Wimbledon Greyhound Stadium** A lot less posh than horse racing but doggone fun (sorry!). Admission is £5 ($8). Starts at 7:30pm. http://www.wimbledonstadium.co.uk

SIX MONEY-SAVING STRATEGIES

1. **Net Savings.** Scan **www.lastminute.com** for fab short-notice discounts of up to 50% on theater, musicals, comedy, cinema, concerts, and even VIP entry to nightclubs. The online ticket brokers, listed above, usually have a few enticing deals, too, particularly **Ticketmaster** and **Firstcall.**
2. **Flock to a Festival.** Time your trip to coincide with any one of a host of festivals for a blitz of entertainment, often at giveaway prices. See our "London Calendar of Events," in chapter 2. There are 20 London festivals covered in the brochure and e-listing compiled by the **British Arts Festivals Association** (✆ **020/7247-4667;** www.artsfestivals.co.uk). Also check with ***Time Out*** (www.timeout.com), which produces a summer festival guide each year. Again, the ticket brokers are good sources of information—it's in their interest to fill in the info gaps.
3. **Interrogate the Box Office.** Most performing-arts venues follow a few basic charging rules: Tickets may be cheaper on certain nights of the week, Monday especially, and for matinees; it's cheaper to see a preview; same-day tickets and standbys cost a fraction of normal prices; so do bad views and standing up; and seniors, students, and children almost always pay less.
4. **Buy The London Pass.** It can't guarantee ticket availability, but an investment of $49 for a 1-day pass does get you up to 50% off at West End theaters, concerts, opera, and ballet. See "Fifty Money-Saving Tips," in chapter 2.

5. **Theater Bargains.** For West End shows, go to the half-price ticket booth on the south side of Leicester Square, W1. Run by the Society of London Theatres (SOLT), **tkts** charges a £2.50 ($4.60) per seat booking fee for day-of-performance tickets (maximum four per person, no returns). It's open Monday through Saturday from 10am to 7pm, Sunday noon to 3pm for matinees. It accepts MasterCard and Visa.
   Note: Scalpers cluster around the official booth. Don't succumb, and report any that try to rip you off to **SOLT,** 32 Rose St., WC2 (✆ **020/7557-6700**).
6. **Go out Early for Some Discount Dancin'.** Nightclubs are keen to catch clubbers early and keep them as late as they can, so the cover is often cheaper at either end of the evening. Look for discount flyers inside the main door of Tower Records on Piccadilly Circus (p. 228) and on club websites. *Time Out* also has a weekly cut-out-and-keep Privilege Pass on its club pages, which will get you a couple of quid off at selected venues.

2 London's Theater Scene

Ticket prices at London's 40 or so West End theaters range from about £10 to £40 ($18–$74). That's a bargain compared to Broadway and many other theatrical venues in the U.S.

There are two fantastic websites for finding out all the theater gossip. Like the half-price ticket booth in Leicester Square, **www.officiallondontheatre.co.uk** is run by the Society of London Theatres. Listings include summary, cast, times, prices, and the date a show is guaranteed to run until. For pretty good reviews of West End shows, surf **www.whatsonstage.com**.

MAJOR COMPANIES

Royal Court Theatre The 10p (18¢) standby is a spectacular deal, so naturally there's a catch: You have to rely on a less-than-full house, it's standing room only, and the view is restricted. But the £7.50 ($14) Mondays are a regular feature and a real steal. The 400-seat proscenium arch theater and upstairs studio of the Royal Court are home to the English Stage Company. Since premiering the plays of the Angry Young Men of the 1950s, it has built a world-class reputation as a forum for challenging (and sometimes boring and ridiculously bad) new writing. The Royal Court recently had a £26-million ($42-million) tart-up, including digging out a new restaurant under Sloane Square. Sloane Sq., SW1. ✆ **020/7565-5000.** www.royalcourttheatre.com. Jerwood Theatre Downstairs tickets £7.50–£26 ($14–$48), £7.50 ($14) on day of performance; standing-room tickets unsold 1 hr. before performance 10p (18¢). Jerwood Theatre Upstairs tickets £13–£15 ($23–$28). Mon evening, all seats in both theaters are £7.50 ($14). Tube: Sloane Sq.

Value Stealing the Show . . . and Dinner, Too!

Mondays at the Royal Court are really special. Two people can enjoy a five-star night out for less than it costs to buy just one Broadway ticket. Not only are all seats £7.50 ($14), but the sexy new Royal Court dining room serves a rather good modern European two-course meal for only £10 ($18). Royal Court Bar & Food is open Monday through Saturday from noon to 10:30pm (✆ **020/7565-5061**).

Kids **Parent Alert!**

ChildsPlay at Shakespeare's Globe is a parent's dream. A drama workshop and story-telling session keep the kids (8–11 years old) happy and elsewhere, while you enjoy the Saturday matinee in peace. Tickets cost £10 ($18).

Royal National Theatre The core repertory company and ever-changing guest stars perform in three auditoria in this huge theater complex on the South Bank. The large open-stage **Olivier,** the traditional proscenium of the **Lyttelton Theater,** and the smaller, studio-style **Cottesloe** put on dozens of productions a year: reworked classics, cutting-edge premieres, musicals, and shows for young people. There's always a lot going on in addition to the productions. **Platforms** are talks and readings by hot names in the performing arts. They take place at lunchtimes in the Terrace Café and on stage in the early evening. Tickets are practically given away at £3.50 or £2.50 ($6.50 or $4.60) for students and seniors. From the end of June through August, the Theatre Square and the National's terraces are abuzz with **Watch This Space,** a free alfresco festival of music, mime, street theater, acrobats, and magic from all over the world. There's something going on every day but Sunday, mostly in the early evening. Try and make it one Saturday for a Waterloo Sunset spectacular (10:15pm). For events info, call ✆ **020/7452-3327.** Otherwise, the box office is open Monday through Saturday 10am to 8pm.

The 1-hour **backstage tour** provides a fascinating glimpse into day-to-day theatrical life. Tours take place Monday through Saturday at 10:15am, 12:30pm (12:15pm on Olivier matinee days), and 5:30pm, and cost £5 ($9) or £4 ($8) students and seniors. It's a good idea to reserve in advance because there are only 30 places on each tour. South Bank, SE1. ✆ **020/7452-3400,** or 020/7452-3000 box office. www.nt-online.org. Tickets £10–£32 ($18–$54); all tickets unsold 2 hr. before performance in the Olivier and Lyttelton theaters £15 ($28); student standby may also be available for £8 ($15) 45 min. before curtain at all 3 theaters. Tube: Waterloo or Embankment (cross over Hungerford Bridge). River services: Festival Pier.

Royal Shakespeare Company The RSC dropped a bombshell when it announced it would not be renewing its contract with the Barbican, where it had spent 6 months a year since 1982. Although the Barbican Theatre is still one of its performance venues, the company now uses various theaters in the West End, such as The Gielgud and the Theatre Royal Haymarket, and has expanded its season. The point of all the hullaballoo was to increase the visibility of this world-renowned company in London. The other news is that the RSC has launched an Academy for young actors in Stratford-upon-Avon, with performances taking place during the summer festival season at The Other Place (www.stratford-upon-avon.co.uk/soaother.html).

All this is rather muddlesome for visitors to London. To see this illustrious company perform you'll need to peruse the various theater listings when you arrive in London, or, better yet, surf the RSC website **www.rsc.org.uk**. The ticket situation has been decentralized, so you'll have to get tickets at the various theaters, just as you would for any other West End show; ticket prices vary according to the show, the theater, and the stars performing. For more information you can call the Ticket Hotline in Stratford (✆ **0870/609-1110**), but remember: it's a long-distance call. Barbican Centre, Silk St., EC2. ✆ **020/7638-8891** for box office. Tickets £15–£34 ($28–$62). Tube: Barbican or Moorgate. Gielgud Theatre, Shaftesbury Ave, W1. ✆ **020/7494-5065** for box office. Tickets £15–£38

Central London Theaters

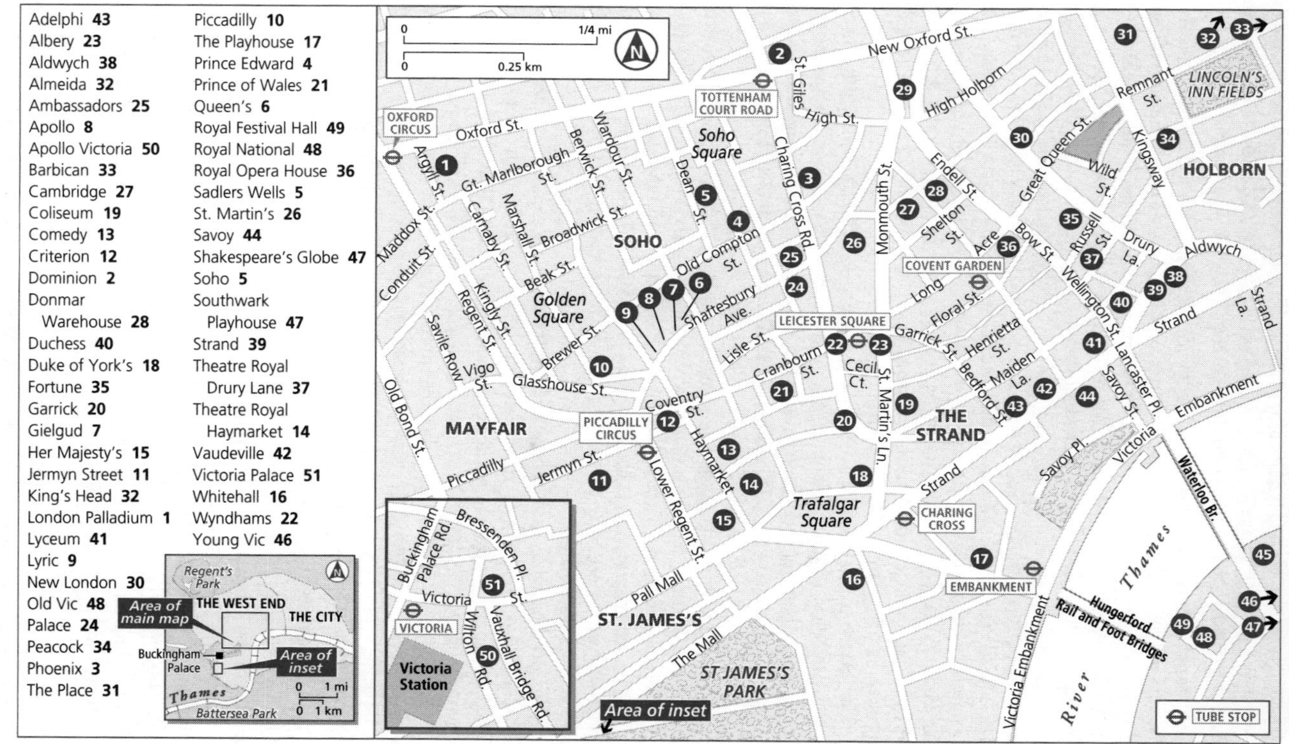

($28–$70), same-day tickets £15 ($28), standby half-hour before performance £15 ($28) seniors and students. Tube: Leicester Sq. Theatre Royal Haymarket, Haymarket, W1. ✆ **0870/609-1110** (Stratford box office) or go in person to theater box office. Tickets £12–£40 ($22–$74). Tube: Piccadilly Circus.

Shakespeare's Globe Theatre Academics and historians will always chew over the authenticity of the reconstructed theater and the re-staged drama. Critics will sniff at crowd-pleasing performances and the theme park atmosphere. But a night out at the Globe is a really fun experience. The replica stands close to the site of Shakespeare's original amphitheater, which burned down in 1613. Constructed from the same materials as the original, four tiers of banked benches encircle the stage where the company performs the Bard's great works as their predecessors would have done in his day. The Elizabethan set shuns lighting and scenery. There are no little luxuries like cushions on the wooden bench seats, many of which are backless, or protection from the elements, hence the summer-only season. Hawkers selling food and drink roam through the audience standing in the central yard. The box office is open Monday through Saturday from 10am to 6pm.

The excellent **Shakespeare's Globe Exhibition** ★ (✆ **020/7902-1500**), in the undercroft below the Globe, is open daily, May to September 9am to noon and October to April 10am to 5pm. Tickets include a theater tour, unless matinees throw off the schedule, and cost £8 ($15) adults, £6.50 ($12) seniors and students, £5.50 ($10) children ages 5 to 15, and £24 ($44) family ticket.

And call to find out about the huge range of workshops (stage fighting, voice work, and so on), lectures, staged readings, and Walkshops—guided tours of the historical sights of Southwark and a quick look round the Globe. Most take place on weekends, others on weekday evenings. Usually £5 to £13 ($9–$25), tickets are free one mid-June weekend to celebrate the birthday of the man with the vision to rebuild the Globe, Sam Wanamaker.

You can dine here, with superb river views: Shakespeare's Globe Café (✆ **020/7902-1576**) is open May to September from 10am to 11pm, October to April from 10am to 6pm; Shakespeare's Globe Restaurant (✆ **020/7928-9444;** reservations essential) has pre- and posttheater menus costing from £18 ($33) during the season and is open noon to 2:30pm, and 6 to 11pm throughout the year. 21 New Globe Walk, Bankside, SE1. ✆ **020/7401-9919.** www.shakespeares-globe.org. Tickets £8–£30 ($15–$55); £5 ($9) yard-standing tickets. Season runs end of April–Sept. Tube: Mansion House and St. Paul's (cross over Millennium Bridge), or Southwark. River services: Bankside Pier.

OFF–WEST END & FRINGE THEATER

Listings magazine *Time Out* carries details for around 60 off–West End theaters and fringe venues, where you'll see some of the most original drama in London—and also some of the worst. The best-known fringe venues are reviewed below. Also check out the Canal Café Theatre under "Comedy & Cabaret," later in this chapter.

Almeida Theatre The Almeida, originally an old science lecture hall in Almeida Street, Islington, got a massive and well-deserved £1.5-million ($2.4-million) makeover and reopened in the spring of 2003. The theater's mission has always been to provoke, and over the decades it has built such a hot reputation that A-list actors gladly play leading roles for £300 ($550) a week. The annual Festival of Contemporary Music, aka Almeida Opera, takes place in June and July. The box office is open Monday to Friday 10am to 7pm, and from 1pm on Saturday. Almeida St., N1. ✆ **020/7359-4404.** www.almeida.co.uk. Tickets £6–£28 ($11–$51). Tube: Angel.

Donmar Warehouse Sam Mendes, who directed the Oscar-winning film *American Beauty,* was only 24 when he took over the Donmar, now one of the hippest and most highly rated theaters in London. Under his artistic direction, this Covent Garden stage produces a huge range of old and new shows, including performances by visiting companies and a cabaret season, Divas at the Donmar. This is the theater where Nicole Kidman bared her all for art, in a play called *The Blue Room.* The box office is open from 10am to 8pm, but phone booking is round the clock. The 20 standing tickets go on sale once there's a full house. 41 Earlham St., WC2. ✆ **0870/060-6624.** www.donmar-warehouse.com. Tickets usually £15–£25 ($28–$46) but vary for each show; standing tickets £5 ($9). Tube: Covent Garden.

The King's Head London's oldest pub-theater produces new writing and neglected classics, some of which have gone on to the West End and Broadway. It also trains up 12 young directors each year. Come for a pint before you see the tiny stage where Hugh Grant and Gary Oldman started their careers. In addition to evening shows, they often stage plays at 1pm for the lunchtime crowd. The box office is open Monday to Saturday 10am to 8pm, Sunday 10am to 4pm. 115 Upper St., N1. ✆ **020/7226-1916.** Tickets £8.50–£18 ($16–$32). Tube: Angel, Highbury, or Islington.

Soho Theatre The evangelistic mission at this newly built theater and smaller studio is to foster new writing and new talent. It has been very successful at both, winning a reputation for high-quality drama. Shows tend to have a 1-month run, alongside Soho Nights—late-pm stand-up comedy every Thursday through Sunday. Downstairs there is also a Café Lazeez (p. 126): A two-course meal in the bar costs £7.50 ($14). The box office is open from 10am to curtain-up. 21 Dean St., W1. ✆ **0870/429-6883.** www.sohotheatre.com. Tickets £12–£15 ($22–$28); matinees and Mon all tickets £5 ($9). Tube: Tottenham Court Rd.

Young Vic The Young Vic has a large main auditorium and a smaller studio, where tickets are no pricier than going to the movies. It not only puts on its own productions, with guest stars for bankability, but hosts touring companies too. The faded decor and inadequate loos are somewhat redeemed by the delicious brasserie menu at its Bright Light Café (p. 154). The box office is open Monday to Saturday 10am to 7pm. 66 The Cut, SE1. ✆ **020/7928-6363.** www.youngvic.org. Main House tickets £9–£18 ($17–$33). Studio £5–£9 ($9–$17). Tube: Waterloo or Southwark.

3 The Performing Arts

OPERA & BALLET

Opera audiences have flocked to Covent Garden ever since the mid–18th century. All the world's great singers, from the legendary Adelina Patti and Maria Callas to the three tenors, have appeared at the **Royal Opera House,** and many famous British composers have premiered works there: Sir Arthur Bliss, Sir Ralph Vaughan Williams, Sir Benjamin Britten, Sir Michael Tippett, and Sir William Walton. **The Royal Opera Company** moved in after World War II. The other big opera venue is the **London Coliseum,** on nearby St. Martin's Lane, which is the home of **The English National Opera.** All the operas staged by the ENO are sung in English, and the productions are generally more cutting edge; its ticket prices are much more affordable than at The Royal Opera. The London Coliseum just had a multimillion-pound refurb, and the Royal Opera House was given a much-needed interior facelift a few years ago.

It was not until the big Royal Opera House refurb that **The Royal Ballet** got a custom-made performance space. The **English National Ballet** presents its season of dance at the London Coliseum. The newly renovated **Sadler's Wells** serves as one of the city's premiere venues for contemporary dance. London is also a regular stop for international dance companies, both classical and contemporary. See "Dance," below, for more on the sizzling modern scene.

MAJOR COMPANIES

The English National Opera The ENO thrills enthusiasts and rocks traditionalists with newly commissioned works and lively, theatrical reinterpretations of the classics. The ENO performs in the 2,350-seat London Coliseum, always in English, during a season lasting from September to July. At Christmas and during the summer, the English National Ballet takes over the auditorium. Show up at 10am on the day of performance and you can usually snag at seat for as little as £5 ($9). The box office is open 10am to 8pm (9:30am–8:30pm, by phone), Monday through Saturday. London Coliseum, St. Martin's Lane, WC2. ✆ **020/7632-8300.** www.eno.org. Tickets £10–£77 ($18–142). Discounted, premium seat day-of-performance tickets: £13–£30 ($23–$55), £5 ($9) standing room; each adult buying a full-price ticket can buy one half-price seat for a child under 18. No under-5s. Tube: Charing Cross or Leicester Sq.

The Royal Ballet Britain's leading ballet company is now firmly ensconced back at the Royal Opera House. The company's repertoire is extremely varied but veers toward the classics and works by its earlier choreographer-directors, Sir Frederick Ashton

Performers in the Park

It might sound like utter lunacy in a place as wet as England, but there's a very strong tradition of open-air theater, music, and dance in London's parks. The **Open Air Theatre,** Inner Circle, Regent's Park, NW1 (✆ **0870/060-1811;** www.openairtheatre.org; Tube: Baker St. or Regent's Park), has been staging summer drama, from June to early September, since 1932. Tickets cost £10 to £30 ($18–$55). **Holland Park Theatre,** Holland Park, W11 (✆ **0845/230-9769;** www.operahollandpark.com; Tube: Holland Park), has opera, and a week of ballet, to the accompaniment of the Royal Philharmonic Orchestra, from June to August under a temporary canopy in the ruins of the Jacobean Holland House. Tickets cost £21 to £43 ($39–$80). Savvy bargain hounds listen to the music for free while relaxing on the lawn outside. Perhaps the most famous open-air concerts are during July and August at the outdoor amphitheater near the Robert Adam–designed mansion, **Kenwood House** (p. 198), Hampstead Lane, NW3 (✆ **0870/890-0146;** www.picnicconcerts.com). This is a magical scene, on Hampstead Heath, by a lake that reflects the spectacular firework finales—a favorite with unstuffy types enjoying popular classics. Tickets are £17 to £20 ($31–$37) for a deck chair, or £15 to £17 ($27–$31) to sit on the lawn. Take the Tube to East Finchley, and catch the courtesy bus. Also call **Somerset House** (p. 171) about open-air concerts and theater in the stupendous courtyard.

(A Month in the Country) and Kenneth Macmillan *(Romeo and Juliet)*. Royal Opera House, Bow St., WC2. ✆ **020/7304-4000.** www.royalballet.org. Tickets evening £4–£85 ($7–$157); 67 discounted seats for each show sold from 10am on day of performance. Tube: Covent Garden.

The Royal Opera The combined talents of the Orchestra of the Royal Opera House, the Chorus of the Royal Opera, and the dozens of guest artists and conductors make The Royal Opera one of the world's premiere operatic venues. Operas are sung in the original language with projected supertitles that translate the libretto for the audience. Royal Opera House, Bow St., WC2. ✆ **020/7304-4000.** www.royalopera.org. Tickets £8–£175 ($15–$324); 67 discounted seats for each show sold from 10am on day of performance. Tube: Covent Garden.

CLASSICAL MUSIC

The city supports several major orchestras—the **London Symphony Orchestra** at the Barbican Centre, the **London Philharmonic** and **Philharmonia Orchestra** at the Royal Festival Hall on the South Bank, and the wandering **Royal Philharmonic,** which always plays in various venues including Holland Park in the summer (see above). There's also a host of choirs, chamber groups, and historic-instrument ensembles and the highly regarded but smaller venues (see below) where they perform. Look out for the modernist **London Sinfonietta,** the **English Chamber Orchestra,** and the **Gabrieli Consort.** London also draws all the top-name international musicians to its top-name venues, including the Royal Albert Hall (see "Major Arts Venues," below).

The **British Music Information Centre,** 10 Stratford Place, W1 (✆ **020/7499-8567;** bmic.co.uk), is *the* resource center for new British classical music, including upcoming concerts. Phone or stop by from noon to 5pm, Monday to Friday, or surf their website. The Centre holds recitals (£6/$11 adults, £4/$7 seniors and students), usually on Tuesday and Thursday at 7:30pm. Call for exact times, then take the Tube to Bond Street.

London Symphony Orchestra London's top orchestra is a major international force under the direction of principal conductor Sir Colin Davis. It stages 85 concerts a year at the Barbican Hall. The sound in the Barbican is much better since the hall's big refurbishment and acoustical tune-up. Barbican Centre, Silk St., EC2. ✆ **020/7638-8891.** www.lso.co.uk. Tickets £5–£20 ($9–$38). Tube: Barbican or Moorgate.

RECITAL VENUES

Don't forget to check out the magical candlelit concerts at **St. Martin-in-the-Fields** (see chapter 7).

St. John's Smith Square This baroque masterpiece, designed by Thomas Archer, is slightly bigger than Wigmore Hall but a lot less comfortable. It hosts chamber groups, choirs, and voice soloists. From September to July, on alternate Thursdays, there are lunchtime concerts, which are a steal at £5 ($9). The box office is open Monday to Friday, from 10am to 5pm. Smith Sq., SW1. ✆ **020/7222-1061.** www.sjss.org.uk. Tickets £5–£18 ($8–$29). Tube: Westminster or St. James's Park.

Wigmore Hall This venerable, vaulted auditorium celebrated its centenary in 2001 and is London's foremost venue for lieder and chamber music. Even the cognoscenti don't mind the cheap seats at the back of the stalls, as the acoustics are superb. All tickets at The Sunday Morning Coffee Concerts, and those recorded for BBC Radio 3 on a Monday lunchtime, are £8 or £9 ($15 or $17)—a great deal. The box office is open

Monday to Saturday from 10am to 8:30pm, Sunday 10:30am to 8pm (5pm from Nov to mid-Mar). 36 Wigmore St., W1. ✆ **020/7935-2141.** www.wigmore-hall.org.uk. Tickets £7–£20 ($13–$38). Tube: Bond St. or Oxford Circus.

DANCE

Set up in 1998, the **London Dance Network** aims to build audiences and win support for creating a National Dance House. It revamped its website last year (**www.londondance.com**), making this a one-stop info shop on everything that's going on in the capital's dance world. Contemporary dance is certainly thriving in London. Top international companies like Merce Cunningham, Twyla Tharp, and Trisha Brown appear at the Barbican Centre, Royal Festival Hall, and Sadler's Wells Theatre (see "Major Arts Venues," below). Smaller venues, like **The Place** (see below), focus on the even more avant-garde. Also worth checking out for the occasional dance events in their programs are: **ICA,** The Mall, SW1 (✆ **020/7930-3647;** www.ica.org.uk; Tube: Piccadilly Circus or Charing Cross); and **Riverside Studios,** Crisp Road, W6 (✆ **020/8237-1111;** www.riversidestudios.co.uk; Tube: Hammersmith).

Dance Umbrella (✆ **020/8741-4040;** www.danceumbrella.co.uk), the internationally acclaimed fall showcase of contemporary dance, runs for 6 weeks from October into November and uses various venues throughout London. Seats are usually available on the day of performance and cost as little as £8 ($12), depending on the venue.

The Place This has been *the* showplace for contemporary dance since it was founded in the late 1960s by Robert Cohan of the Martha Graham Company. Now The Place is the permanent home of the Richard Alston Dance Company and the London Contemporary Dance School. The box office is open Monday to Friday (and Sat performance days) from 10am to 6pm. 17 Duke's Rd., WC1. ✆ **020/7387-0031.** www.theplace.org.uk. Tickets £10 ($18), £8 ($15) students and seniors. Tube: Euston.

4 Major Arts Venues

Barbican Centre The Barbican opened in 1982. Reputedly the largest arts complex in Europe, it is so badly laid out that yellow lines have been painted across its brick-paved walkways and piazzas to help visitors find their way from the Underground. The "brutalist" architecture is grotesque, to say the least, but even detractors agree that the facilities inside are superb. As well as the Barbican Theatre and The Pit, it has two art galleries (p. 183), three cinemas, and several restaurants, bars, and cafes. The newly refurbished concert hall is home to the London Symphony Orchestra (see "Classical Music," above) and hosts other festivals and large-scale events between LSO performances.

Up until 2002, the Barbican Theatre was the yearly London home of the Royal Shakespeare Company (see "London's Theater Scene," earlier in this chapter). The RSC now uses other West End theaters in addition to the Barbican.

Barbican Plus is a program of talks and workshops, often linked to major productions; some cost £5 to £8 ($9–$15), but many are free. Call the box office, open daily from 9am to 8pm, for tickets and to find out what's on. Silk St., EC2. ✆ **020/7638-8891.** www.barbican.org.uk. Tube: Barbican or Moorgate.

London Coliseum Built in 1904, this former variety hall was later turned into London's biggest opera house. A much-needed £41 million ($66 million) face-lift to glam up the dowdy public spaces and improve conditions backstage was unveiled in

Finds Fantasy on Folgate Street

American artist Dennis Severs spent nearly 20 years, until his death in 2000, turning his Georgian terrace house in Spitalfields into a "still-life drama." Each of the 10 rooms is dedicated to a different era in the life of a family of Huguenot weavers, between 1754, when the house was built, and 1914. The half-eaten supper, the wig on the back of the chair, smells, sounds, and flickering candlelight are used to transport you back in time. The house is open every Monday evening: the time varies depending when dusk falls. Tickets are £12 ($22), and you must call to book: **Dennis Severs' House,** 18 Folgate St., E1. (✆ **020/7247-4013;** www.dennisseversHouse.co.uk; Tube: Liverpool St.). Children are not welcome. The house is now open to walk-in visitors without reservations on the first and third Sunday of every month between 2 and 5pm (£8/$15), and the following Mondays between noon and 2pm (£5/$9).

time for the centenary year in 2004. The Coliseum is home to The English National Opera (see "The Performing Arts," above) and hosts touring companies when the ENO isn't performing. English National Ballet has a fleeting Christmas season and comes back during the summer. The box office is available by phone around the clock. St. Martin's Lane, WC2. ✆ **020/7632-8300.** www.eno.org. Tube: Leicester Sq. or Charing Cross.

Ocean Three different performing spaces, with a total capacity of 2,700. Acoustics adjustable at the flick of a switch to suit any kind of music. Wired for live webcasts. It's little wonder that Ocean, which opened in 2001, cost £23 million ($37 million) to build. Located in Hackney in northeast London, it's part of a big neighborhood regeneration plan. The eclectic musical calendar reflects the local melting pot of cultures, with everything from bhangra to blues, classical, country, rock, reggae, jazz, soul, rap, latin, dance, and world music on the calendar. It has six bars and one cafebar. 270 Mare St., E8. ✆ **020/8533-0111,** or 020/7314-2800 box office. £5–£18 ($9–$33). Tube: Bethnal Green, then 8-min. ride on no. 106 or 253 bus.

Royal Albert Hall A £4 ($7) standing ticket to one of the Sir Henry Wood Promenade Concerts at the Royal Albert Hall has to be one of the best buys of the summer cultural season (www.bbc.co.uk/proms). Every year, from mid-July to mid-September, the daily changing performances cover every conceivable spot on the classical music spectrum. During the Proms, the hall takes out all the central orchestra seats to leave an open space for the promenaders. They take over the show on the Last Night of the Proms, a national institution broadcast live into Hyde Park, with patriotic flag waving to the sounds of Elgar's *Pomp and Circumstance.* The rest of the year, this circular hall serves as a venue for a huge range of entertainment, not all of it musical. Sheryl Crow, Burt Bacharach, Tony Bennett, B. B. King, Cirque du Soleil, and the world's top stand-up comedians, tennis players, sumo wrestlers, and amateur choirs—they've all appeared here. The box office opens daily from 9am to 9pm. Kensington Gore, SW7. ✆ **020/7589-8212.** www.royalalberthall.com. Tube: South Kensington or Kensington High St.

Royal Opera House The ROH reopened at the end of 1999 in a new guise as the "people's pleasure palace." The Vilar Floral Hall—a stunning, Victorian atrium—has been restored. And a new "indoor street" called The Link runs through the ROH to the piazza colonnade, finally completed to Inigo Jones's original design. Ticket prices for The Royal Opera, The Royal Ballet, and visiting international opera and ballet companies have come down, but still only a small proportion of them are affordable. The new Linbury Studio Theatre stages unusual repertory. Together with the Clore Studio Upstairs, it also hosts talks and workshops. Tickets cost £8 to £25 ($15–$48), but some events are free. And there are free lunchtime concerts every Monday at 1pm during the season. Tickets are available from 10am on the day of performance at the information desk next to the box office. Preperformance talks are also free. You can tour backstage, usually at 10:30am, 12:30, and 2:30pm, for £7 ($13). For tour information only, call © **020/7212-9389.** No children under 7.

The Link, its coffee bar, and the box office are open from Monday to Saturday from 10am to 8pm, the Vilar Floral Hall from 10am to 3pm. The Amphitheatre restaurant (© **020/7212-9254**), with its terrace overlooking Covent Garden, serves modern European cuisine. But it's a splurge, with main courses costing around £14 ($26). Bow St., WC2. © **020/7304-4000.** www.royaloperahouse.org. Tube: Covent Garden.

Sadler's Wells Theatre Recently rebuilt, this is one of the busiest stages in London and also one of the best, with superb sightlines. It hosts top visiting opera and dance companies from around the world. Each May, Sadler's Wells is one of the venues for the Covent Garden Festival, dedicated to making dance accessible, so there are always some seats within reach of the budget traveler (£8.50–£35/$16–$65). Students, kids, and seniors can sometimes get standbys 1 hour before a performance. Prices are much the same at The Peacock Theatre in Holborn, a satellite venue staging more populist musical theater and dance. The ticket office is open Monday to Saturday 9am to 8:30pm. Rosebery Ave., EC1. © **020/7863-8000.** www.sadlers-wells.com. Tube: Angel.

South Bank Centre This South Bank arts complex is in the midst of a controversial redevelopment plan that seeks to re-landscape the neighboring Jubilee Gardens (where the British Airways London Eye is now) and build shops, a new concert hall, a home for the Museum of the Moving Image (currently closed), and a multiplex cinema to add to the existing **National Film Theatre,** hub of November's London Film Festival (www.lff.org.uk). The **Hayward Gallery** (p. 185) and Royal Festival Hall are to be spruced up and the existing brutalist plazas reconfigured for humans to enjoy. The work will continue into 2007, and probably beyond, but the concert hall will remain open.

The **Royal Festival Hall** comprises three music and dance venues: **RFH1** is the usual venue for big orchestral performances. The smaller **RFH2,** formerly known as Queen Elizabeth Hall, is dedicated to chamber music, semistaged opera, and special events; because of the construction work, it will be closed for part of 2006. The intimate **RFH3** usually hosts advanced students and young performers making their professional debuts. All three stages are lit almost every night of the year, with ballet (including The Royal Ballet), jazz, pop, and folk concerts as well as classical music. If you can, try to make it over for Meltdown in June. The RFH invites a different performer each year to devise their fantasy arts festival, so this 3-week event is uniquely diverse (or perverse, perhaps).

The RFH foyer must be one of London's hardest-working venues. Free informal recitals take place in front of the Festival Buffet cafe, from Wednesday to Sunday, 12:30 to 2pm. On Friday evenings, it's Commuter Jazz from 5:15 to 6:45pm. **Summer on the South Bank** is a fest of mostly free events in the foyers and outdoors on the terraces, from mid-July through August. Booking is not usually required, but check with the box office, open daily from 9am to 9pm. Belvedere Rd., SE1. ✆ **020/7960-4242.** www.sbc.org.uk. Tube: Waterloo, Southwark, or Embankment (cross over Hungerford Bridge). River services: Festival Pier.

5 The Club & Music Scene

COMEDY & CABARET

The all-purpose *Time Out* lists comedy gigs, or surf **www.chortle.co.uk** for longer reviews. Do be careful when you see laughably low ticket prices as they may be for open-mic, talentless spotting sessions. However, some deals really *are* too good to miss. At the **Comedy Café,** 66 Rivington St., EC2 (✆ **020/7739-5706;** Tube: Old St.), there's no admission charge on Wednesday, when new acts perform, and it's only £5 ($9) on Thursday. And the **Soho Theatre** (p. 237) pulls in big names in the laff biz for its late-night weekend shows, Soho Nights; tickets run £6 to £10 ($11–$18).

Madame JoJo's, for decades London's premiere professional drag revue, has revamped itself into a club with a DJ instead of a she-male cabaret. The he-divas only perform on Saturdays now: for more information, see "Dance Clubs & Discos," below.

Canal Café Theatre For a nice evening out, come early and stroll along the canal in this very pretty part of Maida Vale. The Canal Café Theatre is a small but long-established fringe venue above a pub. Performances range from drama to cabaret, but the most famous is the topical sketch show *Newsrevue* (Thurs–Sat at 9:30pm, Sun at 9pm). You can buy tickets in person up to 45 minutes before the show. Food is served until 10pm. The Bridge House, Delamere Terrace, W2. ✆ **020/7289-6054.** Cover £7 ($13), or £5 ($9) seniors and students, plus £1 ($1.85) membership. Tube: Royal Oak or Warwick Ave.

The Comedy Store Launched in 1979, The Comedy Store has nurtured such talents as Dawn French and Eddie Izzard. The Cutting Edge, a topical satirical revue, takes the stage on Tuesday night. An improv group, The Comedy Store Players, performs on Wednesday and Sunday. Best in Stand-Up is on Thursday, Friday, and Saturday. Shows start at 8pm, Tuesday to Sunday, with extra midnight performances on Friday and Saturday. The box office opens at 6:30pm, and 100 of the 400 tickets are always held back to be sold on the night of the performance. Haymarket House, 1A Oxendon St., SW1. ✆ **020/7344-0234.** www.thecomedystore.co.uk. Cover £12–£15 ($22–$28), or £8 ($15) seniors and students. Tube: Piccadilly or Leicester Sq.

ROCK & POP

London has hundreds of live music venues hosting rock legends, pre-fab boy and girl bands, and the sharpest indie sounds. The newest is the technologically marvelous **Ocean,** in Hackney (see "Major Art Venues," above). For big-name gigs, you'll need to book well ahead—sometimes several months. The website **www.aloud.com** is an excellent source of advance info, as are the ticket agencies mentioned at the start of this chapter. But contact the box office directly to avoid the booking fee.

The ever-expanding Mean Fiddler Group owns three of London's premier venues: **Astoria** and next-door **Mean Fiddler W1,** 157–165 Charing Cross Rd., WC2 (✆ **020/7434-9592;** Tube: Tottenham Court Rd.); and **Forum,** 9–17 Highgate Rd., NW5 (✆ **020/7344-0044;** Tube: Kentish Town). Find out what's on where at www.meanfiddler.com; tickets cost £8 to £20 ($15–$37). Two more venues to keep in mind are **Brixton Academy,** 211 Stockwell Rd., SW9 (✆ **020/7771-2000;** Tube: Brixton);

and **Shepherds Bush Empire,** Shepherds Bush Green, W12 (✆ **020/7771-2000;** Tube: Shepherds Bush). Tickets to both are £10 to £25 ($18–$46).

Camden's legendary **Bull & Gate,** 389 Kentish Town Rd., NW5 (✆ **020/7485-5358;** www.bullandgate.co.uk; Tube: Kentish Town), is small and scruffy and serves as the unofficial headquarters of London's pub music scene. Unsigned indie bands play back-to-back, sometimes three or four a night, starting at 8:30pm. Nirvana and Manic Street Preachers are alumni. You'll pay around £5 ($8) for a night at the bottom end of the fame chain (no credit cards).

Also check out the live music nights at the club bars, reviewed below.

FOLK

Cecil Sharp House This was the focal point of the 1960s folk revival. The English Folk Dance and Song Society is based here and continues to document and foster this music. Concerts range from traditional English music to Cajun, Irish, and anything else that's danceable. Tuesday nights at 8pm are the Sharp's Folk Club "singaround" sessions with guest artists; no need to book. 2 Regent's Park Rd., NW1. ✆ **020/7485-2206.** www.efdss.org. Cover £3–£8 ($5.50–$15). Tube: Camden Town.

JAZZ

There is a great gig guide at **www.jazzservices.org.uk**; otherwise trawl the listings magazines. A big freebie favorite is **Commuter Jazz** from 5:15 to 6:45pm on Fridays at the Royal Festival Hall (see "Major Arts Venues," above). The **Lamb & Flag** in Covent Garden (see "Pubs," later in this chapter) also puts on free jazz on Sunday night from 7:30pm. So does **The 100 Club** noon to 3pm on Friday (see below).

Jazz Café The Sunday lunchtime Jazz Jams are the most fun. Aspiring musicians pitch up and get in the groove with the resident band, Tomorrow's Warriors, from noon to 4pm. The cover is a whopping £1 ($1.85). On a regular night, the sounds range from rap to Latin jazz. You must book a table ahead of time, but try to avoid going upstairs; the restaurant is pricey. Music starts at 7pm. Open Monday through Thursday until 1am, until 2am on Friday and Saturday, and midnight on Sunday. 5 Parkway, NW1. ✆ **020/7916-6060.** www.jazzcafe.co.uk. Cover £8–£18 ($15–$33). Tube: Camden Town.

The 100 Club The smoky basement stage hosts jazz sets, swing, jive, rhythm and blues, as well as funk and soul. Every night is different, so give them a ringy-dingy to find out what's on. Don't miss the fab Friday Lunchtime Jazz—admission is free. Open Monday to Thursday 7:30 to 11:30pm, Friday 11:15am to 3pm and 8:30pm to 2am, Saturday 7:30pm to "late," Sunday 7:30 to 11:30pm. 100 Oxford St., W1. ✆ **020/7636-0933.** Cover £9–£10 ($17–$18). Tube: Tottenham Court Rd.

PizzaExpress Jazz Club Unlikely though it sounds, the basement of this chain restaurant is one of the city's most popular jazz venues. The house band, the PizzaExpress All-Stars, shares the stage with leading traditional and contemporary names. Doors open at 7:45pm, with the first set at 9pm. Also check out the more expensive Pizza on the Park (p. 120). 10 Dean St., W1. ✆ **020/7437-9595.** www.pizzaexpress.co.uk. Cover £10–£20 ($18–$38), plus food. Tube: Tottenham Court Rd.

Ronnie Scott's Since it opened in 1959, London's best-known jazz room has featured all the greats, from Ella Fitzgerald and Dizzy Gillespie to Hugh Masekela and Charlie Watts. Book a week ahead for a Saturday show. On Sunday, an independent promoter puts on contemporary and world music. Ronnie Scott's is open Monday to Saturday 8:30pm to 3am, Sunday 7:30 to 11pm. There's a separate entrance for clubbers to get to Upstairs@Ronnies. On Wednesdays and Sundays, the Ratt Club spins some R&B, soul, and hip-hop; 1970s jazz, funk, and soul takes over on Thursday at Starsky & Hutch (no sneakers); on Friday and Saturday, it's Club Latino and the first hour is a salsa lesson. Upstairs opens 10pm to 3am except on Sunday, when it opens 6pm to midnight. 47 Frith St., W1. ✆ **020/7439-0747.** www.ronniescotts.co.uk. Cover £15–£25 ($28–$48), includes admission to Upstaris@Ronnies, £10 ($18) students Mon–Wed; Upstairs@Ronnies alone £3–£7 ($5.50–$13). Tube: Leicester Sq. or Tottenham Court Rd.

DANCE CLUBS & DISCOS

The London club 'n' dance scene is kicking. Even hardcore hedonists will find their heads spinning at the choices.

The hot spots change from week to week, so it's crucial to consult *Time Out* for the latest roster. The magazine's **Privilege Pass,** printed weekly, will buy you cheap entry at a number of venues; for more money-saving tips, see "Entertainment on a Shoestring," earlier in this chapter.

Note: Always check the dress code because many clubs ban sneakers.

GROOVY SATURDAY CLUB NIGHTS

- **Blow Up** 1960s R&B, funk, and soulful jazz for a stylish postpubescent crowd, at The Metro Club, 19–24 Oxford St., W1 (www.blowup.co.uk); advance tickets from Stargreen (✆ **020/7734-8939**). Cover £8 ($15) before 11:30pm, £6 ($11) students and with flyer; after 11:30pm £10 ($18), £8 ($15) students and with flyer. Open 10pm to 4am. Tube: Tottenham Court Rd.
- **Carwash** Every night is glam disco night, so dress sexy because the dress code is enforced. Try to get there by 11:30pm because it gets busy early. At Sound, 10 Wardour St., W1 (✆ **020/7403-8585;** www.carwash.co.uk). Cover £12 ($23). Open 10pm to 3am. Tube: Leicester Sq.
- **Garage City** Underground garage, disco house, and dressy garb, at Bar Rumba, 36 Shaftesbury Ave., W1 (✆ **020/7287-2715;** www.barrumba.co.uk). Cover £7 ($13) before 11pm, then £12 ($23). Open 9pm to 4am. Tube: Piccadilly Circus.
- **Headstart** Techno club with open-doors attitude to guest DJs—big names and newcomers—and live acts, at Turnmills, 63 Clerkenwell Rd., EC1 (✆ **020/7250-3409**). Cover £8 ($15). Open 9pm to 5am. Tube: Farringdon.
- **Rulin** U.S. and U.K. house, and designer streetwear, at the monster club/store Ministry of Sound, 103 Gaunt St., SE1 (✆ **020/7378-6528;** www.ministryofsound.co.uk). Cover £15 ($28). Open midnight to 8am. Tube: Elephant & Castle.
- **SchoolDisco.com** Bizarre glimpse into undeveloped English psyche as 2,000 naughty girls and boys turn up in mandatory school uniform to relive their teenage years, at Hammersmith Palais, 230 Shepherds Bush Rd., W6 (✆ **020/8699-9983;** Tube: Hammersmith). Cover £14 ($25). Open 10pm to 3am.

GREAT VENUES

Also check out the upstairs nightclub at **Ronnie Scott's** under "Jazz," above.

Bar Rumba This club is a classy favorite. It travels through the whole musical spectrum every week—from Latin sounds to cosmic disco house and garage (see "Groovy Saturday Club Nights," above). And get this: Drinks are two-for-one during weeknight happy hour *and* there's no cover charge, so come before 9pm and you can club it up later for free. On Tuesdays, a night of Latin mayhem starts with a salsa class (6:30–8:30pm). Open Monday to Thursday 5pm to 3:30am, Friday 5pm to 4am, Saturday 7pm to 6am,

Sunday 8pm to 1am. 36 Shaftesbury Ave., W1. ✆ **020/7287-2715.** www.barrumba.co.uk. Happy hour Mon–Thurs 5–9pm. Cover £3–£12 ($5.50–$23). Tube: Piccadilly Circus.

The End At this beautifully designed, cutting-edge club, the main sounds are techno, house, garage, and drum 'n' bass. Monday is Trash: dress code is "make an effort," music is anything excessive from 1980s electronica to hi-NRG, cover is a supercheap £4 ($6), and drinks are cheap, too! Thursday night is the gay-ish Atelier (see below). Be prepared for long lines any night. Open Monday 10pm to 3am, Thursday 7pm to 1am, Friday 11pm to 5am, Saturday 10pm to 6am, and Sunday 8pm to 3am. 18 West Central St., WC1. ✆ **020/7419-9199.** www.endclub.com. Cover £4–£15 ($7–$24). Tube: Holborn or Tottenham Court Rd.

Fabric The 15 Victorian brick arches of this minimalist superclub (capacity 2,500) used to be the old cold-storage area for Smithfield meat market. There are three rooms, various bars, a roof terrace, and chill-out rooms. A hi-tech sound system pumps the beat from some of the city's best house, garage, techno, and drum 'n' bass up through the main dance floor. One grumble: Fabric is notorious for its mile-long lines, both to get in and for the unisex bathrooms. Sunday is the gay DPTM night (see below). Open Friday 10pm to 5am and Saturday 10pm to 7am. 77a Charterhouse St., EC1. ✆ **020/7336-8898.** www.fabriclondon.com. Cover £12–£15 ($23–$28). Tube: Barbican or Farringdon.

Hanover Grand Here's the scene: A dress-conscious crowd cavorts around a renovated theater to a maelstrom of musical styles. It's the home of youth, glitter, and glam. Wednesday's Fresh 'n' Funky is a great cheap mid-weeker, £5 ($9) to get in before 11pm, then £7 ($13). Open Wednesday and Thursday 10pm to 4am, Friday 11pm to 4am, and Saturday 10:30pm to 4:30am. 6 Hanover St., W1. ✆ **020/7499-7977.** www.hanovergrand.com. Cover £5–£15 ($9–$28). Tube: Oxford Circus.

Madame JoJo's This was once London's premiere drag-revue bar, but it recently changed hands and turned itself into a mostly straight dance club, spinning a bit of everything from nu-jazz to breakbeats, funk, and deep soulful house. The drag divas strut their stuff on Saturdays only now: cabaret tickets are pricey, and you must prebook. Open Wednesday 10pm to 2am, Thursday 9:30pm to 3am, Friday 10pm to 3am, Saturday 10:30pm to 3am, and Sunday 9am to 3pm (yes, really!) and 9:30pm to 2:30am. 8 Brewer St., W1. ✆ **020/7734-3040.** Cover £5–£10 ($9–$18); £37 ($68) cabaret, Sat only. Tube: Piccadilly Circus.

Scala This is the smallest of the so-called superclubs (capacity 800), and it is certainly the quirkiest. The shabby old cinema reopened in March 1999 as a live music venue, gallery, sometime film-house, and nightclub. Surf the website because the schedule of DJs, promoters, and special events is very eclectic. It's the gay Popstarz on Fridays. Open Thursday 9pm to 3am, Friday 10pm to 5am, and Saturday 9pm to 5am. 278 Pentonville Rd., N1. ✆ **020/7833-2022.** www.scala-london.co.uk. Cover £5–£12 ($9–$23). Tube: King's Cross.

Velvet Room This low-lit late-hour basement joint is the reason so many clubbers turn up for work looking like the living dead. It's much classier and more elegant now than it was in the days when it was called the Velvet Underground. DJs spin out favorite dance hits every night but Sunday. Open Monday and Thursday 10pm to 3am, Tuesday 10:30pm to 3am, Wednesday 10pm to 2:30am, Friday 10pm to 4:30am, and Saturday 10pm to 4am. 143 Charing Cross Rd., WC2. ✆ **020/7439-4655.** Cover £4–£10 ($7–$16). Tube: Tottenham Court Rd.

CLUB BARS

For every action there is a reaction. And the reaction to superclubs has been the rise of the club bar. These are more intimate spaces, but with live music and specialist DJs. Nights tend to end earlier and the cover charge is much less.

Cargo Cargo is billed as a bar, not a club, but it has the feel of a nightclub in the decades up to the 1950s when venues were smaller and dancing, drinks, and food were part of an evening's entertainment. Cargo has updated that concept. Friday's Barrio, which is Latin house, funk, nu-jazz, and soul, is the only weekly fixture. Otherwise the schedule spans every kind of music style. Cocktails are £5 ($8). That's also the highest price for any nosh on the international street food menu. Cargo is open Monday to Friday from noon to 1am, Saturday 6pm to 1am, and Sunday noon to midnight. Kingsland Viaduct, 83 Rivington St., EC2. ✆ **020/7739-3440.** www.cargo-london.com. Cover £3–£7 ($5.50–$13). Tube: Old St.

Notting Hill Arts Club Come before 8pm (6pm on Sun), and it's free to get in. Come early anyway or you'll have no chance at all of getting in to this cupboard-size basement bar that hosts a mix of DJ and live music nights. Wednesday night is Deathdisco, a mix of punk, funk, indie, and glam for indie celebs and punk veterans. Bands take the sort-of stage on Saturday too, at RoTa. But the hottest spot on the dial is Sunday's hard dancing at Lazy Dog. NHAC is open Tuesday to Friday 6pm to 1am, Saturday 4pm to 1am, Sunday 4 to 11pm. The "art," by the way, is minimal and doubtful! 21 Notting Hill Gate, W11. ✆ **020/7460-4459.** www.nottinghillartsclub.com. Cover £5 ($9). Tube: Notting Hill Gate.

The Social The upstairs bar is just a bar. Downstairs is where the action is, with DJs laying on some soulful house, hip-hop, and funk, and the live Acoustically Heavenly night every Wednesday. That's the only time there's a cover charge, but it's worth it because there are always two indie bands or singer-songwriters in the lineup. The stage is high above the hole-in-the-ground dance floor, and you'll have to get there early to get a table. The Social downstairs is open Monday to Saturday 7pm to midnight, closing at 10:30pm on Sunday. 5 Little Portland St., W1. ✆ **020/7636-4992.** www.thesocial.com. Cover £3 ($5.50) Wed. Tube: Oxford Circus.

6 Gay & Lesbian London

Old Compton Street in Soho is the epicenter of gay London life. But there are plenty of bars and clubs elsewhere. To find out what's going on and where, pick up one of the free newspapers you'll find at most of the places listed below: the *Pink Paper* and *Boyz,* for instance. *QX* magazine is another top guide, and there are gay listings in *Time Out.* Lastly, for purely online help, check out the comprehensive **www.gaytoz.com** or **www.rainbownetwork.com**. Otherwise, the **Lesbian & Gay Switchboard** (✆ **020/7837-7324;** www.llgs.org.uk) is a round-the-clock information source on absolutely everything.

Note: Clubbers should check out the gay bars (see below) for discount flyers and jump-the-queue tickets.

GROOVY CLUB NIGHTS

Club nights can change, disappear, or move to new locations, so call first.

- **Atelier** Groovy laid-back house for loungers from the media, music, fashion, and film industries at The End, 18 West Central St., WC1 (✆ **020/7419-9199**).

Cover £5 ($9). Open Thursday 10pm to 4am; happy hour 10 to 11pm. Dress: "Make an effort." Tube: Holborn or Tottenham Court Rd.

- **Coco Latté** Get queue-jump tickets at The Box (see below) and join the mixed crowd for a hot, hot night of garage, techno, and 1970s sounds, at the Velvet Room, 143 Charing Cross Rd., WC2 (✆ **020/7439-4655**). Cover £10 ($18). Open Friday 10pm to late. Tube: Tottenham Court Rd.
- **Crash** Gaining an international reputation as "the dog's balls," music and muscle on two dance floors in a Vauxhall railway arch, at Crash, Arch 66, Goding St., SE11 (✆ **020/7820-1500**). Cover £10 ($18) or £8 ($15) with a flyer. Open Saturday 10:30pm to late. Tube: Vauxhall.
- **DPTM** Three dance floors of Latino house, funky grooves, hip-hop, R&B, soul, and jazz, and a few Sunday celebs, at new superclub Fabric, 77a Charterhouse St., EC1 (✆ **020/7439-9009**). Cover £13 ($25). Open Sunday 10pm until late. Tube: Barbican or Farringdon.
- **Popstarz** Kitsch 1970s and 1980s, plus indie and alternative sounds, at Scala, 278 Pentonville Rd., N1 (✆ **020/7738-2336**). Cover £8 ($15), £5 ($9) with a flyer before 11pm. Open Friday 10pm to 5am. Tube: King's Cross.
- **Trade** Late-late-night techno, lasers, and the seriously body beautiful, at Turnmills, 63 Clerkenwell Rd., EC1 (✆ **020/7250-3409**). Cover £12 ($23) with a flyer, or £15 ($28). Open from 4am Saturday to 1pm Sunday. Tube: Farringdon.

GREAT VENUES

G.A.Y. This colossal club is less about posing and more about a young unpretentious crowd having fun. The biggest night is strictly gay-only Saturday, when there are always some special surprises—big-name personal appearances, for instance. Five hundred queue-jump tickets go on sale at the Astoria box office from the Monday before, with some available on Saturday afternoon at Ku Bar (see below). G.A.Y. is open Monday 10:30pm to 3am, Thursday and Friday 11pm to 4am, and Saturday 10:30pm to 5am. Astoria and Mean Fiddler, 157–165 Charing Cross Rd., WC2. ✆ **0906/100-0160.** www.g-a-y.co.uk. Cover £3 ($5.50) or £1 ($1.85) with a flyer, Sat £10 ($18) or £8 ($15) with a flyer. Tube: Tottenham Court Rd.

Heaven The 2,000-capacity Heaven is London's most famous gay club, though its popularity has drawn a lot of heteros, too. It's like a self-supporting space colony, with three floors of separate bars and dance floors. Big name DJs power up the volume across the full musical spectrum. On a Monday, you'll get cheap drinks, with happy pop, disco trash, and dance downstairs, and indie upstairs. Wednesday is soul and heavy funk, Friday techno and hard house. Saturday is the one strictly gay-only night. Surf the website, and you can print "flyers" to save pounds getting in. Open Monday and Wednesday 10:30pm to 3am, Friday 10:30pm to 6am, and Saturday 10pm to 5am. The Arches, Craven St., WC2. ✆ **020/7930-2020.** www.heaven-london.com. Cover £6–£12 ($13–$23). Tube: Embankment or Charing Cross.

PUBS, BARS & CAFES

These places keep regular pub hours—Monday through Saturday 11am to 11pm, Sunday noon to 10:30pm—unless otherwise stated.

The Box Bar A friendly, comfortable, and recently redesigned cafe-bar where people hang out and graze during the day, and gather for drinks in the evenings. This is one of the places to pick up queue-jump tickets to Saturday night at Heaven (see above). Seven Dials, 32–34 Monmouth St., WC2. ✆ **020/7240-5828.** Tube: Leicester Sq.

Candy Bar Britain's first-ever 7-night lesbian bar has great beer, great cocktails, and great club nights. Gay men are welcome as guests. Open Monday to Thursday noon to 1am, Friday and Saturday noon to 3am, and Sunday noon to 11pm. 23–24 Bateman St., W1. ✆ **020/7437-1977.** Cover Fri–Sat £5 ($9) after 9pm. No credit cards. Tube: Tottenham Court Rd.

Central Station A pub with a difference—later hours and a laid-back crowd here for the cabaret, sports bar, roof terrace, and cruising at the basement's club nights (Mon and Thurs, men only). Open Monday to Wednesday 5pm to 2am, Thursday 5pm to 3am, Friday 5pm to 4am, Saturday noon to 4am, and Sunday 11am to midnight. Happy hour Monday through Friday 5 to 9pm. 37 Wharfedale Rd., N1. ✆ **020/7278-3294.** Cover £5 ($9). Tube: King's Cross.

Ku Bar Great place to start a night on the town as you'll find lots of discount flyers for clubs at this hip West End bar. You can also buy advance tickets on Saturday afternoon for that night's G.A.Y. (see above). All the beer is bottled, so no cheap pints. But there's another hot seller, schnapps shots. On Sundays, Ku Bar doesn't open until 1pm. Happy hour daily noon to 9pm. 75 Charing Cross Rd., WC2. ✆ **020/7437-4303.** Tube: Leicester Sq.

Kudos A well-groomed pampered party crowd gathers at what many think is the best boys' bar in London. Kudos certainly tries hard, with big video screens downstairs for semireal music nights, and DJs on Wednesday and Saturday (no cover). It's also a good place to pick up club flyers and advance tickets. Happy hour Monday through Friday 4 to 6pm, Saturday and Sunday 6 to 8pm. 10 Adelaide St., WC2. ✆ **020/7379-4573.** Tube: Embankment or Charing Cross.

West Central Is it a pub? Is it a club? It's both. There's a decibel and energy level to suit any mood at the three-storied West Central, with some kind of entertainment every night for eyes, ears, and dancin' feet. The basement bar stays open latest, Wednesday and Thursday 10:30pm to 2am, Friday and Saturday 10:30pm to 3am. The main bar opens at 3pm and the plush velvety Theatre Bar upstairs at 5pm. 29–30 Lisle St., WC2. ✆ **020/7479-7980.** Cover (basement bar only) £3 ($5.50). Tube: Leicester Sq.

The Yard This is a friendly spot, attracting a laid-back mixed clientele and a big after-work crowd. There's a blissfully secluded courtyard, behind a set of iron gates, and two bars inside. The Yard opens at noon and is closed on Sundays. 57 Rupert St., W1. ✆ **020/7437-2652.** Tube: Piccadilly Circus.

7 The Drinking Game: Pubs & Wine Bars

The licensing laws in England and Wales restrict the sale of alcohol in pubs, bars, restaurants, and shops to between 11am and 11pm, Monday to Saturday, and noon to 10:30pm on Sunday. Proprietors must make a special application if they want to extend their hours, put on entertainment, and so on, which is why late-openers often charge for entry.

The government has promised to overhaul the whole system, but no one will say when.

PUBS

There's nothing more British than a smoky local boozer. But it takes more than a polished wooden bar, draft beer, overflowing ashtrays, and a few pictures of Queen Victoria to make a true British pub—the atmosphere of the real thing is unique. Public houses aren't just for evening entertainment: locals go almost any time—to meet their mates, swap stories, tell jokes, and put away quite a lot of booze. Pubs serve every sort of alcohol (except fancy cocktails), but beer is the national drink. Expect to pay £1.80 to £2.70 ($3.35–$5) for a pint, depending on what and where you're drinking. It's flat-out impossible to review all the great pubs in London, or even the merely good—surf **www.pubs.com** for another 160 or so to add to this list.

Note: In pubs, you order food as well as drinks at the bar; there's no table service and there's no tipping, either. If you like, you can offer to buy the bartender a drink.

Cittie of Yorke This soaring high-gabled room must have the longest bar in England. You can still see the huge vats originally used to dispense wine and liquors. All along one wall are private wood-carved cubicles, supposedly designed for lawyers from the dozens of chambers in the neighborhood to meet discreetly with clients. The pub dates from 1430, though it was rebuilt in 1923. 22–23 High Holborn, WC1. ✆ **020/7242-7670.** Tube: Chancery Lane or Holborn.

The Dove A perfect riverside pub at Hammersmith, with a terrace where you can watch the local rowers. Along with what must be one of the smallest bars in the world, it has a series of comfortable oak-paneled rooms with copper tables and settle seating. Get here early on sunny weekends. 19 Upper Mall, W6. ✆ **020/8748-5405.** Tube: Ravenscourt Park.

French House This Soho institution became the center of French life in London during World War II when de Gaulle and his circle gathered here. It still attracts a lot of French-speaking visitors. Beer is only sold in half-pints—myths abound but no one really knows why. 49 Dean St., W1. ✆ **020/7437-2799.** Tube: Tottenham Court Rd.

Grenadier This cozy mews pub is always crowded. It was an officers' mess in the Duke of Wellington's time. Come to see the military memorabilia and maybe the resident ghost of a soldier flogged to death for cheating at cards. 18 Wilton Row, SW1. ✆ **020/7235-3074.** Tube: Hyde Park Corner.

Jamaica Wine House This is one of the oldest bars in the City, where Caribbean merchants met to make deals over coffee and rum. Today, young bankers gather at the first-floor bar or downstairs in the cozier cellar to sip good wines, port, or beer. St. Michael's Alley, off Cornhill, EC3. ✆ **020/7626-9496.** Tube: Bank (exit 5).

Jerusalem Tavern This pub pulls a mean pint, supplied by the St. Peter's Brewery in Suffolk. So it's no surprise that the tiny Georgian-style bar, with its open fire, is always packed and getting more so as Clerkenwell zooms up the list of London's coolest neighborhoods. 55 Britton St., EC1. ✆ **020/7490-4281.** Tube: Farringdon.

The Lamb The etched and hinged glass screens stretching round the bar are called snob screens; they were put in so that customers didn't have to see the bartender. Apparently, they were the cat's pajamas at the turn of the last century when such snobby Victorian attitudes really mattered. 94 Lamb's Conduit St., WC1. ✆ **020/7405-0713.** Tube: Oxford Circus.

Lamb & Flag This old timber-framed pub is in a short cul-de-sac off Garrick Street, Covent Garden. The poet Dryden dubbed it the "Bucket of Blood" after he was almost beaten to death here. The Lamb & Flag can be hard to find, but the friendly atmosphere and list of 30 whiskies are ample reward for the effort. The food is good traditional pub grub, and there's free live jazz from 7:30pm on Sunday evenings. 33 Rose St., WC2. ✆ **020/7497-9504.** Tube: Leicester Sq.

London's Best Cocktails

Last seen several decades ago sporting a kitschy paper umbrella and a glacé cherry, the cocktail is making a huge comeback in London, but this time, it's very, very classy (and pretty expensive). Also check out The Bar at Villandry (p. 141) and Soho Spice (p. 138).

- **A White Lady at the American Bar of the Savoy** Best for paying homage to London's first "mixologist," American barman Harry Craddock, who invented the delicious mix of gin, lemon juice, and Cointreau. A splurge at £10 ($18). Dress very elegantly. Open 11am to 11pm. Savoy Hotel, Strand, WC2 (✆ **020/7836-4343;** Tube: Charing Cross).
- **Pimms on the River Terrace of Somerset House** Best for some enchanted evening, weather permitting, and if you can ignore the embankment traffic noise, as you sip the quintessential English summer tipple of Pimms, lemonade, ginger ale, fresh fruit, and mint for £6 ($11). Open 10am to 11pm, April to September. Somerset House, Strand, WC2 (✆ **020/7845-4600;** Tube: Charing Cross).
- **A Dekamron at the Lab** Best for hangin' with the 20-somethings tasting Soho's finest fruity flavors, like this mix of Myer's and coconut rums; papaya, fresh lime, and apple juices; cream; and sugar. One's enough at £6 ($11). Open Monday to Friday noon to midnight, Saturday 4pm to midnight, Sunday 4 to 10:30pm. 12 Old Compton St., W1 (✆ **020/7437-7820;** Tube: Leicester Sq. or Tottenham Court Rd.).
- **A YO! Qualude at YO! Below** Best for drinking horizontally on the 30-foot-wide bed at this crazy beer and sake hall, as the mix of Wyborowa vodka, sake, Baileys, and Frangelico puts you in the mood for a Japanese neck massage or tarot reading. Given away at £3.50 ($6.50). Open noon to 11pm daily. 95 Farringdon Rd., EC1 (✆ **020/7841-0790;** Tube: Farringdon).

Market Porter This pub opens from 6 to 8:30am, as well as at the usual times, to cater for the weird working hours of the porters at Borough Market. It's the place to come for an alcoholic reviver after a dawn start of trawling the antiques at the other almost local market, Bermondsey. Locals bewail the recent makeover, but it still has a good selection of real ales. 9 Stoney St., SE1. ✆ **020/7407-2495.** Tube: London Bridge.

Prospect of Whitby Named after a coal barge that operated between Yorkshire and London, this is an atmospheric pub with a fine view of the river. Once frequented by smugglers, thieves, and "Hanging" Judge Jeffries, it dates back to 1520. Take a cab from the Tube station, or turn right and walk along the river. 57 Wapping Wall, E1. ✆ **020/7481-1095.** Tube: Wapping.

Punch Tavern Charles Dickens and a bunch of his friends founded the satirical magazine *Punch* at this pub next to St. Bride's Church. It's known for its brilliant plush Victorian gin-palace interior and Punch-and-Judy memorabilia. 99 Fleet St., EC4. ✆ **020/7353-6658.** Tube: Blackfriars.

Spaniards Inn This romantic Hampstead Heath pub has a lovely garden in summer and hearthside drinking in winter. Part of it dates back to 1585, and many a famous drinker has dallied here—from Keats and Shelley to Dickens and the highwayman Dick Turpin, who stabled his horse across the road. Spaniards Rd., NW3, Hampstead. ✆ **020/8731-6571.** Tube: Hampstead, then no. 210 bus.

Toucan This pub is so tiny that drinkers can barely raise their elbows to sup their Guinness, so they spill out onto the street. As well as pints of the black stuff, Toucan has a selection of fine Irish whiskeys and Galway Bay oysters on the bar menu. 19 Carlisle St., W1. ✆ **020/7437-4123.** Tube: Tottenham Court Rd.

Windsor Castle It's a risky business meeting a friend at the Windsor Castle—the maze of small wood-paneled rooms are always crowded, and you can circle round hopelessly for hours. Come in the summer and enjoy a drink in the lovely walled garden. 114 Campden Hill Rd., W8. ✆ **020/7243-9551.** Tube: Notting Hill Gate.

WINE BARS

Wine lovers will thank their lucky stars for an alternative to the pub, where belch predominates over bouquet. A bottle of house red or white generally costs £10 to £15 ($18–$28), a great deal to share between two or three people, and most wine bars sell a selection by the glass (from £2.50/$4.60). You can almost always eat there, which is why the full reviews are in chapter 6 (look for the "Wine Bars" category in the "Restaurants by Cuisine" section). For great wine lists at more than manageable prices, try: **Bleeding Heart,** Bleeding Heart Yard, off Greville St., EC1 (✆ **020/7242-8238;** Tube: Chancery Lane or Farringdon); and **Cork & Bottle,** 44–46 Cranbourn St., WC2 (✆ **020/7734-7807;** Tube: Leicester Sq.).

10

Easy Excursions from London

Spur-of-the-moment escapes may be great fun, but you won't be laughing when you realize how much you could have saved by making plans at the same time you booked the whole vacation—especially if you're traveling to a hot spot at a hot time in the summer when discount deals are snapped up very quickly. You can arrange tours, trains, and coaches, as well as get helpful advice, at the **Britain & London Visitor Centre,** 1 Regent St., SW1 (no phone; **www.visitbritain.com**), open Monday to Friday 9:30am to 6:30pm, Saturday and Sunday 10am to 4pm (Sat 9am–5pm, June–Oct).

All the excursions in this chapter are doable in 1 day, but if you'd rather make an overnight trip, contact a local tourist office to book a bed. To help you pick a trip, we've put together a calendar of the must-see annual events ("Calendar of Events for London Excursions," below). Again, the tourist offices can fill in any gaps. Also, have a browse through *Frommer's England from $75 a Day.*

1 How to Save on Day-Trippin'

Don't forget to check out additional ideas and information on special passes under "Fifty Money-Saving Tips," in chapter 2.

- **Play the Train Fare Game** Avoid traveling on Fridays when prices soar to profit from the mass exodus of city dwellers. There are dozens of different fares with varying restrictions (see "The Train Ticket Dictionary," below). So always ask for the cheapest, and then decide if it suits your travel plans.
- **Use your All-Zone London Visitor Travelcard for Day Trips** I've discovered that it's often cheaper to buy an All-Zone Travelcard and pay supplemental rail fares to day-trip destinations than it is to buy a separate BritRail pass (see "tip 10" in chapter 2 and "Getting Around," in chapter 3 for more on London Visitor Travelcards). Simply show your All-Zone London Visitor Travelcard at the ticket window of a London train station, and tell the clerk you want to pay the supplemental fare to your destination. This way, your rail fare does not begin until you reach the end of zone 6. You can get to places like Windsor and Cambridge for less than £6 ($11) return.
- **Train Passes** If you expect to make several trips out of London, call **BritRail** (**© 866/BRITRAIL;** www.britrail.com) about the **BritRail London Plus Pass**—before you leave home, as it is only available outside Britain. This flexipass gets you to Windsor, Cambridge, and Oxford, which we've suggested as excursions, as well as to Brighton, Canterbury, and so on. It's $69 for 2 days of travel within an 8-day period, $129 for 4 days of travel within an 8-day period, or $165 for 7 days travel within a 15-day period. Child passes (ages 5–15) are half the adult price. One big benefit: There are no time-of-day restrictions on these passes.

Tips The E-List for Side-Trip Surfing

We've bookmarked a handful of really handy websites for anyone planning a London-plus kind of vacation. The comprehensive U.K. guide and travel e-zine, **www.britannia.com**, is only marred by the high prices of its short-break packages. Lovers of stately homes must surf **www.nationaltrust.org.uk** and **www.english-heritage.org.uk**, the sites for the leading custodians of Britain's heritage.

- **Bus Deals** The leading long-haul bus line is **National Express** (✆ **0870/580-8080;** www.nationalexpress.com). The **Brit Xplorer** pass, available only to non-U.K. passport holders, allows unlimited travel on a set number of consecutive days: 7 days of travel for £79 ($146); 14 days for £139 ($257); or 30 days for £219 ($405). Special discount cards are often available for under-26s and over-60s; check the website for deals.
- **Car Deals** We beg people on bended knee not to drive in London, but the deals at **easyRentacar** are so good that it does make sense for a puttering-about kind of excursion into the English countryside. Daily rates fluctuate according to demand, so book early and you might only have to pay £14 ($27) to have a Mercedes A-Class for a day. You only get 75 free miles. After that, there's a charge of 20p (37¢) a mile. Booking is online only (www.easyrentacar.com).
- **Take an Escorted Tour** Going with a group can save you money, hassle, and precious time. Frames Rickards (✆ **020/7838-3111;** www.framesrickards.co.uk) offers 1-day coach tours of Bath, Salisbury, and Stonehenge for £55 ($102); and **Trafalgar Tours** (✆ **020/7976-5363;** www.trafalgartours.com) coach trips cost £28 ($52) to Windsor—just as a couple of examples. Both companies include entry to the attractions in their prices.
- **Foot-Following The Original London Walks** (✆ **020/7624-3978;** www.walks.com) can get you a discount on a cheap day-return train ticket. It offers **Explorer Days** every Saturday to places like Oxford, Bath, Canterbury, Salisbury, and Stonehenge.
- **Cheap Sleeps** Several of our hot tips for finding a budget London hotel also apply to stopovers. You can make net savings at the excellent **www.laterooms.com**. Mary and Simon Ette, at **The Independent Traveller** (✆ **01392/860807;** www.gowithIT.co.uk), broker self-catering accommodations, both urban and rural. For leisure deals at chain hotels, check out "The Bargain Business," on p. 106. Outside London, youth hostel dorm beds cost £11 to £18 ($20–$35) a night for adults. For addresses countrywide, including in each of our side-trip destinations, and booking, call ✆ **0870/870-8808** (www.yha.org.uk).

CALENDAR OF EVENTS FOR LONDON EXCURSIONS

February

Cambridge University Rag Week. Students dress up and play the fool to raise money for charity. February 23 to March 3.

March

Festival of Easter Walks. Hundreds of themed walks all over the country, exploring local heritage, landscapes, and wildlife, and led for free by members of the Ramblers Association. Call the London HQ for regional contact details (© **020/7339-8500;** www.ramblers.org.uk). March 29 to April 1.

May

Oxford Eights Week. Intercollegiate rowing championship. Usually end of May.

June

Cambridge Strawberry Fair. Free fest of music, arts, and crafts on Midsummer Common (© **01223/560160;** www.strawberry-fair.org.uk). Usually first Saturday of June.

Encaenia. Begowned university bigwigs and lucky dignitaries process at noon through **Oxford** to the Sheldonian Theatre for the bestowing of honorary degrees. June 19.

July

Cambridge Shakespeare Festival. Open-air performances of uncut texts in beautiful grounds of ancient colleges (© **01223/357851** box office; www.cambridgeshakespeare.com). Early July to late August.

Cambridge Folk Festival. Tents go up in the wooded grounds of Cherry Hinton Hall on the edge of Cambridge for one of the oldest folk festivals in Europe, going since 1965. Very family-friendly celebration of bluegrass, gospel, jazz, Irish (including ceilidh), and world music (© **01223/857851;** www.cam-folkfest.co.uk). Usually from Thursday through Sunday of the last weekend in July.

September

St. Giles' Fair. Street mayhem in Oxford, usually the first weekend in September. Windsor Festival. Concerts and events in Windsor Castle, Eton College, and the Wren-designed Guildhall (© 01753/853888; www.windsorfestival.com). Last 2 weeks in September.

The Train Ticket Dictionary

These are the fares most likely to suit budget-travelers on an excursion from London. You can hunt down fares and book online at **www.thetrainline.com**.

- **Cheap day returns** For round-trip journeys under 50 miles, leaving London after 9:30am. No need to book specific train times. An ordinary **day-return** ticket allows travel during peak times.
- **Network Away Break** No need to book specific trains but not available on some peak services. Return journey must be within 5 days.
- **Super APEX** Selected services only, off-peak. Must be purchased 14 days before departure with fixed dates and times for both halves of the journey.
- **APEX** Selected services only, mostly off-peak. Must be purchased a week in advance with fixed dates and times for departure and return.
- **Super Advance** Must be bought by 6pm the day before departure with fixed times and dates, mostly off-peak.
- **Supersaver return** Walk on, but not within the morning and evening rush hours. Not available on a Friday.
- **Standard return** A no-restriction splurge.

2 Windsor & Eton

21 miles W of London

Surrounded by gentle hills and lush valleys, this pretty riverside town—which the ancient Britons called Windlesore—is famous for two things: an enormous royal fortress and a very posh private boys school. You'll need at least 1½ hours to look around Windsor Castle, and that's at a bit of a trot. Take it easy, and make sure to see St. George's Chapel and Queen Mary's Doll House, too, at a pace that lets you really enjoy them. Then take a well-earned lunch break to refuel before one of these three great afternoon options: visit Eton College, for free unless you look round the museum or take a tour; take a boat trip that goes past the school for a smallish fee; or splurge and head for the amazing Legoland theme park.

When planning your trip, keep in mind the following scheduling considerations:

- Windsor Castle is open year-round, but visiting hours are subject to change at short notice; be sure to verify that it's open, especially in June when there are many official engagements.
- If you want to watch the 11am Changing of the Guard from outside the castle, you need to be on High Street by 10:50am; keep in mind that the ceremony takes place on alternate days August through March and never on Sunday.
- Eton College is open to visitors from late March until early October (closed May 28–June 17), with daily guided tours at 2:15 and 3:15pm.
- Legoland is closed November through March.

A WEEK AT A GLANCE

Monday: Summer evening meetings (races) at **Royal Windsor Racecourse** (**© 01753/865234;** www.windsor-racecourse.co.uk). Admission £6 to £20 ($11–$38), under-16s free. Take the Riverbus to the racecourse from just west of Windsor Bridge, paying your £4 ($7) return fare on board. **Saturday:** in the afternoon, Eton boys get to change out of tailcoats and wing collars into *mufti,* or street clothes. **Sunday:** no Changing of the Guard; St. George's Chapel open for services only; Eton boys in *mufti* after church.

ESSENTIALS

GETTING THERE There are two train stations in Windsor: Windsor Central Station and Windsor and Eton Riverside Station; both are about a 10-minute walk from Windsor Castle. South West Trains operates a direct 55-minute service from Waterloo to Windsor & Eton Riverside Station. From Paddington you can get a Thames Train to Windsor Central Station, but the trip requires a change in Slough. On both, a cheap day return ticket costs about £7 ($13); children pay half that. Call **National Rail Enquiries**

Tips More Side Trips from London

Bath, Brighton, Canterbury, and Stratford-upon-Avon are also popular side trips from London, but unfortunately we don't have room to cover them here. For details on how to get to these towns and what to do once you're there, check out *Frommer's England from $75 a Day,* or browse the "Destinations" section of our website, **www.Frommers.com**. For even more options, look for Frommer's *Best Day Trips from London: 25 Great Escapes by Train, Bus or Car.*

(✆ **0845/748-4950**). **Green Line buses** (✆ **0870/608-7261**) leave from Bulleid Way, near Eccleston Bridge behind Victoria Station, and take around 1 hour. Standard day-return tickets cost about £8 ($15) adults, £4 ($7) children; ask about special excursion fares. If you're driving, take the M4 west out of London to exit 6.

ORIENTATION Windsor is one place where there's little chance of getting lost. The castle is so enormous that you can always take your bearings from it. Eton is just on the other side of the river.

VISITOR INFORMATION The **Royal Windsor Information Centre,** 24 High St. (✆ **01753/743900;** www.windsor.gov.uk), is open daily year-round 10am to 5pm (4pm weekdays and most Sun, Oct–Mar; to 5:30pm July–Aug).

CASTLE HILL

Windsor Castle ★★ Windsor Castle lies on a bend in the Thames, surrounded by 4,800 acres of lawn, woodlands, and lakes. With more than 1,000 rooms, it claims to be the largest inhabited castle in the world, and it is certainly one of the oldest, dating back over 900 years. The **State Apartments,** damaged in a 1992 fire and restored to their original appearance, are open to the public as long as the queen isn't in residence—if you see the Royal Standard flying, then you're out of luck. Room after room is filled with fabulous furnishings, tapestries, and paintings by Rembrandt, Canaletto, Van Dyck, Rubens, and Holbein. **St. George's Hall** is decorated with the heraldic arms of more than 800 Knights of the Garter going back to the founder, the Black Prince. The painter of the extraordinary pagan feast on the **King's Dining Room** ceiling got ideas above his station and put himself into the picture. See if you can find his face, or ask one of the guards to point it out.

But for many visitors, the favorite of all the treasures at Windsor Castle is the spectacular **Queen Mary's Doll House.** Designed by Sir Edwin Lutyens, it took 1,000 craftsmen more than 3 years to create. Everything in it actually works, from the plumbing to a tiny electric iron. Even the bottles in the cellar contain a drop of by-now vintage wine.

Edward IV founded **St. George's Chapel,** located within the castle precincts, in 1475. It's one of the finest examples of late-Gothic architecture in Britain. This is where Prince Edward and Sophie Rhys-Jones got married. Ten sovereigns are buried here, including Henry VIII, who completed the chapel, and his third wife, Jane Seymour. St. George is patron saint of the Most Noble Order of the Garter, Britain's highest chivalric order. You can see banners, swords, helms, and crests of each current member, as well as more than 700 metal stall plates, the oldest of which dates back to about 1390. Sadly, many have been lost, including those of the original founders in 1348. Visitors are welcome at Sunday services and also at daily Evensong, at 5:15pm during school terms. Go to the Henry VIII Gate.

The **Changing of the Guard,** when soldiers march to a military band through the town to the castle's Lower Ward, takes place at 11am, from Monday to Saturday between April and June, and on alternate days the rest of the year. You can watch the marching from High Street but to see the actual ceremony, you must be inside the castle.

✆ **01753/831118** (24-hr. info) or 020/7766-7304. www.royalresidences.com. Admission £13 ($23) adults, £11 ($19) seniors and students, £7 ($12) under-17s, £32 ($58) family; if the State Apartments are closed, admission discounted to £6 ($11), £5 ($9) seniors and students, and £3 ($6) under-17s. Castle Mar–Oct daily 9:45am–5:15pm (last entry 4pm); Nov–Feb daily 9:45am–4:15pm (last entry 3pm). Closed when queen in residence (call to check) and Dec 25–26. St. George's Chapel Mon–Sat 10:45am–4:15pm (last entry 4pm).

. . . AND BEYOND

Have a wander through the cobbled streets, known as Guildhall Island, opposite the castle gates. Then turn down the High Street toward the river, which is where all the afternoon options start. Eton is across the bridge. You can catch the shuttle bus for Legoland from either Windsor Central Station on the left, or back at Windsor & Eton Riverside. And boat tours start just upriver from the bridge on the Windsor bank.

It's about a 10-minute walk from the bridge, past several antiques stores, to the most prestigious "public school" in England, **Eton College** ★ (**© 01753/671177;** www.etoncollege.com). Eton has educated many members of the British monarchy (including Prince William and Prince Harry) and British establishment, including 19 prime ministers. The **Lower School** has one of the oldest classrooms in the world (1443). It costs £3.80 ($7) for adults, £3 ($5.50) for seniors and under-15s to look around the Schoolyard, College Chapel, Cloisters, and Museum of Eton Life. The 1-hour tour, at 2:15 and 3:15pm, includes all these, as well as an ambulatory history lesson from the founding of the school in 1440 to the present day; it costs £4.90 ($9) for adults, £4 ($7) seniors and under-15s. No need to book, but call to make sure of the schedule and opening times: late March to mid-April and July through August, 10:30am to 4:30pm; mid-April through June and September, from 2 to 4:30pm.

For a more leisurely peak at Eton, as well as several river islands, posh houses, and Royal Windsor Racecourse, take a **French Brothers boat trip** ★ up the Thames from Barry Promenade. The 2-hour cruise starts every day at 1:30 and 2:30pm (Mar 24–Apr 10, Apr 30–Oct 2) or at 2pm (Apr 11–29, Oct 3–30). Tickets cost £7 ($13) for adults, £3.50 ($6.50) for children, and £18 ($32) for a family. Cheaper quickie tours, lasting 35 minutes, leave every half-hour from 11am to 5pm and cost £4.50 ($8) for adults, £2.25 ($4) for children, and £11 ($21) for a family ticket. Call **© 01753/851900** (www.boat-trips.co.uk) for info.

Few theme parks are as impressive as **Legoland** ★★ *Kids*, Windsor Park (**© 0870/ 5040404;** www.legoland.co.uk). It took 20 million of the famous Danish toy company's little plastic building bricks just to create Miniland, one of seven different zones offering over 50 attractions and rides—wet ones, high ones, fast ones, and scaled-down ones for little kids. The shuttle bus from either train station is free with a pre-booked Legoland ticket. And it is essential to book, not only to get the £1 ($1.85) discount on at-the-gate ticket prices, but because queues can be terminally long on school holidays. You can buy over the phone, online, and at train stations between Waterloo and Windsor.

One-day admission is £24 ($44) adults, £22 ($41) under-16s (under-3s free). These are peak, at-the-gate prices; you can save several pounds by going "off peak" (week-days, no school holidays), booking online, or purchasing a combined train/Legoland day ticket. Legoland is open daily mid-March through October 10am to 6pm, closing at 5pm Tuesday to Thursday.

WHERE TO EAT

Peascod Street and **Church Lane,** Windsor, are both good cruising grounds for cafes, delis, and good old-fashioned public houses.

Gilbey's Bar & Restaurant ★ WINE BAR This specialist importer sells its French wines at shop prices alongside bottles from its own English vineyard. The bar menu is delicious and reasonable—perhaps a starter of soup with crusty bread, for around £4 ($7), followed by a double-size portion of smoked haddock fishcakes. The set menu is an excellent value and will save you a few pence off the heavier restaurant prices. In the summer, you can eat out in the garden.

82–83 High St., Eton. ✆ **01753/854921.** Bar main courses £7.95 ($15); 2-course set menu £10 ($18). AE, DC, MC, V. Mon–Fri noon–2:30pm; Sat–Sun noon–3pm; daily 6–11pm.

3 Cambridge

55 miles N of London

Cambridge and Oxford compete fiercely in everything. Oxford is grander and older. A thriving town before the first college opened its doors, it has a busy industrial area, now centered around the Science Park. Cambridge has a gentler, quieter air and a more immediately captivating beauty. But behind the lazy romance of this town on the banks of the Cam is a dot.com business boom. Ever since Microsoft set up its European research center here, Cambridge has become known as "Silicon Fen."

Settled by the Romans, the city did not begin to flourish until the 13th century when the first college was founded. Cambridge University now has 31 colleges, the grounds of which are open to the public. Some are worth visiting, others less so, and admission fees can quickly add up. I recommend a trip to the Fitzwilliam Museum, Kettle's Yard, King's College Chapel, and then one or two of the colleges before taking a punt out on the river. During the summer holidays, the colleges are crowded with visitors.

Note: Many of the colleges close during exam periods (May–June) and are open for limited hours during terms, which generally run from mid-January to mid-March, late April to mid-June, and early October to early December.

A WEEK AT A GLANCE

Monday: Fitzwilliam Museum and Kettle's Yard closed. **Saturday:** craft market takes over All Saints Passage, opposite Trinity Hall. **Sunday:** farmers' market in Market Square, plus an art, craft, and antiques market.

Note: There is a general market, selling everything from fish to fruit to fripperies, every day but Sunday in Market Square.

ESSENTIALS

GETTING THERE Trains depart from King's Cross station as often as every 15 minutes; the trains at 15 minutes or 45 minutes past the hour are the fastest, taking about 45 minutes; otherwise, the trip is about an hour. A cheap day return costs £18 ($34). From Cambridge station, take the Cityrail bus to Market Square; fare is 80p ($1.50). Call **National Rail Enquiries** (✆ **0845/748-4950**) for train information. **National Express buses** (✆ **0870/580-8080**) leave from London's Victoria Coach Station, take 1 hour and 55 minutes, and cost £15 ($29) same-day return. If you're driving from London, take the M11 motorway to exit 11.

ORIENTATION Cambridge (pop. 111,000) has two main streets. **Trumpington Road**—which becomes Trumpington Street, King's Parade, Trinity Street, and finally St. John's Street—runs parallel to the River Cam. It's close to several of the city's colleges. **Bridge Street,** the city's main shopping zone, starts at Magdalene Bridge; it becomes Sidney Street, St. Andrew's Street, and finally Regent Street.

VISITOR INFORMATION The **Tourist Information Centre (TIC),** Wheeler Street (✆ **01223/322640;** www.visitcambridge.org/visitors), is behind the Guildhall. It'll tell you everything you need to know about transportation and sightseeing, and has useful maps as well. The office is open all year Monday to Friday 10am to 5:30pm, and Saturday 10am to 5pm; from Easter through September it's also open on Sunday from 11am to 4pm.

The TIC **Accommodation Booking Service** (✆ **01223/457581**) charges a £3 ($5.50) fee for advance and phone reservations—£5 ($9) if you turn up and need a bed that night—and requires a 10% deposit. It operates from 9:30am to 4pm Monday to Friday.

WALKS & TOURS

Two-hour walking tours leave from the Tourist Information Centre at 1:30pm year-round, with additional tours at 10:30am and 2:30pm Monday through Saturday in July and August, and at 11:30am from October through March. Tickets are £8.50 ($16) for adults, £4 ($7) for children under 12, and include entrance to King's College Chapel. For more info on guided tours, call ✆ **01223/457574.**

VISITING THE COLLEGES

You won't have time to see all the colleges. And some are frankly not worth the admission charges of between £2 and £3.50 ($3.70–$6.50), so below are a few recommendations. A great way to see a lot more of them, from the outside, is to take a stroll along **the Backs**—the meadows between the colleges and the Cam. This swath of green takes you up to **St. John's Bridge,** a replica of the Bridge of Sighs in Venice. ***Note:*** Many of the colleges are closed to visitors during Easter Term (late Apr to mid-June).

The undoubted must-visit is **King's College** ★★ (✆ **01223/331100;** www.kings.cam.ac.uk/visitors), founded by Henry VI in 1441. The chapel is internationally famous for its choir and the traditional Festival of Nine Lessons and Carols, which is broadcast every Christmas Eve. It has incredibly beautiful fan vaulting, stained-glass windows, and a screen given by Henry VIII that bears his initials and those of his queen at the time, Anne Boleyn. Behind the altar is Rubens' *Adoration of the Magi,* painted in 1634. A small exhibition hall holds a display about the chapel's history.

Go for a choral service (Mon–Sat at 5:30pm, Sun at 10:30am and 3:30pm, call to check) for the full experience, but only during university terms and during the first half of July. Then, the chapel is open Monday through Saturday 9:30am to 3:30pm, Sunday 1:15 to 2:15pm. During vacation, it's open Monday through Saturday 9:30am to 4:30pm, Sunday 10am to 5pm. The chapel is closed December 26 through January 1, and often without notice for recording sessions and rehearsals, so it's always a good idea to call or check on the website before visiting. Admission is £4.50 ($9) for adults, £3 ($5.50) for students, seniors, and children (children under 12 enter free if visiting with their families).

Founded by Henry VIII in 1546, **Trinity College** (✆ **01223/338400;** www.trin.cam.ac.uk) is the largest and wealthiest of Cambridge's colleges. It has produced 29 Nobel Laureates. Famous alumni include the scientist Sir Isaac Newton; poets and writers Francis Bacon, Lord Tennyson, Lord Byron (who reputedly bathed naked in the large central fountain), Andrew Marvell, and John Dryden; and philosopher Bertrand Russell. Traditionally, students try to run around the 2-acre courtyard in the time it takes the clock to strike 12, a scene you may remember from the movie *Chariots of Fire.* Note the statue of Henry VIII on the Great Gate clutching a chair leg instead of a sword—the result of a student prank. The impressive **Wren Library** was designed by

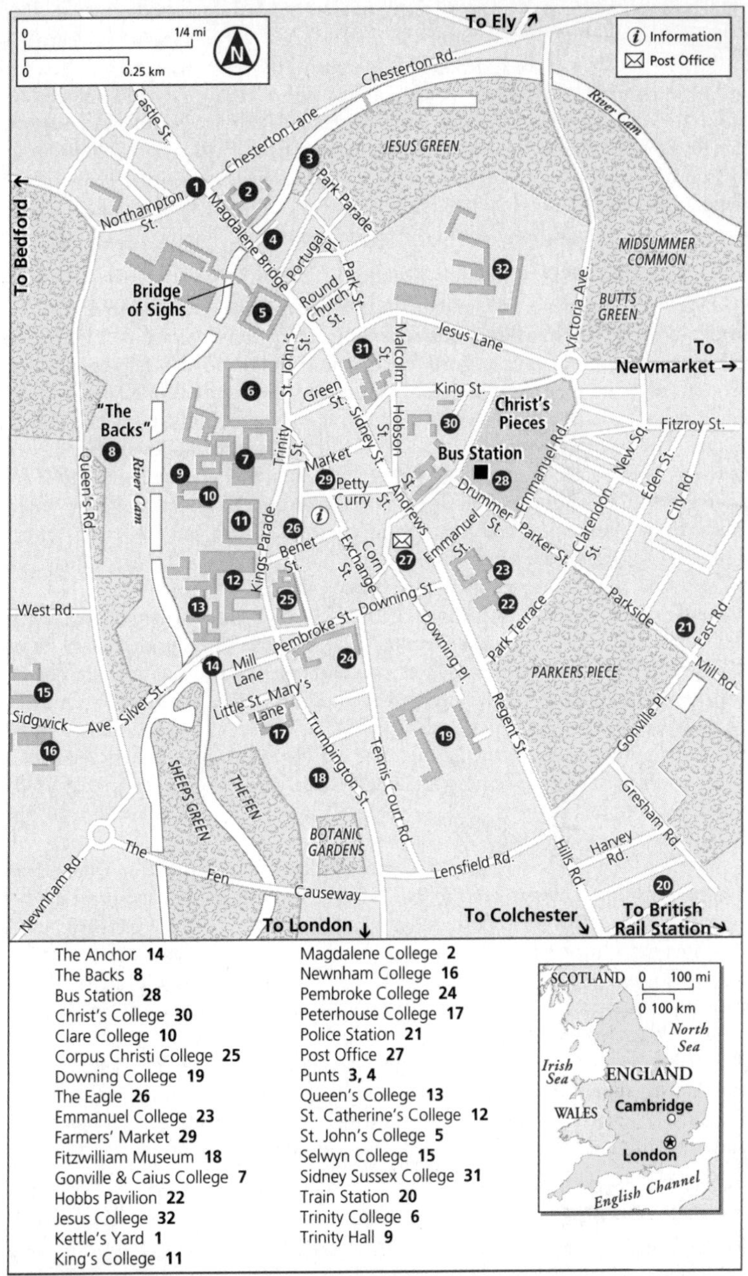
0 1/4 mi
0 0.25 km
N
To Ely
Information
Post Office
Chesterton Rd.
River Cam
Castle St.
Chesterton Lane
JESUS GREEN
Park Parade
To Bedford
Northampton St.
Magdalene Bridge
Portugal Pl.
Park St.
MIDSUMMER COMMON
Bridge of Sighs
Round Church St.
Victoria Ave.
BUTTS GREEN
Jesus Lane
Malcolm St.
To Newmarket
St. John's St.
Green St.
King St.
Christ's Pieces
"The Backs"
Trinity St.
Sidney St.
Hobson St.
Fitzroy St.
Queen's Rd.
River Cam
Market
Bus Station
Emmanuel Rd.
New Sq.
Eden St.
Petty Curry St.
St. Andrews St.
Drummer St.
City Rd.
Kings Parade
Benet St.
Corn Exchange St.
Emmanuel St.
Parker St.
Clarendon St.
West Rd.
Downing St.
Parkside
Pembroke St.
Park Terrace
East Rd.
Downing Pl.
Mill Lane
PARKERS PIECE
Mill Rd.
Silver St.
Little St. Mary's Lane
Sidgwick Ave.
Regent St.
Gonville Pl.
Trumpington St.
Tennis Court Rd.
SHEEPS GREEN
THE FEN
Gresham Rd.
BOTANIC GARDENS
Newnham Rd.
The Fen Causeway
Lensfield Rd.
Hills Rd.
Harvey Rd.
To London
To Colchester
To British Rail Station
The Anchor 14
The Backs 8
Bus Station 28
Christ's College 30
Clare College 10
Corpus Christi College 25
Downing College 19
The Eagle 26
Emmanuel College 23
Farmers' Market 29
Fitzwilliam Museum 18
Gonville & Caius College 7
Hobbs Pavilion 22
Jesus College 32
Kettle's Yard 1
King's College 11
Magdalene College 2
Newnham College 16
Pembroke College 24
Peterhouse College 17
Police Station 21
Post Office 27
Punts 3, 4
Queen's College 13
St. Catherine's College 12
St. John's College 5
Selwyn College 15
Sidney Sussex College 31
Train Station 20
Trinity College 6
Trinity Hall 9
SCOTLAND
0 100 mi
0 100 km
North Sea
Irish Sea
ENGLAND
WALES
Cambridge
London
English Channel

Sir Christopher himself and holds many original works by famous former students. Admission is £2.20 ($4.10) for adults, or £1.30 ($2.40) for seniors and students.

Queens' College (✆ **01223/335511**) is arguably the prettiest of them all. Founded in 1448, it is named for Margaret of Anjou, the wife of Henry VI, and Elizabeth, wife of Edward IV. The most spectacular parts are the 16th-century **President's Lodge** and the Tower, where the great scholar, Erasmus, lived from 1510 to 1514. Other places to stop in include **Magdalene** (pronounced "*Maud*-len"), to view the Pepys Library, the diarist's collection of 3,000 volumes; and **Jesus College,** for the chapel's stained-glass windows designed by Edward Burne-Jones and its ceiling by William Morris.

. . . AND BEYOND

If you enjoy museums and galleries, there are two exceptional **freebies** to visit here in Cambridge. The **Fitzwilliam Museum** ★, Trumpington Street (✆ **01223/332900;** www.fitzmuseum.cam.ac.uk), is an eclectic treasure house of Chinese jades and bronzes, pages from beautiful Books of Hours, and the first draft of Keats's "Ode to a Nightingale," as well as china, glass, majolica, silver, clocks, and a good Egyptian collection. The paintings range from medieval and Renaissance works to contemporary canvases. Feast your eyes on Titian's *Tarquin and Lucretia,* Rubens's *The Death of Hippolytus,* brilliant etchings by Van Dyck, rare Hogarths, 25 Turners, works by William Blake, the Impressionists, and more recent artists Paul Nash and Sir Stanley Spencer. The new Courtyard Café serves coffee, tea, and lunch. Open Tuesday to Saturday 10am to 5pm, and Sunday 2:15 to 5pm. Closed December 23 to January 1.

Kettle's Yard ★, Castle Street (✆ **01223/352124;** www.kettlesyard.co.uk), is a very different kettle of fish. Jim Ede was the curator at the Tate during the 1920s and 1930s. He and his wife Helen acquired this collection of artworks, furniture, and decorative objects, displayed as he arranged them in his home. You'll find work by Ben Nicholson, Christopher Wood, and Alfred Wallis, and sculptures by Henry Moore, Henri Gaudier-Brzeska, Brancusi, and Barbara Hepworth. The gallery, meanwhile, holds exhibitions of 20th-century art. The house is open Tuesday to Sunday 1:30 to 4:30pm (2–4pm in winter), and the gallery Tuesday to Sunday 11:30am to 5pm. Closed December 24 through 28 and January 1.

"Punting," or pole-boating, is a Cambridge tradition, and the venerable **Scudamore's Punting Company** ★ (✆ **01223/359750;** www.scudamores.com) has been operating since 1910. It's important that you call ahead to reserve a punt (you can do it online, too). It costs £14 ($27) an hour to hire a punt weekdays (£16/$30 an hour weekends), and you have to leave a £60 ($111) refundable deposit. Head for the Mill Lane punting station, next to The Anchor pub (see below), or the one by Magdalene Bridge. Both are open daily, from 9am to dusk, April through September, and from 10am October through March. The main boatyard, also in Mill Lane, keeps the same summer schedule, and opens at weekends only, 10am to dusk, from October through March. The Jesus Green punting station operates June through August, 10am to 6pm, and weekends only, from 10am to dusk, in April, May, September, and October. Scudamore's also organizes "chauffered" punting tours.

WHERE TO DINE

Raid the market for picnic provisions, and then head to the Backs for an idyllic alfresco lunch by the Cam. Magical!

The Anchor PUB Looking out on a raft of punts and the willow-fringed river, The Anchor is loaded with atmosphere—beams, sloping ceilings, and odds and ends like cider pots and prints. It serves traditional homemade English pub grub, from battered cod and plaice to lamb-and-vegetable or leek-and-potato pies, or sausage, egg, and chips. Come here for real ale, as well as the usual selection of lagers and bitters.

Silver St. ✆ **01223/353554.** Lunch £2.25–£6 ($4.20–$11). MC, V. Food served Mon–Thurs noon–7:45pm; Fri–Sat noon–3:45pm; Sun noon–2:30pm.

The Eagle ★ PUB This ivy-covered pub has a lovely galleried courtyard that serves as a beer garden. Inside are two bars and three sitting areas with scrubbed wood tables. Burned into the ceiling of the Air Force bar are the names and numbers of wartime officers. The Eagle has culinary aspirations—its five daily specials range from shark steak to Cajun chicken.

Benet St. ✆ **01223/505020.** Lunch £3.50–£5.95 ($6.50–$11); evening main courses £5–£11 ($9–$21). Food served Sun–Thurs noon–9pm; Fri–Sat noon–8pm.

4 Oxford

57 miles NW of London

Oxford contrasts dramatically with Cambridge. It's a modern, crowded, and busy place where town seriously competes with gown. After all, people were living here two centuries before the founding of the first college. Although scholars and students began to congregate as early as the 12th century, Oxford University didn't receive its charter from the Papal Legate until 1214. From 1249, colleges began popping up like mushrooms, starting with University, then Balliol in 1263, and Merton in 1264. Originally, they were men only. The first one for women, Lady Margaret Hall, was established in 1878. In 1975, some of the men's colleges began admitting women, and the rest reluctantly followed.

Wedged between the Thames and Cherwell rivers, Oxford has more than 600 buildings listed for historical or architectural interest. If you really want to uncover the nooks and crannies, the history and personalities, read *Oxford* by Jan Morris.

A WEEK AT A GLANCE

Monday: Ashmolean Museum and Museum of Modern Art closed. **Wednesday:** general market at Gloucester Green. **Thursday:** flea market, same place; also farmers' market the first Thursday of the month. **Saturday:** additional official tour of Oxford at 1:45pm, starting at Carfax Tower and usually including a visit to Christ Church. **Sunday:** same additional tour as Saturday; Sheldonian Theatre closed; no tours of the Bodleian Library.

ESSENTIALS

GETTING THERE Trains depart from London's Paddington Station and make the trip to Oxford in about 1 hour. A cheap day return ticket costs £16 ($30). Call **National Rail Enquiries** (✆ **0845/748-4950**). **National Express buses** (✆ **0870/580-8080**) take 1 hour and 40 minutes; the day-return fare from Victoria Coach Station is £8 ($15). If you're in a car, take the M40 to the A40, which takes you to the A420. Don't drive into the city center, however, as parking and traffic are horrific. There are **Park and Ride** car parks on the main approaches to the north, south, and west sides of the city. Buses run regularly from there into the heart of the city (parking is free; there's a small charge for the bus).

ORIENTATION Known as **Carfax,** the city center radiates out around the crossroads where Cornmarket Street, St. Aldate's Street, Queen Street, and High Street meet. Most of the colleges are to the east, with **Magdalen Bridge** beyond the eastern end of High Street. The bus station and the tourist information center are in the northwest corner of Carfax, while the train station is farther west, across the canal, about a 10-minute walk.

VISITOR INFORMATION The **Oxford Information Centre,** Broad Street (✆ **01865/726871;** www.visitoxford.org), is open year-round Monday to Saturday 9:30am to 5pm, and on Sunday April through October from 10am to 3:30pm. As well as selling maps and providing brochures for local sights and attractions, the center has an accommodations booking service, which charges a £4 ($7.40) fee and takes a refundable 10% deposit. Cheap sleeps are scarce in the middle of Oxford, but the main roads out of town are lined with affordable B&Bs—fine if you don't mind a bus ride or healthy walk.

For more information and a handy what's-on guide, surf **www.oxfordcity.co.uk**. Otherwise, **Oxford University's** website (www.ox.ac.uk) is refreshingly visitor friendly and better than the phone (✆ **01865/270000**) as a one-stop info shop on all the colleges and museums, what to see and when.

WALKS & TOURS

Two-hour tours, costing £6.50 ($12) for adults or £3 ($5.50) for under-16s, leave from the center: Sunday through Thursday at 11am, 1 and 2pm; Friday at 11am and 1pm; Saturday at 10:30 and 11am and 1pm. On Friday and Saturday there are tours of Christ Church at 2pm; the cost is £7.50 or £3.50 ($14 or $6.50). You can pick up more details at the information center.

Citysightseeing Oxford (✆ **01865/790522**), which you can hop on at the train station, travels through the city on double-decker buses and covers all the main sights. You can hop on and off as you like. Tickets cost £9 ($17) for adults, £8 ($15) for seniors, £4 ($7.40) for children, and £20 ($37) for a family of 2 adults and up to 3 children. Buses run every 10 to 15 minutes from 9:30am to 5pm (6pm in summer).

THE DREAMING SPIRES

The Oxford Story, 6 Broad St. (✆ **01865/728822;** www.oxfordstory.org.uk), claims to be the longest "dark ride" in Europe, trundling visitors around the inside of a converted book warehouse. The animatronics are pretty creaky, but they will help put in context what you see during your visit, telling the history of Oxford and student life from the first town-and-gown riots in the 14th century. Open daily July and August from 9:30am to 5pm; September to June Monday through Saturday 10am to 4:30pm, Sunday 11am to 4:30pm. Admission is £6.95 ($13) adults, £5.95 ($11) seniors and students, £5.25 ($10) children (ages 5–15).

A cheaper way to plot out Oxford's dreaming spires is to scale the 97 steps to the top of **Carfax Tower** (✆ **01865/792653**) and have a look out over the rooftops of the colleges and town. It's open daily from 10am to 5:15pm but closes at 3:30pm in winter. Admission is £1.60 ($3) adults, 80p ($1.50) children.

Today there are 45 colleges scattered throughout the city. Most open their quads and chapels in the afternoon only, except for Christ Church, Hertford, New College, St. Hugh's, and Trinity College, which are open in the morning, too. Obviously you can't and probably wouldn't want to visit all of them, so I've picked the best of the bunch for you.

Oxford

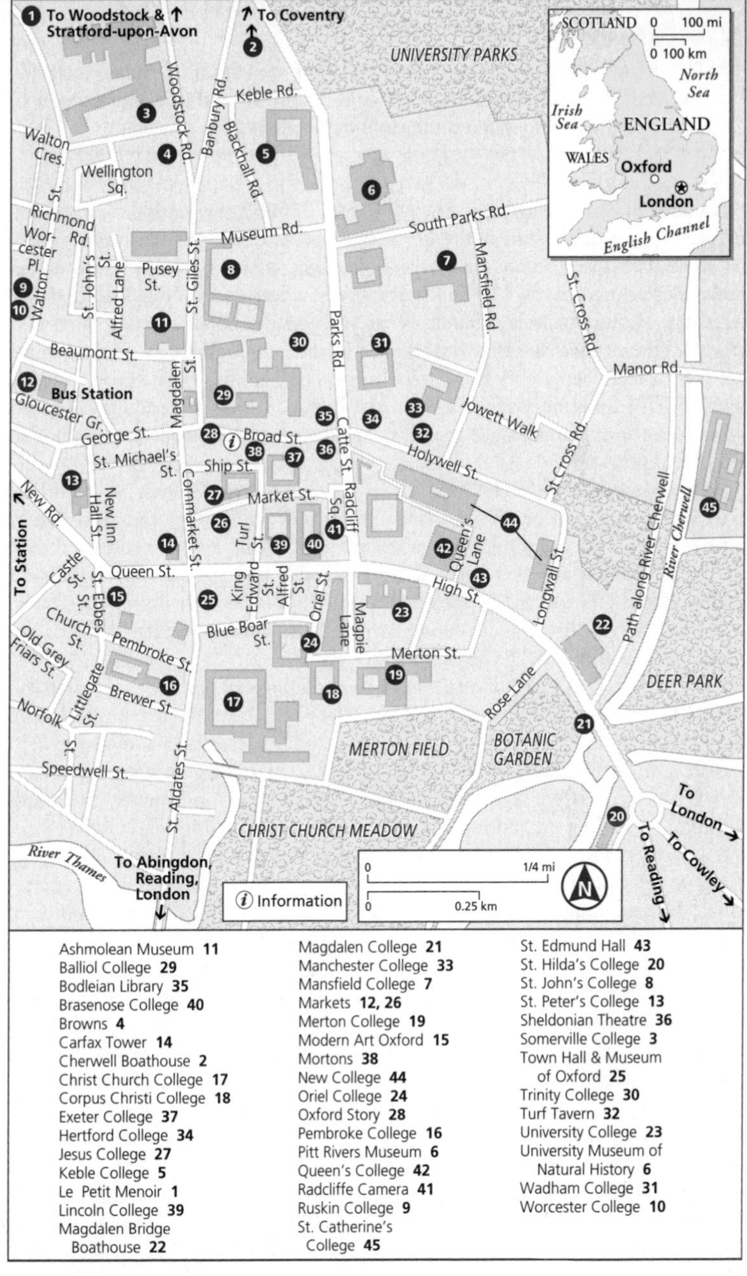

To Woodstock & Stratford-upon-Avon
To Coventry
UNIVERSITY PARKS
SCOTLAND
0 100 mi
0 100 km
North Sea
Irish Sea
ENGLAND
WALES
Oxford
London
English Channel
Keble Rd.
Woodstock Rd.
Banbury Rd.
Blackhall Rd.
Walton Cres.
Wellington Sq.
Richmond Rd.
Worcester Pl.
Walton St.
St. John's St.
Alfred Lane
Pusey St.
St. Giles St.
Museum Rd.
South Parks Rd.
Mansfield Rd.
St. Cross Rd.
Parks Rd.
Beaumont St.
Magdalen St.
Manor Rd.
Bus Station
Gloucester Gr.
George St.
Broad St.
Jowett Walk
Holywell St.
St. Michael's St.
Ship St.
Catte St.
Radcliff Sq.
Market St.
New Rd.
New Inn Hall St.
Cornmarket St.
Turl St.
Queen's Lane
Longwall St.
Path along River Cherwell
River Cherwell
To Station
Castle St.
Queen St.
King Edward St.
Alfred St.
Oriel St.
Magpie Lane
High St.
St. Ebbes St.
Church St.
Blue Boar St.
Pembroke St.
Merton St.
Old Grey Friars St.
Littlegate St.
Brewer St.
Norfolk St.
Rose Lane
DEER PARK
MERTON FIELD
BOTANIC GARDEN
Speedwell St.
St. Aldates St.
CHRIST CHURCH MEADOW
To London
To Cowley
To Reading
River Thames
To Abingdon, Reading, London
Information
0 1/4 mi
0 0.25 km
N
Ashmolean Museum 11
Balliol College 29
Bodleian Library 35
Brasenose College 40
Browns 4
Carfax Tower 14
Cherwell Boathouse 2
Christ Church College 17
Corpus Christi College 18
Exeter College 37
Hertford College 34
Jesus College 27
Keble College 5
Le Petit Menoir 1
Lincoln College 39
Magdalen Bridge Boathouse 22
Magdalen College 21
Manchester College 33
Mansfield College 7
Markets 12, 26
Merton College 19
Modern Art Oxford 15
Mortons 38
New College 44
Oriel College 24
Oxford Story 28
Pembroke College 16
Pitt Rivers Museum 6
Queen's College 42
Radcliffe Camera 41
Ruskin College 9
St. Catherine's College 45
St. Edmund Hall 43
St. Hilda's College 20
St. John's College 8
St. Peter's College 13
Sheldonian Theatre 36
Somerville College 3
Town Hall & Museum of Oxford 25
Trinity College 30
Turf Tavern 32
University College 23
University Museum of Natural History 6
Wadham College 31
Worcester College 10

Fun Fact **Time for Bed**

At 9:05pm every evening, the 7-ton "Great Tom" bell at Christ Church tolls 101 times. The tradition dates from the time when each chime represented a scholar and the tolling marked the closing of college.

Founded in 1458, **Magdalen** ★★ (✆ **01865/276000;** www.magd.ox.ac.uk), pronounced "*Maud*-len," is one of the largest and most beautiful of the colleges—the hall has some particularly lovely carved-wood paneling. Its tower (1492–1509) is a city landmark from which, on May mornings, you can hear the glorious pealing of bells. Magdalen alumni include Thomas Wolsey, Edward Gibbon, Oscar Wilde, and Edward, Prince of Wales. The college is open October through June from 1pm to dusk and July through September from noon to 6pm. The admission charge is £3 ($5.50) or £2 ($3.70) for seniors and students. The Botanic Gardens, meadows, and Grove (where deer have roamed since the 1700s) that surround the college make it a very peaceful retreat.

Built on the site of St. Frideswide's Monastery, **Christ Church** ★ (✆ **01865/276150;** www.chch.ox.ac.uk) dates from 1546 and is both college and cathedral. The latter contains some beautiful medieval stained glass, including a depiction of the martyrdom of Thomas à Becket, and the St. Frideswide and St. Catherine windows by Edward Burne-Jones. Charles I took up residence in the Deanery during the civil war, when Oxford was his military headquarters. Sir Christopher Wren designed **Tom Tower** (1682), at the college gate.

The dining hall at Christ Church has a fine collection of portraits, including those of notable graduates William Penn, W. E. Gladstone, John Wesley, Anthony Eden, and Lewis Carroll. Old Masters, Russian icons, and English glass are on display in the **Picture Gallery** (✆ **01865/276172;** admission £2/$3.20); its entrance is on Canterbury Quad. The college is open year-round from 9am to 5pm Monday to Saturday, and from 11 to 5pm on Sunday. You can visit the dining hall from 10:30am to noon and 2:30 to 4:30pm; the Picture Gallery is open 10:30am to 1pm and 2 to 4:30pm. Times at the cathedral vary depending on choir practices, concerts, and services, of which there are four on Sunday. Evensong is at 6pm weekdays. Admission to Christ Church is £4 ($7) adults, £3 ($5.50) concessions (seniors, people with disabilities)—£1 ($1.85) less if any parts of the college are closed to visitors.

The chapel at **New College** (1379) is one for art buffs: It has some very famous works, including Epstein's *Lazarus* and El Greco's *St. James,* as well as fine stained-glass windows and beautifully carved choir stalls. The paneled hall is the oldest in Oxford.

Corpus Christi (1517) is a small college that somehow managed to retain most of its silver and other valuables through all the turbulent episodes in Oxford's past. It also has a charming sundial topped by a pelican in the middle of the front quad, and in the chapel there's an altarpiece, *The Adoration of the Shepherds,* attributed to Rubens. **Hertford** (1874) has its own Bridge of Sighs. Capability Brown laid out the gardens at **St. John's** (1555). And if you want to tread in Bill Clinton's footsteps, visit **University College,** where he was a Rhodes Scholar in 1968.

. . . AND BEYOND

The attractions below are ranked subjectively by entertainment value. It is up to you how to mix and match them. Bear in mind that the Pitt Rivers Museum is only open for a few hours in the afternoon. The bustling **covered market** ★, which links Market Street and High Street, has fed the burghers of Oxford since 1774. It's a great place to take a breather from nonstop sightseeing, as well as to grab food for a picnic out on the river.

Back on the history trail, let's start with a fabulous **freebie.** Founded in 1683, the **Ashmolean Museum** ★★, Beaumont Street (© **01865/278000;** www.ashmol.ox.ac.uk), is England's oldest public museum. It's the sort of place where you don't quite believe what you're seeing is for real—things like Guy Fawkes's lantern, Henry VIII's stirrups and hawking gear, and the mantle said to have belonged to Powhatan, father of Pocahontas. It has a terrific archaeology collection, too, with Egyptian mummies, casts of Greek sculptures, silver, ceramics, and bronzes. The paintings include works by da Vinci, Raphael, and Rembrandt. The Ashmolean is open Tuesday through Saturday 10am to 5pm, Sunday 2 to 5pm. From June through August, hours extend to 7pm on Thursdays.

Just off Broad Street you'll find the famous 1602 **Bodleian Library** (© **01865/277224;** www.bodley.ox.ac.uk), which contains more than 5 million books. You can visit the gift shop, but tours of the library itself cost £4 ($7.50).The library's **Radcliffe Camera** (1748) is England's earliest round reading room, designed by James Gibbs. The only way Joe Public can look around is to take a separate tour, at 10:30am, 11:30am, 2pm, and 3pm from Monday to Friday, April through September; and mornings only during summer weekends and over the winter. This is a working library and it is also often closed for university ceremonies, so call ahead to make sure the schedule isn't disrupted. Tickets cost £3.50 ($6.50).

To see where the university bestows honorary degrees during the Encaenia ceremony (June 26), visit the **Sheldonian Theatre** (© **01865/277299**). This concert hall was Sir Christopher Wren's first commission, completed in 1669. The interior is made entirely of wood except for the ceiling, which consists of 36 panels painted by Robert Streeter, court painter to Charles II. It's open Monday to Saturday 10am to 12:30pm and 2 to 4:30pm (to 3:30pm mid-Nov–Mar), but call ahead to check. Admission is £1.50 ($2.75) adults, £1 ($1.85) children ages 15 or under.

The **University Museum of Natural History** ★, Parks Road (© **01865/270949;** www.oum.ox.ac.uk), shows off a good collection of dinosaur skeletons and other curiosities in a marvelous glass-roofed Victorian hall. Admission is free. The **Pitt Rivers Museum** ★★ (© **01865/270949;** www.prm.ox.ac.uk), entered from the Natural History Museum, is also free, and it's like taking a tour through the pages of *National Geographic.* General Pitt Rivers gave his collection of ethnic artifacts to the university in 1884, and there are now more than half a million objects in old-fashioned cases crammed into a dimly lit room. The spookiest section is on magic; there's a 17th-century silver phial said to have a witch trapped inside. Most redolent of adventure are the 150 pieces collected during Captain Cook's second voyage, from 1773 to 1774, including a Tahitian mourner's costume. Arranged by type, rather than geography or date, the exhibits demonstrate how different peoples tackled the same tasks. The Pitt Rivers is open Monday through Saturday noon to 4:30pm and on Sunday from 2 to 4:30pm.

Modern Art Oxford on Pembroke Street (© **01865/722733;** www.modernartoxford.org.uk) could hardly be more of a contrast. This leading center for contemporary visual arts holds ever-changing exhibitions of sculpture, architecture, photography, video, and other media. It's open Tuesday through Saturday 10am to 5pm, and Sunday noon to 5pm. Admission is free. Café Varvara is a great place for a breakfast, lunch, or tea-time snack stop. It opens at 9:30am from Tuesday to Saturday, and nothing costs much more than £5 ($9).

Punting, or pole-boating, is as traditional in Oxford as it is in Cambridge. Both the hire companies below are on the River Cherwell and operate every day from March to October only. **Howard C & Son** ★, Magdalen Bridge Boathouse (✆ **01865/202643**), hires out punts, rowing boats, and pedalboats for £9 to £12 ($17–$23) an hour, plus £30 ($55) deposit, from 10am to dusk. **Cherwell Boathouse,** Bardwell Road (✆ **01865/515978**), charges £10 to £12 ($18–$23) an hour for a punt, with a £50 to £60 ($92–$111) deposit, from 10am to 6pm.

WHERE TO DINE

Browns TRADITIONAL BRITISH This large, casual, upbeat brasserie is one of the best places to eat in Oxford. It serves hearty food, including a good traditional cream tea, and has a large convivial bar and a very pleasant outdoor terrace. Mummies and daddies visiting their high-achieving offspring at the university bring them here. There is also a Browns in London (p. 140).

5–11 Woodstock Rd. ✆ **01865/319655.** Main courses £6–£15 ($11–$29). AE, MC, V. Mon–Sat 11am–11:30pm; Sun noon–11:30pm.

Mortons SANDWICHES/LIGHT FARE If you don't want to spend a lot for lunch, stop in at Mortons for a fresh sandwich or a bowl of soup. They make delicious sandwiches on fresh baguettes: Thai chicken, BLT, brie with onion marmalade are some of the choices. You can eat upstairs, in the back garden, or take your sandwich away and picnic elsewhere. They also have a location in the covered market.

22 Broad St. ✆ **01865/200860.** Sandwiches £2.20–£2.50 ($4–$4.60). MC, V. Daily 8:30am–5pm.

The Turf Tavern PUB Tucked away down a cobblestone alley, this delightful pub gets very crowded. It has several bars in a series of long, low-ceilinged rooms decorated with rowing crew portraits and other Oxford memorabilia. The food is traditional grub, ranging from steak-in-ale pie and fish and chips to sandwiches and salads. It also has a good selection of cask ales and a pleasant beer garden.

4 Bath Place. ✆ **01865/243235.** Main courses £5–£7 ($9–$13). Daily noon–7:30pm.

Appendix A: London in Depth

London is the place to see history in the making. Two thousand years of continuous habitation have left their mark on the city's architecture, cuisine, politics, and just about every aspect of culture you can think of. The city is like an ever-expanding time capsule, to which each generation adds its own contribution—from modern streets that still follow the arrow-straight Roman highways, to chic new-wave Indian cuisine that is a legacy of the Empire, to modern skyscrapers wedged in amongst old City churches. This appendix will help you to see beyond the superficial and immerse yourself in a multidimensional London experience.

1 London in the 21st Century

The capital is on the cusp of enormous change. The population has jumped to 7.4 million and is forecasted to top 8 million by 2016. The economy has grown by more than 35% since 1993 (but is currently in a recession that nobody wants to talk about). The public Underground transportation system is failing miserably under the pressure of too many bodies and too little investment. Traffic is so clogged that in 2003 a new "congestion charge" went into effect, forcing commuters who drive into London to pay £5 ($9) for the privilege. Housing is astronomically expensive and in short supply.

Just when Londoners thought it couldn't get much worse, Mayor Ken Livingstone came up with his 20-year plan for London. It involves building new skyscrapers and Tube lines and redistributing some of the wealth from West London by pushing new development east.

Londoners may admire the glossy sentiments, but they ain't holding their collective breath. The wheels of change grind so slowly in Britain's capital that movement is generally imperceptible—unless you're a visitor who's going back for a visit after many years away, in which case you'll see a sleeked-up, more efficiently running city today than you saw back in the 20th century. You'll see that Londoners have rediscovered the South Bank and the entire riverside area from Westminster Bridge to Tower Bridge, and beyond. You'll see a reconfigured Trafalgar Square—suddenly pedestrian-friendly after decades as a traffic island. You'll see new skyscrapers, more passenger service on the river, and gleaming new pedestrian bridges. All kinds of public redevelopment schemes have brought London right up to the nanosecond, making it a better city without sacrificing the hodgepodge of historic charm that has always made London so delectable.

You can thank the mayor of London, Ken Livingston, for many of these improvements—or at least for coercing and shaping the various bureaucracies that rule London. The mayor, who just moved into a fabulous new city hall on the south bank of the Thames, is a scrappy chap, ready to take on anyone. He's had lots of practice, even getting up Prime Minister Tony Blair's nose. The PM, for instance, wants to privatize the Underground. Mayor Ken says, oh no you don't—but let's make it run better by replacing antiquated tracks and equipment over the next few years, which is what's happening right now.

British governments have an expiration date, rather than a set date, for re-election. The prime minister and party pundits read the runes, sniff the air, and poll thousands of voters to find the most propitious moment within their allotted 5-year term to "go to the country." Sniffing the air was a bad idea in 2001, unless you wanted a nose full of burning-cow smoke. Foot and mouth disease ran rampant round the country, forcing the slaughter and burning of hundreds of thousands of bovines and sheep and running roughshod over New Labour's election plans. Instead of sucking up to the voters, Tony B had to suck up to stay-away tourists, trying to persuade them that Britain was open for business.

Then came the September 11, 2001, terrorist attacks. London has had its share of terrorist attacks over the years—crisis is London's middle name. But what's true is that the city is enormously dependent upon tourism, most notably from Americans, and throughout 2002 Americans just weren't traveling as they had done. The same was true during the spring of 2003, when many Americans weren't flying overseas because of the war in Iraq. And then in 2004 and 2005 Americans were dismayed to find their dollar sinking against the British pound, so here was yet another crisis—at least for the Americans, who were shocked at just how bloody expensive everything had become. The news that London ranked second after Tokyo as the most expensive city in the world to visit came as no surprise to anyone who'd been in London recently and paid $15 for fish and chips. The one bright spot was that of all the major overseas tourist destinations, London remained one of the most popular.

In the 2000 election, Tony Blair managed to annihilate the Conservatives. It was the first time ever that Labour won a second term with an outright majority. So it was back to no. 11 Downing Street—no. 10 couldn't accommodate the abundant Blair family. But then a new scandal erupted: Cherie Blair, Tony's Superwoman barrister wife (voted "most powerful woman in Britain" in 2001), got caught in an embarrassing real-estate fiasco. She'd purchased some property on the advice of a chap who turned out to be a crook. Much bigger problems loomed on Tony's horizon in 2003 when he strongly and single-mindedly followed President George Bush's lead and pressed for war with Iraq. His government and a majority of the British population refused to get wholeheartedly behind him on this issue. They are still not behind him, and in the last election, held in May 2005,

Dateline

- **A.D. 43** Londinium settled by Roman invaders.
- **50** London Bridge built across the Thames.
- **61** Boudicca sacks London.
- **190–220** City walls built.
- **350** Saxons invade.
- **410** Romans retreat.
- **457** Londoners take refuge behind city walls.
- **604** First St. Paul's built. Mellitus appointed Bishop of London.
- **886** Alfred the Great takes London from the Danes.
- **1066** William of Normandy (the Conqueror) crowned king.
- **1078** Construction of White Tower begun.
- **1097** William Rufus builds Westminster Hall.
- **1123** St. Bartholomew's Hospital founded.
- **1176–1209** London Bridge built of stone.
- **1192** Henry FitzAilwin elected first mayor of London.
- **1214** King John grants city a charter.
- **1215** Magna Carta signed.
- **1348–49** Black Death sweeps London.
- **1381** Peasants' Revolt.

New Labour lost one-third of its seats. This may be one crisis Tony can't overcome, and he has said that he might be turning over the reins to Gordon Brown in 2006.

Meanwhile, on the royal front, the queen continues to weather her own public-relations storms. She celebrated her Golden Jubilee in 2002, the only monarch besides Queen Victoria to sit on the throne for 50 years. But many of the planned celebrations were PR duds because more and more people see the monarchy as irrelevant and the queen as aloof and out of touch. The poor dear called in the two men behind Britain's most successful breakfast TV show to advise her on how to click with Britain's youth, but guess what—nothing clicked. During her Jubilee year, the queen lost her sister, Princess Margaret, and her mother in the space of a few weeks. And then came yet another royal scandal. Princess Di's former butler was accused by Diana's mother and sister of stealing some of Di's personal effects. Virtually at the last minute, before the case was set to go to trial (and receive enormous media attention), the queen conveniently "remembered" that the butler had, in fact, told her soon after Diana's death that he was removing Diana's property for safekeeping. More than a few eyebrows were raised. Almost everyone assumed that the queen's actions were a last-ditch effort to ward off throne-damaging revelations. But all kinds of nasty royal secrets emerged anyway.

You'd think by now the royals would have learned something about history. But how do you explain what happened in 2005 when Prince Harry, the younger son of Prince Charles and Diana, appeared at a costume party wearing a Nazi uniform? Everyone was shocked by his grotesque insensitivity, and Harry was forced into a public apology. Following that, there were accusations from one of Harry's art teachers at Eton that she had basically created his graduation "portfolio." And then, of course, the country (and world) was subjected to the mind-numbing scrutiny of Charles' wedding to his unpopular mistress, Camilla Parker Bowles—the one Diana referred to as "the third party in the bed." In comparison to the spectacular pomp and circumstance that attended the wedding of Charles and Diana, the wedding of Charles and Camilla was supposed to be almost nothing more than a formality. But what with rumors flying that the queen wouldn't attend and royal historians speculating that the marriage would be illegal and the burning question of whether or not Camilla would ever be

- **1397** Richard Whittington, a wealthy merchant, elected lord mayor.
- **1401** Water piped in from Tyburn.
- **1455** Wars of the Roses begin.
- **1461** Edward of York crowned king.
- **1483** Richard, Duke of Gloucester, imprisons (and possibly murders) Crown Prince Edward V and his brother; crowns himself Richard III.
- **1485** Henry Tudor defeats Richard at Bosworth. Henry VII launches Tudor dynasty.
- **1509** Henry VIII succeeds to the throne. Marries first of six wives.
- **1513** Henry VIII builds navy and opens dockyards at Deptford and Woolwich.
- **1536–40** Dissolution of the monasteries. Church of England established, with king at head.
- **1553** Mary Tudor made queen. Lady Jane Grey, the "Nine Days' Queen," is executed.
- **1558** Elizabeth I (1558–1603) succeeds to throne.
- **1588** Spanish armada defeated.
- **1599** Globe Theatre built.

continues

called "Queen" (she will, unless legislation is changed to prevent it), the little ceremony at Windsor's civil court turned into an international spectacle of absurdity and irrelevance.

On the cultural front, "democratization" has become the 21st-century buzzword among the once elitist cultural institutions that now scoop up millions of pounds from the state lottery. In late 2001, the government persuaded the national museums to ditch their admission charges, a rare example of successful political meddling in the arts. What this means to you, the visitor to London, is that you don't have to pay a hefty £8 ($15) charge to get into lots of London's world-class museums.

When it comes to entertainment, the arts, and dining, few cities can hold a match to London. The restaurant scene is thriving and constantly evolving as restaurant pioneers turn into empire-builders, leaving space at the bottom of the heap for yet more new ideas and new tastes. The new club-bars provide an intimate antidote while giving the stage to new bands. Meanwhile young British artists have moved en masse to East London, pumping up the excitement there.

Shopaholics still want for nothing in London. The city's streets have become the center of the shopping universe, particularly for anything to do with the twin national obsessions: gardening and home decoration.

These obsessions are probably tangled up with soaring property prices. In London, you have to earn at least £50,000 ($92,000) a year to buy a shoebox. It's rumored that Madonna, who's married to British film director Guy Ritchie and lives in London, paid over £10 million ($18 million) for her town house. Housing prices in the capital have become so outrageous that the government has had to promise help to "key workers"—nurses and teachers, particularly—in order to stop a mass migration out of town.

Like any huge multicultural city, London suffers from homelessness, poverty, drugs, crime, and violence. Even in Southwark—which Tate Modern has turned into one of the most visited boroughs and developers have yuppiefied by turning warehouses into apartments—a growing gap between rich and poor is evident. And yet for all its problems, there remains some essential London magic, distilled, in part, from the very problems that make this city on the Thames so frustrating on the one hand and so exciting on the other. As usual, there's never been a better time to visit London.

- **1600** London expands south of the Thames.
- **1605** Guy Fawkes and his Gunpowder Plot to blow up King James I and Parliament are foiled.
- **1631** Inigo Jones builds Covent Garden.
- **1637** Hyde Park opens to the public.
- **1642–58** Oliver Cromwell leads Parliamentary forces during Civil War and later Protectorate.
- **1649** King Charles I beheaded before the Banqueting House in Whitehall.
- **1660** Monarchy restored under Charles II.
- **1665** Great Plague strikes 110,000 Londoners.
- **1666** Great Fire destroys 80% of the medieval city.
- **1675–1710** Wren rebuilds 51 churches, including St. Paul's.
- **1688** Bloodless Revolution: James II banished; William and Mary invited to throne.
- **1694** Bank of England established.
- **1725** Mayfair developed.
- **1739–53** Mansion House built.
- **1759** British Museum founded.
- **1780** In Gordon Riots, mobs protest against Papists.

2 A Look at the Past

EARLY ROMAN, SAXON & DARK AGE LONDON London is very old by any measure. Archaeologists have unearthed evidence of settlements from as far back as 2500 B.C. Scholars hotly debate the origin of the city's name, but most believe it comes from the Celtic words *Llyn Din,* meaning "lakeside fortress."

The British Isles began to feel the heat of Roman attention in A.D. 43. The invaders were great engineers and put in an impressive infrastructure throughout the empire. Some of London's modern streets follow their original roads—Oxford Street, Bayswater Road, and Edgeware Road, for example. As the Romans settled Britain, they transformed what began as a military base into an important trading center, putting up buildings with tiled roofs and mosaic floors. To see what it looked like then, visit the Museum of London, which has a very effective reconstruction.

Two hundred years later, though, the Empire began to crumble, and the Romans pulled out of Britain. The vacuum created by the sudden loss of a national governing force led to inevitable turmoil. The local tribes had to fend for themselves against Anglo-Saxon invasions.

From the 7th to the early 9th centuries, the tribal kingdoms of Kent, Mercia, Northumbria, and the West Saxons fought each other for control of Britain. Meanwhile, the Viking hordes descended, occupying the Saxon suburb that had grown up around Charing Cross, outside the walls (871–872). The Saxon king Alfred the Great fought back, then in 886 made peace with the Danes. Londoners abandoned the settlement and moved back inside the Roman walls. The population had grown by then to around 12,000.

The rapacious Vikings began raiding again in the late 10th century. London resisted at first but finally had to accept Sweni as king in 1013 and later his son Canute. After the latter's death, Edward, the son of Ethelred the Unready, came to the throne. It was he who moved the court out of the city to a new purpose-built palace on the site of today's Westminster Hall. He also spent a tenth of his income rebuilding the nearby abbey of St. Peter. Not for nothing was the king known as Edward the Confessor. When his beloved wife Eleanor of Castile died in Nottinghamshire, her funeral cortege traveled slowly back to London, and Edward had a cross erected at every overnight stop. Only one survives in London—at Charing

- **1801** First census. Population: 959,000.
- **1802** West Indian Dock opens.
- **1826** University College established.
- **1829** Metro Police established.
- **1832** First Reform Bill enfranchises some property owners.
- **1837** Victoria, 18, succeeds her uncle, William IV.
- **1840s** Influx of Irish immigrants, fleeing famine and political repression.
- **1847** British Museum opens.
- **1851** Hyde Park hosts the Great Exhibition, which finances development of South Kensington.
- **1858** The Great Stink. Royal Opera House opens.
- **1861** Prince Albert dies, sending Victoria into deep mourning and 10 years out of the public eye.
- **1863** The first Underground connects Paddington to the City.
- **1877** First Wimbledon Tennis Championship.
- **1882** Law Courts built in the Strand.
- **1888** London County Council established.
- **1889** Great Dock Strike.

continues

Cross, the last stop on the sad journey. You can visit his tomb in Westminster Abbey.

Edward's death on January 6, 1066, sparked a raging battle for the throne between the Saxons and the Normans—his mother's people. The city's merchants and barons sold their support to the Saxon Harold for the promise of certain rights and privileges. But he fell at the Battle of Hastings, and William the Conqueror marched on London, burned Southwark, and forced a surrender.

MEDIEVAL LONDON William had himself crowned in Westminster. He was smart enough to understand the power the bigwigs wielded, and he fulfilled Harold's promises—though that didn't stop them from fighting for more independence. William granted favored Norman barons tracts of land on which they built huge, fortified, stone houses, known as *burhs.* None survive, but street names such as Bucklersbury and Lothbury tell us where they once stood.

Throughout the 11th century, the old Saxon London of wood and thatch slowly transformed into Norman stone. William began the massive, impregnable White Tower (of the Tower of London) in 1078, not only as a fortification against invaders, but also to intimidate his new London subjects.

But the city fathers went on wielding influence in later battles for the throne. King Stephen (1135–54) only held onto his because Londoners attacked Matilda, daughter of Henry I, and prevented her coronation at Westminster. Later, they kept the rebel William Longchamp in the Tower, and King John (1199–1216) in power. That earned them formal right, later enshrined in the Magna Carta and still in place today, to elect their own leader, the Lord Mayor of London. Which is why the monarch has to ask permission to enter the City.

Wars dominated the whole of the 12th, 13th, and 14th centuries: abroad, in the Crusades, and the Hundred Years' War with France; and at home, with the Wars of the Roses, between the House of Lancaster and the House of York for the English throne. Despite all this strife, London continued to grow and thrive, through trade largely, even though London Bridge was the only way across the Thames. The original wooden bridge was replaced several times, then work started on a stone version in 1176: It was to take 33 years to complete and cost 200 lives. It was 940 feet long, with 20 arches, and had a chapel on top of it, dedicated to Thomas à Becket. Timbered houses lined the 12-foot-wide cobbled roadway. It was across the new London Bridge that the

- **1894** Tower Bridge opens.
- **1900** Coca-Cola arrives in Britain.
- **1901** Queen Victoria dies. Edward VII ascends throne.
- **1907** Central Criminal Court (the Old Bailey) constructed.
- **1910** King Edward VII dies and is succeeded by George V.
- **1914–18** World War I. London bombed from planes and airships.
- **1922** BBC begins broadcasting.
- **1936** King George V dies. Prince of Wales succeeds to throne as Edward VIII but abdicates to marry Wallis Simpson.
- **1937** Edward's younger brother crowned King George VI.
- **1939–45** World War II. Air raids and rocket attacks destroy much of the city: 30,000 killed; 50,000 injured.
- **1947–48** New influx of Commonwealth immigrants.
- **1948** London hosts Summer Olympics.
- **1951** Royal Festival Hall opens.
- **1952** King George VI dies.
- **1953** Queen Elizabeth II crowned in first nationally-televised coronation ceremony.

medieval kings of England set out to Crécy, Poitiers, and Agincourt. And they impaled the heads of traitors on the gate at the southern end (one foreign visitor in the 16th c. counted 30 on display).

The River Thames was the city's main highway. It cost only 2p to travel from London to Westminster in 1372. Wharves lined the banks, each one assigned a particular type of cargo. There were a few roads wide enough for 16 knights to ride abreast (dubbed royal roads), but most were narrow, unpaved, and badly maintained.

London's wealth grew out of the wool trade, in particular; sheep outnumbered people 300 to 1. A handful of merchants controlled the market, which was exporting a million yards of cloth to Europe by the 1480s. Other industries flourished, too. In 1422, the clerk of the Brewers Company recorded 111 city trades—drapers, soapmakers, cordwainers, goldsmiths, vintners, haberdashers, and many more. The guilds set standards, trademarks, and prices, and arranged pensions for their members. As prosperity grew, they built impressive halls. Many survive today, though often in 19th-century incarnations: Drapers' Hall, Fishmongers' Hall, and Goldsmiths' Hall, for instance. You can see the companies' banners flying in the Guildhall.

Daily life was hard for most. The Great Plague killed 30% to 40% of the population between 1348 and 1349. At the height of the epidemic, one London cemetery buried 200 dead each day. Drink and religion were the common escape from the grind and the terrors. In 1309, there were 1,334 taverns, each brewing its own individual ale. London had 106 churches in 1371 and several monasteries. Holy Days, royal celebrations, and fairs, like the famous St. Bartholomew fair, provided blessed relief.

The Court had its own pleasures. Jousting tournaments took place in Smithfield and Cheapside, and the king went hunting for deer, boar, and hare in what are now our favorite London parks. Among the wealthy classes, chess was so popular that *The Rules of Chess* was the second book Caxton printed.

Westminster was the center of government, linked to London by Whitehall and the Strand (but primarily via the Thames). From the early 14th century on, the king summoned his nobles to council there. The courts and the treasury were in Westminster Hall, where the exchequer kept the accounts with tally sticks. Notches marked out the money owed along the stick, which was then split in half, one part kept by the exchequer and the other by the debtor. It was burning old sticks that destroyed the original buildings at Westminster in 1854.

- **1955** Heathrow Airport opens.
- **1956** Clean Air Act passed to cut through famous pea-soup smog.
- **1960s** Swinging London—Mary Quant, the Beatles, et al. The controversial Centre Point Tower built. England beats Germany in the Football World Cup in 1966 and dines out on it ever after.
- **1965** Churchill (b. 1874) dies. Greater London Council formed.
- **1973** Britain joins the European Common Market, despite opposition from the old foe France.
- **1974** Covent Garden Market moves out to Nine Elms.
- **1976** Royal National Theatre opens.
- **1979** Margaret Thatcher becomes Britain's first woman prime minister, heading a Conservative government.
- **1981** Charles, Prince of Wales, marries Lady Diana Spencer in St. Paul's Cathedral. Docklands Development Corporation established.
- **1982** The Thames Flood Barrier is completed downstream at Woolwich. Barbican Arts Centre opens.

continues

By the early 14th century, the population had reached 50,000, and living conditions were abysmal. Pigs, chickens, packhorses, and dogs roamed the city, and the streets were open sewers. Many people scraped a living as rakers and gong farmers—digging through the garbage and excrement. There was no clean water supply: It came straight out of the Thames at the Great Conduit in Cheapside. And fires were frequent.

TUDOR & ELIZABETHAN LONDON The modern history of London begins with the Tudors, who ascended the throne at the end of the 15th century. The first was Henry VII, who laid the solid administrative foundations on which his successors built a great nation and a strong monarchy.

Between 1500 and 1600, the population of London rocketed from 50,000 to 200,000. The city got wealthier and wealthier, due largely to the English Company of Merchant Adventurers. They traded wool to the Dutch in Antwerp and shipped back to England all kinds of things—from tennis balls, licorice, and Bruges silks to warming pans, thimbles, and dye for cloth. These 800 or so wholesale traders were the richest men in England. It was they who, in 1571, founded the first financial institution in the city, the Royal Exchange, which went on operating until 1939.

Under the Tudors, England grew in economic and political power. Henry VIII was a powerful Renaissance prince who competed fiercely with archrival Francis I of France. It was Henry who laid down the foundations of the British army and the navy.

But Henry's most significant legacy was separating the English church from Rome in furious response to the pope's refusal to grant him a divorce. It was a huge step, and a very lucrative one, because the king went on to dissolve the monasteries and confiscate church wealth and lands. Frustrated in his desire for a male heir, Henry married six times, executing two of his wives and divorcing two. One died of her own accord, and one outlived him. Anne Boleyn passed through Traitor's Gate at the Tower in 1536 on the way to her beheading. Catherine Howard was beheaded too, but she tested the block first and died proclaiming her love for Culpepper, who'd already got the chop for dallying with her.

Patronage of the arts and architecture was an important way to display power, and Henry VIII invited great painters like Holbein to his court. He built Nonsuch Palace (long gone) and embellished St. James's and Whitehall. Henry's reputation for extravagance was well earned. The

- **1986** Margaret Thatcher abolishes the Greater London Council after battling for years with its bolshy left-wing leader, Ken Livingstone.
- **1990** Tories oust Margaret Thatcher and vote for John Major to replace her. Paparazzi shots of a possibly tearful Maggie leaving Downing Street shoot round the world.
- **1992** Royal family rocked by scandals and Windsor Castle fire. Queen agrees to pay income tax and opens Buckingham Palace to the public.
- **1994** Channel Tunnel officially opens.
- **1996** IRA bombs Docklands in first attack for 17 months. Two die. Prince Andrew and Sarah Ferguson's divorce becomes final. Charles and Diana divorce, too.
- **1997** Tony Blair wins election for New Labour. Princess Diana killed in Paris car crash; nation mourns with huge outpouring of grief.
- **1999** Scotland and Wales win partial self-government. Monica Lewinsky chooses Harrods to launch her book, *Monica's Story*, written by

kitchen at Hampton Court Palace, which you can visit, was 100 feet long and 38 feet wide, and had ceilings 40 feet high. He spent £300,000 ($480,000) a year on food and £50,000 ($80,000) on drink. What is surprising is that, despite his ever-expanding waistline, the king had boundless energy for manly pursuits: He enclosed Hyde, St. James's, and Green Parks for his own hunting and other pleasures.

Henry VIII may have plundered Catholic coffers and estates, but it was his fanatical Protestant son, Edward VI (1547–53), who wreaked the greatest physical destruction on London's parish churches. He presided over the wholesale stripping of sculptures and decoration: One church lost 100 tombs and monuments. The Lord Protector Somerset demolished the cloister of St. Paul's in 1549 and used the materials to build Somerset House in the Strand. In 1550, Edward dissolved the bishopric of Westminster. The church returned to the Dean, but part of its revenues were transferred to St. Paul's; hence the English saying, "robbing Peter to pay Paul." Henry VIII's elder daughter Mary reestablished Catholicism in 1553. She was as hardline as her brother had been, though of the totally opposing view, and many public executions took place at Smithfield.

Her sister Elizabeth ascended the throne in 1558, ushering in not only Protestantism again, but a period of unprecedented colonial expansion and economic growth. A popular queen and master politician, she held England at peace for 30 years while she advanced the nation's interests against those of Catholic France and Spain. In 1588, her navy defeated a large Spanish armada that had set out to invade. Elizabeth gave thanks for this victory at St. Paul's.

Literature and the arts also flourished. Edmund Spenser dedicated his epic poem, *The Faerie Queene,* to Elizabeth. And the statesman and philosopher Francis Bacon; the soldier, explorer, and poet Sir Walter Raleigh; and others of equal versatility wrote pivotal books on history, science, and philosophy. At the same time, the English theater came into its own. James Burbage built the first playhouse, called simply "The Theatre," in Shoreditch in 1576, then the Rose on Bankside in 1587, the Swan in 1595, and the Hope in 1614. Play-going became a central part of London life, with as many as 40 productions a year at the Rose, including works by Christopher Marlowe, John Webster, Ben Jonson, Thomas Middleton, and William Shakespeare, of course, who joined Burbage's company in 1599. Today, Bankside is experiencing

---

Diana biographer Andrew Morton. Prince Edward and Sophie Rhys-Jones marry at Windsor. New Labour makes hereditary lords pitch for parliamentary privileges and ousts 600 of them.

- **2000** First Universal Day of new millennium starts at Greenwich. The fortunes of the much-ballyhooed Millennium Dome fortunes go downhill from there. Ken Livingstone elected as first London mayor. First official meeting between the queen and Camilla Parker-Bowles. Prince William leaves Eton.
- **2001** Foot and mouth disease ravages Britain. Tony Blair trounces the Tories, again, to win Labour a second term with an outright majority for the first time ever.
- **2002** Queen Elizabeth II celebrates her Golden Jubilee.
- **2003** Great Britain backs the United States and sends troops to help fight the war in Iraq.

another cultural flowering, with the rebuilding of the Globe Theatre and opening of Tate Modern.

STUART LONDON Elizabeth's death destroyed the long-standing political stability as an increasingly assertive, and largely Puritan, Parliament sought to build its power and limit that of the monarch. Known as the Virgin Queen, she had no direct successor and the throne passed to James VI of Scotland, who then became James I of England. James believed absolutely in the divine right of absolute monarchy, so he couldn't help but fight with Parliament. He persecuted the Puritans, despite an avowed intention to begin a new era of religious tolerance. And, though it was Catholic-led, he won no friends during the Gunpowder Plot when Guy Fawkes tried to blow him up at the state opening of Parliament.

If the conflict had simmered under James I, it exploded under his son Charles I, who was forced to dissolve several parliaments. In response, Parliament put the king's ministers on trial. It charged Thomas Wentworth, Earl of Strafford, with 28 crimes, and he fought for 18 days in Westminster Hall to defend himself. Charles fled to York. In 1642, he raised his standard at Nottingham, and London prepared for a Royalist attack. Parliament called out trained bands of men. Armed boats patrolled the Thames, and 100,000 men were pressed into digging 18 miles of trenches to link up the 24 bastions. The attack never came. The Royalist and Parliamentary troops waged their battles all over the country instead—at Edgehill, Oxford, Marston Moor, Naseby, and Preston.

Finally defeated, Charles I stood trial in Westminster Hall in 1649 and was condemned to death. He took his last walk through St. James's Park on January 30, flanked by guards with a troop of soldiers in front and behind, colors flying and drums pounding. The procession crossed a gallery at what is now Horse Guards Parade and entered the Banqueting House of Whitehall Palace. Four hours later, the king stepped out of the window onto the wooden scaffold. After saying his prayers, he pulled off his doublet, laid down his head, and the executioner wielded his ax. His last words were: "To your power I must submit, but your authority I deny." Today, a statue of a horseman stands looking down to the spot where he died. At the other end of Whitehall, outside Westminster Hall, there's a statue of Oliver Cromwell, the Puritan general who ruled England from 1649 to 1658, as Lord Protector, after Charles's execution.

Charles I had been a great patron of the arts and invited Van Dyck and Rubens to his court. In 1621, the latter painted the ceilings of the Banqueting House in Whitehall for £3,000 ($4,800) and a gold chain. Under Cromwell, the arts died. He closed the theaters and the city fell under a pall of fear and Puritan gloom. Diarist John Evelyn described Cromwell's funeral in 1658 as the "joyfullest . . . that ever I saw." The crowds impaled his head and those of his generals Ireton and Bradshaw and stuck them up on the roof of Westminster Hall. It's said Cromwell's remained there for 25 years until the wind blew it down and a sentry stole it.

The Restoration brought the Merry Monarch, Charles II, to the throne and brought the city back to life. The theaters reopened, and the king kept a lavish court at Whitehall Palace. Political and social climbers flocked there to curry favor, either directly or with one of the many royal mistresses.

Two major catastrophes interrupted the merrymaking—another Great Plague (1665) and the Great Fire of London (1666). The first victim of Black Death died on April 12, 1665; by December,

110,000 had died. The king and his court left for Hampton Court, and most of the nobility dismissed their servants and fled. The unemployed roamed the city looting and pillaging. Men worked day and night digging mass graves but couldn't keep up with the corpses, which piled up in mounds. The stench of death was horrific. When someone succumbed to the swellings in the groin and armpit (buboes), officials locked up their whole household for 40 days, and marked a red cross on the door, which multiplied the death rate. The innocent-sounding nursery rhyme "ring a ring o' roses" refers to the first telltale marks on the victim's skin.

Eventually, the rat-born plague ran its course and, in February 1666, the king deemed it safe enough to return to London. In the early morning of September 2, 1666, the Great Fire broke out at the bakery of Robert Farriner in Pudding Lane. It raced through the city, fanned by strong easterly winds. Samuel Pepys describes the flames leaping 300 feet into the air, warehouses blazing, and people jamming the river and roads in a vain attempt to flee.

The duke of York (later James II) was put in charge of firefighting, and the king himself helped too. The flames raged for 4 days over 400 acres within the city walls and 60 more outside. It wiped out medieval London, destroying 87 churches, 44 livery halls, and 13,000 half-timbered houses. Ten thousand people were left homeless. From then on, it was decreed that all buildings must be constructed of stone and brick.

Although Charles II realized this was an opportunity to create an elegantly planned city and even invited architects to submit plans, London needed rebuilding immediately. The medieval layout had to stay: To this day, London's streets follow the same routes as in the Middle Ages, hence the traffic jams and average speed of 10 mph. The streets were widened, though, and pavements laid for the first time. The king appointed six commissioners to mastermind the city's reconstruction. Wren was one of them: He rebuilt 51 churches (23 survive today, along with the towers of 6 others) and designed the 202-foot Monument commemorating the fire. St. Paul's was his greatest achievement.

In 1688, England went through a "Bloodless Revolution." James II had succeeded his brother Charles and, after converting himself, tried to bring the whole nation back to Catholicism. It was too bitter a pill for the people to swallow. So they asked his Protestant daughter Mary and her husband, the Dutch Prince William of Orange, to take the throne. The couple did so, first signing a new bill of rights, fixing limits to a sovereign's power. England had taken its first step on the path to constitutional monarchy.

London went through a property boom between 1660 and 1690, especially in Piccadilly, the Strand, and Soho. In 1656, Covent Garden Market opened as a temporary arrangement in the earl (later the duke) of Bedford's garden. In their headlong flight from fire and plague, many of the aristocracy had suddenly woken up to the advantages of living outside London, in the villages north and west of the city—Bloomsbury, Kensington, Hackney, Islington, and Hampstead. As they developed their estates, London began to take on its current form. They built houses and laid out formal squares, like Bloomsbury (1666) and St. James (1665).

18TH-CENTURY LONDON During the 18th century, London's population continued to multiply explosively, from 490,000 in 1700 to 950,000 in 1800. The city transformed in the process, as Mayfair and the West End began to develop. Private and corporate landowners laid out squares as the focal points of their estates.

Wealth flowed back from overseas colonies in America and from those established in the 17th century by the East India Company, the Royal Africa Company, and the Hudson's Bay Company. The Port of London boomed; trade tripled between 1720 and 1780. Because of the congestion on the Thames, it sometimes took 3 or 4 weeks to unload one vessel. As the century progressed, the pivotal role of the river as a main trade and general highway began to decline. Other forms of transport, from the stage and hackney coach to the sedan chair, took over, and more and more bridges began to span the river, like the one built at Westminster in 1749.

Other social developments helped change the face of the city, too. Greater wealth brought philanthropy and a growing concern for the poor. This led to the establishment of major public institutions like the Foundling Hospital (1742), Chelsea Hospital (1692), and Greenwich Hospital (1705); the British Museum (1755); and the Royal Academy of Arts (1768). The authorities set up a rudimentary fire department. And, by 1710, there were already 3,000 pupils at various charity schools, including St. Paul's, Westminster, and Christ's Hospital.

The major social institution, other than the church, was the coffeehouse, where literary and powerful men gathered to debate and gossip about politics and society. Addison, Steele, and Swift all met at Burtons in Russell Street; Samuel Johnson was a regular at the Turks Head at no. 142 the Strand; East India Company merchants packed the Jerusalem Coffeehouse in Cornhill; and the first ever stock exchange started informally at Jonathan's Coffeehouse in 1722. In 1702, London got its first newspaper, the *Daily Courant,* which was reaching 800 readers by 1704. Later in the century the *Guardian, Spectator,* and *Rambler* all published regular editions. Grub Street hacks would anonymously fire off any kind of libel or satire for a fee—a tradition some might say the tabloids uphold to this day.

One word sums up the politics of the age—corruption. Hogarth pictured the scene most acidly in his series, *The Election.* Votes were bought and sold. Politicians stole from the public purse. Riots were common; during the worst, the Gordon Riots in 1780, the mob torched several prisons and attacked the Bank of England and Downing Street.

Life was grim in the 18th century for the poverty-stricken. Silk weavers in Spitalfields hired out looms, employing female and child labor. Workhouses and prison workshops were common, too. To see the seamier side of London life, just take a look at Hogarth's *Gin Lane* or *The Rake's Progress.*

Those who could afford it took their leisure at Vauxhall Gardens (1660) or at Ranelagh Pleasure Gardens (1742). Their favorite fun was horse racing, archery, cricket, bowling, and skittles, as well as less salubrious pastimes like bullbaiting and prizefighting. Freak shows were very popular, too, at Don Saltero's Coffee House in Chelsea. And people flocked to Mrs. Salmon's waxworks in Fleet.

Though the prudish Victorians later hushed it up, London's sex industry has never been bigger than it was behind the elegant Georgian facades. Indeed, it funded much of the building. One in eight women (25,000) in the city was a prostitute in 1796, and each one made more in a night than the average man earned in a fortnight. It was no big deal for celebs and wealthy Londoners to go to brothels, half-heartedly disguised as Turkish baths. As well as the wealthy courtesans of Marylebone, streetwalkers did brisk trade in Covent Garden, adding to the louche atmosphere of this theatrical neighborhood.

David Garrick and Richard Brinsley Sheridan were the best-known actor-managers, both at Drury Lane. Musicians and composers were feted at the courts of the Hanoverian kings (Georges I, II, and III): Johann Christian Bach, Franz Joseph Haydn, and Mozart all performed there. Handel is the composer most closely identified with the London of this period: It was during the reign of George III that the annual performance of his *Messiah* began. Beyond court and the church, Thomas Britton fired a new musical tradition in the city, arranging weekly concerts from 1678 to 1714 in a loft above his Clerkenwell coal house.

Under the Georges, a great many artists rose to prominence, among them Sir Joshua Reynolds (who became head of the Royal Academy of Arts, founded by George III in 1768), Thomas Gainsborough, William Turner, and William Hogarth. Literature burgeoned, too: The celebrity cast list includes the great lexicographer and wit Samuel Johnson, his biographer James Boswell, poet Alexander Pope, and the novelists Samuel Richardson and Henry Fielding. Edward Gibbon's multivolume *History of the Decline and Fall of the Roman Empire,* one of the great achievements of English literature, caused George III to remark, "Always scribble, scribble, scribble. Eh, Mr. Gibbon?"

19TH-CENTURY LONDON In the 19th century, London became the wonder of the world—a wonder based on imperial wealth and power. In 1811, at the age of 58, the Prince of Wales became regent for his father, mad George III. He set up an alternate court at Carlton House and at his extravagant palace in Brighton. At both, the prince entertained his mistresses openly and lavishly. He treated his wife Caroline abominably, banning her from his coronation, which took place in 1820 at the massive cost of over £238,000 ($380,800). Though lambasted for his dissolute behavior, George IV contributed to London's development, working with architect John Nash to introduce urban planning. Together they laid out Regent Street, a grand avenue from Carlton House to Piccadilly and Regents Park.

Plump as a partridge, Victoria ascended the throne in 1837. As the century progressed, the city's transformation into a modern industrial society proceeded apace, shaped by the growing power of the bourgeoisie and the queen's strict moral stance. The raciness of the preceding 3 centuries seemed to disappear, but it actually just went underground.

Extremes of wealth and poverty marked life in Victorian London. Children worked long hours in factories and sweatshops or as chimney sweeps. Immigrants—Irish and European—poured into the foul, overcrowded slums. Thirty percent of the population lived below the poverty line, in the appalling conditions graphically described in many of Charles Dickens' novels. The consumption of gin was huge in the 1820s. In an effort to reduce it, the government abolished tax on beer, and scores of ale houses opened as a result—probably why there are so many pubs in London today.

Parliament passed the first Reform Bill in 1832, and social campaigners pressed for better conditions: Lord Shaftesbury strove for improvements in labor and education, Elizabeth Fry in prisons, and Florence Nightingale in hospitals. In 1870, the Education Act made elementary education compulsory.

The Victorians revolutionized public transport, too. In 1829, Shillibeer launched his horse-drawn omnibus. Underground trains started running from Paddington to Farringdon in 1863, carrying 12,000 passengers that year. And the first electric Tube ran on the Northern Line in 1890. Vast railway networks spread out across the country, all terminating at impressive Central London stations—Victoria, Charing Cross, St. Pancras, and Euston—several of which are virtually unchanged today.

In 1851, Prince Albert put his weight behind a celebratory Great Exhibition, housed in an astonishing iron-and-glass construction, Crystal Palace, built in Hyde Park. More than 6 million people flocked to see this showcase of the industrial and technological wonders of the age. Albert was a great promoter of new advances, like the revolutionary electric lighting that began to replace traditional gas lamps in London houses in 1880.

The middle class enjoyed a fantastic nightlife. By 1850, London had more than 50 stages, producing everything from popular blood-and-thunder melodramas to pageants at Christmas and Easter. The repertoire began to get more upmarket toward the end of the century, with works by Oscar Wilde, Arthur Wing Pinero, James Barrie, and George Bernard Shaw. Actor-manager Henry Irving and actress Ellen Terry lit up the Lyceum in the Strand. But music halls were even more popular—there were over 400 in 1870. People flocked to the Hackney Empire and the London Coliseum to hear Marie Lloyd, Dan Leno, and other stars belt out Cockney tunes and ribald variety shows.

Eating out became an upper-middle-class pastime, too. Once an exclusively male domain, mores slowly relaxed to let women in on the fun. The opening of the first Joe Lyons corner house in 1894 made eating out something the masses could enjoy, too. There were 98 in London by 1910, serving everything from a snack to a five-course meal.

Spectator sports took off in a big way in the 19th century—football, rugby, and especially cricket. The All England Croquet Club put in tennis courts in 1874 to revive its sinking fortunes. The ploy was so successful that the club held its first Wimbledon Championship in 1877. The manufacture of the safety bicycle in 1885 launched a craze, which gave women a taste of liberation: The "New Woman" of the 1890s took to the road on two wheels without a chaperone. Shopping, too, was becoming a national pastime. Department stores opened up to satisfy the urge to splurge—Whiteleys in Queensway (1863, now converted into a shopping mall), Harrods (1860s), Liberty (1875), and Selfridges (1909).

Victoria celebrated her golden jubilee in this energetic capital before ushering in the 20th century.

THE EARLY 20TH CENTURY The early 1900s, during the reign of Edward VII (1901–10), were filled with confidence. Britain was at the height of its power, and Londoners looked forward to a radiant future. Looking back, though, some historians pinpoint this as the start of the economic decline, arguing that Britain was already losing markets and trade to the United States.

At home, the trade union movement gained recruits, and women campaigned vigorously for the vote. They chained themselves to railings and protested at the Houses of Parliament. The courts sent 1,000 suffragettes to Holloway Prison between 1905 and 1914; it took World War I, with its social ramifications, to help women gain the franchise.

Rivalry with Germany had been festering for years, and war eventually broke out in 1914. British men marched off to do their duty, expecting certain and rapid victory. Instead, the war bogged down in the trenches and the slaughter wiped out a whole generation. Back home, 900 bombs fell on London, killing 670 people and injuring almost 2,000. The Great War shattered the liberal middle class's illusion that peace, prosperity, and social progress would continue indefinitely.

The peace imposed on the Germans at Versailles led inexorably to economic dislocation and ultimately to both the Crash of 1929 and the Great Depression of the 1930s. An unprecedented constitutional

What'd Ya Say?

Many Americans are shocked to discover that there's such a thing as British English. Believe it or not, the gulf between the two languages is wide enough to cause some embarrassing and entertaining exchanges. The English use words and phrases you may think you understand, but their meaning is often quite different from the U.S. equivalent.

Troublesome Slang "Mean" is a playground word for nasty, an adult word for "stingy," and a once-cool term of praise. And "homely," isn't "ugly" or "plain," but "cozy and comfortable." Other slang can get you into much worse trouble. In England "pissed" is "drunk," "pissed off" is "angry," a "rubber" refers to an "eraser," and "fag" means a "cigarette" as well as being a homophobe's term of abuse. "Fanny" in English is definitely not what you think it means. *Fanny Hill* might give you a clue—let's leave it at that.

Problematic Pronunciation The letter Z is pronounced "zed." Zero can be "zero," but is more often "nought," or interchanged with the letter "O," especially when people are telling you their phone number. French words can cause hiccups (or "hiccoughs," sometimes), too. The Brits put the emphasis on the first half of "*croi*-ssant" and "*ba*-llet."

Local Customs If you don't line up in London, you're a pariah. Except that the Brits "queue" instead.

Public Transport Whereas a "subway" is an underground pedestrian walkway, the actual subway system is "the Underground" or "the Tube."

Automobiles Very little is the same, except for the word "car:" A truck is called a "lorry," and a station wagon is an "estate car." The hood is the "bonnet," the windshield the "windscreen," and the trunk is the "boot." Drivers "hoot" the horn and "indicate" before they turn. Oh, and gas is "petrol."

Groceries In a supermarket, canned goods become "tins," potato chips "crisps," eggplants "aubergines," green squash "courgettes," while endive is "chicory" (and, conversely, chicory is "endive"). Both cookies and crackers become "biscuits." A Popsicle is called an "iced lolly," candy is "sweets," and a soda is a "fizzy drink." If you want diapers, ask for "nappies."

Clothes Shopping This is a real red-face territory. Repeat after me: Undershirts are called "vests," and undershorts are "pants" to the English. Long pants are "trousers," their cuffs are called "turnups," and, unless you're looking for lacy things that hold up ladies' stockings, ask for "braces," not suspenders. Panties are "knickers" and pantyhose are "tights." Pullovers can also be called "jumpers," "jerseys," or "sweaters."

At Home Most of us know that an English apartment is a "flat," unless it's over two floors, which much-reviled estate agents (realtors) describe as a "maisonette," rather than a duplex. An elevator is a "lift." And the first floor is always the ground floor, the second floor the first, and so on.

crisis further threatened Britain's stability in 1936, when the new and hugely popular king, Edward VIII, abdicated after refusing to renounce his love for the American divorcee, Wallis Simpson. His brother succeeded him as George VI.

Meanwhile, fascism was rising in Germany and threatening the peace with its expansionist ambitions. British and French attempts at appeasement failed. Hitler marched into Poland. And, in 1939, World War II began. The Blitz of 1940 to 1941 and again in 1944 to 1945 killed over 20,000 people in London and destroyed vast areas of the city, but Londoners' spirit proved indomitable. They dug trenches in public parks to resist the expected invasion. Night after night, they ran for their shelters as waves of German bombers flew overhead. One hundred and fifty thousand slept in the Underground, others stayed home, and the defiant continued partying. The royal family remained in London despite the dangers.

Recordings of Winston Churchill's speeches still evoke pride, even among people who weren't born at the time. But for many who were there, the memories are bittersweet: Britain won the war but lost the peace. Unlike Germany and Japan, which received American aid under the Marshall Plan, Britain was impoverished, and her industrial plants antiquated. Dissolution of the empire and a plummeting of national morale followed swiftly.

POSTWAR & CONTEMPORARY LONDON Postwar London was a glum place. Rationing continued until 1953. Only the coronation of Queen Elizabeth II in June 1953, watched by 20 million on their TV screens, seemed to lift the city's spirits. Heathrow formally opened in 1955, the same year Mary Quant launched her boutique on the King's Road. The coffee bar, rock 'n' roll, the new Mini (relaunched in 2001 as the BMW Mini Cooper at 20 times its original £499/$798 price tag), and antinuclear protests all arrived in the 1950s, setting the stage for the Swinging London of the following decade. It was then that young people all over the world went bananas over the Beatles, the Kinks, the Rolling Stones, The Who, Eric Clapton's Yardbirds, and the Animals. Sixties London was suddenly the fashion and arts capital of the world.

The swinging slacked off a bit in the 1970s when the Beatles disbanded. But the trendy movement continued as Terence Conran launched Habitat, Anita Roddick created the Body Shop, and the Saatchi & Saatchi advertising empire was born. In 1976, London finally got its Royal National Theatre, first conceived of in 1848. The Barbican Arts Centre opened in 1982.

Other less-heartwarming developments also took place during the postwar years. The number of West Indians heading for Britain each year rose from 1,000 to 20,000 after 1952 when the United States closed its doors to them. Ultra-conservative politicians like Enoch Powell called for a slowdown in immigration, and London experienced its first-ever race riots in Notting Hill in the summer of 1958. Parliament responded by restricting entry to Britain but prohibiting discrimination in housing and employment. More riots followed in 1981 and 1985, and the race issue continues to fester as the second and third generations still find themselves treated as second-class citizens.

In the 1950s and 1960s, immigrants also began arriving from India and Pakistan. Their communities have also been under attack, but successful Asian entrepreneurs and businesspeople are fighting back and demanding justice. In contrast to other European countries, though, the shocking violence of the 1980s does seem to have helped mold a more honest cross-cultural society than most, despite tabloid references to "frogs" and "krauts" that might suggest the contrary.

Impressions

Every city has a sex and age which have nothing to do with demography. London is a teen-ager and urchin, and, in this, hasn't changed since the time of Dickens.

—John Berger, *Guardian,* March 27, 1987

The post-war economic decline was initially masked by Britain's continuing reliance on preferential trade with former colonies. Most Commonwealth exports flowed through London, making its port one of the busiest in the world. But many of these countries gained full independence in the 1960s and began to build their own industries and diversify. Germany, Japan and the United States were tough competitors, too. Most dockyards closed, and manufacturing jobs went as big companies like Thorne-EMI and Hoover relocated to other areas. Unemployment in the poorer boroughs of London, like Tower Hamlets and Southwark, soared from 10,000 in the 1960s to 80,000 in the 1980s.

The Conservatives rose to power in 1979, with Britain's first woman prime minister at the helm, on the promise of revitalizing the economy. Margaret Thatcher's reforms were ground-shaking: privatization of major industries, from insurance companies to British Airways and British Rail. Maggie also squashed the trade unions and dismantled parts of the welfare state. At the height of her power in the early 1980s, she mobilized British forces to rescue the Falkland Islanders from the Argentine invasion. The return to gunship diplomacy reignited English pride and won the Tories the next election.

Later, fiercely protective of British sovereignty, Maggie refused to agree to a German-backed monetary union within the European Community and opposed moves toward the creation of a federal entity. She angered many backbenchers in her own party in doing so. And, in 1990, the party rebelled and ended the longest tenure of any modern British prime minister, voting to replace her with the Chancellor of the Exchequer, John Major. His tired government limped along, but the Furies were on their tail.

The Tories couldn't seem to keep their hands off dodgy money and dodgy women. They fought amongst themselves, very publicly, about Britain's role in Europe. In 1994, the Channel Tunnel opened. Though considered an astonishing feat of engineering and a success now, then it was a money pit that had to seek repeated refinancing. And the monarchy, of which the political right has always been a loyal supporter, was in such disarray that it prompted louder calls for a republic than at almost any time since the Protectorate.

In 1992, Windsor Castle lit up the night sky as workers struggled for 15 hours to put out the blazing fire. Angry political debate about freeloading royals prompted the queen to agree to pay income tax for the first time. And both her elder sons' marriages crumbled in the full lip-smacking glare of media attention. The next year brought her yet more grief in the shape of published transcripts of taped, almost telephone sex between Charles and Camilla Parker-Bowles. The royal marital farce reached its climax in 1996 with the divorces of Prince Charles and Diana and Prince Andrew and Sarah Ferguson.

The British people were more than ready for change. Tony Blair moved the Labour Party way up the sexiness scale and to the political center, reassuring Middle England that it was no longer the party of high taxation. It worked, and the blessed Tony led his gang to a massive victory in 1997.

After 18 years of Tory rule, it felt like throwing off a particularly smelly and oppressive old dog blanket. The government promised so much to so many, in a new inclusive society: help for the disadvantaged, powerful support to British business, a revitalized education system and health service, backing for the arts, and so on. Blair's golden glow lit up their efforts, even surviving the misjudged sucking up to arts and media luvvies.

A year later, Britain had its dreadful Kennedy moment. Ask any local and they'll be able to tell you where they were when they heard about the death of Princess Diana. The nation plunged into mourning and turned on the royal family for their hidebound reaction. With the prime minister volunteering advice, they have been trying to "get real" ever since.

Appendix B: London's Art & Architecture

by Reid Bramblett

No one artist, period, or museum defines London's art and architecture; rather, the city builds upon the work of artists and craftsmen from its earliest days to the thriving, sometimes shocking art scene today, which could shape the look and view of the city in the future. You can see the art of London in medieval illuminated manuscripts, Thomas Gainsborough portraits, and Damien Hirst's pickled cows and sharks; its architecture from Roman walls and Norman castles to baroque St. Paul's Cathedral and towering postmodern skyscrapers. Read on to learn more about some of the art and architecture that surrounds you in this graceful, exciting city.

1 Art 101

CELTIC & MEDIEVAL (CA. 800 B.C.–16TH C.)

The Celts, mixed with Scandinavian and Dutch tribes, ruled England until the Romans established rule in A.D. 43. Celtic art survived the Roman conquest and Dark Ages Christianity mainly as carved swirls and decorations on the "Celtic Crosses" in medieval cemeteries. During the Dark and Middle Ages, colorful Celtic images and illustrations decorated "illuminated manuscripts" copied by monks. Plenty of these have ended up in London's libraries and museums.

Important examples and artists of this period include:

- **Wilton Diptych,** National Gallery. The first truly British painting was crafted in the late 1390s for Richard II by an unknown artist.
- **Lindisfarne Gospels,** British Library. One of Europe's greatest illuminated manuscripts from the 7th century.
- **Matthew Paris** (died 1259). See examples of the Benedictine monk's illuminated manuscripts in the British Library and Cambridge's Corpus Christi College.

THE RENAISSANCE & BAROQUE (16TH–18TH C.)

While the Renaissance was more of a Southern European movement, London's museums contain the works of many important old masters from Italy and Germany. A few foreign Renaissance artists did come to English courts and had an influence on some local artists; however, significant Brits didn't emerge until the baroque period.

The baroque mixes a kind of super-realism based on using peasants as models and an exaggerated use of light and dark, called *chiaroscuro,* with compositional complexity and explosions of dynamic fury, movement, color, and figures.

Significant artists of this period include:

- **Hans Holbein the Younger** (1497–1543). A German Renaissance master portraitist, Holbein the Younger cataloged many significant figures in 16th-century Europe. You'll find examples in the National Gallery, the National Portrait Gallery, and Windsor Castle.

- **Anton Van Dyck** (1599–1641). This Belgian painted portraits in the baroque style for Charles I and other Stuarts, and set the tone for British portraiture for the next few centuries. See his works in the National Portrait Gallery, the National Gallery, the Wallace Collection, and Wilton House, and Oxford's Ashmolean Museum.
- **William Hogarth** (1697–1764). Hogarth painted and engraved scenes of everyday life. His works such as *The Rake's Progress* (in Sir John Soane's Museum) were morality tales presented as early versions of a comic strip. See other works in the National Gallery and the Tate Britain, and Cambridge's Fitzwilliam Museum.
- **Sir Joshua Reynolds** (1723–92). A staunch traditionalist and baroque painter, Reynolds was the first president of London's Royal Academy of Arts. He liked to depict his noble patrons as ancient gods in compositions cribbed from old masters. Many of his works are in the National Gallery, the Tate Britain, the Wallace Collection, and the Dulwich Picture Gallery, and in Oxford's Cathedral Hall.
- **Thomas Gainsborough** (1727–88). When not immortalizing noble patrons such as Jonathan Buttell (better known as "Blue Boy"), Gainsborough painted quite a collection of landscapes. See works in the National Gallery, the National Portrait Gallery, Cambridge's Fitzwilliam Museum, Oxford's Cathedral Hall and Ashmolean Museum, and Gainsborough's House, a museum in his birthplace in Suffolk.

THE ROMANTICS (LATE 18TH–19TH C.)

The Romantics idealized the Romantic tales of chivalry; had a deep respect for nature, human rights, and the nobility of peasantry; and were suspicious of progress. Their paintings tended to be heroic, historic, dramatic, and beautiful. They were inspired by critic and art theorist **John Ruskin** (1819–1900), who was among the first to praise pre-Renaissance painting and Gothic architecture.

Significant artists of this period include:

- **William Blake** (1757–1827). Blake snubbed the Royal Academy of Arts to do his own engraving, illustrations, poetry, and painting. He believed in divine inspiration, and channeled a vengeful Old Testament God with works filled with melodrama, muscular figures, and sweeping lines. See his work at the Tate Britain.
- **John Constable** (1776–1837). A little obsessed with clouds, Constable was a great British landscapist whose scenes (especially those of happy, agrarian peasants) got more idealized as he aged—while his compositions and brushwork became freer. His best work is in the National Gallery and the Victoria and Albert Museum.
- **J. M. W. Turner** (1775–1851). Turner, called by some "The First Impressionist," was a prolific artist whose mood-laden, freely brushed watercolor landscapes influenced Monet. London and the River Thames were frequent subjects. He bequeathed his collection of some 19,000 watercolors and 300 paintings to the people of Britain. The Tate Britain displays the largest number of Turner's works, and others grace the National Gallery and Cambridge's Fitzwilliam Museum.
- **Pre-Raphaelites** (1848–70). This "Brotherhood" declared art had gone all wrong with Raphael (1483–1520) and set about to emulate the 15th-century Italian painters that preceded him—though their symbolic, sweetly idealized, hyper-realistic work looks nothing like it. They loved scenes from Romantic poetry and Shakespeare as well as the Bible. There were seven founders and many followers, the most important were Dante Rossetti, William Hunt, and John Millais; you can see work by all three at the Tate Britain and Oxford's Ashmolean Museum.

THE 20TH CENTURY

The only artistic movement or era the Brits can claim a major stake in is contemporary art, with many young British artists bursting onto the international gallery scene just before and after World War II. The 20th century showed the greatest artists searching for a unique, individual expression rather than adherence to a particular school.

Important artists of this period include:

- **Henry Moore** (1898–1986). Sculptor Moore saw himself as a sort of reincarnation of Michelangelo. He mined his marble from the same quarries as the Renaissance master to create flowing, abstract, surrealistic figures. Moore did several public commissions (*Knife Edge* [1967] at Abingdon St. Gardens underground garage; *The Arch* [1979] on the east bank of the Longwater in Kensington Gardens), and started working in bronze after the 1950s. Other sculptures grace the Tate Modern and Cambridge's Fitzwilliam Museum and Clare College.
- **Ben Nicholson** (1894–1982). The most famous of Britain's abstract artists, Nicholson is known for his low-relief abstract paintings using layered cardboard and minimalist colors (his most famous are just white). His work is in the Tate Modern and Cambridge's Fitzwilliam Museum.
- **Francis Bacon** (1909–1992). A dark, brooding expressionist, Bacon used formats such as the triptych, which were usually reserved for religious subjects, to show man's foibles. Examples of his work are in the Tate Modern, including *Triptych August 1972* (1972).
- **Lucien Freud** (born 1922). Freud's portraits and nudes live in a depressing world of thick paint, fluid lines, and harsh light. The grandson of psychiatrist Sigmund Freud, this artist has pieces at the Tate Modern, including *Girl With a White Dog* (1950–51) and *Standing in Rags* (1988–89).
- **David Hockney** (born 1937). Hockney employs a less Pop Arty style than American Andy Warhol—though Hockney does reference modern technologies and culture—and is much more playful with artistic traditions. The Tate Modern is the place to see his creations, including *Mr. and Mrs. Clark and Percy* (1970–71).
- **Damien Hirst** (born 1965). The guy who pickles cows, Hirst is a celebrity/artist whose work sets out to shock. He's a winner of Britain's Turner Prize, and his work is prominent in the collection of Charles Saatchi (whose Saatchi Gallery in London displays his holdings).

2 Architecture 101

While each architectural era in London has its own distinctive features, there are some elements, floor plans, and terms common to many.

From the Romanesque period on, most **churches** consist either of a single wide **aisle** or a wide central **nave** flanked by two narrow, less-tall aisles. The aisles are separated from the nave by a row of **columns,** or square stacks of masonry called **piers,** connected by **arches.** Sometimes there is a second level to the nave, above these arches punctuated by windows, called a **clerestory.**

This main nave/aisle assemblage is usually crossed by a perpendicular corridor called a **transept** near the far, east end of the church so that the floor plan looks like a **Latin Cross.** The shorter, east arm of the nave is called the **chancel;** it often houses the stalls of the **choir** and the **altar.** Some churches use a **rood screen** (so called because it supports a *rood,* the Saxon word for *crucifixion*) to separate the nave from the chancel. If the far end of the chancel is rounded off, we call it an **apse.** An **ambulatory** is a corridor outside the altar and choir area, separating it from the smaller chapels radiating off the chancel and apse.

Some churches, especially after the Renaissance when mathematical proportion became important, were built on a **Greek Cross** plan, each axis the same length, like a giant +.

Very few buildings were built in only one style. They often took centuries to complete, during which time tastes would change and plans would be altered.

NORMAN (1066–1200)

Aside from a smattering of pre-classical stone circles and Roman ruins, the oldest surviving architectural style in England dates to when the 1066 Norman Conquest brought the Romanesque era to Britain, where it flourished as the **Norman style.**

Churches were large, with a wide nave and aisles to fit the masses that came to hear Mass and worship at the altars of various saints. But to support the weight of all that masonry, the walls had to be thick and solid (pierced only by a few small windows) and resting on huge piers, which gives Norman churches a somber, mysterious feeling.

Some of the features of this style include:

- **Rounded arches.** These load-bearing arches allowed the architects to open up wide naves and spaces, channeling the weight of the stone walls and ceiling across the curve of the arch and down into the ground via the columns or pilasters.
- **Thick walls.**
- **Infrequent and small windows.**
- **Huge piers.** These are square stacks of masonry.
- **Chevrons.** These zigzagging decorations often surround a doorway or wrap around a column.

White Tower

White Tower, London (Gundulf, 1078), William the Conqueror's first building in Britain, is the central keep of the Tower of London. The tower's fortress-thick walls and archways provide a textbook example of a Norman-era castle. **St. John's Chapel,** located in the White Tower, is one of the few remaining Norman churches in England.

GOTHIC (1150–1550)

The French Gothic style invaded England in the late 12th century, trading rounded arches for pointy ones—an engineering discovery that freed architects from the thick walls of Norman structures and allowed ceilings to soar and windows to proliferate.

Instead of dark, unadorned Norman interiors that forced the eyes of the faithful toward the altar, the Gothic interior enticed the churchgoers' gazes upward to high ceilings filled with light. While the priests conducted Mass in Latin, the peasants could "read" the Bible stories in the stained-glass windows.

The squat exteriors of the Norman churches were replaced by graceful buttresses and soaring spires, which rose from town centers.

The Gothic proper in Britain can be divided into three periods or styles: **Early English** (1150–1300), **Decorated** (1250–1370), and **Perpendicular** (1350–1550). Although each has identifiable features, they all include:

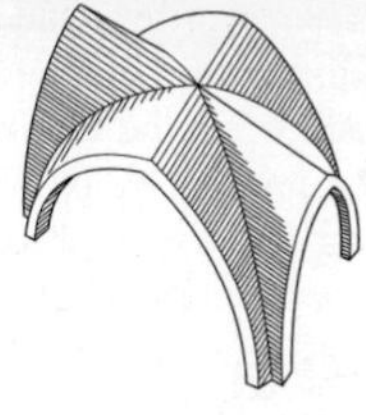

Ribbed Vaulting

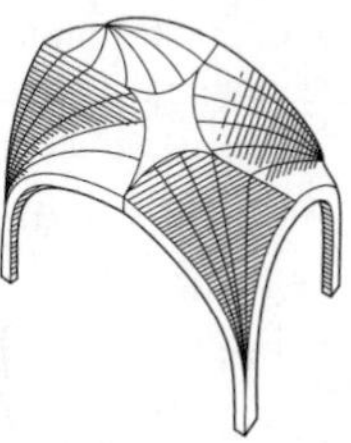

Fan Vaulting

- **Pointed arches.** It was discovered during the Gothic era that pointed arches could carry more weight than rounded ones.
- **Ribbed vaulting.** In Gothic buildings, the square patch of ceiling between four columns arches up to a point in the center, creating four sail shapes. This is called a **cross-vault.** The "X" separating these four sails is often reinforced with ridges called **ribbing.** As the Gothic progressed, the spaces between the structural ribbing became more decorative, often filled with **tracery** (delicate and lace-like carved stone). In the Perpendicular style, **fan vaulting** (cone-shaped concave vaults springing from the same point) was often used.

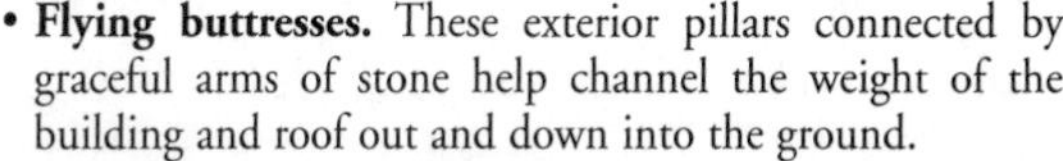

- **Flying buttresses.** These exterior pillars connected by graceful arms of stone help channel the weight of the building and roof out and down into the ground.

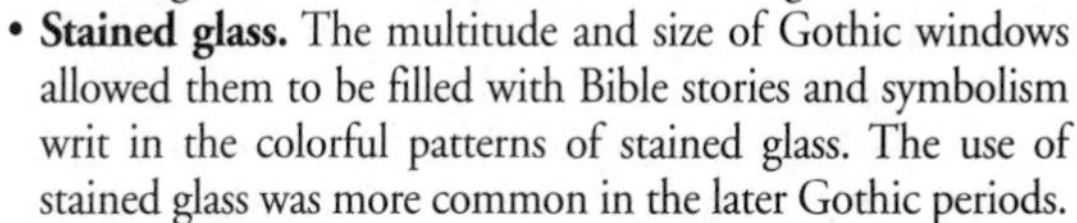

- **Stained glass.** The multitude and size of Gothic windows allowed them to be filled with Bible stories and symbolism writ in the colorful patterns of stained glass. The use of stained glass was more common in the later Gothic periods.
- **Rose windows.** These huge, circular windows, often the centerpieces of facades, are filled with elegant tracery and "petals" of stained glass.
- **Spires.** These pinnacles seem to defy gravity and reach toward Heaven itself.
- **Gargoyles.** These are drain spouts disguised as wide-mouthed creatures or human heads.
- **Choir screen.** Serving as the inner wall of the ambulatory and the outer wall of the choir section, the choir screen is often decorated with carvings or tombs.

Among England's towering Gothic achievements, **King's College Chapel** (1446–1515) at Cambridge has England's most magnificent fan vaulting, along with some fine stained glass. At Windsor are two great examples, the **College Chapel** at Eton College (the stained glass is modern, and the fan vaulting redone in 1957, but the 15th-c. murals are original), and the **St. George's Chapel** in Windsor Castle (a gorgeous nave vault with fan vaulting in the aisles and carved choir stalls).

RENAISSANCE (1550–1650)

While Italy and France were experimenting with the Renaissance ideals of proportion, classical inspiration, and mathematical precision, England was trundling along with the late **Tudor Gothic** Perpendicular style in places such as Hampton Court Palace.

It wasn't until the Elizabethan era that the Brits turned to the **Renaissance** style. Architect **Inigo Jones** (1573–1652), England's greatest Renaissance architect, applied what he'd learned during travels in Italy to several structures, but most English architects tempered the Renaissance style with a heavy dose of Gothic-like elements. Little specifically identifies Renaissance buildings, except:

- **A sense of proportion.**
- **A reliance on symmetry.**
- **The use of classical orders.** This idea specifies three different column types: Corinthian, Ionic, or Doric.

Noteworthy structures in this style by Inigo Jones include the **Queen's House,** Greenwich (1616–18 and 1629–35); the **Queen's Chapel,** St. James's Palace (1623–25) and the **Banqueting House,** Whitehall (1619–22), both in London; and the state rooms of Wiltshire's **Wilton House** (1603), where Shakespeare performed and D-day was planned. Recently, **Shakespeare's Globe Theatre** dusted off one of Jones's never-realized plans and used it to construct the new indoor theater.

BAROQUE (1650–1750)

England's greatest architect was **Sir Christopher Wren** (1632–1723), a scientist and member of Parliament who got the job of rebuilding London after the Great Fire of 1666. He designed 53 replacement churches alone, plus the new St. Paul's Cathedral and numerous other projects. Features as practiced by Wren and others include:

- **Classical architecture rewritten with curves.**
- **Complex decoration.**

St. Paul's Cathedral, London (1676–1710), is the crowning achievement both of the English baroque and of Wren himself. The city's other main Wren attraction is **Royal Naval College,** Greenwich (1696).

A student of Wren, **Nicholas Hawksmoor** practiced a baroque more fanciful than that of his teacher. Hawksmoor left London several churches, including **St. Mary Woolnoth** (1716–24); **St. George's,** Bloomsbury (1716–30); **Christ Church,** Spitalfields (1714–29); and **St. Anne's,** Limehouse (1714–30).

NEOCLASSICAL AND GREEK REVIVAL (1714–1837)

Many 18th-century architects cared little for the baroque, and during the Georgian era (1714–1830) a restrained, simple neoclassicism reigned, balanced between a resurgence of the precepts of the Renaissance and an even more distilled vision of classical theory called Greek Revival. Buildings in these styles are distinguished by:

- **Mathematical proportion, symmetry, and classical orders.**
- **Crescents and circuses.**
- **Open double-arm staircases.**

The chapel in Greenwich Hospital (1779–88) is a fine example of the style, courtesy of the most textbook of Greek Revivalists, James "Athenian" Stuart. The greatest site by Greek Revivalist John Soane is his own house at 13 Lincoln's Inn Fields (1812–13), now **Sir John Soane's Museum**. Other Soane buildings include the **Dulwich Picture Gallery** and the **Bank of England** in Bartholomew Lane. Another example of this style is the **British Museum** (Robert and Sidney Smirke, 1823).

VICTORIAN GOTHIC REVIVAL (1750–1900)

The Romantic Movement swept up many others with rosy visions of the past. Their imaginary and fairy-tale version of the Middle Ages led to such creative developments as the Pre-Raphaelite painters and Victorian Gothic Revival architects, whose buildings can be distinguished by:

- **Mishmash of Gothic features.** Look at the Gothic features described earlier, and then imagine going on a shopping spree through them at random. How to tell the copycats from the original? Victorian buildings are much younger, so they tend to be in better shape. They're also often much larger than original Gothic buildings.

- **Eclecticism.** Few Victorians bothered to get all the details of the Gothic era right (London's Houses of Parliament comes closest). They just wanted the overall effect to be pointy with pinnacled turrets, busy with decorations, and medieval.
- **Grand scale.** The largeness of these buildings was usually accomplished by using Gothic only on the surface, with Industrial Age engineering underneath.

Charles Barry designed the British seat of government, the **Palace of Westminster** (Houses of Parliament) (1835–52), in a Gothic idiom that sticks pretty faithfully to the old Perpendicular period's style. His clock tower, usually called "Big Ben" after its biggest bell, has become an icon of London.

Palace of Westminster

The massive pinnacled and redbrick Victorian mansion, **St. Pancras Station** (George Gilbert Scott, 1867), makes for a quirky entrance to the Industrial Age phenomenon of rail travel. (And, while purely industrial and not Gothic, the station's steel-and-glass train shed was an engineering marvel, the widest in the world at its time.) The **Albert Memorial** (George Gilbert Scott, 1863–72), a massive Gothic canopy by the same architect, was commissioned by Queen Victoria in memory of her husband. Like St. Pancras, the **Natural History Museum** (Alfred Waterhouse, 1873–81), is another delightful marriage of imposing neo-Gothic clothing hiding an Industrial Age steel-and-iron framework.

THE 20TH CENTURY

For the first half of the 20th century, London was too busy expanding into suburbs and fighting world wars to pay much attention to architecture. After the Blitz, much of central London was rebuilt, but most of the new buildings that went up in the City held to a functional school of architecture aptly named **Brutalism.** It wasn't until the late 1970s and 1980s that **postmodern** architecture gave architects a bold new direction.

Identifiable features of postmodern architecture in London include:

- **The skyscraper motif.** Glass and steel as high as you can stack it.
- **A reliance on historic details.** Like the Victorians, postmodernists also recycled elements from architectural history, from classical to exotic.

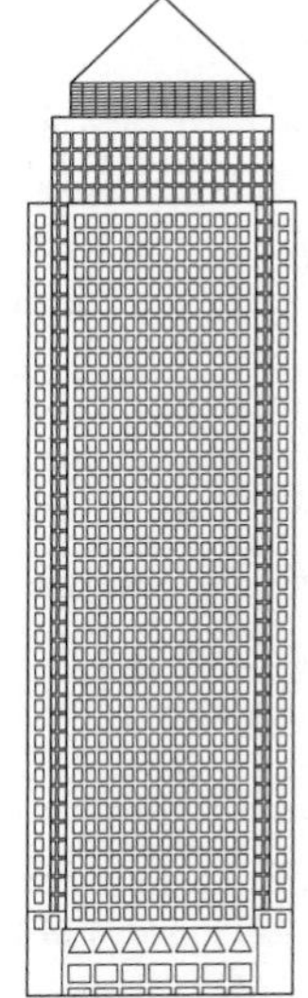

Canary Wharf Tower

The **Lloyd's Building** (1978–86) is *the* British postmodern masterpiece by architect Richard Rogers, who had a hand in the design of Paris's funky Centre Pompidou. Britain's tallest building, **Canary Wharf Tower** (César Pelli, 1986), is the centerpiece of the early 1990s Canary Wharf office complex and commercial development. **Charing Cross** (Terry Farrell, 1991) capped the famous old train station with an enormous postmodern office-and-shopping complex in glass and pale stone.

Index

See also Accommodations and Restaurant indexes, below.

General Index

Accommodations

Restaurants

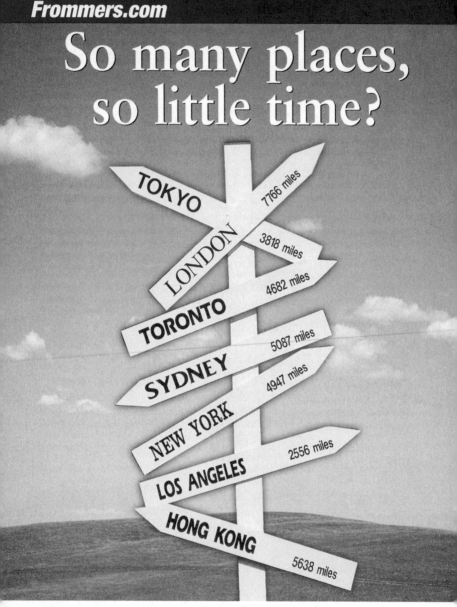

Frommer's® Complete Travel Guides

Alaska
Alaska Cruises & Ports of Call
American Southwest
Amsterdam
Argentina & Chile
Arizona
Atlanta
Australia
Austria
Bahamas
Barcelona
Beijing
Belgium, Holland & Luxembourg
Bermuda
Boston
Brazil
British Columbia & the Canadian Rockies
Brussels & Bruges
Budapest & the Best of Hungary
Calgary
California
Canada
Cancún, Cozumel & the Yucatán
Cape Cod, Nantucket & Martha's Vineyard
Caribbean
Caribbean Ports of Call
Carolinas & Georgia
Chicago
China
Colorado
Costa Rica
Cruises & Ports of Call
Cuba
Denmark
Denver, Boulder & Colorado Springs
Edinburgh & Glasgow
England
Europe
Europe by Rail
European Cruises & Ports of Call
Florence, Tuscany & Umbria
Florida
France
Germany
Great Britain
Greece
Greek Islands
Halifax
Hawaii
Hong Kong
Honolulu, Waikiki & Oahu
India
Ireland
Italy
Jamaica
Japan
Kauai
Las Vegas
London
Los Angeles
Madrid
Maine Coast
Maryland & Delaware
Maui
Mexico
Montana & Wyoming
Montréal & Québec City
Munich & the Bavarian Alps
Nashville & Memphis
New England
Newfoundland & Labrador
New Mexico
New Orleans
New York City
New York State
New Zealand
Northern Italy
Norway
Nova Scotia, New Brunswick & Prince Edward Island
Oregon
Ottawa
Paris
Peru
Philadelphia & the Amish Country
Portugal
Prague & the Best of the Czech Republic
Provence & the Riviera
Puerto Rico
Rome
San Antonio & Austin
San Diego
San Francisco
Santa Fe, Taos & Albuquerque
Scandinavia
Scotland
Seattle
Seville, Granada & the Best of Andalusia
Shanghai
Sicily
Singapore & Malaysia
South Africa
South America
South Florida
South Pacific
Southeast Asia
Spain
Sweden
Switzerland
Texas
Thailand
Tokyo
Toronto
Turkey
USA
Utah
Vancouver & Victoria
Vermont, New Hampshire & Maine
Vienna & the Danube Valley
Virgin Islands
Virginia
Walt Disney World® & Orlando
Washington, D.C.
Washington State

Frommer's® Dollar-a-Day Guides

Australia from $50 a Day
California from $70 a Day
England from $75 a Day
Europe from $85 a Day
Florida from $70 a Day
Hawaii from $80 a Day
Ireland from $80 a Day
Italy from $70 a Day
London from $90 a Day
New York City from $90 a Day
Paris from $90 a Day
San Francisco from $70 a Day
Washington, D.C. from $80 a Day
Portable London from $90 a Day
Portable New York City from $90 a Day
Portable Paris from $90 a Day

Frommer's® Portable Guides

Acapulco, Ixtapa & Zihuatanejo
Amsterdam
Aruba
Australia's Great Barrier Reef
Bahamas
Berlin
Big Island of Hawaii
Boston
California Wine Country
Cancún
Cayman Islands
Charleston
Chicago
Disneyland®
Dominican Republic
Dublin
Florence
Frankfurt
Hong Kong
Las Vegas
Las Vegas for Non-Gamblers
London
Los Angeles
Los Cabos & Baja
Maui
Miami
Nantucket & Martha's Vineyard
New Orleans
New York City
Paris
Phoenix & Scottsdale
Portland
Puerto Rico
Puerto Vallarta, Manzanillo & Guadalajara
Rio de Janeiro
San Diego
San Francisco
Savannah
Vancouver Island
Venice
Virgin Islands
Washington, D.C.
Whistler

Frommer's® National Park Guides

Algonquin Provincial Park
Banff & Jasper
Family Vacations in the National Parks
Grand Canyon
National Parks of the American West
Rocky Mountain
Yellowstone & Grand Teton
Yosemite & Sequoia/Kings Canyon
Zion & Bryce Canyon

Frommer's® Memorable Walks

Chicago
London
New York
Paris
San Francisco

Frommer's® With Kids Guides

Chicago
Hawaii
Las Vegas
New York City
Ottawa
San Francisco
Toronto
Vancouver
Walt Disney World® & Orlando
Washington, D.C.

Suzy Gershman's Born to Shop Guides

Born to Shop: France
Born to Shop: Hong Kong, Shanghai & Beijing
Born to Shop: Italy
Born to Shop: London
Born to Shop: New York
Born to Shop: Paris

Frommer's® Irreverent Guides

Amsterdam
Boston
Chicago
Las Vegas
London
Los Angeles
Manhattan
New Orleans
Paris
Rome
San Francisco
Seattle & Portland
Vancouver
Walt Disney World®
Washington, D.C.

Frommer's® Best-Loved Driving Tours

Austria
Britain
California
France
Germany
Ireland
Italy
New England
Northern Italy
Scotland
Spain
Tuscany & Umbria

The Unofficial Guides®

Beyond Disney
California with Kids
Central Italy
Chicago
Cruises
Disneyland®
England
Florida
Florida with Kids
Inside Disney
Hawaii
Las Vegas
London
Maui
Mexico's Best Beach Resorts
Mini Las Vegas
Mini Mickey
New Orleans
New York City
Paris
San Francisco
Skiing & Snowboarding in the West
South Florida including Miami & the Keys
Walt Disney World®
Walt Disney World® for Grown-ups
Walt Disney World® with Kids
Washington, D.C.

Special-Interest Titles

Athens Past & Present
Cities Ranked & Rated
Frommer's Best Day Trips from London
Frommer's Best RV & Tent Campgrounds in the U.S.A.
Frommer's Caribbean Hideaways
Frommer's China: The 50 Most Memorable Trips
Frommer's Exploring America by RV
Frommer's Gay & Lesbian Europe
Frommer's NYC Free & Dirt Cheap
Frommer's Road Atlas Europe
Frommer's Road Atlas France
Frommer's Road Atlas Ireland
Frommer's Wonderful Weekends from New York City
Retirement Places Rated
Rome Past & Present

IF YOU BOOK IT, IT SHOULD BE THERE.
Only Travelocity guarantees it will be, or we'll work with our travel partners to make it right, right away. So if you're missing a balcony or anything else you booked, just call us 24/7. 1-888-TRAVELOCITY
travelocity
You'll never roam alone